We dedicate this book to you—our readers—
who reached out to us to thank us for reaching out to you.
May our visions and dreams for our community come to pass—
bimheirah veyameinu—speedily and in our days.

May God who blessed our fathers Abraham, Isaac, and Jacob
and our mothers Sarah, Rivkah, Rachel, and Leah bless
Adrianne Onderdonk Dudden, Kay Powell, Stu Copans, Bill Aron,
Phyllis Talmadge, Lionel Koppman, Rebecca Ziplonsky,
Audrey Sideman, Sid Medwed, Norma Harrop, Glenn Richter,
Maier Deshell, our editor, whose firm judgments and gentle
urgings proved invaluable, and most especially,
our first editor Chaim Potok, who helped us formulate the vision—
for their assistance and encouragement in the preparation
of this **Catalog.** May ha-Kadosh Barukh Hu send blessings and
prosperity on all the work of their hands together
with all those who work for peace.
AMEN.

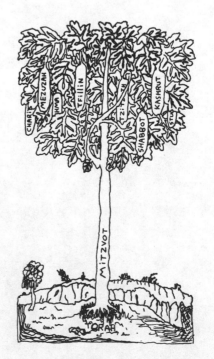

THE THIRD JEWISH CATALOG

Creating Community

COMPILED AND EDITED BY

Sharon Strassfeld · Michael Strassfeld

5740 / 1980 Philadelphia THE JEWISH PUBLICATION SOCIETY OF AMERICA
illustrations STUART COPANS
design ADRIANNE ONDERDONK DUDDEN

Before the word

Before you, friends and readers, lies the end product of a process that began over seven years ago with the publication of *The Jewish Catalog: A Do-It-Yourself Kit* (1973). *The First Jewish Catalog*, as it came to be known, attempted to make accessible to Jews with a variety of backgrounds the richness of Jewish tradition, ritual, and custom. It reflected the attitude of a growing number of Jews who at the time were seeking to rediscover Judaism's meaning and significance in their lives and who, for that matter, are still engaged in the quest. The *Catalog*'s approach was marked by a spirit of eclecticism and joy and yet by a seriousness of purpose. *The Second Jewish Catalog: Sources and Resources* (1976) continued this approach, advancing the discussion of Jewish practices and concepts, seeking always to make them part of modern Jewish life. Thus it treated such new topics as birth, bar/bat mitzvah, prayer, education, and sex.

As we began to work on the third—and final!—volume of the *Catalog*, we were faced with the question of its organizing principle. What have we left out? What now to include? We recalled the observation made by the director of the local federation of Jewish philanthropies of a major city, after reading *The First Jewish Catalog.* He remarked that he liked the book very much, except that there seemed to him to be no underlying feeling for or conception of klal Yisrael—the people Israel. We were puzzled by his comments, but dismissed them as nit-picking. They seemed to echo an often-voiced criticism of the havurot: that they are self-centered, thus selfish, and unconcerned about the larger Jewish community.

Much later, we returned to that conversation, reconsidering our critic's comments. Was the charge true or not? We spoke with friends, associates, and comrades to garner their thinking. That the criticism is fairly representative of many people who know little about havurot became clear. That the criticism is both fair and unfair also became clear.

Certainly, havurot, the *Catalogs*, and the whole "alternative" Jewish movement are all inner-directed and place a high value on satisfying the personal needs of their participants. Partly in reaction to much of the rest of American Jewry, which is wholly outer-directed, the havurot stand in opposition to the participation of people whose Judaism consists solely of supporting Israel, saving Soviet Jewry, or helping others to be Jewish—either physically or spiritually—but who do not spend time being Jewish themselves.

On the other hand, most members of havurot, in some way or another, support the larger Jewish community—either with their bodies or their minds. Tzedakah collectives, which are described more fully in this *Catalog*, are a havurah response to the need to give money. Moreover, some members are actively planning to make aliyah. In addition, whether by marching for Soviet Jewry, teaching in Hebrew schools, or supporting local federations, havurah members reach out beyond their own needs and their own communities to make contact with the rest of the Jewish world.

What we finally realized was that the federation director had been wrong. It became apparent that what sometimes seems clear is really more subtle than it appears; that the criticism had been misdirected because havurot, as well as the *Catalogs*, solidly subscribe to the notion of kol Yisrael areivim zeh bazeh—all Jews feel responsible toward one another. It became important to us to make this statement, not just for the federation director or for some of our readers, but for our own acknowledgment as well, since we continue to struggle with the tension between outer- and inner-directed.

If we had organized the three *Catalogs* from the beginning—that is, if we had realized that there would be three and what their subjects would cover— we would have made different divisions. But we didn't know at the outset, and for that reason there is material in the present volume that would better have been included in *Catalogs 1* and *2*, and material in *Catalog 1* that should have appeared in *Catalog 3*. Still, one could divide all three *Catalogs* in accord with the rabbinic statement: "On three pillars does the world stand, on Torah, on prayer, and on deeds of lovingkindness." *The Third Jewish Catalog*, then, subtitled "Creating Community," grapples with the question of gemilut hasadim—the people Israel and its responsibility to itself and the world. Thus, there is less ritual and more "issues," less "how-to" and more pointers and signposts indicating the Jewish way for ethical living. These are the issues that this *Catalog* treats, in the hope that it will bring us all closer to our goal of tikkun olam—the reordering and repairing of the world.

Sharon and Michael Strassfeld

Contents

"editors" refers to Sharon and Michael Strassfeld

EXILE

SURROUNDINGS

ISRAEL

Contributors

Zalman Alpert is a doctoral candidate in Jewish history at New York University and a librarian at Stern College.

Ronald L. Androphy received his B.A. from Brandeis University and his ordination from the Jewish Theological Seminary. He is rabbi of Congregation Shomray Hadath in Elmira, N.Y.

Albert S. Axelrad is the chaplain, Hillel rabbi, and director of the Bnai Brith Hillel Foundation at Brandeis University. He has been especially active in the causes of fair housing, civil rights, abolition of capital punishment, abortion, and Arab-Jewish cooperation and reconciliation.

Hillel Besdin, a graduate of the Jewish Theological Seminary, now practices as a dentist.

Aviva Cantor is a founding editor of *Lilith*, the Jewish feminist magazine, and lives in New York with her husband and two cats.

Mitchell Cohen is a doctoral candidate at Columbia University. He is editor of *The Jewish Frontier*, the Labor Zionist journal, and his articles and reviews have appeared in *Midstream, Present Tense, New Outlook*, and *Response*. He is currently preceptor in the political science department at Columbia University.

Steven M. Cohen teaches sociology at Queens College and is the publisher of *Response* magazine.

Jonathan Chipman is a freelance writer living in Israel.

Lynn Andrew Ellenson is a financial analyst with the CBS television network. She lives in Los Angeles with her husband, David, and their two children, Ruth and Micah.

Everett Gendler is the rabbi of Temple Emanuel of Merrimack Valley in Lowell, Mass. He is also an organic gardener who grows most of his own food when he is not moonwatching.

Mary Gendler is a family counselor, organic gardener, photographer, wife, and mother. She has written on the role of women in Judaism.

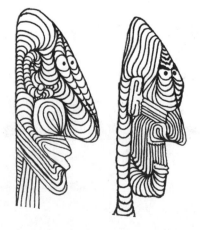

Arthur Green teaches Jewish mysticism and theology in the Department of Religious Studies at the University of Pennsylvania. His book, *Tormented Master: a Life of Rabbi Nahman of Bratslav*, was published in paperback by Schocken Books. He has long been associated with the havurah movement, and was instrumental in the founding of Havurat Shalom in Boston.

Sharon Freiberg Hammerman was born in Greensboro, N.C., and is on the faculty of Ocean County College in New Jersey. She lives in Toms River, N.J., with her husband and their two children, Eytan and Leah.

Barry Holtz was a founding member of Havurat Shalom Community. He is currently chairman of publications at the Melton Research Center for Jewish Education of the Jewish Theological Seminary. He is coeditor of *Your Word Is Fire: the Hasidic Masters on Contemplative Prayer*.

Richard J. Israel is the director of the Bnai Brith Hillel Foundation of Greater Boston. He is a beekeeper and a Boston Marathon runner.

Chava Allon Katz is a graduate student living in Israel.

Marshall Kupchan serves as director of education at Adath Israel Congregation in Washington, D.C., and tries to go camping every summer.

Arthur Kurzweil, the author of *From Generation to Generation: How to Trace Your Jewish Genealogy and Personal History*, is a writer and lecturer.

Lawrence Kushner is the rabbi and storyteller at Congregation Beth El of the Sudbury River Valley, Sudbury, Mass. He has written *The Book of Letters: A Mystical Alef-Bait* and *Honey from the Rock*, both published by Harper & Row. He and his wife, Karen, have three children.

Allan Lehmann graduated from Reconstructionist Rabbinical College and is now the rabbi of Congregation Bnai Israel of Gainesville, Florida. He has been a member of havurot in Boston, New York, Philadelphia, and Jerusalem.

Richard N. Levy is executive director of the Los Angeles Hillel Council. He helped found the Westwood Free Minyan and Bet Tzedek Legal Services, and was on the editorial board of the *Guide to Jewish Los Angeles*.

Sheldon Lewis is the rabbi of Congregation Kol Emeth in Palo Alto. He was an army chaplain during the Vietnam war and is married with three sons.

Avram B. Lyon is the associate dean for continuing education at Pratt Institute. He was formerly the executive director of the Jewish Association for College Youth and the North American Jewish Students Appeal.

Marlen Mertz is a graduate of Brandeis University's program in Jewish Communal Service and is presently the assistant director of the Jewish Federation of Long Beach, Cal. She is an enthusiastic camper who has celebrated Shabbat in many remote wilderness areas.

David Neal Miller is on the faculty of Queens College, CUNY, where he teaches Yiddish language and literature. He has published widely on Sholem-Aleykhem, Y. L. Perets, and Isaac Bashevis Singer.

Alan Mintz is a university teacher of Hebrew literature. He was the founding editor of *Response* magazine and edited *The New Jews*. He is the author of *George Eliot and the Novel of Vocation*.

Jonathan Porath has visited the USSR on eight occasions and is the author of *Jews in Russia: The Last Four Centuries*. He is currently rabbi of Temple Beth Or in Clark, N.J.

Yehiel E. Poupko is executive director of Bnai Brith Hillel Foundation–College Age Youth Services for the state of Illinois.

Shirley Bard Rapoport is a former folk-dance instructor, recreational supervisor, and journalist. Currently a member of a Renaissance recorder group, she also enjoys the needle arts and weaving.

Glenn Richter is the National Coordinator of the Student Struggle for Soviet Jewry.

Barry Rosen is a physician who specializes in family medicine. He took a year off recently to study Talmud and work in a community health center.

Gary and Sheila Rubin's most significant accomplishment to date is Ari, born May 15, 1978. They helped found Project Ezra, for which Sheila is secretary-treasurer and past president. Gary works at the American Jewish Committee's Institute on Pluralism and Group Identity.

Zalman Schachter Shalomi heads Bnai Or in Philadelphia and is a professor of Jewish mysticism and the psychology of religion at Temple University. He has spearheaded the trend to do-it-yourself Yiddishkeit and has been called the "zayde of the *Jewish Catalog*."

Daniel Siegel is a poet, author, and lecturer whose most recent volumes are *Between Dust and Dance* and *Nine Entered Paradise Alive*.

Hank Skirball works for the Reform movement in Israel.

David Slotkoff is employed as a social worker in Flatbush, Brooklyn, and is compiling, editing, and designing a booklet about the neighborhood.

Bernard Steinberg is a freelance writer living in Israel.

Lucy Y. Steinitz is completing her doctorate in gerontology at the School of Social Service Administration of the University of Chicago, where she also teaches social research to social-work students.

Joseph B. Stern teaches Bible and Talmud at Hebrew College, Brookline, Mass., and is concerned with the study of Jewish law and its application to political and social issues of our time. He and his wife live with their two sons in Newton, Mass.

Meyer J. Strassfeld is the rabbi of Temple Sinai in Marblehead, Mass. He is the past president of the Massachusetts Board of Rabbis and the Marblehead Ministerial Association. He is Jewish chaplain at Boston City Hospital and University Hospital.

Trude Weiss-Rosmarin is the editor of *The Jewish Spectator* and the author of *Judaism and Christianity: the Differences* and other books.

Linda Weltner is a writer whose essays have appeared in the *New York Times* and the *Boston Globe*. She is an antinuclear activist who lives in Marblehead, Mass.

Arnold Jacob Wolf is director of the Bnai Brith Hillel Foundation and Jewish chaplain at Yale University. He is a teaching fellow of Pierson College, Yale, as well as a writer and a provocative thinker.

Jonathan Wolf, who is famous for his practice of the mitzvah of hakhnasat orkhim—making guests welcome—teaches Jewish thought and practice at Lincoln Square Synagogue and other shuls and campuses. He helped found the Jewish Vegetarians of America and directed social-policy work at the Synagogue Council of America.

JUSTICE

JUSTICE/CHARITY SHALL YOU PURSUE

Deuteronomy 16:20 צדק צדק תרדף

Tzedakah

Traditions

It is a positive mitzvah to give tzedakah to poor Jews. If possible, one is obliged to meet each poor person's needs. . . . Anyone who sees a poor person begging and avoids him and does not give him tzedakah has violated a prohibition (Rambam, Mishneh Torah, Hilkhot Matenot Aniyim 7:1–2).

THE IMPORTANCE OF LANGUAGE

What's Jewish about this quotation? Of course Hebrew terms are used and the phrasing is halakhic, but what is peculiarly Jewish about saying that it is a good thing to provide for the needs of the poor? Let's start by examining the Hebrew terms and legal phraseology; for what might appear to be external and superficial—names and style—might really show themselves to be deeply significant.

Leaving the words mitzvah and tzedakah untranslated in the quotation above (and thereby risking not being understood by some readers) is not an attempt to be obscure; neither were they entirely a matter of preference for Jewish language. Compare the following two sentences: "One ought to give to the poor," and "It is a mitzvah to do tzedakah." The first might be said to be the equivalent of the second, but Jewishly there is a world of meaning missing from it.

A mitzvah is a religious imperative, an obligation that involves much more than virtue or altruism. Mitzvot pervade the entire range of Jewish life— from honoring one's parents to eating matzah, from not stealing to not doing work on Shabbat. Some mitzvot seem to be a matter of simple sekhel—the pure common sense of living. These, such as the command to visit the sick or the prohibition against murdering, are things that we would certainly follow anyway. But for the person who regards the framework of halakhah seriously in making life-style decisions, they attain a larger importance as mitzvot, as substantive demands for holiness in every part of life.

Tzedakah is usually and incorrectly translated as charity. Both words, tzedakah and charity, denote giving alms to the needy. But their connotations are so different that the English term is not helpful in our understanding of the ways of tzedakah. Charity is one of the words that, through centuries of Christian theological use, makes the English language an inept vehicle for expressing Jewish ideas. Charity, from the Latin *caritas,* refers to the love of God for creation or to the love of one person for others. Charity, then, as normally used, refers to the tangible expression of that love. This principle of free, unrestricted love finds its closest Jewish parallel in the word rahamim— usually translated as "mercy," an English equivalent with its own problems. Rahamim is part of the fundamental polarity of din—strict judgment—and rahamim—pure mercy—which forms the universal balance by which the world endures.

Tzedakah is not the same as rahamim; it is *not* charity. Gratuitous actions of loving-kindness are certainly positively valued in the Jewish tradition, but they are not what tzedakah is all about. The word tzedakah comes from a root meaning to be just and ethical. Tzedakah then, in a general sense, means behavior that is just. This is not an expression of one's free will, as is charity. Instead, tzedakah is the fulfillment of one's obligation.

Specifically, tzedakah has come to mean the obligation to see to the needs of fellow human beings who are unable to meet their own needs. One could easily object and ask: If the basic conceptual difference between tzedakah and charity is that charity is freely given and tzedakah is obligatory, then wouldn't charity be the higher, more virtuous form? Indeed, this claim is a considerable one and not to be taken lightly. But such are the questions that make up part of the most basic divisions between Christian and Jewish life and thought.

We can begin to answer the question by considering the process of tzedakah. Obviously, the most important aspect of almsgiving, be it charity or tzedakah, is its result. What is accomplished? Concepts by themselves don't save people's lives; they have to lead to action. What's important here is that if people need things in order to live, they must receive them. They should not be dependent upon the hope that there will be some virtuous people somewhere who will express their love for humanity. The poor should be supported because as human beings they have the right to a decent life, and those with the wherewithal have the obligation to provide them with their needs. There is nothing wrong with altruistically doing more for others than one is obliged to do. That is, in fact, more virtuous than yotzeh—which is the fulfillment of one's obligation but the refusal to do one bit more. But what we are speaking of is supporting and maintaining human beings who need help. Jewish law and tradition see this as essential. Such activity is not an example of lovingly (charity) doing more than what is demanded; this is tzedakah: rightness, justness, and therefore obligatory behavior, doing precisely that which is demanded.

HOW TZEDAKAH WORKS

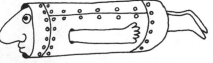

Let's examine the basic laws and norms that define what tzedakah traditionally is. As we saw in the quotation from Rambam, it's a mitzvah to give tzedakah and a prohibition not to; but what, how much, to whom, how, when, etc. do you give?

The rule of thumb is to supply each poor person with what s/he lacks: food, clothing, household necessities, or whatever. But this rule leaves a host of new questions in its wake. What is a legitimate lack? I don't happen to own a helicopter at present—does that mean that I "lack" one and that you are commanded to supply me with one? You need $200 right now to cover the rent, buy a winter coat for your kid, and handle immediate day-to-day grocery

Hillel the Elder brought a riding horse for a poor man who had formerly been wealthy, as well as a servant to run before him. Once when he could find no servant, Hillel himself ran before the man for three miles (Ketubbot 67b).

A poor man came before Rabbi Nehemiah. The rabbi asked, "What do you usually eat?" "Fatted meat and old wine," he replied. "Would you be willing to live on lentils with me?" He shared the rabbi's diet and soon died. Someone said, "Pity that man, for Rabbi Nehemiah killed him." On the contrary, one should rather pity Rabbi Nehemiah, for there was no need for that man to have spoiled himself so much (Ketubbot 67b).

expenses—I have $200 and more, but that's still a lot of money for me. Am I obligated to give that much to you? There are a lot of poor people in the community, in the country, in the world; how are priorities set?

Different people have different needs. This is true not only in a physical sense, where some need to be fed more calories than others, but also in a social sense. People are accustomed to various standards of living, and when they lose their means of livelihood, it takes different kinds and amounts of maintenance to support them in ways that give them self-respect. Tradition provides that, ideally, each person should be "provided for in the manner to which he has become accustomed." There are stories in the Talmud where this is taken to the extreme.

As we have seen, the specific needs of each person must be taken into account. But the extent of the obligation is limited: "You are commanded to support him, but you are not commanded to make him wealthy" (Rambam, Ketubbot 7:4).

Just because there are some people who can provide for the entire needs of a poor person—or for that matter, of many people—that does not mean that they are the only ones who are able to participate in the mitzvah of tzedakah. One is commanded to support the poor "as far as the hand reaches," i.e., according to one's own means. A contribution of one-tenth of one's income and property is considered to be an average amount, a fifth is mitzvah min hamuvhar—a choice mitzvah—and giving less than a tenth is considered miserly. You should not give more than one-fifth of your income lest you risk becoming poor yourself and thus become an unnecessary burden upon the community.

Even though tzedakah of less than 10 percent is considered meager, it still technically fulfills the requirements for the mitzvah, which specify a minimum annual contribution of a third of a shekel, or about one-third of a dollar. This amount ought to present no obstacle even to the very poor to do the mitzvah, for the poor themselves are not exempt from giving tzedakah. In fact, even those who are supported through tzedakah must give what they can, for it requires more than money to do the mitzvah.

In addition to the amount given and the attitude of the donor, there are several other criteria for determining the value of a particular act of tzedakah. In his "Laws of Gifts to the Poor" the Rambam presents the following scale:

There are eight degrees of tzedakah, one higher than the other. The highest degree of all is where one strengthens the hands of an Israelite who faces poverty, giving him a gift or a loan or entering into a business partnership with him, or giving him a job in

order to strengthen his hand and so prevent him from becoming an object of tzedakah. It is with regard to this that Scripture says: "Then thou shalt strengthen him: Yea, though he be a stranger or a sojourner; that he may live with thee" (Lev. 25:35) The meaning is, strengthen him before he falls and needs to be supported by others.

A lesser degree is when one gives tzedakah to the poor, but neither the giver nor the receiver knows of the other. For in this case the duty of giving tzedakah for its own sake has been carried out. In the Temple, for example, there was a secret chamber into which good men would secretly place money and from which the poor would take secretly. Not very different from this is where a man gives money to the tzedakah kupah (fund). But a man should only give money to a tzedakah kupah if he knows that the directors are trustworthy, wise, and reliable like Rabbi Hananya ben Teradyon.

A lesser degree is where the giver knows to whom he has given but the poor man does not know to whom he is indebted. The famous sages, for example, would go in secret to throw some money into the houses of the poor. This is the desirable way of giving tzedakah when the directors of the kupah are unreliable.

Less than this is where the poor man knows to whom he is indebted but the giver does not know to whom he had given. Some of the famous sages would wrap up their contributions to tzedakah in a scarf slung over their shoulder so that the poor could come and take it without suffering embarrassment.

Less than this is when the giver gives money directly to the poor man but without having to be asked for it.

Less than this is when he gives after the poor man has asked him to do so.

Less than this is when he gives the poor man less than he should but with a cheerful countenance.

Less than this is when the giver is glum (Rambam, Hilkhot Matenot Aniyim 10:7–14).

Here the Rambam deals with many of the important issues of tzedakah. He keeps in mind the purpose of tzedakah. His highest level is the kind of giving that eliminates the need for tzedakah. He is concerned with the proper allocation of funds and agrees to the value of communal philanthropic organization only when it is clear that those in charge are scrupulously honest. The cheerfulness of the giver as well as the proper amount of the donation figure in his scheme, but his most pressing concern is to alleviate the inevitable embarrassment that occurs when one is forced to become dependent upon the contributions of others. He recommends the "anonymous donation," but even goes further, suggesting a "double-blind" situation in which neither the donor nor the recipient knows the identity of the other.

SETTING TZEDAKAH PRIORITIES

The questions of how and how much to give are complex, requiring delicacy and sensitivity. Far more complicated and potentially heartbreaking, however, is the problem of to whom to give money. No one, no matter how wealthy and benevolent, can single-handedly give to everyone who needs. What criteria can you use to decide how to allot your tzedakah money?

First of all you start with yourself. You have a responsibility to yourself and to your community to see that your needs and those of your spouse and minor children are provided for. Then you look to the people nearest you. If your parents are needy, providing for them takes precedence over providing for all others (see Honoring Parents in *Catalog 2*, p. 84). Then come your grown children, then your siblings, and then the rest of your relatives. Of course this only applies to poor relatives. Giving gifts to materially comfortable relatives may be a fine way to cement family ties, but it is no substitute for tzedakah to the poor. Tzedakah continues in concentric circles moving away from yourself: after your relatives come those who live near you and then the poor of your town in general. "The inhabitants of your town take precedence over the inhabitants of any other town" (Sifrei Devarim 116).

One must give tzedakah cheerfully, with joy and a good heart, commiserating with the poor person about his troubles and saying words of consolation to him (Shulhan Arukh, Yoreh Deah, 349:3).

Shammai says . . . receive everyone cheerfully (Avot 1:15). How? This teaches that if a man gives his comrade all the good gifts in the world but with a downcast face, Scripture accords it as if he gave nothing. However, if he receives his companion cheerfully, even if he gives him nothing, Scripture accords it as if he gave him all the good gifts in the world (Avot de Rabbi Natan, 13).

Catalog 1 refers to *The First Jewish Catalog* (Philadelphia: Jewish Publication Society, 1973). *Catalog 2* is *The Second Jewish Catalog*, published in 1976.

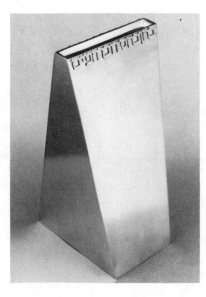

The only real requirement for a pushke is that its contents be reserved for tzedakah—i.e., the money must not also be used for a petty cash fund. Money pledged to tzedakah is special, and it should be treated that way. That doesn't mean that a pushke has to be a big deal—an empty jar is fine. But since the pushke is an object connected with a mitzvah, many people like to have something special to use. This is called hiddur mitzvah—the beautification of the mitzvah—which is the impetus for having beautifully made ritual objects. Use your imagination and make your own!

There is one important additional item that must be mentioned here. The same paragraph of the Sifrei provides that "the poor of the Land of Israel take precedence over the poor of other lands." At first this pronouncement appears ambiguous. Does this mean that residents of Eretz Yisrael take absolute precedence over any indigent of the rest of the world, presumably even including poor relatives and neighbors? Or is this clause rather meant to fit somewhere else within the system, and if so, where?

Not surprisingly, as is frequently the case when we have problems understanding the details of a traditional text, there is a commentary in one of the classical codes that discusses and resolves the question. In the Bayit Hadash, the seventeenth-century commentary to the fourteenth-century code of Jewish law, the Arbaah Turim, R. Joel Sirkes clarifies the question by saying that after the poor of one's own city come the poor of other places; and of all those other places, the poor of the Land of Israel have priority (Bayit Hadash to Tur Yoreh Deah 250).

So we see that when it comes to Israel the question of priorities for tzedakah is not a new one. Eretz Yisrael has always played such an important role in Jewish spiritual life that it could never be considered merely some other place (see the section on Israel). Jews, always understanding the mitzvah of tzedakah as an imperative to express tangible care for other Jews, have appropriately felt special concern for Jews living in the place in the world that can be called most Jewish. The question that Rabbi Sirkes considered did not originate with him, nor has it decreased in importance since his time; that is, the tension that Jews in the Diaspora have always felt between their responsibilities to the needs of their own communities and the needs of the Jews residing in the Land of Israel has not diminished. At one extreme is the statement that "the poor of the Land of Israel take precedence over the poor of other lands." At the other pole comes the interpretation of the Bayit Hadash, which, in effect, says that the poor of one's own community take precedence even over the poor of Israel. Neither extreme should be allowed to eradicate the other entirely. Rather, we should understand the situation as a dynamic tension within which we must make continuing judgments about how we can best fulfill the mitzvah of tzedakah.

HOW AND WHEN TO GIVE

How and when do you give tzedakah? Traditionally two methods stand out: the pushke (or for our Galitzianer friends, the pishke) and giving directly to beggars. A pushke is simply a coin box reserved for the purpose of tzedakah giving. They are frequently made for and distributed by particular tzedakah causes. The most common one is the familiar blue box of Keren Kayemet Le-Yisrael, the Jewish National Fund, of Plant-a-Tree-in-Israel fame. In addition, every yeshivah usually distributes its own pushke. Synagogues frequently have really nice brass pushkes that make a fine clink when you drop in a coin, pushkes which the shammash—sexton—shakes at each weekday service to remind people that "it is good to give a coin to the poor before each service" (Shulham Arukh, Yoreh Deah 249:14). These pushkes are sometimes elaborately decorated, and many of them are beautiful in a simple way.

Pushkes are for small regular giving. It's a good idea to associate tzedakah-giving with frequent regular periods, as well as special occasions. On Friday evening before Shabbat candlelighting (and before holidays too) it's traditional to put money in a pushke. Jews like to compound mitzvot, so whether it be at prayer or before Shabbat or before studying Torah, giving tzedakah heightens the consciousness that the act is a mitzvah.

Beggars are a very different story. For most of us, the picturesque shnorrer of Sholem Aleikhem stories exists—only in Sholem Aleikhem stories. We usually refer to people who ask for money on the street as panhandlers. Our society regards them as low-life types who are nuisances at best, and drunks, addicts, or muggers at worst. They are a far cry from my favorite toothless beggar in Jerusalem who gums his way through a mi-she-berakh ("May you be blessed") for you when you drop a coin in his cup.

So it's usually a surprise for us to hear that, according to Jewish law, beggars should not be refused. Even when one honestly has nothing to spare at the moment, the person who asks should be neither ignored nor abused, but rather consoled and related to with the dignity befitting a fellow human being.

But aren't they all a bunch of drunks anyway? Isn't their request of money for a cup of coffee really a petition for a shot of liquor? This may be true, of course, and I admit that my personal attitude when confronted by panhandlers is rather ambivalent. But let me cite the Jewish law that states that one who asks for tzedakah in order to eat is to be immediately given something, without first checking to find out if he is a charlatan (Shulhan Arukh, Yoreh Deah 51:10).

Special occasions are good times to set money aside for tzedakah. Special times mean significant ones, whether they are happy or sad. Thinking about those in the world who need your help and acting on those thoughts adds an extra dimension to the uniqueness of the time. There's no need to list the possibilities—births, anniversaries, or lehavdil (to keep the two far apart) deaths and yahrtzeits.

There's one occasion for which there's a special traditional way of giving tzedakah. When someone you know is going on a trip, give him or her some money to be given to tzedakah upon arrival (see "The Tale of the Shaliah/ Messenger"). That person becomes your shaliah mitzvah—mitzvah messenger. This custom developed when travel was particularly dangerous. It was thought that if the traveler was on a special errand to perform a mitzvah, then the chances for a safe trip would be vastly improved. Even if this isn't taken seriously, the custom transforms the voyage itself into the stuff of mitzvah. Seymour "Epi" Epstein of "Be Happy It's Adar" fame (*Catalog 1*, p. 136) has been known to carry a few Israeli pounds (now shekels) in his wallet so that whenever he runs into someone about to go to Israel, he is able to turn the person into a shaliah.

Remember, the traveler becomes *your* agent; give him/her instructions accordingly, if you wish, specifying what should be done with the money.

ORGANIZING

Until now we have been dealing almost entirely with the individual and his/her responsibilities. Tzedakah is, however, by its very nature a societal concern. Jews have everywhere and always organized themselves for philanthropic purposes. The Rambam wrote that he had never seen or heard of a Jewish community that had no kupah, no fund for the poor (Rambam, Hilkhot Matnot Aniyim 9:3). Individual one-to-one acts of tzedakah must not be disparaged by any means. In terms of quantity and organization, however, a community can achieve significant things far beyond the power of any single individual. Ideally, the community as tzedakah agency can facilitate higher and higher qualitative levels of tzedakah. An organized community can help people to self-sufficiency, the highest level of tzedakah. Furthermore, through the kupah, giver and receiver are unaware of each other's identity, thus preserving the anonymity that the Rambam rated so highly.

Such a system, like any social system, is to be guarded carefully to keep it far from corruption and abuse. For all the Rambam's extolling of the kupah, it must be remembered that he was careful to caution that one "should only give money to a tzedakah kupah if he knows that the directors are trustworthy, wise, and reliable." As with dealing with any system capable of both great benefit and great misuse of power, concerned people must find their way through the possibilities of "working within the system," acting as an individual and developing alternative institutions that attempt to better reflect the values and concerns of the community that develops them (see "Tzedakah Collectives").

Our role in attempting to respond to the mitzvah of tzedakah is that of striving to do tikkun olam—to help to perfect the world. In so doing we are in a sense sharing God's work. We become partners with God in the creation of the world. In Birkhat ha-Mazon—Grace after Meals—there is a line that gave me a good deal of trouble some years ago. "Hu noten lehem lekhol basar—God gives bread to all flesh." How, I would ask, could we have a line in our liturgy that is so blatantly untrue? My teacher answered that there really is sufficient nourishment in the world to feed everyone. The failing is not God's, but that of humanity which has never learned to distribute the wealth that it receives. I'm no longer sure that the answer is totally satisfactory, but the perspective on tzedakah that it provides is important. In this way we are able to make seriously our role of having been created betzelem Elohim—in God's image.

Here's a form that contains some suggestions for giving tzedakah as an individual, as a family unit, or as a communal collective. For other ideas, see the section on Israel.

NAME:_____ ADDRESS:_____ AGE:_____
OCCUPATION:_____ HOME PHONE:_____ BUSINESS PHONE:_____
WHAT EVENINGS ARE YOU GENERALLY FREE FOR MEETINGS: M T W Th Sun. Aft. Sun. Eve.

Please indicate the causes below which you would want to support, and estimate the *percentage* of your contribution which you would like to see given to each. (This is just a partial list to get organizing started; we've grouped them for convenient consideration.)

Humanitarian Projects

____ World hunger relief organizations (UNICEF, Oxfam, etc.)
____ Medical research (cancer, etc.)
____ Media (NET, WBAI, etc.)
____ Other:

Political Projects

____ Environment (Sierra Club, etc.)
____ Legal aid (ACLU, NAACP, et al.)
____ United Farm Workers
____ Women's movement (NOW, etc.)
____ Consumer groups (Nader, Common Cause)
____ American Indian organizations
____ Other:

Establishment Jewish Organizations

____ United Jewish Appeal—l Federations
____ Nat'l Conf. on Soviet Jewry
____ Defense orgs. (ADL, AJComm, etc.)
____ UJA Israel Emergency Fund
____ Hillel Foundations
____ Jewish Higher Ed. (Brandeis U., Jewish Theol. Sem., Yeshiva U., etc.)
____ Jewish Agency for College Youth
____ Other:

Alternative Jewish Organizations

____ Jewish Student Appeal as a whole, or particular groups supported by JSA:
____ N. Am. Jewish Students Network
____ *Response* magazine
____ Jewish Stud. Press Service
____ Yugntruf
____ Yavneh
____ Stud. Struggle for Soviet Jewry
____ Project Ezra
____ Ad Hoc Jewish Comm. on Hunger
____ *Lilith* magazine
____ Natl. Havurah Coordinating Committee
____ Council for the Jewish Poor
____ Individual schools or yeshivot
____ Others:

Special Projects in Israel

____ Independent social welfare projects (e.g., aid to Sephardic communities)
____ Political alternatives in Israel (Shinui, Yozma, Moked, etc.)
____ Schools and orphanages
____ Pardes
____ Mosad Heschel
____ Magen David Adom
____ Other:

maybe we should tell him to use paper money.

The sages would sometimes tie money in a cloth bag, then throw it behind their backs for poor men to pick up, so that the poor should not feel shame.
— Maimonides

The tale of the shaliah/messenger: irises and gym shoes

WHERE, WHY, AND HOW THE REVELATION BELTED ME

Last fall friends and acquaintances in Boston began gathering for Israel. Crisis, again, as usual, was hanging in the air. It seemed apparent that millions of new pages would be written in papers and analyses about whatever chunk of history was going to come crashing down on the Holy Land any day. For myself, the urge began to chomp away at me, the psalm-craving to go back to Eretz Yisrael, though I had just finished a year in Jerusalem that previous August. I would go, I decided, stam—just because I wanted to go (or had to, or should, or whatever). To me this was kosher Jewish thinking—the more reasons given for the trip, the less chance of gathering the aromas and sounds and stirrings of holiness waiting to be ingested in the Holy Land.

Daniel (Danny) Siegel recalls his experience as a tzedakah-agent in Israel. Fellow-travelers, take note, go forth—and do likewise.

My tenth trip. You know how you feel when people tell you, "Oh, I've been there eighteen times. Just last year I was over for Sukkot, Purim, and the summer. Ho, hmmm, hum." It is the "repetition syndrome" which teachers, assembly-line workers, and secretaries suffer from (to say nothing of occasional neurosurgeons, professional fund raisers, and other assorted busy individuals). What I would do while in Israel was unclear to me, though a month in Jerusalem, no matter how unplanned, could be awesome, enjoyable, or at least fun.

As was my custom, I visited my well-wishers, telling them to "Give me a buck for tzedakah." I would give it out as the occasion presented itself *somewhere* in Israel. Apparently some friends adjusted their palms to the cost-of-living index, as fives and tens and twenties began inundating my pushke. I usually consider ten dollars a nice sum to take with me, but by the time this occurred to me for trip number 10, I was rated by Dun & Bradstreet at well over $150. So I decided to steamroll a little, making the rounds of aunts, cousins, parents, in-laws, friends, and passersby, saying, "I'd really like a thousand dollars."

I left the U.S. with more than $900, and more arrived while I was there, so I reached $955, or 5,730 Israeli pounds. Which is harbeh lehem—a lotta tzedakah-bread.

Except for three people who specified where I should give their money, I was on my own, a shaliah—messenger—to the Holy Land.

I assured all that I would stretch every bill and coin. I would sanctify their money by giving exclusively to those who were reliable, hated bureaucracy, and could use it as directly as possible to bring some assistance, joy, and the sense of Ma Rabbu Ma'asekha—How great are Your Creations, O Lord— to the recipients.

No one I asked felt that she/he was being "hit." Each considered it a privilege to take part in the mitzvah with me. No receipts, no questions of income tax deductions, no hesitations like "Well, I already hit my 10 (or 20) percent for the year."

A family of eight in Oklahoma spent the better part of a late evening working out how much they could send me.

Some never let me finish my description of "The Plan." My wallet "swole up as the mighty waters" before I could say, "I'll send you a report."

Oh, there might have been one or two who play-grumbled. But I assured them (taking the last seven dollars from their hand) that even the most grumbly giver with the most obnoxious intent is moving heaven and earth. And I threw in a quote and some trumped-up page number from the Talmud to bolster my argument.

Reviewing my preparations, I see now that the friends and relatives and strangers created a mitzvah hevra—fellowship—that would go wherever I would go, speak with me, and give me some insight into the work at hand.

So it was me, Dan Quixote, the thirty-five or so of them, and a few others against the Montefiore windmills. The "few others" included my rabbi, my forebears, and some Russian Jews.

My rabbi: When he was in love and had found the woman with whom he chose to live his life, my rabbi gave a thousand dollars to Israel in place of buying his fiancée an engagement ring. I think he said it was in the late 1940s. (I was, fifteen years ago, his favorite, his hope, his most intimate prayer to God.) I remember that: his ring of love was a gift to Israel.

My forebears: Sometime in the last century, Usher Zelig Siegel took to wife a certain Sarah Golda, whose family name is forgotten. They begot a multitude of children, among them Zeev David, called Velvel, my zaydeh. I pilgrimaged to Keansburgh, New Jersey, to supplement the old pictures and conversations with my father and aunts and cousins. His dry-goods store is now a gun and ammunition shop, but the cop who grew up with my father said, "He would take a nickel on a pair of gloves, and let them pay the rest whenever they could. He was a kind man." I remember that.

His son, my abba, has carried on where Velvel left off. It is fit and proper to praise his generosity. Now that I am past the age of rebellion and crankiness toward my parents, we can sit and recall and work out insights into tzedakah, because he is my master in this domain of mentshlikhkeit. I am his child, and again and again, I return to childhood when I wonder how his vision and foresight have been acted out by me, whether I am worthy of him and his parents and grandparents, all the way back to Abraham. When I bring to mind my years of knowing him, a constant flow of tzedakah acts-and-intimations gushes forth.

Some Russian Jews: Crossing into Russia from Finland, the border guards took half, more than half, of our siddurim and calendars and mezuzot, and Magen Davids. They were entitled to them—they are Russians and we are Jews, sixty-four Jews with a pittance of thing-gifts for our friends in the Soviet Jewish community. Stripped to the bare heart. I remember that feeling of being scared: twenty Yiddish phrases and a few tchatchkes to give. Over there, you give someone a three-dollar prayer book and your thanks are in tears. Whoever gave me a three-dollar gift that moved me so much? *That* question has stuck in my kishkes.

These thoughts and questions are everyone's, I thought.

As the plane approached Lod I thought, Ki tireh arom vekhisito—When you see the naked, clothe them! Isaiah, I hear you. We hear you.

A note about being a shaliah
Being a shaliah is an ego-safeguard. Wherever you go and however you choose to distribute your funds, you are constantly aware of the fact that you are just the representative of those who sent you. When speaking to the recipients, you simply say, "It's from my friends."

WHAT HAPPENED TO THE GELT

It immediately became clear to me that there are two distinct psychologies of giving out tzedakah money: Big Gelt and Small Gelt. If you have $500,000 to distribute, you go to different places, talk to different people, and give out different proportions and quantities than if you have $955. You are constantly aware of the fact that $50 too much here means next week there may not be anything left to give, just when you are discovering that the next week's encounter is the one that needs $50 the most. As a result, I determined to watch carefully each grush and to proceed with a sharpened sense of spontaneity vs. overprudence.

Just as I had chosen to collect the money through straightforward, friendly means, so also I decided to search out the people and places of my mission through my friends, by word of mouth and suggestions from whomever I knew or got to know well enough to be touched by his grasp of what I was about.

I started with flowers at Life Line for the Old. Life Line (Yad LaKashish) was discovered by my mother about five years ago. During one of my previous visits, she, the mitzvah-searcher-outer par excellence, put her Jewish-motherly foot down and declared that I *must* go—in the tone of voice of "No questions, no wise remarks, kiddo!"

"Tell Mrs. Mendelow I sent you," she said.

Life Line is workshops for the elderly. It is food for invalid old people who are unable to get out. It is a choir and tree planting and a hevra of dignity. None of the pathetic foolishness of basket weaving is to be found in its precincts, and indeed the handiwork that they produce has won awards in various countries, not because a bunch of doddering old fools made them, but because they are joy-forever things of beauty. The American custom of stashing away

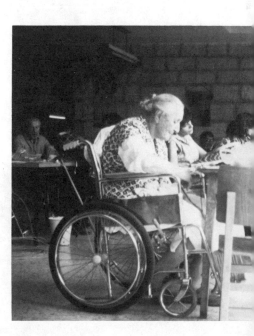

aging parents in (ugh) convalescent homes to let them die out of the way, stripped of their well-deserved majesty and treated like infants—all this is foreign to Mrs. Mendelow. He who would wish to learn what mentshlikhkeit is would do well to visit her and the young old people of Life Line. My Shabbat tablecloths are from their workshops, as are my sweaters and a few of my toys.

So me and my friend, see, we marches in with a flower for each one to take home for Shabbat.

Big man, you say! A flower! Tzaddik—righteous one! Ten lousy bucks and he thinks he's turned the world on its ear! One lousy rose or chrysanthemum or iris per person. Whoopie-do!

And to spite my cynic self, the next day (Friday; Thursday at Life Line . . . closed Friday) I did the same for my hevra at Hadassah. There is a certain woman on the staff of Life Line who for the last seven years has made the rounds of the soldiers at the hospital, bringing fruit and cigarettes and candy and other things for anyone there from the Israeli army. After being introduced to the people in the military office and obtaining a list of who was in what ward, the lady, my friend, and I, bundled in flowers, began to walk the corridors.

It couldn't hurt, could it, fellas? I know they're soldier boys, and tough, and Israelis, and this is sort of twinkie, but the lady said, "Don't worry. It's all right."

Big man—tzaddik, with a wad in his pocket, doing cheap-ticket-to-paradise mitzvahs. Flowers for everyone!

Until you talk to the boy (that's all he is, a boy) in the eye clinic with a bandage, and he tells you he writes, and you say, I write too. And he tells you he wrote a story about a soldier who was badly wounded, the only survivor in his tank, and his girlfriend comes to see him in the hospital. But he dies. And she never makes peace with it all. And cracks.

And then he says, "It's the other way around. My girlfriend died in a car crash, and I don't know what to do."

Big man!

And the mother, who is all war mothers, standing over her son (the one with the head wound, the paralyzed one), trying to feed him.

Here.

Here are some flowers for your son.

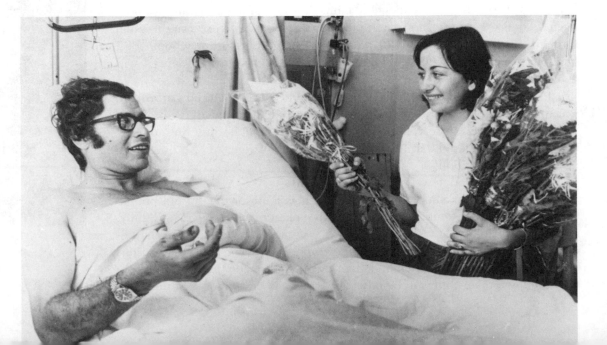

See, Shimon, she says, they brought you flowers (Who? Oh, just some friends from America). See, Shimon, say thank you.

Is there anything we can do?

Pray.

Tears.

Hers, I think.

Big man. A dime's worth of flowers!

I decided then not to do any more of these mitzvahs alone. I wanted others, preferably three or four others, standing with me, because I am not so sure I can stretch that far—even for the hevra.

By Sunday I had called my friends and flipped through the note cards of recommended tzaddikim, adding here and there a few names suggested by my people in Jerusalem. Spontaneously (I would try spontaneity again and see how far it would go) I picked Mrs. Eva Michaelis. It was a name my mother had given me, because she knew she was edel—refined, devoted, kindly, a decades-long crusader for the retarded. Her most recent project is Magen, making a home for older retarded people whose parents are too old and too ill to take care of their children. I began to like one-way conversations: "Speak to me, Mrs. Michaelis. Say anything." And she would take up her evangelical theme, displaying verbally her struggles with the government and Welfare Department to get the proper funds, then passing to some miracles, saving children from the Nazis at the outbreak of the war, meeting Eichmann (you mean Eichmann's henchmen? No, Eichmann), and stepping out to get me coffee and cookies.

"I cannot give to your building fund," I explained. "My hevra wants more direct, more immediate results, and they want the funds to be under your personal control." We gave her 250 pounds for anything she liked, like cab fare for Irene Gaster, seventy-seven, who is a little shaky on her legs. Nevertheless, she personally went to interview the forty candidates for Magen.

Ms. Gaster: founder of almost everything in Israel having to do with the retarded, denouncer of psychiatrists who are too quick to label, thereby condemning someone to retardation, anathema-hurler at agencies and institutions-gone-bad, Lover of Children Class-A with four Oak-Leaf Clusters. When a child who could not learn to feed himself was sent to her, more likely than not she would teach the child to feed himself. If the child was a bed-wetter at age ten (and therefore disturbed), she stopped the bed-wetting. More miracles, please, Gveret Gaster. Oh, here's another one, and another, and another (with absolute humility and a tinge of modest pride). "And I never took a penny from anyone. And this is all I own [hand sweeps the air in the apartment on Ramban Street]. And Miss Szold said I would never get anywhere—that was when I first arrived. And now we have this Magen (take some more tea) project."

I was doing well. In the course of less than one Jerusalem week I had discovered three of the thirty-six righteous people. If I could just find another two or three I would have fulfilled my mission. I had seen with my own eyes and the eyes of the hevra and all-the-time holy people, rubbed my hands in theirs, and felt warmth and hope and the mysterious glory of what it is to be a creature of God.

I also tzedakah-alchemized one hundred pounds into gasoline. Boris is my only friend in Jerusalem who has a car. I said, "Here's a hundred pounds for benzine—put yourself at Bracha Kapach's disposal till the gelt runs out." Rebbetzin Kapach (or, as the Sefardim would say, "Ha-Rabbanit") is the utmost Yemenite, the woman I was looking for but didn't know was true until I saw her and watched her walk around Jerusalem doing her acts of gentle loving-kindness. Four of the hevra had asked me to find someone to whom they could send clothes, so this was a priority. This rabbanit-rebbetzin gives clothes, Shabbat food, love, weddings, a jar of hot sauce and Yemenite bread, books, or whatever is needed all over Jerusalem and into the boondocks on the hillsides of Judea—the most extensive far-stretching private mitzvah-matchmaker I was to meet, coordinating the givers and the receivers with enthusiasm and uplift as I had never seen before. Mickey and I went Shabbat-flowering with her, into the homes of large-families-in-two-rooms that are around, if you look for them. On the way back to her house she saw some children she knew who should have been in school. Why not, she asked. No gym shoes, the two girls said. I don't know if they needed gym shoes for gym class or whether it was teenage fashionable to wear the casual style and therefore embarrassing to come to school in some other kind of shoe. Either way, the twenty-five newly arrived dollars were searing the seams of my pocket, and I understand that within a day, as if by magic, they were transformed into sneakers for the girls.

I didn't see, but I heard about a person she found who goes with an elderly blind lady to the hairdresser on Fridays, to fulfill the old woman's wish of being presentable to the Shabbat Queen.

Through another lead I entered the bowels of Israeli bureaucracy (just once, to see what it was like): the Welfare Department. The assistant director, Aharon Langermann, understood me and the hevra immediately and assured me that 350 pounds from the fund would be used individually, directly, and personally for anything that comes to him that will not be taken care of by the Red Tape Machine.

A widow needed a loan. OK. The money will be recycled when she has finished with it.

Sara Pearl, mother of the soldiers all over Galilee. I couldn't get to Safed, but I called and told her husband the hevra believes in her. The check is for whatever she wants.

Hadassah Levi's day-care center for young retarded people in Ramat Gan. Swings for them. Let me give her the title of The Most Loving Person in the World. Take my word for it.

Yaakov Maimon, inventor of Hebrew shorthand, recorder for the Knesset, who at the time was 72½ years old and dressed like out of a movie, rumpled hat, thick glasses; he shlepped me up and down and up and down steps visiting families (Iranian, Indian, Algerian, Moroccan) to whom he brought tutors in English for the children. For over twenty years before he died he did this, bringing truckloads from the university and other parts of town, dropping them off, picking them up, remembering each name and making sure each one is working well, becoming a part of the family.

Mickey's cousin, Rabbi Mordechai Gimpel Ha-Kohen Wolk, scion of great rabbinic houses, devoted to children, particularly those in large families, placing them in good yeshivot, throwing weddings and simhas and worrying for their welfare. He is the full embodiment of the life of Torah. Listening to his tales and his quotes, following his hands, you understand a hint of Hillel.

The list is longer. This is not a lyrical exposition or highfalutin dissertation. If you want more, you'll ask, or you'll go.

COROLLARIES

The next step is to do Big Gelt projects. To raise $1 million to be put at your disposal, all you have to do is convince 200 people to throw a $5,000 wedding for their kids instead of a $10,000 jobbie, or 400 people to throw a $2,500 Bar Mitzvah instead of a whopper for 5 grand. With the remaining money you

Shaking your kishkes
Everyone should be a shaliah sometime. Even if you are going to be in Israel only a week. Even if you won't be in Israel for a while but want to do it in Minneapolis, L.A., or Aberdeen, South Dakota. The moral insight and imaginative investment will be proportional in at least a 100 to 1 ratio to the quantum of money put in the pot. By giving your own money, you treat yourself to the feeling that you are not as tightfisted as you thought you were, recession or no recession. You will become more aware of the privilege of mitzvah-doing and of allowing others to join you. As the Talmud informs us: He who encourages others is even greater than he who does it himself.

So you will say: Well, I'm not all that good. I'm only part time, and Wolk and Kapach and Maimon and Levi and Gaster and Michaelis are too much—I'm not those people. Which is exactly right, and exactly the point. Part time is good enough. And you may never consider despair again.

take them, their wives, their sons and daughters, and all their dear ones to Israel for a tzedakah junket, a spree of tzaddik-touching.

Next: find yourself a local millionaire and surprise him with a $10 proposal. Tell him you are not a foundation, institution, or home for anything, but on the contrary, think you can get a lot of mitzvah mileage out of $10. If you get $1,000, don't panic. Just check your matchmaking files and start asking more friends about more people.

HEAVY CONCLUSIONS

The risk and emotional drain are immense. You are in unaccustomed touch with those who suffer from circumstance, misfortune, or the will of God in its less pleasant manifestations—and with those whose lives are, hour by hour, tied to these people. Spiritual exhaustion is a possibility to be considered. So too are the dangers of surprise. In distributing irises and gym shoes you are never certain who will be there to meet you in the next house or corridor or on the park bench.

For nine trips I loved wandering the streets and alleys of Jerusalem. I used to watch the sun throw different shadows and light-cartoons on the buildings and street corners and trees. I believe I saw an entirely different city on this visit, shimmering with an extraordinary glow of holiness I had missed without the hevra's help.

When we at long last recurriculum our Sunday schools and Hebrew schools and day schools, we must include—aside from courses on risk, joy, fear, loss, uncertainty, failure, Big Think, and death—lectures and labs on tzedakah and mentshlikhkeit (see How to Be a Mentsh). By the very fact of having reached Bar or Bat Mitzvah, a Jewish child becomes obligated to fulfill the mitzvah of tzedakah. Why should we spiritually orphan our children, sending them insensitive as the cattle of Nineveh into the world, only to have them discover at age twenty-five or thirty-three or forty-one that they have missed out on this unique privilege for years? Let them begin with their 10–20 percent from the earliest age, and let us teach them the ins and outs of finding the righteous ones and the creativity of giving. Too few people consider that a hat, a hand gripped firmly on someone's arm, or an inexpensive three-dollar prayer book can give a sense of startling and sublime joy to another person. Mentshlikhkeit should be a word in every Jewish child's vocabulary.

According to the Torah, each Jew is required to write his own Torah. By doing these acts, by conscientious and energy-charged consideration of the swirl of people around us, we can do just that. By being a shaliah or mitzvah-doer or just plain old part-time giver.

And of course, by retelling the signs and wonders of the people we meet along the way.

Danny has now made the trip to Israel six times and has prepared a tzedakah report that he distributes to all contributors and other interested people. Below is Danny's report for the year 1979.

1979 Tzedakah Report

To the tzedakah hevra, and other interested individuals: Shalom and Yasher Koach! Our fifth distribution of funds is complete, and we have continued to exceed our previous efforts. The list of recipients is longer and more varied, and you placed at my disposal more money than in the past. This summer, as your shaliah-messenger, I have given out $9102. Previously our fund had distributed the following amounts: $955, $1667, $2930, and $6396. In all, we have been fortunate to disburse $21,050.

I will begin with the details of this summer's distribution. An asterisk (*) indicates people and projects mentioned in previous reports.

I. Interest-free loans (גמילות חסד)

$1750 A. Interest rates in Israel are outrageously high. A friend told me of attempts to obtain loans at 17%, 22%, and 34%. Often the person in need of a loan cannot obtain one, even at those rates. Therefore, we allocated funds to certain individuals for immediate needs: $500 to one to purchase a piece of medical machinery for his infant daughter, so she would be able to sleep at home, rather than spend each night in Shaare Zedek Hospital. Another $1250 was given to a lawyer in the process of setting up private practice, to assist him in buying a reference library. $200 has already been returned and recirculated to another. That $200, plus another $1050, will be paid back to Beth Huppin, who is in Israel for the year doing tzedakah work (to be explained below). The other $500 will be given to Hadassah Levi's Meon Ha-Tinok (IIIA below).

$351 B. Contributions to existing free-loan societies
1. $150—Director wishes to remain anonymous.
2. $100—Gomayl Le-Ish Chessed: Dr. David Weiss, Radak St. 21, Jerusalem, 669-363 (office 428-726). Dr. Weiss is a world-prominent immunologist and cancer researcher, and a well-known lecturer on Jewish topics. The fund he is involved with has been functioning for 18 years, without a single default.
*3. $101—Kupat Gemillut Hassadim: contact Muki, Shivtei Yisrael St. 7, Ramat Ha-Sharon, 03-470-084. Muki continues to assist people with immediate or long-term financial demands. When I saw him in August, it was clear that his fund is functioning at full strength, each lira being used and recycled regularly.
C. Dr. Weiss informed me that there are between 250 and 300 registered free-loan societies in Jerusalem alone. American Jews, particularly the younger generation, are generally unaware of the magnitude (or for that matter, even the existence) of this mitzvah. I refer to you to *The Second Jewish Catalog*, page 424 ("Free Loans"), for a partial listing of these organizations in North America.

II. Individuals who wish to remain anonymous

$590 Contributions of $100, $200, and $250 were made to certain people who are helping others, but who do not wish to be listed by name. An additional $40 was used for a gift for someone, the nature of which must remain unspecified.

III. For the retarded

$1520 *A. Meon Ha-Tinok, Hadassah Levi, Director, Ma'alay Ha-Tzofim St. 4, Ramat Gan, 03-721-565. Hadassah Levi continues to stagger the imagination with her efforts in behalf of the retarded. Meon Ha-Tinok, her home for infants with Down's syndrome (most of whom have been abandoned by parents in

the hospital at the time of birth), now has nearly forty children. The horror stories from her contact with the "outside world" continue to mount in number. In turn, her efforts to counteract the misunderstanding and outright cruelties visited on these children reach heroic intensity. Her other project, Meon Ha-Yeled, a day care center for retarded children (recently moved to a new, better facility) also continues to flourish. Three or four USY groups visited Meon Ha-Tinok this summer and contributed over $700 of their own money for her work. I consider a visit to Meon Ha-Tinok an extremely high priority for anyone visiting Eretz Yisrael.

$262 *B. Alumin (עלומים), school for the retarded: contact Lorraine Lemberger, 51 Shahal St., Jerusalem, 662-284. Last year, Lorraine and a coworker reached me toward the end of the summer, and the fund could give her at that point only $36. This year I was in touch with her shortly after I arrived, and could therefore offer much more. Also, this year I had the chance to visit their summer activities and could clearly see that their work is full of human devotion—though their budget for materials is pathetically small. Each teacher (there are 9, I believe, for 60 students) gets approximately $14/year for supplies beyond the basic paper, pencils, and crayons normally provided. Besides our contribution, USYers gave more, including many toys they had brought with them, and a basketball and soccer ball. For those planning to go to Eretz Yisrael, toys of all sorts should be included in your baggage. They can be put to great use here and in other places.

$200 *C. The Irene Gaster Hostel for Retarded Adults, Mrs. Eva Michaelis, Director, Lloyd George St. 4a, Jerusalem, 665-945. This project, as you may recall from previous reports, is being forced to move from its location because of pressure from the neighbors who do not wish to have retarded adults around. The search for a new place has been extremely difficult. Objections and legal snarls spring up everywhere. The latest report is that Mayor Kollek will give the hostel a piece of land, and they will have to build their own building—an enormous expenditure of funds. (Our contribution goes toward more immediate concerns, of course. We have always tended away from having our money swallowed up in a large fund. Funds for a building must be found through large contributions and foundations.) I was present at the hostel during a pre-Shabbat program, with kiddush and other blessings, music, singing—it was extremely moving.

$300 D. Akim (אגודה לקידום ילדים מפגרים — אקי"ם), Curt Arnson, 37 Borochov St., Jerusalem, 416-277. Akim is the national organization for retarded people in Israel, though the check was written to Curt, so that he would have exclusive supervision of the funds. While at the post office with a friend, I mentioned my work in Eretz Yisrael, and the friend said I should be in touch with Curt. We called, and within an hour I met him and listened to his enthusiastic plans. He is the father of a retarded child, and has established a substantial reputation for achieving significant goals with these children.

IV. Miscellaneous individual projects

$200 A. To a nameless, small volunteer organization of paratroopers working to provide Bar Mitzvahs, summer camping, and other benefits to orphaned children—children of their haverim who have died in the wars. Contact: Arele Marmarosh, Ha-Nassi Ha-Rishon St. 13, Rehovot, 054-75912. Approximately 10 to 15 paratroopers are involved. I was called on a Friday afternoon by a friend asking whether or not I might be interested in contributing on behalf of the tzedakah hevra. I had known Arele from USY Pilgrimage work. The meeting was brief, the emotions touched were very deep.

$100 *B. The Daniel Kuttler Charity Fund: contact Daniel or Charlotte Kuttler, Keren Ha-Yesod St. 7, Jerusalem (a few doors away from the United Synagogue building), 233-991. Besides other mitzvot, the Kuttlers continue their Hakhnassat Kallah project of lending out wedding dresses to needy brides. If you wish to send one, label the package "Used Clothes." Long-sleeved dresses with high necks are preferred, since most of the weddings take place in the Ashkenazi Orthodox community. Bridesmaids' dresses are also of use to them.

$268 *C. The Rabbanit Bracha Kapach, 12 Lod St., Jerusalem, 249-296. The rabbanit was awarded the Israel Prize last year for her work—a variety of mitzvot providing for the underprivileged elements of many neighborhoods in Jerusalem and environs. She helped some 600 families for Pesah, provides summer camping for many children, and continues to distribute used clothes from the warehouse she has beneath her apartment. If you wish to send clothes, label the packages "Used Clothes." Maximum weight is 22 pounds per package. She can also use wedding dresses (sleeves need not be as long as for the Kuttlers), which she puts at the disposal of needy brides. An amazing woman. A giant!

$320 D. Ilan (ארגון ישראלי לילדים נפגעים — איל"ן). Ilan is the national organization for handicapped children. Our funds went to purchase a refrigerator for a newly established sheltered workshop for people with cerebral palsy. Contact: Rachel Gur-On, 16 Shivtei Yisrael St., Jerusalem, 286-555 (next door to Life Line for the Old). This is a small project, providing work and skills for people who need such facilities and teachers. I had met Mrs. Gur-On previously, and now she has her own project. It was a wonderful feeling—lite as it sounds—simply to write a check for what they needed. It took less than a week for me to hear of this project, and shortly thereafter the transaction was completed.

$100 E. Si Levine, Jerusalem, 666-864. Si, an old hero for many people from USY days, is involved in wide-ranging personal mitzvot. I put the money at his disposal to use as he saw fit.

$150 *F. Gemillut Chessed Fund, supervised by Dr. Pesach Schindler (Director of the United Synagogue in Israel), 2 Agron St., Jerusalem, 226-386. As in years past, I gave to Pesach's fund, to use the money at his own discretion—no questions asked, of course, as to where it goes.

$100 G. Subsidy to Michael Schudrich, a seminary rabbinical student, for buying materials (candlesticks, books, etc.) and to have some tzedakah money for a trip from Israel into Eastern Europe. He may be reached at (212) 749-8000 for details of his extraordinary experience, including a tie-in with the Holocaust Commission's visit to Auschwitz.

V. Larger projects with personal contact with certain individuals

$350 *A. *Yad Ezra, Ha-Rav Sorotzkin St. 15, Jerusalem, 526-133 (contact Shmuel Katz there, or at home—817-767, or Yehoshua Lendner, Ron Hotel, Zion Square, 223-471). This section is to emphasize how impressive—inspirational—the work of Yad Ezra is. I had seen some of their work last year, but this year I was, to put it quite simply, overwhelmed, moved more deeply than in any other work in the past few years. All aspects of this project were started by one Jew: Reb Osher Freund. Projects include a 750,000 pound free-loan society, distribution of 2,000,000 Israeli pounds of free food for Pesah (קימחא דפיסחא), free dental and medical services (including X rays), enough dishes to be lent out for simhas to*

provide for a half dozen weddings, free lodging in Meron for 300+ people for vacations (נופש —a wonderful Hebrew word), discount supermarket and clothing store in Bnai Brak, discount and free food distribution throughout Jerusalem, and other projects. I saw the distribution of food one night: 4 minibuses, each to make two rounds, loaded with crates of fruits and vegetables. All the work is done by volunteers. But most impressive of all (in the category of Life Line for the Old and Meon Ha-Tinok—redeeming the lives of broken people)—occupational therapy for about 50 people from mental institutions. Printing presses for the men, sewing machines for the women, producing hallah and matzah covers, Shabbas-Yontiff dresses for children, and more. There is here a sense of hevra and devotion to others (religious, nonreligious, Jew or non-Jew—whoever) that is unbelievable (though our tzedakah hevra is used to hearing that word). All this through the vision of Reb Osher. And this year I had the chance to meet him. I hesitate to write more, other than to say it appears that every person he reaches is certain that Reb Osher cares for him or her personally. Sublime, exquisite. In the fullest, truest sense of the word—tzedakah. Yad Ezra should be on everyone's itinerary in Israel.

$450 *B. Micha (מחנכי ילדים חרשים-אלמים — מיח"א), Sylvia Feiner, Director, Akiva St., Jerusalem, 232-031. My contact: Toby Wolinsky, Lincoln St. 12b, Jerusalem, 227-502. Micha-Jerusalem (there are four Michas—all independent, and of varying quality) specializes in training preschool deaf and hearing-impaired children. They too can use toys, if you wish to bring some with you. $300 of the $450 was given directly to Toby, to use for her particular work within Micha.

$200 *C. Life Line for the Old—Yad La-Kashish, Director, Myriam Mendelow, 12 Shivtei Yisrael St., Jerusalem, 287-829. The greatest place in the world for old people to work (we have not found or heard of another like it anywhere). Thirteen workshops produce beautiful products: toys, clothes, Shabbat tablecloths, wall hangings, whatever—often from the hands of people who had given up, wished to die in fragments, abandoned to loneliness and uselessness. This is the fourth summer USYers have visited (about 2500 people), and, again, it was inspiring. The $200 was used for a party, given in honor of Sally Mendelsohn and David Lowenfeld (longtime friends of Yad La-Kashish), who wanted a wedding party given there on the same day they were getting married in Chicago. It was a fraylach event of the first order, complete with Yad La-Kashish choir, blind guitarist, accordionist, singing, dancing, speeches. There is now a contact in the United States: American Friends of Life Line for the Old, One State Street Plaza, New York, NY 10004. Mrs. Arthur Hertzberg is the national chairperson.

$200 D. Yad Sara, contact Uri, 4 Ezrat Torah St., Jerusalem, 813-777. This is a three-year-old organization of volunteers that lends out medical supplies (wheelchairs, hospital beds, oxygen, vaporizers, etc.—at no cost, of course), to those who can't afford them. They now have 18 centers in Israel, almost all of them working out of people's homes, thus allowing for late-night calls. One can well imagine how long the process is trying to get the bureaucracy to provide this equipment. As Uri said, "By the time they get the wheelchair, they will no longer need it." Their sense of infinite caring is a great healer.

$200 *E. Keren Peulat Yaakov Maimon, contact Dr. Kurt Meyerowitz, Keren Kayemet Le-Yisrael St. 21, Jerusalem, 639-970. Dr. Meyerowitz and his friends continue to carry on the work of the late Yaakov Maimon, who, as you recall from previous reports, coordinated thousands of volunteers—Jews helping Jews, tutoring, assisting in many ways. Nowadays they are concentrating on volunteer work in certain areas of Jerusalem, bringing tutors to many and providing other activities which will allow people to function better in Israeli society.

$100 F. Delet Petuchah, same address as above, contact Mrs. Meyerowitz. This is a recently established center of activities for old people. It is around the corner from Dr. Meyerow-

itz's apartment, providing opportunities for the old in the area to get out of their homes and to enjoy a variety of activities.

$300 *G. Zahavi (זכויות המשפחה ברוכת ילדים — זהב"י), contact Dr. Eliezer Jaffe, 37 Aza Rd., Jerusalem, 661-908 or 637-450. This is the Israeli grass-roots organization for families with 4 children or more. There are 80,000 such families in Israel. (One out of every two soldiers is from such a family.) Working on many fronts, they seek out discounts and reductions for large families, work with individual families, and work as a lobby in the government to get legislation favorable to this particular element of Israeli society. Our contribution went toward the purchase of 10 copies of the *Michlal Encyclopedia*, an excellent reference set for schoolchildren. Contributions of $30 to Zahavi may be earmarked for this particular project.

$150 H. Matav (מטפלות בית — מט"ב) = Homemakers. Contact Mrs. Jaffe, same address as above. Matav functions essentially the same way as Homemakers over here, easing certain household chores and strains by bringing in help for a variety of jobs. Matav is a significant force in holding families together under the day-to-day strain of just keeping a household functioning.

$100 *I. Americans and Canadians in Israel (AACI) Jerusalem Scholarship Fund, contact Mr. or Mrs. Meyer Bargteil, 4 Ben Tabbai St., Jerusalem, 664-278. This group, working with a personal, delicate touch, provides scholarships (I believe at $50 apiece) for war orphans. It is very carefully administered, with no overhead.

$100 *J. The Central Library for the Visually Handicapped, contact Uri Cohen, Ha-Histadrut St. 4, Netanya, 053-25321 or 32422. This place contains a vast and growing library of Braille books and tapes. They are distributed throughout the country. The money provides for materials, typists, and readers for the tapes.

$100 *K. Civic Center Organization, contact Tova Baskin, Kiryat Segal 6/28, Netanya. I had met this woman a couple of years ago at a get-together in memory of Yaakov Maimon. She explained the work to me: volunteers organizing to get the street kids' energies channeled into more constructive activities than just wandering around. She speaks with great enthusiasm of the spirit of the people working there.

VI. Miscellaneous: trees and flowers, music and hope

$600 *A. Salary (our third year) for a music teacher to provide music therapy for a young lady in an institution for emo-

tionally disturbed children. I get periodic reports, and significant progress has been made with the young woman. The work is arduous, the progress slow, but there are moments of comfort and hope in the music and human contact.

$16 B. Flowers for a pre-Shabbat visit with friends, making the rounds at Hadassah Hospital to wish people a good Shabbat. The hospital staff there (and at Shaare Zedek and Bikur Holim) is always cooperative, and the effort is most appreciated by the patients. It is also one of the least expensive mitzvot to be done during a trip to Israel.

$25 *C. Trees—5 of them, one for each year we have done the project. Planted outside Jerusalem, with a view, for those who wish to see them. I planted them in honor of Rabbi Chaim Pearl, rabbi of the Conservative Synagogue-Adath Israel of Riverdale; the bookkeeper at the shul; and the shul itself—their unhesitating support and assistance made the project function that much better this year than in the past. The last two: one for the tzedakah hevra and, well—I couldn't resist—one for me, your most grateful shaliah.

I am available at all times for resource ideas and consultations concerning these people. In the past month I have been contacted by two individuals concerning bequests totaling approximately $125,000. It is clear that people are seeking out appropriate places for larger sums of money.

This report is not a solicitation of funds. A number of people do send me money during the year, after reading the report, and the funds are put to use here and in Israel. (Among other things, I have managed to finance 3 *Encyclopaedia Judaica*s—on a free-loan basis, with regular return payments.) Some would feel uncomfortable that I might be shnorring. Therefore, I want to make it unmistakably certain that people understand this is just a yearly report.

More and more, as I do one-day seminars or weekend institutes, I attempt to schedule one talk on tzedakah. Unfortunately I still feel that this kind of work, done in different forms by many people, is not getting the proper widespread publicity and exposure. Once entrée is given to appropriate audiences the response is always positive, but the entrée is often hard to come by. This work is not meant as a replacement for federation giving, nor was that ever its intention. Rather it is an examination and attempt to carry out the mitzvah of tzedakah through careful examination of potential recipients. The methods of giving are not mutually exclusive.

This summer was different in at least one significant way: after having given out some $5000, I found that there was still a significant quantity of money left, and I did not feel the need to scrimp on contributions: $9102 was a grand sum of money!

As in the past, the work was profoundly moving to me. I am grateful for your allowing me to do this work. I am again and again amazed how many people there are doing so many things we consider impossible. The old-time terms "devotion, love, exquisite, caring, concern, sublime" keep coming to mind. People I had known from past years suddenly turned a new corner in their work or speech or gestures, and I would rush into a new realm of reverence. We can only stand back and gaze in wonder at this work, religious in the full sense of the word, a Kiddush ha-Shem. In a lyrical sense, we see clearly the image of God reflected in the faces and hands and footsteps of these wonderful creatures.

Yes, I am grateful. To have been ushered into their presence, to converse with them, watch their faces, has been a joy, and, as you know, a great privilege.

If you want to get in touch with Danny, write to him
c/o **United Synagogue Youth**
155 Fifth Ave.
New York, NY 10010

יישר כחכם, שנה טובה ומבורכת, ונזכה למצוות !

May we continue to do mitzvot together in the coming years,

Family tzedakah

I will never forget the image of our then two-year-old daughter huddled in a corner of the sandbox at a public playground, hanging on for dear life to her bucket and shovel, unable to enjoy playing in the sand herself for fear that, if she did, someone might snatch her possessions away from her. No one did, and she left the playground with shovel and pail intact, having had a thoroughly miserable time. Sound familiar? Ever do it (actually or symbolically)? For most of us, the answer to both questions is probably yes.

What does it mean to share? And, one step further, what does it mean to give? Let's go even one more step: how does it *feel* to share? to give? In the United States we are brought up with the notion of "ownership" and "private property." "That's mine! Give it back or I'll tell on you!" And if you don't, Mommy or Daddy or the police will see that you do. So we believe that we have a right to have that which, by one means or another, becomes "ours." At the same time, we hold it a virtue to share. We share with our friends, our family, our schoolmates, our fellow workers. "Come on, give half of your candy bar to your sister, be a nice girl." For one thing, if you share with someone this time, maybe the next time you need something they might share with you. Besides, you want to be "nice," don't you? If you're not, people won't like you, and then what?

But what about sharing with people whom you don't know, whom you will never know? Why share with them—from guilt? from compassion? from a sense of human togetherness? What claim have they on us? And anyway, how much should we share? With whom? Do we share mainly with those who are "our kind," who are the same color, religion, ethnic group, political persuasion, etc.? Or should we give to people who are "different"? Do we give through large agencies who have broad access and even broader bureaucracies or to small, particular groups who are probably not tax deductible? Do we share locally so that we have a more immediate sense of what's being affected or do we share with Africans whom we will never see?

These and many more questions, I imagine, we have all grapple with in one way or another. Tzedakah is an ancient and venerable mitzvah within Judaism. Many of us practice it in our own lives in some form. Our children learn about it both through our constant urging them to share with their friends and siblings and often more formally at religious school in the form of tzedakah boxes or other giving projects.

What I find has *not* happened, at least among people I know, is the custom of actively involving children in family decisions about where money set aside for tzedakah should go. It seems to me that in so splitting the formal giving, we miss a golden opportunity—both to educate our children in values (social, political, and religious) and to gain for ourselves the freshness of their insights and understanding.

How would this work? Any number of ways. Here are a few suggestions. You yourselves will undoubtedly invent many more.

1. The parents can decide, given their evaluation of the family's budgetary needs, what sum of money they can afford to give away. Children and parents can then decide where the money should be given. The ideas for where to give can come from:

    a. a list composed by the parents; the parents can explain what/who the different places/people are and why they feel them worthy.

    b. a list composed by both parents and children (this might work better with older children); each person who puts an item on the list can explain it.

    c. a more formal list, like the one in the section on Tzedakah Collectives (see below).

Mary Gendler describes how her family treats tzedakah-giving

2. The family can, as a whole, decide what proportion of their money they can afford to/should/want to/will anyway give away.

3. Besides certain decisions that the parents might want to make on their own, there can be a certain sum of money set aside that will be available either for a family group decision or for a children's group decision or for an individual child's decision.

4. Children can decide on particular chores or jobs for which they can get paid—either by their parents or outside the home. The money for these particular jobs will be dedicated to tzedakah. This money can then either be put into a collective family "pot" or disposed of individually by the one who earned it.

5a. The family can check around their neighborhood or area and discover projects that need help. Then as a family they can volunteer a certain amount of time—a day a week, a month, or whatever, working as a family. Or:

5b. The family can, as a whole, make a pledge to volunteer a certain amount of time a week or a month to help others, and then each person can find his/her own project. Some way to make sure that the family was meeting its quota would need to be devised.

6. Make a tzedakah pushke at home, a kind of Jewish piggy bank. Loose change, money left over, a regular sum, money from something you wanted but decided not to get—these and other sums can be stuck in. Keep it in an obvious place and urge the children to get in the habit of contributing to it. Every two months or six or whatever, break it open and decide what to do with the funds.

7. Do any or all of the above with other families or groups or people involving adults and children.

With all of these projects, be sure to schedule enough time as a family (or group) to talk. You will have many things to talk about: What does giving and sharing mean anyway? How do we do it at home? Is it working? How do we do it with others? With whom should we share? How much? Does it feel different to share time than to share money? And how much money do we have anyway? Where did/does it come from? Should I have to deprive myself of things in order to share or can I just give what's left over? How much do I/we need anyway? Which things that I have do I really need and which do I just want? And what's the difference? What is our life-style that we need/want these things? Are we living the way we really want to live? What is our responsibility to others? To ourselves? Where does it begin and where does it end?

Obviously, I could go on and on. It may even be like that with your family: once you start really talking and sharing, you might never stop. Family money is often a source of mystification to children. This could be a very natural way of sharing fact, values, and beliefs. Certainly children learn many wonderful things from religious school, but the most basic, firmly rooted "knowing" comes from the things that they experience at home. Who knows, family tzedakah, sensitively executed, might even one day replace "family therapy"!

Tzedakah collectives

yeder mentsh hot zein peckel.

Every man has his burden

SOME HISTORY

Starting in 1973, East Coast members of havurot have come together for retreats three times a year at Weiss's Farm in New Jersey and other locations. At one retreat a group of people met to study and discuss the issue of tzedakah. They raised some complex and difficult problems, and from their discussions grew the proposal for the formation of tzedakah collectives that appears here.

The given is that, as pointed out above, Jews must give tzedakah, and people who do not do so shirk a sacred and profound responsibility. But the ambivalence felt by many people toward the vast fund-raising operation of the Jewish community cannot be ignored on a number of counts, among them these:

1. There appears to be little accountability for the use of funds.

2. The priorities of the allocating agencies frequently differ radically from the priorities of the giver.

3. The possibility of influencing these allocating agencies is small if the amount of tzedakah money you have at your disposal is small.

Other more general problems include defining, according to the scheme set out by the Sifrei Devarim, just what one sees as one's primary community. With the fragmentation of modern-day existence, where do we owe our first allegiance—in what corner of the many communities of which we are members? And what about non-Jewish tzedakah, cultural tzedakah, etc.?

The proposal was made at Weiss's Farm to encourage people with similar tzedakah priorities to come together in small groups. The members of these groups could then pool their tzedakah money and decide communally on allocation priorities. Not only would groups become more conscious of the mitzvah of giving tzedakah but their pooled money would carry more political weight than individual small gifts can.

Accordingly, a small group of organizers worked to create tzedakah collectives in Boston, Washington, Philadelphia, Los Angeles, and New York.

Each group differs in small and large ways from any of the others. But all came up against similar problems, which each group solved in its own specific way. Here are some of them:

1. Should everyone give the same amount of money? Should everyone give the same percentage of his/her income?

2. How should decisions be made on where to give money—by consensus? by vote?

3. If by vote, does everyone's vote have equal weight? Should people who give more have a more weighted vote?

4. What if someone refuses, on moral grounds, to support an organization? Is one blackball vote enough to end consideration of that project?

5. What if there are different factions who want to support different Jewish angles (i.e., only Israel projects or only local communal projects)?

6. Are we willing to support only new projects, or are we willing to support ongoing functioning of an organization. (Do you *really* want to buy

the paper clips for an organization? On the other hand, can an organization work without paper clips?)

The Derech Reut Tzedakah Collective, which has been operative for the last five years, was one of the groups that confronted these issues. Reut decided to require all members to donate a minimum of 3 percent of their gross income (most members make additional contributions to tzedakah outside the collective). Each member, because s/he gives the same *proportion* of income to the group (even though one person's donation may total $300 and another person's donation may total $3,000), is given an equally weighted vote. There is a certain amount of lobbying that ensues because of people's varying loyalties and interests, but Reut members will not support a group that any one member refuses, on moral grounds, to support.

Essentially, Reut functions in the following manner. Before Purim (or in the spring, whenever we get up enough energy and feel we've recovered from the last year's giving process) we begin to meet to consider group decisions that have to be renegotiated in light of the previous year's experiences. By the end of spring we begin looking around for new proposals, projects, groups, fledgling ideas to investigate and nurture. By the fall we are ready to begin our interviewing process.

From fall through Hanukkah we interview new groups, solicit updates on groups we've given money to in the past, and try to prioritize our giving objectives for the year. Before December 31 (to coincide with the IRS's Rosh ha-Shanah) we have one marathon meeting that lasts as long as it takes to complete all our work, and we make all our allocation decisions at that one meeting. People come prepared with budgetary figures and progress reports of various groups to bolster their opinions.

The question of whether or not to support the Jewish federation has been an ongoing discussion in Reut, as well as other tzedakah collectives. This question has been handled in different ways by different groups. Fabrangen in Washington requires its members to set aside one-third of their donation to be given to any one group on a list of five large-scale fund-raising organizations. Among those organizations is the federation. Thus members who do not choose to support the federation need not do so, as their names are not listed among the givers when the donation is made.

Reut, on the other hand, decided, after careful soul searching some years ago, not to support the federation-UJA campaign. The decision was made because it was felt that the federation does not adequately support (or in some cases does not support *at all*) the projects our havurah community is most committed to, and it then becomes our obligation to support these projects. Furthermore, it was felt that the federation fund-raising strategies represent an approach alien to our attitudes toward tzedakah. And finally, it was decided that those people who wanted to support the federation could do so privately outside the group (which some members have done).

For information about tzedakah collectives contact:

Arthur Kurzweil
251 W. 101st St.
New York, N.Y. 10025

The money machine: Jewish federations

The Jewish charitable world is divided into three parts: overseas, national, and local needs. The United Jewish Appeal is charged with funding services for Jews overseas, including:

1. health, educational, and social services in Israel

2. relief and rescue of Jews in oppressed lands (i.e., their physical and spiritual support, transportation, and resettlement)

3. support for Jewish communal life in overseas communities unable to maintain basic Jewish communal services and structures

In roughly 225 American cities, towns, and regions, local federations raise the bulk of the monies for major support of local services and for partial support of Jewish national agencies. Although the scope of services found in a local community generally is directly proportionate to the size of its Jewish population, the services funded by federations in larger cities include a mix of the following:

1. Jewish hospitals; mental health services; care for the blind, deaf, handicapped, and orphans; and other health-related services ostensibly geared to a predominantly Jewish clientele

2. YMHAs and YWHAs, Jewish community centers, camps, and other social and recreational facilities

3. social-work agencies and programs for troubled children, adults, families

4. employment and vocational guidance services

5. care for the aged (both homes and social services)

6. Jewish community councils or other local intergroup-relations agencies

7. Jewish education

8. Jewish campus life (primarily local Hillels) and other youth-related services

Federation history and function

The federation movement developed during the first half of this century, when many community agencies performing social services pooled their efforts to create unified fund-raising bodies. With full responsibility for communal fund raising and the allocation of those funds for local and national needs, federations developed as the central planning organizations in the local Jewish communities.

As a result, in addition to raising funds, the federations influence the development of local Jewish communal institutions. The planning and allocation process effectively determines which specific agencies shall flourish and which shall be forced to retrench. These decisions are partly based on how much influence is wielded by those with vested interests in specific institutions and partly by more altruistic considerations. Federations try to respond to what they perceive to be the changing needs of the population they serve. Since Jewish communities undergo geographic shifts, this procedure may mean the reduction of services in inner-city neighborhoods where Jews no longer reside and the expansion of services in the suburbs or other areas of increased Jewish residence. Demographic shifts—for example, the rapidly growing proportion of the Jewish population that is over sixty-five— also bring about the reassessment of allocation priorities. Finally, shifts in Jewish public opinion with regard to the significance of federation-supported services also influence the direction of funding.

The organization of the federation

The decision makers charged with setting priorities can be divided into the lay (volunteer) and professional leadership. The leaders influencing federation policies are found in both the central communal structures (the decision-making bodies of the federations themselves) and also in the diverse agencies funded by the federation. The complexity of interrelationships between and among these decision makers increases proportionately with communal size: in large cities where there are many institutions, federation leaders may well operate to protect or increase funding for a general sector of service (e.g., Jewish education, or Y's, or hospitals, etc.). But beyond these decisions, affiliated with each institution are influential lay and professional leaders who develop the program and influence of that institution.

The central federation structures charged with making these decisions are usually twofold (although in smaller communities one such body may be responsible for all allocation decisions).

COMMUNAL PLANNING

One committee, with its supporting staff, is responsible for "communal planning" (it is often called the Communal Planning Committee or the Inclusions Committee). Its purpose is simply to make decisions about whether to assume a specific agency's budgetary request as a federation responsibility in light of several considerations: the demonstrated effectiveness of the agency; the significance of its activities in the general scope of perceived Jewish needs of the local community; and, not least important, the influence of its lay board members or others already involved in the federation's activities.

DISTRIBUTIONS

Once included as a member agency, the organization's budgetary requests are considered by the Distribution Committee, which makes recommendations for the federation's allocations. These recommendations are in turn sent to a

larger body, the board of trustees of the federation, for final shaping and approval.

In large and intermediate cities, where there are large numbers of such agencies, the Communal Planning Committee and Distributions Committee employ several subcommittees, each evaluating a different group of agencies. These subcommittees comprise additional winnowing-out bodies through which requests for funding must pass.

The allocation process more closely resembles that of a politically stratified state legislature than the ideal form of the ostensibly "objective" peer review process employed by academic grant agencies. Agencies are initiated and their budgets are expanded or cut back as a result of decisions made by lay leaders and professionals of varying degrees of influence and expertise. The disparity between the most and least influential of those interested in the decision-making process is probably greatest in large cities. Smaller communities involve a greater proportion of their active leadership in the decision-making process, are less likely to be heavily stratified by class, and thus are less subject to the rule of a plutocratic elite.

A community of social-work professionals has developed around the federation and its institutions. These professionals wield a considerable degree of influence over the policies pursued by the federation and the agencies in which they work. That is, they may initiate or sabotage specific programs, and they can control the flow of information to each other and to the volunteer leaders. Thus they can enhance the influence of some leaders (by making them privy to the inner workings of their organization and bringing them into the social circle of decision makers) and diminish the influence of other leaders (through analogous means). Moreover, they are often looked to by lay leaders to recommend other individuals to the boards and are thus often effectively able to preclude the assembling of lay leadership opposed to the professional's style, personality, or policies. That federations are heavily involved in social service has resulted in a social-work fraternity in and around the federations whose ticket of admission is an MSW—a master of social work degree. As a consequence, Jewish cultural or identificational training has in the past not been at a premium; in recent years, though, there has been greater recognition of the criterion of a Jewish background.

The influence of lay leaders in the federations is probably greater than that of their counterparts in other Jewish communal organizations. A fund-raising agency relies on those individuals who can give funds and/or influence others to give. As a consequence, a balanced partnership usually develops between lay and professional leadership in a local federation.

OTHER FEDERATION ALLOCATIONS

In addition to allocating funds directly to UJA for overseas needs and to deciding how to divide up funds for local use, a small percentage of federation funds (perhaps no more than 4 percent) is allocated to national agencies. Agencies ranging from the American Jewish Committee to the North American Jewish Students Appeal each receive a large proportion of their budget by making requests to individual federations.

Since each federation is not totally responsible for the budget of any national agency coming to it for funds, federations seek to coordinate their funding of national agencies through the Large City Budgeting Conference (LCBC). The LCBC consists of delegates from the sixteen largest communities, who consider many national agencies and make budgetary recommendations to one another and to the scores of smaller federations. This committee is the only true embodiment of a national federation communal decision-making body, and even it is empowered only to *advise* its constituent members. It operates within and is a creation of the Council of Jewish Federations and Welfare Funds (CJFWF), the umbrella organization for nearly two hundred local federations. In addition, the CJF board meets quarterly for three to five days at a time.

The CJF is a vehicle for national expression of aggregate federation concerns and is the instrument through which federations (1) exchange ideas, sensing new directions in policies and structures; (2) develop nationally funded bodies (such as the Institute for Jewish Life or a task force for pro-Israel public relations); and (3) through resolutions, express their aggregate opinions on national and communal issues about which there is a large degree of consensus. To encourage the sharing of developments, programs ideas, etc., CJFWF conducts a massive General Assembly every November, at which three thousand delegates and observers from local federations and other interested agencies gather. While on the one hand the CJFWF is the only institution capable of achieving national coordination of any sort, on the other hand it is genuinely incapable of coercing a constituent member federation to adopt policies, allocate money, or support issues with which that community honestly disagrees.

Criticisms

In recent years Jewish federations have drawn a variety of adverse comments from a number of sources within the Jewish community. These are usually substantive and/or procedural in nature.

    1. Substantive objections are those pertaining to allocation priorities.

        a. Rabbis, Jewish educators, students, intellectuals, and others have voiced objections to what they regard as insufficient funding of Jewish education, campus youth, and other cultural-Jewish-identificational endeavors of American Jewry. Let's call this the "cultural criticism."

        b. On the other hand, not too many years ago Jewish Defense League activists, the Council of Jewish Anti-Poverty Workers, and other inner-city Jews called for more attention to the problems of the Jewish poor and aged. Let's call this substantive objection the "poverty criticism."

    2. The procedural criticisms are those entailing objections to the composition of decision-making bodies and/or the methods they use to arrive at their decisions. The procedural criticism can also be divided into two categories. They are either "reformist" or "radical" in nature.

        a. The reformist objection decries exclusion of some "out groups"

(e.g., rabbis, women, poor people, students, intellectuals, etc.) from the decision-making process.

b. The radical-procedural criticism calls for systematic change, objecting to allegedly undemocratic features of federations and seeking new procedures for the selection of decision makers and the process by which they make their decisions.

CULTURAL CRITICISM

The cultural criticism has been voiced by rabbis, Jewish educators, and organized Orthodoxy for many years, and most recently, has been taken up by Jewish intellectuals and student activists. Essentially, this group makes two major charges:

1. Far too much of the federations' allocations are made to hospitals, Y's, and recreational facilities of low Jewish identificational content.

2. Far too little of the federations' monies are allocated to Jewish education, Jewish cultural life, the arts, and scholarship.

EDUCATION AND HOSPITALS: THE INDICTMENT

Critics have focused on Jewish hospitals, noting that federations in the large cities allocate as much as one-quarter of their budgets to Jewish-sponsored hospitals. These funds, however, comprise only a small portion—perhaps 2 percent—of the hospitals' budgets. Moreover, comparable hospitals in the same region flourish financially without organized Jewish communal support. According to the critics, reasons that once may have justified Jewish communal support of hospitals are no longer operative: Jewish patients formerly could not obtain quality medical care from nonsectarian institutions; Jewish doctors could not obtain training elsewhere; the religious needs of Jewish patients were not properly attended to by nonsectarian hospitals (today, in contrast, critics suggest that non-Jewishly sponsored hospitals sometimes have been more sensitive to Jewish religious needs that their federation-sponsored counterparts); or that anti-Semitism required American Jews to make a visible philanthropic response to general social needs.

With respect to Y's, Jewish camps, and other recreational facilities, the critics charge that such facilities are often primarily geared to providing recreation or social services but are not particularly capable of—or seemingly interested in—heightening Jewish identification or promoting Jewish cultural life.

In charging that Jewish education, arts, and culture are grossly underfunded, critics contend that

1. the organized Jewish philanthropic community is obligated to support these aspects of Jewish life

2. Jewish education, culture, etc., suffer in part because of underfunding

3. individuals typically involved in running and contributing to federations are less likely to be interested in supporting Jewish cultural life because they themselves are of established upper-class lineage and are so "Americanized"

4. the professionals in and around federations are drawn from a social-work milieu that is unreceptive to communal ethnic and religious needs. As a result of all this, critics say, Jewish pedagogy is primitive, the Jewish arts are underdeveloped, and genuine American Jewish cultural life is stagnant.

FEDERATION RESPONSE

Federation officials respond to these criticisms in a number of ways. Chief among them is the argument that the Jewish charitable world is entirely voluntaristic, that individuals are not subject to taxation, and that a large number of federation contributors are indeed more interested in Jewish hospitals than Jewish cultural life; in fact, the membership on boards of Jewish hospitals and boards of federations often overlap to a large extent. The officials will concede the validity of some of the antihospital arguments and point out that over the last few years federation allocations to hospitals have remained stationary—or declined—and that the *proportion* of funds allocated for that purpose has declined drastically. They also point to the much-increased expenditures for Jewish education (for both capital and operating expenses), and suggest the support of the arts and culture is a high-risk venture not likely to win support in financially hard times.

POVERTY CRITICISM: THE INDICTMENT

The poverty criticism entails objections to federations' alleged failure to provide services to the neglected Jewish poor, frequently the aged. This objection also attacks the practice of service to non-Jewish clientele and federation aid recipients. (See World of Our Fathers and Project Ezra.)

FEDERATION RESPONSE

The response of the federation to the first portion of the criticism is that it indeed devotes substantial portions of its funds to social service. Moreover, the "discovery" of the Jewish poor a few years ago has spawned a dramatic increase in services to this target population. As to the second part of the criticism, federation supporters cite the huge multiplier effect of matching federal, state, and city funds that are received to match Jewish communal funds. The price of accepting governmental aid is the agreement to serve a clientele without regard to religious or ethnic origins. However, the federation officials maintain that even with this stipulation, the increased funds received through government grants make possible a much higher level of services to the Jewish poor and aged.

REFORMIST CRITICISM: THE INDICTMENT

The reformist criticism entails objections to the allegedly restrictive social circles to which federation lay and professional decision makers belong. Critics charge that federations are typically run by wealthy upper-middle-class businessmen and professional men. The composition of boards of trustees, critical committees, and upper-echelon professional ranks largely supports this charge.

That there are a few "outsiders" in key positions does not invalidate this criticism. Rather, especially in the large cities, the informal circles of wealthy male philanthropists who socialize with each other outside as well as inside the boardrooms effectively disenfranchise even those with token influence.

FEDERATION RESPONSE

The reformist criticism is voiced by many groups, and to each group the federation's advocates offer reasoned rebuttals for their alleged exclusion from positions of power. The Orthodox are underrepresented because they fail to contribute large amounts to the federation campaigns. The poor and middle class are excluded for the same reason. Students are not found on federation boards because they are so transient, staying in their college community for only four years, while influence in a federation comes from years of steady work. Women are not to be found in these positions ostensibly because (as some federation leaders have actually said):

1. Their presence might lead to sexual affairs.
2. They are ill equipped to handle complicated financial matters.
3. They are not interested in taking on typically male roles.

CRITICS' REJOINDER TO THE FEDERATION RESPONSE

The critics in turn respond that the Jewish community suffers when large groups of potentially valuable contributors to the decision-making process are effectively excluded. They suggest that those skilled in raising funds (i.e., wealthy business people and professionals) may not be the only ones adept at allocating those funds. Moreover, large city federations make little effort to raise funds from small contributors—in effect narrowing the circle of participants in the Jewish charitable community.

RADICAL CRITICISM: THE INDICTMENT

The radical critics attack the allegedly undemocratic procedures of federations. Specifically, they charge that

1. decision makers are not democratically selected by a board constituency but are selected and advanced by self-perpetuating boards

2. the boards themselves are dominated by a small group of influential lay members as well as a small number of the key executives of an agency

3. budgets, minutes of meetings, reports, and other pertinent items of information are only available to the most persistent contributors or interested parties

As a result, the radical critics have called for regular communitywide open hearings on federation policies, free elections to federation boards, and the enactment of freedom-of-information provisions to ensure the full disclosure of most informational materials at a nominal cost to all interested parties.

FEDERATION RESPONSE

Federation officials typically respond to these suggestions with the rebuttal that such changes would make the federation operation highly inefficient, consume enormous lay and professional energies, and "hinder motivational mechanisms" which inspire lay volunteers to devote time to the federation.

Despite the mixed reputation enjoyed by federations among the young and intellectual communities, it is true that changes along the lines suggested by the above criticisms are occurring, though quite slowly. Hospital allocations are indeed declining. Y's and other facilities serving non-Jewish clientele have been moved, been shut down, or had their budgets slashed. In fact, more money is now being allocated for Jewish identificational and cultural life than ever before. More nonprofessional, nonbusinessmen are to be found in positions of influence than five years ago. However, it remains to be seen whether these changes will occur rapidly enough, or be far-reaching enough, to broaden the activist philanthropic base and counteract potentially disastrous demographic trends in the Jewish community.

How to raise money

How do you get money when you need it for a good project idea you've dreamed up to benefit the Jewish community, whether local, national, or international? There are ways to get money for a project and there are ways you can lose support—sometimes without even realizing you've done it. The following is my advice (*free*), based on my experience in raising money and sitting on allocations committees.

Money is not really money. It is many things, including power. It is a crude form of energy and, like most energy, it is in short supply. This is particularly true in the Jewish community. Allocations committees of the various Jewish communities are faced with that classic of all economic problems: insatiable demand and limited resources.

Contrary to popular belief, there are very few bad programs that come before allocations committees, the members are often asked to determine which of several very good proposals has the most importance to the Jewish community. So if you don't believe in your project, don't propose it. Sit down and think it over very carefully. Remember, at this point there are two factors to consider:

1. Your own sincerity, which others will judge with a sharp, experienced eye.

2. The relative value of your project to the community when weighed against other pressing demands. If you are not sincere in your belief, the decision makers will know it immediately and you will not only fail but also damage your image in the community, thus affecting your ability to find funding for other projects in the future.

I have seen wonderful, important, and valuable projects, presented by the most sincere, well-meaning people in the world, fail miserably, while projects of less importance and value receive commendations, praise, and funds. The worthiness of a project often has little to do with its being funded. What does matter is knowing how to go about soliciting support.

The politics of power

The ability of a group or individual to get money from the Jewish community is generally the result of power relationships built on and nutured between yourself (or your group) and those who make decisions in the community.

The first step in acquiring support is to determine the structure of the decision-making body within the community. This can often be confusing since names, titles, committees and subcommittees, and other bureaucratic camouflage may cloud and confuse your perception of the loci of power. I am familiar with several Jewish communities where the basic organizational structure would lead us to think that power sits in a particular committee. But when I began working with these communities I rapidly discovered that, in fact, real decision-making power was in a different committee altogether. Committee names mean very little; people with power mean everything. So after determining the worthiness of your project, the next step is to find out where the centers of power and decision making really are.

It has long been recognized by UJA, Israel Bonds, and every other major fund-raising body in the United States that the most successful attempts at fund raising are those done on a peer-to-peer basis—that is, fund raising by people in the same age, social, economic, and educational and cultural bracket. That is why fund-raising bodies often run campaigns within professional groups (e.g., pharmacists, dentists, jewelers, etc.) or within social settings (e.g., clubs, lodges, and chapters).

This presents a special problem for persons coming before allocations committees of Jewish welfare funds and federations. It is not unusual for these allocations committees to be made up of the most wealthy and/or politically powerful men in the community. Because these men (and a handful of women) usually move in circles far removed from that of the average member of the Jewish community, making a presentation before an allocations committee can be an uncomfortable experience, both for you and the committee, akin to being out of one's element and swimming in a foreign sea.

There are, however, ways of alleviating this potentially uncomfortable situation. First of all, remember that they are as uncomfortable as you are and will be trying (although sometimes not very hard) to find a common ground. Second, well before such a meeting takes place it is in your interest to develop a relationship with an amicus curiae, a friend of the court. Ideally, this will be a member of the allocations committee or someone whose position the allocations committee members respect. The makeup of a committee is usually so broad that someone on it will have an interest in your project. It is to him/her that other members of the committee will usually look for advice concerning your proposal. If through a series of meetings and encounters you can convince that person of the efficacy of your project, you will have someone who can argue for your project on a peer-to-peer basis, when the doors are closed and the decisions are made.

The next-best advocate for your project is a member of a different committee within the decision-making process whose status is equal to or greater than that of the members of the allocations committee. After that would come an advocate from the Jewish community whose credentials are unquestionable even though s/he is not part of the decision-making process. While there may be only one member of the allocations committee within whose area of interest your project falls, you should not confine your approach to that one individual alone. Attempt to make positive contact with all members of the committee.

Contact on primary and secondary levels

Ideally you and a member or members of the committee will work together directly, on a primary level. This may take some doing and require a good deal of preliminary work. For example, on several occasions I have arranged for my first contact with a committee member to be preceded by phone calls over a three- or four-day period, from friends of the committee member telling him/her about the "wonderful" project they have just heard about. By the time we meet s/he is already positively disposed to the idea of the project.

Sometimes primary contact is impossible. If so, it is imperative that you develop a very thorough secondary contact system to ensure a positive hearing.

Professionals

Since the power of Jewish welfare and federation executive directors and professionals varies from city to city, it is impossible to make any general statement concerning their position. In some cities they control everything and in others they control nothing. With that in mind, I will make a few observations.

First of all, as with any institution, the longer an executive director serves as the chief professional of the organization, the more direct and indirect power (influence over lay leadership) he amasses. Second, very rarely will the lay leadership approve a resource plan of which the executive director vehemently disapproves. Third, most executive directors enjoy being helpful and having their names associated with a good idea. They also hate being patronized. Look for and actively seek the help of these Jewish professionals. Take their advice, with as much or little salt as common sense would dictate. But under no circumstances should you patronize or ask them to rubber-stamp your ideas.

Professionals can, and often do, serve as amici curiae for a project but rarely will they do so alone. Usually they will sound out committee members to find additional support before they themselves will back a proposal.

Nothing will anger an executive director or committee chairperson more than to feel that you have sidestepped them and not "followed the process." There is a thin line between seeking help and playing politics, so be careful when undertaking direct contact with committee members.

Budget formulation

The key factor in putting together a budget is that it should reflect clarity of thought and be self-explanatory. Committees have little time to spend trying to figure out what you mean by Item 3 in your budget or why "widgets" costing $17.50 each are necessary for the project. Keep explanations short and to the point. Do not hesitate to footnote a budget item if you think it might be confusing. If you can, get the help of a federation professional in putting together your budget. Remember, s/he knows the format preferred by the committee, as well as which items might prove confusing and therefore need greater clarification.

Our last suggestion on budget formulation is that budgets should reflect quantities, not only of money but of participants, paper, etc. in relation to a specific time period. The more general your plans and figures, the more open to misinterpretation you leave yourself.

Ideally you might like $5,000 for your project, but in a squeeze you might be able to get by with only $3,000. You have heard that it is unlikely that the committee will fund you at your full request. How much should you ask for: $3,000? $5,000? $7,000 or more? First of all, keep in mind that the people you are dealing with know their business. If you request a minimum figure for a project costing twice as much and show no other source of income, the decision makers will question your practicality and hence your ability to carry out such a project. On the other hand, inflating your budget with unnecessary or overpriced items will lead to obvious questions about your sincerity. In short, the best course of action is honesty. Your budget should reflect the ideal project/program you are undertaking. Trying to con the experts will get you nowhere.

Presentations

It is very much to your advantage to make a presentation before a decision-making body. Presentations are often difficult to arrange because there are a vast number of agencies, programs, or individuals also seeking interviews. Different communities have different arrangements. You may be asked to go before the Inclusions Committee first or a special subcommittee of a larger committee. You may be asked to give many presentations or absolutely none at all. Processes and committees are as varied as the number of communities. However, each will have a process that you must follow. In any event a presentation is valuable since it gives the decision makers a chance to see who you are and answer any questions they might have. Very often the questions asked by decision makers at such presentations may seem irrelevant or only tangentially concerned with what you want to talk about. Remember, however, the decision makers are evaluating not only the project, but also the people who plan to carry out that project.

In most communities full committees usually meet in order to agree to decisions delegated to subcommittees or to vote on the recommendation by a member of the committee appointed to investigate the program/project. So keep in mind that your preliminary meetings will be setting the stage for the disposition of the committee.

Your written presentation to the decision-making board should be short and to the point. Do not be so verbose that the committee has to wade through ten pages to find out what you want.

Never send a "bare" proposal; always include supporting data and material such as cost estimates from companies, newspaper articles about past programs/projects, and pictures. (A good 8×10 picture really *is* worth a thousand words.)

Verbal presentations should follow your written presentation. Your opening statement should be short and to the point, but not curt. Do not assume that anyone at the meeting has read or remembered any of your written material. Explain everything but do not go into massive detail. Again, if the committee wants to know something they will ask.

There will usually be one person at the meeting who will play devil's advocate; s/he may even take pleasure in being hostile. Avoid direct confrontation with an antagonistic member of the committee while making a presentation before that committee. Losing your cool will not help your image or the committee's impressions of your program/project. Never yell, scream, shout, or sermonize. These individuals can sometimes be dealt with by first

A foundation director once gave me a formula to follow in writing proposals which I have found very useful with federations as well as foundations:

1. What is the situation?
2. What do you want to do about it?
3. Why do you think your plan of action will affect the situation?
4. Who is going to do it?
5. How much will it cost (budget)?

All of this should take a maximum of four pages! In fact you might want to include in your cover letter a one-sentence summary of each point to further assist the committee in getting your message. If they want information, they will ask for it.

agreeing that you can "see their point" or "understand their feelings," and then adding your "but," "however," or "It is our understanding."

Listen to what people tell you—not only to their words, but also to the implications of their words and questions. Direct your answers to the basic problems implied by a series of questions. Don't try to answer every question, item by item.

Remember, the uniqueness of your program/project is your advantage and you are an expert on that uniqueness. Do not try to be an expert when you are not. In other words, don't be a phony. Finally, it is a good policy to invite members of the committee to meet with your group or project. This could involve a meeting at a certain physical location, with the group planning to carry out a project—a sort of "on-site inspection."

Some of the best thinkers in the Jewish community make the worst presentations. If you are working with a group, analyze your "troops" to see who makes the best impression on the decision makers, and let that person (or persons) make the presentation. Different people are good under different circumstances. A person who is great on a one-to-one basis may be terrible in front of a group and vice versa. Choose your best people for any particular situation. If two or more people are going to make a presentation, make sure that they are well rehearsed. Nothing will destroy your presentation faster than one presenter correcting another presenter or other signs of internal strife. Internal dissention and strife should be settled at home, not in front of a committee.

Follow-through

Your job is not over when you have obtained funding. You must remain in regular communication with the decision makers—not only for re-funding purposes, but also for future projects you might wish to undertake. The Jewish community finds it very distasteful to be involved with someone who is only after money. If you can involve people in your projects, so much the better. At the very least you should submit regular written reports and invite on-site inspection. It is extremely important that your last report include some form of evaluation, a critical aspect of your project/program. It is not enough to say a project was successful; you must explain what factors contributed to its success or failure. What was its value to the community?

Sponsors

Slightly different from mass appeals is the sponsorship method, which offers a more secure base of support.

On a regular basis the Jewish community takes to its bosom and adores different Jewish public figures. These figures are then asked to travel around the country lecturing to different Jewish groups, where, inevitably, they build up a following of supporters. If one of these public figures becomes interested in your project, you can approach him/her to act as your sponsor.

The person would then contact a key follower in each major city and explain the project to him/her. If that person is enthusiastic, a "parlor meeting" of other people who might be interested in such a project could be organized. Again, peer-to-peer fund raising is very effective, and the parlor meeting utilizes this technique

Organizing a system of sponsors is tricky and very time consuming. Jewish organizations doing fund raising in the same parts of the country are apt

While it is in your interest to avoid confrontation, this in no way means that you shouldn't stand up for what you believe in and fight for it. Do not sell your soul. They won't like what they have bought and you won't like what you have sold. The way to fight is to build a sound, irrefutable case for your project. But you needn't yell and scream about it.

A good proposal, written or verbal, has a planned beginning, middle, and end. People usually remember this while writing but tend to forget it when making a verbal presentation. If you have an objective, make sure you don't forget it. In fact, it is also a good rule of thumb never to walk into a meeting (especially when dealing with the Jewish community) unless you have a good idea of what you want to accomplish by the time you walk out of it. In order to achieve this goal—rehearse. Look at your plan/project through the eyes of others and see your weakness. Develop arguments and counterarguments.

to think you are stepping on their toes and may react hostilely. Also, if you want to get started on the project right away this is not the way to do it, since it may take two years to organize the effort. This method, with slight modifications, has a better chance of working for a small project. Under these circumstances it is not necessary to have a national public figure sponsor it. Instead you need one or a few local philanthropists (not charismatics) who will back the project and attempt to get their peers involved. Parlor meetings followed by publicity that lists the sponsors is the basic approach. This publicity is gratifying to the sponsors and encourages other people to become involved. Naturally, as with any of these approaches, constructive communication with the sponsors is important. Many of these projects set up an overseeing board of sponsors. As always, it is easier to get support for a project that can be self-sustaining after the initial investment instead of requiring yearly support.

Foundations

Foundations exist for the purpose of giving away money, which is to your benefit. All of them have their own pet interests and concerns, however, which make them more likely targets for certain projects than for others. Also, in tight-money situations, foundations are no better off than the rest of us. They will fund fewer projects because they will be working with a smaller amount of cash.

There are hundreds of thousands of foundations. Many are family foundations that were set up to bypass certain tax situations; these frequently do not fund new projects but exist simply to support the family's favorite charities. There are many other foundations, however, that actively seek to fund new projects.

There are three foundation libraries (that's right, a whole library devoted exclusively to foundations) as well as sections in general libraries that can provide the same information. (Starred libraries in the list below are foundation libraries.) They will help find you a foundation and are generally kind about helping you with advice for proposals, specific approaches, etc. They have a total listing of all foundation directories. Such libraries can be found at:

A word about mass appeals
Mass appeals for financial help are usually the least effective way to raise money. Some points, however, might prove helpful in making an impact.
1. Target a particular population, e.g., rabbis, secular school principals, Men's Clubs and Sisterhood presidents, etc.
2. Your mass appeal letter should be no longer than *one* page.
3. If possible, have someone of importance in the community sign the letter.
4. Don't try to say everything in one page! Be specific in your description. Offer further information.
5. Enclose a self-addressed return envelope.
6. And don't expect a quick response.

There are certain consulting firms whose sole purpose is to get funding for your project. They take a cut off the top (their fee might be 10 percent or 25 percent of whatever they raise for you). Look under "Foundations" in your phone book for specific consulting firms. In general, keep in mind that foundations can be a costly method of fund raising. If you do all the legwork yourself it will involve months of time. At best it will be time (= money) well invested.

Alabama
Birmingham Public Library
　2020 Seventh Ave. North
　Birmingham 35203

Arkansas
Little Rock Public Library
　Reference Dept.
　700 Louisiana St.
　Little Rock 72201

California
University Research Library
　Reference Library
　University of California
　Los Angeles 90024

San Francisco Public Library
　Business Branch
　530 Kearny St.
　San Francisco 94108

Colorado
Denver Public Library
　Sociology Div.
　1357 Broadway
　Denver 80203

Connecticut
Hartford Public Library
　Reference Dept.
　500 Main St.
　Hartford 06103

District of Columbia
*Foundation Center
　1001 Connecticut Ave. NW
　Washington 20036

Florida
Jacksonville Public Library
　Business, Science and Industry
　Dept.
　122 N. Ocean St.
　Jacksonville 32202

Miami Dade Public Library
　Florida Collection
　One Biscayne Blvd.
　Miami 33132

Georgia
Atlanta Public Library
　126 Carnegie Way NW
　Atlanta 30303

Hawaii
Thomas Hale Hamilton Library
　Humanities and Social
　　Sciences Div.
　2550 The Mall
　Honolulu 96822

Illinois
Donors' Forum
　208 S. La Salle St.
　Chicago 60604

Iowa
Des Moines Public Library
　100 Locust St.
　Des Moines 50309

Kansas
Topeka Public Library
　Adult Services Dept.
　1515 W. Tenth St.
　Topeka 66604

Kentucky
Louisville Free Public Library
　4th and York Sts.
　Louisville 40203

Louisiana
New Orleans Public Library
    Business and Science Library
    219 Loyola Ave.
    New Orleans 70140

Maine
University of Maine at Portland-
    Gorham
        Center for Research and Advanced
        Study
        246 Deering Ave.
        Portland 04102

Maryland
Enoch Pratt Free Library
    Social Science and History Dept.
    400 Cathedral St.
    Baltimore 21201

Massachusetts
Associated Foundation of Greater
    Boston
        One Boston Pl., Suite 948
        Boston 02108
Boston Public Library
    Copley Sq.
    Boston 02117

Michigan
Henry Ford Centennial Library
    15301 Michigan Ave.
    Dearborn 48126
Grand Rapids Public Library
    Sociology and Education Dept.
    Library Plaza
    Grand Rapids 49502

Minnesota
Minneapolis Public Library
    Sociology Dept.
    300 Nicollet Mall
    Minneapolis 55401

Mississippi
Jackson Metropolitan Library
    301 N. State St.
    Jackson 39201

Missouri
Kansas City Public Library
    311 E. 12th St.
    Kansas City 64106
Danforth Foundation Library
    222 S. Central Ave.
    St. Louis 63105

Montana
Eastern Montana College Library
    Reference Dept.
    Billings 59101

Nebraska
Omaha Public Library
    1823 Harney St.
    Omaha 68102

New Hampshire
New Hampshire Charitable Fund
    One South St.
    Concord 03301

New Jersey
New Jersey State Library
    Reference Sec.
    185 W. State St.
    Trenton 08625

New York
*Foundation Library
    888 Seventh Ave.
    New York 10019
New York State Library
    State Education Dept.
    Education Bldg.
    Albany 12224
Buffalo and Erie County Public Library
    Lafayette Sq.
    Buffalo 14203
Levittown Public Library
    Reference Dept.
    One Bluegrass La.
    Levittown 11756
Rochester Public Library
    Business and Social Sciences Div.
    115 South Ave.
    Rochester 14604

North Carolina
William R. Perkins Library
    Duke University
    Durham 27706

Ohio
*Cleveland Foundation Library
    700 National City Bank Bldg.
    Cleveland 44114

Oklahoma
Oklahoma City Community Foundation
    1300 N. Broadway
    Oklahoma City 73103

Oregon
Library Association of Portland
    Education and Psychology Dept.
    801 S.W. 10th Ave.
    Portland 97205

Pennsylvania
Free Library of Philadelphia
    Logan Sq.
    Philadelphia 19103
Hillman Library
    University of Pittsburgh
    Pittsburgh 15213

Rhode Island
Providence Public Library
    Reference Dept.
    150 Empire St.
    Providence 02903

South Carolina
South Carolina State Library
    Readers Services Dept.
    1500 Senate St.
    Columbia 29211

Tennessee
Memphis Public Library
    1850 Peabody Ave.
    Memphis 38104

Texas
Hogg Foundation for Mental Health
    University of Texas
    Austin 78712
Dallas Public Library
    History and Social Sciences Div.
    1954 Commerce St.
    Dallas 75201

Utah
Salt Lake City Public Library
    Information and Adult Services
    209 E. 5th St.
    Salt Lake City 84111

Vermont
State of Vermont Department
    of Libraries
        Reference Service Unit
        111 State St.
        Montpelier 05602

Virginia
Richmond Public Library
    Business, Science and Technology
    Dept.
    101 E. Franklin St.
    Richmond 23219

Washington
Seattle Public Library
    1000 4th Ave.
    Seattle 98104

West Virginia
Kanawha County Public Library
    123 Capitol St.
    Charleston 25301

Wisconsin
Marquette University Memorial Library
    1415 W. Wisconsin Ave.
    Milwaukee 53233

Wyoming
Laramie County Community College
    Library
        1400 E. College Dr.
        Cheyenne 82001

A short bibliography
1. There are lots of books. A good one is *The Art of Fund Raising*, by Irving R. Warner (New York: Harper & Row, 1975), which costs $7.95. It's full of ideas and advice.
2. A brochure entitled *What Will a Foundation Look for When You Submit a Grant Proposal*, by Robert A. Mayer, is available free from any of the foundation libraries (those starred on the list).

Finally, as with every other type of fund raising, the best way to get money is through a personal contact. If you know someone who sits on the board of a foundation, has dealings with one, etc., make contact through that person. If you don't know any such person, find one and cultivate him/her.

All of the above is my own de-romanticized picture of the money-power game. I've left out the foundation route for raising money simply because the topic is massive and each foundation has different requirements.

None of this should discourage you. Unlikely projects get funded every day. It's all really a matter of going about it properly. And remember, if you don't get funding from one source, try another. If it's a good project and a service to the Jewish community, it's a mitzvah to keep plugging away.

Social action

Jewish tradition has never made distinctions between ritual or "religious" responsibilities and ethical/social obligations. Among the laws of the Torah one finds mitzvot concerning the building of the Tabernacle and the treatment of foreigners, commandments about sacrifices and regulations about giving testimony and helping the poor. Similarly, the rabbis of the Talmud discussed not only the laws of prayer and kashrut, but also the relations between employer and worker and the obligation of tzedakah. Judaism has never been simply a religion of sacraments and liturgies, but rather a vibrant and compassionate culture, a people constantly aware of political and human realities.

The Jewish ideal is in some senses a political one: not the perfection of individual souls, but tikkun olam—the repairing of the world. We are bound to commit ourselves to creating a more just, more whole world. This can take place only through the interactions between people and between communities, and so Jewish teachings have always been concerned with personal morality, social responsibility, and "political" questions of leadership, power, and control of property.

When the rabbis were faced with a social injustice they did not simply rely on platitudes; nor did they act blindly:

The rabbis enforced the rule that on the sabbatical year all debts would be canceled. Hillel saw that the people were not lending to each other. He attempted to "set it right" (lit., perfect) by instituting a prozbul, whereby the debts could be collected (Gittin 36).

We can see from this that the rabbis did not feel locked into the status quo, and so they used the legal norms available to right the wrong. We see such concern for ethical behavior throughout our tradition. Perhaps the following statement in the Talmud makes the claim most clearly:

Whoever can protest against the sins of his or her household and does not, is seized and held accountable for the sins of his or her household; against the sins of their townspeople and does not, is held for the sins of their townspeople; and of the whole world, he or she is held responsible for the sins of the whole world (Shabbat 54b).

Jews throughout the ages have been caught up in "causes"; the Bar Kokhba rebellion, the false messiahs of the Middle Ages, the struggles of the Maccabees, the tantalizing promises of early Zionism, and, since Emancipation, political ideologies of every sort from Karl Marx to Ayn Rand. Jews have

Is such the fast I desire,
A day for men to starve their bodies? . . .
No, this is the fast I desire:
To unlock fetters of wickedness,
And untie the cords of the yoke
To let the oppressed go free;
To break off every yoke.
It is to share your bread with the hungry,
And to take the wretched poor into your home;
When you see the naked, to clothe him,
And not to ignore your own kin (Isaiah 58:5–7).

Our teacher Rabbi Abraham J. Heschel has taught: "In a free society, although each person may not be guilty, *all* are responsible."

No Jew is an island, and to the Jewish conscience all questions of politics, ethics, power, and wealth are ultimately moral, ultimately Jewish issues, as it is said: "*Tzedek tzedek tirdof—Justice, justice shall you pursue.*"

gotten themselves mixed up in strikes and revolutions, electing candidates and gathering petitions for just about everything. In recent years many Jewish leaders in America have called for Jews to become involved in causes like the civil rights and anti-Vietnam War movements, while other prominent Jews have strenuously warned against it. Those who feel ambivalence are caught in this tension, while those who support the Left watch in dismay as leftist groups, whom they formerly felt so much a part of, repulse them by their indiscriminate support of Arab terrorists and by their stand on Israel.

The point is, however, that there is really very little choice for most Jews but to align ourselves, as individuals, with one political movement or another, at least for a time. The Jews of the United States (and France and Russia and South America, not to mention Israel) are passionately political, and in the heart of even the most assimilated the instinctive Jewish formulation can usually be found; the moral progress of each person and the well-being and just operation of the institutions of society are eternally bound up together.

One interpretation of the role the Torah assigns to Jacob's descendants, that of being "a kingdom of priests and a holy people," is that this is a two-part job: to be holy, observing laws of study and purity, and to be priests of justice and human cooperation, advertising and acting out the ethics of Judaism. And this second role can be accomplished only by becoming a community—a political entity—whose internal rules and behavior toward others exemplify the universal ideals we preach.

Some problems of social involvement

Some issues are listed below, but this is not meant to serve as a comprehensive list of all areas of social action. There are issues, both "Jewish" and "non-Jewish," that will not be mentioned at all. Issues are constantly changing, disappearing, reappearing in new guises. There are, indeed, a number of areas that the Jewish community and its organizations have only begun to deal with, if they are dealt with at all. Surprisingly, for example, the area of Arab Jewry has received little attention beyond the passing of resolutions.

There are a number of other issues we must confront when considering social action. For example, how do we react to the corruption that exists in certain Jewish organizations and some Jewish leaders? Whether within the nursing-home industry or Israel investment groups, such signs of corruption have become all too apparent. There are many questions raised by these situations. Should the Jewish community act when a prominent member appears to be involved in wrongdoing? Should it rely on the legal system to enforce justice? Should it refuse "tainted" money or accept it but not honor the donor? Should the possibility that organized crime is involved in the kashrut industry be of concern to the Jewish community? Should the exorbitant prices charged for kosher-for-Pesah products be of concern to rabbinical organizations? Are Jewish organizations accountable to their constituents?

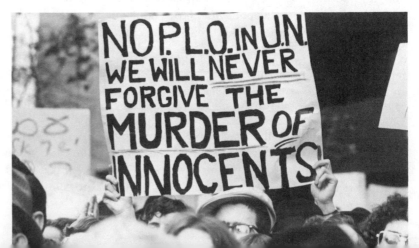

In the area of non-Jewish issues not confronted by our community, the list is overwhelming—whether it be the environment, civil rights, nuclear energy, corruption in government, or consumerism.

One of the issues that different groups and individuals have struggled with is the priority of Jewish issues over non-Jewish ones. There are no easy answers to this dilemma, for no one can be involved in everything. There is a natural pull to Jewish concerns, for if we don't care for/support our own community, who will? Yet should we concern ourselves only with ourselves— even in a broad sense? Does a non-Jew who is starving to death have a greater claim on us than a Soviet Jew seeking to leave Russia? Does a Jew in a decaying neighborhood have a greater claim on us than an Ibo of Nigeria? There are only shades of shades of gray in such troubling questions. The two major Jewish events of the century have brought us to opposing conclusions. The State of Israel has taught us the power of the Jewish people acting in unity, and the absolute necessity for Jews to be able to rely on themselves rather than on others during times of crisis. The Holocaust, however, taught us the powerlessness of people isolated in ghettos of their own or other people's making. To quote the oft-repeated words of Pastor Martin Niemöller:

In Germany they first came for the Communists and I didn't speak up because I wasn't a Communist. Then they came for the Jews, and I didn't speak up because I wasn't a Jew. Then they came for the trade unionists, and I didn't speak up because I wasn't a trade unionist. Then they came for the Catholics and I didn't speak up because I was a Protestant. Then they came for me—and by that time no one was left to speak up.

This leads us to a second point: self-interest. Much of political concern is really a concern with what's good for you (narrow sense) or what's good for the Jews. While civil rights, women's liberation, equality for all are important issues, how do we deal with the realistic implications of these stands? To rectify old injustices, we can all be in favor of hiring more women for university positions, but how do we feel when a competent male friend can't get a job only because we've righted the wrong for women? This whole area of quotas is surrounded by conflicting needs, and it is this conflict that led to a split by the major Jewish organizations over the issues in the Bakke case. Is protecting your neighborhood in Forest Hills really racism or legitimate self-interest? Each must answer the question for him/herself.

Finally there is the question of effectiveness. What good does it do if I go to a demonstration for Soviet Jewry? Or so what if I don't eat meat twice a week; *that* won't help anybody in Bangladesh! Again, the answers are not simple. However, we've seen movements that began small (the antiwar movement of the 1960s) and have grown and become powerful. The Soviet Jewry

In answer to all of these questions it is worth responding to them in Jewish fashion, with three questions:

If I am not for myself, who will be for me?

If I am for myself alone, what (kind of person) am I?

If not now, when? (Hillel, Ethics of the Fathers 1:14).

An afterthought: We believe what this whole section is about is concern for human beings and this can take many forms and wear many labels. That concern is neither liberal nor conservative, just as the "Jewish tradition" is neither liberal nor conservative. Judaism stands for justice, against injustice—terms unrelated to those labels. All of us continue to seek guidance, support, and even justification for what we do from the Jewish tradition, and this is just as it should be: "Turn [study] the Torah this way, turn the Torah that way—for everything is in it" (Ethics of the Fathers 5:25).

Plug in where you will so we can all look toward the day when "righteousness and justice shall walk the earth."

movement existed years before it became widely known. Obviously, if everyone had given up in the beginning none of these movements would have gone anywhere. (Imagine if everybody had told Herzl that he was a nut, and he had given up!) On the other hand, some causes are clearly hopeless and continue to remain so. The whole system of Jewish law is based on the idea that there is a correct way to act, to live, to do business. In Jewish terms, if it is wrong to eat too much meat, it is wrong whether or not the food you don't eat will go directly to a hungry person or not. The kabbalists believed that the whole world was linked together in a delicate balance, that each act, even the simplest, had cosmic ramifications that could tilt the world balance. This theory is reflected in the Mishnah, which says: "If you destroy one life it is as though you have destroyed the entire world, and if you save one life, it is as though you have saved the entire world" (Sanhedrin 5:1).

Getting involved

One place to plug in is through the local social-action committees of your synagogue or other Jewish organization. These groups vary greatly in size, interest, commitment, and quality. Not every synagogue or local chapter of Bnai Brith (etc.) has such a committee. If yours doesn't, see if you can generate enough interest to begin one.

Various national groups can be contacted on any number of issues (see the section below on Soviet Jewry, for example); check the chapter on the Jewish Establishment in *Catalog 1* (pp. 262–74) for organizations with areas of specific expertise. Another good place to begin is your local community relations council. This is usually an umbrella group that represents many different organizations. If you are interested in working, however, you can in most cases get a place on a committee. In fact, the committee on Israel is the group that will be doing most of the day-to-day work concerning Israel political action. In any event, the professionals who work for the council will be valuable resource people even if your commitment is to your local social-action committee.

The local community relation councils are affiliated on a national level with

National Jewish Community Relations Advisory Council (NJCRAC)
55 W. 42nd St.
New York, NY 10036

NJCRAC can be helpful in all areas of social action, and each year they publish a comprehensive booklet on the positions of the major Jewish organizations (all members of NJCRAC) on the major issues of that year—along with program suggestions. It's called the *Joint Program Plan for Jewish Community Relations* and is available from NJCRAC.

OTHER USEFUL ADDRESSES

1. **Social Action Dept.**
   United Synagogue
   155 Fifth Ave.
   New York, NY 10010
2. **Commission on Social Action**
   Union of American Hebrew Congregations
   838 Fifth Ave.
   New York, NY 10021
3. **Social Policy Committee**
   Synagogue Council of America
   432 Park Ave. South
   New York, NY 10010
4. **Religious Action Center**
   2027 Massachusetts Ave. N.W.
   Washington, DC 20036

Saving Soviet Jewry

Any connection between the Soviet Jewry protest movement of today and the small, loosely organized student group that first demonstrated in 1964 is purely coincidental. Then the few scholars and professors who took part always seemed to be out of place at a "student" rally. I remember the late Abraham Joshua Heschel towering above the massive steps of Columbia's Low Library invoking the prophets to protest Soviet injustice, seemingly the solitary member of the Jewish establishment who would join in the early "Children's Crusade."

Mass rallies and protests, involvement on the highest political levels, the existence of an infrastructure of local and national organizations were then beyond the realm of possibility. Equally improbable was the possibility that the Jackson Amendment (which linked the Soviet Union's trade status with its record on Jewish emigration) would become the law of the land, or that a president of the United States would be elected on a platform of human rights. Indeed, Soviet Jewry has become the bellwether of Soviet intentions in fields extending far beyond our own Jewish concerns.

Paralleling this growth in numbers has been the increased level of sophistication and effectiveness of the activities in behalf of Soviet Jewry. Political contacts and pressures, ways of working with the media, and new forums for protest have been developed and implemented.

What follows is a catalog of the most noteworthy programs in operation in behalf of Soviet Jewry, arranged into the following categories: political action by members of Congress and American public officials, mass action, peer-group action, ongoing contact with Soviet Jews, pressure on Soviet of-

The cause of Soviet Jewry has become, second only to the survival of Israel, the most widely supported concern of the American Jewish community. Up to two hundred thousand protesters have participated in the annual Solidarity Day rally in New York City, and many more have participated in local projects at the grass-roots level.

ficials and representatives, direct aid to Soviet Jews, and consciousness-raising activities. A bibliography and directory follow.

Choose the level of activity at which you would like to become involved and stick to it. The Soviet government is counting on the American people *not* having the stamina to see this issue through to its satisfactory conclusion. Let's you and me prove them wrong.

Political action by members of Congress and American public officials

Involve your congressperson in the congressional Adopt-a-Prisoner Project. More than thirty members of Congress in the greater New York area have assumed responsibility and undertaken regular efforts in behalf of Soviet Jewish Prisoners of Conscience in Soviet labor camps. Contact the National Conference on Soviet Jewry (NCSJ), National Jewish Community Relations Advisory Council (NJCRAC), Greater New York Conference on Soviet Jewry (GNYCSJ), and Union of Councils for Soviet Jewry, (UCSJ) for congressional assignments and further details. (See "Directory of Organizations" for addresses.)

For address of the president, etc. and suggestions for establishing a "telegram bank," see How to Make Waves.

They decided to learn ballet so they could go to America with the Bolshoi and then defect.
But He's 57 Shh!

Since 1972 the United States Congress has emerged as a potent major forum for political action in behalf of Soviet Jewry. Congressional support of the Soviet Jewry movement is vital not only for critical legislation such as the Jackson-Vanik Bill, but also because members of Congress, if properly encouraged and motivated, can effectively bring pressure upon the Soviet government to ameliorate the condition of specific Soviet Jews and Soviet Jewry as a whole.

1. Soviet Jewry is not exclusively a Jewish concern; it is an American issue. The rights of cultural and religious minorities, freedom from economic and political discrimination, and the ability to emigrate from the country of one's birth are mainstays of the American tradition.

2. Don't allow a politician to feel that s/he is getting your support too cheaply. Make demands for concrete action on his/her part. Some specifics will follow.

3. Be certain the congressperson knows that what you want is not merely a favorable vote on a specific issue, but leadership in aiding Soviet Jewry as well.

4. No matter how much work has been done on Capitol Hill in the past, each November brings new faces to Washington who must be familiarized with the issues and your concern. Some are new to the problem of Soviet Jewry. Others have limited their Jewish concerns to defending Israel. Seek them out and focus your attention upon them. Remember to send letters of appreciation to members of Congress acknowledging their efforts. Many people ask their representatives for favors but few show their thanks.

Other suggestions for action by congresspeople include the following:

1. Introduce resolutions in behalf of Soviet Jews and make frequent insertions in the *Congressional Record*.

2. Spearhead efforts with the United States Postal System regarding the nondelivery of mail and packages to Soviet Jews and with the Red Cross concerning conditions in Soviet labor camps.

3. Host receptions in behalf of visiting Soviet Jews to the United States.

4. Join in rallies and demonstrations including New York's "Congressional March" on Solidarity Day.

5. When visiting the Soviet Union as a member of a congressional delegation, raise the question of the treatment of Soviet Jews.

6. Place phone calls to the Soviet Union to attempt to speak with Soviet Jews or with Soviet government officials. Unfortunately, this has lost its effectiveness in recent years because Soviet authorities have maintained a deliberate policy of cutting off phone contacts with Soviet "dissidents."

7. Intervene in behalf of specific Soviet Jews.

8. Visit your local congressperson when s/he returns to your home district. Since they usually meet only professional lobbyists, the efforts by concerned nonprofessionals have a special effect. This is particularly vital in the "hinterlands," far away from the urban Jewish population centers. Your work there has an even greater effect.

In addition to federally elected officials, involve the governor, state senators and assemblymen, and city and county officials. Many visiting Soviet delegations come into contact with these state and local politicians. Proclamations, City Council resolutions, and local efforts are especially helpful and widely reported in the press. These groups are particularly sensitive to their local constituencies, so don't let them forget us!

Mass action

Mass rallies and demonstrations used to be the exclusive focus of the Soviet Jewry protest movement, but now they have been supplemented by many other programs and avenues of work. However, they're still crucial, the most effective way of retaining media interest and political support, in addition to providing sympathizers with the opportunity to express their concern and, at times, their frustration and anger. As a leading member of the American Soviet Jewry establishment put it: "Whether in Washington or the Kremlin, they know how to count heads."

In recent years the nationwide Solidarity Day for Soviet Jewry held in the spring has produced hundreds of thousands of marchers all across the continent and has been widely reported by the national news media.

The National Conference on Soviet Jewry is the central clearinghouse for fixing the date of Solidarity Day, Solidarity Week, and other nationwide projects. Word on these activities is communicated by NJCRAC through local community relations councils (CRCs) of the federations. *Keep in close contact with them for various action alerts!*

Don't allow people to be lulled into inaction while anticipating the next mass rally. Keep them busy with programs and projects on an ongoing basis.

The word about these rallies gets back to the Soviet Union and is a source of great encouragement. Be certain to go to the demonstrations held in your community and bring your friends. Often it is good to gather with thousands of other fellow Jews and friends not only for the sake of Soviet Jews, but for our own neshamot—souls—as well.

For advice on demonstrations, see How to Make Waves.

Peer-group action

A recent development in behalf of Soviet Jewry has been the formation of a series of peer professional matching groups to work for the rights of their

Two examples of action: On the May 9 anniversay of the Soviet defeat of the Nazis in World War II, groups of civil libertarians, public officials, and humanitarians sent public telegrams to Brezhnev and Dobrynin calling for amnesty for Soviet Jewish political prisoners.

President McGill of Columbia University announced that the university had adopted Oriental scholar Vitaly Rubin from Moscow and would not meet with Soviet representatives until Rubin was allowed to leave the Soviet Union to accept an academic appointment at Columbia. A year later Rubin, a hardcore case, received permission to take the appointment. He attributed his release to the work of Columbia University in his behalf.

Prisoner of the Soviet Secret Police
VLADIMIR SLEPAK
☆ SOVIET JEW ☆

LET MY PEOPLE GO!

Student Struggle for Soviet Jewry

Elie Wiesel tells about an incident that happened on one of his trips to the Soviet Union during the early years of the Soviet Jewry protest movement. He was asked how many American Jews had attended a certain rally held in their behalf. Wiesel, wanting to encourage them with a figure greater than the 25,000 who had actually come, said with pride: "One hundred thousand!" "That's all?" the Moscow Jew asked disappointedly. "Out of so many millions of American Jews, only 100,000 came out for us?"

professional counterparts in the Soviet Union. Among the most active committees are the following:

New York Legal Coalition for Soviet Jewry and
New York Medical Committee on Soviet Jewry
8 W. 40th St., Rm. 602
New York, NY 10018
(212) 354-1316

Medical Mobilization for Soviet Jewry
164 Main St.
Watertown, Mass. 02172
(617) 924-7726

Long Island Medical Committee for Soviet Jewry
91 N. Franklin St.
Hempstead, NY 11550
(516) 538-5454

A Useful Suggestion: The GNYCSJ has published a booklet entitled *The Conscience of Congress, 1974–1976,* detailing the efforts by representatives from the New York area in behalf of Soviet Jewish prisoners of conscience. (It is noteworthy that both Jewish and non-Jewish members took part.) Use it as a guide for programs that should be implemented and demanded of your local member of Congress.

These committees have undertaken projects, as for example in behalf of Dr. Mikhail Stern, a Soviet Jewish endocrinologist falsely accused of bribery and given an eight-year sentence. A petition signed by several thousand doctors in behalf of their colleague in the Soviet Union was presented to the American secretary of state. As a result of intense Western pressure, Dr. Stern was released after serving less than three years and now lives in Israel.

New York Women's Coalition for Soviet Jewry
8 W. 40th St.
New York, NY 10018

is an association of prominent women leaders. They sponsored a "trial" of the Soviet Union in which the wives of congressmen, city officials, prominent women's organization presidents, and others participated in marking the United Nations Human Rights Day. The transcript of public hearings is available from the GNYCSJ.

Other committees include the following:

New York Legal Coalition for Soviet Jewry
8 W. 40th St., Rm. 602
New York, NY 10018

Committee of Concerned Scientists
9 E. 40th St.
New York, NY 10016

New York Mental Health Committee on Soviet Jewry
8 W. 40th St., Rm. 602
New York, NY 10018

National Lawyers Committee for Soviet Jewry
10 E. 40th St.
New York, NY 10016

National Business Advisory Council on Soviet Jewry
10 E. 40th St.
New York, NY 10016

Information and details are available from the NCSJ and GNYCSJ.

Professional groups and societies can be extremely effective. Here are some of the ways your group can help:

a. Contact specific Soviet officials, such as the director of the Soviet Ministry of Health, protesting the condition of specific Soviet Jews.

b. Feature the stories of Soviet professionals in your specialized magazines—i.e., medicine, dentistry, and other professional journals. Letters to professional journals are frequently published.

c. Pass resolutions in behalf of Soviet peers. For example, library societies took the lead in protesting the imprisonment of Raiza Palatnik, a Jewish librarian from Odessa.

d. When visiting the USSR, raise the question of the condition of Soviet

Jews in your specific profession with the appropriate Soviet ministry officials. This has been very effective, but requires proper briefings and preparations. (Be certain to check with national Soviet Jewry groups *before* making such contacts.)

The movement to involve non-Jews and Christian clergy is being led by the National Interreligious Task Force on Soviet Jewry. They can be reached at

1307 S. Wabash, Rm. 221
Chicago, IL 60605
(312) 922-1983 and 341-1530

or

% American Jewish Committee
165 E. 56th St.
New York, NY 10022
(212) 751-4000
(contact Rabbi James Rudin at the AJC's office)

Sister Ann Gillen is the executive director. These people do exemplary work and are in the process of organizing in local areas.

Ongoing contact with Soviet Jews

The two major forms of communications between the Jews of the West and Soviet Jews are letter writing and phone calls. Both can serve to "protect" individual Soviet Jews by letting the KGB know that their condition is being monitored and scrutinized in the West. Equally important is the fact that the image Soviet Jews have of themselves as Jews is largely determined *before* they leave the Soviet Union. Therefore ongoing contact with them before emigration is critical.

Not unexpectedly, both letters and calls are subject to waves of Soviet governmental harassment and interference. If either letters or calls do not get through, refer to the "Followup" sections below. The Soviet government must be sensitized to the fact that the interest and concern of people in the West are constantly growing and that threats to the freedom of communication will not be tolerated.

One additional form of peer pressure has been the organized protests of individuals bearing the same surname as a Soviet Jewish prisoner. Recently New Yorkers with the name Feldman demonstrated in front of the Soviet Mission to the United Nations in behalf of Soviet Jewish prisoner of conscience Aleksandr Feldman.

Prisoner of the Soviet Secret Police
GRIGORY GOLDSTEIN
SOVIET JEW
LET MY PEOPLE GO!
Student Struggle for Soviet Jewry

MAIL

Writing to prisoners of conscience (POC): The NCSJ has published a definitive resource book (with provision for constant updating) on the POCs in Soviet labor camps. This basic program handbook contains background material, charges leveled against Soviet Jewish activists, lists of POCs with short biographical profiles, a listing of the addresses of labor camps and their commanding officers, recommendations for sending letters and packages, and a bibliography. Entitled *The Prisoners of Conscience: A Resource Book*, it was compiled and prepared by Sheila Woods and Isabel Cymerman and costs $1 per copy. The Student Struggle for Soviet Jewry (SSSJ) also makes available updated lists and information.

Contact a Soviet Jewry group for advice on choosing a POC. By coordinating efforts, you can assure contact with every POC in each labor camp.

The following guidelines are suggested:

a. Individuals (or groups) should write to just one POC. A steady correspondence is preferable to a single letter.

b. Soviet authorities try to discourage new contacts with a POC. Although first letters may not get through, *persistent* sending of letters has often resulted in receipt by the POC.

Note of Caution: To ensure that certain phone lines remain open, don't make calls to the Soviet Union without checking first with a sponsoring organization.

c. Initially the correspondent should send *many* letters, all short, and mail them at the same time to the prisoner. The first few letters will not be delivered but will serve to establish the writer's identity with the prison authorities.

d. Sometimes POCs are allowed to write only one letter per month (depending upon regime—prisons in the Soviet Union have different rules of strictness) and naturally prefer writing that letter to their family. Don't be discouraged if your letters are not answered. If you do receive a reply it may be after some delay, and from a third person writing in behalf of the POC.

e. Don't give up! The letters are a major way of indicating to prison authorities that the prisoner's well-being is followed in the West.

f. Send copies of your letters to your congresspeople to encourage their continued concern.

Adopt-a-Family: In addition to POCs in Soviet labor camps, other Soviet Jews have also indicated that they would like to be in contact with the West. These include the families of the POCs themselves. The Adopt-a-Family program matches Soviet Jewish families with American by family size, ages of children, and profession. The American family who is "adopting" receives a biographical data form about the "adoptee," including names, addresses, birthdays, academic training, name of spouse, children's names, birthdays, education and occupation, and additional information where available. Details and names of Soviet Jewish families are available from each of the national organizations. This has been popularized among many of the Soviet Jewry groups as Project Yachad and is a most worthwhile form of contact.

TELEPHONE: PROJECT INQUIRY

The Soviet government has systematically cut the phone lines of virtually all Soviet Jewish activists, in violation of the 1965 Montreux Convention and of the terms of the International Telecommunications Union, of which the Soviet Union is a member. One method of response to this policy is to call Soviet offices and institutions in America—ostensibly to ask for information on an individual who cannot be reached because of a disconnected phone. The raising of such questions will serve to protest the illegal activities of the Soviet government. Protest letters should also be written. Information calls and letters can be addressed to the following:

Embassy of the USSR
1125 16th St. NW
Washington, DC 20036
(202) 628-7551

Consulate of the USSR
2790 Green St.
San Francisco, CA 94133
(415) 922-6642

Soviet Mission to the United Nations
136 E. 67th St.
New York, NY 10021
(212) 861-4900

The SSSJ has a complete listing of the addresses and phone numbers of worldwide Soviet embassies and offices where similar letters and calls can be addressed. Call Soviet officials to express your indignation and concern. The calls should not be obscene or threatening. The Soviet authorities should be made to understand that the cutoff in communications will not be tolerated by the American Jewish and general communities.

Phone numbers of selected Soviet Jews are available through the NCSJ, SSSJ, and NJCRAC. If such calls are initiated and not completed, detailed specific data concerning the particular attempted conversation should be recorded. The NCSJ and SSSJ have prepared a "data form" to collect such information, and it is available from them.

This information is vital to the building up of a case protesting such Soviet action to the State Department, American Telephone and Telegraph, and the Soviet authorities.

Pressure on Soviet officials and representatives

During the past few years, increased numbers of Soviet citizens and government-sponsored groups have been visiting North America. Each Soviet performance, showing of a Soviet film, exchange program, sports event, and cultural exchange presents an opportunity to focus attention on the plight of Soviet Jews.

All Soviet visitors to the United States should be confronted with an American protest, particularly in areas far from the main centers of urban Jewish population. If a Soviet official is greeted with signs, pickets, questions, and press coverage, as was done at the University of Oklahoma in Norman, Oklahoma, then the Soviet government will realize that no corner of America is unaware of their policies regarding the Jews and minority rights.

A few caveats:

a. The point should be made that we are not protesting the policy of détente and cultural exchanges, and in fact we welcome visitors from abroad. However, we feel the necessity to share with them our concern about an issue that will, if not resolved, separate our countries even further.

b. Demonstrations should be vigorous but nonviolent. The distribution of handbills and "freedom programs," presentation of parallel competing events and picketing should be the focus of activity. Sample programs are available from the national organizations.

c. Be as creative as possible; old formats and activities are less newsworthy. A few examples:

—At a recent Bolshoi Ballet presentation Bnei Akivah and SSSJ conducted an open-air counter dance performance.

—On the occasion of the visit of a Soviet track team, a billboard in Russian was erected, bearing the legend: THE JEWISH PEOPLE STILL LIVES: LET OUR PEOPLE GO. CALL 555-9632.

—More than two hundred Jewish and non-Jewish concertgoers walked out of a performance of the Leningrad Orchestra and joined in a counter concert staged by local music students outside Carnegie Hall.

In recent years, the numbers of American cultural groups, political leaders, and business people traveling to the USSR has also increased. The visits of American public and private delegations should be the occasion for a thorough airing of the American concern for Soviet Jews. Keep the local community relations council and the national organizations informed so that all members of local delegations can be appropriately briefed.

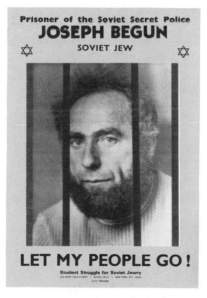

Prisoner of the Soviet Secret Police
JOSEPH BEGUN
SOVIET JEW

LET MY PEOPLE GO!
Student Struggle for Soviet Jewry

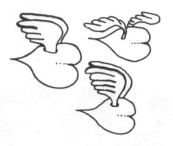

REMEMBER: The Soviet government does not distinguish between art and politics. Art is an extension of politics. Americans should not feel that demonstrating at Soviet cultural and artistic programs is inappropriate. Were it not for such protests, the Panovs would still be in Leningrad!

A Suggestion: Plant a question about Soviet Jewry at a university press conference, particularly on the occasion of a visiting Soviet scholar or visitor. Constantly remind Soviet officials of your interest. If the Soviets are not embarrassed to put Jews in prison for wanting to be Jewish, don't be afraid to ask a public question that might seem to be too "delicate."

Write to the Soviet Union: Communicate your concern about the condition of Soviet Jewry by letter directly to Soviet officials. The following would love to hear from you:

**President Leonid Brezhnev
The Kremlin
Moscow, USSR**

**Roman Rudenko
Procurator General
15A Pushkinskaya
Moscow, USSR**

Lt. Col. Andre Verein [head of Moscow OVIR—Visa office]
**Kolpachny Pereulok 9
Moscow, USSR**

Andrei Bykov [head of Leningrad OVIR—Visa office]
**26 Zheliabova Ulitsa
Leningrad, USSR**

**Dr. Boris Petrovsky
Minister of Health
Rehmanovsky Pereulok 3
Moscow K-51, USSR**

**Dr. Anatoli Alexandrov
Chairman, Academy of Sciences
Leninsky Prospekt 4
Moscow V-71, USSR**

General Karpov [head of Moscow KGB]
**Committee for State Security
Moscow, USSR**

Yuri Andropov [head of KGB]
**Dzerzhinskovo Ulitsa 2
Moscow, USSR**

Direct aid to Soviet Jews

Under certain circumstances it is possible to supply direct financial and material aid to families of prisoners and to Soviet Jews in the USSR, although new customs regulations and taxes have made the cost of mailing such materials prohibitive (e.g., a $250–300 tax on $100 worth of goods).

The following are some suggestions:

a. The Soviet Jewry organizations maintain a direct aid fund (tax deductible) to Soviet Jews. Contact them for procedures.

b. The SSSJ, NCSJ, and GNYCSJ sponsor Project Sefer to send books of Jewish interest to the Soviet Union. For a modest cost (up to $7) book parcels can be prepared.

c. Each year the Soviet Union is visited by more than 100,000 Americans, many of whom are Jewish. Committed and responsible Jewish tourists should be encouraged to visit Soviet Jews. These kinds of contacts are essential in supplying Soviet Jewry with the continued encouragement and education it needs for its own existence. In addition, American Jews can see firsthand the depths of emotion and commitment to Judaism long since forgotten on our side of the Atlantic.

Prior to their departure, tourists should be briefed properly through the SSSJ, GNYCSJ, and NJCRAC. Consult *Catalog 1*, pp. 82–89, for helpful travel suggestions. Proper orientation is essential, so don't leave this part of the trip to the last minute.

Consciousness-raising activities

It is critical to create a climate of opinion where the topic of Soviet Jewry becomes wide public knowledge and where actions in behalf of Soviet Jewry become acceptable and encouraged. Many of these consciousness-raising techniques, though well worn, have proved to be useful. Use your own creativity to come up with some new ones.

The NJCRAC publishes a yearly *Joint Program Plan for Jewish Community Relations* with many helpful suggestions as to the conduct of American Jewish public policy relating to a variety of areas, including an extensive section of Soviet Jewry. If you're in doubt as to the appropriateness or advisability of a particular course of action, the *Joint Program Plan* will convey the views of the major Jewish organizations.

Here's a brief version of the *Joint Program Plan*'s calendar of activities for the programming year:

August 12	Anniversary of the Stalinist execution of Jewish intellectuals, writers, and actors. Appropriate demonstrations featuring Yiddish literature and culture in communities and camps
Rosh ha-Shanah	Greeting cards to Soviet Jews and demonstrations
Yom Kippur season	Memorials in solidarity with Soviet Jews who hold public gatherings to commemorate the Yahrzeit at various sites of World War II massacres, e.g., Babi Yar in Kiev, Ponari in Vilna, Rumbili in Riga, etc.; commemoration services in synagogues or at Jewish cemeteries; dedication of special monuments at central locations
October	Sunday prior to Simhat Torah observance in solidarity with Soviet Jewish youth
Hanukkah	Anniversary of the Universal Declaration of Human Rights (December 10) and the anniversary of the first Leningrad trials (December 15)
Solidarity Sunday	Date of nationwide gatherings and demonstrations
Pesah	Symbolic acts of solidarity with Soviet Jews; places of honor at family Sedarim, using the Matzah of Hope declaration
Shavuot season	Teach-ins and university-related activities appropriate to the traditional devotion of this period to study
June 15	Anniversary of mass arrests leading to the Leningrad trials; sponsorship of programs focusing attention on the prisoners of conscience

Where to go for more books and bibliographies

The subject of Soviet Jewry has begun to be included in more Jewish high school and university curricula. It has also become a subject of much self-study. A good text for informal Jewish groups (high school classes, mini-courses, synagogues, etc.) is *Jews in Russia: The Last Four Centuries*, by Jonathan D. Porath (New York: United Synagogue of America, 1973). It is a collection of basic informative source material, with "Questions to Consider" following each selection. The appendix (pp. 163–76) lists over fifty suggestions for classroom and out-of-class activities.

The Board of Jewish Education of New York
426 W. 58th St.
New York, NY 10019

has published *A Master Listing on Soviet Jewry for Teacher and Students* (New York: Board of Jewish Education, 1975), which contains an annotated bibliography, with sections on tsarist, Soviet, and contemporary Russian and Soviet Jewries; lists of informational books, pamphlets, and brochures; source material written by Soviet Jews; guides to action programming; lesson plans; and a footnote on media. The bibliography is suitable for the university level and provides a good survey of books currently available.

A highly recommended collection of basic Soviet Jewry programming materials, adaptable for schools and information groups, is *The Challenge of Soviet Jewry: A Guidebook for Programs and Projects* put out by

Bnai Brith Youth Organization
1640 Rhode Island Ave. NW
Washington, DC 20036

This is a comprehensive 61-page educational guide containing a map, action program suggestions, appropriate songs, sociodramas, projects, useful addresses, a listing of Soviet synagogues and prisoners of conscience, and a detailed bibliography.

Some suggestions:

a. Do a term paper, MA thesis, or doctorate on the subject of Soviet Jewry. More and more schools and universities are accepting and encouraging such proposals.

b. Get some free advertising: write to the letters-to-the-editor pages of the local newspaper and various periodicals.

c. Let your car, mail, and body carry the message. Use bumper stickers, rubber stamps, T-shirts, bracelets, etc. (check the SSSJ catalog). Remember, the more visible an issue is, the more acceptable it becomes to publicize it. But be ready to defend the message you're carrying.

d. Organize a Soviet Jewry telephone hotline, a phone number supplying up-to-date information; make Soviet Jewish POCs members of synagogues, havurot, and other groups; stock school, university, synagogue, and private libraries with books and materials on Soviet Jews; present appropriate books and texts to public libraries and universities; voice Soviet Jewry concerns on TV and radio talk shows; produce your own cable TV Soviet Jewry show; conduct a "Soviet Jewry Walkathon" and sponsor a walking participant or take part yourself; set up POC information booths at schools and universities, on the streets, in shopping centers; compose prayer and liturgical modes for use in services (including silent kavvanot); organize mini-courses on the subject. Etc., etc., etc.

Prisoner of the Soviet Secret Police
JOSEF MENDELEVICH
SOVIET JEW

LET MY PEOPLE GO !
Student Struggle for Soviet Jewry

National Conference on Soviet Jewry (NCSJ)
10 E. 40th St.
New York, NY 10016
(212) 354-1510

has published a *Selected Bibliography of Recent Materials.*

American Jewish Committee
165 E. 56th St.
New York, NY 10022

has put out two very complete and authoritative bibliographies: *Jews in the Soviet Union (1967–1971)* and *Jews in the Soviet Union (1971–1975).*

The American Jewish Committee's listings cost $1.50 each and are well worth the money for any serious student of the Soviet Jewry scene.

Over the past few years there has been a dramatic increase in the number of books about Soviet Jewry. For a concise and authoritative history of Soviet Jewry by an outstanding Jewish historian, see the essay "Outline of the History of Russian and Soviet Jewry, 1912–1974" by Leon Shapiro (included in A. M. Dubnov, *History of the Jews of Russia and Poland,* vol. 3 [New York: Ktav, 1975]), pp. 413–496. *The Last Exodus* by Leonard Schroeter (New York: Universe, 1974) is the definitive work on the emigration movement in the USSR. *The Soviet Cage* by William Korey (New York: Viking, 1973) and *Courts of Terror* by Telford Taylor (New York: Knopf, 1976) give rich insights into the oppressive aspects of Soviet life, while *The Russians* by Hedrick Smith (New York: Quadrangle, 1976) gives an overall view of the broader Soviet society.

In addition, contact the national Soviet Jewry organizations for their own listings and program guides.

News and information

The situation regarding Soviet Jewry is constantly changing. The following will keep you up to date on events in the Soviet Union, and the response of American, Israeli, and world Jewry.

a. The NCSJ publishes a biweekly *News Bulletin* reporting on the current activist scene in the USSR, followup in Israel, and American efforts in behalf of Soviet Jews. A subscription is $3 a year.

b. The SSSJ sends out a *Soviet Jewry Action Newsletter* with the latest information and activist happenings, with focus on action that should be undertaken by American Jews.

c. The GNYCSJ's publications include *Freedom Line, In Brief,* and *Update,* which come out periodically, providing brief progress and news reports on the situation and detailed news of the prisoners.

d. A most informative biweekly *News Bulletin* is put out by

Scientists' Committee of the Israel Public Council for Soviet Jewry
4a Chissin St. Entrance B, 4th Fl.
Tel Aviv, Israel

The *News Bulletin* features correspondence from the Soviet Union, reports and a news roundup from the Soviet Jewish world, and happenings in Israel and around the world. Each issue is complete with pictures and documents.

e. The UCSJ issues a monthly newspaper. Now approaching its tenth year, *Exodus* is available at

944 Market St., Rm. 701
San Francisco, CA 94102

It has news and programmatic materials and sells for $5 a year.

Directory of organizations

The following is a basic listing of Soviet Jewry organizatons. Each local community will have its own group, which is usually tied in to one of these national agencies. Check with your local community relations council and federation for details.

1. The National Conference on Soviet Jewry (NCSJ) was organized in 1971 as heir to the American Jewish Conference on Soviet Jewry. The National Conference is the central policy-making body of the organized American Jewish community, and on its plenum are represented members of the Conference of Presidents of Major American Organizations and the representatives of local welfare funds and community relations councils.

> 10 E. 40th St.
> New York, NY 10016
> (212) 354-1510

2. The National Jewish Community Relations Advisory Council (NJCRAC, sometimes referred to as NACRAC) is the advisory body that coordinates national programs through the local federations and community relations councils. It introduces and implements national policy on the local level.

> 55 W. 42nd St., Rm. 1530
> New York, NY 10036
> (212) 564-3450

3. The Greater New York Conference on Soviet Jewry (GNYCSJ) was founded in 1971 to replace the loosely associated New York Conference on Soviet Jewry, with responsibility of serving as the community coordination body for eighty fraternal, religious, and educational constituent organizations. The GNYCSJ initiates citywide programs and, because of its scope and staff, is a central address for Soviet Jewry concerns.

> 8 W. 40th St.
> New York, NY 10018
> (212) 354-1316

4. Ever since its creation in 1964, the Student Struggle for Soviet Jewry (SSSJ) has been the mainstay in sustaining interest in the Soviet Jewry issue. It focuses on the activists and the families of prisoners and publishes a wide variety of information and program guides.

> 200 W. 72nd St., Suites 30-31
> New York, NY 10023
> (212) 799-8900

5. The Union of Councils for Soviet Jewry (UCSJ), a loose confederation currently consisting of fifteen local Soviet Jewry groups across the country, evolved as a more action-oriented and independent Soviet Jewry organization. They focus exclusively on the Soviet Jewish activists and prisoners and were the first to develop the person-to-person programs with Soviet Jews that were later adopted by other national Jewish organizations. UCSJ maintains close ties with Congress.

> 2920 Arlington Blvd.
> Arlington, VA 22204
> (703) 920-1020

The member councils include the following cities and regions: San Francisco, southern California, San Diego, Cleveland, Pittsburgh, Detroit, Cincinnati, Omaha, St. Louis, Philadelphia, Washington, D.C., Long Island, Brooklyn, Boston, Denver, Alabama, Connecticut, Chicago, Lansing, Minneapolis, Miami, Seattle, and Harrisburg. A complete directory is available from the UCSJ office.

Note:
These groups all emphasize different things and have differences related to their origins. SSSJ and UCSJ were early organizations in the Soviet Jewry field. They have moved from an antiestablishment position to a nonestablishment position or even a cooperative position with the other "more establishment" latecomers. These organizations adopt programs from each other, so you can contact any of them about the suggested programs. Yet there are still some antagonistic feelings—especially among rival groups in local communities—and you should step carefully.

May the day come soon—in our lifetime—when this chapter is irrelevant.

How to make waves

Demonstrations

December 24, 1970. The Soviet government, expecting no outcry on a holiday eve, announced the death penalty and long prison terms for members of a desperate group of Jews who had sought to escape the USSR. Within one hour a hearse pulled up near the Soviet Mission to the United Nations in New York and deposited two coffins. Students and rabbis appeared, lifting the caskets to their shoulders. Other youths, holding flaming torches and signs, flanked them as they marched to the door of the heavily guarded mission. The entrance was locked, as they had expected, and the demonstrators read a short, strong statement before being moved away by police. That evening millions of Americans saw this Jewish response to Soviet oppression on television and heard it on their radios. Photos were flashed to newspapers around the world. This demonstration helped to crystallize the massive public opinion that led to the commutation of the death sentences.

WHY SHOULD JEWS DEMONSTRATE?

In this media-oriented world in which Jews are still a small minority, a public manifestation can project your message to many people in a very short time with little cost. If Jews are not seen publicly backing their own causes, it is more difficult to ask for help outside the Jewish community. A demonstration generates political pressure and provides a useful outlet for the people involved.

THE PRELIMINARIES

Begin by formulating your publicity, political, and organization goals. This will determine where and how you'll demonstrate. If you're protesting White House indifference to the plight of Soviet Jews and you're in San Francisco, it's probably better to go to the Federal Building than to the Soviet Consulate. You'll want a place where you stand out, where you're not made invisible by a large crowd. You'll also want a locale that's accessible to reporters. It's better to rally in a small hall and overflow than to be lost in a large auditorium.

What are the range of demonstrations?
  a. from being for to being against an issue
  b. from small demonstrations to large rallies
  c. from immediate response to delayed action
  d. from peaceful actions to use of force

Choose your time carefully. If your local TV station film crew ends work at 5 P.M., then you'll want to demonstrate at least two hours earlier. If your "troops" will be watching the Super Bowl at 2 P.M., then choose another time. An immediate response to an issue will usually get media coverage. Keep in mind the following things:

1. Determine your constituency. Make a list of those you can count on to show, keeping it for future reference. Check with other groups who share your interest for their support; if you want their help, find out if they expect a hand in decision making or sponsorship. To avoid disappointment, figure out the number of people you can expect to show up—be optimistic yet realistic—and tailor your demonstration to that number.

2. How will you demonstrate? The press likes movement; add a dash of creativity. Spend time beforehand thinking of dramatic, eye-catching ideas.

3. Think of legal requirements. Check with local police or lawyers—cities vary widely in the need for permits. If there's a question, know the legal consequences of your action.

4. Who's doing what? If possible, break up into committees (such as publicity, contacts, demonstration site) with good communication between chairpersons and members and among chairpersons themselves. Select a competent coordinator; make sure s/he knows who's responsible for what. One or two people may have to do all the work; make sure your press and demonstrator lists are up to date and supplies for signs are on hand.

COUNTDOWN

1. *Contacts*: Write and/or phone the people on your list. Post clearly written flyers on bulletin boards and lampposts. (Write PLEASE POST and DON'T LITTER on flyers.) Announce the demonstration at organizational meetings. Keep a notation of what response you get and who needs a followup call. Utilize phone-in radio shows and radio "community bulletin boards" to publicize.

2. *VIPs*: If you think that big names—in the political, entertainment, scholastic worlds, etc.—will help you, choose deliberately and suggest what they speak about so as to avoid unnecessary duplication and to elicit specific promises of support. In a campaign year, try to be evenhanded in selecting politicians from various parties. If Mr. or Ms. Big Name has a tight schedule, find out when s/he will arrive and tell that to the press, which often will not stay long. If you can, get Big Name's remarks printed in advance to hand out at the rally.

3. *Media*: A press release should list the name and address of the sponsoring group and the name and phone number of a press contact. It should tell who, what, where, why, when, and how. If it's not going to be a large rally, two releases before your action will probably be enough. Try to speak to the news director of your TV and radio stations and editor of your newspaper. See if there is any specialized press (such as financial) that may be interested. Big fancy press kits are unnecessary—just one or two basic sheets. Don't tell outrageous lies ("Thousands will be there!" when one hundred will show up); it will redound against you next time. Tell the press to come fifteen minutes after you've told the "troops" to arrive; the media will see you at your strength. Remember that media coverage is largely the reason for having the rally. The person in charge of the press is very crucial to the operation. They should try as best they can (without being a nuisance) to make sure the press will be there. Most TV stations have only two or three film crews, so try not to conflict with other major events. If one film crew is covering a major address by the governor, the second one will inevitably have to leave (or will

never arrive at) your demonstration in order to cover a fire or other emergency. Sundays are very slow news days—which is why so many demonstrations take place then.

4. *Visuals*: Signs tell your story; 2′×3′ oak tag is usually sufficient. Use clear, plain, bold, black lettering; *thin, light-colored letters appear blank on TV or in news photos.* If you're demonstrating outside, use waterproof markers or paint. Brainstorm for slogans that are simple but tell your story. Check whether sticks can be put on your signs; police say no in New York City, for example. (The objection to sticks is they might be used as weapons if the demonstration gets violent.) If sticks aren't allowed, punch holes (strengthen them with reinforcements) and put in string so signs can be worn around the neck. Some places will allow you to use long cardboard tubing (like the core of a roll of wrapping paper) to which signs can be stapled. Put holes in large signs to allow the wind to pass through. Stars of David or Israeli flags bring immediate recognition. Use easy-to-make or easy-to-get things that tie in to the theme of the rally and/or make for a good photo, such as shofars, tallit, drums, prisoner suits and bars, chains, gallows, doves, black clothing, yellow stars, fake Bolshoi ballet programs, etc. Women in England presented a Soviet delegation with a goat representing scapegoated Jews. Motorcades might attract attention. Timed tie-ins, like birthdays and anniversaries, might prove useful. A simple bit of guerrilla theater acted out on the street can involve the public and can be repeated many times.

5. *Think ahead*: Run through scenarios of what might happen when you demonstrate. What are your contingencies for rain, adverse public or police reaction, medical problems? How have you arranged for lost children and bathroom facilities? Check out the area at which you'll demonstrate. You may want a legal observer; the local bar association will sometimes provide one.

AT THE DEMONSTRATION

1. Be there before your "troops." Survey the scene, remove obstructions such as garbage cans, and talk with the police. Have with you extra oak tag, markers, string, scissors, masking tape, and batteries for your bullhorn. Bring the permits. If there is a sound system, check it out and adjust it before the demonstration begins.

2. Be in control of your group. Appoint captains—if necessary, with visible identification such as armbands. If the rally is large, you'll have established separate squads with a headquarters and communication by hand signals, runners, or walkie-talkie.

Make sure someone is taking photos for your group—for publicity and for documentation, should trouble arise. Call or meet with all your key people the night before the demonstration.

3. Remember—you're dealing with humans. Despite a game plan, most demonstrators never act with military precision. Children get hungry or must use the bathroom. Cars break down. The guy with the bullhorn never shows up. Be flexible and improvise.

4. Find out who's in charge of the police squad, in case you need to speak with him. Appoint press spotters who can give out press statements, and make sure your press spokespersons know their subject, can speak to the point (perhaps fifteen to twenty seconds for radio and TV), and won't be thrown by surprise questions. If the press doesn't show up within about fifteen minutes after the time listed on the press release, call again to remind them.

5. Set up your visuals and tie-ins carefully as a background or as a centerpiece around which demonstrators can march. Make sure your most important signs are included in some of the scenes that are photographed; this makes a "story" and so creates a greater likelihood of appearance on TV or in the newspaper.

6. Chant, sing, read psalms, pray. Silence seldom attracts attention. Keep up the noise even if it means repeating yourself several times. If it's a serious demonstration, be serious. This is no time for socializing. Not *every* demonstration should end with Israeli folk dancing. If folks want to stand and talk, ask them to do it around the corner.

7. Movement is important. March around in picketing style (making sure the outside of your circle faces oncoming traffic so drivers can read your signs) or from one place to another. Walk slowly, with dignity, heads and signs high. Leave room for pedestrians.

Recently there has been a lamentable practice of having a dozen speakers address a rally, i.e., every local politician who is in attendance. This is boring and, when political necessities do not require it, should be avoided. If you want to, march a short distance away and break up.

8. End on a high note. Finish either at a set time or when you detect a rapidly deteriorating participation of your demonstrators, not when almost everyone has gone home.

ILLEGAL AND VIOLENT DEMONSTRATIONS

A demonstration can have force without being violent or illegal. But there may come a point where you seem to have no other option—you feel you must show that Jews are willing to engage in illegal acts in defense of their cause or else the media will not carry your message. Think before you act. This is a difficult situation that requires careful judgment. There are two types of demonstrations of this nature: (1) civil disobedience and (2) violence.

Civil disobedience involves disobeying a law in a nonviolent manner— for example, chaining yourself to the gates of the Soviet Mission, marching

Finally, in terms of violence on your part: A violent demonstration has grave consequences:

1. It alienates public opinion.
2. It gives the police a free hand to beat you up.
3. It ensures that many sympathizers will be afraid to attend or let their children attend the next demonstration even if it is billed as nonviolent. Violence is resorted to only by those who feel that in no other way will their cause be heard.

where you are not allowed to, or staging a sit-down and refusing to move on request. The fact that you are willing to be arrested for a cause shows people that it is very important to you. From your point of view you must decide:

a. Is this issue important enough to use this tactic? If used too often this technique loses its force.

b. Are you and enough other people willing to be arrested and possibly have an arrest conviction on your record or pay a fine or (though this is very unlikely) spend time in jail? Just because many arrested demonstrators have been let off by the courts does not mean that you will be.

c. Will this tactic generate sympathy or antipathy for your cause? If you decide to use this tactic, then

1. Arrange for legal aid beforehand. Know what the legal consequences of your action are likely to be; know what your bail might be. Have a legal observer or equivalent on hand, and have that person follow anyone arrested to jail to help. Have some dimes ready for calls to lawyers and family.

2. Give those demonstrators who do not wish to participate in the civil disobedience a chance to stand aside or leave.

3. Remove earrings, eyeglasses, watches, and other items that might be lost or prove painful or dangerous.

4. Have someone at a designated phone so s/he can call a lawyer and answer calls from families or friends.

5. When arrested you can stand and walk quietly to the patrol wagon or you can go limp, forcing the police to carry you. The latter tactic has the virtue of slowing down the arrest procedure—which can be useful in giving the press enough time to cover the arrests. Also, if your numbers are large it makes the whole procedure difficult for the authorities. On the other hand, it can provoke the police into more violent arrest procedures. You should realize that the police bear the brunt of your action, and their response is crucial in terms of how the demonstration looks and the safety of the demonstrators. As much as possible, you should inform the police of your plans (e.g., we will go quietly if we are arrested one by one, etc.). The "limp tactic" also carries the risk that you will be charged with an additional offense—"resisting arrest." A careful decision should be made between these choices, though you could leave it up to individuals to decide. In any case you should not march quietly together to the wagon so that the whole procedure is over in five minutes— the arrests will have no impact if they're over too quickly.

6. In case of violence, whether provoked or unprovoked, you should try to get out of the way if it is safe to do so. If you are in danger of being clubbed, you should lie flat on the ground with your face down. Clasp your hands and place them on the back of your neck. In this position the most vulnerable parts of you body are protected; it is also more difficult to hit someone who is lying on the ground. Try to get the badge number of policemen involved in the violence; they are supposed to wear them on their chests.

FOLLOWUP

The first thing to do after any demonstration is to check on how the media covered your event. If you think your point was greatly misunderstood, write or call the news director or editor; see if they'll air or print your response. Don't be surprised that little of what was filmed or taped is aired; that's normal. If your story was not reported—or if no media representatives showed up at your demonstration—figure out what might have gone wrong so you can avoid this situation next time. Then

1. Review all aspects of your preparation and demonstration.
2. Thank the people involved—from the "troops" to the big shots. Keep

your list of demonstrators and press contacts updated. Form an action squad of people ready to hit the streets at very short notice. Try to form coalitions with other groups for future work.

3. Follow up promises of help by big shots and others. Demonstrations are only means, not ends. Make it clear to legislators that your concern is a political issue and your group will exercise its power in the voting booth.

HOW TO HAVE A DEMONSTRATION WITH ONLY TWENTY PEOPLE

A frequent problem is the inability, for any number of reasons, to mobilize large numbers of people. Despite this fact, there are a number of things you can plan. Here are a couple:

1. Use a gimmick. As mentioned above it is good to utilize something that is photogenic—a coffin, people in striped prisoner clothes, etc. One effective demonstration during the Leningrad trials was staged by a small group of people who chained themselves together and walked through the downtown shopping area of Boston. It provoked comments/interest (other people went alongside leafleting) and was worth a photo and story in the press. To have an eye-catching photo accompany a newspaper story significantly increases the number of readers. This kind of demonstration requires only a small number of participants and no one will ask why there aren't a thousand people there.

2. Build your demonstration around an event of local interest. The dedication of a park ("Soviet Jewish prisoners can't stroll freely in a park" or "Israel has turned its desert into parks") is a local historical event. Don't be obnoxious. Try to think of how you'd feel in the other person's shoes. To ride through Boston the day before the annual reenactment of Paul Revere's ride shouting "The Russians are coming" would offend no one. To disrupt the official ceremony the next day would offend many. The basic principle is: if you can't get the press to come to you, go where the press will be. Line one block of a presidential campaign motorcade as solidly as you can with your people and signs, hoping the press and the candidate will take notice as they go by. Similarly, fill one section of a political rally with your people (perhaps softly chanting a slogan in the brief silence before the candidate speaks—you want to gain notice, not dislike). Often the candidate will feel that s/he has to make a remark about your issue since s/he is on the spot. Even if the press only carries the candidate's remark (whether the candidate means it or not is irrelevant on this level), you will have achieved the publicity you desired. Remember that the camera crew is looking for visual shots and might pick up your large sign. (If you can get permission to hang it from a nearby building, all the better.) Make sure that at least the key words are legible from a distance. But above all, remember that it is better to have done nothing than to offend a lot of people and create bad publicity.

Your second and third demonstrations
1. Review what went right and wrong with your first demonstration and plan accordingly.

2. The biggest problem with continued demonstrations is sameness. The press is bored, the people that come are bored, you're bored. Therefore avoid repeating exactly the same demonstration. Use a different theme, different route of march, different rally site, different speakers, etc. To prevent boredom, don't overload the demonstration with speakers. Besides famous types (famous and eloquent is best, of course), try to choose people who speak well. Different speakers also give the press something different to focus on. Consider introducing the people on the platform and letting each be applauded, rather than having them all speak. Naturally if Senator Q came from Nebraska to your rally in Florida, you have to let him/her speak. This whole area of limiting speakers takes some finesse (you do want them to *be* there), but remember that the politicians want to attend the rally for their own political reasons. They walk in Saint Patrick's Day parades etc. without getting a chance to speak. It's part of politics to be seen at these kinds of events.

Leafleting

Another small-group activity is leafleting. Setting up a table at a shopping center or main pedestrian thoroughfare can be very effective. Again, something visual—a photograph or someone dressed as Stalin standing nearby—will attract the attention of passersby. To get a table often requires a permit, so check it out. Even without a table (which also lets you display additional material) leafleting can be effective. Some hints:

A Suggestion: Multiply the effectiveness of the letters you write. Send carbon copies of the letters you send to other government officials, to your representative, and to your senator. Mark them FOR YOUR ATTENTION and ask them to follow up on the specific issue.

A few words about telegrams

a. They should not all look the same. Vary the text. Individualized telegrams have a tremendous effect.

b. A nearly instantaneous emergency response to a crisis by small numbers of people is far more effective than a thousand individuals responding two weeks later.

c. Let the people in power know how you feel. Public opinion is molded by those who care enough to tell their representatives what is important to them.

A Note: For further details, contact your local community relations council or

National Conference on Soviet Jewry
10 E. 40th St.
New York, NY 10016
(212) 354-1510

1. Be pleasant and presentable. People will avoid you if you look like a panhandler or a nut.

2. Try to make eye contact; most people are too embarrassed to refuse something if you catch their eye first (next time you try to avoid someone in the street, see how you act—and then prepare countermeasures).

3. Begin with pleasantries like "Hello!" and end with "Have a nice day!" Personalize if you can. "This flyer [on green paper] will go well with your blouse/shirt, etc."

4. Space your leafleters across the sidewalk to prevent the old end-run routine: people walking near the curb to avoid contact with the leafleter. Also spread them out so if large crowds pass by you have a second line of leafleters.

5. Avoid long conversations with people who stop. You'll miss too many people. Explain this to them and get their names and addresses for later contact or give them yours.

6. Don't get discouraged. Don't expect to give a leaflet to everyone and don't be upset by hostile comments.

7. Go where the crowds are. But again be sensitive. No one will object to your handing things out at a sports event (it's neutral), but you're likely to suffer from leaflets-in-the-mouth disease if you appear with your leaflets at a rally to Free the Albigensian Nine, etc.

Telegrams and letter writing

Write directly to American government leaders expressing your concern about the issue:

The President
The White House
Washington, DC 20500

The Hon. Secretary of State
Department of State
Washington, DC 20520

The Hon. (your senator)
United States Senate
Washington, DC 20510

The Hon. (your representative)
United States House of
   Representatives
Washington, DC 20515

The telegram is a significant political weapon that can be used with great effectiveness. It is estimated that one personal letter to a public official is worth the political impact of twenty-five signatures on a petition, while one telegram is equivalent to a hundred signatures. The special rate for public-opinion messages (e.g., to the president) is $2.00 for 15 message words. Slower and cheaper is a mailgram, which costs $2.50 for 100 words.

Organize a local *telegram bank*. Get the authorization of friends, neighbors, relatives, and others to send a number of telegrams per year to American or Soviet officials under their own name. Prepare a form for their signature:

I authorize _____ (name of individual or group) to send _____ 10
_____ 5 _____ (fill in number) of telegrams in behalf of Soviet Jews in my name in time of crisis.

Bill the telegram to the following phone: _____ which is listed under the following name: _____ and address: _____
_____

My home address is: _____
My home senators' names are: _____, and my home representative is: _____.

Signature: _____
Return to: [name of individual or committee]

Aiding Russian immigrants

Russian Jews who leave the Soviet Union are brought to the United States by HIAS (Hebrew Immigrant Aid Society). The majority of the Russian Jews who come here are aided in their settlement by HIAS in communities outside of New York or by its special organization in New York—NYANA (New York Association for New Americans). Despite the important work done by both HIAS and NYANA, volunteer groups in individual communities are valuable and necessary. Because of the size of the present immigration and hoped for future immigration, more help and local assistance are needed to ensure that the new immigrants will adjust and adapt to their new surroundings. In addition, the agency workers usually do not have local contacts or the knowledge and use of community resources in all areas. Therefore community volunteers have a chance to fill a unique position in settling Russian Jews.

Initial contact

Volunteers wishing to find out if there are Russian Jews in their own communities should consult the local rabbis. Since Russian Jews often make their initial contact with the local Jewish community through the rabbis of the area synagogues, the individual rabbis will probably have the names and addresses of any Russian Jews in your community. When you contact the rabbis, make sure that they understand who you are and what you are doing. It is vital to have their support and help because they have constant access to the community and its resources. You may also contact local federation agencies to find out additional names, but they may not be able to give out names for confidential reasons. Try anyway because some federations will.

Another very important way to attract Russian Jews who may be in the area is to place a large sign in the front of the synagogue or other Jewish building. This could be a welcome sign for Russians, with the name of volunteers or Yiddish- and Russian-speaking people in the community whom the Russians should contact for help.

Using existing Jewish communal institutions

The rabbis, the synagogues, and other local Jewish communal service organizations (the YM–YWHA or community center), as well as the family service

A word of caution for volunteer groups
It is very helpful to set up an organized group of volunteers to share the work of settling the Russian Jews within a given community, but it is very difficult to set up an ongoing group of the Russians. They are basically unaccustomed to such groups and require individual attention. Each family—in fact, each individual—presents his/her own problems and adjustment difficulties and will require individual attention. One quickly notes that these people, like many other immigrant groups before them, want to move quickly into the mainstream of American life and leave behind both the old life and ties to the old land. They may say they feel that they have very little in common with other Russian Jews except perhaps a common hometown in Russia. While this may not be entirely true, it is often better to plan joint social, religious, and cultural activities for American and Russian families. There may be strong feelings of rivalry and competition; they may feel that not everyone receives equal help and attention. So don't play favorites—help each family according to its needs.

agencies and Jewish day schools, can be most helpful to volunteers in many areas. They can provide physical space for programs and classes, materials, financial resources, professional guidance and personnel, counseling services, and religious programming, as well as volunteers.

The volunteer group may operate out of a synagogue, community center, or family agency, but a neutral place like the latter two is probably more desirable. This not only serves to eliminate competition among different religious movements for affiliation by the Russians but also helps attract the largest base of support from the Jewish community. Experience has shown that if one synagogue or movement administers the volunteer project, the thrust is limited—and so is the participation by all segments of the Jewish population. It is also extremely difficult to try to work with all affiliations, since there is little agreement on priorities or methods. If this can be done, it is much fairer to the Russian Jews, who should have a chance to learn about and make their own choice of affiliation and religious life-styles.

It is vital to establish effective channels of communication through the local synagogue bulletins, newspapers, day-school newsletters, and social-service agencies. Once the volunteer group has identified itself in the community, the public will know whom to contact if they wish to help. In addition, the volunteers can obtain quick responses to requests for furniture, tutors, and volunteers.

It is not necessary for the volunteers to speak Russian, though of course it is helpful. Many of the older immigrants speak Yiddish and some speak German. The Russians, particularly the children, do learn English quite quickly, and those more fluent in English can translate for the others. Language should not be a barrier to any volunteer wishing to help.

Hospitality and initial setting up of households

HOUSING NEEDS

The rabbis will be able to give you a list of the names of sympathetic Jewish and non-Jewish landlords in their areas. Have the rabbis or one of the volunteers approach the landlords about the availability of apartments. Explain the importance and the value of helping to settle the Russian Jewish immigrants in the community. Advertise in synagogue bulletins and local Jewish and non-Jewish publications to let people know that apartments and rooms, both furnished and unfurnished, are needed for these immigrants.

FURNITURE

Advertise that you are looking for used furniture. Offer to pick it up. Be prepared, however, for people who want you to pick up the furniture immediately, "like yesterday." Finding furniture is not hard—even very specific items—once you have set up good channels of communications. If you get offers but do not need the furniture immediately and have no place for storage, let the furniture go—there will always be more. To move the furniture, enlist the aid of the Russians in both the physical labor and the rental of a small truck (it usually costs between $15 and $25).

Many of the adults are reluctant to accept used clothing for themselves but do appreciate children's clothing, particularly winter clothes. You will receive many offers of clothing. Some of it will be in good condition and others fit only for the garbage. If you do take clothing, you will need a storage area and rack. Also be prepared to wash and iron much of what is donated. Many immigrants would rather buy one new item themselves than be given several secondhand items. Respect their feelings. If there is limited personpower, avoid getting involved with clothes unless there are special requests from the immigrants themselves.

DISHES, POTS, PANS, LINENS, BLANKETS, ETC.

A brief notice in the bulletin newsletter, or an appeal at a Sisterhood meeting about these needs should start the word going out and the responses coming in. Advertise for specific requests. If you receive kosher dishes, let the donors know that they may not remain kosher. Try to explain to the Russian the laws of kashrut. However, do not expect them to accept it or attempt to obligate them to observe this ritual.

Enlisting the aid of volunteers from existing organizations

Have the youth groups and the men's and women's organizations set up committees to welcome and help settle the Russians. If possible, provide an information booklet in Russian about the local community. Some of the Russians may need and appreciate an individual guide when braving the supermarket, the drugstore, and other local stores. A list of essential stores and bargain shops can be compiled by these volunteers. In addition, they may help the Russians to master the local transit system or take them for job interviews. Volunteers may also interpret and help the Russians to answer job advertisements in the newspapers and to write their résumés, as well as helping them practice for driving licenses.

The youth groups may provide free baby-sitting services while the parents are in classes, at work, or shopping. The youth groups, in particular, should invite their counterparts to join them and get involved in the local youth activities. The adults generally are too busy at first to join the Jewish organization, but invitations should be extended after the families have settled in.

Consultants in various professions

Put together a list of professionals that a new resident might need: doctors, dentists, social workers, lawyers, and teachers. Give each family the telephone number and address of the nearest municipal hospital's emergency room. The immigrants generally qualify for Medicaid since they arrive on a special refugee visa. It has been found that many of the immigrants have serious dental problems requiring costly and extensive care, so try to locate sympathetic (preferably Yiddish-speaking and/or Russian-speaking) dentists and oral surgeons.

Emotional and mental stresses and pressures may be expressed in physical health problems, so have doctors, psychiatrists, and social workers available for consultation. The social and financial upheavals experienced by the immigrants, as well as physical and mental ones, must be taken into account. It is important to realize that while there are certain specific difficulties faced by any new immigrant, each person has his/her own normal problems, and these may become exacerbated by the move.

Providing educational opportunities

In the New York metropolitan area NYANA sends Russians to English classes for four months; but the immigrants usually need and request more classes. For these people, set up voluntary English classes that will meet once a week or more for as many hours as possible in a synagogue or other community building. Advertise the need for teachers and tutors. High school or college students from youth groups or community centers are particularly good teachers for children. If there are a large number of immigrants in an area, you may be able to get a teacher and materials from the board of education. Regular English teachers and special English-as-a-second-language teachers are particularly helpful but not necessary. Often materials for both children and adults are available from the public school or the local library. Generally the children learn quickly in school but may need tutors in special subjects, particularly if they attend day schools and have a dual program of Judaic and general studies. Individual tutors may teach children and adults in their own homes as well. English classes are also offered in some public schools.

There have been some attempts to organize adult education courses about basic Jewish history, concepts, etc. given in Russian. Usually the immigrants will only attend classes in which English is taught. In the first year or two, they are occupied with adjusting to a new life, job, culture, and surroundings; they have little interest or time for basic courses in Judaism; such classes are more appropriate at a later time. By discussing upcoming Jewish holidays during class, the teachers in the English classes can provide a beginning knowledge of Jewish history and ritual.

JEWISH AND SECULAR EDUCATION FOR CHILDREN

Jewish day schools and yeshivot have extended a welcoming hand to Russian Jewish children by offering full scholarships for the first year (or until the parents are working and can pay part of the tuition). Individual synagogues or groups may wish to sponsor a Russian child in a day school.

Most of the children have little or no Jewish background, but the parents want to provide their children with the Jewish education that was not available in Russia. In addition, many of the parents are reluctant to send their children to public schools, despite the cost of private schools. If the child does go to public school, try to have the parents enroll the child in an afternoon or Sunday religious school program. Where there is a day school available but the parents still choose the public school, they may be feeling reluctant to involve themselves in any type of Jewish education. In such instances, be patient; wait until the parents are more receptive or can express their feelings and reservations about Jewish education. All Russian immigrant children, those in day schools and public schools, should be invited to community and synagogue holiday celebrations.

JOB TRAINING

Check out the technical and commercial courses available in your community. Some hospitals run training programs for various positions, such as record clerks and technicians. Local industries may also offer in-service training programs. In addition, there are other training programs for which Russian immigrants may qualify.

Council of Jewish Manpower Associations
299 Broadway
New York, NY 10007
(212) 233-8333

helps to place people in on-the-job training programs in many occupations. Under this program employers are subsidized for up to 50 percent of an employee's salary for up to six months.

JOBS

People wish to be self-sufficient and so want to find jobs quickly. Use local contacts to find out about jobs. Bulletins and community newsletters can be utilized effectively to advertise to the community what skills the immigrants have and to enlist job openings. Approach local merchants and members of the synagogues to see if they need extra clerks, stock people, or delivery people, or to find out if they are willing to train a new person. Contact hospitals and nursing homes to determine the availability of semiskilled or unskilled jobs. If possible, try to interest the women, men, and teenagers in baby-sitting jobs as an additional source of income. Women may also be interested in being paid companions to older or ill people or in doing housework. If there are seamstresses in your group of immigrants, advertise that their skills are available at a reasonable price.

Try to match up Russian- and Yiddish-speaking Americans in various professions with their Russian immigrant colleagues. There may be retired or older doctors in your community who speak Russian and can translate medical terms into English and train the immigrants in American techniques. The licensing exam for both doctors and dentists is extremely difficult. The opportunity to meet practicing professionals and watch them at work can be beneficial. Most professions require licensing; if posible, therefore, find out the guidelines and requirements for foreign professionals. This information can probably be obtained from the state employment office.

Note: Many Russian Jews come to America with inflated job and economic expectations. As they learn more English and begin to understand the American job market, they can try to obtain jobs that better utilize their skills. Many expect to get jobs comparable to the jobs they had in Russia, but this is usually not possible. Many of the Russians cannot easily comprehend the open and competitive nature of our labor market. They are accustomed to being assigned a job and remaining in that one job. They have difficulty maneuvering in our free-enterprise system where jobs are gained through personal initiative and where upward mobility is an expected way of life.

Religious life, activities, and orientation

It is often difficult for the Americans working with the Russian Jews to get satisfactory answers to two questions: (1) Why did these Jews come to the United States rather than Israel? (2) Since many of these Jews know very little about Judaism and were not terribly persecuted as Jews in the USSR, why did they want to leave?

At present the only people allowed to leave Russia are Jews seeking the right to emigrate to Israel. Unlike the refuseniks, many Russian Jews leave Russia because they believe they would have a better life in the West rather than for reasons of religious persecution. In fact, most Russian Jews experience little overt or personal persecution until they apply for exit visas to Israel.

Upon arrival in the United States, Russian Jews seek out synagogues for friendship, kinship, financial help, and job opportunities; perhaps some seek spiritual or religious guidance, but this is basically an unknown area for them. Therefore one successful approach in working with Russian Jewish immigrants is to provide them with friendship, hospitality, and financial, educational, and occupational help first, while at the same time being cognizant of the need to help them learn about Judaism. By so doing, one conveys to the Russian Jews that the American Jewish community accepts the responsibility of helping them become part of the community. To accomplish this, here are some suggested activities:

1. Invite each of the local rabbis to go to one or more Russian homes to place mezuzot on the doors. A real celebration with singing, dancing, wine, cake, etc. can be planned for the housewarming.

2. Distribute Shabbat candles and candlesticks to each family and provide the blessings in English, Hebrew, and Russian/Hebrew transliteration.

3. Arrange for Russian families to visit American families for Shabbat dinners and perhaps Havdalah ceremonies. Encourage the Russian families to reciprocate by inviting American families to their homes.

4. Try to teach, by example and explanation, the laws of kashrut and explain what would be appropriate if they invite people who keep kosher to their homes.

5. Publicize Jewish community or religious activities in Russian by having one of the Russians translate the regular publicity. Follow up with personal calls and explanations and offer to go with them to some event. The Russians are not accustomed to such organized religious activities and may not understand its purpose—so be explicit. (See the accompanying flyer in Russian about Misha Alexandrovitch.)

6. During the summer, scholarship money for camp (day or sleep-away camp) may be available from the local Jewish federation or other organizations in the community. For the older teenagers and college students, jobs at a Jewish summer camp can provide a good exposure to a positive Jewish experience.

7. If there is interest, arrange for one or two lectures or even a class in elementary Hebrew or a course in basic Jewish concepts and rituals. If there are individuals in the groups who are more interested in learning about Judaism, have individuals within the congregations help these people learn Shabbat blessings, prepare for an aliyah to the Torah, learn Hebrew, put on tefillin, etc.

8. Organize special holiday celebrations or involve the Russian families in ongoing community celebrations whenever possible. Do not be frustrated or disheartened if they turn you down or disregard any of your efforts in this area. Synagogue attendance and observance are usually alien to them, and though they may know the names of the holidays, the practices and history behind the holidays are usually unfamiliar to them. Note that the Board of Jewish Education of New York has published a series of booklets in Russian on each holiday; see list of publications for addresses. Some suggestions:

Rosh ha-Shanah and Yom Kippur: Invite the Russian families to participate in home and synagogue observances. Although both holidays are occasions for large public gatherings in Russia, most of the Russian Jews have never witnessed a service or participated in the home rituals of eating new fruits, dipping the apple in honey, etc.

Sukkot: Invite Russian Jewish families to a sukkah meal during the holiday. The children can help decorate the sukkah.

Hanukkah: Arrange a party for both American and Russian children with dreidel games, food, and music (preferably with someone who can sing in Hebrew, Yiddish, and Russian). Transliterate the Hebrew blessings into Russian (see the example) so that everyone, adults and children, can sing the blessings while lighting the candles. It is an exciting and beautiful experience to witness the miracle of Hanukkah lights with the Russian Jews. Inexpensive candles and menorot ($1.00–$1.25), available from most Jewish bookstores, can be given to each family. Include the transliterated blessings so each family can light their own candles every night.

HANUKKAH BLESSINGS IN RUSSIAN TRANSLITERATION

Свечка зажигается в воскресенье вечером.

Все правила 1, 2, 3 положенно говорить только в первую ночь (воскресенье вечером). Все остальные дни только первые две молитвы говорить 1, 2.

Каждую ночь кроме первой

1. Барух ато адоной, элохэйну мэлэх хоалом ашер кидышану, бымицвосов выцивану лыхадлик нэйр шэл ханука.
2. Барух ато адоной элохэйну мэлэх хоалом ше осо нисим лавотэйну ба емим хахэйм базман хазэ.
3. Барух ато адоной элохэйну мэлэх хоалом шэхэхиану выкиману выхигиану лазман хазэ.

Все три говорить в первую ночь

После произношения молить надо зажигать свечи слева направо.

Purim: Invite Russian families—particularly the children—to community or synagogue megillah readings. This is a Jewish celebration that everyone can understand!

Passover: Arrange to have each family attend at least one Seder with an American family. This is a very meaningful learning experience for both families. Try to include the broadest range of families—Orthodox, Conservative, and Reform—so as to provide a variety of experiences. In all cases the American families should be warm, understanding, and Jewishly committed people who can respond to the Russian Jews, regardless of their own practices. If it is hard to place a large family, try to arrange for a communal Seder or have the family attend an ongoing community Seder. Or have the Russians attend a Seder at a Jewish nursing home, where there is greater possibility that Yiddish- and Russian-speaking people will be present. Several different editions of Haggadahs are available in Russian (see the list of publications below).

One or more community organizations can arrange to deliver Passover packages to each family. The packages can be simple—wine and matzah—or they may include gefilte fish, eggs, kosher chicken, Passover cakes, cookies, candies, etc. Give proper explanations as to preparations for both the Seder and the special foods eaten during Passover.

Shavuot: At this time and throughout the year show slides or films about Jewish holidays and life in Israel. A night of Israeli music, slides, food, and dancing would be a good learning experience.

Many more religious activities can be arranged, but it is very important to keep several things in mind. As in any social situation that requires great adjustment and emotional adaptation, one must first establish trusting and meaningful relationships with the new immigrants. This may take a few weeks, months, or even years, depending on the individual people involved. In addition, the priorities of the American Jewish community may differ radically from those of the Russians. Whereas the Americans may want the Russians to fulfill themselves as Jews, for example, by having their sons circumcised, learning Hebrew, observing kashrut and Shabbat, etc., these may very well not be among the top priorities of the Russians. Finding a job (which may mean working on Shabbat and holidays), learning English, providing a home for a family, and trying to regain a stable way of life in a new country are major priorities for any new immigrant, Russian Jews included. Therefore, go slowly and be cognizant that you may alienate some people if you try to force them to move more quickly toward Judaism than they are ready to. Your values and way of life have been adopted by you through your own choice. Give the immigrants time to adjust to the radical changes in their lives; support them physically, materially, and emotionally. When they are better settled and established, then they will be more ready and willing to study and learn about Judaism.

Volunteer organization

The number of volunteers working with Russian Jews is growing, and two groups have been organized in the New York area to coordinate group programs. Contact them for further details:

Brighton Beach Committee
℅ **Mrs. Pauline Bilus**
293 Neptune Ave.
Brooklyn, NY 11235
(212) 769-1618 or 332-7000

Manhattan Committee
℅ **Jacob Birnbaum**
Student Struggle for Soviet Jewry
200 W. 72nd St.
New York, NY 10023
(212) 799-8900

Useful Russian-language and information publications for Russian Jews

1. The Board of Jewish Education of New York—in conjunction with Amanah Press—has published a series of Jewish educational materials written in Russian. The series includes thirteen books, a Russian-Hebrew Haggadah with historical background and commentaries in Russian, plus individual books on Shavuot (with a Georgian text available in addition to the Russian), Yom Kippur, Rosh ha-Shanah, Tisha b'Av (with a separate Ekhah—Lamentations—booklet), Hanukkah, Purim, a Yom ha-Atzmaut Collection (Israel Independence Day), the Book of Jonah, and laws and customs. Most books cost $1.00–$2.50, with the exception of the Hagaddah, which is $5. Contact

Eileen Roth
℅ **Board of Jewish Education**
426 W. 58th St.
New York, NY 10019
(212) 245-8200, ext. 858

2. The Greater New York Conference on Soviet Jewry will shortly be making available eighteen book titles in Russian. The books are of Jewish cultural content, including the works of S. Y. Agnon. Contact

GNYCSJ
8 W. 40th St.
New York, NY 10018
(212) 354-1316

3. The Student Struggle for Soviet Jewry has a list of selected titles that have been published in Russian. Thy also have a map of Israel printed in Russian. Contact them at

SSSJ
200 W. 72nd St.
New York, NY 10023
(212) 799-8900

4. Rabbi Pinchas Teitz has published a number of religious books and articles in Russian, including a Haggadah and essays on the holidays. (One difficulty with the Haggadah is that the Russian script is pre-1917 and therefore difficult to read.) He can be reached at this address:

Rabbi Pinchas Teitz
607 Park Ave.
Elizabeth, NJ 07202
(201) 353-4446

5. There are a series of Russian-language publications coming out in Israel with increasing frequency. One of these is *Nedelya*—a weekly that deals with social, political, and economic problems in Israel. The address to write to in Israel is

Nedelya
King George St. 38
P.O. Box 4601
Tel Aviv, Israel
(03) 248-261

6. *Tribuna* is a Russian newspaper published in Israel. The address is

Tribuna
Herzl St. 113
Tel Aviv, Israel

7. *Klub* (Club) is a popular weekly Russian magazine published in Israel; it appears every Thursday. The address is

P.O. Box 36372
Tel Aviv, Israel
(03) 269-386

8. *Vozrozhdenie (Revival)* is an elegant Russian-language magazine published in America with a strong Jewish religious orientation. Subscriptions are $10 a year. Inquiries and subscriptions should be addressed to

B. Haskelewitch
701 Empire Blvd.
Brooklyn, NY 11214
(212) 756-8786

9. The Lubavitcher Hasidim have religious books in Russian which may be obtained by contacting them directly at their headquarters at

770 Eastern Pkwy.
Brooklyn, NY 11213

or through FREE, an organization that works closely with these Hasidim. Contact **Mrs. Felice Gross** at **(212) 873-3279.**

10. The Jewish Occupational Council is the umbrella organization involved in research, planning, and dissemination of information concerning the vocational situation in Jewish communities. There are several publications available that describe workshops on the newly arrived Russian Jewish immigrants and the absorption and settlement process in communities throughout the United States. They can be reached at

Jewish Occupational Council
114 Fifth Ave.
New York, NY 10011
(212) 989-1920

11. *The Essentials of Judaism* by Rabbi Dr. Leo Jung is available in a Russian-language edition. It may be obtained from

Union of Orthodox Jewish Congregations of America
116 E. 27th St.
New York, NY 10016
(212) 725-3400

12. Dvir Publishing House in Tel Aviv has produced a number of Russian translations of Hebrew masterpieces, including the poetry of Bialik. Check with Jewish bookstores in the United States or in Israel for specific titles.

13. *OF SPECIAL NOTE* is "Which Promised Land? The Realities of American Absorption of Soviet Jews," the November 1, 1974, edition of *Analysis*. It is still the most thorough and honest discussion available on the subject of Russian Jews. This issue of *Analysis* may be obtained from:

Synagogue Council of America
432 Park Ave. South
New York, NY 10016

Ask for No. 47 Special Issue, November 1, 1974 (16 Heshvan 5735).

Useful Addresses
1. **United Hebrew Immigrant Aid Society (HIAS)**
   200 Park Ave. South
   New York, NY 10010
   (212) 674-6800

2. **New York Association for New Americans (NYANA)**
   200 Park Ave. South
   New York, NY 10010
   (212) 674-7400

3. **Student Struggle for Soviet Jewry (SSSJ)**
   200 W. 72nd St.
   New York, NY 10023
   (212) 799-8900

4. **Greater New York Conference on Soviet Jewry (GNYCSJ)**
   8 W. 40th St.
   New York, NY 10018
   (212) 354-1316

World of our fathers: Jewish poor and elderly

The rapid transition of the American Jew from poor ghetto neighborhoods to middle-class suburbia has encouraged the myth that all Jews are rich. Although sometimes Jews would also like to believe that, it's not true. Jewish defense organizations have repeatedly denied and disproved accusations of a "Jewish money" conspiracy, but it was only recently that they learned how false that image really is.

According to the *National Jewish Population Study* of the Council of Jewish Federations and Welfare Funds, there are approximately 750,000 poor American Jews. In an article called "The Invisible Jewish Poor" (1972), Ann Wolfe wrote that it took the publication of Michael Harrington's book ten years earlier (*The Other America: Poverty in the United States*) to

alert most of us to the fact that we were a country in which poverty, in its extreme, existed side by side with affluence. For a reason that is not altogether clear, the Jewish community did not recognize the relevance of this phenomenon to its own people.

The initial call to action, however, was sounded outside the established Jewish community. In 1971 S. Elly Rosen, executive director of the Association of Jewish Anti-Poverty Workers, testified before the Congressional Ad Hoc Sub-Committee on Manpower and Poverty. He charged that significant numbers of poor Jews lived in New York and that they were systematically being denied participation in the federal antipoverty program. In a subsequent investigation by the Office of Economic Opportunity, most of Elly Rosen's allegations were found to be true.

But far more significant than the government actions taken to correct these injustices was the combined effect of Elly Rosen's testimony and Ann Wolfe's article on the American Jewish community. Suddenly Jews saw a "new" crisis with which to contend. What was really new, however, was their awareness of it.

Who are the Jewish poor?

No one really knows who the Jewish poor are. For various reasons statistics on the Jewish population are scarce. Government poverty statistics, for example, classify the poor into categories of "Blacks," "Hispanics" (Spanish surnamed), "American Indians," and "Others," which include Jews along with all white ethnics. In addition, census takers are not allowed to ask about religious affiliation, on the principle of separation of church and state. (In traditional Jewish paranoid fashion, the Jewish community has supported the omission of the "religious question," figuring the less that is known about Jews, the less the evidence that could be found against them.)

To some extent these obstacles were overcome by several local Jewish community studies in the early 1970s and by the publication of the 1976 *National Jewish Population Study.* Unfortunately, the latter project (which can safely be called one of the greatest shams in federation history) offers us only the crudest national statistics: that 19.4 percent of all Jewish households have incomes of less than $6,000 annually, while 66.7 percent of the elderly fall in the "under-$6,000" category. More specific are some of the earlier regional findings: in November 1972, for example, the Federation of Jewish Philanthropies of New York released a monograph entitled *New York's Jewish Poor and Jewish Working Class: Economics Status and Social Needs,* which reported that

1. 140,300 families (including 272,000 individuals, or 15.1 percent of the Jewish population in New York City) are poor or near-poor.

2. 190,300 families, including 423,000 individuals, are between the near-poverty level and the Bureau of Labor Statistics' moderate level of living. This is almost one-quarter of New York City's Jewish population and constitutes the Jewish working class.

Ann Wolfe suggested that there is an even greater percentage of Jewish poor in New York, claiming that approximately 250,000 New York Jews subsist below an annual income of $3,500, with another 150,000 living at near-poverty incomes below $4,500 a year—a total of 400,000 Jews.

Unfortunately, even less is known about poor Jews in communities outside New York. A federation task force reported in 1973 that there are about 55,000 poor Jews in Los Angeles. In a 1975 study by the Combined Jewish Philanthropies of Greater Boston, 7 percent of Jewish families in the Boston area were found to have incomes under $3,000 annually. Chicago's Jewish federation stated that there are close to 25,000 poor and near-poor in that metropolitan area—and that figure could be low. Over half the people served by Philadelphia's Jewish Family Service (3,000 out of 4,800) are poor. A Welfare Planning Council Study (1968) done in South Beach near Miami found that about 34,000 Jews living in an area of some thirty square blocks had an average annual income of $2,460. Toronto has approximately 6,000 Jewish poor. And Montreal's federation reported that 15 percent (16,500) of that city's Jews live in or near poverty, with a large proportion of them younger working poor.

About two-thirds of the Jewish poor and near-poor in America are aged, the reverse of the general population, where approximately three-quarters of the impoverished are under sixty years of age. The remaining poor Jews are single individuals and families with one parent or a disabled head of household, or families with many children. Included in the last category are many Hasidic families. There are about 80,000 Hasidim in New York, and they constitute the third largest poverty group in that city. In addition, there are a small number of impoverished black Jews, numbering between 500 and 4,000 in New York City, with up to several more thousand nationally (statistics vary widely and wildly).

Other Jews who require increasing attention (especially during any economic recession) are the immigrants from Russia, who need funds and social services to adjust to American life (see Aiding Russian Immigrants).

When a poor man gets to eat a chicken, one of them is sick.

THE PROBLEM

The Jewish poor share the problems of all poor people in America. They all suffer from ill health, the effects of poor housing, and lack of opportunities to improve their situation. Most poor Jews live in urban areas, in inner-city neighborhoods that were once Jewish. (In New York this means parts of the Lower East Side, the South and West Bronx, Brooklyn, and upper Manhattan; in Boston, Roxbury, Mattapan, Dorchester, and a bit of Cambridge; in Chicago poor Jews are found mostly in Albany and Hyde and East Rogers Parks; in Cleveland they're in the Mount Pleasant area of the East Side; and in the Los Angeles area they live in Fairfax, Venice, the San Fernando Valley, and Boyle Heights.) These neighborhoods are breeding grounds for criminals and drug addicts. The remaining Jews live in isolation and fear, frequently without protection or support from Jewish communal or religious institutions.

RELIGIOUS NEEDS

There are problems caused by religious needs that are unique to certain groups of Jewish poor. Ann Wolfe points out that Hasidic Jews place little value on secular education and therefore cannot benefit from the economic advantages that a college degree may bring. Paying for private Jewish education adds to the drain on their resources. Strict observance of Shabbat and holidays precludes their taking on certain jobs or accepting overtime wages or part-time supplementary work. Orthodox and Hasidic families oppose birth control on religious grounds and tend to have large families. In Williamsburg, Brooklyn, the median family size is 6.3 children, compared to the average Jewish family size of under two children. Observant Jews have the added expense of kosher (or glatt kosher) food. Jewish festivals (like Sukkot and Pesah) require special foods and ritual objects. As a result an Orthodox family may be living in poverty although earning more than the official poverty income level.

Mr. Blumenthal is eighty-six years of age, his wife is eighty-four. They live on his social security of $1,380 a year. Of the $115 he gets a month, he pays $60 a month rent for the four-room apartment they have lived in for the past 38 years, plus the telephone and electric bills. He is left with $35 a month to buy food and clothing and maybe a newspaper once in awhile. Their shul—the Stone Avenue Talmud Torah—closed. Mr. Blumenthal cries every day as he says his prayers. It was his shul that died. "Where did everybody go?" (Arnold Fine, "I Remember When," *The Jewish Press*, May 12, 1972).

The elderly

The situation of the elderly poor is more acute, both because of their numbers and their relative helplessness. Let's consider, for example, the problem of housing.

Most elderly poor live in either public housing projects, decaying tenements, or neglected proprietary nursing homes. Thus the specific problems facing an old Jew in the inner city vary according to his/her residence; each type of housing threatens the stability and happiness of aged residents in its own way.

PUBLIC HOUSING PROJECTS

Changing neighborhoods with large Jewish populations, such as the Lower East Side of New York, are among those with the largest number of public housing projects in the country. From the outside these structures appear to offer decent, if not luxurious, housing for their inhabitants. They are tall and impressive; in some cases architectural amenities such as indented rather than unrelieved straight walls have been added. But first impressions of these buildings quickly fade when one discovers the frightened and lonely existence of the old Jews who live inside them.

First, the Jewish aged are isolated in such projects. Since public housing projects are run by a government committed to equal rights for all, Jewish residents cannot arrange to live in one section or floor of a building by themselves because it would constitute discrimination on the basis of religion. While such laws are unquestionably necessary to preserve our democratic society, the result is that Jews in housing complexes must be scattered throughout a vast project rather than situated among neighbors with whom they share their heritage and life-style. Frequently the customs of their non-Jewish neighbors seem strange and frightening to them; this causes spiritual alienation and personal loneliness.

The second problem arises from the first. Because the Jews are isolated, they have no one to accompany them as they go out to shop, which makes them easy prey for gangs of adolescents who are too young to pick on stronger victims. More dangerous are the drug addicts who need cash or goods to support their habits and who find the elderly vulnerable targets for assault and robbery. Furthermore, many of the old people are too weak to operate complicated dead-bolt locks, so that their apartments can be easily burglarized while they are out. As a result, the Jewish aged in public housing projects live in constant fear of attack on their persons and property.

Vandalism is rife in public housing. In the corridors of a project there is rarely an unbroken doorknob, an intact lightbulb, an unlittered hallway, or an elevator that does not reek of urine. Worst of all, mailboxes are frequently damaged or broken in such a way that they cannot be locked. Elderly residents, whose sole income is often their social security checks, must drag themselves down to their mailboxes on the day they expect their check to arrive so that they can receive it directly from their letter carrier; they fear that if they do not meet the mailman their check will be stolen out of their broken mailboxes. (To relieve this problem, some elderly have their checks deposited directly into their savings account, which has only been possible in the last few years.)

TENEMENTS

But if life is lonely and sad for those who live in housing projects, it is worse for tenement dwellers. These Jews live in five- or six-story walk-up buildings that are often seventy years old, in terrible shape, and infested with vermin. Archaic pilotless gas stoves often leak, broken windows go unrepaired, and fire is a constant danger. Although there is no law that prevents Jews in tenements from living near each other, in practice most of the Jews who lived in any one house have fled from the area, leaving those who remain behind as isolated and friendless as the Jews in public housing projects.

Old Jews in the tenements generally get along well with the blacks and Puerto Ricans who live near them. It is not unusual to find Jews whose neighbors shop, cook, and look out for them. Yet both Jewish and non-Jewish residents must face the appallingly high crime rate in the tenement districts. Both also must endure the high rents and low level of services imposed on them by their (sometimes Jewish) landlords. But because of their cultural isolation and physical infirmity, the Jewish elderly suffer more severely in these conditions than their younger neighbors.

NURSING HOMES

It is too easy simply to condemn all nursing homes as an unmitigated evil that brings terror to the minds and bodies of all aged persons. Our society has

An elderly woman from Mattapan in Boston told Yona Ginsburg (*Jews in a Changing Neighborhood*, 1975):

I was held up four times. The first two times they only took my money; the last two times they beat me up and threw me on the street. They cut my coat with a knife because they thought I had my money in the inside pocket. Last time I was attacked by a black at the entrance of this building. He pointed a knife at me and asked for money. He beat me. No one was around and I was scared to death. After the first two times I said to myself, "It happened twice; they only took money; it doesn't have to happen again." But now I am so scared, I'm afraid to leave the house.

We
should
see
with eyes
that are no
**** eyes, and hear ***********
*   with ears that
*   are no ears. For
*then, when someone
comes to ask our advice,*
we may hear them giving
themself the answer to their
question. - Rabbi Pinhas via M. Buber

Beginning in 1970 small groups of students and concerned citizens began to investigate nursing-home care for the aged. From their reports the passage of new legislation and some legal litigation against nursing-home owners has ensued. One early result was a report by Townsend that makes for particularly valuable reading, not only because it contains a wide range of information, but also because it includes personal reactions by the students working in several homes. One of its most useful contributions is a list of questions to ask and areas to explore when considering a nursing home for an aged person. Some of these questions:

Does the home offer progressive stages of care? ... Does the home require a complete physical before entrance or immediately upon arrival? Is

been forced to deal with the severe problems of caring for the sick and infirm old person who either can no longer be cared for at home or is not wanted there. Nursing homes developed out of necessity, not desire. (Significantly, most nursing-home patients have no close kin in or near the cities in which they reside who *could* take care of them. Thus they are not abandoned in any conventional sense.) Nevertheless, poor Jews living in proprietary nursing homes (i.e., homes run for profit) tend to live in horrible conditions.

Since the introduction of Medicare and Medicaid payments in 1965, nursing homes have become increasingly important as inpatient facilities serving the elderly in the United States. Presently there are over 17,000 nursing homes in the country, 80 percent of which are proprietary; they house 5 percent of the total elderly population—or one million persons. Because elderly Jews comprise a higher proportion of all Jews than do the aged in general (12 percent of Jews are over 65 compared with 10 percent nationally) and because Jewish families are relatively small and geographically scattered (thus precluding many of the informal supports that frequently prevent institutionalization), the proportion of Jews in nursing homes appears considerably higher than average. Poor Jews, who lack the financial resources often needed to sustain independence in the community, are especially vulnerable to institutionalization.

In their *Citizens' Action Guide to Nursing Homes* (1977) Linda Horn and Elma Griesel describe a litany of nursing-home abuses that have been identified time and time again in newspapers, documented reports, public records, and consumer letters:

> unsafe and unsanitary physical conditions
> poorly trained or untrained nursing-home personnel
> low salary levels and high turnover rate for personnel
> insufficient staff to meet patient needs
> lack of medical care and/or medical provision
> lack of nursing care and/or supervision
> inadequate food service
> poorly controlled and uncontrolled drug practices
> no protection of residents' legal rights
> no opportunity for resident involvement in decision making
> lack of rehabilitative and preventive health care
> lack of social and recreational services
> physical and mental abuses
> inappropriate placement according to level of care needed by patient
> lack of cost accounting and cost controls

Unfortunately, the very act of being institutionalized causes severe harm to most patients: confronted with the trauma of relocation and loss of personal freedom, close to half of all nursing-home residents die within their first year there. Although old people have the legal right to sign themselves out of nursing homes, they are seldom properly informed about this or physically capable of doing it. Often hospitals and doctors commit elderly patients to institutional care after the old men and women have been in a hospital for several weeks and have lost their apartments because of nonpayment of rent. In these cases the individual has nowhere else to go but to a nursing facility. In the home the aged person feels disoriented and stripped of all dignity. One woman, after being forced into a home, remarked: "They're just putting me here to die, aren't they?"

In many nursing homes old people suffer unspeakably horrid conditions. Filth and vermin are everywhere. Elderly men and women find themselves thrown into a small room crowded with five or six other persons. Few physical or mental distinctions are made in assigning people to a room. The continent must live near those who cannot control themselves and endure the stench

created by those who sit all day in their own filth. Day after day the sane must hear the uncontrolled screaming of people who are mentally ill. Perhaps most frightening of all are the physically and psychologically fit who simply stare blankly into space because they have nothing else to do.

But the horrors of nursing homes do not end with the wretched conditions of these institutions. The staffs of these homes, often underpaid and recruited from the lowest segments of the population, regularly rob, cheat, and beat the patients. Women who enter homes with diamond rings, often the only memento of their dead husbands, commonly "lose" them within a week. Fine clothes are taken away from the old people and rags are given to them to wear. Any cash the elderly receive must be spent quickly or the nurse's aides or maintenance personnel will appropriate it for themselves. Obviously these conditions exist only because the owners of these homes (often Jews who are very prominent in philanthropic and communal causes) care more about their profit margins than about the human beings entrusted to their callous care.

An explanation for the origin of these problems

How did this situation come about? American Jewry did not intentionally abandon its poor and aged members and condemn them to occupy the poorest and most dangerous sections of our large cities. Why did this problem remain hidden from Jewish consciousness for such a long time in the United States?

It is ironic that, for the most part, Jewish poverty is rooted in the great economic success of the American Jewish community. As Jews prospered they desired the physical comforts that their growing resources could now acquire. They found those luxuries in the affluent areas of the city and in its expanding suburban ring. Geographic mobility out of the inner city accompanied social mobility out of the working class. Only those too poor to move did not participate in this out-migration. The largest group of this nonmobile population was the elderly poor.

Other aspects of mobility also work against the interests of the aged. As modern executives and professionals move from place to place their ties to their extended families weaken. Nieces, nephews, cousins, and especially grandparents lose their importance in families of the mobile middle class. The suburbanite tends to concentrate his/her affection on spouse and children—the unit that moves along—rather than on other relatives who remain behind. Again, the elderly suffer from this neglect more than younger relatives, who can turn for attention to their own conjugal units.

The economic success of Jews in the United States has received a lot of attention, most of it favorable. But American Jews must realize that social mobility has its costs as well as its rewards. The overconcentration on the benefits of upward mobility has obscured its debilitating effect on the portion of the community that did not prosper. The outward migration of mobile Jews devastated urban Jewish communities. Strong communal institutions left the

there also a questionnaire to be filled out dealing with the patient's hobbies, favorite pastimes, etc.? . . . Does the owner require entrance contracts that fail to promise a return of property if a patient leaves the home? (Always get an entrance contract checked by a lawyer.) . . . How many patients are bedridden? (If large numbers are confined to their beds, it might indicate a lack of staff.) . . . Is there an in-service training program . . . ? (This shows a willingness on the part of the home to improve the quality of care.) . . . Is there a good rapport between the staff and the patients? . . . Are the patients clean? Is their hair neat, clean, and combed? Are their finger- and toenails clean and cut? Is there an extra charge for washing hair or for cutting nails? . . . Are the bedrooms neat and clean? . . . Are the emergency buzzers within reach of the patients? Do the nurses respond to these calls quickly? . . . Is there any urine smell in the home? Or a heavy coverup smell? . . . Does the home have a regular dietician? (Ask to see the kitchen.) . . . Are there different diets for patients who require them? . . . Does the staff eat the same food as the residents? . . . How many residents use the dining room? Do they seem to enjoy their meals? . . . Do the bedridden patients receive hot food? . . . At what hours are the meals served? (Some homes serve all the meals within one shift to save money.) . . Does the home charge extra for hand feeding? (This is ridiculous, since the need for being fed may well be the reason for institutionalization in the first place.) . . . Are the surroundings cold, impersonal, hard to adjust to? . . . Is there a sprinkler system and fire extinguishers? Is there a heat and smoke sensor system, with an automatic direct alarm line hooked up with the local fire station? Does the staff have regular fire drills so they know what to do in case of fire? . . . Are there handrails along the halls? Guardrails in the bathrooms? . . . Does the home provide occupational therapy? Physical therapy? Recreational therapy? . . . Is there a therapist who works often enough to fulfill the patients' needs? . . . Are visitors encouraged to come? (If visiting hours are restricted at all, perhaps the nursing home is trying to hide something.) . . . Do the patients seem happy? Would *you* feel happy leaving your mother there? (Townsend, *Old Age: The Last Segregation* [New York: Grossman, 1971], pp. 207–209).

city and moved to the suburbs along with their wealthy supporters. Economic centers dried up when their affluent customers lived and shopped elsewhere. The most politically aware and socially active members of the community abandoned entire urban areas, leaving those who stayed behind without articulate representatives or political clout. Most poignant, the friends, relatives, and especially children of the inner city dwellers fled from the remaining Jews, leaving behind isolation and loneliness. The community turned its attention to other things and the elderly poor were forgotten.

This is not to argue, of course, against social mobility: American Jews have made great economic gains and have earned the amenities that accompany wealth. But our successes must not mask our failures. Because American Jewry has advanced so far, it must assume a greater responsibility for those left behind.

Question: Do you know where your mother/father/grandparents live? When was the last time you visited them?

Jews and the antipoverty program

Despite the fact that the federal "war on poverty" began over fifteen years ago, government programs have been, by and large, insensitive to the problems of the Jewish poor. Although there are approximately 750,000 poor American Jews, Jewish participation in welfare and poverty programs has been minimal, a situation the Commission on Urban Affairs of the American Jewish Congress explains in the following way:

REASONS EXTERNAL TO THE JEWISH COMMUNITY

1. The first part is simple. Government antipoverty programs are geared to youth. Delinquents cause trouble, grow up to cause more trouble, and become a menace to society. Since little old ladies are virtually harmless and their poverty affects no one but themselves, the government pays very little attention to them. In New York City, for example, less than 1 percent of the money funneled through the New York Council against Poverty has been devoted to senior citizens' programs. In brief, these programs were designed to help poor people escape poverty, not to help those who cannot escape it survive. Although the needs of the aged are being increasingly acknowledged by Congress, they are still not a priority item. And since most of the Jewish poor are over sixty years of age, they are most neglected.

2. Under the federal guidelines of the Economic Opportunity Act (1964), antipoverty funding is directed toward *communities* of poor people. The individual is helped by these programs only if s/he lives in these officially designated areas, which were measured in terms of births, juvenile delinquency, and number of welfare recipients—all indices that do not apply to the majority of Jewish poor. Theoretically, local and national governments do recognize that poor people (e.g., many Jews) live outside these poverty areas. Nevertheless, with the exception of a few development projects there has been almost no attempt to reach out and serve the isolated poor, most of whom are unaware of the benefits the poverty program can provide.

3. Another reason Jews have been bypassed by federal antipoverty programs is that they are not officially considered a minority group. The Metropolitan New York Coordinating Council on Jewish Poverty is attempting to correct this condition by obtaining minority status for all Jews whose primary language is Yiddish. They would then be eligible for certain benefits and programs they cannot now receive. (In New York State, approval for some programs has already been granted.)

Jewish poor and elderly

1. Many Jews are eligible for welfare but have not applied for it. Public assistance carries a stigma that most poor Jews want to avoid. Some don't want to admit not having "made it" like many of their former neighbors who rose to the middle class and moved away. Since traditional Jews have always taken care of their own, many elderly and Orthodox Jews cannot become reconciled to asking goyim—non-Jews (the historic enemy)—for help.

2. Another problem is that poor Jews are not organized—especially the aged poor, who are scattered and often ill or housebound. Resigned to poverty, they feel that it is simply a burden that one accepts. They reject confrontation and power politics as frightening or alien to Judaism.

3. In addition, Jewish social welfare organizations are hesitant to become involved in the poverty program. The Commission on Urban Affairs of the American Jewish Congress places the blame squarely on Jewish community (New York) politics:

Originally they [Jewish communal organizations] viewed the program as a threat to their dominance in the social welfare field. By the time they overcame this reluctance, it was too late to play more than a minor role. They have not pushed for senior citizens' programs, they have not demanded more representation on the Council against Poverty, they have not submitted projects to be funded, they have not pushed for more citywide programs and they have played no role in organizing the Jewish community on a local level so that it could participate in local programs.

Communal responses to the poor: historical and contemporary models

In earlier centuries the average Jewish community was so small that the entire community, acting as a unit, could provide for all the social and religious needs of its members. As the communities grew, however, it became apparent that a more organized approach was necessary in order to meet the needs of the poor and ill. The models in medieval Europe were the Christian guilds, religious orders, and pious associations. Out of the Jewish community emerged the Hevra Kadisha (see the chapter on Hevra Kadisha).

The Hevra Kadisha was an agency for prayer, study, and philanthropy. The typical Hevra Kadisha tried to handle all communal needs; it concerned itself with charitable activities like burying the dead, caring for the poor, and helping the sick, as well as with organizing study and prayer. In *Communal Sick Care in the German Ghetto* (New York: Ktav, 1979) Jacob Marcus notes that the Young Men's Society in Vienna (1763) was organized to further the study of Torah, clothe and support the local poor, help impoverished wanderers, outfit poor brides, contribute funds for building synagogues abroad, send aid to Palestine, ransom captives, help the sick, study Mishnah, and light candles in behalf of the deceased.

The Hevra Kadisha still exists within some Orthodox communities today, notably in Israel and among the Hasidim and the K'hal Adath Jeshurun ("Breuer") community in Washington Heights, New York. It is still a relevant model for the local Jewish welfare organization and offers a welcome alternative to modern bureaucracy and impersonalization—in both densely settled communities and smaller havurot. Most importantly, the Hevra Kadisha embodies the traditional stress on self-help, human dignity, and interpersonal fellowship.

Historically the care of the poor and the sick gradually came under the

Blanche Bernstein, of the New School for Social Research, gives other reasons why many aged poor have not become welfare recipients. She suggests that some might be receiving monetary allowances from children who do not want their parents to be subjected to the humiliation of welfare. Others may have several thousand dollars in savings, which renders them ineligible for welfare. They use these assets either to supplement their monthly incomes or, more likely, as security against some future catastrophe or as an inheritance to be left to their relatives. Bernstein points out that those elderly who do not receive welfare lose not only cash assistance but also their eligibility for Medicaid, food stamps, and homemaker services if needed.

aegis of the Kehillah, the local communitywide organization of European Jewry. Although already existing in larger towns through most of the Middle Ages, the Kehillah reached the height of its influence in seventeenth- and eighteenth-century Poland. Kehillot were involved in local government, community representation, and civil service or public welfare, under which the Hevra Kadisha performed certain specific functions (such as burial of the dead).

As a result, most Jewish immigrants to the United States brought with them a tradition of communal welfare. In fact, the first Jews to arrive in America in 1654 were allowed to remain only by the decree of the Dutch West India Company stipulating that the incoming Jews "not become a charge upon the deaconry or the Company." Two months later the company reiterated that the "poor among them [the Jews] shall not become a burden to the Company or the community, but be supported by their own [Jewish] nation."

Because of this stricture no Jew was permitted to beg on the streets of New York. The lack of Jewish names on the records of the city's poorhouse indicates that most of the Jewish poor were serviced by private funds and were spared from entering city institutions. For example, at Congregation Shearith Israel in New York, established in 1655, one could ask the president directly for sums not exceeding three or five dollars, but above that sum the president had to consult with the Junta or the board of trustees. Soon a host of institutions developed, including a Jews' Hospital and an orphan asylum as well as the Hebrew Benevolent and the German Hebrew Benevolent Societies. This pattern was repeated in the early Jewish communities across the United States.

Between 1881 and World War I over two million Jews came to America. The overwhelming majority were poor—crammed into the miserable sweatshops and overcrowded tenements of the Lower East Side. But only in 1908, when Police Commissioner Bingham charged that 50 percent of the criminals in New York City were Jews, did the Jewish community become aroused. As part of their rebuttal to Commissioner Bingham the wealthy "uptown" Jews called for the establishment of an extensive communal organization. What developed was the New York Kehillah, which promised to absorb immigrants and help the impoverished (that is, the potential criminals). For a time its efforts succeeded. But by 1917 there was an alternative to the Kehillah in New York (which, in fact, the Kehillah helped create): the Federation of Jewish Philanthropies.

Through the years federations across the country have grown in strength, increasing the number of people for whom they provide educational and human services. The largest, New York City's Federation of Jewish Philanthropies, consists of a network of 130 constituent agencies that spend a total of over $500 million a year.

A complex organizational structure with vast economic resources necessarily finds it difficult to serve the individual client according to his/her needs. The casework agencies in particular try to overcome the numbers game by attempting to address themselves to the specific needs of each individual. In most American cities it is this kind of agency—the Jewish Family Service— that has the most direct contact with the Jewish poor. In Baltimore, for example, 33 percent of the JFS funds are used for servicing impoverished Jews; in Cleveland 40 percent of the JFS caseload is poor people; in the Miami area the figure is 25 percent; in Los Angeles, 55 percent; in Boston, about 50 percent; etc. The kind of services offered usually include counseling, financial aid (cash relief or rent subsidies), homemakers, friendly visitors, rabbinic services, child protection and foster family care, and relocation of Jews from deteriorating areas.

Traditional approaches to poverty

Jewish poverty is very different today from what it was in the past. When we think of the Jewish poor we think of the aged, the Hasidim, and the newly arrived immigrant, but in biblical times it was the widow, orphan, and traveler who comprised the needy.

The prophets proclaim the necessity of social change because of the many injustices and wide disparity of wealth in their society. In Proverbs, however, the blame is thrown back on the poor: "Negligent hands cause poverty, but diligent hands enrich" (Proverbs 10:4)—which sets a precedent for the more familiar cry that the poor became that way because they're lazy. Whatever the cause of poverty, we are obliged to help relieve it.

What is being developed in these examples is the concept of tzedakah (originally "righteousness," now "charity" or "philanthropy"). The first laws about tzedakah are based on an agricultural life-style. The rabbis derived a number of obligations to the poor from the Bible: (1) leket—the prohibition against gleaning fallen produce; (2) peah—the obligation to leave a corner of the field unharvested; and (3) maaser—a tithe contributed every third year for the orphan, widow, stranger, and Levite. The poor are entitled to the fruits of the sabbatical (seventh) year (Exodus 23:11), which is also the time for a release of debts (Deuteronomy 15:1–2, 7–11). The release of Israelite slaves and the return of ancestral lands to their original owners every fiftieth (jubilee) year was designed to reenforce tribal solidarity and prevent the permanent establishment of a landed gentry (Leviticus 25:8–17).

The halakhah (Jewish legal code) is concerned about how much is given to the poor and the way tzedakah is implemented. Even if one has given beyond the prescribed quota, "it is forbidden to turn away a supplicant person empty-handed" (Matenot Aniyim 7:7). The way in which giving charity is judged depends on the extent of kindness associated with it. Humiliation, embarrassment, and bureaucratic red tape should be at a minimum, as suggested in Maimonides' "Eight Degrees of Benevolence" and in the talmudic passage, "The person who gives alms in secret is greater than Moses" (Baba Batra 9a). (See Tzedakah above.)

The Jews are commanded to be kind to strangers, remembering that we were once strangers in Egypt (Exodus 22:20). We are not to mistreat widows or orphans: "If you do mistreat them," God tells us, "I will heed their outcry . . . and I will put you to the sword, and your own wives shall become widows and your children orphans" (Exodus 22:21–23). God protects the needy: "[He] upholds the cause of the fatherless and the widow, and befriends the stranger, providing him with food and clothing" (Deuteronomy 10:18). (See also Psalms 132:15 and 146:7). We are urged to follow God's example: "If . . . there is a needy person among you . . . do not harden your heart and shut your hand against your needy kinsman" (Deuteronomy 15:7). "Happy is he who is thoughtful of the wretched" (Psalms 41:2).

Despite these early attempts to reduce economic inequality, the warning of Deuteronomy rings true: "There will never cease to be needy ones in your land, which is why I command you: open your hand to the poor" (Deuteronomy 15:11).

These are the things for which no limit is prescribed: the corner of the field, the firstfruits, the pilgrimage offerings, the practice of kindness, and the study of Torah. These are the fruits of which a man enjoys in this life, while the principal endures for him in the hereafter, namely, honoring father and mother, practice of kindness, early attendance at the schoolhouse morning and evening, hospitality to strangers, visiting the sick, dowering the bride, attending the dead to the grave, devotion in prayer, and making peace between fellowmen; but the study of Torah excels them all (Mishnah Peah 1:1, Shabbat 127a).

Communal responses to the elderly poor: a case study of JASA

The Jewish community, in both its established and grass-roots manifestations, has not totally forgotten its elderly poor. The last few years have seen the growth of projects designed to aid the elderly. The community needs not so much to alter its perspective on aging as to augment already excellent organizations aimed at old, poor Jews. To illustrate this point let's take a look at the program for the aged of the Jewish community of New York City, where the majority of aged Jewish poor live and where projects for the elderly are most developed. New York's example can be applied—with certain modifications—across the country.

The major established organization responsible for aid to the aged in New York is the Jewish Association for Services for the Aged (JASA), a constituent agency of the Federation of Jewish Philanthropies of New York. In every way JASA is a professional, skillful agency, providing a wide range of excellent services to clients in the New York area. About one-quarter of JASA's $4 million budget comes from the federation, with the balance from various levels of government. (These sums exclude expenditures on housing.)

Note: While JASA is not unique in the services it provides, it represents a notion of comprehensive community care for the Jewish aged that ought to be more common than it is. Readers outside New York, however, may also want to take a careful look at the Council for the Jewish Elderly in Chicago, which concentrates all its services within one geographical neighborhood, with the purpose of helping older people remain independent residents of that community as long as possible. In addition to evaluation and counseling programs, personal assistance at home, a noon meal program, neighborhood bus transportation, and a wide range of social activities, the Council for the Jewish Elderly focuses on alternative housing options and maintains a temporary residence for the elderly (for periods of crisis or transition, or while younger family members take a vacation), independent apartment units, and a group living residence (commune) in nearby Evanston. Additional information about any of these projects can be requested from

Jewish Federation of Metropolitan Chicago
Public Relations Dept.
One S. Franklin St.
Chicago, IL 60606
(312) 346-6700

JASA attacks the problem of poverty among the Jewish aged on many levels. Perhaps most basic, it offers multiple services to individual old people, including help with life plans; mental health counseling; referral services; aid in securing government assistance such as social security, food stamps, and Medicaid; help in deciding on whether there is a need for medical or nursing care and advice on which institution would be best in any particular case; and emergency financial help. JASA also sponsors self-governing senior-citizen associations that provide the aged with meaningful outlets for their organizational talents and fruitful places in which to spend their time. In addition, the agency developed sponsors and owns two large housing complexes where the elderly can find not only decent places in which to live but also competently planned and well-run social services for all residents. Finally, JASA operates many special projects such as community Passover Seders and an experimental program to service old people in need of medical care in their apartments so that they can avoid going into nursing homes. For all of its activities JASA relies on an experienced administration, a fine professional staff, and a core of dedicated case aides and volunteers.

Because JASA receives government funds it must maintain a nonsectarian intake policy in all of its district offices. However, JASA by policy establishes its offices in sections with large Jewish populations. Also, due to the nature of the agency's sponsorship and reputation, it attracts a largely Jewish clientele. The proportion of Jews in JASA's caseload approaches 90 percent.

The New York federation also sponsors not-for-profit nursing homes that provide model institutional care for elderly residents unable to maintain themselves in their own apartments. They include modern physical therapy units, classes and social groups led by trained professionals, and excellent medical treatment. These facilities are immaculately clean and physically attractive. Conversations with residents indicate that they enjoy being there.

Like any nursing facility, the federation homes have their problems. Nurses' aides do not always treat the old people with particular care; racial tensions at times flare up between residents and staff. Also, many of these homes do not serve kosher food, precluding the possibility of their use by traditional Jews. Still, the level of care practiced in federation homes far exceeds that rendered in scandalous profit-making institutions.

Federation community centers offer further services to old people. The Educational Alliance in the Lower East Side, for example, includes an outreach unit staffed jointly by the Alliance, JASA, and the Jewish Family Service. Elderly people with personal problems can received skilled casework and psychiatric help, besides participating in a variety of trips, entertainment events, and parties. However, the problem with federation efforts for the elderly lies not in their quality but in their scope. While senior citizens enrolled in JASA, not-for-profit nursing homes, or community center programs receive excellent services, not enough old people utilize these resources. Many are helped; more are not.

JASA's projection is that there will be 340,000 aged living in the New York area by the end of the 1980s, slightly less than half of whom will be "poor" or "near-poor." In 1974 the figures were 310,000 Jewish aged living in the New York area, slightly less than half labeled "poor" or "near-poor." Through its social services, group programs, housing projects, and special programs such as the Passover Seders, JASA served some 42,000 elderly New Yorkers and their families in 1979/80, which means that the major federation vehicle for aiding aged Jews in New York reached only 12 percent of its potential clientele and, worse, only 25 percent of those who desperately needed its assistance. To serve 42,000 clients is undoubtedly a signal achievement, but to leave over 100,000 poor Jews unaided is a serious failure. The federation must augment JASA's outreach capability if it is to produce an effort capable of solving the problem of poverty among Jewish elderly.

Smaller still is the proportion of infirm Jewish old people living in not-for-profit nursing homes. While construction of decent communal-sponsored nursing facilities has remained dormant for the last few years, poorly conceived and terribly maintained private homes have been built at an alarming rate. In fact, since the introduction of Medicaid by the federal government, nursing homes run for profit have become both lucrative and attractive for enterprising businessmen who share none of the concern that federation-sponsored institutions demonstrate for patients in their care. The profit motive in these cases works directly against the best interests of the old people. While homes under communal auspices offer the best care, most patients end up in facilities whose chief reason for existence is money, not service.

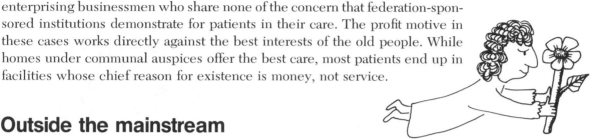

Outside the mainstream

Two predominantly nonfederation efforts also deserve special mention. They are both grass-roots organizations, initially founded outside the established Jewish community by small but dedicated groups of students and part-time volunteers. Deserving high acclaim is The Ark in Chicago, which has been able to sustain its initial idealism for nine years of high-quality professional services that continue to gain the respect and the support of community leaders, Ark volunteers, and neighborhood recipients. More widely known, and very much a part of our own personal experience, is Project Ezra in New York (see Project Ezra below for more details).

The Ark, a storefront operation in Chicago's Albany Park, was created in 1971 in response to two diverse social problems. The more obvious of these, that of the isolated Jewish poor, was for all practical purposes going untreated by Chicago's Jewish community. Second, its founders were concerned with disillusioned Jewish youth who needed an immediate and viable means with which to express their resurgent Jewish identity. Utilizing this corps of young Jewish activists, The Ark (named after the biblical ark that sustained life during a period of crisis) began with the creation of a free medical clinic, modeled on similar ghetto-area clinics operated by political groups but espousing the traditional Jewish ideals of mitzvot—good deeds—and hesed—loving-kindness—as their central tenets. Today a small staff plus over one hundred volunteers provide free legal, nutritional, social, medical, and dental services to approximately twenty-five hundred Jews each year. A visitor is immediately struck by the warm, individualized, and truly heymish—homey—environment of the center.

The Ark has five principal sources of funding. As a beneficiary agency of the federation, it receives approximately 40 percent ($80,000) of its annual budget from the organized Jewish community. Added to that are profits from its thrift store, an annual fund-raising concert, a few small government grants, and donations from over twenty-five hundred individual contributors. While working together with other Jewish organizations and institutions in the community, The Ark continues, in the words of one of its board members, "to trade efficiency for effectiveness and [to] use Jewish volunteers in the place of paid staff to the greatest extent possible."

Like The Ark, New York's Project Ezra also works closely with traditional federation agencies (especially JASA) in order to provide important volunteer-based services not currently offered by the established Jewish agencies. An outgrowth of the student movement of the late 1960s and early 1970s, Project Ezra seeks to break down the isolation of lonely aged Jews on the Lower East

Side. Operated by a small, part-time paid staff and a slightly larger young board of directors, it recruits student volunteers to visit old people weekly on an intimate, one-to-one basis. Strong ties are forged between the elderly and their college-age visitors. From this unique relationship the aged gain friends who are interested in them as human beings and bring them meaningful relationships in their later years; the young are given contact with a kind of Jewish life lost to their generation, in addition to the inestimable satisfaction of knowing that they have made an old person happy.

Ezra also runs special projects for its aged clientele, such as parties related to each of the major Jewish holidays. It sends speakers to affluent synagogues and Jewish organizations to acquaint the general community with the problems of the urban Jewish poor. In addition, it conducts tours of the Lower East Side to give uptown and suburban Jews a feeling for the section's rich history and present problems (see Tours, "Lower East Side"). Finally, it works with synagogues in the area, cleaning their premises and restoring their beautiful but deteriorating buildings.

Ezra's problems of scope resemble those of the federation. It serves about 80 clients on a weekly basis and its outreach activities may involve 250 old people in some way in the course of a year. But 9,500 aged Jews live on the Lower East Side. Student projects such as Ezra do marvelous work for the elderly and offer young people unique opportunities for mixing with another generation, but their impact on the total problem of Jewish poverty remains limited.

Eliciting government aid

The federation's resources for eliminating poverty among aged Jews are also severely limited. Altogether the New York federation raises about $20 million to spend on all its programs (the total spent by federation agencies is much higher, of course, because many of them receive government aid). These funds must be divided to meet educational, health, family service, youth activity, and community action needs, as well as to help the aged. But even if all of the $20 million were spent on the problems of the elderly, it would only be enough money to construct one decent housing project. If the federation wanted to augment the income of the aged poor, its entire resources would be exhausted by giving merely $150 to every old poverty-stricken Jewish person in New York. The entire federation budget would probably be inadequate to build and operate even one fully serviced nursing home.

The Jewish community itself, then, cannot eradicate the suffering of its senior members. Its resources, however impressive, are simply too meager for the enormousness of the task. Sufficient resources to provide livable housing, adequate relief, and humane nursing care can come only from government aid.

The Jewish community should actively work for government action in two areas. First, it should monitor present public antipoverty programs to make sure that Jews receive a fair share of assistance in proportion to their numbers in the poverty-stricken population. The problems of the Jewish poor and elderly poor at least match the conditions of other disadvantaged groups; they should not be deprived of any resources devised to combat poverty.

Second, the organized Jewish community must lobby for new welfare measures that would benefit its poor citizens. The Jewish aged single parents and disabled poor who cannot work to support themselves desperately need higher incomes and social security payments, desperately need—but cannot afford—better medical care, more decent housing in safe areas, and vastly improved nursing facilities. Only the government can provide these, and Jews, as American citizens, must urge that it do so.

But the responsibility of the federation will not end with increased public advocacy. Although the federation does much to aid the poor and the elderly poor, and in any case does not possess the ability to remove their problems, it could still do more to ameliorate the plight of these people. Too much Jewish money is still spent on nonsectarian hospitals and suburban community centers where crisis situations do not exist; not enough is spent on the poor and elderly whose condition is truly desperate. While the federation obviously cannot afford to allocate millions of dollars for housing for the poor, it certainly can find the thousands of dollars necessary to hire more social workers and case aides or to pay for kosher food in its own homes for the aged. In fairness, it must be stated that the federation's priorities for the poor and elderly are changing, but this is certainly not happening fast enough to reach most of our old people in the few years they have left to live. The responsibile Jewish community must press its philanthropic leaders to allocate a greater proportion of communal resources to the crisis-ridden poor and to use their prestige in the general community to fight for public aid for the Jewish poor.

Although it is the elderly poor who are obviously isolated, the rest of the Jewish poor are more subtly excluded. As is true of other groups, the Jewish community too divides itself along income lines. Some of us are in the position to offer jobs, education, recreational facilities, and hospitality (especially on holidays) to the less fortunate members of our community. We must begin to seek out those who can benefit from the resources we control, with the ultimate goal of enabling others to become self-sufficient—the highest form of tzedakah.

Resources

All Jewish Family Service agencies welcome volunteers in most of their work. If you are interested in volunteer work or in further information about the poor and/or the elderly poor, contact the organizations below, where examples from three cities are given. For a complete national listing of Jewish health and welfare agencies under the aegis of the Council of Jewish Federations and Welfare Funds, write for their booklet, which is available for $4 from Council of Jewish Federation Welfare Funds, 315 Park Ave. South, New York, NY 10010.

Isolation and loneliness
The problems of housing, physical security, low incomes, and nursing care must be solved jointly by established Jewish organizations and government agencies. But the fifth problem, isolation and loneliness, can be solved only by the solid commitments of the mass of American Jews. The causes of loneliness lie in the breakup of extended family ties. Certainly no federation agency or grassroots organization can replace a family. But we can resolve to get closer to our old people and to meet them as friends rather than as clients or patients. If we cannot recreate the trigenerational family, can't we at least attempt to forge again a trigenerational community?

In order to do this, communities will have to create Ezra-type organizations for the purpose of bringing Jews of different ages together in warm social relationships. Young and middle-aged people in such a program would benefit from the aged Jews' wisdom as much as the elderly would enjoy and appreciate the attention of younger people.

New York:
Jewish Association for Services for the Aged
40 W. 68th St.
New York, NY 10023
and
244 Graham Ave.
Brooklyn, NY 11206
services 16,000 persons, 95 percent with annual incomes under $3,500

Federation of Jewish Philanthropies of New York
130 E. 59th St.
New York, NY 10022
umbrella organization of all federation-sponsored agencies in the city

Project Ezra
197 E. Broadway
New York, NY 10002
student organization serving Jewish aged on the Lower East Side

Chicago:
Council for the Jewish Elderly
1015 W. Howard St.
Evanston, IL 60202
a model federation agency providing a wide range of services to the aged in East Rogers Park

The Ark
3509 W. Lawrence Ave.
Chicago, IL 60625
free medical/social/legal unit serving poor Jews in the Albany Park area

Los Angeles:
Bet Tzedek Legal Services
163 S. Fairfax
Los Angeles, CA 90036
provides free legal services to a predominantly Jewish clientele; receives government and federation funds

Israel Levin Senior Citizens' Center
201 Ocean Front Walk
Venice, CA 90291
a multipurpose senior center made famous by Barbara Meyerhoff's heartwarming book and award-winning documentary film, *Number Our Days*

Jewish Family Service
6505 Wilshire Blvd., Suite 614
Los Angeles, CA 90048
umbrella organization for services to the poor and aged

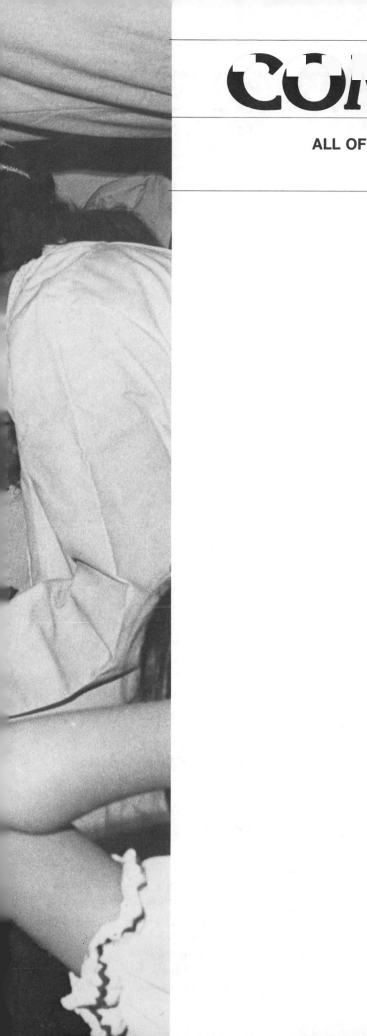

COMMUNITY

ALL OF ISRAEL IS RESPONSIBLE ONE FOR THE OTHER

כל ישראל ערבים זה בזה Shavuot 39a

Dissonance and harmony: lashon ha-ra

The most fundamental question about the nature of community must be: What is it that exists prior to any particular aspect of communal life? What is it that makes a community a community? The Hafetz Hayyim, one of the great sages of the modern era who was vitally concerned with speech, argued that a community in its simplest definition is a collectivity of people who speak *to* each other *about* each other. A community may or may not exchange goods and services, it may or may not worship or study together, yet prior and essential to any other function is the fact of the community's basis in spoken communication. The word community as we use it, then, is actually shorthand for "speech-community." And because it is so basic, speech has both a demonic and a liberating potential. Unwatched and unregulated, speech takes the form of slander and rumor and becomes a means for the majority to maintain control over the individual; disciplined and monitored, speech can permit a community to heal the wounds of its conflicts and permit a person to change his/her life without being hounded by past sins.

Judaism possesses a highly evolved ethics of speech that amounts to a vision of what it means to live a responsible life in community. The Hafetz Hayyim, who codified the law of speech and was active in promulgating the concern, did not invent these notions; they are embedded in the Talmud, the midrashim, and medieval codes. His achievement was of a second order of creativity but significant nonetheless; for in retrieving the legal materials governing speech from the recesses of ancient sources and in fashioning them into a coherent code, he did nothing less than restore to the Jewish past its availability and its relevance.

VARIETIES OF UNDESIRABLE SPEECH

What does Judaism have to say about speech? To begin with, under the general rubric of speech Jewish law comprehends a truly immense number of different modes of prohibited speech, each with its own derivation from Scripture and its own set of conditions: verbal abuse, public humiliation, defamation of character, swearing false vows, slander, talebearing, profanity, blasphemy, informing, cursing, false flattery, mockery, and of course, lying. The very exhaustiveness of this catalog reveals a stubborn realism about the multifarious ways evil enters human affairs through the agency of speech. It further reveals a determination to make the law operational, not by depending on the eloquence of general moral maxims, but anticipating the concrete occurrence and specific permutations of the offense. Of all these prohibitions and transgressions, however, we believe it is slander and talebearing that best represent this entire constellation of law and touch most directly on the daily business of life.

Lashon ha-ra

In prohibiting the circulation of ungrounded rumors, false tales, and defamatory information of any sort, Judaism hardly distinguishes itself from most other legal and ethical systems, which also view suppression of such practices as essential to the health of society. In Judaism this is taken for granted and hardly requires statement; rather, the great burden of discussion and investigation in Jewish sources centers on a more subtle question, the question of circulating information about someone that, though negative, is nonetheless true. This practice, referred to as lashon ha-ra—literally, "evil talk," or slander—is prohibited.

Lashon ha-ra occurs every time we originate or pass on a story about a person's past which, though true, has the effect of undercutting his/her present efforts. It is present every time we disseminate information about a person's family or spouse that would adversely affect our judgment of that person. And its exists every time we reveal something about a person that s/he would want kept secret. We indulge in a particularly serious form of lashon ha-ra when our disparagement of a person's talents and capacities in his/her work results in a loss of professional reputation and a deterioration of business. When we are told about someone we have not yet met, we are commonly put in possession of information that makes it nearly impossible to form a fresh opinion of the person when the meeting eventually takes place. The restrictions on lashon ha-ra, then, apply not only to cases where the discussant is known beforehand, but to *all* slighting expressions about a person's moral, intellectual, or professional character.

We could bear our burden lightly if direct expressions of disparagement were the only kind from which we are enjoined, for we are all adept at the kind of subtle innuendo that manages to be effective without being obvious. But in Jewish law such indirection, called "the dust of lashon ha-ra," is prohibited too. The rabbis were fully conscious of the heights of ingenuity we reach in utilizing implication, gesture, and context for the purposes of lashon ha-ra. To impugn a man's generosity, for instance, one need only dilate on the size of his fortune and leave the rest to the imagination. The rabbis understood the possibilities present in the style of an utterance—the tone of voice, gestures, and the whole arsenal of nonverbal skills we have become so adept at using—all of which can turn the ostensible content of a statement inside out. The rabbis were especially sensitive to the significance of situational factors in determining the ultimate import of a communication. Praise is a good example. One should avoid praising someone in public, we are told, because a large gathering is bound to include enemies of the person; moreover, one should avoid excessive praise because it tempts the listener to balance the picture by matching virtues with vices. Most of all, one must beware of indiscriminately revealing kindnesses that have been done for one and not for others.

The story is told in the Talmud of the man who comes to a strange city and has the good fortune to receive generous hospitality from a certain resident of the town: "Next morning he goes out into the street and says: May

We will use the Hebrew term lashon ha-ra because, while lashon ha-ra is actually something we do every day in ordinary conversation, "slander" suggests the kind of criminal intent and litigation we would hardly associate with our own lives.

If you don't open your mouth, no flies will get in. -yiddish proverb Trans.- Leo Rosten

the Merciful One bless so-and-so, who labored so much on my behalf. Whereupon people will hear it and come and plunder him" (Arakhin 16a).

It is not only the speaker of lashon ha-ra who places himself in transgression, but the recipient of the communication as well. The Talmud (Arakhin 15b) reflects on the essentially triangular network of relations set in motion by lashon ha-ra: "The talk about third (persons) kills three persons: him who tells (the slander), him who accepts it, and him about whom it is told." Some commentators take the killing here in its literal sense: if the calumny transmitted to the recipient refers to something done to him by the third party (the person spoken about), forces of conflict will be unleashed that will climax in the murder of the third party, the punishment of the murderer (the recipient), and the revenge taken by the relatives of the slain man on the original speaker. Other commentators take this image of primitive violence figuratively: while the death referred to in the case of the subject of the slander represents potential real suffering, the deaths of the slanderer and the recipient are moral and religious—they have ceased to be alive to the consequences of their actions; they have become like lepers who no longer have a place in the community of people.

In Jewish legal sources the recipient of lashon ha-ra is the subject of special attention. It goes without saying that he is enjoined from passing on what he has been told; his special responsibility is to refuse to believe the slander. Now, the rabbis were perceptive enough to realize that once a choice piece of information has been deposited or a seed of doubt planted, it is immensely difficult to withhold our tacit assent, for we invariably believe that if it was said at all there must be some truth to it. However, the rabbis were characteristically less concerned with what people "believed" (in the sense of having an inner conviction about) than with the actions taken on the basis of those beliefs. Thus while there is little hope of controlling the imagination and suspicion, there can be every expectation that a concerned Jew will decline to act on the basis of the slander—that he will continue to act, in other words, as if he had never heard it.

There are situations in which the norms of the community make it nearly impossible for such self-restraint to be practiced; when lashon ha-ra has become the habitual ethic of a group, its members are given the special designation of "masters of lashon ha-ra" and henceforth their company is shunned, for this is no longer an environment in which a decent man can expect to receive support for ethical behavior.

PERMISSIBLE LASHON HA-RA

Asking anyone to observe all these prohibitions is asking a great deal, and the strain would be greater if it were not for certain areas of leniency that make the law workable. To begin with, there are times when a person is positively commanded to speak lashon ha-ra. For example, if the "negative truth" you are to communicate will prevent future injury or loss of money—if it is information about various forms of violence and dishonesty—then you must not hold back. This is not a trifling matter, however, and before proceeding to act, a person must not only have observed the dishonesty or violence firsthand but must also have good reason to believe that transmission of the information will indeed make a difference. A similar imperative (as well as a similar set of cautions) applies where the judicious disclosure of information might reconcile quarreling parties and further the cause of peace. Leniency also obtains in cases where the subject of lashon ha-ra is either a Jew who has rejected the Jewish community, or a Jew who has repeatedly committed immoral acts

and refuses to change; each of these types, by virtue of his/her actions, is located outside the Jewish speech-community and therefore outside the orbit of its reciprocal responsibility. Finally, there is a partial exemption from these injunctions when a story classifiable as lashon ha-ra is told in the presence of three or more persons and without any warning against repeating it, the assumption being that under such circumstances the story is destined before long to become common knowledge.

Hokheah tokhiah: confrontation

At once the most distinguished and the least conspicuous aspect of the laws of speech is aimed, paradoxically, at promoting confrontation rather than inhibiting it. According to the rabbis, Leviticus 19:17—"Reprove [hokheah tokhiah] your neighbor"—unambiguously commanded a Jew to reproach his fellow for a wrong act. Though hedged in by numerous conditions and contingencies, the commandment to reproach is a central institution of Judaism and one that reveals a great deal about the underlying rationale of the entire network of laws regulating the Jewish speech-community.

The image of community in Judaism is not romantic. Life is lived with intense interaction, intense concern, intense participation, and, more than occasionally, intense criticism and conflict. It has been the constant goal of Jewish law, understanding all this, to make life livable by limiting the costs of conflict without limiting the intensity of community. In this connection, the laws of lashon ha-ra play an important role, functioning to restrict the sphere of conflict to the disputants themselves and preventing the accusations of either party from being picked up in gossip and bruited about until they gain universal currency as well as thorough distortion. The only thing to be achieved by keeping such stories in circulation, it was understood, is the formation of invidious coalitions, which, fueled by furtive communications, eventually lead to total communal breakdown. Thus while the rabbis knew that conflict cannot and should not be eliminated from the life of a vibrant community, they also knew that the secondary consequences of conflict, the "fallout" that reaches beyond the disputants, can and must be controlled.

The commandment to reproach is significant for just this reason: its fulfillment redirects the urge to speak *about* people toward the goal of speaking *to* people. As a reaction to disappointing behavior we are asked to take our sense of offense directly to the source of the disappointment, rather than enlisting others in our outrage and putting in motion a story that will have a life of its own. We are asked to break the circuit of indirection and mediation and to attempt face-to-face encounter. Probably because they recognized that it is natural to make snide remarks to a friend and unnatural for a person to speak directly to an opponent, the rabbis made the latter course a positive commandment.

The ability to criticize without further enflaming a conflict is a delicate art, one which even in the time of the rabbis was already considered to be at a low estate:

Rabbi Tarfon said, I wonder whether there is anyone in this generation who accepts reproof, for if one says to him: Remove the mote from between your eyes, he would answer: Remove the beam from between your own eyes! Rabbi Eleazar ben Azariah said, I wonder whether there is anyone in this generation who knows how to reproach! (Arakhin 16b).

Since later scholars did not consider their generations to be much superior to those of the talmudic jurists, they exerted themselves in trying to improve

Speech is hard, but who can keep quiet?

Yiddish proverb, Trans. Leo Rosten

the art of criticism. The occasion for criticism must be rooted, not in feelings of personal grievance, but in the definite knowledge that something objectively wrong has been done, something in clear violation of the Torah. The entire enterprise of reproof is not to be undertaken unless there is good reason to believe that it will succeed. Moreover, reproof is undertaken in gradual steps, in a spirit of solicitude rather than accusation, with respect and dignity. And so the rabbis proceeded to design an "art of reproof" whose ultimate aesthetics, they realized, depended upon the insight of each generation.

The laws of reproof, like all the laws governing speech, leave many unanswered questions about the specific application of these regulations to the new circumstances of contemporary life, circumstances that earlier codifications would hardly have anticipated. How would the law apply to

1. therapists, counselors, and advisers whose professional responsibility is to be a receptacle for other people's confidences, much of which would come under the category of lashon ha-ra? Is this relation proper only when therapist and client operate within different communities? What are the ethics of a therapist's or doctor's discussing a case with colleagues or in a journal? The U.S. Supreme Court has recently taken up this matter, but what is the Jewish view?

2. teachers and students, workers and managers who are asked to evaluate each other's performance? Does the ban on public embarrassment apply to negative evaluations of professors' teaching in widely circulated course-evaluation books? Or is it permitted because it prevents "injury" to a student in the form of a useless course? What considerations should we keep in mind each time we sit down to write a recommendation or an evaluation?

3. journalists, TV broadcasters, and investigative reporters whose job it is to air doubtful private doings in public? Which disclosures protect the public and which exploit its thirst for sensationalism? What are the limits of human dignity in the public exposure of a misdeed?

4. the contemporary definition of an apostate and of a Jew who has rejected his community, that is, of those persons who are not protected by the laws of speech?

5. our communal organizations and philanthropies and how they are run? Are the pressure tactics often used in fund raising justified? Is the publication of lists of big givers and small givers permitted under the law?

The responsibility to (carefully) reprove someone

Everett Gendler discusses how to administer reproof.

Now we should look at the specifics of how one ought to go about administering reproof. Let's take a look at the rest of the hokheah tokhiah quote in the Bible:

You shall not hate your kinsman in your heart. Reprove your neighbor, but incur no guilt because of him. You shall not take vengeance or bear a grudge against your kinsfolk. Love your neighbor as youself; I am the Lord (Leviticus 19:17–18).

A curious section, this one. Starting with hate, it ends with love—as nice a succession as one might wish. The path between the two points, however, is a bit bumpy and in places takes some surprising turns, so perhaps a careful look is in order.

At first glance it all seems so appealing. Feeling hostile toward someone close to you? Angry about something? Don't keep it in: "Reprove your neighbor." Somebody you're living with didn't scrub the pots and pans to your satisfaction? Should you raise the issue? Oy, another hassle about housekeep-

ing! Ignore it and redo them yourself? Oh, how the resentment smolders: here I am stuck doing somebody else's work!

In fact, living within any community doesn't always make it easy to issue the reproof, to share the anger. Nor is it always necessary. If through genuine understanding there are irritations you can comfortably overlook without harboring resentment, that's great. Maimonides called that midat hassidut—the most generous response (Hilkhot Deot 6:9)—and there's no need to fight it.

But if the irritation persists, and resentment builds, and little things become more and more annoying, then it's better to have out. You've got to reprove your neighbor/housemate/friend/lover/spouse or you'll really end up bearing a grudge, taking vengeance, or splitting.

Yet for some it doesn't come easy, this sharing of displeasure. It feels hard, even threatening, and there is sometimes the fear that criticism will not be accepted or that it will destroy a relationship. This does sometimes happen, and it is one of the risks.

On the other hand, to avoid sharing dissatisfaction will falsify a relationship, while criticism offered in the right spirit almost always strengthens it.

So what is the right spirit? The tradition offers several suggestions.

1. First of all, most of all, do it privately, not publicly (Maimonides Hilkhot Deot 6:7). So serious is the sin of publicly embarrassing someone that it is considered the equivalent to bloodshed.

2. Calm speech and soft language that convey caring for the person will be more easily heard (ibid).

3. Avoid name calling, which would embarrass or hurt the person, since the appeal should be to sensitivity, not to shame. (Talmud, Arakhin 16b; Maimonides, Hilkhot Deot 6:8).

4. Finally (or perhaps first), try to take a look at yourself to see if there are ways in which you embody what you criticize in the other person. OK, so you scrub the pots shiny bright. How's your desk? Your closet? Is that your pile of stuff cluttering the coffee table? Etc., etc.

5. And always keep in mind that Maimonides' dictum, "If you can overlook it without resentment, great!," applies to yourself as well as to others. So don't be overly strict with yourself. Remember midat hassidut!

Rabbi Nathan said: Don't reproach your neighbor for an imperfection which you yourself have (Bava Metzia 59b).

Said Resh Lakish: First correct yourself, then correct others (Bava Metzia 107b).

Rabbi Yose bar Hanina said: Reproof leads to a state of love. . . . Love without reproof is not true love. Resh Lakish said: Reproof leads to a state of peace. . . . Peace without reproof is not true peace (Genesis Rabbah 54).

SOCIAL IMPLICATIONS

"Reprove your neighbor," however, is more than just a private precept relating to interpersonal feelings. It is also a social injunction that relates to commitments and convictions, the ideas and ideals by which we try to live.

For the sins which we have committed before Thee with utterance of the lips.

The Talmud makes this very explicit:

If one could have influenced his/her household and failed to speak out, one is implicated in household misdeeds. In the case of one's city, the same obtains: could one have influenced by speaking out but instead maintained silence, s/he is implicated in municipal misdeeds. With rulers and officials of one's party or nation, the same is true: by default through silence one bears responsibility. Yet further, to the ends of the earth itself, this responsibility extends: that ever we attempt by clear and forthright speech and action, to prevent that from happening which ought not to occur (Talmud, Shabbat 54b–55a).

Nor is one relieved of the responsibility to protest merely because protest appears futile.

R. Zera said to R. Simeon, "Let the master rebuke the member of the exilarch's household." "They will not accept it from me," was his reply. "Even though they will not accept it, yet you should rebuke them," he responded (ibid. 55a).

For, as emerges in the subsequent discussion, how can one be sure that one's words will have no effect? Since such certainty is not given us, there is no responsible alternative other than to try.

POLITICS

As with the interpersonal, so in the realm of the political. Name calling and personal abuse ought to be avoided. A calm, insistent appeal should be tried first and is more likely to achieve constructive results than ranting. On the other hand, in matters of general public concern public, not merely private, discussion is warranted. Maimonides, in fact, urges that where there are unrepented misdeeds that violate basic religious or moral precepts, those who perpetrate them and refuse to heed private appeals be denounced publicly. In such cases of gross injustice, the prophetic example ought to be followed even though those denounced suffer public embarrassment (Hilkhot Deot 6:8).

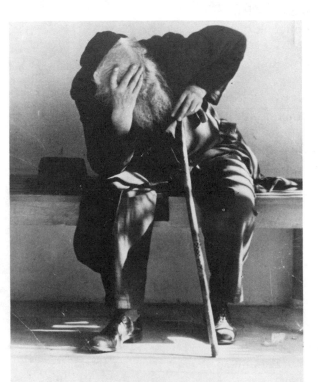

How long should one try? Results are not usually instantaneous.

To what point shall one carry reproof? Rab said: Until the reprover be beaten. Samuel said: Until he be cursed. Rabbi Yohanan said: Until he be rebuked. The same point was at issue between tannaim. R. Eliezer said: Until he be beaten. R. Joshua said: Until he be cursed. Ben Azzai said: Until he be rebuked (Arakhin 16b).

In short, the question discussed by tannaim around 100 C.E. was still under discussion by amoraim 150 years later without consensus!

Maimonides is of the opinion that one should persist either until he is struck or until the reproved person states unequivocally: "I will not hear it" (Hilkhot Deot 6:7). On the other hand, one commentator on the Shulhan Arukh (Magen Avraham on Orah Hayyim 608) cites an opinion that one should not reprove a person who will retaliate by seeking to injure the reprover: "As one is commanded to say that which will be obeyed, so one is commanded not to say that which will not be obeyed. . . . 'Reprove not a scorner lest he hate thee' (Proverbs 9:8)" (Yevamot 65b).

It would seem, then, that the question is even now not finally resolved, and *you'll* have to figure out the fine points and particulars for your own individual case, perhaps reciting to yourself hazak ve-ematz—be strong and of good courage!—as you decide.

A final thought about tokhaha—reproof. Though it is directed *toward* persons, it need not be directed *at* persons and shouldn't be overpersonalized. For example, sometimes certain courses of action entail certain consequences, regardless of who pursues them or with what intent. (Might nuclear power and mechanized, mass-tract farming be examples in our society?) To spell out those consequences and proclaim them widely is also a form of reproof.

But if you do not obey Me and do not observe all these commandments, if you reject My laws and spurn My rules, so that you do not observe all My commandments and you break My covenant, I in turn will do this to you: I will wreak misery upon you . . . I will set My face against you . . . I will break your proud glory. I will make your skies like iron and your earth like copper, so that your strength shall be spent to no purpose . . . nor shall the trees of the land yield their fruit.

And if you remain hostile toward Me and refuse to obey Me, I will go on smiting you sevenfold for your sins (Leviticus 26:14–21).

This passage, commonly refered to as "the Tokhaha," is directed toward the community of Israel as a whole, not at particular persons, and tries to prevent ill effects by warning against courses of action that will surely entail such consequences. In our own time and place such warnings before the fact, free of denunciation or blame, yet truthful to our situation, may be among the most valuable ways of fulfilling the ever-applicable command, "Reprove your neighbor."

As for the dangers of smugness or self-righteousness, again some critical self-scrutiny will help. Remember the high-level energy conference in Washington, D.C., when those who gathered to urge energy conservation upon the nation departed in so many private jets that Washington National Airport was jammed for hours, and then they wondered why we weren't immediately convinced by their words? Well, the likelihood is that each one of us could in other areas find some embarrassing similarities with ourselves. Have you doubts? Try it and see!

oose tongues *are* worse Wicked hands.
Than
— yiddish proverb
—Trans. Leo Rosten

PERSONAL FREEDOM AND THE TRADITION

It need hardly be said that within this complex of prohibitions and regulations there is much that would not only be difficult for a modern person to comply with but would also conflict with the sense of personal liberty. For citizens of Western secular democracies, the place of the law is to attempt to restrain physical aggression, not to regulate private moral life. Judaism, of course, would have it otherwise, for Jewish law attempts to encompass the entirety

of experience—civil, moral, ritual, criminal—within a system that comprises positive commandments as well as negative injunctions. In contrast to the libertarian resentment of law as a restriction of personal freedom, Judaism welcomes law as an opportunity for the enactment of value concepts. The Hafetz Hayyim wrote his work about speech with the hope, we might conjecture, that if religiosity was returned to its ethical bearing, Judaism might yet prevail over the gathering crisis.

We, the children and grandchildren of the Jews who emigrated from towns like the Hafetz Hayyim's Radin, have observed the process of secularization proceed apace, as each of the areas of experience that were once mediated by Judaism has been "liberated" from tradition. Not all of us have considered this liberation to be without its disappointments, nor does the reduction of Judaism to a synagogue ritual somehow strike us as a fair trade. We sense in the Jewish community today a desire to know what exactly was bartered away, what Judaism has to say about a number of aspects of life— community, family, personal growth, social responsibility—that we have not been in the habit of thinking within Judaism's jurisdiction. There is a further desire to know whether Judaism has anything to say that differs from the modernism which formed our minds but does not always sustain us in the exigencies of modern life.

The laws of lashon ha-ra are a good instance of Judaism's opposition to certain prevailing notions of modern life. Politics and advertising, for example, have given us a vigorous distrust of words publicly spoken; we no longer expect speech to have much to do with either truth or action. Speaking, to our minds, has become an essentially inconsequential activity, one that is less than an action and often less advisable than silence. Moreover, we judge ourselves and others less by what we *say* than by what we *feel*. Spoken words have become an untrustworthy medium that cannot be counted on to convey feelings.

In contrast to such attitudes, Judaism holds speech to be a form of action as significant as physical aggression or violence. The rabbis used the verse from Proverbs 18:21, "Death and life are in the power of the tongue," to stress that speech is potentially both a lethal weapon and an instrument of salvation. It was taught that it is through the quality of our talk about people that we create the solidarity of community or give way to the primitive state of nature. An acknowledgment of the extreme capabilities of speech was incorporated in a prayer added to the Eighteen Benedictions (Shemoneh Esrei), the central prayer of the daily liturgy. Composed during the Roman occupation of Palestine, the prayer, "For the slanderers let there be no hope, and let all wickedness perish . . . ," is a petition for protection against the kind of national persecution that can result merely from the license of ungoverned talk. Similarly, the prayer following the Shemoneh Esrei begins: "O my God! Guard my tongue from evil and my lips from speaking guile."

Even in more mundane and less momentous circumstances speech always remains consequential; spoken words are far from hot air that floats away, leaving behind "real" feelings. Every work a person pronounces, according to the rabbis, ascends to heaven and is recorded under his name in a book; no matter how he protests that his words do not adequately represent him—he intended better, he meant something else—he is nevertheless judged by everything he has uttered. Though he may add to the record by speaking more or by speaking better, nothing can be erased. With such an image, the rabbis sought to underscore the ultimate responsibility we bear for what we say, a responsibility that cannot be selectively assumed precisely because the consequences of our words cannot be selectively applied.

In addition, Judaism is particularly at odds with the contemporary emphasis on the all-importance of self-expression. It is a widely held assumption that the goal of individual development is total expressivity, the capacity to convert feelings directly into words without first relaying them through the processes of conscious deliberation. There is nothing to fear from such spontaneity, it is argued, for nothing that is genuinely felt can be genuinely harmful.

Judaism, in contrast, refuses to consider expression or discourse exclusively from the point of view of the speaker, as his/her right or need. As it is seen in Jewish sources, speech is social and communal in nature, drawing together the speaker, the listener, and the spoken about into an ineluctable web of relationship. The needs of self-expression, like any form of self-actualization, must therefore be balanced against the potential costs to others, a calculation that cannot always be decided in favor of immediate release. Commenting on the verse in Psalms 12:5, "By our tongues we shall prevail; with lips such as ours, who can be our master?" the rabbis declared that a preoccupation with self-expression, especially in the form of lashon ha-ra, was evidence of the progressive displacement of the sovereignty of God by the sovereignty of the self, a process that could, in the end, lead only to apostasy.

Far from being indifferent to an individual's growth, the rabbis were passionately concerned with a particular form of self-development called teshuvah—turning (see As the Jew Turns in *Catalog 2*, pp. 253–61). Teshuvah is the process whereby a Jew, out of a sense of remorse, reassesses his/her past behavior, commits him/herself to change, and makes good a commitment by changing his/her life and returning to the path outlined within the Jewish tradition. Now, the rabbis did not for one moment underestimate the extreme difficulty of effecting such a change; they knew it is difficult enough for a person to contend with the regressive forces within him/herself without having those difficulties overlaid with the weight of communal gossip and skepticism. The laws of speech were therefore seen as a way of holding the community at bay long enough for a person to sort out his/her deeds. For it is in the very nature of lashon ha-ra to associate a person with past misdeeds and to circulate this image as if it were a complete and enduring account of the person's life. And as the image is cycled through the everyday conversations of the community, it attains, quite apart from the usual distortions and exaggerations, a virtual life of its own, a sovereignty that can hardly be expected to yield to encouraging developments in the life of its real subject. Lashon ha-ra is always directed toward the past and always committed to an image of people in which hope has been reduced.

A Jewish community can become truly communal only when its solidarity ceases to be based on shared secrets and on acts of exclusion and victimization. And a Jewish community can become truly Jewish only when it achieves a self-restraint necessary to liberate the individual's potential for return and reintegration.

It is written in the Talmud:

Why was the First Temple destroyed? On account of idolatry, sexual promiscuity, and bloodshed. But the Second Temple, during whose time Jews occupied themselves with Torah, mitzvot, and deeds of loving-kindness, why was *it* destroyed? On account of forbidden speech. This teaches us that forbidden speech alone is equal in severity to idolatry, sexual promiscuity, and bloodshed (Yoma 9b).

With the destruction of the Second Temple came the exile that has become our enduring condition. But the Hafetz Hayyim did not look back over the history of his people without an eye of hope. If the Jewish people had been exiled on account of their violation of the purity of speech, he asked, for repenting this same sin might they not one day be redeemed?

Lashon ha-ra

The story of how the Hafetz Hayyim came to be called by that name is an interesting one. The wide and successful distribution in the West of his book *The Dispersed of Israel* was based on the fact that the Hafetz Hayyim was already a famous and immensely popular figure in Eastern Europe—virtually a household name. This fame, oddly enough, was achieved under conditions of anonymity. In 1873 a young Talmud scholar from the town of Radin named Rabbi Israel Meir ha-Kohen published a compilation of the talmudic laws governing slander and talebearing. Determined to see the book judged on the truth of its message rather than the personal authority of its author, Rabbi Israel Meir suppressed the fact that he was the author and released the book simply with the title *The Book of the Hafetz Hayyim*, the Hebrew phrase referring to the character-type spoken of in the verse from Psalms (34:13) that he considered the core of the Jewish teaching on the matter:

Who is the man who is eager for life [hafetz hayyim],
  who desires years of good fortune?
Guard your tongue from evil,
  your lips from deceitful speech.
Shun evil and do good,
  seek amity and pursue it.

To say that the book was a success would be a considerable understatement, for it seized the imagination of Eastern Europe as only a handful of popular ethical treatises ever had and became what would be the equivalent of today's best-seller. Although the religious intelligentsia knew the author was Rabbi Israel Meir (he had received the prepublication imprimaturs of several famous rabbis), the masses had little inkling of this. So when speaking of the work's author they employed the traditional Jewish practice of calling a writer by the title of his most important work. Thus Rabbi Israel Meir became known in the cities and villages of the Pale of Settlement simply as the Hafetz Hayyim.

Why should such a book be so popular? And why should its author choose a moment of mass communal disintegration to discourse on such a subject as Judaism's attitude toward speech?

The Hafetz Hayyim believed that if religion was to survive the crisis of the modern age, it would only be because of its moral authority over Jewish life and that that authority could be rescued only by once again making Jewish law expressive of a vision of an ideal Jewish society. Judaism, in short, would have to be forced to fulfill its promise of making people into mentshen and of making the Jews into a holy people. Business practices, the treatment of the poor and the dependent, communal organizations, personal relations—the Hafetz Hayyim sought to reexamine all these areas of Jewish life in the light of the Torah's demand for concern and justice. Judaism had in the past spoken effectively of these matters, and, he argued, it had the potential to do so once again.

Communities within synagogues

Jews must gather, not because they are friends or even because they agree, but simply because they need each other to go on being Jews. Hermits are noticeably absent from our history. What is more, tzaddikim—the pious ones, the ego models for the Jews—who could probably live their Jewish lives without the support of a group, don't want to. They teach us by their example that there is intrinsic value in performing mitzvot—commandments—as a group. The very act of working with the congregation for the sake of heaven is a mitvah in itself. And so it has been until our own era—a time in which the gathering together of Jews has become so efficient and the groups so large and the means so technocratic that the very institution of the synagogue itself threatens to destroy the religious life it purports to sustain.

The synagogue is the only institution claiming as its reason for existence the perpetuation of religious Judaism in America. It is the only place offering any form of worship experience. It is clearly the chief employer of rabbis and teachers of Judaism. It assumes the awesome responsibility of educating the vast majority of Jews and their children. For all but a very few Jews the synagogue is the sole vehicle for religious life and response. Indeed, its promised goals exhaust virtually every activity religious Jews of our time feel it is important for Jews to go on doing. And despite all this, few would disagree that most synagogues are irrelevant, boring, and probably secular.

Some problems / some responses

... the two essential secrets of moral education—intimacy and activity (Herbert Read).

Whatever the classification of the institution, whatever its type or structure, two qualities, intimacy and activity, seem essential to any process or setting intended to nurture human growth. Consequently, they are valuable criteria to apply to present and future models of the synagogue.

Everett Gendler suggests some of the problems and possibilities for responding to the problems that challenge synagogue life in America. (Note that most of this is not Everett-fantasy. It is based on his own work as well as his own dreams.)

Applying them, let's see what we can imagine for future models that would work in behalf of greater intimacy and more activity within synagogue structures.

Problems

At present, rabbis, cantors, teachers, and youth leaders do most of the creative work, including leading services, teaching, working with youth, conducting weddings, etc. Where laypeople exercise their capacities, as in administration or fund raising, it often duplicates what they already do daily in their work; hence it does not explore their full potentialities. Adult study sometimes boils down to merely listening to lectures, for services are too often performances. Underlying much of the problem is what we might designate as the TV cultural stance: passive and vicarious experiencing. This is a societywide problem of great seriousness, with political consequences as well, and one might hope that the synagogue can offer something to counter this tendency.

Possible responses

Here we merely list, with a few words about each, a number of possibilities. There are many others.

1. Involve members creatively in personal services and celebrations, not just by assigning pages to be read. Examples:

   a. At Bar/Bat Mizvah ceremonies, encourage the family to select some supplementary readings for the service—readings that have special meaning for them. If a tallit is to be worn, let the parents present it with some personal words. Etc. Let the rest of the congregation/community search out how it wants to welcome the new adult.

   b. At weddings it would be good to involve the couple in planning the ceremony in some detail, with a combination of elements of the traditional liturgy and readings/pictures/dance movements of special significance to the couple. The hatan/kallah might want to actively involve their families in the ceremony by, for example, inviting members to recite the concluding seven blessings or by substituting their own variations for them. Here again some family members might want to sing, others to recite poetry, others to dance; all are appropriate.

   c. At namings invite parents to participate by expressing hopes, fears, and expectations. At synagogue namings, be sure the child is physically present. Etc. Again, as in Bar/Bat Mitzvah, it can be important for the synagogue community to welcome the new member.

2. Encourage small groups to plan and work out their own holiday celebrations in home settings, parks, forests, and beaches. Synagogue staff should be available as resources, but should at most merely encourage, not dictate or direct, such activities.

3. Ask members to contribute to both regular and special services, and specify that this does not mean bringing food for the Oneg Shabbat. A few examples:

   a. For Shabbat Shirah, invite musical contributions from members who play instruments or sing (and who are comfortable with such activities on Shabbat). They'll be shy at first, but a few may emerge the first year, and lovely things can begin to happen and grow the following year.

   b. For Lag b'Omer, let those who love gardening bring sheaves of grain from the previous year, or new shoots or sprouts, or whatever the season suggests in your area. These should be distributed among the worshipers, and then, to the accompaniment of appropriate music, they can be lifted and danced with like the offerings of ancient times.

4. Invite members to "share their thing" with religious-school students

when these relate to the purposes and aims of the school. For example, members with interests or skills in rock collecting, crafts, gardening, space shots, photography, etc. can enrich the school offerings on either a regular or special basis.

5. Work toward adult study with material accessible to all for active discussion and experimentation. The latter is especially important in such inquiries as worship or Jewish mysticism, for example.

All of the above possible responses, by implication, suggest working within current structures for *less* dependence on staff, *less* dependence on rabbis, *more* self-development, *more* self-expression, *more* self-reliance. Now let us move into restructuring the structure by confronting the *enormous* problem of . . .

SIZE

The problem—one thousand member families!

Here are some very well-known facts that most Jews apparently regard as immutable or trivial when in fact they are neither. Synagogues try to get as many members as they can. Since families shop for the best religious school, the nicest service, and the most attractive rabbi, the more members a synagogue has—it is almost universally assumed—the better it is. Furthermore, since more members mean more dues, which means more money, which means more services, which means the more you get for your money, success and size of membership are understood to be directly related. The synagogues that have the most members usually have their pick of the rabbis, and certainly they have the most clout within national organizations. Those synagogues that *say* they want to remain small and intimate (250 families times the average family size is roughly NINE HUNDRED PERSONS) are usually ambivalent: when confronted with an influx of prospective new members they do not help them form a new congregation, and when not confronted with an influx of prospective new members they seem to wish they were. The number of congregations who have limited their membership to a fixed number of families

I see. You want to start a young parent group, and write a blessing for changing pampers.

can be counted on one hand. Everett Gendler in his article "Yesh Birera" (*Response*, No. 72 [Fall 1972]) observed that:

> Synagogues are almost never selective in membership. Financial needs combine with a commendable spirit of hospitality to make the synagogue open to all who can afford it. This means, in practice, however, that each synagogue tends to have such a mixture of people in it that, attempting to meet the needs of all of this quite random grouping, there develops a distressing uniformity among the institutions.

The amassing of members, it is claimed, is the only way to meet the ever-rising costs of maintaining the institution. The irony, of course, as Arnold Jacob Wolf has noted, is that synagogues are able to remain within a budget only by predicating it on the quiescence of a majority of their members, for surely no congregation could satisfy even a significant minority of its members if they chose to pray and study weekly—even though that is what they are allegedly paying for and encouraged to want. There is no religious community; there is just another monster organization.

Possible responses

What are some possible responses? Everett suggests a few and adds a word or two about each, in the hope that they strike some chords of recognition in others.

1. Alternative institutions: This is an important option, but is developed in "Communities without Synagogues." (So skip to the next chapter if you're a rebel type.)

2. Small groupings within present large syngogues

a. One might have neighborhood clusters where people meet periodically in living rooms for co-op Shabbat meals with table ceremonies and their own service. Holidays are other natural occasions, as well as changes of the seasons, phases of the moon, or whatever may seem appropriate to the members of such clusters. The energy crisis as well as other trends in the U.S. today may give some impetus to such small, nearby personal support and worship groups.

b. Affinity or interest groups within the synagogue are another possibility. People might be encouraged to join together for self-directed study, prayer, or social action, assisted by the rabbi or staff if so desired, but determined by the persons themselves. Such self-initiated activities should be regarded as legitimate extensions of what the institution already offers, not as competition with already-established programs or services. What better way to give institutional recognition to the varieties of temperaments, interests, and theologies that are the actuality of our synagogue membership today?

3. Where attendance at services is already small, help the officiants come down from the bimah and join the congregation. Rearrange the chairs for more face-to-face contact. If necessary, unscrew and rearrange some of the pews, perhaps with ceremony. Invite persons to bring readings, music, dance movements, and other contributions to the regular service. Etc., etc., etc.

4. If planning a new building, beware of gigantism. Aim for more modesty and less cost.

5. If a small synagogue, take advantage of the necessities dictated by size and enlist the human resources that are surely part of the membership. It is surprising and wonderful to discover how many unexercised capabilities people have.

But let's develop the community idea a bit more.

The structural model for the synagogue is not the commune or the council or the fellowship; instead, it is that definitive form of American technocracy: the corporation—complete with paid executive professionals, a board of directors, hierarchies of committees, interorganizational political in-fighting, and an annual meeting of dues paying sharcholders!

If we didn't let Spot dog or Willie Cat in, I think we could fit 5 people in our living room.

A fantasy

Imagine for a moment a very tiny congregation. An extended family. Such a group would not be a committee, since it would not exist for the sake of any larger organization. It would be a social clique only by accident, and indeed the homogeneity that tends to characterize such cliques could only stultify and monotonize a group that hopes to be challenged and even changed. It would not be a study group since the primary goal would not be intellectual growth. Nor would it be anything like an encounter/sensitivity group, since the focus would not be each other but a common search. No, the members would understand their common association as a mutual attempt to perform acts of primary Jewish importance, which they cannot or probably would not do alone and yet which they cannot go on being Jews without. They come together because of and for their being Jews. They may be friends but that is clearly irrelevant to their common experience and search. The group would, we suppose, be a tiny congregation in the fullest sense of the word "congregation."

Since such a group must have a constant membership over a significant span of time—at least four seasons—considerations of size and makeup are crucial. We can say that the size of the group must be large enough to ensure diversity yet small enough for each member to be and feel like an integral part. To put it another way, the group must be small enough that when a member is absent each person will sense somehow that the group is incomplete, not ready yet, not whole, lacking some irreplaceable part—even though it is not until they scan the faces present that they know who is absent. And from a purely pragmatic standpoint, the group must be small enough so that all can physically gather in the living room of the member who has the smallest home.

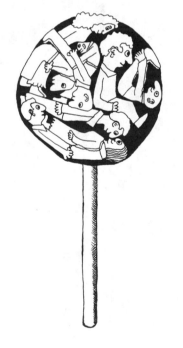

Deal with your rabbi lovingly but honestly.

Forming a synagogue community—some models

The profile of a typical family group might run something like this: one or two families express cautious interest to the rabbi about maybe getting into "one of those family group things." The rabbi then serves as a kind of impresario, arranging for an evening get-together of at least five and not more than nine couples. It is billed as an opportunity for some families who might be interested in the havurah adventure to learn more about the idea and each other. It is just an informal discussion to decide if they should consider scheduling another one.

The second model for forming a group within the synagogue is simply for a synagogue member to begin to discuss on a one-to-one (or, where couples are involved, on a two-to-two) basis what s/he is looking for. When there are five to eight couples (or between ten and twenty people) who seem to be moving in the same direction you are, call a meeting at your house. Chat about your needs, direction, goals—and then begin to make decisions about the future.

THE FIRST MEETING

Go around the room asking each person to present a brief extemporaneous biographical sketch of his/her spouse. So much for openers. Then you might encourage each person to describe as concretely as possible how s/he would

envision a family group working. What would it do? Why would it do it? How many families should it embrace? How often would they meet? Not until everyone has had a chance to contribute to the collective fantasy is cross-examination allowed. The host/leader/rabbi may or may not wish to add his/her own ideas. Larry Kushner suggests that the group then study a little Torah. Have people bring a Bible or xerox a short passage and study it—even if it is only for fifteen minutes. From the very first meeting a tradition will have been established of meeting over or through something that transcends one another. Even if the group decides not to continue, the encounter will not have been a total loss.

You have gathered because you are Jews and you are doing what Jews have done for millennia. That fact authenticates the Jewishness of the group from its very inception. Then break for coffee.

THE SECOND MEETING

At the end of the first meeting two families will probably love it—the next meeting cannot take place soon enough for them. And a few families are frightened or just generally don't sense that they have anything in common with (what they perceive to be) the majority. This is why it is a good idea to invite up to nine families—well over the ideal number of five. In this way the group can lose four families and still be composed of families who were all present at the original gathering. It is obviously much harder to bring in a fourth or fifth family once whatever-it-is has already got going.

Groups that should have been great have failed because their members tried to solve some difficult social task before they had established a common religious base. (Which, we suspect, is why most committees in most congregations fail.)

So at the second meeting, five couples, who ideally have had few previous social relationships with one another, meet at a different home. (A rotating cycle of homes is thereby initiated.) This is the hardest and most important meeting. Somehow the group should not talk too specifically about future plans and goals, even though that seems to be the leading topic on everyone's agenda. You have not gathered to plan another organization. The logistics will come after you have been Jews. Depending on the group, you might discuss some communal mitzvah to undertake, study some Torah, or even try a weekday Evening Service. Only then will planning the group's (possible) future be seen in the proper perspective.

The idea is that "we have gathered because WE are Jews right HERE and right NOW and we are going to do something about THAT first. Then we will decide when we shall meet again and what we shall do for our children. And which book we shall study. And if we shall go on a weekend retreat."

Communities within synagogues

If Jewish materials would throw light on these subjects, they should be introduced, but it is not necessary that all the study be concerned with specifically Jewish things. The subjects should be of concern to the Jewish members—itself a definition of "Jewish subjects."

SOME POSSIBILITIES FOR GROUP DIRECTION

1. A group might decide to meet every other week as adults to study a common text. Monthly they could meet for part of a Shabbat—perhaps dinner, songs, and a creative service, or an afternoon of play, concluding with Havdalah.

2. The group might attend functions at the synagogue as a group.

3. The group could gather together for events in the celebratory cycle—building a common sukkah, having a Seder the second night of Pesah, or writing and staging a Purim spiel—play.

4. The most important single thing a would-be family group can do is to share a family retreat weekend. Here levels of experience reach profound heights and depths, and, as has already happened at Larry Kushner's synagogue many times, enough spiritual energy is generated to last a year or more. Every family group that has gone on a retreat has left the weekend planning "next year's retreat."

5. A group might decide to daven—pray—together every other week and attend synagogue together during the alternate weeks.

6. Groups could meet to share social action concerns, for example, the world food crisis or Israel.

7. A group might concern itself with doing service to the Jewish community—visiting the elderly, making sick calls, visiting mourners, etc.

8. A group could meet around a religious task—rewriting the Haggadah, writing prayers, doing a group painting, or creating a Jewish music group or choir.

9. Dick Levy suggests that a group might meet to begin a bet midrash, where teachers and students would equally pursue understanding the material available, either Hebrew or English texts. Taking the idea one step further, he suggests that the synagogue might want to begin to function in part as a "free university," somewhat on the model of such groups in large cities. Thus "scholars" might offer courses that they might not feel ready to offer at the university and with special expertise might also lead study groups in their areas of interest.

10. Dick Levy suggests also the idea of forming a coffeehouse in the synagogue. He feels that there are few synagogues that have facilities conducive to dropping in when one is in the neighborhood. Unless one comes to the building for a specific purpose, there is no place where one may meet people, work informally on a project, or just come in for refreshment and respite. Most Jews who are used to synagogue life do not think of a synagogue as providing such a "drop-in center," but it is to be hoped the members would not feel fettered by such inhibitions. A coffeehouse would provide an inducement to use the synagogue as a center. Members of action groups could conclude their day in worship, mingling with afternoon study groups at the end of their session and all present meeting their neighbors over refreshments in an atmosphere reflecting the seasons of the Jewish calendar. It could be a place where, along with the coffee, there flowed discussion, study, drama, and music—both rehearsed and spontaneous; where good books and shared worship could conclude a day spent in each other's company. The coffeehouse could be a symbol of a synagogue that belongs not to a board or a rabbi but to its members, and is open for their use not merely on Friday evening, not merely when a meeting is called, but at all times. It would be a symbol of a synagogue in which members relate to each other, not as planners or spectators, but as persons striving to form a community with each other—and might even become a model for other people, striving to bring the world that *is* a little closer to the world that *could* be.

Synagogue affiliation

A tendency might arise for groups in the synagogue to become independent institutions of their own, losing their tie to the synagogue community as a whole. To prevent this, as soon as the group is formed its members could name one or two representatives to a planning council, each of whom might serve for a period of six months to a year, then relinquish his/her seat to another member of his/her group. Rotation would discourage the planning council from becoming a permanent mediator between synagogue and membership, like present boards of trustees, but would instead give many members a chance to see the workings of all groups in the synagogue.

Dick Levy also suggests some problems to beware of.

The role of the rabbi

Along with the role of counselor, gradually developing from the trust that members come to place in him/her, the rabbi's primary role as adviser and participant with the groups of the synagogue could develop.

S/he would lead one or more of the worship groups, preach, or lead discussions according to his/her and the group members' wishes. The rabbi would lead one or more of the study groups, or invite members or visitors to lead them; s/he might be an automatic member of any action group in which s/he wished to participate. It is hoped that no group would embark upon a project to which, after discussion, the rabbi still had strong objections; but this question should be decided by the members. The rabbi would be free to act as an individual and speak apart from the synagogue, but it would be hoped that s/he would attempt to involve the members in as many projects of concern to him/her as possible. The rabbi would be encouraged to leave time for his/her own study and writing.

Part of the rabbi's newly acquired role of priest and pastor might be more widely shared with other members than at present. Members might be encouraged to conduct funeral services, for example, in cases where the family is closer to them than to the rabbi, and a few especially knowledgeable members—assuming the planning council could vote them authorization satisfactory to the state—might even perform wedding ceremonies.

Finally, the following are descriptions/balance sheets of two experiments that have gone on in different parts of the country during the last few years. The first is Beth El, in Sudbury, Mass., where Lawrence Kushner was and is the rabbi. The second is Congregation Solel in Highland Park, Ill., where Arnold Jacob Wolf was the rabbi (he now works in Hillel at Yale University).

THE SUDBURY ADVENTURE: A POSTCORPORATE CONGREGATION

For several years now members of the Sudbury experiment have been into reorganizing the congregation. The principal form for communal involvement has become the small family congregation. Of course the older structure is still dominant—and it may remain so—but its perpetuation per se is no longer essential for the religious needs of the congregation. At Beth El in Sudbury we have five such groups. They are at different stages of self-awareness. They have formed around different nuclei and for ostensibly different reasons. Nevertheless, they provide examples of how such groups might form and relate to an extant synagogue structure.

One group began as an experimental parent-child religious education venture. Parents and their sixth-grade children met weekly to discuss the weekly parashah. They participated in a weekend retreat together. But for a year after their rabbi stopped "teaching" the class, the group continued to meet weekly to study, celebrate, worship, and do mitzvot.

Another group has begun—again, around religious education for children—as a sort of family-center first grade. Six families planned and arranged a year-long series of weekly meetings, which exposed their children to a broad range of Jewish activities, from building a sukkah to visiting an old-age home; from studying Hebrew to holding communal Shabbat meals. All the parents understand that unless what they do is substantially meaningful to themselves as adults, and not some charade they act out for their children, the tiny group will fail.

Another group of four families has formed a year in advance for the approaching group Bar/Bat Mitzvah of their children. They too constitute a miniature congregation. And a new group of families with first-graders has formed, as well as a group of families who all have a fifth-grader.

The congregation itself becomes a kind of confederation of semi-independent religious family groups. It serves as a central clearinghouse, enabling families at similar places or headed in similar directions or with similar needs to get in touch with each other. They look to it for teachers as they need them. Rabbinic assistance. A library. A community magazine. Groups may dissolve after a year or two, their members, as often happens, seeking new inputs or just needing a period of relative uninvolvement. How such groups will ultimately relate to the formal structure of the synagogue is still unclear. One thing is certain: without exception, members of the havurot have all become more active in the larger parent community than they had previously been. And because they have come to the synagogue through the path of Torah and tefillah—prayer—and mitzvot—commandments—they are able to lead their congregation in the same path.

All the groups we have had at Beth El thus far had families whose children were of similar ages. In principle it does not seem necessary, and yet the formation of a parallel miniature group for the children has obvious advantages.

Our experience has obviously been limited to a span of only a few years, and I cannot say whether or not groups can or should try to continue over a longer period of time than two years. On the one hand, stability, permanence, and security are not to be discarded lightly in these times; on the other hand, where veterans of two different groups have participated in a new third-group synthesis, the results have invariably been very exciting.

In any case, what has been created is a sense of organic human interconnectedness where before there was only the golem of an institution existing for its own sake and rarely for the sake of heaven.

BALANCE SHEET OF AN EXPERIMENT: CONGREGATION SOLEL

A look back at what Congregation Solel has done—or failed to do—in the first ten years of its life might be of interest to the synagogue community. I have recorded as many of the Solel experiments (some innovative, a few borrowed) as I can remember, together with a rough rating scale and a few personal comments.

1. *Lay participation in congregational services**** Every service includes a creative prayer (which is often a meditation, still more often, unfortunately, a sermonette) by a member of the congregation and a reading selected by a member from anywhere in Jewish literature (Buber, Maimonides, Kaplan, *The Rabbinic Anthology,* Saul Bellow), to follow the Torah reading. The service, then, becomes a responsibility of persons other than the rabbi, and the congregation has the privilege of reacting to many individual different

Three stars indicate an almost unqualified success, two a highly qualified success, and one a relatively complete failure. Of course, the rating and comments are only mine; other, more influential members of our congregation might well have directly opposing views.

expressions of Judaism. While many of the "prayers" are preachy or cliché-ridden, some are superb and a few blasphemous.

2. *A statement of principles for religious action** Hammered out with great tension over many months, our high-sounding principles have led to very little action. It is much better, we know now, to begin with specifics, no matter how difficult and controversial, than with abstract notions that can lead nowhere.

3. *No fund raising*** We do not believe that the community is obligated to pay for our synagogue and school, so we have no bazaars or fund-raising projects. We find that our members would rather pay annual dues somewhat higher than most if they are spared endless pleas for money on Yom Kippur, annual meetings, etc. What they will not give, we cannot spend; what they will give pays for most, but not all, of what we should have.

4. *The bulletin as magazine*** Our bulletin is not a mere house organ reflecting endless self-concern. It is written and edited, not simply pasted together. It is a controversial reflection of what some of our members and some of our readers think about many subjects. Many others, however, could not care less and never contribute to the Solel *Pathfinder*.

5. *New-members' dinners*** We invite each new family to a small informal dinner. We discuss, in an open-ended way, the program of Solel. Some are hooked, others begin to see clearly that they made a mistake in joining.

6. *Tzedakah*** We collect tzedakah at every service for causes not internal to Solel (Maot Hittim, Union Institute, American Indian Center, the Jewish Council on Urban Affairs). With a soft-sell approach, our intentions are better than our contributions.

7. *A 22-year Bible study course*** With ten of the twenty-two years behind us, and with about a third of the original thirty students (plus ten or twenty new ones), we have reached the Minor Prophets. The course has been of most benefit to the rabbi.

8. *Employment for the underprivileged** With enormous effort and the expenditure of considerable intelligence, we failed to upgrade more than a handful of black workers into skilled or semiskilled responsibilities. The social agencies we made contact with failed to come up with many real applicants, except members of their own staffs, whom we refused.

9. *Rotation of responsibility*** No officer can serve more than two one-year terms, no board member more than one three-year term. Every Solel member will serve on the board, if he can, within a very short time. There has been and can be no inner clique, no dominant voices, no persistent monolithic leadership. What we lose by amateurism we gain in democracy.

10. *No sermon titles*** Sermons are de-emphasized, their subjects never announced; often we have discussions or debates or films instead of sermons. When we do have sermons, they are subordinated to prayer.

11. *Youth as full-fledged members** Our utopian hope that our teenagers might serve as full members of all committees has largely failed of fulfillment. Except for Religious Action (and one member of the Finance Committee) the kids could not care less. They are are too busy studying and living simply to discuss.

12. *No kavod*** No plaques adorn our building, no honors attach to responsibility. No one is "Man of the Year." When the president of the congregation leaves office, we have a party to lampoon him; outside of that, nothing. Our leadership must be motivated intrinsically, or they will soon stop working.

13. *No one-shot lectures*** Our study program is books, homework, discussions, seminar papers. We do not let famous guests come in to lecture us and then flee—except sometimes.

14. *Shoah weekend**** One weekend a year, on the anniversary of the Warsaw Ghetto uprising, we all think about the Holocaust, kindergartners through old-timers. Questions of chosenness, death, Zionism, compassion fill our whole weekend from sunset on Friday till sunset on Sunday. It is a sad, resonant weekend.

15. *No Bar/Bat Mitzvah**** Our elimination of the ridiculous Bar/Bat Mitzvah ceremony has been a complete success. No one quits our school at thirteen, our services are not cluttered up with preadolescent mouthings, and we can teach Hebrew as a living language, not a nostalgic fake-out.

16. *Same holiday sermons every year*** I have felt it important to consider the same problems each holiday season: Prayer, Human Responsibility, Turning, Congregation, Jewish Peoplehood. Some have found the sequence repetitious, a few indispensable. It is good for me.

17. *Religious research committee**** An entirely self-generated group is studying the Sabbath (historically, theologically, sociologically). Their research may never be conclusive; their spirit hovers over almost the whole congregation and makes us attend where we would otherwise have been ignorant. It is important that the rabbi consult with, but not be a member of, the committee in order to free them for their own work.

18. *Magazines for the membership** Another brilliant idea that never came off as planned; we subscribed for several years to a different Jewish magazine (*Commentary, Judaism*) for each member of the congregation and then discussed an article every month. But some members were offended at our "forcing" Jewish education on them, and even more just plain refused to read the articles that would be discussed. Still, several dozen became subscribers on their own after the trial year, and we did have a lively all-temple discussion program for a while.

19. *Confirmation*** Our Confirmation exercises are what Confirmation used to be at the turn of the century, in a few liberal congregations anyway: a Shavuot service and statements written and spoken by the confirmands about problems in Jewish theology. We have no cantatas, no rigmarole, no canned speeches, no ceremonialism, no elaborate formalities. It worked perfectly when we had thirty confirmands; now, with a hundred or so, it freezes most of the kids out, though it still avoids outright phoniness.

20. *Cocurricular program**** Members of the congregation volunteer to help our students to express themselves on Jewish themes in art, music, drama, dance, discussion, writing, etc. after each religious-school session.

21. *Limited membership*** Our congregation voted to limit itself to 425 dues-paying families when it had less than 200. A few years later the chips were down, but fortunately we stuck to our decision. We now have over 65 on our waiting list. For the congregation, the limitation has been absolutely essential in working out our program. But I have doubts that we are treating fairly people waiting to get in when it appears they will have to wait five or ten years.

22. *Original services produced by members*** One of our most incredible successes has been the original liturgy produced by about 150 different members of the congregation, serving over the years on fifteen or twenty different worship committees. Five Evening Services on the Sabbath, a High Holiday Family Service, a Summer Service, a Pesah Haggadah, and a Home Service have already been published. Several other projects are on their way. The results are always stimulating and often learned; the process is, however, far more important than the results. Many Jewish laymen have learned through responsible creativity what Jewish prayer is all about. The rabbi functions as a resource and proofreader, but no page of any of the services is mine. Not

A hundred kids find what they do very much worth doing, and the school profits from their boundless creativity.

unexpectedly, most of the liturgies are both more radical and more traditional than is customary in Reform Judaism.

23. *Parents in school*** Our school year begins with parents studying with their children's teachers what their children will study the rest of the year, and talking over with the rabbi and Religious School Council what our goals are and what problems we expect. The project is successful for those parents who come; most do not.

24. *Solel summer gateways**** Working with inner-city families, a hundred of our own women organized and led a day-camp school for black youngsters and some of our own. Extrapolating from the cocurricular experience (No. 20), it has achieved enormous success in eliciting response, talent, and brotherhood. The program has been imitated in other congregations and churches all over the area, and bids fair to continue until the Messiah comes.

25. *Humor in congregational life**** The truth is that Judaism is important, while Congregation Solel is a joke. So we laugh at ourselves in our annual meeting (where the rabbi is a kind of stand-up comic and the committee, humorists), in our Bulletin, and whenever we get to believing our own PR.

26. *Hebrew**** Our youngsters who want to learn Hebrew (about one hundred) study it for seven or eight years, mostly under Israeli teachers, and then go to Israel for a summer of study and travel planned and subsidized by the school. The best of our graduates know how to speak Hebrew and write Hebrew and read Hebrew by then, though the specific skills of the Bar/Bat Mitzvah may elude them.

27. *Controversy**** Everything is up for grabs at Solel: sermons, policy, personnel, ideology, social action. We have had heated arguments over hundreds of big and small decisions, but we have never had a split in the congregation. I believe we have proved that dissent is not necessarily dissension and that what American Judaism needs is not conformist rigidity but experiment, debate, and unashamed innovation.

28. *Equality of women*** Women have been almost everything men have been at Solel. School policy, adult study, service to community have been mostly women's work. But men have kept officers' roles and board pretty much for themselves without, in most cases, doing enough studying to know what the women have learned about Judaism and the synagogue.

29. *Rabbi as teacher**** I teach two Confirmation, two adult, and one or two children's classes weekly, and five others every month. That plus two Sabbath services, counseling, and some community teaching is a full-time job. It means that this rabbi has no time (and no skill) for administration, no time for (and no interest in) running the congregation. I give direction, if at all, by what I teach and what I am, not by physically or spiritually inflicting my presence on lay committees. Since I need not often be with them, we can have over sixty committees working, and since I need not "approve" of what they are doing, they feel free to accomplish what they can. They make no more mistakes, in the long run, than I do, and they produce much more than I could.

30. *Modern Jewish thought*** Each year we have selected a different contemporary Jewish theologian (Buber, Heschel, Herberg, Baeck, Rav Kook, etc.) to study for eight months. Sometimes we have been in over our heads, but the work of the congregation has been powerfully influenced by our ten years of consecutive study.

31. *Lay choir*** We do not pay people to sing at us (except on the High Holidays, when they seem required to help boost our morale). Our own people study, write, speak, sometimes compose, and always sing the service. We are less impressive aesthetically than some synagogues and almost all

churches, but our music is our prayer, and our choir and congregation are the same people. Unfortunately, for some of us it is still too hard to free up and sing out.

32. *Youth**** Our youth group studies Hebrew, tutors youngsters in the inner city, discusses religion with a rabbi, and assists in our school *every week.* This leaves them little time for "socials" (though on Purim they go on well past midnight), invidious electioneering, or the gimmickry of a youth group on the make. But they have had time to help build Union Institute, work for civil rights in our community, study Judaism, and collect food for the hungry, and they have come to care for each other in the deepest possible way.

33. *Confirmation committee*** A lay committee has the responsibility for working out all details for our Confirmation exercises except the program of the service. Amid incredible cacophony, they do.

34. *Teachers**** Our teachers are humanist, Orthodox, existentialist, Reconstructionist, Conservative—everything! On principle, we do not choose teachers who believe the same thing about God, Shabbat, war, or Judaism. By working with many different but authentic Jewish persons, our children learn the various options from which they may select. And we challenge each other by seeing the same world from sharply different perspectives.

Our synagogue has no party line, no religious "principles" except the principle that nothing Jewish is to be ruled out, and nothing human is irrelevant.

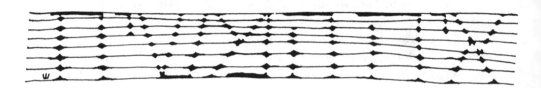

Our calendar and our minds cleared precisely for study, prayer, and work, we have a chance of becoming a community—with God's help.

35. *Contested elections** In the very earliest days of our congregation we nominated more candidates than could be elected, hoping to have congregational elections that would debate the issues. A great idea, it never worked. We lost our nerve and simply expanded the board to fit the number of candidates.

36. *Selma, Montgomery*** Our congregation sent what I believe was the largest group of any civil rights marchers from any "church" in the Midwest. We went because going was already implicit in what we had been doing in our own community before the march and were to continue doing long afterward.

37. *Blood bank**** We donate our blood for use by anyone we know of who needs it. The congregation that bleeds together . . .

38. *Open building** It was decided to open our building to any legitimate community need that requested it; in fact that was one of the reasons we built our synagogue in the first place. The building has in fact been used by CORE, the UJA, Pioneer Women, Summer Gateways (see No. 24), and several peace groups. But I have the feeling we still prefer to keep our building mostly for ourselves. In any case, we have not permitted others to take it over on more than an occasional basis, and I think that was a defeat for a very noble idea.

39. *No sisterhood, brotherhood, etc.**** How lucky to lack what could have done us no good! Proper Sisterhood functions have been properly assumed by a proper service committee. With bowling, book reviews, female fund raising, and hoopla out of the way, we have a little time to try to be Jews. With no invidious electioneering and no organizationalism, we have scope to do what we are in business to do.

Communities without synagogues

How do you make bread? It all depends. Do you want something rich and nourishing or a light and airy slice to frost with butter? Will you be pleased with a plain and tasty loaf or satisfied with nothing less than a braided work of art? Do you have the time to nurture and knead it, or would a quick bread, whipped up in half an hour, better suit your schedule and your palate?

There really is no recipe for forming a religious community either. The only essential ingredient we can think of is the wish to search for the formula in the company of others. Still, the members of the Alternate Religious Community (ARC) of Marblehead, Mass., a group of thirteen adults and thirteen children, have had five years to think about the subject, and we'd like to share some of our observations with those who may be interested in beginning the adventure.

Membership

First, every individual who becomes a member of the group should do so because of his/her wish to take part. With small numbers, there really is no room for people who are there simply to be agreeable to a friend, for people who challenge the group to prove that the concept of a religious community makes sense.

Once you have gathered together, there are certain important issues that ought to be discussed. Do members believe in an authoritarian structure, or are they thinking about a group of people who will share leadership responsibilities? Do they wish to maintain the tradition relatively intact, or are they seeking new interpretations of the tradition? Compromise seems possible when people agree that change is possible, but even then it requires goodwill and a cooperative spirit. If some members perceive the group as a more intimate setting for celebrating in traditional ways, while others have very different goals, serious and intractable conflicts will arise.

Rabbi / scholar figures

The Alternate Religious Community of Marblehead has a rabbi as a participating member, and the presence of at least one Jewish scholar can prove an invaluable source of information and enrichment for any religious group. A community is not a school, however, and unless the group wishes to become a study group or a minicongregation, the teacher-pupil model of interaction is not a very productive one. If the group is to offer each member the chance to make his/her own unique contribution, it is important not to allow respect for scholarship to outweigh appreciation for the experimental and nonacademic insights that make all of us truly human.

This vision of equality between the rabbi and his/her companions seems to us equally applicable whether the community operates independently or seeks synagogue affiliation. A synagogue and a community can benefit from such an interchange only if the synagogue can respect the autonomy of the havurah and the rabbi is willing to share his/her knowledge without expecting to lead the group (however gently) in the direction s/he chooses. (If you are interested in synagogue affiliation you ought to take a look at Communities within Synagogues.)

Clarification of such issues will result in a self-sorting process that is far less painful at the beginning than later.

Goals

Now that those who remain have reached a tentative agreement on structural matters, what are the group's real goals? Should celebration be the focus for the first year? Are there clear educational aims for children or adults that dictate areas of concentration? What are possible topics for discussion if the group decides to concentrate on new definitions of a Jewish life-style? Goals change as people change, and such agreements, naturally, will have to be reevaluated as time goes on.

Pursuing goals, however, should not be confused with forming the kinds of relationships that are achieved in the process of working together. Getting to know one another, building an extended family, forming a close-knit community that can respond in times of trouble—these result from sharing common goals. Rarely if ever can they be achieved as ends in themselves, and never quickly. Unrealistic expectations can lead to disappointment, anger, and eventual withdrawal.

For this reason we suggest that no group exact commitment as a precondition for membership. Such attitudes as an open mind, an interest in the group's stated goals, and a willingness to give the concept a try are important,

but commitment is a curious quality. It is difficult to commit oneself to the unknown. If the group's activities grow naturally out of everyone's wishes, and if people compromise yet go away feeling that their ideas have been given a fair hearing, members will discover, often with surprise, the extent of their commitment to the community that they have helped bring to life.

Participation of children

The Alternate Religious Community includes children, but to set goals that are primarily child-centered seemed to us a mistake. No matter how many activities invite the children's participation, no community can survive without time set aside for the adults to develop their own bonds and common understanding.

First, the children will only value a group that they see their parents enjoying and holding in high esteem for themselves. To join something for a child's sake is a subtle form of coercion that will be resisted one way or another, and if children are to feel part of the community, they must experience their participation as an act of their own volition. Second, children are apt to model their behavior upon that of their parents, and the enthusiasm, caring, and religious pleasure (or lack of it) in the adult community will be reflected in the children's attitudes toward each other and the group as a whole.

The magic recipe

So a handful of compatible people, with a rough idea of where they're going, begin to meet in people's living rooms. Perhaps they make and break bread, try to find ways to dance and sing and celebrate together, and begin devising religious ceremonies that seem relevant to personal needs and concerns. Friends, that's the easy part.

We have found (but sometimes ignored this, to our sorrow) that a very special feeling can be imparted to the most ordinary proceedings if time is set aside at the beginning of every meeting for members to share passages from books, listen to records, or hear poetry that is meaningful to them. We have found it liberating not to limit that kind of sharing to Jewish sources,

The real challenge is how to keep regular meetings from bogging down in endless arrangements and unavoidable personal differences, and turning what began as pure delight into sheer drudgery.

A community needs music as well as words, practicality as well as spirituality, administrative ability as well as emotional openness, and the very diversity of contributions is what keeps a group as infinitely variable as a kaleidoscope.

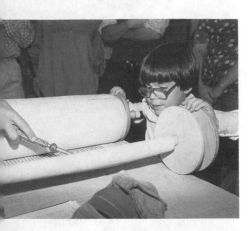

All that matters is to begin and to resist the pressures to rush to completion. For the trip will be a long one, we hope, with many interesting detours, and the traveling far more memorable than the arrival.

but to allow people to bring in anything that affects their own spiritual lives or has broadened their understanding and made them feel more whole, more caring, more alive.

From that sharing has come our conviction that the most important quality any religious community can foster is a spirit of tolerance and acceptance.

It has taken awhile, but we are beginning to recognize that a group of thirteen (twenty-six with children) is too large for many things, and there are times when activities and discussions should take place in small groups, with a final coming together for sharing.

It has been difficult, but we have struggled to listen and not argue when members share their feelings of discomfort about what is happening, and we have tried to accept merely being heard when we fervently wished we could convince everyone else of our point of view. And we are learning to pay attention, not only to the waxing and waning of the moon, but to fluctuations in people's energy levels, for sometimes members who have been very involved may wish to take a more passive role and need to be given that freedom.

Regularity of meetings is important, for members have to know that the group will not suspend itself for any length of time; we have found a kind of security in ending each meeting with a clear understanding of when the next meeting will be. There have also been times, however, when issues under consideration required more attention, and in response we have met more frequently. Weekends and three-day retreats offer a leisurely opportunity for exploring complex issues as well as deepening relationships, and at least one a year seems to be necessary to renew the feeling of being part of a very momentous undertaking.

There are certain problems that threaten the well-being of any community and must be resolved, though every group will find its own unique solution. How responsive must others be when one member has an overriding concern, or finds him/herself in pain because of personal difficulties? What degree of intimacy can be realistically expected with such a large number of people? When are confrontations best avoided? When should they be encouraged for the growth and health of the group? How personal can the content of meetings be without transforming the religious community into an encounter group? What does "religious" mean anyway?

In coming up against such problems we've learned a few hard lessons. There's no such thing as "the group," for example, so there's no sense in blaming *it* for everything that goes wrong. What has been created is each person's responsibility, and it is his/her responsibility to work for constructive change. We realize that small groups place a burden on members that large congregations do not. There is an interdependence that makes each person's actions echo through the consciousness of others. There is no question but that such closeness limits the freedom of those who would like to believe that their acts will have no consequences.

Don't let us frighten you, though. There will always be others to direct our lives for us, to tell us what to feel, what to believe, to define our limits and our limitations. Members of an alternate religious community, however, take the responsibility for their lives into their own hands and head for a destination that will only slowly emerge from the unfolding of their own natures.

Be lighthearted about experimentation and willing to call some of your ventures failures. Be willing to take risks, trusting in the group's ability to take a second chance. Whatever the outcome, value the opportunity to work alongside friends, celebrate together, experience and accept disappointment, and grow in understanding.

An alternate route

All of this is only one model for forming a community. It is not at all necessary for a community to have its main focus around the celebrating cycle. Other possible focuses include political action, social service, and self-education. A different group will emerge if the group exists basically for an external purpose, e.g., running a day-care center. This kind of project often leaves little time for interpersonal and intergroup development. Naturally there are groups that function on two levels, e.g., run a service open to everyone yet primarily provide a focus for religious, educational, etc. development as a group. Again, the earlier the group agrees on its main purposes, the fewer conflicts you'll encounter; people with different ideas will either leave the group or compromise with other members.

A few practical words

1. *Meeting places*: The amount of space available will limit the number of people or families in a group, for most living rooms won't comfortably hold more than twenty people, even if half of them sit cross-legged on the floor. Certainly you want to have enough space for people to eat together, even if it's buffet style with plates on laps.

But place is not as restrictive a limitation as it might seem at first, for people own more than their own living rooms. On Friday nights beaches are empty, and moonlight, candles buried deep in the sand, and a hallah passed from hand to hand can create a moment more beautiful than any indoors. In addition, you might begin to explore other options. Harvard University has an arboretum open to the public; most towns have conservation land; there are parks as well as backyards, riverbanks as well as playrooms. We have danced outdoors, done dramatic improvisations with the children, and even filmed the story of the Exodus in public places.

Go outdoors. Not only is there space but a kind of grace, too: the benediction of fresh air and sparrows, sunshine and flowering weeds. We've usually agreed on an indoor location in case of unexpected bad weather, but if you dress warmly anything this side of a downpour usually enhances the celebration.

Special spaces can be created. A living room can be emptied of furniture and folding tables set up so that a formal Passover meal can be served. Retreat houses can be rented from ski clubs in the off season or borrowed from other religious groups. An attic or cellar can be cleared and used. Use your ingenuity. You'll be astounded at the results.

Should you decide you want to open your community to noncommunity members for certain events/celebrations, you might want to think about acquiring a permanent place. Some people only want to pray with the community every other week and prefer to "shul-hop" the other times. They should not have to make frantic phone calls to members of the community to find out whose house will be serving as base during any given week. Some suggestions for acquiring a permanent base:

a. Before you invest money in yet another edifice, check out existing facilities. Synagogues, community centers, etc. can prove surprisingly generous about lending space to Jewish groups (the Upper West Side Minyan in New York has been immeasurably helped in this way by Congregation Anshei Chesed).

b. Renting a finished basement (preferably with an outside exit) could be another alternative.

c. If these options fail, look into getting an apartment that can be supported by the community at a reasonable cost. Don't get in over your head financially. To help defray rental costs you might think about how to use the apartment creatively when the community is not using it. Rent out rooms to students. Organize a drop-in center. The Chapel Hill, N.C., Hillel runs a day-care center. The New York Havurah rents space with

Communities without synagogues

We don't own a Torah (and couldn't read it if we had one), but anything that seems essential to your religious experience can be acquired.

Actually, you can do all this and more without children. They're just the excuse for not having to act grown up all the time.

A relaxed body leaves room for new energies to emerge and grow.

the Havurah School. The Boston Havurah used to run a Hebrew school. Etc. If you hunt around you'll turn up some new group needing space.

2. *Holy places*: The biggest mistake you can make is to think that synagogues have cornered the market on religious spaces. The best altars, we've found, are those you create by imagination. Indoors, a fireplace, a driftwood menorah on a low table, or a hanging candelabrum can create a focal place for prayer or meditation. A candle, its halo shimmering in the air, turns any spot into a place of reverence. A piece of sculpture or child's drawing, even shells or polished rocks, by serving as a reminder of the unseen and eternal, can create a religious mood.

Outdoors, the base of trees, the tops of dunes, the flat planes of rocky cliffs under blue skies, all create natural sanctuaries for times of worship.

3. *Acquiring things*: With all the money you're saving by not building a synagogue, there's no limit to the kinds of Jewish articles you can buy or make. You'll love owning your own shofar. We found a beautiful one for under fifteen dollars, and it adds another dimension to its power when ten-year-olds become expert at blowing it. Records and books are easily available, and even Hebrew teachers can usually be found at nearby universities.

4. *Sharing things*: The larger Jewish community is a spectacular resource. There is no reason the alternate Jewish community and the established Jewish community cannot cooperate in creating a multifaceted Jewish culture. The resources of the larger community provide an opportunity for the havurah to concentrate on the things it does best.

In the past year various members of ARC have attended concerts, taken part in weekend retreats, attended services on Simhat Torah, learned Israeli dancing, and attended a wide range of lectures. All were offered by community centers, temples, and other Jewish organizations.

In return we have worked with a local temple wishing to raise the issue of an affiliated havurah with its members, spoken to groups about forming religious communities, and welcomed visitors to some of our meetings and celebrations. An alternate religious community need not go it alone; it can serve as a vehicle for engaging in more honest dialogue about Judaism with its friends and neighbors.

5. *Doing things*: Sometimes it's hard to break out of preconceptions about how to learn. There's more to education than formal study, particularly when you're working with children. If you mix kids and adults together, then divide them into small groups, you can

    a. paint murals on large sheets of paper taped to walls or floors
    b. make Hanukkah menorot out of wooden spools and wood scraps
    c. write a collective poem
    d. improvise a "what if" play (e.g., what if Ahasuerus gave a beauty contest and nobody came)
    e. make up your own set of commandments
    f. plan a Shabbat service
    g. make a movie
    h. create a new dance
    i. make peanut butter, hallah, hamantashen, granola, or ice cream and eat it all up

6. *Surviving*: There's a big difference between considering yourself important and taking yourself too seriously. There's a lot of heavy work in building a community, or a better world, and you'll find more energy for it if you take time off to enjoy yourself and replenish inner supplies. Take time to walk in the woods together, do a facial massage late on a Friday, ride bicycles, swim, etc.

Retreats

All of us who celebrate/understand/are sensitive to Shabbat understand the importance of celebrating within a community. Similarly, it is clear that by removing ourselves as much as possible from that which surrounds us during the week we come closer to relinquishing the life that binds us normally and to creating an authentic Shabbat experience.

Retreating merges both these needs. We can totally remove ourselves from our normal everyday environment and spend Shabbat with a community of people. And because of this, retreats can be exhilarating, revitalizing, challenging, and beautiful.

Unfortunately, though, as with many things, it is possible to blaspheme the notion of retreat. What is in a reality a seminar, a vacation, an institute, a conference, a fund-raising event, etc. should never be called a retreat. Retreats are very special entities that carry with them certain expectations, assumptions, and attitudes these other events simply do not. Retreats assume that a group of people is open to each other as people, and as Jews, and chooses to isolate itself (sometimes with a retreat leader[s]) for a minimum of twenty-five hours to experience an authentic Jewish Shabbat. The assumption is that the psychology of Shabbat as well as the traditional structure surrounding Shabbat can combine to create a deeply important religious experience for the community.

There are, of course, "heavy" as well as "light" retreats—that is, there are retreats where the spiritual search is more intense than at others. Whether heavy or light, however, there must be a real commitment to a search in order for there to be a retreat. Volleyball is fun. But if, out of twenty-five Shabbat hours, you spend ten sleeping or napping and six playing volleyball or swimming you will have missed something important.

The following are some suggestions from different people about how to organize/be a leader for/participate in a retreat. None of this is dogma. They are suggestions that ought to function as take-off points for you.

It is told: Once on the evening after the Day of Atonement, the moon was hidden behind the clouds and the Baal Shem could not go out to say the Blessing of the New Moon. This weighed heavily on his spirit, for now, as often before, he felt that destiny too great to be gauged depended on the work of his lips. In vain he concentrated his intrinsic power on the light of the wandering star, to help it throw off the heavy sheath: whenever he sent someone out, he was told that the clouds had grown even more lowering. Finally, he gave up hope.

In the meantime, the Hasidim, who knew nothing of the Baal Shem's grief, had gathered in the front room of the house and begun to dance, for on this evening that was their way of celebrating with festal joy the atonement for the year, brought about by the tzaddik's priestly service. When their holy delight mounted higher and higher, they invaded the Baal Shem's chamber, still dancing. Overwhelmed by their own frenzy of happiness they took him by the hands, as he sat there sunk in gloom, and drew him into the round. At this moment, someone called outside. The night had suddenly grown light; in greater radiance than ever before, the moon curved on a flawless sky (Martin Buber, *Tales of the Hasidim*, pp. 53–54).

Zalman Schachter Shalomi shares his experience.

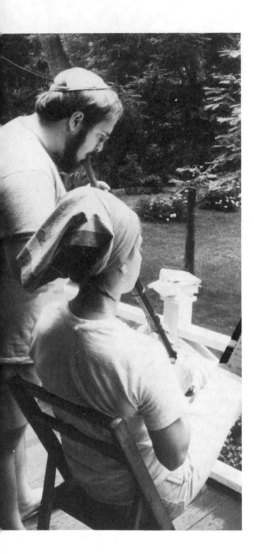

How to conduct a retreat

THE GIVENS

I take it that the group will be on a cultural island so that a high degree of control over the facilities where the meeting, the eating, and the sleeping will take place is possible. I take it also that it will be possible to control wake-up and lights-out times and so forth. In such a retreat (which can also be conducted in the synagogue proper) it is important that the desiderata be observed. One of the prime necessities, then, is to break the regular social set. People who pursue the social games they play at home will gain little from the retreat. It is a good idea to run a few briefing meetings with the people who are to be participants. These briefing meetings could be held in the congregation prior to going to the retreat place.

Briefing

The briefing has to deal with the tendency of retreatants to be beset by the disease mavenitis. A maven is one who has become an expert on things and who, instead of entering into an experience, stands on the outside and derives all his psychological kicks from the fact that he can judge the retreat leader, the speaker, and everyone else. People with mavenitis should be discouraged from the tendency or from coming.

What you are attempting to do is change life for the retreatants in a very significant way. Any organism tries to adapt its environment to its own pattern, and this group will resist change, especially if the changes are brought about with too serious an attitude. The entire thing has to be dealt with like a game in which people try different roles. Obligatory implication may seem to be a threat—that is, a person who has an experience may feel threatened if he has to repeat the experience. This threat can be reduced by inviting the people to play "the retreat game" for this particular weekend only. (Not until the postmortem, which is a necessary final component of the retreat experience, should the question, "What is to be extracted and learned and integrated into a person's life?" be considered.) However, if the threat is completely removed, if it is understood that people are just playing the retreat game and there is to be no learning and abstraction from it, this too would be a bad set and the retreat game would be impeded by it. The retreat demands that at least some attention be paid to the possibility of transferring the experience to home grounds.

This is the game contract that should be read to everyone signing up for the retreat:

"I am going to the retreat in order to explore the retreat game. I want to get the greatest amount of joy out of a new role. I will play from Friday afternoon to Sunday afternoon (Sunday evening to be spent on a postmortem). I understand that for me to pursue my social games at the retreat would be hindering the intention of the retreat. I also understand that it is very necessary for me to step out of my regular social game (the father game, the mother game, the family game, the employee game) in order to be able to see the meaning of these other games in the sight of God and Judaism. As a responsible adult I will observe rules dealing with silence and movement. I will "play ball" with the persons in charge of the services and the liturgy. My main concern in the retreat is to find out how I can serve God better and make my Judaism more meaningful. I will take care of all my obligations, which involve setting up the place, cleanup, paying costs. I will prepare all the readings that the retreat leader suggests."

It is also most important during the briefing session(s) prior to the retreat to get people to spell out specifically why they want a retreat, what they think it is, what they hope to gain. Conflicting desires among the group members, nonretreat types of goals, or unrealistic expectations should be pointed out, discussed, worked through.

THE OPTIMAL LAYOUT OF THE RETREAT PROPER

There are several areas that need attention. The interpersonal area, the use of eating time and the menu, the services, the study sessions, and the verbal interaction. Basically we are dealing with three time blocks on the Shabbat, one time block before Shabbat, one Saturday night, and two time blocks on Sunday, with the evaluation session at the end.

Time blocks

The time block before Shabbat is a time for becoming acquainted with the surroundings, unpacking, and settling down; for taking a shower, rushing around, setting tables, and—giving some time to meditation prior to Shabbat, just to consult with one's values and to remember why one is there.

The time block right after Shabbat on Saturday night has to offer a break, an outlet for detaching from the Shabbat experience.

This leaves two sessions for Sunday: one early Sunday morning, to begin with a service, and the other one from Sunday noon time into the afternoon for evaluation.

For the detaching session Saturday night something of a social nature ought to be planned; if any cultural presentation is desired, this time block would be a good time for it.

Shabbat

Before any other Shabbat activity begins, preparations for the blessing of the candles ought to be made. Every "household" and every single person ought to have two candles to light. The lighting must be done before the service, and people should be encouraged to share the prayers they add to the blessing. Candlelighting ought not to be at the service proper but rather at the place where the group, the community-for-the-weekend, will partake of their meals.

Then the service itself. The chairs ought to be arranged in a V pattern, with a clear aisle in between, so that two groups will be facing each other. The aisle is necessary so that whatever has to be done responsively can be handled as an antiphonal reading by the two groups, instead of as the usual responsive reading. What the reader usually reads is said by one group and what the congregation usually responds is said by the other group. In this a simple chant could be followed. It would be nice, although halakhah doesn't require it, for people to wear their tallitot—prayer shawls—during the service, to give them a sense of wrappingness and change of the regular role.

A prelude before the service might be in order. Incense or a fragrant spray or other olfactory stimuli should be set up before the people come in.

Even better than an organ prelude would be something that everyone could replicate at home, such as a fine recording. Some suggestions: a Rachmaninoff piano concerto, the lento of the Piano Concerto No. 23 by Mozart, the lento of *The American Quartet* by Dvorak, the Adagio for Strings and Organ by Albinoni. Generally, it ought to be music that aids in recollection.

Before we start moving into specifics, I want to spell out one more thing: learning at a retreat occurs on several levels. One level is, of course, the academic and didactic. It is not, however, the most important level, especially for a retreat. The other levels therefore need very careful planning and consideration. These levels are the aesthetic and liturgical. I don't want to call any of these "spiritual" because this is not a word that best describes the process (especially not for early retreats). Here we are working mainly on positive and negative feedback situations to things that are body-linked and sense-linked. Primary process work is the most important to us.

After this prelude there is a reading that concerns itself with the theme for the weekend. It would be best not to use a biblical passage, for biblical passages have to be expounded before they can really be accessible to people. A medieval text from Nahum Glatzer's *The Judaic Tradition* (Boston: Beacon, 1969) would be better. Afterward, observe some silence, which is to be spent in meditation.

Then follow the service of the prayer book. Participation in regular conversational tone is the best. Shouting or overly quiet reading will not bring about the proper involvement. The least amount of direction that the service is given, the better it will be. If any introductions as to the meaning of particular passages, etc. have to be made, all this ought to be done before, so that the pace of the service itself is not interrupted or changed by didactic material. The Kiddush should not be said in the place of the service but rather the dining hall.

Since community is more important to Jewish values than angels, before greeting the angels by singing "Shalom Aleikhem" at the table, there ought to be some time spent by everyone saying "Gut Shabbes" to everyone else who participates in the retreat. The warmer and the friendlier the greeting, the better. The phrase "Shabbat Sholom" is a bit too clipped in its rhythm, and a slow "Gut Shabbes" is to be preferred because it gets up the proper parasympathetic response rather than the adrenal sympathetic response.

The walk to the dining hall should not be used as a time for talking but rather for singing by the group.

The meal: Until Birkhat ha-Mazon—Grace after Meals—is over, no talking is to be encouraged. It should be made clear that the meal will be held in silence except for group singing. The song tempo must not be a USY/NFTY 2/4 quickly sung dance or a 4/4 march, but rather a very slow 3/4 melody such as "Hiney Ma Tov u-Mah Naim" or "Avinu Malkenu." If no special didactic presentation is planned for after dinner, this is a good time for the retreat leader to take the group to the library and assign to each one of the retreatants a book that the retreatant uses as a study base during free moments of the retreat.

If there is a featured speaker, a theme, or a text-centered study session, it would be a good idea to begin the presentation right after the dishes of the main course have been cleared, while the people are still seated at the table. Shabbat dinner should be prolonged as much as possible for conversation and song; dessert and tea can be given after the presentation. This is followed by Birkat ha-Mazon and then not more than fifteen or twenty minutes of informal socializing before curfew, so that the group can be up early enough in the morning for a study session before the service.

Shabbat morning: The wake-up procedure should involve one person who will undertake to go from room to room to knock on doors. It would be much nicer if s/he would hum a melody or sing it—but not too boisterously. And when the party or parties within the room answer, they should say something of a devotional nature: "Bless you the blessed Lord," or "Give praise to God, to whom all praise is due," "Great is Your faithfulness." This way the whole devotional nature of the day is set by the wake-up period. The breakfast ought to be light; otherwise it will impede the prayer of the morning. On the other hand, it should include butter or whole milk to stave off hunger pangs for the rest of the morning.

Following breakfast, a study session should be held before services. This session should concern itself with something of a devotional nature, so that the insights derived from the study session can be used in meditation prior to the service.

A sermon is unnecessary for the service because much work is being done as part of the retreat. Yet it is important, for the sake of transferability (see "On Transferring") and because it is really right, for a devar Torah to be offered before or after the reading of the Torah. If it's offered before the reading of the Torah, raise some questions that the text answers, sensitize the readers to any answers in the text that deal with problems to be discussed at the retreat.

As many of the people should be called to the Torah as a feasible. It makes sense to call more than the usual seven, even, if need be, to have them double up so that all can be called to the Torah to recite the blessing over it. The family of the one called to the Torah should rise when s/he is called and remain standing during the aliyah, so that they share in the aliyah.

I usually make a mi-she-berakh for the person who had the aliyah, invoking a blessing for him/her. If I have any knowledge of his/her life, and if it does not touch anything that is too intimate, I invoke God's blessing for the person who had the aliyah according to the life situation of that person. If it is a student who wants to get a scholarship, I spell this out in the mi-she-berakh. The same with a person about to engage in a new business venture. If it is a special occasion in the person's life, i.e., a birthday or an anniversary, I mention it in the mi-she-berakh. If the person who is conducting the retreat is called, I try to thank God for this person who came so far to share wisdom and knowledge with us.

The service is then concluded and Kiddush should be served, despite the fact that it may yet be too early for lunch.

The discussion session can begin before lunch or, if the service takes longer (as it well might with increased participation), held off until after the main course of the meal. There is much to be said for either mode; how to plan time depends greatly on the understanding of the director or retreat leader. Friday night is a far better time for nighttime talk, for mood setting, for explorations that deal with the emotive. Shabbat morning, after the group has had a night's rest, is a time for greater clarity by virtue of their having been cut off from the world for several hours; they are now ready for good conceptualization. Thus new words and concepts to be taught to the group are best to be kept for Saturday morning. For Saturday afternoon one has to get back into nighttime talk.

Shabbat afternoon/evening: Early Shabbat afternoon presents the greatest danger to discipline; this is part of the makeup of a retreat. The novelty has worn off, the need for breaking the routine is very great. Very little can be done with the people at this time. They will absolutely have to take a walk, play a sport, nap, etc. to get a second wind. If you don't get a second wind, then the retreat will not reach the depth it has to. The best way to deal with the situation is to plan a Shabbat afternoon nap. This will provide the needed break without shifting the pace. It will also prepare the people for the third session of the Seudah Shelishit.

Assuming that the difficulties of the afternoon have been safely passed (even if there has been some breach of pace, it is still possible to bring the group to the next situation), there is a nighttime-talk situation—the Minhah and Seudah Shelishit block. The service should be kept short. There is little new material, yet the pace requires it. Sit around after the Minhah service, preferably in a buffet-style situation, where one takes a bit of hallah with a bit of herring and something to drink it with.

Close physical proximity is important here—this too has to be a huddle. The image: a prehistoric group or David and his friends in the cave with the sun setting outside. Discourage the use of artificial light at this point because you want the fullness of the sunset and the ebbing away of the day to be experienced by the group.

The psychological set in the briefing ought to contain something like the following: on Shabbat we receive an additional soul called the neshamah yetairah. This additional soul is about to leave. Everytime Shabbat leaves it is a deathbed situation. The Baal Shem Tov said: "Why is it that the Shabbat meals on Friday night and Shabbat noon are usually eaten with one's family, whereas the third meal is taken in the synagogue?" And he answered: "This is a deathbed situation. We die from the Shabbat and give up our additional soul. No Jew wants to die alone: he wants to die with a minyan—religious quorum. So we eat the third meal in public to 'die' in God's presence." Having a quorum present means that the Divine Presence is there. All the anxiety is death anxiety, is time anxiety, is anxiety at having to let go, becoming passive to the inevitable. Use very little verbalization with the group; perhaps a good poem or an inspirational paragraph could be read and then a melody (at the most two or three) should be chanted—slowly. Suggestions:

1. "Avinu Malkenu," but without the words. Maybe only once or twice you can sing it with the words, but most of the time the repetition ought to be without the words. People should be encouraged to close their eyes and hold hands during the singing.

2. "Hava Nagila" hummed—but *very* slowly.

3. "Going Home," "Shenandoah."

4. *The Union Hymnal* has a fine melody to "Joy of Lord, we hail the day that Thou dost call Thine own." Again, slowly.

5. "Thou Shalt Rest."

When it is good and dark outside and people are in the same mood, do the Birkat ha-Mazon, this time without using books; it is surprising how much people know by heart, and I am sure that there is at least one person that can manage to say the Birkat ha-Mazon by heart. If not, there can be even a loose paraphrasing of it in the vernacular, to which the others will reply with "amen," and a concluding prayer of thanksgiving for the Shabbat spent together. The evening prayer can then be said (again, without prayer books, right at the table). When it is completed the group stands.

Havdalah: The Havdalah ceremony has been given so much prominence— often a greater prominence than the Kiddush. There is much to be said for making the Havdalah simple. The requirements for the Havdalah are the "drink of the country," and coffee or soft drinks fill that requirement. Two candles can be held together or even two cigarette lighters—to show the coming weekdayness. A little vial of perfume or cologne or a flower could provide the fragrance instead of elaborate spices. And here there is a real transfer possibility for the Havdalah: a couple going out on Saturday night could celebrate the Havdalah before having a nosh exactly the same way without having to set up a fancy scene for it.

Now as to the content of the Havdalah. The words of the traditional Havdalah are very good when said slowly and with feeling: "Behold God, He is my salvation. I shall trust and never fear, for my strength and my song is the Lord."

Sing the usual songs after Havdalah—"Eliyahu ha-Navi," etc. There ought to be a tension releaser, like "Everybody Loves Saturday Night." Really emphasize and clarify that we are now moving into a weekday period and that the Shabbat is over.

A break. Cigarettes, pipes. However, if it is close to the middle of the month all this ought to be postponed for the experience of Kiddush ha-Levanah—the Blessing of the New Moon. A Kiddush ha-Levanah service can be adapted to the particular group. Mention ought to be made that we Jews are a moon people, that in a sense we live by the moon, we wax and we wane.

We are far more with the Dionysiac than the Apollonian. All of which leads to Kiddush ha-Levanah.

This ceremony is completed with the beautiful passage, "At the house of Rabbi Yishmael they taught that if Israel merited to see the face of the Father in heaven only once a month, it would be enough." We are not worshiping the moon but identifying with it, making clear that we have no light of our own; that all light is from the Holy One, blessed be He.

Then the cultural presentation, the larks, the jokes. It should not go too long. The Sunday morning session ought to be stressed as something not to be missed.

Sunday

You are now moving into the home stretch of the retreat and that is very important. For Sunday morning, plan a little lesson before worship. After breakfast the speaker should finish up. Then comes lunch and the postmortem.

The retreat leader should make sure that s/he keeps a log and shares it with the next person who takes the retreat, so that a permanent record is created.

And finally the retreat must be followed up several weeks later to see how much was transferred.

ON TRANSFERRING

Before beginning

1. Perhaps you cannot picture yourself being able now, or later, or ever, to observe the Shabbat completely and perfectly. (Perhaps no one ever does.) Perhaps your present situation (your work, your family, your background, your outlook, your readiness) prevents you from making a great or sudden change in your pattern of Shabbat observance. Perhaps the members of the family are in varying situations and will therefore find it best to begin at different points. The important thing is to make a start. Begin now.

2. Ask yourself: What work have I performed on the Shabbat but can now regularly abstain from? ("Regularly" may mean less often than "always" but it must mean more often than "sometimes.")

3. Ask yourself: What forms of "keeping holy" have I neglected on the Shabbat but can regularly observe from now on? (Again, if not always then at least sometimes.)

4. Remind yourself that "a little is a lot, if done with the right kavvanah—intention of heart."

Hershel Matt suggests ways for following up a retreat—for transferring at least part of the Shabbat experience to your own life.

After a start has been made

1. Ask yourself: Am I seeking God's help to keep me from becoming discouraged because of my difficulties thus far?

2. Ask yourself: Can I do more in seeking to derive blessing from the Shabbat? Are there additional aspects, approaches, dimensions? Is there a deeper level of piety at which I can observe?

3. Ask yourself: Am I seeking God's help to keep me from becoming satisfied with my accomplishment thus far?

BEFORE SHABBAT

Reserve new or special garments, utensils, or delicacies?

Prepare especially festive meals?

Clean the house?

Set the table with special service?

Bathe and dress in special clothes?

Invite friends or strangers to share part or all of our Shabbat?

AS SHABBAT BEGINS

Seek to put aside weekday concerns?

Designate money for tzedakah—charity?

Put away all other money?

Kindle the candles before sunset, pronouncing the berakhah?

Welcome Shabbat with further prayer?

Bless the children?

AT SHABBAT MEALS

Wash the hands, pronouncing the berakhah?

Pronounce ha-Motzi over the hallah?

Sing zemirot—table hymns?

Eat leisurely?

Discuss words of Torah?

Say the Birkat ha-Mazon—Grace after Meals?

Share in after-meal tasks, to relieve any one family member of household duties?

ON SHABBAT EVENING, MORNING, AFTERNOON

Refrain from going to work?

Refrain from shopping and commercial pursuits?

Refrain from traveling outside my neighborhood?

Refrain from work in and around the house?

Attend services in synagogue or pray at home?

Study Torah privately or with others?

Spend time appropriately with family—studying, reading, telling stories, playing games,
    singing, taking a walk, showing special affection?

Take a nap?

Visit with friends or relatives living in the neighborhood?

Seek not to give in to anger, hate, grief, despair, cruelty, ridicule, etc.?

AS SHABBAT DEPARTS

Delay its departure with song, sigh, story, study, and prayer?

Pronounce Havdalah—using wine, spices, candle?

If not, could we do it now?   If so, how can we begin?   What have we done?

Family retreats

Everett Gendler is concerned with family retreats and has offered some advice on how to plan a successful (albeit non-traditional) retreat that involves different age groups while offering an important experience for all.

"Consultation with the children": let's be clear about that phrase. It *does* mean finding out what they want; it does mean responding to their preferences. It also means stating your adult preferences and expecting some response from the children to those preferences and desires and needs. In short, it should be a reciprocal process, not exclusively one-way in either direction.

It's a tough assignment, this one, but a productive one: putting something together with appeal for a wide range of ages. That we shy away from it is a bad sign: further evidence of the disintegration of both our society and ourselves. All these rigid separations and categories: adults, children, preteens, teens, postteens, adolescents, kids, young adults. Who can chart them? Who can keep track of them? There are differences, of course, no mistaking that. But how basic are they? Even more important, how exclusive are they? Which of us is not part child and part adult—part infant and part adolescent, part youth and part oldster? I fear for us and for our society if any one of us manages definitely to exclude all parts except those "proper to one's actual age."

Yet it must be admitted that multiage retreats often fail. Why? My own impression is that the problem is not so much age range as lack of discipline. Discipline in the sense of "behavior in accord with rules of conduct" does not mean an arbitrary imposition of unreasonable rules or a tyrannically structured period of time. It means that by common consent there shall be agreed-upon periods when all present will try to focus attention in a particular direction (substitute kavvanah if that's a more acceptable term). It means that after taking into consideration every person's needs and interests, some schedule, however loose, will be worked out and adhered to. It means that chores and tasks—meal preparation, cleanup, etc.—will be equitably shared. (Be careful of stereotyped male-female work divisions. Men can prepare food and care for kids too.)

It also means that sleeping arrangements for the children are thought about, discussed, and agreed on. Among the questions that need to be asked: Shall they sleep all together dormitory-style, in smaller groups, or by family units? If in small groups, what shall determine who sleeps in which group? (Be alert to cliquish or excluding tendencies.) What time are lights to be put out? What time shall talking stop? What is the procedure to be followed if some wake up early while others are still asleep? Etc.

OK. So there's an agreed-upon minimum discipline, some reasonable rules of procedure, which presumably everyone can see the sense of since everybody, including the children, has had some part in working them out. What? You think it too energy demanding, time consuming, and complicated to include the children in this decision making? Let me simply suggest that if there were some way of calculating the time, energy, and complications involved in *coercing* children to do things that they feel are being imposed upon them, and if this were compared with what it takes to do it the cooperative way suggested above, in time and energy as well as spirit you're far ahead if you proceed in consultation with the children.

PROGRAMMING

As with discipline, so with the substance of the programming. Everyone will gain from listening and responding to one another. Children, I think, have something of value to learn from us. Adults, I know, have something of value to learn from children.

I do not mean to idealize children and childhood, yet at times I have seen a child drawing with such gentle yet persistent enthusiasm that the delicate effects have been almost snowlike in their purity and sparkle. I have seen children unafraid to ask the simple questions—where does a seed come from?—and to each response pose the same question once more, until we, like they, are brought face to face with the ultimate mystery of life and its origins. I have seen a child so fascinated by what to me was the random pattern of small pebbles in a piece of rough, "ordinary" sidewalk that her attention forced me to notice and feel the textures, the variety, the contrasts.

Children often like to move. We could learn from that, and would do well to include plenty of movement in a service. Children like to sing. We could learn from that, and would do well to include plenty of singing in a service. Children like to discover, to find things, to experience. Except for the sound of nonsense syllables, they like to know what is being talked about. That's not a bad cue for us, to personalize and exemplify and experience some of what the prayer book is pointing to or talking about. A few examples of the latter may help.

Ma Tovu can introduce the Shabbat morning service. It can be sung. It can be swayed to. So sing and sway. It draws attention to *where we are*. So notice where you are and share some of what you notice with one another. That is, establish a sense of setting, be it indoors or outdoors.

Nishmat Kol Hai says literally: "The breath of all life proclaims Your name blessed, Lord our God." So focus a while on breathing, notice how it proceeds. Do we breathe or are we breathed? There's quite a difference. Now, how does that connect with what the prayer is saying? Invite comments, and the likelihood is that children will have some fine insights.

Hai ha-Olamim, the Life of the Universe. Another phrase that often goes by unnoticed. So notice. With the children, look around for signs of life, for signs of the Life Force making itself manifest: trees, flowers, grass, bushes, etc., etc. Relate them to the prayer.

Such activity need not degenerate into mere busyness or breathless hyperactivity. It can be calm, reflective, yet active and involving. It can also have a nice literalism about it, and there is much to be said for acting out in simple and basic ways some of the words and metaphors of prayer.

Torah portion? How about asking the children to prepare in advance a skit or playlet for presentation at the time of the Torah reading, drawing the theme from the Torah portion?

And once more, remember: include the children in the planning of the service and the Torah reading.

Such materials can serve as amusements for the children and can help them fill stretches when the adults have something they want to pursue by themselves. When such times arise, do not feel guilty. Children as well as adults have needs to be within their peer groups. Feel free to plan programs to which the children are not invited, but provide supervision for them while you are otherwise engaged. For such occasions it is often desirable to ask some of the teenagers in the group to assume special responsibilities for the younger children. If by chance the group does not include any teenagers, then it might be desirable to invite one or two along to help out.

Cordelia

The depths of solitude that she can reach
On any cool, green morning, as she swings
In long slow rhythms through the backyard peace.
I watch her waken daily in its sway,
Lulling herself from sleep, until she sings
Plain nonsense as her greeting to the day.

If, rarely, I can touch that central quiet,
I find it by old music; fine fierce words
And in the dark. I've never seen the light
Even of winter evenings on such calm
As that my child's morning rite affords.
I only watch; nor can I match her song.
(Mary Baron, *Letters for the New England Dead*)

Anything and everything seems to fascinate her. Is she a lunatic? An enviable lunatic! One for whom a pebble has value must be surrounded by treasures wherever she goes (Par Lagerkvist, *The Dwarf*).

A few other suggestions might be helpful. Don't forget plenty of paper, crayons, paints, clay, perhaps spools and chunks of woods, hammers, nails, etc., etc. Wonderful hours can be spent either on Sunday or Shabbat (if your children's observance level permits) using such materials. Games and athletic equipment are also worth including, and of course include a copy of *Catalog 1*.

Materials and activities need not be simply diversions or mere imports from the familiar world of home. They can also help bring the surroundings in which the group finds itself into finer focus. For example, if the leaves are on the trees, children (and adults, for that matter) might take a walk, gather leaves, return, and iron them between pieces of wax paper. These could then serves as meditation material at a service. Or they might gather especially interesting rocks, pebbles, shells at the seashore, acorns and pine cones in the forest, etc., etc.

One other theme for possible shared activity might be mentioned: food. It is, after all, pretty basic and receives rather extensive attention from Jewish tradition. Why not, then, do some food things together? On various occasions we have done some of the things listed below—possibilities are almost limitless.

Bring wheat berries and a small flour mill, and grind the flour that you'll use to break bread. If someone thinks to begin sprouting wheat berries a couple of days before the retreat, the sprouts will expand everyone's appreciation of the marvelous grain cycle. Even if you omit grinding the wheat, baking bread is a superb project for everyone to participate in, and ha-Motzi—the blessing over bread—has new life.

Or bring raw peanuts—you can generally get them at a candy store that makes its own candy. Have the kids sample them raw. Then roast them (mix with a small amount of peanut oil—say, one cup of peanuts to one tablespoon of peanut oil, sprinkle them with salt, and roast at 350° for fifteen to twenty minutes). The difference in taste is astonishing. If you then grind the peanuts in your small flour mill (most have another attachment for grinding nuts) you can make your own peanut butter, which is fun indeed. Once again, the berakhah—blessing—has quite a new taam—flavor.

Or bring the various ingredients for a granola cereal—honey, molasses, rolled oats, pumpkin seeds, sunflower seeds, sesame seeds, raisins, etc.—and prepare that together one morning, bringing it freshly roasted out of the oven just in time for breakfast. Yum!

Sprout seeds for salads. (And again, be sure to start at least two days before the retreat begins so that they can be observed and ready before the weekend is over.)

Make ice cream together. It's not too hard, and everyone turns out to be a willing participant in this one—too willing at times!

All of the above and more can be planned "for the children." And since each one of us, I hope, is still part child, by such activities we come closer not only to our children but to ourselves. What more could one hope for from a family retreat?

More about retreats

If you want to run a retreat that is less structured than the first model outlined above, we suggest adapting some of the forms that seem appropriate to you. Keep in mind the following:

1. While you must have some person/persons coordinating the entire thing, they need not be retreat leaders in the classic sense. They could simply coordinate time/place/program/food/equipment, etc. Which brings us to the second point . . .

2. You *must* assume that retreatants have skills they can share with others. Find out who the "hidden" are and set the pattern early on for people to share their skills with others. If someone knows how to lead davening (no, it need not at all be a rabbi or Jewish professional) then s/he should not only be

urged to lead davening at the retreat but should teach the skill to others. Ditto for reading from the Torah, making Kiddush, leading Birkhat ha-Mazon after meals, making Havdalah, putting on tallit and/or tefillin, etc. If there is no time before the retreat begins for sharing such skills, plan the program using the local experts but allow time in the program for them to share their skills.

3. It can be a nice idea to spend the Friday before the retreat doing things to prepare for Shabbat. People could make tallitot, kippot, hallah covers, candles, as well as hallah and other food.

4. Allow time for non-"head" kinds of activities. Every activity need not be a discussion, lecture, etc. Shabbat is a time to invite a friend for a long walk in the woods, to sit around singing, to dance and jig, etc. Bring sports equipment if your level of observance permits this on Shabbat.

5. Everyone should help set up and clear away meals. Except in special situations, it is highly undesirable to have a retreat in a hotel, where retreatants are waited on. People should be concerned/involved with the food for Shabbat. This might mean buying prepared foods or having a cook prepare the food ahead, but making retreatants responsible for serving the food at the retreat. Remember, a retreat is not a vacation. It is an attempt to build community through a Jewish experience.

6. Don't overprogram. Allow a one- to two-hour free block of time on Shabbat afternoon if at all possible. A typical program might look something like this:

    a. Friday
       day: activities related to Shabbat preparation
       just before Shabbat: retreatants shower, don fresh clothes
       Shabbat: lighting of candles
                 Kabbalat Shabbat services
                 meal with singing and devar Torah (see Giving a Devar Torah in *Catalog 2*)
                 large group presentation
                   or
                 small group discussions of different Jewish areas of interest
                 curfew

    b. Saturday
       Shabbat: wake up
                 services and Torah reading
                 lunch (or, if the service ends early, discussion groups and then lunch)
                 discussion groups
                 free time, one to two hours
                 discussion groups
                   or
                 lecture
                 third Shabbat meal—Seudah Shelishit
                 Havdalah

7. Above all, if you bring in "experts," "leaders," "professionals," etc. to do your retreat, make sure they are as professional as they claim to be. Far too many people charge excessive fees and do not have the necessary skills to create a Shabbat environment.

8. Many Jewish camps now make their facilities available for retreats during the noncamp season. A resource listing of such camps can be found in the Jewish Education section in *Catalog 2* under "Informal Education—Camping" (pp. 184–85). Also check the retreat centers given in the Jewish Yellow Pages in *Catalog 2* on p. 447.

Some general advice—no matter what style retreat you're planning

1. Keep the food simple. Menus should be simple to prepare, filling, easy to execute. Save the Cordon Bleu stuff for your next orgy.

2. Plan absolutely every detail. Don't forget the Shabbat candles need holders and matches, that Havdalah needs spices, that stands for washing before meals need wastepaper baskets nearby, etc.

3. Remind people ahead of time to bring their ritual paraphernalia—kippot, tallitot, etc.

4. Make sure there are enough xerox copies of everything to go around.

5. Provide songbooks and/or Birkat ha-Mazon—Grace after Meals—booklets.

6. Where possible, keep fruit or cakes/cookies and other varieties of noshes around for people who get the hungries or the munchies frequently.

7. If sports activity is planned during the retreat, make sure to bring appropriate equipment. If you plan on playing music at any point, make sure to bring a record player or tape recorder.

8. For additional retreat suggestions, see *Catalog 1*, p. 33.

So, with all of this, we believe we can begin to build a stronger community if we sound the shofar and retreat!

Hevra Kadisha

The Hevra Kadisha—the burial society—was once a basic institution of Jewish communal life. Unfortunately it has dwindled into virtual nonexistence in contemporary Jewish communities.

Historically, the Hevra Kadisha was one of a whole network of hevrot—societies—concerned with a variety of communal needs, all guided by the basic imperative of hesed—the practice of kindness to both the living and the dead. Among these hevrot were those for lehem la-reevim—feeding the hungry; hakhnasat kalah—providing dowries for poor brides; and gemilut hasadim—free loan societies. Any activities that could conceivably touch upon death were, in some communities, the concern of the Hevra Kadisha, e.g., bikur holim—visiting the sick and the dying; nihum avelim—comforting the mourners; seudat havraah—providing them with with a meal of consolation upon their return from the cemetery; and financial assistance to bereaved families where necessary to help them through the immediate crisis arising from a death. The Hevra Kadisha also involved itself in the broader needs of the community by charging a fee for its services, scaled to the means of the family, which then went into a fund for the poor.

Perhaps one aspect of the revitalized community that many of us envision for American Jewry is the reestablishment of the human sharing and mutual responsibility that was embodied in these hevrot. Too often the simple acts of human kindness that all Jews are commanded to perform are seen as part of the job of the rabbi, and the rest of the community regards itself as being exempt from visiting the sick or the mourners.

But to turn over these areas to the domain of the rabbi is to abandon the responsibility for the community that is the foundation of Judaism. A rabbi should not be expected to perform *your* duties. If a member of the community is sick, it is *your* responsibility to pay a sick call. If a person dies, it is *your* responsibility to comfort the mourners. It goes against the very grain of Judaism to abandon these responsibilities.

Here we are going to set out a model for forming one specific type of hevra—a Hevra Kadisha or burial society. Thumb through the rest of this book for other hevra possibilities—e.g., Project Ezra, Visiting the Sick, and even Social Action! You'll be surprised at the areas ripe for hevra development.

Some history

In biblical times burial was performed by the immediate family of the deceased or all the residents of the particular town. All activity in the town would cease. By the time of the Talmud, society had grown sufficiently large and complex so that it was no longer feasible for the whole town to cease its activities each time a death occurred. Special groups that assumed responsibility for burying the dead were set up, and the rest of the townspeople were relieved of this obligation (see Moed Katan 27b). The oldest known Hevra Kadisha as such, however, was one in sixteenth-century Prague. Among its regulations, drawn up by the Maharal of Prague, were that no fees were to be charged for burial, that all Jews were to be buried by the hevra, and that a fixed system was to be established for the allocation of graves.

The name Hevra Kadisha—Holy Society or Holy Brotherhood—does not refer to death at all but to the spirit of holiness in which duties can be performed as mitzvot. An alternate name for these groups—Hevra Gemilut Hesed Shel Emet—Society for True Kindness—also reflects the religious concern that served as their basic motivation.

The crucial principle underlying the formation of such groups was that, according to halakhah, a corpse is assur be-hanaah—forbidden as a source of any financial benefit. One could not, therefore, make a commercial venture of the burial of the dead: it had to be done without pay as a religious duty.

It was also considered a "true kindness" because the person benefiting from the kindness, i.e., the deceased, obviously had no means to repay the act. Since no ulterior motive could be attributed to the act, it was considered the highest form of "true kindness."

Thus to be admitted into the Hevra Kadisha was one of the highest honors a Jew could attain. Its membership was often restricted to the most respected members of the local community. The Hevra Kadisha saw itself as following in the tradition of Abraham, who was concerned with acquiring a cave in Machpelah in which to bury Sarah (Genesis 23:9). An even more significant example was the burial of Moses:

Moses went up from the steppes of Moab to Mount Nebo, to the summit of Pisgah, opposite Jericho, and the Lord showed him the whole land. . . . And the Lord said to him, "This is the land which I swore to Abraham, Isaac, and Jacob, 'I will give it to your offspring.' I have let you see it with your own eyes, but you shall not cross there." So Moses the servant of the Lord died there, in the land of Moab, at the command of the Lord. He buried him in the valley . . . and no one knows his burial place to this day (Deuteronomy 34:1–6).

God Himself performed the duties of burial for Moses, and we see God's act as a model showing us the importance and the holiness of the act. And it was this act that made the task of the Hevra Kadisha both an honored and an awesome one.

Because of the paradigm of the burial of Moses, his Yahrzeit—death date—has become a special day for many Hevrot Kadisha. Tradition fixes this day as the Seventh of Adar. On this day the members of the hevra would fast, asking forgiveness from the dead for any unintentional disrespect. After the fast an elaborate feast was held in the evening, at which the members of the hevra were treated royally by the rest of the Jewish community. In some communities this annual fast/feast was held on a different day because of varying traditions. In some communities the reading of the haftorah of Ezekiel's vision of the valley of the dry bones was reserved solely for members of the hevra.

Function of Hevra Kadisha

Essentially the duties of the Hevra Kadisha consist of the preparation of the body for burial and the burial itself (see Death and Burial in *Catalog 2*, pp. 172–81). These may be divided into five steps:

1. Shemirah—guarding the body after death.
2. Taharah—washing the body, including both cleaning the body and a ritual pouring of nine kavim (about 6 gallons) of water over the body. (See *Catalog 1*, pp. 167–71, Tumah and Taharah.)
3. Levishah—dressing the body in white shrouds, preferably of linen. A man is also dressed in his tallit.
4. Hotzaat hamitah—carrying the body to the place of burial.
5. Kevurah—burial and filling in the grave.

A model for forming a Hevra Kadisha

How does the Hevra Kadisha work in contemporary society? What follows is a description of my experience as a member of a Hevra Kadisha in Boston.

Essentially, our Hevra Kadisha performs all the traditional tasks of the Hevra Kadisha—shemirah, taharah, and occasionally the burial itself. But there is one basic difference. Whereas the Hevra Kadisha in prewar Europe and in the State of Israel function as autonomous bodies with full responsibility for all aspects of burial, we function as subcontractors to the Jewish funeral homes in the area. Taharah, shemirah, shrouds, and the traditional coffin are merely options that funeral directors make available to those families who wish them. Thus on numerous occasions we have faced the anomaly of being called to perform a traditional taharah on a body that has been embalmed (embalming is forbidden under Jewish Law) or of placing the body after taharah in a heavy mahogany casket inlaid with plush satin (see below—hillul ha-met). For the most part, our job begins and ends with taharah. For more traditional families we will, on request, arrange for shemirah, serve as pallbearers, and participate in the filling of the grave. But even in those cases the context in which we work—the room in which we prepare the body, the hall in which the funeral takes place—is that of the commercial funeral home. In only one case, the funeral of a pious patriarch who lived on a farm in an outlying region, did we bypass the funeral home completely to perform taharah and the funeral in the man's own home.

We also found it necessary to pay the members a modest fee for each taharah performed. Many of the members turn this money over to charity, but others do not (cannot). In this respect we fall short of the ideal of a purely religious, noncommercial hevra.

Another problem we have faced and one that is peculiar to the modern situation is that of education concerning death. Modern man is afraid to talk about death. Our culture attempts to deny the reality of death and makes a fetish of youth. As some observers have commented, we have overcome the Victorian taboo on sex but have substituted for it, unwittingly, a taboo on death. Yet if death is the conclusion of every life, it must be confronted in a clear and realistic way, not only when it takes place, but as part of the educational process—the study of Torah that has always been the center of Jewish communal life. As we did in Boston, perhaps the Hevra Kadisha might stimulate public discussion of this subject within the synagogue, both on the ethical and philosophical dimensions of death as well as the specific customs relating to burial and mourning.

There is appalling ignorance within the American Jewish community regarding the authentic traditions on these matters. Too often bereaved families are at the mercy of funeral directors with little respect and no commitment to the tradition, coupled with a vested interest in selling as expensive a funeral as possible. (For an excellent collection of essays on a variety of problems relating to death, see Jack Reimer, *Jewish Reflections on Death* [New York: Schocken, 1975].)

Hillul ha-met (dishonoring the dead): what to avoid

Jewish law is concerned with a number of ways in which the dead may be dishonored or their bodies desecrated. The following list includes several practices, all common in modern life, that tradition views negatively. Some are forbidden, while others are permitted under certain circumstances (consult a rabbi).

1. *Autopsy:* The principle here is that the body's integrity is not to be disturbed. In some cases the benefit to the living or the saving of a life may outweigh this consideration.

2. *Organ transplant:* Same reasoning as in No. 1.

3. *Embalming:* The basic objection is the same as above. This is sometimes difficult to avoid, as when a funeral must be delayed for the arrival of a relative or when the body must be transported elsewhere. Rabbinical advice is required.

4. *Viewing the body:* This is a pagan, death-denying custom, to be categorically avoided.

5. *Extravagance:* Elaborate clothing or caskets of metal or hardwood are against the tradition, which calls for extreme simplicity. The desired end of the body is to perish naturally. In talmudic times there were problems with elaborate funerals. Hence an early tradition was formed: poor and rich are equal in death.

6. *Affronts to modesty:* The dead are not to be left lying naked. Even during the washing process they should be treated modestly and reverently, and washed only by people of the same sex.

Procedures

How can you organize a Hevra Kadisha in an area where there is none? First find at least three men and three women who are willing to commit themselves to (a) overcoming whatever emotional aversions they may have to handling dead bodies—and those may be very deep; and (b) coming whenever they are called on short notice. Naturally the larger the group, the less ironclad the commitment any one person need make. Second, work out an arrangement with the local funeral home to allow the hevra to perform taharah at the request of a family. At this point it is wise and useful to work with the local rabbi. Third, learn how to perform taharah and the various customs connected with it. A good description of the procedures to be followed by the Hevra Kadisha is to be found in Maurice Lamm, *The Jewish Way in Death and Mourning* (New York: Jonathan David, 1969), or, for those who read Hebrew, in Yehiel Michael Tukatzinsky, *Gesher Ha-Hayim.* Fourth, arrange to have available all the necessities for performing taharah: a room with a large table and running water; buckets for the nine kavim; sponges; towels; and most importantly shrouds and simple pine coffins. If such coffins are not immediately available, the funeral director may order them; or else commission a local carpenter to make them. Takhrikhim—shrouds—may be ordered from

> Miriam Funeral Supplies
> 48 Canal St.
> New York, NY 10003

The more serious difficulty to overcome, however, is to make the general Jewish public aware of the problems so that reform in funeral practices may embrace the entire Jewish community, not just those who know about and insist on the traditional forms. (For a discussion of this problem, see *Catalog 1,* pp. 172–79; and Samuel Dresner, *The Jew in American Life* [New York: Crown, 1963], chapter 2, "The Scandal of the Jewish Funeral.")

A final word
Being part of a Hevra Kadisha is a mitzvah. But to look at it another way, being part of a hevra is sharing the basic idea of people who are willing to commit their time and effort to fulfilling a communal responsibility.

As Jews we have a responsibility to one another. And as Jews we must seek to fulfill that responsibility in Jewish ways: "Simon the Just was one of the last survivors of the Great Assembly. He used to say: Upon three things the world is based; upon the Torah, upon worship, and upon the doing of righteous deeds" (Pirkei Avot 1:2).

Visiting the sick

Thus Abraham and his son Ishmael were circumcised on that very day; and all his household, his homeborn slaves and those that had been bought from outsiders, were circumcised with him. The Lord appeared to him by the terebinths of Mamre (Genesis 17:26–27, 18:1).

The Talmud comments on the fact that God appeared to Abraham by explaining that God paid a sick call on Abraham while he was recovering from the circumcision. "The Holy One, blessed be He, visited the sick, as it is written, The Lord appeared to him by the terebinths of Mamre" and so *you* must visit the sick!" (Sotah 14a).

Bikur holim—the commandment to visit the sick—is thus seen as a very important mitzvah, with God setting the precedent for us.

History

Visiting the sick became a well-established norm of Jewish life. In the Talmud we find many references to such visits made by scholars and disciples.

Since the Middle Ages one of the principal institutions established by every Jewish community has been the Bikur Holim Society. In addition, Jewish communities established communal infirmaries and hired communal doctors. These physicians were paid a specific amount per year for their service to the poor. They were permitted to collect a set fee from those who were not classified as poor by the community.

During the Middle Ages it was the custom to visit the sick immediately following the Shabbat morning services. This was the responsibility of everyone; most particularly, it was the responsibility of the lay leadership. The modern practice of the rabbinic "pastoral visit" did not exist. Rabbis simply fulfilled the mitzvah that was the obligation of every Jew.

In modern times the landsmanshaften and fraternal orders in America continued the duties of the Bikur Holim Society. Many of them also hired doctors to serve their membership at specified fees.

At the present time visiting the sick as a communal mitzvah has been relegated to rabbis and Jewish chaplains, who usually make these visits only when the patient is in the hospital and not at home as the halakhah also requires. It is time for us to revitalize this mitzvah and realize that it is viewed by the tradition as a very serious obligation incumbent upon every one of us.

Traditional concerns

Like many other social and personal obligations, the sages surrounded the concept of visiting the sick with religious significance. They indicated that this mitzvah is important enough to be numbered among those commandments "the fruits of which a man enjoys in this life while the principal endures for him to all eternity" (Peah 1:1).

On the other hand, they were also alert to the fact that a visit could at times cause pain and suffering (Nedarim 40a). They therefore set up rules as a guide for sick visits.

WHOM TO VISIT

One is obligated to visit family, friends, and non-Jews, whether they are in the hospital or at home. *Sefer Hasidim* (pp. 361, 367) indicates that this mitzvah crosses class lines and even a great person must visit a humble one: "If a poor man and a rich man become ill at the same time, and many people go to the rich, you should go to the poor first, even if the rich be a scholar."

There are certain people one should not visit. For example, do not visit an enemy unless you have come to apologize. (I would also suggest that when you plan such a visit, you should inform the patient as well as the family before you go.) Also, don't visit people to whom such a visit would be disturbing because of the nature of their illness (Nedarim 41). For example, a patient who is not permitted to speak should not be visited lest by the visit you inadvertently bring about embarrassment or injury. Instead, see if you can be of help in some other way. You may want to speak with the family and/or doctor.

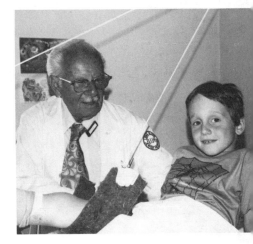

TIME OF VISIT

1. Don't visit the sick immediately after they have fallen ill for they become frightened, thinking that it must be a serious illness when it might really be a simple illness (Jerusalem Talmud, Peah 18b). This rule, however, does not apply to relatives and close friends, who should visit immediately because the patient will want the comfort of their presence.

2. Wait until the third day to visit an acquaintance who is a patient. If the illness is serious, however, do not wait at all (Jerusalem Talmud, Peah 18b). Anyone entering a hospital may be considered, in this sense, to have a serious illness, unless s/he entered for testing. It is considered exemplary to visit more than once—even a few times a day, as long as it does not disturb the patient (Nedarim 39b). In any case, do not make your visit too long as this cannot be considered in the best interests of the patient.

3. Do not visit during the first three hours or the last three hours of the day because you may find yourself refraining from praying for the patient's recovery (see "Purpose of the Visit" below). The reason for this is quite interesting. It is felt that in the early hours the patient usually feels fine and the visitor will not feel the need for prayer; and in the late hours the sickness often appears so serious that the visitor gives up on the efficacy of prayer. In addition, I have found that in the morning hours the visit interferes with the activities of the staff, and in the evening the patient is exhausted.

Rabbi Akiba stated that when one neglects to visit a sick person, it is as if one sheds the patient's blood (Nedarim 40a). This is interpreted to mean that the absence of such a visit indicates that one is not praying for the person's recovery.

Purpose of the visit

The purpose of bikur holim is twofold: (1) aiding and comforting the sick and (2) praying for the sick. Try to render any service, such as straightening the pillows, bringing reading material, alleviating anxiety and concern. Speak only pleasant and comforting words. Do not bring sad news or weep for the dead in the patient's presence (Moed Katan 26b).

Prayer: The essence of the mitzvah of bikur holim is to pray for the patient. At the bedside the prayer can be said in any language, while at the synagogue it is traditionally said in Hebrew. The traditional prayer during the weekday is "Hamakom yerahem alekha betokh shear holei yisrael [May the All-Compassionate have mercy upon you among the other sick of Israel]." (One always couples private needs with the needs of others in the community.) On Shabbat or Yom Tov one says: "Shabbat (Yom Tov) hi melizok urefuah krovah lavo [It is the Shabbat (Yom Tov); therefore on this day we make no supplication, but may his/her healing come very soon]."

Viddui: When possible and advisable the rabbi or an elder member of the family should recite the viddui—the confession—with the patient. It should be pointed out to the patient that this does not mean there is no hope for recovery. It is intended to ease his/her mind and reduce anxieties while the patient asks God's forgiveness. The prayer is as follows:

I acknowledge before You, O Lord my God and God of my fathers, that life and my death are in Your hands. May it be Your will to heal. But if death is my lot, then I accept it from Your hand with love.

   May my death be an atonement for whatever sins and errors and wrongdoing I have committed before You. In Your mercy grant me of the goodness that is waiting for the righteous and bring me to eternal life.

   Father of the orphans, Protector of the widows, protect my loved ones with whom my soul is bound.

   Into Your hands I return my spirit. You will redeem me, O ever-faithful God.

   Hear, O Israel, the Lord our God, the Lord is One.

Mi-she-berakh: In addition to praying at the bedside of the patient, one should arrange for the recitation of Mi-she-berakh in the synagogue at the time of the reading of the Torah. The text for that prayer is as follows:

May He who blessed our fathers Abraham, Isaac, and Jacob bless the sick person, ———. May He in His mercy restore him/her to perfect health and speedily send him/her a healing of soul and a healing of body: and let us say amen.

It is customary to use the name of the mother of the sick person instead of the father in this prayer, i.e., "Samuel son of Sarah" (not "son of David"). One

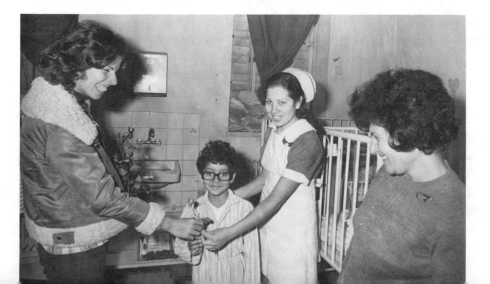

of the reasons for this is that in Hebrew the word for compassion is rahamim and the word for womb is rehem. We pray that God will show compassion and love, just as the mother's womb engendered love and protection.

In shul one can also recite the special prayer of Veyehi Ratzon, which appears as an insert to the Refoeinu—May You Heal Us—prayer in the week-day Amidah—The Silent Devotion. This special prayer for healing found its way into the Amidah in medieval times and is used today:

> May it be Your will, Lord our God and God of our fathers, to send with speed a total healing from heaven, a healing of the soul and a healing of the body of the sick, ———, among the other sick people of Israel.

Tehillim: Another manner of praying for the very sick in the synagogue is to recite specific psalms, such as Psalms 6, 9, 13, 16, 17, 18, 20, 22, 23, 25, 30, 31, 32, 33, 37, 38, 39, 41, 49, 55, 56, 69, 86, 88, 90, 91, 102, 103, 104, 107, 116, 118, 142, 143, or 148.

Follow any of these with Psalm 119. The verses of this psalm follow the order of the Hebrew alphabet; each letter of the alphabet has eight consecutive verses. Thus verses 1–8 of Psalm 119 all begin with the letter alef; verses 9–16 begin with the letter bet, etc. The name David, for example, can be spelled using verses 25, 41, and 27. The custom is to choose verses from this psalm to spell out three things:

1. the name of the sick person
2. his/her mother's name
3. the words קְרַע שָׂטָן —may the evil decree be abolished.

All this is followed by a Mi-she-berakh.

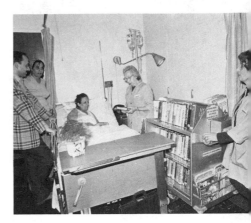

Shinui Hashem: When a person is very seriously ill the above tehillim procedure is followed by a special prayer instead of the Mi-she-berakh. In this prayer an additional name is given to the sick person. This was intended as a device to confuse the Angel of Death, who wouldn't know the person's new name and so could not claim the soul. Additional names usually used were Hayim (life), Hayah (life), Rephuel (God cause recovery), and Alter (old). This prayer in the Ashkenazic version is found at the end of the regular Book of Psalms. The Sephardic version is as follows:

> And his/her name in Israel shall be known: (new name).

> *For a man:* As it is written (Genesis 17:5), "And you shall no longer be called Abram, but your name shall be Abraham, for I made you the father of a multitude of nations."

> *For a woman:* As it is written (Genesis 17:15), "As for your wife Sarai, you shall not call her Sarai, but her name shall be Sarah."

> May it be Your will, Lord our God and God of our Fathers, that the change of this name make naught all harsh and evil decrees; tear away from him/her the evil decisions. If death was decreed upon (old name), but on (new name) it was not decreed. If harm was decreed upon (old name), but on (new name) there is no such decree. S/he is like a different person, a newborn individual. Like an infant born to good life, length of years, and fullness of days, as it is written (Isaiah 38:5), "I have heard your prayer, I have seen your tears. I hereby add fifteen years to your life."

Suggestions for the community

The mitzvah of visiting the sick needs revitalization with as much emphasis as possible on communal involvement.

I make the following suggestions with the hope of reestablishing the halakhic norm that this mitzvah is incumbent upon *every* person.

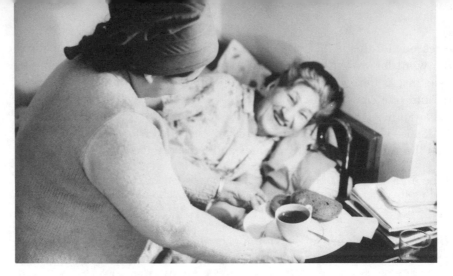

1. A large Bikur Holim Committee should be established in each synagogue, temple, havurah, etc. A report should be given at every board meeting so that other members may also visit. These members should be taught the essential components of this mitzvah, including the prayers.

2. The names of the sick for whom prayers should be recited should be posted in each synagogue so that members of the community may include their names in the Amidah prayer, as indicated above.

3. When the Mi-she-berakh is recited at the Torah service, the family name should also be used, thus calling it to the attention of the congregation.

4. People who have been seriously ill, both men and women, should be encouraged to come to services where they can recite the Birkhat ha-Gomeil. (For full prayers, see *Catalog 1*, p. 157.) In congregations where women are not given aliyot to the Torah the woman could recite the prayer while her husband receives the aliyah, or else she could recite it by herself at an appropriate time.

5. Although we stress the desirability for a renewal of communal involvement, the chaplaincy program should be strengthened and expanded to cover all hospitals, nursing homes, etc. Until we as a community can reclaim this mitzvah as our own, we ought to make sure that at least we have professionals who represent our care and concern when one of our "family" is ill. Local Jewish federations should be encouraged to make the creation of chaplaincy programs an important priority.

Suggestions for friends

1. Visit during the hours assigned by the hospital.

2. Knock on the door before entering; do not enter suddenly.

3. Before visiting a very sick person check with the family as well as the nurse. Ask if you are allowed to visit and whether there are any specific suggestions or restrictions.

4. Do not visit on the day of an operation and for a few days after the operation without first checking with the doctor or family.

5. Visit or say hello to all other patients you pass on the way to the one you are visiting and to the patients next to the one you're visiting.

6. When you bring books be sure they are not heavy in weight or in content, neither too serious nor too funny (especially for a person whose stitches have not been removed; otherwise the possibility of having someone *back* "in stitches" may become all too real).

7. It would also be wise—especially when the patient must remain in the hospital a long time—to check with the family and arrange the visits so that there are not too many visitors at the beginning and not too few near the end of their stay; the former tends to exhaust and the latter to depress the patient.

8. If there are too many people visiting already, come back later or wait until they leave. A patient often feels that s/he must "entertain" visitors (such as keeping the conversational ball rolling) despite the visitor's insistence to the contrary. Too many visitors could be a strain for the patient, although the patient might try to hide it. For the same reason, be sensitive enough to leave *before* the patient is thoroughly exhausted.

9. If necessary, introduce yourself. Unless it is too difficult for the patient to talk, try to involve him/her in the conversation. Don't be embarrassed to speak loudly and slowly or to sit very close when the needs of the patient require it. Don't be ashamed to ask the patient to repeat something a number of times. If s/he can't talk, leave after wishing him/her a speedy recovery and perhaps sitting with him/her quietly for a few moments. Sitting quietly with any patient shows that you really care.

10. Avoid case histories (documented hearsay) about some acquaintance of long ago who suffered the same symptoms and had the same treatment. (Not only is "Who made you an M.D.?" valid here, but also "What good does such information do the patient?"—who should be encouraged to have faith in his/her own doctor and treatment.) Other topics to avoid: What are those tubes for? What did the tests show? Why aren't they letting you out of bed? Etc. Do not criticize the food, the doctor, the nurses, the room, or other hospital services. It can only prove disheartening to someone who is already in an emotionally strained state.

11. Don't debate with the patient. Even the most innocent topic can be an emotional one for reasons unknown to you. Steer the conversation elsewhere when such situations arise. To find suitable topics of discussion, keep your eyes and ears open. If you see flowers or a photograph on the patient's table, comment on it. This may start a conversation about the patient's family or friends. Try to focus on topics of the patient's interest rather than your own.

12. If a patient asks for physical help (for example, wants you to turn him/her around in bed or help him/her into a wheelchair), check with a nurse before doing anything.

13. In addition to visiting the sick, spend some time with the family whenever possible.

AS MY GRANDMOTHER USED TO SAY (iN YiDDiSH, OF cOURSE), YOUR health comes fiRST. YOU Can always hang yourself later.

Suggestions for the patient

1. Do not be ashamed to ask people to leave when you are tired or indisposed.

2. Do not be ashamed to refuse to discuss your case, the diagnosis, the prognosis, the doctor, etc.

3. Do not apologize for your appearance.

4. Ask for books and magazines from the book cart.

5. Feel free to discuss with your doctor any questions related to your condition.

6. Feel free to request kosher food and visits from the Jewish chaplain (if one is assigned to the hospital). Also ask the chaplain's assistance in obtaining a lulav and etrog, mahzor, etc. See if the chaplain can arrange for someone to come to blow shofar or read the megillah for you.

And may God grant to all the sick of Israel a speedy recovery.

Project Ezra

The idea of a community of people forming a group to care for its elderly can only be seen as beneficial to all. The concepts represented by Project Ezra and the services it performs are easy to adopt in communities throughout the United States. The following is a brief how-to for forming your own such group.

Assessing the situation

To organize such a project you must create a core group that will explore the types of services, if any, being provided for the aged in your community. Some questions to be asked:

1. How many aged are currently being reached?
2. What is the nature of the services provided?
3. Do those served reside in certain neighborhoods?
4. If so, can you be *sure* that there are no Jews in need of service residing outside these neighborhoods?
5. Do the agencies engage in active outreach to find their clients, or do those served come on their own or via referrals from other organizations?
6. What percentage of those in need are receiving service?

The best place to look for answers to these questions is your local Federation of Jewish Philanthropies, in particular the Jewish Family Service, which, unless there is a particular office set up to deal with the aged (such as JASA in New York), is the agency most involved in this area. If there are still unanswered questions, particularly concerning those *not* reached by family service agencies, other places to look for answers include settlement houses, community centers, local offices for the aged, etc.

Finding the elderly

You will probably find that most agencies do not do active outreach to find clients. You may decide, therefore, that this should be a function of your group—to find those isolated, homebound individuals in need of help.

There are several ways to go about this. First, if you are dealing with an area where there are public housing projects, speak to the manager of each building. The manager is usually familiar with the old Jews living in these buildings since they pay their rent to the housing office. You may be able to obtain lists of residents. If a manager is reluctant to supply you with lists for an entire building, try to get lists of the one-bedroom apartments. Most of the elderly live alone—certainly not more than two together—and therefore would be in the smaller apartments.

If there are no large apartment buildings and your area of concern consists of small apartment buildings, tenements, or even three-family houses, the initial stage of finding the people in need of help is more difficult but certainly not impossible. Contact synagogue rabbis, local shopkeepers, and especially kosher butcher shops and bakeries and ask if they know of any elderly Jews living alone who might like someone to visit them. Finding these people is often a long, tedious, and frustrating process, but if you are determined to help them you must also be prepared to put in long hours. Few agencies have the time, energy, and willpower needed for doing this kind of outreach to the elderly.

Knowledge of other languages is helpful, sometimes necessary: Yiddish for communicating with old people when you find them, often Spanish to ask their Puerto Rican neighbors for help in finding them. In many instances these Spanish-speaking people already provide services, such as shopping and mailing letters for their elderly Jewish neighbors.

Since many of these people live in unsafe neighborhoods and are often mugged or robbed, police stations have statistics that may also help you find isolated elderly Jews. Also, mailmen may be able to direct you to old people, who often wait downstairs for their social security checks.

Making contact

You must be extremely patient during all stages of this initial process. Many people don't have telephones, so you will have to write informing them when you plan to visit. These letters should be in both English and Yiddish. When you arrive at the door, knock long and hard: many of the elderly are hard of hearing or walk very slowly and may take up to five full minutes to answer the door. Identify yourself in a loud, clear voice. A few Yiddish words—even "Shalom Aleichem"—will often help alleviate their fear of strangers.

Once inside, explain again what the nature of your visit is, i.e., that you represent a new organization that can provide a volunteer to visit once a week for an hour or two and help the person with shopping, going to the bank, writing letters, filling out forms, etc. Make it clear that you are not offering to send a social worker, nurse, or housekeeper and that the person coming is basically offering an understanding ear and friendship. You'll probably want to design a simple questionnaire with certain basic questions, e.g., name, address, phone (if any), name of doctor or hospital, souce of income (social security, pension, welfare, etc.), services already received (including social worker, visiting nurse, housekeeper, food stamps, Medicare, Medicaid, etc.), services not presently received but desired (stress that you are not promising to provide any or all of what is asked for), names of relatives or person to contact in emergency. This last piece of information is often the one the elderly are least willing to divulge. Many have been abandoned by their families and harbor hostilities toward them. They often will ask that their relatives not be contacted or will not tell you they have family in the area. *Don't* push for any information: Remember, you are there as a friend to offer help but never to force the elderly Jew to accept it. Your first concern should

be what these people want and what they feel is best for them, *not* what you think they should want.

After the initial interview, stress the fact that you will try your best to send them a visitor (if they decide they want one), but that it could take a few weeks since you're just beginning to work. Start small. The worst thing anyone can do for these elderly people is make unrealistic promises that cause them to raise their expectations and then lead to disappointments. Never say you'll do something unless you're sure you will be able to.

Volunteer recruitment

Now that you've found the people to serve, you must find the volunteers to visit them. There are no easy ways to get volunteers. Often students are the best source of volunteer help since they have free time during daylight hours and look for worthwhile causes in which to become involved. Contact Hillel rabbis, heads of Jewish organizations, etc. Prepare written publicity—such as flyers—to distribute in person or by mail. The best time to contact students is the beginning of the semester (within the first three or four weeks) before they commit their time to other activities.

Plan to speak on campus either in the evening or some other time when most students are free, such as club hour. Advertise extensively and well in advance of the speaking date. Place ads in the school paper; put posters and flyers in the student union, Hillel house, dormitories, and other conspicuous places where they will be seen and attract people to the speaking engagement.

Prepare a well-organized presentation of your program with specific details on responsibilities of volunteers and goals of the program as a whole. Visual aids, such as slides or films, are very effective. If you do not have your own, the Synagogue Council of America has published *A Guide to Aging Programs for Synagogues*, which has a film bibliography at the end:

> **Synagogue Council of America**
> **432 Park Ave. South**
> **New York, NY 10016**

This publication also contains addresses of offices of the Administration on Aging throughout the United States and National Voluntary Organizations.

When you are speaking, remember to be enthusiastic about the program you are describing. One of the special aspects about Project Ezra is that the volunteers are an integral part of a project staffed and governed by a group of students and young professionals. The volunteers feel that the project is "theirs" and that without them there could be no project.

At the end of your speech, while you answer questions, pass around cards on which people can sign up, indicate which day(s) and how often they would be willing to volunteer, and if they are interested in helping find the old people, visiting, office work, etc. Also distribute literature with your address, phone number, and a description of your program. If you have no literature in the beginning stages, print flyers with your name and phone number, some basic information about the program, and a call for hep.

Although student groups often prove to be the best source for volunteers, they are by no means the only groups to approach. People with flexible work commitments, e.g., those who do housework or retired people, can be excellent sources for volunteers. Synagogue groups, Bnai Brith chapters, Brotherhoods, Sisterhoods, young adult groups, and youth groups all have many people to whom you can speak. Follow procedures similar to those outlined above for dealing with students. Even people unable to offer time every week can help with special programs or be on call for emergency situations.

Orientation and supervision of volunteers

You will have to call the volunteers. Don't wait for them to call you. Set up group orientation sessions with eight to ten people (maximum) at a time. After a general orientation to the problems of the elderly, allow the potential volunteers to voice their anxieties or ask questions, but don't spoon-feed them. Often a general orientation before the initial visit followed by an individual evaluation afterward can prove most productive. You are basically introducing two people to each other; you do not want to control the relationship.

It is essential, however, that the volunteer report regularly, telling the date and length of visit, what was done (talking, shopping, escorting, filling out forms, etc.), the reaction of the elderly person to the volunteer, any other areas where help may be needed, and any significant changes in the relationship as it progresses. Group followup meetings, where volunteers discuss their experiences and problems with each other and with the supervisor(s), are also important. The more contact between the staff and the volunteers, and between volunteers and volunteers, the better—for the volunteers and for the project as a whole. Other possibilities for following up on the relationship include on-site visits, where a staff person actually goes on a visit with the volunteer and discusses it afterward; regular telephone contact with volunteers; and a monthly newsletter, preferably written by volunteers, where volunteers can ask questions, discuss problems, and be informed about other activities of the project in addition to their individual visits.

Special projects

Special projects can be loosely defined as anything outside the one-to-one visiting that forms the heart of the project. The purpose of special projects is to allow the elderly group to have contact with peers on a social level and provide activities or entertainment. Theater parties, movies (if these are in Yiddish, it's even better), picnics, coffee hours, craft classes, lectures, etc. are all possibilities.

When programming for the elderly, remember always to plan activities for them, not for yourself. Ask yourself if an old person would truly enjoy a certain event, what problems will be involved in its planning and execution,

Always look for ways to expand and improve your project. Continued critical evaluation is important and necessary for continued success. Don't be discouraged in the early stages. Volunteers *are* hard to find and hard to keep. Students structure their extracurricular activities around their school schedules, so be prepared for volunteers leaving at the end of each semester and especially before the summer. If we can be of any help, please contact us:

Project Ezra
197 E. Broadway
New York, NY 10002

etc. Older people are just as intelligent as younger ones, so don't treat them as if they were preschoolers (you may like crafts, for instance, but they may not appeal to some of the elderly). Also, an activity can be directed to some of the older people and not to others. To cope with varying needs, you might consider having a planning committee of both younger and older people.

Inevitably you will not please everyone. This is the problem with any group activity. You will have to learn through some trial and error, seeking feedback on all programs and activities from everyone who attended. People's handicaps must also be considered. For example, someone who is hard of hearing or blind might not enjoy a theater party but might prefer small group activities like crafts or large parties with a meal and entertainment.

Synagogues provide a good base for programming and often can sponsor events for the people you serve. A synagogue in the suburbs, for example, may sponsor a picnic where it supplies transportation for the elderly and offers a day in the sun, with refreshments and perhaps some entertainment. The best events, sponsored by outside organizations in conjunction with your activities, are those where the elderly are integrated into a multigenerational group and made to feel important and wanted. One idea is for a family from the synagogue, children, parents, and even grandparents, to "adopt" an aged person for the afternoon. Of course, any continued contact, through followup telephone calls or letters, is especially heartening for these people.

Synagogues can also have programs for the aged in their own communities. Many senior-citizen clubs are synagogue-based. For further suggestions in this area, see *A Guide to Aging Programs for Synagogues.*

Plan all activities thoroughly and well in advance. People must be reminded, and often more than once, of commitments they have made. There is no such thing as too much planning or too many reminders. Once a commitment is made to the old people, it *must* be carried through. The last thing you want to do is raise false hopes.

Working with the aged is not easy but can be very rewarding, both for the older people receiving the services and for the younger people providing them. Plan well. Don't promise what you can't provide. Continually evaluate your programs and assess your goals. There are no easy solutions for the large and complex problems of the isolated elderly. However, we must show these people that the Jewish community has not forgotten them and has not forsaken them; we must show them that there are Jews of all ages who care enough about them to visit every week for a few hours; we must affirm our commitment to making their lives a little less lonely.

Bet din

The only institution that is noted for its considerable impact upon Jewish society is the bet din, commonly known as the rabbinical court of justice (literally, house of law). At certain periods and in many areas the bet din served as a pivotal communal institution, developing and changing through the ages and producing in the process a massive record of adjudication in a dynamic system of law that stands on its own among the great legal traditions of East and West. It embraced the whole spectrum of religious and ritual laws, as well as criminal and civil law whenever principles of morality, equity, justice, and human dignity were involved in the intent and execution of the law.

The bet din can be credited for its unique role in Jewish history in grappling with the dilemma presented by two contending forces: the wish to preserve tradition and the wish to cope with change within the halakhic framework. The bet din constantly sought to incorporate in its legal process the highest norms of morality and principles of justice before rendering the appropriate ruling on a given case. Hundreds of thousands of cases attest to the creativity of the bet din. Many of the cases that came up before the bet din at various times in history involve issues of state and society, the klal and the prat. Because the bet din attempted to deal with the tensions within society in mediating the strained relationships between individual and community where there was a clear conflict of interest, it affected the very lives of people and families, business and commerce, and the impact of some of its decisions went beyond the confines of the local community. No wonder this institution has been the subject of intensive study by scholars who marvel at its legacy of change, legal creativity, and evolving jurisprudence.

The birth of the bet din can be traced to early biblical times, when Moses established the judicial hierarchy in the desert, but its structure, function, and character as an institution have varied from era to era from one region to another. Throughout most of the past the bet din enjoyed wide acceptance and was thoroughly respected by the overwhelming majority of the Jewish people. This was due to the foundation upon which it stood, the Torah, and to the unique authority the bet din possessed in interpreting the laws of the Torah as they applied to ever-changing life situations.

But the bet din ought to be looked at from another perspective: the enduring national identity of the Jewish civilization. It exemplified the judicial autonomy of the Jews and thereby gave substance and meaning to the Jewish nation's independence when it was denied political control over its own territory and over the Diaspora.

After the destruction of the Second Commonwealth in 70 C.E. the persisting ideal and the life-force of the am ha-Sefer—the people of the Book—was to live by the laws of the Book. The Jewish society did not recognize the system of justice that was prevalent in pagan societies, in feudal social systems, or in church-dominated state courts in Christendom or Islam. This deep aspiration for judicial autonomy permeated every Jewish community. Because only within such an autonomous judicial system, the particular brand of Torah justice—mishpat—can prevail; only here can value-laden notions such as tzedek—righteousness, yosher—fairness and equity, and shalom—peace among the litigants be fully realized.

Historians point out various forces nurturing such aspirations that were in fact fulfilled in the course of time. Whether it was because of the corporate fact fulfilled in the course of time. Whether it was because of the corporate nature of social systems in centuries past, whether it came as a result of specific character arrangements with church or secular state authorities for reasons of social control or tax collection, the fact remains that all these forces combined generated a living, autonomous, and fully functioning system of law that governed the lives of the Jewish people for centuries. The effectiveness of the bet din and its legal creativity in many instances correlated with the degree of autonomy it was permitted to exercise in civil and criminal cases and to a large degree upon the willingness of Jews, especially in modern times, to resort to the bet din to adjudicate disputes. But the effectiveness of the bet din also depended on stature and personality of the individual rabbis who served on these courts as dayanim—judges.

The respectability and acceptability of the bet din at some times went beyond the confines of the Jewish community. The records of history show numerous instances of non-Jews adjudicating their disputes in the only court known for its impartiality, fairness, and justice, devoid of the greed and self-interest so prevalent in other judicial systems. Scholars have noted those interactions at the crossroads of history: in Holland, Spain, Italy, England, and elsewhere. Some suggest the possibility that in time certain principles of law established by the bet din became precedents to be cited or to be emulated by other judicial systems (in both public law and private law), such as principles regarding evidence, judicial procedures, real estate, commerce, civil criminal law. Noteworthy were legal principles that were well developed in talmudic law close to two thousand years ago and that today we have come to take for granted. Enlightened jurists of modern times have sought to incorporate in the judicial system certain progressive legal doctrines that were thrashed out in the halls of talmudic academies. Those doctrines were tested and applied after exhaustive deliberations during hundreds of cases that had come before the various battai dinim centuries before. Concepts such as due process of law, self-incrimination, double jeopardy, arbitration, conciliation, and many other legal doctrines were studied by generations of rabbis and students in their quest for the ultimate measure of justice and truth. Indeed, the evolving Jewish jurisprudence may have had an impact on the development of society that went beyond the Jewish community.

We are familiar with the burden of responsibilities placed upon each individual Jew in terms of commandments to be fulfilled, mitzvot that must be performed in our everyday life. Similarly, an overriding responsibility is placed upon the Jewish community wherever it may be, namely, the communal obligation to establish a bet din. It is derived from a specific biblical commandment to "appoint magistrates" in every city and "they shall govern the people with due justice" (Deuteronomy 16:18). In the fifth century B.C.E., Ezra recognized that the restoration of the Second Commonwealth rested in

What emerges from the voluminous record of legal decision is the fact that the sages of the past and some of the leading rabbis of the time lent to the institution of the bet din the prestige and the needed authority which in time of political decline became the only authority over klal Yisrael—principally because of the quality of justice it dispersed, the ideals it pursued, and the sense of continuity it gave to the Jewish people.

part on the fulfillment of this law, which became part of his numerous enactments.

The proper status of a township can be derived from the Talmud, which lists ten communal institutions: a charity organization, a synagogue, a public bath, a physician, a school for children, etc. First on the list is the court of law, the bet din (Sanhedrin 17b). Indeed, the Talmud cautions one to avoid residing in a town where these communal institutions are lacking. Thus by examining the letter and spirit of the law we can conclude that the Torah places upon us a positive communal obligation to create a bet din. Initially there were differences of opinion as to whether this obligation applied only to the land of Israel or not, but later authorities agreed that this obligation is placed on Jews everywhere (Shulhan Arukh, Hoshen Mishpat, chapter 1).

Jewish judicial system

Moses was the first to establish the hierarchial judicial system (Exodus 18, Deuteronomy 1). Judges had to be elected on their proven merit as men of ability. They had to be men who were wise, discerning, and experienced. Their reputation had to prove them "capable men who fear God" and are incorruptible. In the second chapter of the Mishneh Torah, concerning the laws of the Sanhedrin, Maimonides eloquently capsulizes the unique qualities that a judge ought to possess to be eligible as a candidate for any judiciary.

Ezra revised the system to meet the national needs of his time, and later, during the Second Commonwealth, this system was so refined that it could meet the standards of any judiciary in a modern democratic state.

The bet din remained the backbone of Jewish society, the most durable institution in the Jewish community. In the first chapter of Sanhedrin in the Talmud we find a thorough description of the system. The bet din was composed of at least three judges, and its jurisdiction extended to all civil disputes: dinei mamonot—monetary matters, such as torts, damages, etc., and family law. This court had to be established in any community where there were no more than 120 inhabitants. For larger communities, above the minimum of 120, a small Sanhedrin—Sanhedrin Ketannah—consisting of twenty-three judges had to be established. This court had extended jurisdiction over capital cases that could involve capital punishment (which was a judgment rarely given). Above it stood the seventy-one judges of the Great Sanhedrin—Sanhedrin Gedolah—who had specific authority in certain national issues. Its jurisdiction covered trials of national leaders accused of a crime; the selection of a king; the recruitment, training, and supervision of judges to serve on the small Sanhedrins; and the declaration of war. It really had a dual role as the highest court in the land, presided over by the av bet ha-din—chairman—and as the legislative body under the leadership of the nasi—president—authorized to make new laws binding on all Jews. (For a full description, see Sidney B. Hoenig, *Great Sanhedrin*, New York: Yeshiva Univ., 1966.)

After the destruction of the Second Commonwealth the only body that remained was the local bet din. Although it lacked the specific authority that was passed down from the Great Sanhedrin, it continued to function "in the name of the sages of old" as "agents" and thus was authorized to adjudicate in all civil matters. A further revision took place in the larger communities outside Israel, especially in Babylonia, in Spain during the Golden Age, and later in other Western European Jewish centers. An elaborate system of community elections was devised, and many of the contemporary regulations, bylaws, and procedures are reflected in the responsa literature of the time.

Each community developed its own tradition regarding the bet din. Most communities elected a bet din for one year, and each maintained its independence from any other bet din. There was no central bet din that exerted jurisdiction over all the Jewish people. The government usually recognized the bet din as a legitimate communal institution, and in some countries it was formally chartered by the government.

In the Ottoman Empire the Jewish community constituted a separate millet—ethnic/religious community—with the hakham bashi as its recognized head. As such, the Jewish community throughout the empire was authorized to create communal institutions, among which was the bet din. Under the British Mandate over Palestine the system was further institutionalized with the creation of the chief rabbinate and its various local battai dinim, which became well established in the larger cities, and the Upper Court in Jerusalem, where the chief rabbis presided over the Bet ha-Din ha-Gadol.

In the State of Israel the bet din attained its official status as a state institution. Special provisions have been formulated regarding eligibility to serve on the court, the process of nomination, and procedures for final election. The status of the rabbinical judge—dayan—is similar in every respect to that of his counterpart in the state secular judicial system—bet ha-mishpat—except that the jurisdiction of the bet din is limited to personal status (marriage, divorce). The rabbinical courts in Israel were established on the old and tested model, which consists of the local city bet din and the statewide bet din, the Bet ha-Din ha-Gadol seated in Jerusalem and presided over by the chief rabbis of Israel. This system permits proper supervision and allows for the orderly appeal process. The idea of reviving the Sanhedrin (of twenty-three or seventy-one judges), although hotly debated, was shelved for the time being. Meanwhile, the present system grinds in its judicial mill matters of personal status (including the definition of a Jew) and the unending task of adjudicating family disputes, suits of nonsupport, inheritance, status of marriage, custody, and divorce.

It is these various courts with their long tradition of adjudication and developing jurisprudence, whether in Eastern or Western Europe, North Africa or modern Israel, that have given us the enormous literature of accumulated jurisprudence. Most cases were duly recorded, all decisions were generally preceded by careful deliberation, and then most cases were thoughtfully written up. All the arguments were well supported by quotations from authorized texts or the opinions of authorities of previous generations; established precedents were duly mentioned and thoroughly considered before a decision was rendered on a given case. Thus a vast literature was accumulated that is, in fact, a literature of case law or legal precedents through which the intricacies and the development of the Jewish society over past centuries is vividly portrayed. Much of this literature came to us in a form known as responsa—in Hebrew, sifrut sheelot uteshuvot (literally, queries and replies). Many still in manuscript form and probably scores of other thousands were lost during the Holocaust and in earlier dislocations. But over 300,000 are available in various collections. These responsa were written by more than three thousand rabbinic authorities; many were collected or edited by the disciples or colleagues of various heads of talmudic academies. This custom of sending inquiries was mentioned in the Talmud, and it began to increase in posttalmudic times, spanning a period of more than twenty centuries.

In essence these thousands of individual responses are recorded decisions rendered in individual cases on specific communal issues, or pertaining to personal or interpersonal problems submitted by private individuals or by rabbinic judges who sought direction from greater rabbis when faced with difficult issues that came up before their own bet din. In thousands of such cases a rabbi in a small community would write to the rabbi of a "great city" or to a recognized rabbinic authority in the region or to the great rabbi of a distant land who was acknowledged by his peers to be a person of great learning, a man who was in possession of the oral law tradition and thus was recognized as the authority in Jewish law of his generation (gedolei ha-dor).

As a literature of jurisprudence, the responsa seem to incorporate a unique methodology, deriving from its own coherent, built-in value system, procedural rulings, and laws of conduct that were made applicable to real-life situations. It has promulgated a set of operating principles, both legal and moral, that became part of its developing jurisprudence. All of the responsa are based on actual cases to which these principles have been variously applied as circumstances have changed in the long historical process.

In communities where this jurisprudential tradition grew, the responsa were generally accepted as a matter of law by the questioning individual or by the particular community whose religious leader sought direction from a greater rabbinic authority. At times the decision called for certain community sanctions to be applied, and in most cases the decision was self-enforcing because the inquirer, by posing the question, obligated himself to abide by the decision. He sought direction for the sole purpose of knowing what the law was and which path to follow.

Lay courts

Another variation developed side by side with the bet din, and it has a similarly long tradition. By talmudic times, after the Romans had crushed all semblance of political independence following the Bar Kokhba revolt in the second century C.E., the formal courts and many of the great dayanim were destroyed. The sages in their wisdom devised an alternative that could still maintain their judicial independence. This alternative was modeled on the traditional bet din but functioned as a court of arbitration. Each litigant would choose one representative (not necessarily a person versed in law), and the two litigants would agree on the choice of a third to serve as chairman—the av bet ha-din. Under this sort of voluntary arrangement, the Talmud states, "since this one chooses one dayan and the other chooses another dayan and both choose one more, . . . the true judgment will emerge" (Sanhedrin 23a).

Like the bet din, this institution evolved in the course of time. Generally this court could be created either as an ad hoc arrangement or as a permanent communal institution like the bet din or as an integral part of the bet din itself. The members of the court, chosen by the two litigants, were and continue to be civil experts rather than rabbinic scholars. Although procedures varied, generally each litigant chose a layman to serve as an arbitrator, and both selected a third impartial person (usually a rabbi, but not necessarily so) to serve as chairman. The selection of the third member was an issue extensively debated. One rabbi insisted that both litigants must do the selection, while others maintained that the two chosen members had to agree between themselves on the selection of the third member.

In some communities and at various times a court of arbitration was established, modeled on the traditional bet din, where recognized laity rendered decisions with dignity and fairness, compassion and understanding. Leading rabbis from time to time would express their reservations about the "lay courts," which were prevalent in many communities, and this concern is reflected in various responsa. Indeed, there were many instances where Jewish law was misinterpreted or ignored by ignorant men. But as time went on the

What is significant about this court is that it was effective and durable as a social institution. It had no power of enforcement except for the signed statement that each litigant deposited with the "court" (shtar borrerut) stating his voluntary submission of his case and a promise to abide willingly by its final decision.

practice of inviting the local rabbi to sit on the court spread; this custom recognized his expertise in matters of testimony and evidence and his knowledge of the moral rights and wrongs of the Jewish tradition.

Other durable judicial methods that made a considerable social impact were conciliation and mediation—both products of the unique Jewish approach to law and to the process of adjudication. In a sense the Jewish tradition has fostered a philosophical outlook that has governed the development of the entire judicial process. This philosophy, already present in talmudic times, and becoming fully developed over centuries of judicial experience, represented the idea that people are limited in their ability to arrive at the absolute truth and to render strict justice. The aim was (and is) to arrive at a compromise and to bring about peace and conciliation among the warring parties.

In any adversary procedure there must be one who "wins" his case. The "loser," an unavoidable casualty of strict justice, comes out feeling bitter, defeated, and angry. From a Jewish ethical perspective this is a calamity, a travesty of divine justice. The function of the bet din (referred to in the Bible as Elohim—God [see Exodus, chapters 21–26]) is to emulate divine attributes and, of equal importance, to strive for tzedek—righteousness—and to seek to establish shalom—peace among the quarreling parties. This can be achieved only in a conciliation process where each party gives a little and where both litigants come to accept the decision of the court.

Decline of the bet din

Despite its accumulated jurisprudence and the lofty ideals it set for the Jewish community, the bet din's role as a communal institution in modern times steadily declined. The post-Emancipation years generated a momentum for greater integration with the progressive societies, and Jews began to resort to the local secular court systems. The bet din lacked the power of enforcement and was helpless in cases involving a Jew and a non-Jew. Thus since the nineteenth century the bet din in most of western Europe and in the United States—though still functioning as a communal institution—has been limited to religious, ritual, or family matters; in these cases the competence of the rabbinic authority is an absolute requirement for the observant Jew. In countries where a Jewish communal structure existed but where Jews did not enjoy the same status as did Jews in the West (such as Eastern Europe, Asia, and North Africa), the bet din continued its traditional role.

Today the improved quality of justice in the secular state's courts, the sense of complete equality, and the rapid integration of Jewry into the general society of the West has diminished the role of the Jewish communal court so popular in the centuries before. Religious affiliation is weaker and social conditions have changed to such an extent that the rabbinic court is often looked upon as a relic of the past useful only for divorce (if the couple is religious), for disagreements about kashrut supervision, or for acrimonious disputes within or among the clergy in a given synagogue. For this purpose various rabbinic bodies or synagogue organizations maintain under their auspices a bet din of limited scope. This is the general picture in the United States today: rabbinic decisions on significant issues tend to be the prerogative of a few acknowledged leading rabbis known as gedolei ha-dor, who are recognized by reputation and accepted by the observing public as leading authorities on Jewish law. Their response to a given question is generally adhered to by the majority of Orthodox Jewry as guidelines to follow in their daily lives.

The Conservative movement has institutionalized a procedure by establishing a special Law Committee of the Rabbinical Assembly, which deliberates the issues and presents its findings in the form of a decision agreed upon by the majority of the committee members. The dissenting views accompany each decision, and every rabbi in the movement is free to follow either the majority or the minority opinion in his own congregation.

Two models

While this general pattern does describe the declining role of the bet din in the United States, it is important to note that there are a few exceptions. Two such examples are the Jewish Conciliation Board of New York and the Rabbinical Court of Justice of the Associated Synagogues of Massachusetts.

The Jewish Conciliation Board was founded in 1920 by a lawyer and a rabbi who managed to synthesize secular American law and rabbinic principles of halakhah steeped in the ideals and values of the Jewish tradition. This board (known earlier as the Jewish Court of Arbitration) came into being to fill a gap that became evident in the tension between people in the process of social adjustment: the barrier of language, the awesome impersonal character of the American judicial system, the clashing and sometimes totally different values (American mores versus traditional Jewish mores), the nuances of what Jewish morality demands of a fellow Jew because of yosher—fairness, uprightness, equity—in contrast to "rights" and "wrongs" in the strict secular legal framework.

In the course of a half century, thousands of cases have been brought before the Jewish Conciliation Board for adjudication and thus a magnificent institutional landmark was created. Because the Jewish Conciliation Board succeeded in creating harmony, in restoring broken relationships, in redressing some wrongs, and in maintaining personal dignity and communal stability, it must be seen as a valuable service that even today continues to be capable of rendering Jewish justice in a communal setting.

Another bet din that stands out as an exception to the general pattern in the United States is the Rabbinical Court of Justice in Massachusetts. The record of this bet din in the last decade gives one food for thought about the possible expanding role of the bet din as an institution in the contemporary context of the American Jewish community.

This bet din, an organ of the Associated Synagogues of Massachusetts, saw fit to extend its activities beyond the confines of personal status (conversion, divorce, etc.) requiring a religious act by rabbinic authority. In 1968 the bet din became involved in broad social and community issues of far greater significance to many outside communities than the limited personal and local concern. A few examples will illustrate this point.

An ongoing bitter dispute between non-Jewish tenants and their Jewish landlord was threatening communal stability and could have erupted in violence. It had all the ingredients for continued acrimony with ugly racial overtones that augured serious communal strife. Such an issue could only be seen as a hillul ha-Shem—desecration of God's Name—with its implications for the damaged ethical reputation of the Jewish people.

The bet din was able to bring the opposing sides together and so avoid the dire consequences to the community, since there was not at that time an acceptable state judicial authority that could resolve the dispute. During the long and delicate negotiation process the bet din reviewed halakhic precedents, together with the cumulative wisdom that comes from centuries of arbitration experience, and was able to hammer out a formal agreement that enabled both parties to proceed harmoniously to resolve their dispute.

There is nothing in this agreement that suggests a hint of talmudic terms or a citation of rabbinic authorities to buttress its legal credibility. All of the thirty-three articles were written in the "cold," yet lucid, language of the law and were in turn cited by the supreme court of the commonwealth and by other district courts as a model agreement for tenants and landlords. The rabbis of the court who labored on the precise phrasing of the various articles were engaged, in their private deliberations, in dynamic sessions of talmudic studies. They interpreted basic principles in Baba Batra (a talmudic tractate that deals among others things with real estate, partnerships, leasing of property, relations of neighbors, tenants and landlords, inheritance and contracts), principles that were developed in later codes.

This landmark agreement earned the bet din the dignity and the needed prestige to go beyond the case in question. It was in a position to advocate the establishment of a permanent Community Landlord–Tenant Relations Court, which was sorely needed in the local urban setting. Subsequently this gave the needed impetus in a difficult political struggle to the final successful creation of the Housing Court under Massachusetts law.

Another issue, national in character, was then absorbing the nation's youth and generating enormous agitation among the Greater Boston college community: the war in Vietnam and the public protest against national policy. Non-Jews had little trouble in finding a moral basis for advocating civil disobedience. Many students advanced their arguments and justified their actions on moral and religious principles. They spoke of a higher law that supersedes arbitrary human law. Secularists wrestled with the legality of the war on constitutional grounds challenging the right of government to draft soldiers and prosecute the war.

But what about the Jew? Was there a religious basis on which an observant Jew could reject the law of the state? Could he evade military duty? Should the community offer sanctuary or give support to those who opposed the war? Could opposition to the war be based on Jewish religious beliefs? If so, which ones, and how could a Jew articulate the principles of Judaism to a local draft board?

Swept up by the events of the time, the bet din of Boston found itself involved in a national issue. A sort of a "class action" was brought by students and academicians, who sought authoritative clarification and resolution of their problems. Pressed to find out if there was a "Jewish position" regarding these critical issues that would support an antiwar claim from a religious viewpoint, the bet din wrestled with the issues for ten months. It had to mobilize all the legal doctrines and ethical precepts of the Jewish tradition and subsequently published a cogent response to the seven major "questions" and seven minor ones (i.e., what constitutes murder in war) presented to them. During these ten months of exhaustive deliberations a careful study of the ramifications of the questions was undertaken and a "Responsum on the Question of Conscience" was issued. In this responsum all the questions were carefully considered in light of Jewish law. Principles were clearly defined, and the "Jewish religious view" was expounded in clear, concise language complete with citations and references from the Jewish tradition. Indeed, "Responsum" was a noble attempt and a significant document that emerged out of stormy period—significant not only for what it actually says but for its broader implications. First, individuals joined in a community of interest and collectively presented to a local bet din some of the most difficult and timely questions that had to be resolved. And second, a rabbinic court in the United States rose to the challenge and addressed itself to highly charged social and political issues of the times.

Another significant issue came before the bet din in 1972: "Class Action and Enquiry on Matters concerning Kashruth and Food Considered Dangerous to Life or Human Health" (see the title page of the brief). The opening part of the brief states that

This CLASS ACTION AND ENQUIRY came as a result of recent Congressional Hearings, the publication of scientific data, newly released governmental regulations, a pending civil suit filed at the United States District Court against some Federal agencies and numerous press reports relating to the current methods and practices of:

    (a) raising beef cattle and poultry;
    (b) processing of those meat products;
    (c) Government control and inspection of the food in the United States of America.

All this and many more have raised disturbing questions as to the suitability of certain food and meat products for the consuming public. . . .

2. Since many of the issues involved Biblical imperatives and many problems which touch upon some basic principles in Jewish Law, the guidance of Rabbinical Authorities will be sought to illuminate and direct observant Jews and the Jewish Community at large as to the alternatives and choices they must make in order for them to live in accordance with the HALACHA.

3. The petitioner avers and declares that, to the best of his knowledge and the information contained in the attached exhibits, as part of this Brief presented to The Rabbinical Court of Justice of The Associated Synagogues of Massachusetts, the following presumed facts from the Brief serve as a basis for probable cause to require the response of The Rabbinical Court to the questions raised.

Eleven questions were posed before the sitting tribunal. Questions 1, 3, and 5 were presented as examples of queries—sheelot—that generate rabbinic or court responsa:

Question one: How do we define "HAZARD TO LIFE"— סכנה —to which Jewish Law with all its ethical precepts apply? (Such as the laws concerning the protection of life— בדיני סכנת נפשות ; the saving of life— פקוח נפש ; the prohibition against doing harm or causing a hazard to fellow man, etc.— דין מעקה ועניין לפני עור לא תתן מכשול.

Do we say that "HAZARD" denoted *immediate danger*— סכנה בעין —that may come as a direct consequence of one particular act, or could it apply to situations when the consequence of the act is not presently apparent, but the *cumulative effects* of many such acts, i.e., smoking, excessive drinking, narcotics, D. D. T., etc., may threaten the life in future times? סכנה לאחר זמן משום : „מה לי קטלה כולה, מה לי קטלה פלגא", או משום „אסור חבלה."

Question three: The Talmudic dictum "RULES CONCERNING DANGER TO LIFE ARE MORE STRINGENT THAN RITUAL PROHIBITIONS"— חמירא סכנתא מאסורא — is the basic principle upon which many rules and legal precedents have been established. If we apply the same principle to present-day food matters that are known to be dangerous (such as a discovery of contaminated food with micro-biological poisoning), does it obligate Rabbinical Authorities to declare them as "prohibited"— אסור סכנה משום סכנה —and to remove the official "Kosher" insignia from such products?

Question five: The Talmudic legal "assumption"— חזקה —states that "all cattle are presumed to be fit" in their normal state of nature. This "assumption" is so strong that it is sufficient to pass all cattle as fit and "kosher" for slaughter, thus relieving the detailed Rabbinical meticulous inspection (בדיקה) on each individual animal. Only when a "fault" appears (ריעותא) and there is some question about the "looks" of the animal, the legal "assumption" breaks down and inspection must follow to determine the nature of the fault. . . .

Question nine: As seen earlier under SECTION C, the Government ordered *a seven-day withdrawal period* as in the case of DES because of the apparent danger. This rule, however, rests on *voluntary compliance.* The reality is such that it is impossible for

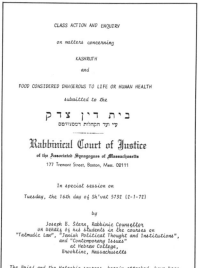

the individual farmer to establish separate feeding lots or store the clean (without the DES) feed. Also, we have seen in SECTION F, it is almost impossible to enforce such a rule. Based on this information, we, therefore, have definite "doubts" as to the observation of these government rules designed to minimize danger to the consumer. Consequently, when should supervision begin (השגחה) according to Jewish Law? Should it be confined to the period between slaughter and sale at butcher's store, or *should it start at least seven days prior to slaughter* as prescribed by the Government?

The brief proceeds to present to the bet din all the relevant data concerning the issues in the case, as well as supportive evidence in the form of medical and scientific testimony—including official government reports and the records of congressional hearings on the matter. The brief then concludes the formal presentation with the following statement:

KEEPING IN MIND ALL THE INFORMATION PRESENTED ABOVE, it was attempted to establish in the Brief the premises, laws, some Halachic precedents, and basic principles which apply to our cases. First and foremost, the Biblical imperative to "preserve life"— שמירת הנפש ; then the laws concerning the avoidance of danger and the prohibitions in Jewish Law against subjecting others to danger— לא תעמוד על דם רעך   אסור משום סכנה ; then references were made to some dietary laws with special regard to "mixing" of permitted with prohibited matter— אסור תערובת —and the subsequent application of these laws to our cases, and also to laws regarding the "torn" animals— אסורי טריפה —dealing with special injuries, imperfections, and certain diseases which render the animal as unfit— טריפה —to be eaten by observant Jews under Jewish Laws.

Regrettably, the death of two members of the court—Rabbi Grolinkin, the venerated chairman of the court, and Rabbi Korff, the court administrator—prevented the process from reaching its legal conclusion. However, the most important ramification of the cases handled by the bet din in Boston is that a local Jewish court established a precedent for functioning as an "activist court" and showed that it was ready and willing to take up issues that went beyond the limited domain of family matters. The example of this court and the Jewish Board of Conciliation of New York should be taken to heart by Jewish communities everywhere.

The challenge for the future

In reviewing this ancient and revered institution in Jewish history, can we possibly perceive the need for and the relevance of a viable modern bet din in the context of present-day American Jewry? At first glance the answer to this question must be negative, considering the reality of our time. The vagaries of our communal existence, the solidification of our sectarian movements, the emerging differences of our religious experience with their concomitant ideologies, the clashing views of rabbis and the specter of rivalries and fierce opposition among old established institutions certainly militate against the establishment of a bet din that would be credible and accepted by all the members of the community on issues other than ritual and family matters.

While the idea is not rejected by community leaders as they probe further into this matter, any religious leaders are reluctant to be involved in any judicial civic process because of the mistaken notion that dina de-malkhuta dina—the law of the state is the law—precludes such activities by a bet din in a constitutional democracy, where all citizens are treated equally under an enlightened judiciary. Opinions such as these may be expressed: "Why stand out and be accused of lack of confidence in a system where Jews gained so many of their liberties," or "It is impossible for Jews to rise above self-interest," or "This will never work out."

What is true about the general (state or federal) courts in the United States can be said about the bet din: as an institution, it is shaped to a great degree by the dominant personalities who determine the direction, mode of operation, and the degree of effectiveness of each court. The two examples cited may well be due to the dynamic and determined leaders who could infuse the court with their vision, provide it with the needed direction, and broaden the scope of the bet din beyond parochial considerations.

A recent case in California may be cited to discourage any attempts in this direction. A New York–based poultry firm in the process of opening a branch on the West Coast ran an ad in the local press, saying that their processed chicken is truly kosher because the temperature of water used in removing the feathers is acceptable in Jewish law (citing the ruling of a "great" New York rabbi whose rulings are accepted by most Orthodox Jews), whereas the water used by the California processor is so hot that it is not acceptable in Jewish law. The California bet din, which had grappled with the problem years before, concluded that the higher temperature is still permissible and does not render the chicken unkosher. (The skins of chickens raised in California tend to break up at lower temperatures.)

Here we have a clear issue of Jewish law pertaining to the processing of chickens and another issue (also basically halakhic) dealing with the extended jurisdiction of a bet din from one city to another. In theory the way to settle this problem is within the framework of Jewish law. But a $1 million civil suit ensued. The California-based firm sued for damages arising from the allegations that their chickens were not kosher, and the New York firm entered a counterclaim on the constitutional grounds that interstate commerce is protected against any restriction of trade. The justification for resorting to a state court was its inherent power to enforce the law, a mechanism lacking in the bet din. However, we can still wonder whether a credible community tribunal could have done the same in settling the case and thereby avoided a hillul ha-Shem.

Certainly some part of the failure of the modern-day bet din can be attributed to a lack of leadership by some rabbis. This lack may be due to rabbis' endemic, built-in fear of getting involved in an issue that might result in a decision that could evoke criticism and subject them to merciless attack by opposing rabbis. Also, some rabbis would be reluctant to "sit in judgment" or "accept the judgment" of others, invoking the Talmud concerning the cessation of the judicial semikhah in Israel since the dissolution of the Great Sanhedrin, and would claim that we are not qualified or "authorized" today to act as a bet din. Lay leaders may express their serious reservations on many grounds. Some show their disinclination to establish another communal agency, others take strong aversion to anything that might resemble the European Kehillah of yesteryear.

Despite these problems modern Jews who are proud of their heritage and who consider themselves to be active Jewish citizens ought to take a fresh look at this ancient marvel of the Jewish tradition, the bet din. It seems clear that the revitalization of the bet din could create an important force in American Jewish life.

The two institutional models and the examples cited above should turn our attention to the social implications of such cases. Considering these implications, we might do well to push for the creation of similar institutions in every Jewish community. Imagine the intellectual force that would be generated, the renewed interest in learning that would occur, and the prestige that would be accorded the Jewish tradition were this to happen!

Under Jewish law, the bet din is the guardian/advocate of the widowed and orphaned, the mentally incompetent, the impoverished and the alien—the whole class of unprotected individuals who do not possess the means or the knowledge to claim their rights in society. The bet din also is the protector of society and the force for justice and morality. Can we possibly envision the reestablishment of this institution? I believe so, and to this end I circulated a proposal to the leaders of the Greater Boston Jewish community. I present a portion of this proposal below as a possible model for implementation in other communities.

Bet din

The COUNCIL will establish a COMMUNITY COURT OF MEDIATION AND ARBITRATION. This court can be confined to the settling of disputes within the Jewish community or it may be offered as a service agency to the public at large as an alternative system of justice. This COMMUNITY COURT can be presented as a court of arbitration composed of eminent, respected members of the community especially in the fields of law and jurisprudence.

The federal and state governments in the recent past have shown increasing interest in organized communal participation in the administration of justice as they grope to reform the civil and criminal justice systems in America. In response, the Institute for Advanced Studies in Justice, Washington, D.C., has undertaken a major study under grants given by the National Institute of Law Enforcement and Criminal Justice and the Law Enforcement Assistance Administration of the Department of Justice entitled "The New Justice—Alternatives to Conventional, Criminal Adjudication."

An additional major study was done by Abt Associates, Cambridge, Mass., under a similar federally funded grant entitled "Neighborhood Justice Centers: An Analysis of Potential Models." Another major study has been undertaken by the American Bar Association. . . .

These are examples of federal and state attempts to revise a burdensome and inefficient criminal justice system in the United States. In the process, many studies and experiments have been undertaken to create models for alternative systems to the conventional criminal and civil adjudication. Many people have expressed their enthusiastic support for these community justice centers, . . . and the mediation concept has been endorsed by the U.S. Department of Justice, the American Bar Association, judges, lawyers, and other criminal justice professionals across the nation. It should be noted that in many communities throughout the land, experiments of this nature have been initiated by various organizations for the ultimate purpose of developing community-based, nonformal judicial structures that can dispense justice fairly and impartially. . . .

Many courts welcome these ventures and invite participants to settle their claims in such community structures. Within Massachusetts, support is also beginning to grow. Mediation programs have been praised by the Chief Justice of the District Court Department, the state Committee on Criminal Justice, and a special court committee set up to examine these programs.

The Greater Boston Jewish Community, in creating such an agency, will at the same time contribute a valuable public service in offering a prestigious form of mediation while utilizing its great human resource of trained and experienced lawyers. This will reduce backlog in the courts and free judges to hear more serious criminal cases. This is a unique area where the Jewish community can develop a model based upon the rich, juridical experience of our people in the past that can be implemented in American society.

The Jewish tradition yielded a vast amount of responsa literature because of the hundreds of thousands of questions that were asked. Let's begin the process of posing the questions, creating the issues, and facilitating the mechanism for judicial deliberation in every community.

Community leaders ought to challenge rabbis and other learned Jews to take an active role in serving on such a court. Community educators may wish to develop study material from classic Jewish texts that have relevance to issues that come before the court. People will respond positively to studying about issues that relate directly to modern questions of living. Students or lay leaders might initiate an issue by submitting to a local rabbi a question that could generate public discussion and attention and a possible rabbinic response.

For further reading, see the following:

Agus, Irving A. *The Heroic Age of Franco-German Jewry: The Jews of Germany and France of the Tenth and Eleventh Centuries.* New York: Bloch Publishing, 1969. See Chapter VII, "Community Organization," especially section C on the "Judiciary Prerogative of the Community," and section E, on the "Supreme Judicial Authority," pp. 202–14.

————. *Urban Civilization in Pre-Crusade Europe: A Study of Organized Town-Life in Northwestern Europe . . . Based on the Responsa Literature.* Vol. 2. New York, 1965. In this study, Professor Agus gathers actual cases pertaining to the role of the bet din from the responsa of the time, in Chapter VII, pp. 421–553.

Baron, Salo Wittmayer. *A Social and Religious History of the Jews.* 17 vols. Philadelphia: Jewish Publication Society, 1952–1980. See the Index volume (1960) under Courts, p. 35; Judges and the Judiciary, p. 81; and Self-Government, pp. 137–38.

————. *The Jewish Community.* 3 vols. Philadelphia: Jewish Publication Society, 1942. See Chapter XVI on "Law Enforcement," Vol. 2, pp. 208–45; and Vol. 1, pp. 157–374.

Chigier, M. "The Rabbinical Courts in the State of Israel." *Israel Law Review,* Vol. II, no. 2 (1967), pp. 147–81.

Cohn, Haim H., ed. *Jewish Law in Ancient and Modern Israel.* New York: Ktav Publishers, 1971.

Elon, Menachem. "The Sources and Nature of Jewish Law and Its Application in the State of Israel." *Israel Law Review,* Vol. 2, no. 4 (1967), pp. 515–65; Vol. 3, no. 1 (1968), pp. 88–126; and Vol. 3, no. 3 (1968), pp. 416–57.

————, ed. *The Principles of Jewish Law.* Special publication of *Encyclopaedia Judaica,* 1975. See descriptions, pp. 561–662.

Finkelstein, Louis. *Jewish Self-Government in the Middle Ages.* New York, 1924; reprint ed., Westport, Conn.: Greenwood Press, 1972.

Herzog, Isaac. *The Main Institutions of Jewish Law.* London, 1965–1967.

————. *Judaism: Law and Ethics.* London: Soncino Press, 1974. See especially Chapter 12, "The Administration of Justice in Ancient Israel: The Reconstruction of the Judiciary by Ezra," pp. 107–16; Chapter 13, "The Bet Din," pp. 117–26; and Chapter 15, "The Sanhedrin," pp. 135–46.

Hoenig, Sidney B. *The Great Sanhedrin.* New York: Bloch Publishing, 1953.

Katz, Jacob. *Tradition and Crisis: Jewish Society at the End of the Middle Ages.* New York, 1961; paperback ed., New York: Schocken Books, 1971. See Chapter X, "The Kehilla's Range of Activities," pp. 91–102.

Levitats, Isaac. *Jewish Community in Russia, 1772–1844.* New York, 1943; reprint ed., New York: Octagon, 1970.

Rabinowitz, Jacob J. *Jewish Law: Its Influence on the Development of Legal Institutions.* New York: Bloch Publishing, 1956.

Shohet, David M. *The Jewish Court in the Middle Ages.* New York, 1931.

Yaffe, James. *So Sue Me: The Story of a Community Court.* New York: Saturday Review Press, 1972. Describes actual cases that came before the Jewish Conciliation Board in New York.

Many studies on the development and function of the bet din are available in Hebrew. Two of the most significant are recommended here:

Assaf, S. *Batei Ha-din Ve-sidreihem Aharei Hatimat Ha-Talmud.* Jerusalem, 1924. And the three-volume study by Menachem Elon (now a member of the Supreme Court of Israel and for many years the director of the Jewish Law Institute, Faculty of Law, Hebrew University in Jerusalem), *Hamishpat Ha-ivri* (Jewish Law: History, Sources, Principles), Jerusalem, 1973. See especially, in Vol. 1, the Introduction and Chapter 1, "Jewish Law—A Law of Life and Practice," pp. 3–42.

For study in depth, begin with at least two of the primary sources on the bet din as codified by Maimonides and Joseph Karo's Shulhan Arukh. See Maimonides, *Mishneh Torah,* The Law of Sanhedrin (on the judicial system, procedure, and punishments), Chapters 1–8, 11, and 20–26. Most interesting is Maimonides' codification of the selection and qualification of judges—see Chapter 2; on judicial conduct that can still serve as a model for our time, read Chapters 20–23; and, on the relationship of a judge to his fellowmen and the dignity of the judicial office, see Chapter 25. This work is available in an English translation published by Yale University Press in its Judaica Series.

Those who can read Hebrew can compare the treatment of the subject with Karo's Code, *Hoshen Mishpat,* Chapters 1–27.

Those interested in specific issues of Jewish law in the context of comparative law may write to the author of this article at

Hebrew College
43 Hawes St.
Brookline, MA 02146.

ROUTES

THESE ARE THE GENERATIONS

Genesis 5:1 אלה תולדת

Living after the Holocaust

> *Editor's Note:* The Holocaust is a difficult subject that has already been much abused in our times. The following chapter is a radical approach to understanding the Holocaust. It is presented to make us question many of our assumptions. For some the answers will lie here; for others this will be far from what you seek. Nonetheless, as the first real attempt to concretize the belief espoused by many that "after the Holocaust nothing can be the same," it commands our attention.

Mitzvot and rituals out of the Holocaust — some fragments of a prebeginning creation

A MODERN MIDRASH

Twenty-six generations before the creation of the world, the twenty-two letters of the alphabet descended from God's crown. They gathered around God, each one vying to be the instrument of creation.

The first to step forward was Tav. "Master of the Universe, it is through me that you will give the Torah to Israel by the hand of Moshe. Let it be Your will to create the world through me."

But God answered, saying, "No, it will not be you because in the days to come I will place you as a sign of death on the foreheads of men."

And Shin came forward. "Master of the Universe, create Your world through me since Your own name, Shaddai, begins with me."

But God answered, saying, "You are the first letter of the word sheker— lie—and I will not create My world through you."

And Resh stepped forward begging to be chosen. "I who am the first letter of the word rahamim—mercy—should certainly be chosen to create Your world."

But God answered, saying, "No, for you, Resh, stand at the head of the word ra—wicked—and you cannot be chosen."

And so it went. Each letter successively came before God begging to be chosen—only to be told of its evil essence and its unsuitability to serve as God's tool.

Until it came to the turn of the letter Bet. When Bet came before God, he pleaded, "Master of the Universe, may it be Your will to create the world through me since every person daily will praise You through me, saying "Barukh—Blessed be the Lord forever and ever." And God granted the petition of Bet, saying "Blessed be he that comes in the name of the Lord." And God created the world through Bet as it is written ".Bereshit—in the beginning—God created the heaven and earth."

And when, in the beginning, God pondered the creation of the Kingdom of Night, lo, the letters that had eagerly rushed to His aid earlier in cosmic time, each one vying to be the instrument of creation, could not be found. Their deafening clamor, once heard at the creation of the Kingdom of Light, was no more. All that could be heard was the chaotic, primordial spirit of God, fluttering over the vast emptiness. And God summoned all the letters to appear before Him, but lo, they had all abandoned their stations in the four crowns that uphold the universe. And so the spirit of God hovered over the world, searching and searching for His lost letters, calling out, wailing like a lost dove, "Where are you, where are you? What has become of My beloved ones?"

But the holy letters did not answer Him. As He cried in despair, the angel Katriel came before Him and said, "Master of the Universe, do You not know where Your letters can be found? They have all fled to the one sanctuary left on earth."

And God did not know whereof Katriel spoke. And so Katriel took Him to Jerusalem, to the Wall, and there, in its cracks and holes hewn out of rock by centuries of prayer, there had the letters taken refuge.

And God said to the letter Tav, "It is My will to create the Kingdom of Night through you because I have set you as a sign of death upon the foreheads of men."

Tav replied, "Oh, Master of the Universe, true, in Your eyes I may be a sign of death. But since the receiving of the Torah at Sinai, the people of Israel have made of me a sign of the Torah. I am the first letter of the word Torah. I shall not be the tool to create the Kingdom of Night."

God then said to the letter Shin, "You are the first letter of the word sheker and so you are the symbol of lying and deceit. Therefore it is My will to create the Kingdom of Night through you."

And the Shin replied, "True, as You see it I stand for lying and deceit; but the people of Israel, through their actions, have understood that I am the first letter of the word shalom. I am the sign of peace. And so the Kingdom of Night cannot be created through me."

God then said to the letter Resh, "You are the first letter in the word ra— evil. You are the symbol of evil and wickedness. Therefore it is My will to create the Kingdom of Night through you."

And the Resh replied, "True, as You see it I stand for evil and wickedness, but the people of Israel, through their actions, have understood that I am the first letter of the word rahamim—mercy. I stand for love and kindness and mercy. Through me the Kingdom of Night cannot be created."

And so it went for each and every letter. Each letter was told of its evil essence and its suitability to be God's tool in creating the Kingdom of Night; and each letter rebelled, telling God that they no longer belonged to the evil qualities, for the actions of the people of Israel had transformed them into holiness.

All this, all this and it seemed as if God would have no means by which to create the Kingdom of Night—until it came time for the letter Alef. All the letters had rebelled except for Alef, for God had a power over Alef that He did not have over the other letters. All the other letters are of this world and the world above, of God and of person, spiritual and physical. But the letter Alef is only of God and of the world above—completely spiritual. It has no sound; it cannot be pronounced. It is *all* God, *all* spiritual. The only letter that the people of Israel heard at Sinai was the silent Alef, the first letter in God's name, the first letter in the word emet—truth. So God took the holiest letter of all, the humblest letter of all, the letter of Sinai, the letter of His name, the first letter of emet—truth. He took away Alef from emet and left met—death. And with Alef, God created the Kingdom of Night.

Two prayers

Please recite these two prayers before reading any further.

"Holy brothers and sisters of Moriah, forgive us for violating your dignity, sanctity, and privacy; but all that we do—seeing, hearing, and thinking—we do only for the sake of the honor of your memories."

"Were all the heavens parchment, all the oceans ink, every blade of grass a quill, and all persons scribes, the Holocaust would still remain veiled in terrifying mystery."

The First Prayer: Whenever we look at those all too familiar pictures of martyred Jews in varying states of life and death, in varying states of dress and undress, in varying states of emaciation and torture, in varying states of . . . we violate their dignity and privacy. The Jewish tradition bids us not to look on the face of the dead; the dead cannot turn away from staring eyes as can the living. Furthermore, the tradition tells us that a dead person should never be left naked. We who violate this by viewing movies and photographs, and through the written and spoken word, are in need of penance. So before you begin any encounter with the Kingdom of Night, please recite this prayer.

The Second Prayer: The moment one begins to study the Holocaust, a betrayal has been committed. If one begins, one must conclude. If one talks of Vilna, one must talk of Lublin. If one talks of Poland, one must talk of Lithuania. If one talks of a victim, one must talk of all victims. If one begins, one is doomed to failure. All must be told, and having not been told, a betrayal has been committed; a betrayal of all that is left out; of all those incidents, cities, and persons that stand on the threshold of memory and the verge of speech crying out, "Do not silence us. Tell our tale." This prayer, too, is one of penance for silencing the forgotten and unspoken voices that we are doomed as humans to omit—an affirmation of our own limitations. So please recite it whenever concluding any discussion, movie, or book that deals with the Holocaust.

The need

What should one do in one's personal life because of the Holocaust? What to do in one's personal life to commemorate the Holocaust and to signify that one is a post-Auschwitz Jew is the ever-present question for all Jews and Jewish organizations. This is not the place, nor is there any need, to detail the constant reckless injudicious use of the Holocaust and its martyrs for the sake of almost every Jewish cause and position, from the far Left to the far Right and through the Center. This is the situation, not because the Holocaust overwhelms us (as in fact it does), but rather because we have not systematized and personalized our response to it. Lacking a coherent set of rituals and mitzvot to meet our need for integrating the Holocaust into our Jewish lives has led us to the present condition of frantic search and hasty application of overdetermined metaphor and unbalanced equation. Today, whoever says "I am a Jew" takes his/her stand in the Holocaust—and we have not ritualized our "in-Holocaust-standingness."

So then maybe there is a reality, a truth that responds to our original question. There is the reality of survivorship—not the survivorship of Jews, but the survivorship of the totality of the Jewish way of life, the whole tradition, the Torah. It is not only the Jewish people who must and do take their stand in the Holocaust, but Judaism, the very Torah itself, with all its mitzvot, rituals, teachings, ethics, and celebrations. You know, we three—Israel, Torah, and God—are one, and what happens to the part happens to all, to the whole. It was not just the Jews living in the Kingdom of Night who experienced its deportations, ghettos, selections, mobile killing units, labor camps, ovens, chambers, gases, bullets, fires, starvations, medical experiments, tattoos, freezings, burnings, beatings, whippings, hangings, shots, dismemberments, soaps, lampshades, days, nights, weeks, months, winters, springs, summers, falls, years, millennia, blacks, reds, yellows . . . but the very same all of us—all of the Torah and all of God. Of God there is nothing I can say. Of the Torah and what it says to our lives, there is much to say.

Response by Judaism

What does it mean to say that Judaism, the Torah, takes its stand in the Holocaust? With its all-encompassing endurance in time, everything that comprises Jewish living entered the Holocaust Kingdom. All of the Torah—its Shabbat, kashrut, holidays, life cycle, rituals, mitzvot bein adam le-haveiro u-vein adam la-makom—commandments between people and commandments with God—did not abandon the Jewish people, but entered the Kingdom of Night together with the Jews; and as one was affected, so was the other. As Jews emerged different from what they were when they entered, so too did the Torah. The mitzvah for us is, no matter how painful, to confront the reality that the Torah, too, has been changed. Painful it is, for it would be comforting to think that there is one thing—the Torah—that survived the Holocaust unchanged. Had that been the case, had the Torah, given in the presence of Radical Good not changed, it could not have survived its encounter with Radical Evil. Had it remained unchanged, the Torah would not be a survivor and would not be here. It is here because it, more than God, was able to say imo anokhi be-tzarah—I am with you in distress (Psalms 91:15). To treat the Torah as if it were the same, as if it had not survived the Holocaust, would be to deny its loyalty to and dependency on the Jewish people. This change, this alteration in all that is Torah, takes place because the living soul of the Torah enters historical time. The Jewish people change and are changed by the events they experience. The very same is true for Torah, which enters all Jewish historical experiences.

Some suggestions on how to relate

What is necessary then is to begin to integrate the survivorship of the Torah of the Holocaust into Jewish ritual life. The following are some fragments incorporating some of Jewish ritual life. This is not meant to be a prescriptive list. What this list does is to formulate some beginnings you and your community can choose from and utilize as a basis for developing rituals suited to your own selves and your own Jewish living after the Holocaust.

Rituals

SHABBAT

Shabbat is the celebration of God's creation and of humankind's partnership in that creation. As a testimony to the one Creator God, Shabbat is a statement of harmony and purpose in the universe, and consequently of God's commitment to that harmony and purpose. Is there anything in the Jewish tradition more antithetical to the Holocaust than Shabbat? Can a Shabbat that experienced the Holocaust be the same as the pre-Holocaust Shabbat?

The Shabbat Queen is now in mourning. Therefore, prior to welcoming her Friday night by singing "L'Kha Dodi," chant Isaiah 40:1, "Comfort, oh comfort My people."

The Shabbat following Holocaust Memorial Day, the 27th of Nisan, should be a taanit—a public day of fasting.

ROSH HA-SHANAH

The Day of Judgment takes on a new dimension of judgment. It is not just humankind that is being judged, but God; the Holy One, blessed be He, is on trial. Consider including in the service some of the following: Rebbi Levi Yitzhak of Berditchev's "A Trial with God"; a selection from the Book of Job; Abraham's dialogue with God prior to the destruction of Sodom and Gomorrah.

The shofar should be blown at the very beginning of every service to awaken God to the fact that we are now praying and He is now on trial.

Along with the reading about the akedah—the binding of Isaac—which since the Holocaust becomes the most relevant portion of the Torah, we should read, on the second day of Rosh ha-Shanah, selections from a diary written during the Holocaust.

YOM KIPPUR

The possibilities here are too frightening to set down on paper at this time. Let us begin at least to think about the issue of God in need of forgiveness.

SUKKOT

The sukkah symbolizes the wandering of the Jews in the desert. We reenact their sufferings by leaving our permanent residences and entering temporary ones. The sukkah is truly the symbol of the exiled and wandering Jew. Now it must also encompass our wanderings in the Kingdom of Night. Therefore let one wall of the sukkah remain as a memorial. Use it to hang pictures of your family, your family tree, and the town your family came from. Use it to learn more about the history of your own family and your people. They must become to the best of our ability symbols of all those habitats of wanderings, those sukkot of the Holocaust, in which our families lived. Each time we enter the sukkah let us recite, "So did our families live when we left Egypt, and so was done to our families in the Kingdom of Night—ko asu avoteinu be-tzaitam mi-mitzrayim ve-kho na'asa le-avoteinu be-mamlekhet ha-hoshekh."

Traditionally on each night of Sukkot we invite a different guest to eat with us, one guest for each of the nights: Abraham, Isaac, Jacob, Joseph, Moses, Aaron, and David (see *Catalog 1*, p. 127). Along with them we must also invite each night one martyr of the Holocaust. Pick the guest yourself: you will find his/her name in any number of the books on the Holocaust or among your own family.

PESAH

For the seder night: a caution

Elijah, who ascended to heaven on a fiery chariot; Elijah, who never died; Elijah, prophet of redemption; Elijah, angel of the covenant. It is he who throughout Jewish history appears wherever there are Jews. It is he who has been found wandering in the destroyed places.

When I arrived at Auschwitz, on the 9th of Av, little did I know or expect what would happen. In the late afternoon, as the sun set on the verdant Polish countryside and cast its fiery red light on fields ripe with God's bounty, I saw walking toward me on a dusty farm road adjacent to the camp an old man dressed in sandals and a torn and dirty white robe. And I knew, I knew immediately that it was he, Elijah the prophet. He walked toward me. I walked toward him. I introduced myself: "I am Yehiel Ephraim, son of Barukh Aron." He said, "Yes, I know. I was at your brit." I asked him what it was he was carrying. He opened his pouch and took out a bottle of wine and matzah. I asked, "What are you doing in Poland, and why in the middle of summer are you carrying wine and matzah?" And this is what he answered: "In 1941, in the month of Nisan, I prepared, as in every year past, to make my usual Passover visit to the homes of the Jews of Poland, of Europe. And as the sun set on the 14th of Nisan and it became the 15th, I eagerly waited for the Jewish people to extend to me their annual invitation by setting aside for me a cup of wine at the Seder table and opening the door. But as that night dragged on, the millions of invitations never came. I checked the calendar. I was not mistaken. It was the night of the Seder, and so I said to myself, 'Maybe the Jewish people have forgotten that it is Passover, and if they have, then they have forgotten to prepare wine and matzah, and I, who have been invited into their homes for thousands of years . . . they would surely welcome me even if I came uninvited.' So I took some wine and matzah and set out to visit all the holy Jews' homes in which I had been an honored guest in years past. And so I came to Poland, and I came to the first house, a house that I had visited many times in the past. From the outside it no longer shined with the light of Passover. The voices I heard were strange. I knocked on the door. The faces were not Jewish. The language I could not understand. No Hebrew or Yiddish was spoken. And so I went from house to house, from village to village, from city to city throughout all the lands and provinces of Poland and so did I find wherever I went. So I thought to myself, the whole people can't have disappeared. Somewhere they are lost, and I will search for them until the end of time to bring them the wine and matzah of redemption. And that is why you now find me in Poland, walking its dusty roads with wine and matzah in hand. Tell me, do you know where my lost Jews are?"

And so this coming Passover when you fill Elijah's cup with wine of redemption and when you open the door of your home to invite him in, be it known to you that he may not come. For Elijah, prophet of redemption, is still looking for his lost Jews somewhere in the forsaken lands. This I know, for thus I was told.

How can one even confront Passover, the holiday of redemption, in this post-Auschwitz life? Is it not now a mockery to thank God for redemption? Some possibilities:

1. When the cup of Elijah is poured, empty it immediately into another cup and in its place let there be a cup of salt water.

2. Prior to the Hallel and after the blessing of Thanksgiving, let there be a recitation of the statistics of the Holocaust, country by country.

3. Let there be matzah over which we recite, in paraphrase of the Passover Haggadah, "Ha lahma anya . . . Behold the bread of affliction which our family ate in the land of Europe; whoever was hungry then received no food, whoever was in need then received nothing; they were slaves then and were not redeemed, they were in exile then and were not brought up to Jerusalem."

SHAVUOT

On this day that celebrates the revelation of Radical Good at Sinai, how can one possibly cope with the ritual other than by the study of Torah? Let that still be the case for the first day, but for the second, let there be time devoted to the study of those mystical texts, Lurianic and Sabbatean, that discuss the problem of evil in and from God.

TEFILLIN

Having entered the Kingdom of Night, tefillin can never be the same. As the most intimate and personal form of marrying oneself to God, of entering into covenant with God, tefillin, worn when this covenant was so radically broken, speaks to us out of its living soul and cries, "I am not that which I once was; if I am bound the way I was, then it is not I you are wearing." Tefillin, heretofore worn only in the presence of God, were then and there worn in the presence of crematoriums and murdered children—in the presence of Satan. Should not these tefillin bring about a new covenantal relationship?

When we wear tefillin, as we bind the straps around our fingers as rings of marriage to God, we recite the following verses from Hosea (2:21–22):

> I will espouse you forever:
> I will espouse you with righteousness and justice,
> And with goodness and mercy,
> And I will espouse you with faithfulness;
> Then you shall be devoted to the Lord.

Let us now add the following verses to signify that we bind God to ourselves, so that what has happened will never happen again. "You shall not render an unfair decision: . . . judge your neighbor fairly. . . . Do not profit by the blood of your neighbor: I am the Lord. You shall not hate your kinsman in your heart. . . . You shall not take vengeance or bear a grudge against your kinsfolk. Love your neighbor as yourself: I am the Lord" (Leviticus 19:15–18).

TZITZIT / TALLIT

In the Torah, *after* the Exodus took place, tzitzit were worn. They were not worn prior to Sinai; tzitzit were not objects of our enslavement in Egypt and our redemption, and yet tzitzit became the ritual of remembrance. How much more so now after the Holocaust, after the tzitzit saw and heard and felt and lived everything that was there, how much more so must they be said to have changed and to embody, in a new way, the ritual of remembrance?

For these reasons tzitzit/tallit are a tremendous challenge, for tzitzit and tallit are the ritual embodiment of remembrance. Let there be sewn to every tallit and to every garment that bears tzitzit—a yellow star.

THE SIDDUR

This holy prayer book of ours, orphaned by God's deafness, is a sad reminder that none of its prayers were heard or fulfilled in those years. Pick any page or any line and you will see that after the Holocaust there are problems. The living soul of the siddur itself knows this and I will tell you how I know it. I have seen and held the holiest siddur in all the world. It is a siddur that is in the museum at Auschwitz. It once belonged to someone who died there. Its pages are all white because its letters rebelled and flew away. There are no answers to this problem, but there must be a way to keep the siddur and yet be faithful to the letters that have flown away.

1. Therefore, let us no longer read "Blessed are You, Lord our God, King of the Universe, who forms light and creates darkness, who makes peace and creates all things." Let us say, rather, the authentic and original verse from Isaiah 45:7, "I form light and create darkness, I make weal and create woe."

2. Let us punctuate the Shema this way: "Hear (Listen to) Israel! Lord our God, God who is one." Indeed, let us explore the possibility of using different kinds of punctuation at other points in the traditional prayer book. For instance, a statement like "A great love has God loved us" might end in a question mark. The possibilities for this are infinite.

Some general kinds of suggestions

1. There is nothing to say in the form of prayer about the Holocaust. So on Holocaust Memorial Day let us enter the synagogue, tear our clothing, put ashes on our heads, and sit on the floor in absolute silence.

2. Let every synagogue choose by lottery, from a list of all the names of all the destroyed Jewish cities of Europe, the name of a city that will become part of the synagogue name. It will then be the responsibility of that synagogue to concentrate its memorial and remembrance on that city. Each synagogue will become expert in the history of that city and all the details of its life, death, and tragedy.

3. Whenever we mention the Holocaust, we are obliged to remember the Gypsies and the homosexuals and the millions of non-Jews, for they too suffered in the Holocaust and there are so few left to remember them.

4. Those of us who are not physical survivors but just spiritual survivors of the Holocaust may not have the right to say the traditional prayers for the dead, which are filled with affirmations of faith and divine justice. Namely, Kaddish or El maleh—God full of mercy.

5. Every Jew has the obligation to make a pilgrimage to Auschwitz.

6. Yad Vashem—the Holocaust memorial in Jerusalem—has a Yad Vashem Holocaust light. Every Jewish home should have such a memorial.

And after all this let us realize that ultimately nothing has been accomplished, and let us recite: "Were all the heavens parchment, all the oceans ink, every blade of grass a quill, and all persons scribes, the Holocaust would still remain veiled in terrifying mystery."

May our souls be bound up in their souls. תהי נשמותנו צרורות בנשמותם.

Genealogy

Reviving a tradition

Genealogy has always been an important part of Jewish tradition. Even people who aren't familiar with Genesis as a whole know about the famous "begat" paragraphs. The Bible is endowed with hundreds of genealogies, some long and spanning many generations, others quite short. In fact, hardly a character in the biblical drama is introduced without some mention of his/her genealogy for at least a generation or two.

Genealogies in the Bible appear to serve several different functions. Many document priestly families—documentation that was vital to the functioning of the Temple. As Ezra (2:62) relates, when priestly families came back to Zion, they looked for their written genealogies—but could not find them. Another function of biblical genealogies appears to be individual identification, providing the reader with a context in which to approach a biblical personality. A third function, which can easily apply today as well, is simply the belief that to identify a person (yourself or someone else) as the son or daughter of So-and-so is to underline the bond of family and people. Genealogical identification is part of the glue that binds a person to his/her tradition. Jacob is not merely the individual person. He is the son of Isaac and Rebekah and the grandson of Abraham and Sarah; he has a responsibility to their name and their ways as well.

Similarly, we do not speak of God, but of "our God" and "God of our fathers." We also speak of the God of Abraham, Isaac, and Jacob, reciting a genealogy each time we utter those words. When we are called to the Torah, we are not identified before our community and God by merely our briefest name. Instead, our name includes our father's name (and in some shuls our mother's name as well). The implication is that we do not exist in a vacuum but are a link in history, the history of our family and our people. Even in death our gravestones identify us by a short genealogy: "Rachel bat——."

Historically the custom of maintaining our Jewish genealogies disappeared after the destruction of the Second Temple. These genealogies were not only of the priests (though it is interesting to note that settling questions of priestly genealogy was within the jurisdiction of the Great Sanhedrin) but also of the ten social groups who returned from Babylonian exile. These ten groups, which included priests, mamzerim—nonlegitimate children, gerim—converts, etc., had restrictions put upon them, largely as to who was permitted to marry whom. Clearly this situation invited corruption, and the Talmud even records an instance of an individual who attempted to imitate a Babylonian accent in order to claim Babylonian descent!

It appears that only two genealogical customs are still widely observed (besides the naming customs already mentioned): (1) the Kohen, Levite, and Yisroel designations continue to be maintained; and (2) the question of mamzerim arises when a woman remarries without a legal Jewish divorce and then bears children. Documentation for both of these designations is almost impossible. Those who claim kohanim status in your synagogue, quite frankly, might easily be in error (though, on the other hand, it is rather fascinating to think that if the designation is correct, then it has been passed down from generation to generation since the time of the Second Temple and before).

It could be argued that there should be no encouragement of widespread genealogical interest among Jews (or any people), since genealogy has often been corrupted. From Temple times to Hasidic dynasty scandals to the relatively recent notion of yichus (which may have had a good origin but became more of a notion of "marrying up" financially), genealogy has often been mistaken for a current appraisal of one's self-worth. This corruption of yichus leads to the other quite prevalent corruption: the idea that if you marry into a family with good yichus, you too suddenly have it.

However, the good most certainly outweighs the bad. Genealogy is an excellent antiassimilation technique. When a child knows the recent history of his people through the history of his family, it becomes real and personal.

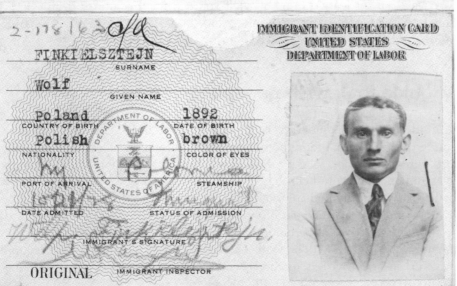

BALTIC AMERICA LINE

NEW YORK,	*8—10 Bridge Street.*
CHICAGO, ILL.	*315 So. Dearborn Street.*
PITTSBURGH, PA.	*Union Trust Building.*
DULUTH, MINN.	*29—31 East Michigan Street.*
SAN FRANCISCO, CAL.	*433 California Street.*
SEATTLE, WASH.	*1222—3 Alaska Building.*

AGENCIES IN ALL PRINCIPAL CITIES

Przechowuj pieczołowicie tą kartę. Ona przedstawia dowód legalnego przybycia do Stanów Zjednoczonych Ameryki Północnej.

B. A. L. FORM. 175. 3000-8-28.

IMMIGRANT IDENTIFICATION CARD
UNITED STATES
DEPARTMENT OF LABOR

FINKIELSZTEJN
SURNAME

Wolf
GIVEN NAME

Poland   1892
COUNTRY OF BIRTH   DATE OF BIRTH

Polish   brown
NATIONALITY   COLOR OF EYES

PORT OF ARRIVAL   STEAMSHIP

DATE ADMITTED   STATUS OF ADMISSION

IMMIGRANT'S SIGNATURE

ORIGINAL   IMMIGRANT INSPECTOR

In fact, Jewish history might be better taught not just by doing it through family history, but by working backward—from the present to Bereshit! When children learn Jewish history they often do not make it through to the present. Somehow the story never gets finished. If it does, there is usually little feeling that the history in the book is *our* history. But if the child can see how s/he got from the last generation to the present one, and how his/her parents got from place to place—and why—then genealogy will have served to strengthen Jewish identity. It was not until I discovered my Mitnaged roots on one side of the family and my Hasidic roots on the other side that I began to understand not only the conflict between Hasidim and Mitnagdim, but my own personal Jewish character as well.

Jewish genealogy can also be a powerful tribute to the victims of the Holocaust. I have traced the names of one hundred Holocaust victims—cousins of mine on my father's side. Suddenly the unfathomable notion of six million becomes real. It is not just a huge number; it includes the names and faces (through the photographs I have gathered) of people I would know today—had it not been for their Nazi murderers. My family tree also shows so plainly how fate allowed me to have been born while others in my family died. These cousins of mine have no gravestones; my family tree has become their memorial.

No genealogy will ever be able to stretch back to Adam and Eve. But through genealogy it is easy to understand and truly believe that we all share the same ancestors. A family genealogy quickly spreads across national boundaries. One discovers that each of us has many cousins in many countries, with different beliefs, levels of observance, occupations, and financial status. Along with our differences comes the realization that we are all of the same origin.

Finally, genealogy offers roots—allowing not only for a way to look back, but providing a way to go forward. A knowledge of who you were permits an understanding of who you are and who you want to be.

This, then, is the proposal: to sit with your parents or children, your grandparents or grandchildren, and to ask and to answer. Document your genealogy and family history. Who were your ancestors? What did they do? Where were they from? How did they live and die? Where did they go? Learn about "the old country," the towns your family lived in. Find out how to do further research in the libraries, archives, and record halls, which *very likely* have information on your family. Chart your family tree as far back as you can—and as wide (I have recently made contact with a cousin who survived the Holocaust and lives in Warsaw—as a Jewish historian). If you cannot go very far back, at least document what you can for the future. It will be that much easier for the next generation, and you will be preserving important information that might otherwise be lost.

Finally, *one more suggestion:* look carefully at the old pictures, letters, and names of generations past. If you examine them closely enough, you will surely discover yourself.

A guide to Jewish genealogy

A guide to Jewish genealogy is difficult to write for the same reason that a guide to the solving of any mystery must be difficult: each case will turn up different clues. These clues will send you in so many different directions that it is impossible to predict what your problems will be or in what order you will discover additional information. Dozens of complex other factors, over which you will have no control, will emerge.

So this guide can't be tailor-made for everyone. Some sections will be of no use to you; others will be vital. There are, however, certain rules that apply to everyone who wishes to engage in the exciting process of constructing a family tree and/or writing a family history:

RULE 1: BEGIN NOW.

This rule is the most important rule of all, and it is meant quite literally. The worst enemy of the genealogist is time. While the genealogist is a time traveler as the Jew is a time sanctifier, it is also time that must be conquered.

In practical terms this means that very early in your career as a genealogist you will hear someone say to you: "You should have started this last year. Aunt Zelda's cousin knew everyone back then, but she died six months ago." Every genealogist has a collection of these sad tales. Since your greatest resource is PEOPLE, you must begin to talk with them now. The sooner you begin, quite frankly, the better your chance of speaking to the people who will be able to help you. And the fact of the matter is that your most valuable contacts will be older people.

RULE 2: WRITE DOWN EVERY BIT OF INFORMATION YOU LEARN, EVEN THE MOST UNIMPORTANT-SOUNDING STORY.

You have undoubtedly seen enough TV mysteries and read enough whodunits to know that the silliest clue will turn up missing evidence. Genealogy is an unsolved mystery. When you begin to treat it that way, you will be on your way to solving each problem that arises.

For example, let's imagine that you are told that your great-great-aunt died during a smallpox epidemic in Pinsk. That clue plus a lot of research will lead you to the approximate date of her death. Dates are often determined this way. You might be told that your great-grandfather remembered when the Williamsburg Bridge in New York was built. Suddenly you know when he was in New York! That date in turn will lead you to records which you never dreamed existed.

RULE 3: BE AS ACCURATE AS POSSIBLE.

It is here that most "professional" (I dislike the term; all it means is money) genealogists will take issue with me. Most genealogy books insist on *total* accuracy. Every name, date, and fact must (according to them) be documented, verified, etc. They will warn you, for example, not to take the family legends too seriously, for they are probably false or contain falsehoods. To me this is absurd. While you want your family tree and history to be as accurate as possible, I believe strongly that there is a dimension of accuracy in all family legends. A family legend contains "truths" that documents could never contain. Any student of Aggadah could verify that!

So while you want to search for the truth, I urge you to keep your mind open to the many levels of truth. Don't accept everything you find as true—but don't discard it either. Only one person may recall the name of your great-great-grandmother; it may be the wrong name—but it will be all you have.

Conversely, do not accept something as true just because it was found in an official document.

RULE 4: BE PREPARED FOR REJECTION.

Some people will think you are crazy. Others will think you are wasting your time. Still others will think you are wasting *their* time. Genealogy either grabs you or it doesn't. So be prepared for some of your best sources of information to give you the cold shoulder. Your grandmother might not want to talk about

This guide will give you concrete instructions on what you can do—so, begin now!

Remember, every clue is important.

Most genealogists will accept an official government document as "more true" than a person's word. We know better!

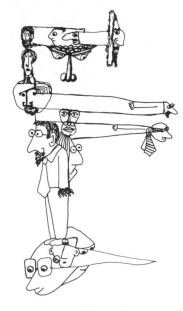

Important Note: This guide to Jewish genealogy is geared to Americans who are of Eastern European descent, but others of varying places of origin can certainly use the principles and most of the sources for their own research.

"the old days." Here's where psychology will come in handy. Try it. But be prepared to be rejected.

You might have to telephone or write some people you've never met. It is possible that they couldn't care less and will never answer your letters.

Be prepared for this—and push on.

RULE 5: BE PATIENT.

Genealogy is a long process. It will take you months and years to exhaust all possibilities. Of course you can stop any time and decide that you have all the information you want. But as a hobby genealogy can be a long, enjoyable pastime. It may have to be. Sending for information, receiving answers to inquiries, and putting all of the pieces of your family history together can take a long time. Don't be discouraged. Your efforts will pay off. Genealogy is not a matter of just sitting down and writing out a family tree. It takes time and effort. Be patient.

Now you're ready to begin. Your first step is to decide on your goal. There are two options:

1. Decide whether you're going to do a genealogy or a family history. A genealogy is different from a family history in that it begins with you and works backward in time. A family history begins with one ancestor and works forward.

To construct your genealogy, you would first chart yourself, then your two parents, your four grandparents, your eight great-grandparents, and so on. To construct a family history you would first start with, say, your great-great-great-grandparents, then their children, then their children, and so on.

A genealogy looks like this: ▽ you

And a family history looks like this: △ your ancestor

Ultimately you may want to do both, which, while it is an enormous job, is also the most sensible. This is because in a genealogy you only document "parents"—that is, parents, grandparents, etc. But in a family history you also document uncles, aunts, cousins, great-aunts, etc.

When you put both a genealogy and family history together, you get this:

2. Decide whether you want to do both sides of your family at once (that is, your mother's side and your father's side) or whether you want to do one

at a time. I recommend both at once, systematically (which will be illustrated shortly). Again, this is because you are fighting time. It is best to cover as much territory as possible.

ORGANIZE!

To be a successful genealogist you must be organized. Your biggest time waster will be searching for material you already have. Therefore I recommend that you purchase certain materials before you actually set out to begin your hard research:

1. file folders—a must; you'll need a good supply and a big envelope to hold them all

2. a looseleaf notebook—also a must; since you will want to discard notes, rewrite notes, and keep notes, looseleaf is best

3. a comfortable notebook—get whatever size you find best for you to carry, take notes in, and keep with you when you interview or search public records

4. envelopes and stamps—since a genealogist depends on the mails, a good supply is essential

As soon as you have any material, label a folder and put the information in the folder. Nobody can teach you how to file or how to label your folders. Only your own system will work for you. There are only two rules for filing:

1. Be specific, not general. For example, if your name is Cohen, you better not have a folder labeled "Cohen." It won't tell you anything.

2. NEVER have a "Misc." folder. You will be tempted to use it, and there is nothing more counterproductive for a filing system than a Misc. folder. In the end you will be searching through an overstuffed Misc. folder for things that should have had their own file.

TALKING TO BOBBEH, ZAYDEH, AND OTHER STRANGERS

One of your richest sources of information will be word of mouth. While documents often will supply the hard data and plenty of factual information, much of your other information and leads will come from people.

Interviewing people, whether they be grandparents, cousins, or strangers, is not as easy as it might sound. For the most effective interviewing, consider the following advice:

1. Start with people closest to home, which means your parents, then your grandparents, and so on. Often they will know very little, but they will undoubtedly be able to suggest someone who does know more about the family (see the next section for directions on what to ask, etc.).

2. Never ask general questions like, "Tell me about the family." Be specific! If you want to know about your great-grandfather, don't say: "Tell me about my great-grandfather." Instead, ask: "What was his name? What was his occupation? Where was he born? When did he die?"

3. Never lead a person. In other words don't say: "Didn't he live in Poland?" Instead, ask: "Where did he live?" This is especially important when verifying information. If someone tells you that your grandmother had four brothers, don't ask someone if your grandmother had four brothers. Instead, try: "How many siblings did Grandma have?" It's too easy for someone to answer yes and leave you with false assumptions.

4. Your greatest sources will be old people, so be sure to consider their situation. Don't tire them out with too many questions. While some folks can talk on for hours, others might have enough after a few minutes. Use your

Undoubtedly many people will fail to take this advice about setting up an organized system for filing. It will be their loss and will contribute to frustration—which may lead, sadly, to abandoning the project.

REMEMBER: Genealogy is akin to solving a mystery. There will be many "false leads," blind alleys, and time wasters—and you will need all the time you can get. So ORGANIZE!!!

Beware of genealogical sexism
Sexism is a sneaky disease that creeps into every aspect of our lives. Genealogy is no exception. Raise your consciousness and beware of the following:

1. Children take the surname of their fathers, as wives take the surname of their husbands. Therefore be particularly careful to document maiden names. In fact, when you construct your family tree, write in all maiden names. In other words, your mother will be listed by her parents' surname—not your father's.

2. Don't trace only your father's ancestors. This is especially tempting because his surname is also yours, most probably.

3. Undoubtedly your genealogy will be lopsided to include more documentation about men than women. This is an unfortunate situation that reflects our male-biased tradition. For example, a gravestone will often say "Isaac ben Abraham" and forget about Isaac's mother! The solution to this is in our hands: in other words, we must prevent this from happening in the future!

4. Keep in mind that you are not simply a member of one family—you belong to a huge number of families. In fact, if you just go back to your great-great-grandparents' generation, you belong to sixteen families. The reason you don't *feel* that you belong to that many families is due to sexism in names. Only one name gets to be yours: your father's father's father's name. That's sexism!

own judgment but don't forget to start with the most important questions first to save time.

5. Psychology will come in handy with some people, especially older people. They may not want to talk. Straining a memory can be a difficult process, especially when people do not remember. It can become an emotional scene when a grandmother cannot recall her own grandmother's name. She will be able to picture her, talk about her, recall events as if they had happened yesterday, but the name might just not be there. Be gentle. Suggest that it will come back to her soon. Go on to something else. Again, use your best judgment!

6. Be persistent but respectful. If a person is not interested in talking to you, try to impress the person with your sincere interest and try, politely, to convince them to talk with you. Don't take the first no for an answer—but don't annoy someone who isn't interested either. Strike a balance.

7. Some people will love to talk, others will hate it. Be prepared for rejection—and keep the name of a "talker" handy. When you're discouraged you'll often want to call that person up after being rejected by someone who doesn't want their time "wasted."

8. Your research will take you to strangers, both members of your family and others. You will speak to cousins you never knew existed and people outside your family who might know more about you than you know.

9. Don't be surprised if some people, especially strangers, are suspicious. There are many crooks in the genealogy business who are selling phony "coats of arms," etc. People are wary of this and will want to know if you are selling something.

10. Some people will resent you for asking what they think are personal questions. Expect it, but don't let this scare you. Most people are more than happy to tell you about "the good old days" and talk about themselves, their relatives, and others. You are putting *them* on center stage!

11. There is one exception to the rule to ask specific questions: when *all* your specific questions are exhausted, then you are ready to ask people things like, "Tell me about life in the shtetl." Here's where the folklore in all its richness will flow forth.

12. Get yourself a cassette tape recorder for your interviews—both for telephone and in person. A telephone jack for a cassette recorder costs only a few dollars. You need not tell your interviewee that the phone call is being taped—unless you plan to play it for others. If it is just for your own use, you can keep it to yourself. But of course *any* playing of the tape for others without the person's knowledge is quite unethical.

Some people might be inhibited by a tape recorder. Others will suddenly become hams. A tape recorder is a tool; it can be used or abused. Be guided by your best judgment. It might inhibit a person from telling you personal stories—or it might inspire people.

13. A tape recorder can also be a way of documenting your family history. Imagine what you would give to hear a tape recording of your great-great-

In *all* cases be honest. If you must call a stranger on the phone (and you will!), introduce yourself, tell the person exactly what you are doing, briefly tell why you are doing it, and then feed their ego a bit. Suggest that they *will* be very helpful and suggest also that you were told they would know A LOT.

grandparents! So if you tape your grandparents, you are ensuring that experience for future generations.

14. Finally, assure people that you will get back to them to share your findings—and follow through. If someone is nice enough to give you information, return the favor by sharing your material with them. It will give you an opportunity to say thank you again. And while we are on the subject of thank-you's, write thank-you notes to people who have helped you. It is the least you can do.

WHAT DO YOU WANT TO KNOW?

You will have to decide how much and what kind of information to gather about your family. The following are some suggestions and comments about what you should search for.

1. *Names:* First and foremost your family tree and history will be composed of names. Here you will have to make certain decisions. We have already discussed the importance of using maiden names. In addition, you will probably want to include middle names as well as first names and surnames. There will also be the issue of English names, Yiddish names, and Hebrew names. I suggest that you document all three. In other words, your great-grandfather could very well have been called Abraham, Avrum, and Avruhum; your family tree will be richer if it includes all three names. The most complete name information will also allow you to spot naming patterns after your tree is complete: who was named after whom, how the names changed, etc.

2. *Dates:* Many dates will concern you, but the most important ones are birth dates, death dates, marriage dates, and dates of immigration from country to country (especially dates of arrival in America, which will aid in later searches). Since the accuracy of these dates is important, not only for its own sake but also to aid in later document searches, do your best to find the accurate dates in all cases. Listen to the way people tell you dates to determine their probability. For example, if your grandmother tells you that her oldest brother was born on April 4, 1892, it is much more likely to be true than if she hesitates and says: "He was about six years older than me, so put 1892." One interesting aspect of dates is that many people use Jewish holidays to remember dates by. Often someone will say: "He was born on the second day of Hanukkah when we first came to America." A quick library check or a hundred-year or perpetual calendar will solve that mystery.

3. *Place of birth:* This is vital not only for future record searches but also for general historic interest. If you know that your great-great-grandfather was born in Pinsk in 1842, then you are on your way to learning what it was like at the time and place of his birth. What did he face as a boy? What was his life like? You can find out from reading history books on the period.

4. *Place of death:* This is also important for general historic reasons, but it's vital to attempt to locate burial site. Gravestones can provide a storehouse of genealogical information because they frequently include dates of birth, parents' names, and names of spouses and/or children.

5. *Occupation(s):* Was your great-grandmother a weaver? Was your great-great-grandfather a rabbi? Was your great-uncle a cattle herder? How did your ancestors make a living?

6. *Motives of immigrants:* One of the most inspiring questions to ask people is: "Why did your father bring you to America?" Often you'll get this answer: "Why do you *think*?" That often means, "I don't know; we just came" or "It was bad 'over there.' Didn't you know that?" But if you press the question you will get stories that otherwise might not have been told.

If all efforts fail, estimate dates and preface them with "ca." (meaning "approximately")—e.g., "ca. 1820."

Another equally inspiring question, though much more difficult and painful to answer is: "Why *didn't* Grandma's brother come to America?" Be prepared for a sad story, but one that's important to your understanding of your family history. Suddenly you will get the sense that it was often strange twists of fate that allowed you to be born and others either to die or never be born.

7. *Routes of immigration:* Try to find out how your immigrant ancestors came to America. What was the name of the boat? Where did it start from? What port did it land at? Get any information regarding this that you can because it will then allow you to send for the actual records of immigration (see below).

8. *Stories:* You are hunting for any stories, tales, and family folklore that you can gather. Learn how to be a good listener and an equally good questioner.

9. *Religious and political affiliations:* Were your ancestors Orthodox? Hasidic? Freethinkers? Were they Marxists? Zionists? You will soon discover that you come from a line of radical thinkers or pious scholars or people who were as committed to their causes as you are to yours.

Many more questions will arise, but it is best to narrow your scope. Don't get too scattered in your information gathering. Everyone's life can be a book; you don't want that. Direct yourself to the goals you set for yourself and you will have a greater reward at the end.

10. *Languages:* What languages did they speak?

11. *Anti-Semitism:* Was there much in your ancestors' lives? Many people will say: "Everyone was a victim of anti-Semitism!" but you may also get some fascinating stories from this question.

WHAT KINDS OF GENEALOGICAL SOURCES CAN YOU USE TO FIND YOUR FAMILY?

While you are busy interviewing family members, you will also want to begin to use public records for your research. Most people cannot believe that U.S. records and other documents contain information about *their* family—but they do! Here are some sources you will be able to use:

1. city directories
2. census records
3. citizenship records
4. birth, marriage, and death certificates
5. wills
6. steamship passenger lists
7. cemeteries
8. obituaries
9. military records

A complete description of all sources and how to obtain them would be impossible here. Suffice it to say that you can find a vast quantity of material about your family in public documents in the U.S. The following Jewish genealogical sources will help you to investigate these sources.

Jewish Genealogical Publications

There are four items of specific Jewish genealogical interest that every Jewish family historian should be aware of. While I must confess my bias in favor of the first two listed here (since they are partly the result of my efforts), all four are worthwhile and should be consulted.

1. Arthur Kurzweil, *From Generation to Generation: How to Trace Your Jewish Genealogy and Personal History* (New York: Morrow, 1980). This guidebook is a detailed "how-to" and "why-to" to help you trace your family history book. It will take you step by step *backward* in history to show you how to successfully trace your own Jewish genealogy. The book includes hundreds of useful sources and methods of discovering your Jewish heritage. The myth is that Jews cannot trace their roots. This book proves that we *can*!

155 E. 93rd St., Suite 3C
New York, NY 10028

Toledot, which means "genealogy" or "generations" in Hebrew, is a quarterly journal dedicated to helping its readers trace their own family histories. Published quarterly since summer 1977, *Toledot* has published important and vital articles for the Jewish genealogist. Perhaps the most important series of articles published to date in *Toledot* has been a town-by-town catalog of each of the nearly one thousand Jewish communities whose records have been microfilmed by the Mormons—in Hungary, Germany, and Poland. The Mormons (Church of Latter-Day Saints) have copied a huge collection of Jewish records (sometimes going back to the 1700s). *Toledot* has cataloged that collection. Subscriptions to *Toledot* are $8 for one year, $14 for two years; slightly higher in Canada, and overseas.

3. Dan Rottenberg, *Finding Our Fathers: A Guidebook to Jewish Genealogy* (New York: Random House, 1977). Rottenberg's book was a first for Jewish genealogy. Although it's a good introduction to the field, it sometimes falls short in its many sources, which simply will not be useful. The book is padded with a lot of information that seems helpful but isn't. Nonetheless, it is worth investigating for the ideas it might give you and the standard sources, which will certainly be of use.

4. David Kranzler, *My Jewish Roots* (New York: Sepher-Hermon Press, 1979). A good introduction to the subject. The book is better for general Jewish historical background than it is for genealogical resources, but the basic information is often useful. Both this book and Rottenberg's should be looked at by the ambitious Jewish family historian, though neither should be relied upon too heavily.

Additional sources that can help with your research

There are many libraries and historical societies that can help you with your research. But don't expect anyone to do your research for you! These organizations can alert you to sources and assist you in working with the materials they have, but they cannot do your work. If you have specific requests they might tell you by mail whether they have the material you want; but general questions can only receive general answers. Though none of these organizations have the staff to undertake research for people, they are quite helpful and I recommend that you call on them for your research needs.

1. **New York Public Library**
   Genealogy and Local History Division
   Fifth Ave. and 42nd St.
   New York, NY 10018

This library, staffed by helpful and friendly librarians, is one of the finest sources of genealogical material and free research advice. Their collection is vast and their knowledge is excellent.

2. **YIVO Institute for Jewish Research**
   1048 Fifth Ave.
   New York, NY 10028

The YIVO library and archives are part of a scholarly research institution devoted to Judaica. They have an extensive collection of material on Eastern European Jewish life, and the archives has material cataloged by town. This is a superb source of information on the European origins of your family. The library has many helpful sources including a collection of memorial books. The staff at YIVO are anxious to assist in genealogical research by making their collection available.

3. **Leo Baeck Institute**
   129 E. 73rd St.
   New York, NY 10021

The Leo Baeck Institute is devoted to research, maintains archives and a library, and operates a museum centering around German Jewry. If your family is of German Jewish origins, be sure to consult the Leo Baeck Institute when doing your research.

4. **American Jewish Archives**
   Clifton Ave.
   Cincinnati, OH 45220

The American Jewish Archives is a wonderful source of American Judaica. Of special interest to the Jewish genealogist is Rabbi Malcolm H. Stern, who is the staff genealogist of the American Jewish Archives (see below).

5. **American Jewish Historical Society**
   2 Thornton Rd.
   Waltham, MA 02154

The AJHS is devoted to American Jewish research and maintains the largest library of American Judaica. Depending on the history of your family in the United States, this society could be of great help with your research.

6. **New York Public Library—Jewish Division**
   Fifth Ave. and 42nd St.
   New York, NY 10018

This division of the New York Public Library is not only a fine source of all aspects of Jewish research but also has a collection of memorial books and some family histories already written.

7. **Rabbi Malcolm H. Stern**
   ℅ American Jewish Archives
   Clifton Ave.
   Cincinnati, OH 45220

Rabbi Stern is genealogist for the American Jewish Archives. His specialty is early American Jewry: he has researched the genealogies of individuals who settled in the United States before 1840 and traced the families of those people to the present. Rabbi Stern is happy to share his research with interested individuals.

8. **National Archives**
   National Archives and Records Service
   General Services Administration
   Washington, DC 20408

Send for free guides to genealogical sources, which will describe the National Archives and its many services. Also, a guide to its complete holdings, *Guide to Genealogical Records in the National Archives,* is available for $1.65. It will give you a detailed survey of all their records. The National Archives is a major source of American genealogical records.

Europe and abroad

Needless to say, genealogy research using sources in the United States is infinitely easier than research of records and sources overseas. However, at some point you will have exhausted all domestic possibilities for information and will want to explore European sources. Since most American Jewish families come from Europe, this guide is generally geared to that situation. However, most if not all of these sources can also be of help if your situation differs.

One of the first things to determine is whether or not you can deal directly with the country of your origin. In other words, while Great Britain probably will be able to supply some records to you, you are not likely to have much luck with the Soviet Union.

Abandon any mistaken notion that you might have that there could not possibly be any records of your family ancestors in Europe. It is incorrect to assume that "everything was destroyed." It wasn't. Much of it was, but it is worthwhile checking into how much is still available.

If you think your family has a long history in the United States, it would be worth your while to contact Rabbi Stern.

The following are the major sources for family history and genealogy information:

1. **Israel Archives Association**
   P.O. Box 1149
   Jerusalem, Israel

This association coordinates the activities of all archival activity in Israel and offers a guide to all of the archival collections throughout Israel for $10: *Guide to the Archives of Israel* (1973). The guide indicates the enormous amount of historical research and collection taking place in Israel. Many of the archival organizations can help in locating information pertaining to individuals and locations throughout the world. The archives that would be of most help to genealogists is the following one:

2. **Central Archives for the History of the Jewish People**
   Hebrew University Campus, Sprinzak Bldg.
   P.O. Box 1149
   Jerusalem, Israel

It is worthwhile to write for the guide to their collection, which is divided by country and then by city. To give you an example, let us say part of your family comes from Somlyo, Romania. The archives guide indicates that they have the mohel book for that town between 1855 and 1888 (a mohel book is a record of circumcisions). This means that if any male members of your family were born in Somlyo during those dates, the archives would have some information for you! The archives collects records of Jewish communities all over the world: all surviving marriage, birth, death, divorce, mohel, and debt records and various other documents. By the way, this would be a good source of memorial books for specific towns since the archives collects them too. It would be worth your while to check this guide for information on your towns.

3. **Mormon Church**
   Genealogical Society
   50 E. North Temple
   Salt Lake City, UT 84150

Odd as it may sound, the Mormon Church may be the best source there is for Jewish genealogical research! One of the precepts of the Mormon Church is that their members undertake genealogical research, based on the Mormon belief that if you can document your ancestors you can baptize them by proxy. Because of the seriousness of this belief, the church has undertaken a huge effort to microfilm records in every corner of the world in order to aid their members (and others) in research. The Mormon Church has made a multimillion dollar investment in this research, and all of their efforts are available to the general public. An enormous number of Jewish records have been microfilmed by the Mormons and are available to anyone doing research.

While the Mormon Church has its main offices in Salt Lake City, where they house their collection as well, copies of the index to the collection have been reproduced and are available for viewing in many branch libraries of the church around the country. By going through the index to the Mormon collection, you can see whether they have reproduced records from the towns and cities you are interested in. If so, for a minimal fee the church will send to the branch closest to you a microfilmed copy of the records you would like to review.

4. Finally, I would suggest getting a copy of *How to Find Your Family Roots,* by Timothy Field Beard (New York: McGraw-Hill, 1977). This is the most thorough guide, country by country, to sources around the world. While many of Beard's sources will not be useful, it still remains the best book I know of on the subject of world records.

Don't believe the myth that Jewish records simply were not kept—or that if they were they were all destroyed. Through public and private records I have traced one branch of my own family back to the late 1700s and another to the 1500s. I have found public documents about my family in Polish and Hungarian records, and I should add that my family does not come from famous people. But they were in the records—and I found them!

A Final Word: The best piece of advice I can give you is to begin NOW. Don't wait! Interview your oldest family members, begin to read the Jewish genealogy sources mentioned in this article—and establish *your* family's link with Jewish history.

Yiddish

Note: All addresses are given at the end of the chapter.

From its beginnings—around the year 1000—through the end of World War II, Yiddish was *the* language of Ashkenazic Jewry. It is a fusion language, drawing its components from the Hebrew-Aramaic of traditional Jewish culture as well as the Romance, Germanic, and Slavic tongues of the coterritorial peoples with whom the Jews came into contact in their various eastward migrations. The era of modern Yiddish—beginning in the nineteenth century—saw its development into a national Jewish language, with its own literature, press, theater, and educational system. A 1935 census estimated that there were almost eleven million Yiddish speakers throughout the world. The events of World War II effected the destruction of the Eastern European Yiddish-speaking community; this and the linguistic assimilation in the Americas and elsewhere have reduced the language community by more than two-thirds. Though it has all but ceased to be the mame-loshn—the language learned at a mother's knee—a renewed interest in Yiddish (as a manifestation and reflection of Jewish culture) has recently led to the growth of Yiddish studies and other nonacademic activity.

Learning Yiddish I: courses

The special joy of learning Yiddish is, in fact, an advantage that we have over the native speaker, who learned Yiddish at his/her parents' wishes, rather than as an act of free will.

Children know the best way of learning a language: they listen to their parents, to their families, to other adults; through trial and error they eventually master the language to an extent and with an ease rarely attainable later. Some of the younger generation of Yiddish enthusiasts learned this way, having grown up in Yiddish-speaking homes—traditionally religious homes where Yiddish was spoken as a matter of course, secularly Jewish homes where Yiddish was a matter of love and ideology, immigrant homes where Yiddish was spoken of necessity. Those with homegrown Yiddish are admired and, let's face it, envied by the rest of us who have chosen or will soon choose to "break our teeth" regaining our birthright. If Yiddish was a secret language in your home for remarks you weren't supposed to understand (sound familiar?) or if it wasn't spoken at all, what is to be done? Relax: Yiddish *can* be learned, well and with relative ease; and part of the fun is in the learning.

WEINREICH SUMMER PROGRAM

How do you learn Yiddish? One way—the best way—is to spend a summer at the Uriel Weinreich Summer Program, sponsored jointly by the YIVO Institute for Jewish Research and Columbia University. The sponsors try to be very academic and detached about their course (and it is of the highest academic caliber), but the students and teachers know better: the Weinreich Program is two-thirds intensive Yiddish course, one-third summer camp/community/havurah. A summer at the program turns a nonspeaker into a sort-of speaker, a sort-of speaker into a competent speaker, and a competent speaker into a maven.

It's difficult to be objective about the program, since many younger Yiddishists have either taught there or have graduated from it. It is a life-changing experience. Go, if you can. The program includes language instruction in the mornings, special seminars (on, for example, Yiddish theater or Yiddish folklore) in the afternoons, film showings, field trips, etc. The tuition is somewhat high, but scholarships are available and relatively easy to come by. For information write YIVO.

QUEENS COLLEGE SUMMER PROGRAM

The only other summer course in Yiddish we know about is offered by Queens College of the City University of New York. It's also fairly intensive: five days a week for six weeks. This is a good compromise for people who cannot devote the entire day to learning Yiddish and the instruction is excellent. For information, write Queens College.

UNIVERSITY COURSES

Many colleges and universities offer Yiddish courses during the academic year, though their number is still appallingly low—fewer than a dozen. This is a good place for some activism: try to interest a faculty member in offering a course and then help him/her persuade the powers that be that it's a good idea. That's the way credit courses were established at most of the colleges currently offering Yiddish. There's often some administrative resistance (inertia? budget-mindedness? just a touch of anti-Semitism?), and Yiddish courses have found a variety of homes. Some are in Jewish Studies programs, others in German departments, others in Hebrew departments, one in a linguistics department, at least one in an English department, and so on. Student response is often overwhelming: over seventy students signed up for a tutorial at the University of California, Santa Cruz, which was limited to eighteen, and the Queens College Summer Program has had almost five hundred students for years. Administrators like these numbers and—except in the severest of crises—tend to continue proven successes. Yiddish courses are currently offered at Bar Ilan University, Baruch College of the City University of New York, Brandeis University, Brown University, Columbia University, Duke University, Hebrew University, Jewish Theological Seminary of America, Ohio State University, Queens College of the City University of New York, Rutgers University, the State University College at Brockport (N.Y.), SUNY at Buffalo, SUNY at New Paltz, SUNY at Stony Brook, and the universities of Arizona, California at Los Angeles (UCLA), Haifa, Manitoba, Pittsburgh, Texas at Austin, and Washington. Please let us know of others in your area.

For information about informal courses in Canada, write the National Committee for Yiddish of the Canadian Jewish Congress.

Less formal noncredit courses in Yiddish are also offered by Bnai Brith Hillel foundations and similar campus-based organizations. Their quality and intensiveness varies, of course, but the enthusiasm is uniformly high: instructors who are volunteers or exploited graduate students and students who are taking time from credit courses make for successful learning communities. Informal courses are offered by the Bnai Brith Hillel Foundations at Boston University; Harvard University; Indiana University at Bloomington; Princeton University; University of California, Berkeley; the University of Chicago; and the Bureau of Jewish Education/College of Judaic Studies in San Francisco. Again, please let us know of other courses in your neighborhood.

Practicing Yiddish with a mouth full of cookies: Yiddish clubs and reading circles

Good bets: colleges with a large Jewish population, synagogues and temples, Jewish community centers, and Y's.

Quite a few campuses, campus communities, and community groups sponsor Yiddish clubs. Most are independent, so you'll have to do a bit of digging.

Yugntruf has a network of chapters and reading circles; write for contacts. A leyenkrayz—reading circle—is a unique institution: a group of friends gather, usually in someone's house or apartment, to take turns reading from a Yiddish story, novel, poem, etc. Occasionally there's a special speaker (we've had poets, musicians, politicians). Always there are refreshments.

If there isn't a student-faculty reading circle in your area, you might want to try a leyenkrayz sponsored by the Ykuf, former Jewish Communists and fellow travelers. It's quite an experience. You'll be the youngest person there, sometimes by over a half century; you'll be greeted with warmth, curiosity, and often a bit of bewilderment, and will be asked to explain yourself at every turn. Not for the timid, but an adventure! One elderly gentleman at the San Francisco leyenkrayz told me about fighting in the Red army during the Russian Revolution, another about moving to California in the 1920s to set up a chicken farm in Petaluma, another about organizing the dockworkers and longshoremen on the Pacific Coast. Not exactly a group of our contemporaries and certainly not a model for the life-style of our generation, which we'll have to work out for ourselves, but a living slice of Jewish history well worth experiencing before the demographic imperative takes its toll. For details, write Ykuf. The Arbeter-Ring also has a network of reading circles; the one

in Philadelphia is the most active and has hosted a considerable number of younger Yiddish enthusiasts.

Maurice M. Rosenthal helped organize quite a different type of Yiddish club in Albuquerque, New Mexico (and you thought you were isolated!). He recounts his experiences and those of the club in a booklet called *Guidelines for a Yiddish Club*. The booklet goes into some detail about the practical organization of a club in the "outback" and is especially valuable as an inspiration and source of brainstorming. The Albuquerque club put on a full-scale amateur production of Sholem-Aleykhem's *Tevye*, for example, and Rosenthal gives details and photographs of the performance. His sections on records, books, and organizations are outdated, however, and are superseded by this *Catalog*. The booklet is available at $3 postpaid from Yugntruf.

The National Council for Yiddish and Yiddish Culture has announced plans for compiling a central listing of Yiddish clubs and reading circles; a letter to them might turn up something in your neighborhood.

If all else fails, organize your own club. We'll be glad to advise, and you can be president.

Print to fit: the Yiddish press

Imagine yourself in the subway (or bus, BART, MTA, Muni), sitting opposite a row of riders, each with his/her reading matter. You don't feel like reading yourself, so you decide to study the faces and habits of the people across the aisle. One man takes out a battered copy of the *Daily News* (a picture tabloid); his female companion is engrossed in the *National Enquirer*. No intellectuals, they. Next to them is a bearded student reading, say, *Socialist Revolution*, and next to him another student reading the *Atlantic Monthly*. At the end of the row is a woman with Isaac Bashevis Singer's latest novel. You, on the other hand, have only a copy of the *Forverts*. Not to worry: your *Forverts* contains, in somewhat uneasy juxtaposition, elements of all the above journals and many more.

The Yiddish press has always been simultaneously splendid and horrific, serving a readership perfectly comfortable with finding social or literary critique of real sophistication cheek by jowl with scandal and true confessions. This uniquely Jewish turn of mind has survived and flourished in New York's most wonderful and awful Yiddish newspaper, the *Forverts* (*Jewish Daily Forward*). On the front page, under a masthead flanked by quotations from Karl Marx, is a page of wire-service news rewritten to emphasize its Jewish import, in an outlandish language called "potato Yiddish." It is, for the most part, English transliterated into Yiddish characters with an unhealthy admixture of Germanized Yiddish, all in a spelling system abandoned by the bulk of the Yiddish publishing world decades ago. Interestingly, this butchery of the language is, or was, the product of conscious choice and not ignorance. The *Forverts*'s editor from 1903 until his death in 1951 was Abraham Cahan, a serious author and careful stylist in both Yiddish and English. He thought to Americanize the immigrant masses by gradually sneaking in so much English that the transition to English in Latin characters would be easy—a program designed to put the *Forverts* out of business years ago.

Fortunately for us Cahan's program was not successful, and the *Forverts* quickly filled an important place in Yiddish life. Today there are columns and features on the inside pages that make the paper, for all our grumblings, very precious to us. Among the features to look out for are the stories by Isaac Bashevis Singer (on Thursdays and Fridays), those by Chaim Grade (on Sundays), the commentaries on traditional Jewish problems and contemporary Israel by Mordkhe Shtrigler (on Sundays, Wednesdays, and Fridays), and the often satirical columns by Avrom Shulman (irregularly scheduled). Of special

A kindersher saichel iz oicher a saichel.

A child's wisdom is also wisdom

The *Forverts* offers sporadic student discounts on subscriptions—worth a try—and subscriptions to the Sunday edition only.

interest is a column ("Shprakhvinkl—Language Corner") on popular language and folklore by Wolf Younin, appearing Mondays, and one ("Perl fun der yidisher poezye—Pearls of Yiddish Poetry") on Yiddish literature by A. Forsher, appearing Sundays.

As is the tradition in Europe (and now in Israel as well), Yiddish newspapers represent specific political positions and do not—except, perhaps, on the news pages—even strive for objective disinterestedness. The *Forverts* is a social-democratic paper and unabashedly so. One longtime, and bitter, competitor is the *Morgn-Frayhayt* (*Jewish Daily Morning Freiheit—Morning Freedom*), once party-line Communist and now vaguely fellow traveler. They stray far from the Communist position on Jewish matters, supporting Israel and advocating cultural and political rights for Jews in the Soviet Union, for example, and this independence cost many *Frayhayt* editors and contributors their Party membership. Unlike the excellent Ykuf publications (see the section on Yiddish periodicals below for a discussion of *Yidishe Kultur*), however, the *Frayhayt* makes rather dull reading for the outsider and does not boast the intellectual vigor and excitement of the *Forverts*. Its Yiddish is light-years better than that of their social-democratic antagonists, however.

The third Yiddish newspaper in New York is the weekly *Algemeyner Zhurnal* (*Algemeiner Journal—General Journal*), a pro-Lubavitch paper that is trying to attract modern Orthodox and secular readers. It features heavy coverage of religious news in Israel and the United States, with (currently) much emphasis on the continuing "who is a Jew" controversy. It is written in a respectable, if somewhat ponderous, Yiddish. Feminists and the non-Orthodox might be put off by the total absence of photographs of women and the near-total absence of photographs of non-Orthodox Jewish men (exception: important politicians, especially in the company of Orthodox Jews). For all that, however, it provides a literate and cogent view of the news from a perspective shared by many Jews.

Lastly, we would like to recommend an excellent Yiddish newspaper published in Israel, the *Letste Nayes—Latest News*—edited by Mordkhe Tsanin, an outspoken and consistent advocate of Yiddish among his often-hostile countrymen. The *Letste Nayes* publishes, in a Yiddish ranging from impeccable to very serviceable, news of Israel and the world without a hint of ethnic quaintness; here Yiddish is the workaday language of communication, taken (delightfully) quite for granted as the contemporary language it is. This makes the paper great for increasing one's vocabulary: what better way is there to learn sports terminology than by reading Olympic coverage? Subscriptions are prohibitive to all but the affluent, but a separate subscription to the Friday edition only is available, and single copies are on sale at the larger agencies—in New York, at Hotaling's in Times Square and at the newsstand on Broadway and 96th Street, among others.

There are Yiddish dailies and weeklies in dozens of foreign cities. Try asking for a Yiddish paper when you travel to Paris or Montevideo or Montreal or Mexico City. You'll find one (or more) in each. For a complete list, see *The Jewish World Press* and the section on Yiddish periodicals in the *American Jewish Year Book*.

The future and the golden chain: Yiddish periodicals

The Yiddish press, by turns dynamic, brassy, opinionated, literary, political, and reflective, has left relatively little room for a general-interest periodical literature. There's no Yiddish *Time* or *Life*, *Better Homes and Gardens* or

Sports Illustrated, but elements of each are to be found in the daily press. Instead, Yiddish periodicals have addressed themselves to more narrowly defined readerships (the trend, incidentally, in contemporary American magazine publishing) and compete with the daily press for contributions of intellectual distinction. Every group and grouplet of the Yiddish world has one journal or a dozen, each reflecting its particular sensibility and world view (Zionist, Bundist, Communist, anarchist, territorialist, Orthodox, Hasidic) and each boasting a large or small—but fiercely loyal—readership.

There are two fairly complete listings of Jewish periodicals, both of which indicate the language of publication; between them they tell about over a hundred Yiddish magazines and journals that you can choose from. *The Jewish World Press*, $3 from the World Jewish Congress, is particularly good on foreign periodicals; "Jewish Periodicals," an annual feature of the *American Jewish Year Book*, limits itself to the United States and Canada. Editors of Yiddish journals, particularly in exotic corners of the world, always welcome inquiries from young people. One distinguished journal in Argentina wrote that currency controls made it easier to send me their issues free, and signed me up for a lifetime subscription! If you can, try writing the editorial offices in Yiddish, even if your Yiddish is weaker than weak; they'll appreciate your efforts. Always say that you're a student, if you are: it might mean a spontaneous discount.

I've put together a list of some of the more important Yiddish periodicals. It should be a good starting point in finding a group that reflects *your* sensibility and world view. After all, you also have the right to become a fiercely loyal reader.

1. *Di Goldene Keyt—The Golden Chain*, Avrom Sutskever, editor. Quarterly. Probably the best journal in Yiddish, certainly the best place to read the latest poetry. Contributions from around the world, but with an Israeli emphasis. Graphically attractive. The book reviews and scholarly reviews are uneven, but one doesn't read *Di Goldene Keyt* for these. The literary contributions are almost uniformly excellent. *Di Goldene Keyt* can hold its own with any literary journal anywhere. Subscriptions are $14 a year from *Di Goldene Keyt*—no student discount no matter how heartfelt your letter; single copies on sale at Cyco Publishing House for $4 after student discount.

2. *Di Tsukunft—The Future*, Khayim Bez (Bass), editor. Ten issues a year. *Di Tsukunft* was founded in 1892 and has become a bit stodgy with the passage of time. Nonetheless, it gives *Di Goldene Keyt* a good run for its money, with less distinguished poetry but equally good prose fiction, as a rule. The book reviews are uneven, the scholarship decidedly middlebrow but honestly so. This is the bastion of those heroically dedicated, broadly knowledgeable older men and women who educated themselves in a society that had little use for Jewish culture, who grew up with many of the Yiddish poets, writers, and activists they write about, whose works are central to the American Jewish experience. Unfortunately this retrospective orientation does not motivate the editors to seek out the works of younger Yiddishists (in contrast to, say, *Di Goldene Keyt, Oyfn Shvel*, and *Yugntruf*). Still, an important journal. Subscriptions are $7 a year from *Di Tsukunft*.

3. *Sovetish Heymland—Soviet Homeland*, Aron Vergelis, editor. Monthly. A friend of mine, a Yiddish instructor and recent immigrant from the Ukraine, told me that he routinely tears out the first and last ten pages of any Soviet periodical: most of the scurrilous propaganda is clustered there. It might be a good idea to do that with *Sovetish Heymland*, the only Yiddish periodical the Russians permit to be published in a country of over three million Jews, many of whom speak Yiddish. (Actually there's also the *Birobidzhaner Shtern*, a skimpy newspaper of translations from *Pravda* that is virtually devoid of Jewish content.) But to ignore *Sovetish Heymland* altogether would be to deprive yourself of a first-class literary magazine, graphically the most handsome in Yiddish anywhere. More importantly, the prose fiction, both contemporary and reprinted, is the most consistently good in the world—this despite the loss through emigration of many Soviet Yiddish writers and despite the freedom and affluence of the United States. Perhaps Yiddish fiction thrives in adversity. Another important feature of *Sovetish Heymland* is works by Yiddish writers murdered by Stalin, many appearing in print for the first time; this takes some courage on the editor's part. Well worth a subscription at $6.40 a year from Four Continent Book Corp.

A proof of the relevance for its readers of Yiddish periodical journalism is to be found, paradoxically, in the graphically and typographically undistinguished appearance of the majority of Yiddish periodicals: one assumes that they are read, since they'd do no good for anyone's coffee table.

4. Two literary journals with contributions exclusively by Israeli-Yiddish writers (many of them recent immigrants from the Soviet Union—which is why this listing follows that of *Sovetish Heymland*) are the *Yerusholayimer Almanakh—Jerusalem Almanac*—and *Bay Zikh—At Home*. They are both sold as single copies only and are available at Cyco. Prices vary.

5. *Yidishe Kultur—Yiddish Culture*, Itche Goldberg, editor. Ten issues a year. The journal of the American fellow travelers, *Yidishe Kultur* reflects the sensibilities of its knowledgeable and humane editor, Itche Goldberg. Current literary contributions of mixed quality; excellent reprints of older Yiddish literature; sound critical and review articles, especially those written by Goldberg or reprinted from the works of pre-Stalin Soviet critics. Scorned by many and not a little dangerous to have in your possession during the McCarthy era, it is controversial in Yiddish circles to this day. Subscriptions are $10 a year from Ykuf.

6. *Oyfn Shvel—On the Threshold*, Mordkhe Schaechter, editor. Quarterly, at least in principle. Activist, lively, engaged, encouraging to Yiddish-speaking youth, edited by a distinguished linguist. The editor's column, "Laytish Mame-Loshn," is a forum for the defense of a pure and contemporary Yiddish. His suggestions for neologisms, chastisement of sloppy writers and speakers, ex cathedra tone (designed, one suspects, to stir up the readership and provoke them to thought) have created tempests of dissent or approbation, as well as personal attacks upon him bordering on the maniacal. Regrettably, perhaps, the sociopolitical content of the journal has all but disappeared (it is the organ of the Freeland League, the Jewish territorialist movement), and the quality of the literary contributions ranges from almost awful to simply awful. Nonetheless, a valuable journal. Subscriptions are $5 a year from the Freeland League.

7. *Yugntruf—The Call of Youth*, Gitl Schaechter, editor. Quarterly. Why be modest? *Yugntruf* is the only journal in Yiddish edited entirely by young adults, and a damn good journal it is. Unlike most student publications, which bud, flower, and wither in short order, *Yugntruf* has been published continuously for fourteen years, new generations of editors and contributors replacing the old. Strictly neutral politically (though it publishes political polemics by individual contributors that the establishment Yiddish press wouldn't dare touch) and strictly neutral religiously (secularists and Orthodox work side by side on the editorial board), *Yugntruf* has provided a forum for the best and brightest of the Yiddish youth movement. The journal is not unflawed: if *Di Tsukunft* shows its age, *Yugntruf* shows its youth. There are, alas, no geniuses on staff, and the literary contribution cannot (yet) compete with those in the "adult" journals. The language too is a bit untried and contrived (with exceptions, like the folksy prose of a former editor, Rakhmiyel Peltz), but this is a positive sign rather than the reverse: it shows that *Yugntruf* is attracting co-workers not just from the "tooth breakers" who are struggling for a not-yet-attained mastery of the language. Subscriptions are $2 a year for students and young adults, $4 for the almost-young, from *Yugntruf*.

8. *Di Yugnt-Shtime—Voice of Youth*, edited by a collective. Irregular. One of the most active of the partisan Yiddishist youth organizations is the Yugntbund (Jewish Socialist Youth Bund), a socialist, non-Zionist group that publishes *Di Yugnt-Shtime* as its official organ. With sections in English and Yiddish, it is a lively, aggressively Bundist, very articulate journal—a challenge to the many Yiddishists who disagree with it. Whether you applaud its positions or consider them misguided, *Di Yugnt-Shtime* is well worth reading and representative of an influential direction of Jewish thought. In English (mostly) and Yiddish. Subscriptions are $2 for four issues from the Jewish Labor Bund. The senior organization also publishes a journal, more mellow and perhaps less interesting for that very reason, *Undzer Tsayt—Our Times*. Ten issues a year; $7 per year from the Jewish Labor Bund.

9. *Kinder-Zhurnal—Children's Journal*, Bella Gottesman, editor. Quarterly. *Kinder-Tsaytung—Children's Newspaper*, Yoysef Mlotek, editor. Quarterly. Two magazines, friendly competitors, written for the Yiddish school systems and edited by competent and dedicated individuals. They should be good, but unfortunately they are not. Little thought is given, it seems, to the children who will have to use materials: there is no grading of texts by difficulty or appropriate age level, insufficient glossing of difficult words, and little of interest to an American child of the 1980s. Graphics are all too obviously lifted from books printed thirty years ago or earlier; articles focus upon famous authors' deaths rather than upon their childhood and youth; and much space is devoted (especially in the *Kinder-Tsaytung*) to self-puffery. Subscriptions to the *Kinder-Zhurnal* (much the better of the two), at $3 a year, are available from the Sholom Aleichem Folk Institute; to the *Kinder-Tsaytung*, at $2 a year, from the Arbeter-Ring.

10. *Yidishe Shprakh—The Yiddish Language*, Mordkhe Schaechter, editor. Three times a year (but in reality an annual with one triple issue); *Yivo-Bleter—YIVO Leaves*, between editors at press time. Annual, at least in principle. Two scholarly publications from the YIVO Institute for Jewish Research, the former devoted to the

Yiddish language, the latter to Yiddish and Eastern European Jewish studies. Both are of high quality. One hopes, incidentally, that *Yivo-Bleter* will actively seek contributions from the younger generation of Yiddish scholars; it's become a bit musty of late. This is a shame, since the freshest Yiddish scholarship is being driven onto the pages of English- or Hebrew-language journals, rather than remaining in the language of the texts or culture upon which it is based. *Yidishe Shprakh* is $5 a year; *Yivo-Bleter*, $6 an issue. Both from YIVO.

Hunting the Yiddish record

Records have become big business, and record companies have hired away executives from General Motors and ITT. As a result, there are few producers or marketers of phonograph records who love, or even know, their contents. Add to this the tendency of records to go into and out of print with bewildering speed, the profusion of companies (and the obscure labels on which many Yiddish records appear in the first place), and the apparent indifference of libraries to the recorded word or piece of music, and the result is an exasperating near-chaos.

There have been some brave attempts to bring some order into the world of Yiddish records. In 1964 Eleanor G. Mlotek published her excellent *List of 55 Recommended Yiddish Records* ($1.50 from the Arbeter-Ring), with complete contents and index to the more than five hundred songs they contained. Unfortunately all but a handful of the listed records are now out of print.

We have done a good deal of detective work, and the "Model Collection of Yiddish Records for the Slightly Affluent" is the result. As we go to press all the listed records were available for purchase. Though many Jewish bookstores and general record stores carry some records, there are four major sources of Yiddish records:

1. J. Levine, a book and record shop on Eldridge Street on the Lower East Side. Rabbi Kastel, the man in charge of record sales, is friendly, spirited, and willing to fill mail orders originating outside New York. The shop is dangerously browsable, and all records are sold to students at $5. At times one can do a bit better at a discount house, but that price for an import or limited pressing is unbeatable.

J. Levine has the added advantage of being two doors down from the House of Menorah, a wholesale distributor with an immense of stock of Yiddish records and sole distribution rights for a number of major Israeli labels (including CBS–Israel). They resolutely won't sell to retail customers, but will arrange for J. Levine to pick up any record they stock and sell or ship it to you. Sol Tischler, the proprietor and a vastly knowledgeable man on the subject of Yiddish recordings, will—if you call ahead to make sure that he's not too busy—be happy to advise you of new or neglected treasures.

2. The Arbeter-Ring—Workmen's Circle, bulwark of the Yiddish establishment. Its Education Department maintains a bookshop that also sells Yiddish records. They stock labels too obscure even for J. Levine and issue a series of house-label recordings. The stock is constantly changing, and the Arbeter-Ring will fill mail orders but will not special-order any record: what they have is all you can get. A "Record List" is published occasionally, cataloging, more or less, the records on hand. If you're in New York it's best to drop by.

3. What we call "Yiddish record shops." These are larger commercial record stores that have substantial collections of Yiddish records. They are, in New York, Sam Goody, King Karol (less good for browsing, but especially efficient on mail orders), and Music Masters Uptown. Check the Jewish Yel-

A half-fool is a very wise man.

A halber nar iz a gantser chochem.

Your help in keeping the listing up to date, as well as suggestions for additions or deletions, would be most appreciated.

low Pages in *Catalog 2* for possibilities in your area. In any case, these "Yiddish record shops" will order only the major labels (for Yiddish records, that means Folkways and Vanguard), although they stock some of the more obscure labels as well.

4. The record companies themselves. This is particularly attractive for Folkways records, which are rather sparsely distributed outside of the major urban centers, and for many of the smaller labels, some of which *only* sell directly to retail customers through the mails.

5. For Yiddish sheet music write

Norman Warrenbud
455 FDR Dr.
New York, N.Y. 10002

Actually, *any* record store is equipped to order Folkways or Vanguard records, but they are increasingly reluctant to do so.

A MODEL COLLECTION OF YIDDISH RECORDS FOR THE SLIGHTLY AFFLUENT

In this list we have indicated what we feel to be the least complicated way to obtain each record.

Happy listening.

Folk and art songs

1. Ruth Rubin. *Yiddish Folksongs Sung by Ruth Rubin.* Private label. Five 7″ LP disks. $10 for the set from Ruth Rubin. Ruth Rubin has the voice, manner, and singing style of an archetypal Jewish grandmother—simple, unadorned, a cappella. But don't let this fool you: Dr. Rubin is an esteemed ethnomusicologist (one of the first field collectors for the Library of Congress), and both the selection and annotation—including full texts and translations—are excellent. This series has a special bonus: Shmerke Kacerginsky, the partisan author of a number of songs of armed resistance against the Nazis, himself sings two of his songs, the well-known "Yugnt-Himne" and the unfortunately less well-known "Fun Getos Oshventshim." An acquired taste, perhaps, but my favorite of all Yiddish records.

2. Ruth Rubin. *Jewish Folk Songs.* Folkways 8740. $6.98 from Folkways or at discount from Yiddish record shops. Another collection by Dr. Rubin. The sound quality is somewhat less good but still acceptable.

3. Ruth Rubin. *Jewish Life: The Old Country.* An ethnographic collection. Folkways 3801. $6.98 from Folkways or at discount from Yiddish record shops. An assemblage of field recordings by Dr. Rubin. Not always easy listening, but essential for the student of Yiddish folklore.

4. Ruth Rubin. *Jewish Children's Songs and Games.* Folkways 3801. 10″ LP. $5.98 from Folkways or at a discount from Yiddish record shops. A delightful selection of Yiddish children's songs (complete with texts, transliterations, and translations), accompanied by Pete Seeger on the banjo. Ruth Rubin and Pete Seeger—what a combination!

5. Mark Olf. *Yiddish Folk Songs for Children.* Folkways 7234. 10″ LP. $5.98 from Folkways or at discount from Yiddish record shops. An interesting selection, balanced between better-known and seldom-heard songs for children. Unfortunately, Olf, who accompanies himself on the guitar, is not an accomplished singer, though his "folksiness" does compensate to some extent for his lack of technical polish. This is a record to learn new songs from, not to play for listening pleasure.

6. *Theodore Bikel Sings Jewish Folk Songs.* Elektra EKS-7141.

7. *Theodore Bikel Sings More Jewish Folk Songs.* Elektra ELK-165. $5 each from J. Levine, usually more expensive at Yiddish record shops.

It has become fashionable to pooh-pooh the considerable talents of Theodore Bikel or to dismiss him as too commercial or overslick. Nonetheless, his performances are professional and enjoyable; they demonstrate obvious gusto and love of the material. The all-time best-sellers of Yiddish folk song, these two records have introduced more than one generation to Yiddish music. The orchestral accompaniments are distracting and—as anyone who has heard Bikel's excellent guitar playing can testify—

he'd have done better to have accompanied himself. Texts, transliterations, and translations are provided.

8. Chava Alberstein. *Yiddish Folksongs*. CBS (*Israel*) S-62969.

9. Chava Alberstein. *Margaritkelekh*. CBS (Israel) S-63603. $5 each from J. Levine. Two records by a talented young folksinger, a sort of Israeli Joan Baez, who accompanies herself quite excellently on an acoustic guitar. The selections are sound and balanced, the performances competent and at times inspired. (Her recording of Leyvik/Gebirtig's "Leyg dayn kop oyf mayne kni" can move one to tears even after repeated listenings.) Her diction is sometimes troubling, and the inclusion of texts and translations (into English and/or Hebrew) would have been a plus, but these are still leading candidates for anyone's record library.

10. Chava Alberstein, Mike Burstein. *Yiddish Folksongs*. CBS (Israel) S-62960. $5 from J. Levine. Not bad at all, but Chava's better without Mike.

11. *Isa Kremer Sings Yiddish Folk Songs*. Greater RC 98. $5.98 from Greater Recording Company. A record too good to go out of print, this masterful if ancient recording has appeared on who knows how many obscure record labels and keeps returning to the surface. Isa Kremer was considered the foremost interpreter of Yiddish song several generations ago, and this record (with piano accompaniment by Vladimir Heifetz) shows us why. Most of the songs are not in the current standard repertoire, a definite advantage. Earlier editions were accompanied by complete Yiddish texts and transliterations; unfortunately they are not a part of this latest package.

12. *Nekhama Lifshitz Sings the Songs of Her People in the USSR*. Collector's Guild CGL-634. $5 from the Arbeter-Ring. When Lifshitz left the Soviet Union the imports of her singing were, predictably, withdrawn from the market. So this is the only recording currently available of a superb singer whose formal training does not get in the way of her folk quality. The orchestra, conducted by A. Kaptzan, is a minor distraction. Though this record is no longer in print in the technical sense, the Arbeter-Ring has a limited supply on hand; when it is exhausted, the opportunity to purchase this very special record will have slipped by, perhaps permanently.

14. *Netania Davrath Sings Yiddish Folk Songs*. Orchestra conducted by Robert DeCormier. Vanguard VSD-2127. Available at discount from Yiddish record shops. I admit to a prejudice against singers with operatic voices and training who "slum" by singing folk songs: the two styles often conflict to the benefit of neither. Netania Davrath is a happy exception, and her renditions of thirteen songs from the standard repertoire are pure and delightful. Wonder of wonders—even the orchestral accompaniments are not too ostentatious. Approximate English translations on the record jacket but no texts.

15. Raasche. *Jewish Folk Songs of Europe*. Accompanied by mandolin, balalaika, and guitar. Folkways 8712. $6.98 from Folkways or at discount from Yiddish record shops. An unusual record by a young folksinger with the voice one more often associates with Sephardic song. Indeed, Raasche sings a number of Judezmo (Ladino) songs—an excellent counterpoint to her selection of Yiddish standards. The accompaniments are lively and tasteful ("Tum Balalayke" accompanied by a balalaika, for instance), and her diction is easy to understand. The inclusion of texts, transliterations, and translations make this album particularly valuable for the student or teacher.

16. *Masterworks of the Yiddish Theatre, vol. 1*. Greater RC 64. $5.98 from the Greater Recording Company.

17. *Aaron Lebedeff Sings Fifteen Favorites of the Yiddish Theatre*. Greater RC 46. $5.98 from the Greater Recording Company. Effetes beware! These are schmaltzy reissues dubbed from masters of old 78's which the Greater Recording Company, a vest-pocket operation in Brooklyn, has apparently managed to corner. Represented are a number of matinee idols of Second Avenue during its years of greatness—among them Boris Thomashefsky, Leon Blank, Peisachke Burstein, Aaron Lebedeff, and Maurice Schwartz. One record is devoted entirely to Lebedeff, whose performances have aged quite gracefully. There's no high art here—but also none of the trashiness the theatrical tradition was prey to in its Catskill decline. It was, for me at least, quite a surprise to discover how nice many of these old songs really were. The Greater Recording Company is a bit laconic in replying to orders and inquiries. No texts, translations, or liner notes of any kind.

18. *Jan Peerce Sings Songs from "Fiddler on the Roof" and Ten Classics of Jewish Folk Song*. Orchestra conducted by Vladimir Gorschmann. Vanguard VSD-79258. Available at discount from Yiddish record shops.

19. *Jan Peerce on Second Ave.: Love Songs from the Golden Era of Yiddish Theatre.* Orchestra conducted by Gershon Kingsley. Vanguard VSD-79166. Available at discount from Yiddish record shops. The two records by Jan Peerce provide an experiment of sorts: is the undeniable attractiveness of reissued theater songs only a result of nostalgia, or can they stand independently when sung by an operatic singer with serious accompaniment and contemporary stereophonic packaging? Make your own decision. If you like these records, keep them; if not, your Aunt Sadie will love them.

20. Emil Horowitz [Gorovets] and others. *Jewish Folk Songs.* Monitor MF-309. $5.98 from Monitor Records.

21. Misha Alexandrovich, Emil Horowitz [Gorovets], Z. Shulman. *"If I Were Rothschild" and Jewish Folk Songs.* Monitor MF-332. $5.98 from Monitor Records.

22. Emil Gorovets. *First Concert in America.* $6 from Arbeter-Ring. Soviet performances of Yiddish folk music are remarkably similar in style and manner. Typically the singer is accompanied by a discreet pianist. Typically too the performances are polished and technically correct but oddly unengaged and distant from the material. The problem isn't the familiar oversinging of the American opera singer, but rather a Victorian hothouse-y feeling to the whole enterprise. Perhaps the omnipresent Soviet oversight leads them to de-emphasize the ethnic and folk qualities and to emphasize the more formal qualities of Yiddish song—personal risk being ultimately more important to the singer than artistic risk. These records present a number of Soviet Yiddish tenors (Alexandrovich and Gorovets have since emigrated) in recitals of Yiddish song. The selections are, for the most part, felicitous and a bit off the beaten path for the American listener. The first record contains two songs ("Kumt tsu forn keyn Kopresht" and "Lekhayim far sholem") by the poet Yoysef Kerler, who now lives in Israel.

23. *Emil Gorovets.* Galton (Israel) D-5804. $5 from J. Levine. An object lesson in what happens when a formal singer is permitted freedom of expression. This record of Gorovets's own compositions on contemporary themes is less disciplined than his Soviet recordings—but infinitely more dynamic.

24. Itsik Manger. *The Megilla of Itzik Manger.* Music by Dov Seltzer. Original Israeli cast recording with Pesach Burstein, Lillian Lux, Mike Burstein. In Yiddish with English commentary. CBS (Israel) S-70050. $5 from J. Levine. A delightful recording of a similarly delightful musical comedy, a playful rewriting of the Purim megillah from the common person's point of view—not exactly deflating the heroism but restating it in human terms. *The Megilla* is in the style of a Purim play—Purimshpil—the folk drama put on by Jews in Central and Eastern Europe for centuries. The Israeli cast recording is preferable to the American cast recording from a purely technical point of view; since both are available from CBS (Israel), be sure to specify the record number.

25. Shmuel Rudenski and the original Israeli cast. *A fidler oyfn dakh.* CBS (Israel) S-70020. $5 from J. Levine or the Arbeter-Ring. The best of a number of recordings of *Fiddler on the Roof* in Yiddish.

26. *Mayn sheyne leydi (My Fair Lady).* Makolit (Israel) 12050. Available to students for $5 from J. Levine. Our spies in Israel tell us that, although nothing can compare to our own Sheva Zucker's *Mayn feir Yivo*, this is nonetheless quite good—more than a mere curiosity. I wonder what they do with "The Rain in Spain"?

27. Sidor Belarsky. *Amol iz geven a mayse.* Artistic Enterprises B-107. $4 from the Arbeter-Ring, $5 from J. Levine.

28. Sidor Belarsky. *Yiddish Song Recital.* With piano accompaniment by an unnamed accompanist. Artistic Enterprises B-103. $4 from the Arbeter-Ring. Although he has been in the United States since 1930, Sidor Belarsky retains the straightforward approach of his Soviet operatic training. His records are in the process of being reissued, and it is difficult to say what exactly is in print. The situation should be clarified before long.

29. Raasche and Alan Mills. *Raasche and Alan Mills Sing Jewish Folk Songs.* Folkways 8711. $6.98 from Folkways or Yiddish record shops. There's no sexism here: Chava is better without Mike in No. 10, and here Raasche is better without Alan. Includes texts, transliterations, and translations.

30. Mark Olf. *Jewish Folk Songs.* 2 volumes. Folkways 6826, 6827. $5.98 each from Folkways or Yiddish record shops. Uninspired performances, but Olf's good diction and the accompanying texts, transliterations, and translations make these records good teaching/learning tools.

31. Norbert Horowitz, Rita Karpinovich [-Horowitz], Rokhl Horowitz. Concertina accompaniment by Allan Atlas. *Songs from The Wall: Ghetto, Partisan, Folk and Love Songs.* Folkways 3558. $6.98 from Folkways or Yiddish record shops. Only in the vaguest sense a cast recording of the John Hersey–Millard Lampell Broadway play, this record is more properly a collection of Yiddish songs, the majority of which are non-Holocaust folk songs, but all of which are tinged by the interspersal of ghetto ("Yisrolik") and partisan ("Shtil, di nakht iz oysgeshternt") songs, hauntingly sung by Rita Karpinovich, Norbert Horowitz, and their young daughter, Rokhl. The concertina and accordion accompaniments are perfect. A beautiful and important record. Includes texts, transliterations, and translations.

32. *Songs of the Vilna Ghetto.* Produced by the House of the Ghetto Fighters of Kibbutz Lohamei Hagetaot and performed by various artists. CBS (Israel) 63345. $5 from J. Levine. On the one hand, this record presents an excellent selection of ghetto and resistance songs and strikes the right balance between sorrow and defiance. On the other hand, some (indeed most) of the performances are slick and superficial. Chava Alberstein and Nama Hendel, for example, give fine performances, while Shimon Israeli and the chorus of the CBS Israel Orchestra sing the "Partizaner lid" with the passion and conviction of just another recording gig—an inexcusable blasphemy. There are texts and a booklet in Hebrew, English, and Yiddish, but no transliterations or translations of the songs themselves.

33. *Yiddish Songs of Work and Struggle.* Performed by members of the Jewish Student Bund. Private label. Available from the Jewish Socialist Youth Bund. This is an excellent recording of Yiddish labor songs, an important portion of the Yiddish folk song treasure—and one underrepresented in the sea of lullabies and love songs that comprise the other records. (Ruth Rubin's are an exception.) The performers are youthful, spirited, and stirring, if not always entirely professional. Regardless of your emotional reaction to the ubiquitous Red flags and workers' blood in these songs, this is an essential record. Complete texts, transliterations, and translations are enclosed.

34. The Pennywhistlers. *Folksongs of Eastern Europe.* Nonesuch H-72007. $5 from J. Levine or at discount from Yiddish record shops.

35. Paul Robeson. *Favorite Songs.* Monitor MPS-580. $5.98 from Monitor Records. Neither of these is really a collection of Yiddish songs, but both contain a sprinkling of Yiddish songs and both are extraordinary performances (though quite different from one another). The Pennywhistlers is a group of seven women who usually perform Eastern European (Serbian, Macedonian, Bulgarian, Russian, etc.) songs in an a cappella manner somewhat reminiscent of women singing while harvesting grain in the fields. Their Yiddish songs wind up sounding like these too and are hauntingly beautiful reminders of the closeness between the Jewish and Slavic folk traditions; "Di arbuzn," a wonderful song comparing the singer's love to ripe watermelons, is clearly Slavic in inspiration.

Paul Robeson sings two Yiddish songs on his record, "Vi azoy lebt der keyser" and "Zog nit keynmol," the latter stirringly and to great effect. One can glimpse the fervor of the American fellow travelers here and get a retrospective taste of how great their disappointment must have been.

36. Lazar Weiner. *Musical Settings of Yiddish Poetry.* Bianca Sauler, soprano; Lazar Weiner, composer, at the piano. Private label. $5.50 postpaid from Naomi Smith.

37. *The Yiddish Art Song.* Leon Lishner, bass; Lazar Weiner, piano. $7.50 postpaid from the University of Washington Press. The Yiddish musical tradition has, for the most part, been a folk tradition, in which even composed songs were written in the folk vein (often set to the music of older folk songs) and then quickly absorbed into the folk tradition. The works of Lazar Weiner, foremost composer of the Yiddish art song, defy this process, since their musical idiom is so different from that of other Yiddish composers—more like Poulenc than Gebirtig. They take some getting used to,

A man should live if only to satisfy his curiosity

Yiddish proverb

trans. Jarecki/Maurice Samuel

but the settings of poems by Segal, Krul, Rolnik, Glatshteyn, Leyvik, Mani Leyb, and others are delicate and true to the poetry they complement. Weiner has made a courageous choice to remain with Yiddish texts, rather than to seek a broader audience in another language; he deserves our respect and his work merits our attention. The performance on the first of these recordings is distinctly better than those on the second; Bianca Sauler has a fine, young soprano, Leon Lishner a bass well past its prime.

Recitations and "word concerts"

1. Herts Grosbard. *Vort-konsertn oyf plates.* EAV (Educational Audio Visual). 10 disks. $8 each from the Arbeter-Ring. This is a remarkable series of readings by the Yiddish Olivier, an artist who added the term *vort-konsert*—word concert—to the Yiddish language. The records are no longer in print at the manufacturer, but the Arbeter-Ring has a fair sampling of the remaining disks (hence their relatively high price). In abbreviated form, the contents are as follows: vol. 1: Elyezer Shteynbarg and A. Lutski; vol. 2: Moyshe Leyb Halpern; vol. 3: Itsik Manger, Yankev Glatshteyn; vol. 4: Y. L. Perets, Sh. An-Ski; vol. 5: H. Leyvik, Arn Tseytlin; vol. 6: Sholem-Aleykhem; vol. 7: Kadye Molodovski, Y. Y. Segal, Y. L. Perets, Elyezer Shteynbarg, Moyshe Nadir; vol. 8: Mani Leyb, Kadye Molodovski, Elyezer Shteynbarg; vol. 9: Itsik Manger ("Velvl Zbarzher shraybt briv tsu Malkele der sheyner"); vol. 10: Kh. N. Byalik. An indispensable collection.

2. Sholem-Aleykhem. *"If I Were Rothschild" and Jewish Folk Songs.* Recited by E. Kaminka. Monitor MF-332. $5.98 from Monitor Records. This is record no. 21 from the first part of this listing. In addition to the songs described earlier, Kaminka recites "Ven ikh bin Rotshild" in good, straightforward Yiddish. Unless you're also buying it for the music, volume 6 of the Grosbard collection is preferable. No text or translation.

3. *Itsik Manger leyent Itsik Manger.* CBS (Israel) 62693. $5 from J. Levine. A fine recording in which the Yiddish folk poet reads from his own works. No text or translation.

4. Avrom Sutskever. *The Poetry of Avrom Sutskever.* Folkways 9947. $6.98 from Folkways or Yiddish record shops. The Yiddish modernist poet and editor of *Di Goldene Keyt,* Israel's foremost Yiddish periodical, reads from his works. Edited and annotated by Professor Ruth Wisse of McGill University.

5. I. (Tsuny) Rymer. *Stories by Sholem Aleichem.* Private label. $5 from the Arbeter-Ring. Rymer is a talented amateur interpreter of Sholem-Aleykhem's works, made more interesting (but more difficult for the beginner) by Rymer's authentic Ukrainian-Yiddish accent—close to what must have been the author's own Yiddish. He reads "Esther," "What a Succah," "Milkhiks," "On Account of a Hat."

6. I. Rotblum. *Yiddish Literature.* Private label. $5 from the Arbeter-Ring. Uninspired readings of Mendele's "Dos kelbl," Sholem-Aleykhem's "Kidalto vekidasto," Perets's "Sholem-bayis," and selected poetry by Yankev Glatshteyn. A good selection.

7. Gustave Berger. *Sholom Aleichem.* Folkways 9907. $6.98 from Folkways or at discount from Yiddish record shops. An excellent reading, with much vigor and with no vulgarity, of three stories, in Yiddish: "Der daytsh," "A mayse mit a grinhorn," and "Mister Grin hot a dzhab." Recommended.

8. Menasha Skulnik. *Stories of Sholem Aleichem.* Caedmon TC-1173. Available at discount from Yiddish record shops. Menasha Skulnik is a gifted reader, and here he reads—in English—five stories by Sholem-Aleykhem translated by Charles Cooper: "Happy Millionaire," "A Matter of Advice," "It's a Lie," "Chanukah and Pinochle," and "High School." It's a shame that Skulnik didn't read half as many stories, but in both languages.

9. Sholem-Aleykhem. *Di kleyne mentshelekh.* Stories read by Shmuel Rudenski, Shmuel Segal, Elye Goldenberg. 2-record set. CBS (Israel) 62702/3. $7 from J. Levine or the Arbeter-Ring. Newly arrived from Israel, this record contains Yiddish readings of several Sholem-Aleykhem stories. I haven't heard it yet, but the readers are accomplished Yiddish actors and should do a good job.

10. *Ikh hob lib yidish/I Love Yiddish: A Mini-course Based on Thirty-Two Gems of Poetry, Folksong, and Humor.* Presented by Emanuel S. Goldsmith. Audio Heritage AH-760723. $6.95 from Audio Heritage or the Arbeter-Ring. This is no more

Az Got vil ainem dos hartz opstroissen, git er im a groissen saichel.

IT was supposed to say "Es iz shver tsu trogen, un avekvarfen tut bang." but he mixed up the signs. THAT'S why he's crying.

When God wants to break a man's heart, He gives him a lot of sense.

it's too heavy to carry and too precious to throw away.

a "minicourse" than any other record, and Professor Goldsmith does himself a disservice with the come-on, especially since the record brings together a very enjoyable cross section of Yiddish poetry, folktales, songs—all declaimed and sung with enviable enthusiasm. Most important, because the selections obviously reflect one sensitive reader's tastes, they give the impression of connectedness despite the thematic and formal diversity of the collection. Complete texts, transliterations, and translations are enclosed.

11. Dzigan. *Lakht mit mir*. Galton (Israel) 5761. $5 from J. Levine or the Arbeter-Ring. A representative comedy album by a well-known Yiddish comedian who went on a hunger strike to encourage the Israeli television authority to permit him to perform in Yiddish. Comedy is a matter of taste, but Dzigan is widely popular and has none of the decadent Catskill vulgarity with which many American albums are tainted. Intelligent fun.

Yiddish flicks

There's a Yiddish film called *Lekhayim* that I've always wished I could have seen. It was only one reel long, silent (the Yiddish was in the titles), and probably not very good. Not many people ever got to see it; perhaps no one now alive remembers it. But *Lekhayim,* filmed in Russia in 1910, was nonetheless a milestone—the first Yiddish film.

Between one hundred and two hundred Yiddish films have been made since then, a process described in a very interesting article (in Yiddish) by Dovid Mates, "Tsu der geshikhte fun yidishe films," in the *Ikuf-Almanakh 1961* ($7 from Ykuf). Many other Yiddish films have shared *Lekhayim*'s fate: victims of neglect, willful destruction, or the inevitable disintegration of the old nitrate-based film stock. But over fifty have survived, all interesting and a few genuine masterpieces.

Just as Yiddish literature has flourished in the most diverse locations, so have Yiddish films been produced wherever larger groups of Yiddish speakers have lived. (The most fertile areas were Russia, Poland, and the United States.) And like Yiddish literature, the films most frequently have more in common with one another than with the cinema of the dominant cultures, having not only a culture and language in common, but also a shared filmic language. For all their family resemblances, however, Yiddish films span the artistic gamut: some were shot outdoors (in part: *Grine felder—Green Fields*) or on location (in part: *Der dibek—The Dybbuk*); others were made under carefully controlled studio conditions (*Mirele Efros*). Still others were essentially filmed versions of stage productions (*Got, mentsh un tayvl—God, Man and Devil—*and *Keynig Lir—King Lear*)—not necessarily unfortunate, since the productions were often distinguished. Qualitatively, too, the films range from the campily trashy *Ketskil honimun—Catskill Honeymoon—*through a vast middlebrow assortment of dramas and musical comedies (*The Cantor's Son* and *Yankl der shmid—The Singing Blacksmith*) to a few films that are the equal of any movies ever made.

We have assembled a model list of a half dozen Yiddish films you might want to sample. The descriptions have been adapted from the catalog of the Rutenberg and Everett Yiddish Film Library (more about them later), and we've added comments from our own perspective:

1. *Der Dibek—The Dybbuk*, Poland, 1937, 120 minutes; studio/outdoor production; directed by Michael Waczinski; based on the play by Sh. An-Ski. A brooding mystery-melodrama about passion, piety, and superstition in a nineteenth-century Polish shtetl. A mystically minded yeshive-bokher, learning that the love of his life, pledged to him since before his birth, is to be given to another man, invokes the aid of the supernatural to prevent the match. He dies in the ecstasy of the attempt, and his soul takes possession of his beloved's body. The wedding, din toyre—rabbinical trial—to which the dead father's soul is summoned, and the final exorcism are unforgettably numinous. Interesting portrayal of the Hasidic rebbe who performs the exorcism. This is my candidate for finest Yiddish film. It was produced, incidentally, by a socialist

collective with decidedly capitalist American backing of over $1 million, and it's good to remember that the Jewish society which produced *Der dibek* was a modern urban one: the shtetl milieu was no less exotic to the actors and producers than it is to the audience of the 1980s. A second tidbit: the romantic leads married one another in real life and are alive and well and living in New York City.

2. *Grine felder—Green Fields,* USA, 1937, 95 minutes; studio/outdoor production; directed by Edgar G. Ulmer and Jacob Ben-Ami; based on the play by Perets Hirshbeyn; starring Michael Goldstein and Herschel Bernardi. Romance about the legendary youth of the great Hasidic master Leyvi-Yitskhok of Barditshev. Wandering across the Pale of Settlement in search of "true Jews," the orphaned, otherworldly young scholar happens upon a family of simple Jewish peasants, who take him in as a boarder and tutor for their children and eventually induce him to marry their daughter. Interesting juxtaposition of the two opposed life-styles. *Grine felder* shows what a strong influence a film's director can have, even when he remains faithful to the text. Hirshbeyn's famous play raises important questions about the respective roles of scholarship and a life close to the soil—questions vital to the former Jewish collectives in Europe and to the present ones in Israel. The film version emphasizes the—admittedly quite funny—machinations of the families' designs on the young scholar. This is a case of comic relief overshadowing the basic drama, not unusual in American films of the 1930s.

"No! Please!"
she pleaded
"It wasn't Ham.
It was Smoked Turkey!"

3. *Mirele Efros,* USA, 1939, 91 minutes; studio production; directed by Josef Berne; based on the Jacob Gordin play; starring Berta Gersten. Set in Grodno at the turn of the century, this film shatters the stereotype of East European Jews as invariably poor and rehabilitates the much-maligned Jewish mother as well. Mirele, a noble, pious widow and a successful businesswoman in her own right, is virtually evicted from her own home by the spiteful, self-seeking woman her son marries—the wife she herself chose for him before discovering the woman's true character. An elaborate, sophisticated production of a stage classic, with a fine cast. Includes a marvelous depiction of a traditional tnoim—betrothal.

4. *Yankl der shmid—The Singing Blacksmith,* USA, 1938, 95 minutes; musical, studio production; directed by Edgar G. Ulmer; based on the play by Dovid Pinski, starring Moyshe Oysher and Herschel Bernardi. Oysher plays a tough, swashbuckling, illiterate shtetl blacksmith who falls in love with his polar opposite—a sweet, refined young woman who, to everyone's surprise, needs no persuasion from the local shatkhente—matchmaker—to agree to the match. The blacksmith is tamed by the marital bliss that ensues, until a former flame of his youth shows up and tries to spoil things. Includes some wonderful caricatures of familiar types and, of course, a feast of Oysher's singing. Wonderful middlebrow entertainment, *Yankl der shmid* should be projected on the largest possible screen and shown as late at night as possible to a boisterous, popcorn-eating audience.

5. *Tevye,* USA, 1939, 80 minutes; studio/outdoor production; directed by and starring Maurice Schwartz; music by Sholom Secunda; based on the novel by Sholem-Aleykhem. A moving adaptation of the episode in Sholem-Aleykhem's familiar novel in which one of the daughters falls in love with the intellectual son of a local peasant. Their courtship and marriage pit Tevye's affection for his daughter against his deep, and ultimately triumphant, loyalty to tradition. But the girl too is torn, and when her parents and sister are arbitrarily expelled from the town she decides to cast her lot with them once again. The film is studded with memorable scenes—Khavele's showing her uncomprehending father the volume of Gorki that her suitor has given her; the colorful Ukrainian wedding and Tevye's mournful havdole after it; Tevye gently teaching psalms to his grandchildren when the expulsion order arrives—all of which owe their power and subtlety to Schwartz's bravura performance and direction. A great film by any standard, and miles above its derivative, *Fiddler on the Roof,* in its authenticity.

Missing from the film, of course, is Sholem-Aleykhem's marvelous narrative, where Tevye tells his story in the first person, simultaneously endearing him and distancing him from a more sophisticated reader; this results at times in our taking Tevye's point of view as that of the story itself—rather than permitting us a bit of ironic breathing room. This is an excellent film nonetheless. (There is, incidentally, a Soviet *Tevye* adaptation that reportedly emphasizes the social aspects of tsarist anti-Semitism.)

Each of these films is available from the Rutenberg and Everett Yiddish Film Library, located on the Brandeis University campus. Rental price for one showing is $55 per film (including shipping but not return); four films "in one season" may be rented for a total of $180. All of the above-mentioned films— and virtually all in their collection—have English subtitles. These are sometimes provided only on a need-to-know basis, however: dialogue not essential

to the plot is often left unglossed—to one's general frustration even if there's no sacrifice of intelligibility.

The Yiddish Film Library, which has obtained a spectacular collection of Yiddish films once belonging to pioneer producer/director Joseph Seiden, is systematically rescuing their treasures from disintegration by refilming them on stable stock and is also systematically making them more accessible to those who have not (yet) learned Yiddish by retitling them. They deserve our admiration.

Two commercial distributors also have Yiddish films for rent: Audio Branden (Macmillan) and Contemporary Films (McGraw-Hill). The former rents a number of charming, if dated, Molly Picon musicals, as well as an interesting Soviet compilation of scenes from Sholem-Aleykhem stories performed by the Moscow Yiddish Art Theater (*Laughter through Tears*, USSR, 1933).

We didn't lose count in promising descriptions of a half dozen Yiddish films. The sixth, and in many ways most exciting, was made by a young Yiddish filmmaker in 1975 as his master's thesis at NYU. It's called *Dos mazl*—*Luck* or *Happiness*—and retells a Yiddish folktale. While the tale itself is simple and charming, the movie is quite sophisticated in structure: children, obviously very American and not wholly attentive, are listening to an old storyteller at what appears to be (and in reality is) a summer camp. As he spins his tale the children almost, although never entirely, "believe themselves into" the Eastern European world of the story. (The transformation is never complete, and one of my favorite scenes has a young girl, dressed now in clothes of the shtetl, smile to the camera, exposing her 1970s orthodonture.) There are plays-within-plays, dreams-within-dreams, and everything, of course, comes out as it should. Music and dialogue in Yiddish; subtitles in English. For rent at approximately $50 from Josh Waletzky. Essential.

Yiddish radio: the great unknown

It is possible that radio people are so dedicated to the broadcast medium that they have abandoned the written word: that's the only explanation that comes to mind for their unique and near-unanimous disinclination to reply to our letters and phone calls or to send their promised schedules. So here you're pretty much on your own. Which is a shame, since there's a good amount of fine Yiddish programming beaming through the ether, if only one is lucky enough to intercept it.

The home of Yiddish broadcasting, "the station that speaks your lan-

It's good to have an honest, upbeat ending to this section: Josh, as well as at least one other young film person, is planning additional Yiddish films. Look for news of them in the supplements to *The Yiddish Catalog*, available from Yugntruf.

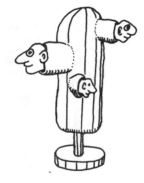

There's a final radio alternative: make your own Yiddish radio programs. Many universities have student stations, and at least one Yugntrufnik, Perl Teitelbaum, broadcast her own show on the radio station at SUNY, Buffalo. Instant fame!

guage," is WEVD in New York, FM (98 MHz). The station was named after Eugene V. Debs, symbolizing its fiery Jewish-socialist past; now it presents programming for and from all segments of the Jewish community. But if you tune to WEVD and hear Spanish or Croatian or Urdu, you haven't made a mistake—the station lends its airwaves to other national groups as a public service and as a way of making ends meet.

For people new to the Yiddish world there's a particular joy in listening to Yiddish radio, understanding first one word here and there, then getting the gist of the broadcast, and finally noticing the words and expressions that you *don't* understand, rather than the other way around. For beginners the content of a program doesn't really make much difference; just the fact that it's there is sufficient. As your Yiddish improves, however, so will your selectivity, especially since the quality of programming on WEVD varies tremendously. As a rule the afternoon programs assembled by the station itself are only fair to middling; the public service spots for a mind-boggling array of Jewish causes and institutions are often more interesting than the programs they interrupt. WEVD does feature some really excellent programs, though, and the following guide, somewhat edited, was prepared by Dovid-Elye Fishman:

1. *Di "Forverts"-sho—The "Forward" Hour*: a variety hour sponsored by the *Jewish Daily Forward,* Sundays at 11 A.M. Guest performers sing Yiddish favorites. The repertoire is limited and may begin to bore you after a year's listening; one wishes the singers were encouraged to explore the not-so-well-known numbers. Zvee Scooler is genuinely hilarious as the grammayster in a rhymed comic review of the week's events.

2. *Der vekhentlekher program fun Yidishn Kultur-Kongres—The Weekly Program of the Congress for Jewish Culture*: a weekly feature with Khayim Bez, Sundays at 2:45 P.M. Bez speaks interestingly about Yiddish literature and culture, topics about which he is well informed. His Yiddish, though rich in vocabulary, is relatively easy to understand—his diction is clear and he speaks slowly.

3. *Lomir lernen a blat gemore—Let's Study a Page of the Gemore*: a weekly Talmud shiur with Rabbi Pinchas Teitz, Saturdays at 9:30 P.M. This is a fine example of genuine Gemore Yiddish. The terminology, intonation, and dialect are those of the Lithuanian yeshives and provide a glimpse into the world and mind-set of a large group of Yiddish speakers with whom most not-so-Orthodox Jews are not privileged to come into contact.

4. *Nayes fun der vokh—News of the Week:* Shelomo Ben Israel commentary on the news of the week, Sundays at noon. This may well be the best-informed, most intelligent radio analysis of Jewish news in *any* language. Highly recommended. Ben-Israel has picked up about a dozen German words somewhere along the line and sprinkles them liberally into his commentary, but this annoying mannerism shouldn't deter you.

A complete program guide is usually available from WEVD. The rest, as we said, is the great unknown. Rumor has it that Yiddish programs are or were being broadcast on the following stations in the U.S.: WADS, Ansonia, Conn.; WAVA, Arlington, Va.; WIBF, Jenkintown, Pa.; WNEB, Worcester, Mass.; WTOW, Townsend, Md.; WSAY, Rochester, N.Y.; and KCSM, Northbridge, Calif. Miami and Chicago are also rumored to have broadcasts in Yiddish. Check them out. (Fortunately, Canadian Yiddish broadcasts are documented by the Canadian Jewish Congress, from whom we could learn a bit.)

There are also Yiddish broadcasts on international shortwave radio, all receivable on the East Coast and several receivable (if the weather is right) farther west. For schedules write the Israel Broadcasting Authority, Embassy of France, Radio Bucharest, and call (they won't tell their address!) Radio Moscow Information. In Israel there are regular Kol Yisrael broadcasts, as well as Moscow's "Radio Station Peace and Progress" and the missionary "Trans-World Radio Monte Carlo," which will try to convert you in your favorite language.

Learning Yiddish II: book learning

Student One: "Yidn zaynen haynt a folk fun draytsn milyon."
Student Two: "Yidn voynen af ale kontinentn."

This isn't a secret code, but it does identify every student who's used Uriel Weinreich's *College Yiddish*, the best textbook for the serious student. (The students are repeating the first two sentences from lesson 1.) Weinreich, son of one of the founders of the YIVO, was an eminent linguist who wrote *the* book (and, as we'll see, the dictionary) when it comes to Yiddish texts. *College Yiddish* is intelligent, comprehensive, admirable. It is also a bit creaky, showing its age—almost thirty years. A magnificent compendium of Yiddish grammar and syntax, *College Yiddish* sometimes seems more like a reference book than a modern textbook: the most difficult concepts—articles and adjective declination, for example—are taught full steam ahead, rather than spread over a number of noncontiguous lessons. Mixed bag that it is, *College Yiddish* is the best we've got and is light-years ahead of any competition. All university courses use it; so should you, even if it's a bit scary at first. It's available from YIVO (ask for the student discount—$6 plus postage). A Hebrew edition has been prepared by the Hebrew University of Jerusalem.

Dovid-Leyzer Gold, professor of Yiddish at Haifa University, wrote a correspondence course in Yiddish based upon Weinreich's text that's been published by the University of Wisconsin Extension. Though dry as dust, this guide through *College Yiddish* breaks down the lessons into more assimilable units.

YIVO also has a set of language laboratory tapes for *College Yiddish*, professionally recorded and almost worth the $100 they cost. Try talking your department, Hillel foundation, or rich uncle into buying the set. Texts are included.

There are other textbooks, but their usefulness is limited. One beginning text is Jean Jofen's *Yiddish for Beginners*. Several schools use it to ease students into Weinreich, since it's less formidable and the model conversations are fun. The book is full of inexcusable mistakes, however, and should be used with care. It's also available from the Arbeter-Ring; it costs $2.75. Another possibility is Yudl Mark's *Invitation to Yiddish*, a manual with two LP disks, available from the American Jewish Congress or the Arbeter-Ring for $8. Advantages: excellent dialogues in excellent Yiddish. Disadvantages: emphasis on spoken Yiddish, little emphasis on grammar, almost none on reading or writing. The records very nearly defeat their purpose by presenting conversations at a n u n u s u a l l y s l o w p a c e (yawn), losing thereby most of the intonation. Worth having, nonetheless. The last of this group is a set of six cassettes with a manual by Wolf and Sylvia Younin. Wolf Younin is a gifted reader and the author of an interesting weekly column ("Shprakhvinkl—Language Corner") in the *Forverts*, and the Younins' *Let's Learn Yiddish* is a lively, if not terribly rigorous, set of 48 lessons; it was, by the way, broadcast on WNYC-FM in New York awhile back. $25 (!) from the Arbeter-Ring.

You'll probably also want a dictionary fairly early in your Yiddish learning. The best by far is Uriel Weinreich's *Modern English-Yiddish, Yiddish-English Dictionary* (New York: McGraw-Hill, 1968). It costs $23.50 at bookstores, or $12.50 for students from YIVO. Did you ever wonder how to say "beatnik," "show-cause order," "stampede," or "walrus" in Yiddish? They're all there.

Another worthwhile dictionary—though some of my purist colleagues might wince at the thought—is Alexander Harkavy's 1898 *Yiddish-English*

P.S.: Don't let the criticism deter you. It really *is* worth the trouble to work through *College Yiddish*.

Avoid, at any price, Harkavy's *English-Yiddish, Yiddish-English Dictionary* written in 1891, however: he hadn't yet mastered English.

Dictionary or his 1928 *Yiddish-English-Hebrew Dictionary.* (The former is $7.50, less 20 percent student discount, the latter $8.50 less discount at Cyco.) Harkavy's spelling is hopelessly out of date—there was a major spelling reform in 1935/36—and he is rather overfond of heavily Germanized words—daytshmerish, in Yiddish—but he has many words not to be found in Weinreich. Harkavy is indispensable for reading texts from the late nineteenth and early twentieth centuries because of his rich fund of localisms and vulgarisms. (Weinreich was a bit of a prude.)

A third dictionary is the all-Yiddish *Groyser verterbukh fun der yidisher shprakh,* the Yiddish OED. Three volumes have appeared to date (with one in preparation), and the dictionary is still in the middle of alef, the first letter! A treasure and a tribute to the editors, who worked without aid of computers or graduate student slave labor. $25 per volume (less 20 percent discount) from Cyco.

Yiddish spelling is sometimes a bit tricky. Two good guides are Mordkhe Schaechter's *Kurs fun yidisher ortografye* and Max Weinreich/Mordkhe Schaechter's *Yidisher ortografisher vegvayzer.* The Yiddish words of Hebrew origin are treated in Y. Levin's *Verterbikhl fun hebreish-yidishe verter,* a blessing for students of Yiddish who don't have a background in Hebrew. The *Kurs* ($2.50) and the *Verterbikhl* ($1) are both available from Cyco at a discount; the *Vegvayzer* can be gotten from Cyco or the Benyumin Schaechter Foundation for the Advancement of Standard Yiddish for $4 less discount.

If the *Groyser verterbukh* is the Yiddish OED, Nokhm Stutchkoff's *Oytser fun der yidisher shprakh* is our Roget's *Thesaurus.* The *Oytser* is the treasure that its name implies. It's not always easy to find the words you want—the index is an exercise in omissions and typos—but the treasure is worth digging for. Good browsing at $12 less discount from Cyco or $10 net from YIVO.

Along these lines, there's a pocket guidebook in the Dover Say-It-In series written by the ubiquitous U. W. There are English, Yiddish, and transliterated Yiddish versions of many useful phrases. Take it with you on the next trip to Europe, Israel, Latin America, South Africa . . . Available at bookstores or directly from Dover Publications at 95¢ postpaid.

If, on the other hand, you're planning a quick getaway to Mars or Pluto, must reading is the terminological guidebook to *Space and Astrophysics* being readied for publication by Mordkhe Schaechter and Shaye Mallow. The first of this projected series of terminological guides is tastier and more down to earth: *Food/Mit a gutn apetit!*, available from its author, Mordkhe Schaechter, at $1.50 postpaid.

At least two textbooks are in preparation: an intermediate Yiddish language text called *Yiddish II,* by Mordkhe Schaechter, and an introductory Yiddish literary reader by Dovid-Noyekh Miller. The second edition of *Yiddish II* is available for $8 from Mordkhe Schaechter; information about the reader is available from the author at Queens College.

A word of warning: keep miles away from the textbooks published by and for the Yiddish school systems. *Fun with Dick and Jane* is a bore in any language.

If you live in Nome or Tuscaloosa, or if you already are pretty far along on the way to learning Yiddish, you might want to go it alone using one or more of the books we've just described. But think of taking a course. It will be more fun, easier to learn by far, and—if you're lucky—the kind of experience that's hard to talk about without sounding a bit oversentimental. Good luck.

HUNTING THE YIDDISH BOOK

Our section on buying Yiddish books doesn't begin in New York or Tel Aviv, but rather in a none-too-respectable storefront in San Diego. Sailors come and go, exchanging three science fiction books or mysteries for one in return. Old men—a bit healthier looking than their counterparts on Broadway and 42nd Street but otherwise much the same—slink in to buy books from behind the counter. A young Yiddish student is also in the shop, checking the racks of used books. Among them he finds an autographed copy, in Yiddish, of H. Leyvik's *Der goylem—The Golem.* A treasure! The book costs a dime.

Most hunters of Yiddish books have similar if less picturesque stories of extraordinary catches or of big ones that got away. In other words, the search for out-of-print Yiddish books is much the same as for antiquarian books in any language, except that—fortunately—the bookseller is less likely to know the worth of his/her wares. There is no guidebook to these stores: if another Yiddishist has already visited a certain shop it's a safe bet that the Yiddish books of value are already gone. Besides, the hunt is (nearly) as much fun as the books it flushes out.

Anyone fortunate enough to live in the Detroit area has an opportunity to do a bit of concentrated hunting at the Brandeis Book Sale. For more information, contact Mrs. Ned Mellen of the Brandeis Book Sale (Southfield). There are also Brandeis Book Sales in Chicago—another major event—Boston, and in other cities, though on a smaller scale; check with the local Brandeis Women's Committee or with the main office at Brandeis University.

Even if you don't live in Detroit, you don't have to be resigned to hunting randomly for that specific Yiddish book you need: virtually any book in print, and a large though ever-shifting selection of out-of-print titles, may be ordered from the Cyco Publishing House in New York. Cyco's manager, Yankl Gutkowicz, might grumble a bit when you ask for the 20 percent student discount to which you are entitled, but he is as knowledgeable and helpful as any bookseller I know. The bookstore—really an assemblage of rooms on the fourth floor of a building that houses a number of Yiddish organizations—is properly heymish—homey—not a bit like the impersonal formica and chrome of Brentano's.

Then there's the Lower East Side in New York, a visit to which calls for the time-tested Jewish skills of haggling and striking a bargain with the bookseller. Few books are marked with prices, and those prices are only points of

One of our correspondents describes the Detroit Brandeis Book Sale:

The Brandeis Book Sale is an annual event in Detroit, which generally takes place around September or October, in the parking lot of Northland Shopping Center (8 Mile Road and Greenfield, in Southfield, Michigan). It is housed in a large tent in which are thousands of books of all kinds, arranged on tables by subject matter. The sale lasts for about five days following a "preview night." There is a charge to get in this first night (though being there then definitely has its advantages), and after that, entrance is free.

Several tables of Yiddish (and Hebrew) books are always laid out, at which a great variety of Yiddish originals, as well as various translations of works into Yiddish, may be found. Prices vary with each book (collections may also be purchased as a whole), and the overall value of what can be found is probably unlike anything in the area (as people behind full shopping carts will attest to). In fact, many of the books to be found at the Brandeis Book Sale seem to be the very things people are running all over New York trying to find.

departure. In fact, I've often thought that a bookseller would be somewhat disappointed if a customer voluntarily paid the first price demanded. A good first stop is the shop of Bernard Morgenstern, whose sklad—storage room— which is accessible only by prior appointment, is a treasurehouse of Yiddish books. The only difficulty is that Morgenstern knows full well the worth of his stock, and spectacular bargains are thus out of the question. Another good bet is Philipp Feldheim, whose prices are lower but whose stock cannot compare with Morgenstern's. The Hebrew Publishing Company is particularly strong on folklore collections (tales of the wise men of Khelm, for example) and early sheet music of Yiddish theater songs. Their Yiddish collection is not available at their Fifth Avenue address but at a picturesque and ancient storage room, access to which is by appointment only. A good source for Yiddish books in English translation, or for English books about Yiddish, is Bloch Publishing Company, which offers a discount to faculty but not to students. J. Levine, recommended in the section on Yiddish phonograph records, extends a 20 percent discount to students.

Yiddish books printed in Israel may be obtained at reduced prices (computed in Israeli currency and then converted to dollars) from the bookstore of Y. L. Perets Farlag in Tel Aviv. The books take forever and a day to arrive here, however, and the hassle is probably only justified by a major purchase.

The National Council for Yiddish and Yiddish culture has announced the formation of an international Yiddish book club (Book-of-the-Month Club, step aside). Write to them for more information, mentioning that you are a student.

Addresses

Algemeyner Zhurnal (The Algemeiner
    Journal)
    404 Park Ave. South
    New York, NY 10016
    (212) 689-3390
All Languages Typewriter Co.
    119 W. 23rd St.
    New York, NY 10011
    (212) 243-8086, 222-6683
Alveltlekher Yidisher Kultur-Kongres
    25 E. 78th St.
    New York, NY 10021
    (212) 879-2232
American Association of Professors of
    Yiddish (AAPY)
    Academic 1309
    Queens College, CUNY
    Flushing, NY 11367
    (212) 520-7067

American Jewish Congress
    15 E. 84th St.
    New York, NY 10028
    (212) 879-4500
American Jewish Theatre
    Henry Street Settlement Arts for
    Living Center
    466 Grand St.
    New York, NY 10002
    (212) 288-2346
    Contact: Stanley Brechner, Artistic
    Dir.
Arbeter-Ring (Workmen's Circle)
    Education Dept.
    45 E. 33rd St.
    New York, NY 10016
    (212) 889-6800
Association for Jewish Studies (AJS)
    Widener Library
    Harvard University
    Cambridge, MA 02138
    Contact: Professor Charles Berlin,
    Exec. Sec.

Audio Brandon Film Center, Inc.
    34 MacQuesten Pkwy. South
    Mount Vernon, NY 10550
    (914) 664-5051
    Branches in San Francisco; Los
    Angeles; Dallas; La Grange, IL
Audio Heritage
    Sepher-Hermon Press, Inc.
    175 Fifth Ave.
    New York, NY 10010
Banner Records
    68 W. Passaic
    Rochelle Park, NJ
    (212) 695-6117, (201) 843-2670
Bar Ilan University
    Ramat Gan, Israel
    Contact: Professor Joseph Bar El
Barnes and Noble/Barnes & Noble
    Sales Annex
    Fifth Ave. at 18th St.
    New York, NY 10003
    (212) 255-8100
    Discourages mail orders.

Bernard M. Baruch College, City
University of New York
155 E. 24th St.
New York, NY 10010
Contact: Dr. Jean Jofen, Dept. of
German and Scandinavian
Behrman House
1261 Broadway
New York, NY 10001
(212) 689-2020
Ben Bonus Theater Company
(212) 686-3535
or reach them through the
Education Department of the
Arbeter-Ring
Bloch Publishing Co.
915 Broadway
New York, NY 10010
(212) 673-7910
Bnai Brith Hillel Foundation
National Office
1640 Rhode Island Ave. NW
Washington, DC 20036
(202) 393-5284
Bnai Brith Hillel Foundation
Boston University
233 Bay State Rd.
Boston, MA 02215
(617) 266-3880
Bnai Brith Hillel Foundation
Harvard University
1 Bryant St.
Cambridge, MA 02138
(617) 876-6138
Bnai Brith Hillel Foundation
Indiana University at Bloomington
730 E. 3rd St.
Bloomington, IN 47401
(812) 336-3824
Bnai Brith Hillel Foundation
Princeton University
Murray-Dodge Hall
Princeton, NJ 08540
Bnai Brith Hillel Foundation
University of California, Berkeley
Lehrhaus Judaica
2736 Bancroft Way
Berkeley, CA 94704
(415) 845-7793
Bnai Brith Hillel Foundation
University of Chicago
5715 S. Woodlawn Ave.
Chicago IL 60637
Bnai Brith Hillel Foundation
University of Wisconsin—Madison
611 Langdon St.
Madison, WI 53703
(608) 256-8361
Bnai Yiddish
387 Grand St.
New York, NY 10002
(212) 989-3162
Contact: Yitskhok Koslovsky
Brandeis University
Dept. of Near Eastern and Judaic
Studies
Waltham, MA 02154
(617) 647-2000
Contact: Professor Marvin Fox,
Chm.
Professor Joshua
Rothenberg
Brandeis Book Sale (Southfield)
22347 Essex Way Ct.
Southfield, MI 48034
(313) 354-2369
Contact: Mrs. Ned Mellen

Brown University
Dept. of German
Providence, RI 02912
(401) 863-1000
Contact: Professor Werner
Hoffmeister, Chm.
Bureau of Jewish Education/College of
Judaic Studies
639 14th Ave.
San Francisco, CA 94118
(415) 751-6983
Contact: Annette Singer, Registrar
Caedmon Records
505 Eighth Ave.
New York, NY 10018
(212) 594-3122
Camp Boiberik
3301 Bainbridge Ave.
Bronx, NY 10467
(212) 655-7336
in season:
Rhinebeck, NY 12572
Camp Hemshekh
25 E. 78th St.
New York, NY 10021 (212) 535-
0850
in season:
Mountaindale, NY 12763
(914) 434-8310
Camp Kinder Ring
45 E. 33rd St.
New York, NY 10016
(212) 889-6800
in season:
Hopewell Junction, NY 12533
(914) 226-9564
Canadian Jewish Congress
1590 McGregor
Montreal, Que., Canada
CBS Records
International Division
51 E. 52nd St.
New York, NY 10019
(212) 975-6160
Contact: Earl Price
Information on wholesale
distribution, a last resort if
J. LEVINE and HOUSE OF
MENORAH cannot help.

N. Chanin Foundation
45 E. 33rd St.
New York, NY 10016
Collector's Guild
507 Fifth Ave.
New York, NY 10011
Columbia University
Dept. of Linguistics
Philosophy Hall
New York, NY 10027
(212) 280-5529
Contact: Professor Marvin Herzog,
Chm.

Congress for Jewish Culture
see: ALVELTLEKHER YIDISHER
KULTUR-KONGRES
Contemporary Films/McGraw-Hill
1221 Avenue of the Americas
New York, NY 10020
(212) 997-2183
Cyco Publishing House
25 E. 78th St.
New York, NY 10021
(212) 535-4320
Contact: Y. Gutkowicz, Dir.
Miriam Daniels Productions
Loch Sheldrake, NY 12759
(914) 647-3230
Davke
Shloyme Suskovitsh, Ed.
Brandsen 1634, Piso 7°
Dpto. A
Buenos Aires, Argentina
Dover Publications
180 Varick St.
New York, NY 10013
(212) 255-3755
Duke University
Dept. of German
Durham, NC 27706
(919) 684-8111
Contact: Professor A. Tilo Alt
Elektra Records
1855 Broadway
New York, NY 10023
(212) 484-8030
Dr. Shifra Epstein
Curator, Ethnography Dept.
Israel Museum
Jerusalem, Israel
Farband (Tsienistisher Arbeter-
Farband/Labor Zionist Alliance)
575 Avenue of the Americas
New York, NY 10011
(212) 989-0300
Phillip Feldheim
96 E. Broadway
New York, NY 10002
Aaron Fishman Foundation for Yiddish
Culture
3340 Bainbridge Ave.
Bronx, NY 10467
Contact: Professor Joshua A.
Fishman
Folksbiene Theater
Central Synagogue
123 E. 55th St.
New York, NY 10022
(212) 755-2231
Folkways Record and Service Corp.
43 W. 61st St.
New York, NY 10023
(212) 586-7260
Four Continent Book Corp.
149 Fifth Ave.
New York, NY 10010
Embassy of France
Cultural Section
972 Fifth Ave.
New York, NY 10021
(212) 737-9700
Freeland League
200 W. 72nd St.
New York, NY 10023
(212) 787-6675
Contact: Mordkhe Schaechter
Di Goldene Keyt
Avrom Sutskever, Ed.
Rekhov Weitzman 30
P. O. Box 303
Tel Aviv, Israel

Sam Goody
235 W. 49th St.
New York, NY 10019
(212) 246-1708
Greater Recording Co.
164 Manhattan Ave.
Brooklyn, NY 11206
(212) 387-0880

Hebrew Actors' Union
31 E. Seventh St.
New York, NY 10003
(212) 674-1923
Hebrew Publishing Co.
84 Fifth Ave.
New York, NY 10003
(212) 925-3700
Hebrew University of Jerusalem
Yiddish Dept.
Jerusalem, Israel
Contact: Professor Khone Shmeruk,
Chm. (courses)
Avrom Nowersztern (publications)
House of Menorah
36 Eldridge St.
New York, NY 10002
(212) 925-7573
Contact: Sol Tischler
Indiana University Press
10th and Morton Sts.
Bloomington, IN 47401
(812) 337-4203
Israel Broadcasting Authority
Yiddish Section
9 Heleni Hamalka
Jerusalem, Israel
Jewish Daily Forward
45 E. 33rd St.
New York, NY 10016
(212) 889-8200
Jewish Daily Morning Freiheit
35 E. 12th St.
New York, NY 10003
(212) 254-9480
Jewish Labor Bund
25 E. 78th St.
New York, NY 10021
(212) 535-0850
Jewish Publication Society of America
117 S. 17th St.
Philadelphia, PA 19103
(215) 564-5925
Jewish Socialist Youth Bund
25 E. 78th St.
New York, NY 10021
(212) 535-0850
Contact: Yankl Jacobs
Jewish Teachers Seminary

69 Bank St.
New York, NY 10014
(212) 741-0220
Contact: Dean Meir Ben Horin
Jewish Theological Seminary
Broadway and 122nd St.
New York, NY 10027
(212) 749-8000
Contact: Dovid-Hirsh Roskies
Dr. Jean Jofen
1684 52nd St.
Brooklyn, NY 11204
Kinderbuch Publishers
see: YIDISHER KULTUR-
FARBAND
Kinder-Tsaytung
Yoysef Mlotek, Ed.
see: ARBETER-RING
Kinder-Zhurnal
Bella Gottesman, Ed.
see: SHOLOM ALEICHEM
FOLK INSTITUTE
King Karol
Mail Order Dept.
126 W. 42nd St.
New York, NY 10036
(212) 354-6880
Ktav Publishing House
75 Varick St.
New York, NY 10013
(212) 966-6980
Labor Zionist Alliance
see: FARBAND
Language and Culture Atlas of
Ashkenazic Jewry
560 Riverside Dr.
New York, NY 10027
(212) 280-3925
Letste Nayes
M. Tsanin, Ed.
52 Harakevet St.
Tel Aviv, Israel
J. Levine Co.
58 Eldridge St.
New York, NY 10002
(212) 966-4460/4461
Contact: Rabbi Philip Kastel
MLB Enterprises
2424 N. 51st St.
Philadelphia, PA 19131

Modern Language Association of
America (MLA)
62 Fifth Ave.
New York, NY 10011
(212) 691-3200
Monitor Records
156 Fifth Ave.
New York, NY 10010
(212) 989-2323
Bernard Morgenstern
150 E. Broadway
New York, NY 10002
(212) 267-1332
Mouton
Commercial Dept.
P. O. Box 482
The Hague, Netherlands
Music Masters Uptown
25 W. 43rd St.

New York, NY 10017
(212) 279-6862
Music Sales
Mail Order Sales Dept.
33 W. 60th St.
New York, NY 10023
(212) 246-0325
Musterverk fun der Yidisher Literatur
Ateneo Literario en el IWO
Pasteur 633, 3er. Piso
Buenos Aires, Argentina
47-6624
Contact: Shmuel Rollansky, Ed.
National Committee for Yiddish
Canadian Jewish Congress
1590 McGregor
Montreal, Que., Canada
(514) 931-7531
National Council for Yiddish and
Yiddish Culture
575 Avenue of the Americas
New York, NY 10011
Contact: Meyer Bass, Exec. Sec., or
the youth delegates via
YUGNTRUF
92nd Street YMHA
92nd St. and Lexington Ave.
New York, NY 10028
(212) 427-6000
North American Jewish Students
Appeal
15 E. 26th St.
New York, NY 10010
(212) 689-0790
Oyfn shvel
Dr. Mordke Schaechter, Editor
see: FREELAND LEAGUE
Y. L. Perets Farlag
Rekhov Allenby 31
Tel Aviv, Israel
Perivale Press
13830 Erwin St.
Van Nuys, CA 91401
Queens College, CUNY
Yiddish Program
Academic 1309
Flushing, NY 11367
(212) 520-7067
Contact: Dr. Joseph C. Landis,
Chm.
Rabinowitz Book Store
30 Canal St.
New York, NY 10002
(212) 267-2406
Radio Bucharest
Bucharest, Romania
Radio Moscow Information
(202) 232-3756
Mary S. Rosenberg
100 W. 72nd St.
New York, NY 10023
(212) 362-4873
Ruth Rubin
45 Gramercy Park N.
New York, NY 10010
Rutenberg & Everett Yiddish Film
Library
Lown Judaic Center
415 South St.
Waltham, MA 02154
(617) 899-7044, 237-3451
Rutgers University
Dept. of Hebrew
New Brunswick, NJ 08903
(201) 932-1766
Contact: Professor Curt Leviant,
Chm.
Benyumin Schaechter Foundation for
the Advancement of Standard
Yiddish

3328 Bainbridge Ave.
Bronx, NY 10467
Contact: Professor Mordkhe
Schaechter
Dr. Mordkhe Schaechter
3323 Bainbridge Ave.
Bronx, NY 10467
(212) 231-7905
Schocken Books, Inc.
200 Madison Ave.
New York, NY 10017
(212) 685-6500
Service Bureau for Jewish Education
see: YIDISHER KULTUR-
FARBAND
Shalom Yiddish Musical Theater
Town Hall
123 W. 43rd St.
New York, NY 10036
(212) 921-9447
Sholom Aleichem Folk Institute
3301 Bainbridge Ave.
Bronx, NY 10467
(212) 881-3588
Naomi Smith
310 W. 97th St.
New York, NY 10025
Sovetish Heymland
Arn Vergelis, Ed.
Kirova 17
Moscow, USSR
Exclusive agent for Western
Hemisphere is FOUR
CONTINENT BOOK CORP.
State University College at Brockport
Dept. of Foreign Languages
Brockport, NY 14420
(716) 395-2211
Contact: Professor Martha O'Nan,
Chm.
Stonehill Publishing Co.
388 E. 57th St.
New York, NY 10022
(212) 935-1425
Strand Book Store
828 Broadway
New York, NY 10003
(212) 473-1452
SUNY at Buffalo
Dept. of Germanic and Slavic
Buffalo, NY 14261
(716) 831-9000
Contact: Professor Byron J.
Koekkoek, Chm.
SUNY at Stony Brook
Dept. of Germanic and Slavic
Stony Brook, NY 11794
(516) 246-5000
Di Tsukunft
Khayim Bez, Ed.
25 E. 78th St.
New York, NY 10021
(212) 535-4642
Martin Kenneth Tytell
116 Fulton St.
New York, NY 10007
(212) 233-5333
UCLA
Dept. of Germanic Languages and
Literatures
Los Angeles, CA 90024
(213) 825-4321
Contact: Professor Janet R. Hadda
University of Arizona
Dept. of German
Tucson, AZ 85721
(602) 884-4111
Contact: Professor Max Dufner,
Chm.

University of Chicago Press
5801 Ellis Ave.
Chicago, IL 60637
(312) 753-3344
University of Haifa
Lexicographical Center for Jewish
Languages
Haifa, Israel
Contact: Professor David L. Gold,
Dir.
University of Manitoba
Dept. of Near Eastern and Judaic
Studies
Winnipeg, R3T 2N2, Man., Canada
(204) 474-8880
Contact: Professor Neal P. Rose,
Chm.
University of Pittsburgh
Dept. of Germanic Languages and
Literatures
Pittsburgh, PA 15260
(412) 624-4141
Contact: Professor John Neubauer,
Chm.

University of Texas at Austin
Dept. of Germanic Languages
Austin, TX 78712
(512) 471-3434
University of Washington
Jewish Studies Program
Seattle, WA 98195
(206) 543-2100
Contact: Professor Edward
Alexander, Chm.
University of Washington Press
Seattle, WA 98105
(206) 543-4050
Vanguard Recording Society
71 W. 23rd St.
New York, NY 10010
(212) 255-7732
Der Veker
Dr. Elias Schulman, Ed.
45 E. 33rd St.
New York, NY 10016
(212) 686-1536
Josh Waletzky
122 Dean St.
Brooklyn, NY 11201
(212) 858-5512
WEVD Radio
1700 Broadway
New York, NY 10019
(212) 757-0880
Working Papers in Yiddish and East
European Studies
Dr. Joan Bratkowsky, Ed.
see: YIVO INSTITUTE FOR
JEWISH RESEARCH
Workmen's Circle
see: ARBETER-RING
World Jewish Congress
Cultural Dept.
15 E. 84th St.
New York, NY 10028
(212) 879-4500

Yedies fun Yivo
see: YIVO INSTITUTE FOR
JEWISH RESEARCH
Yedies vegn yidish/Yiddish Studies
Newsletter
David Neal Miller, Ed.
see: AMERICAN ASSOCIATION
OF PROFESSORS OF YIDDISH
Yerusholayimer Almanakh
Yoysef Kerler, Ed.
Shderot Eshkol 6/12
Jerusalem, Israel
Yeshiva University
Dept. of Jewish Studies
500 W. 185th St.
New York, NY 10033
(212) 568-8400
Contact: Professor Gella Fishman
Der Yid
260 Broadway
Brooklyn, NY 11211
Yiddish
Dr. Joseph C. Landis, Ed.
see: AMERICAN ASSOCIATION
OF PROFESSORS OF YIDDISH
Yidishe Dramtrupe (Yiddish Drama
Group of Montreal)
Saidye Bronfman Centre
1590 Ave. Docteur Penfield
Montreal H3G 1C5, PQ, Canada
(514) 931-7531
Contact: Dora Wasserman
Yidishe Kultur
Itche Goldberg, Ed.
853 Broadway
New York, NY 10003
(212) 228-1955
Yidisher Kemfer
Mordkhe Shtrigler, Ed.
575 Avenue of the Americas
New York, NY 10011
(212) 741-2404
Yidisher Kultur-Farband (Ykuf)
853 Broadway
New York, NY 10003
(212) 228-1955
Contact: Itche Goldberg
Yidishe Shprakh
Dr. Mordkhe Schaechter, Ed.
see: YIVO INSTITUTE FOR
JEWISH RESEARCH
YIVO Institute for Jewish Research
1048 Fifth Ave.
New York, NY 10028
(212) 535-6700
Contact: Yadja Zeltman, Courses,
Summer Program, Scholarships
Dina Abramowicz, Librarian
Yivo-bleter
see: YIVO INSTITUTE FOR
JEWISH RESEARCH
Ykuf
see: YIDISHER KULTUR-
FARBAND
Yugntbund
see: JEWISH SOCIALIST
YOUTH BUND
Yugntruf—Youth for Yiddish
3328 Bainbridge Ave.
Bronx, NY 10467
(212) 654-8540
Contact: Sore-Rukhl Schaechter,
Chm., Executive Comm.
Perl Teitelbaum, Chm., New York
Comm.
Yugntruf (journal)
Gitl Schaechter, Ed.
see: YUGNTRUF—YOUTH FOR
YIDDISH

DISPERSION

THESE ARE THE WANDERINGS

Numbers 33:1 אלה מסעי בני ישראל

Jewish tours

What follows is a brief survey of resource guides to some "Jewish" cities in the United States and Canada. The Lower East Side of New York and Los Angeles—the two Coasts, or poles, if you will, of American Jewish life—are treated at length, with detailed tours. (Only the Lower East Side—rather than all of New York—was included because New York itself, to do it justice, would require an entire book. Try running through the Manhattan phone book under "Jewish," "Israel," or "Hebrew," and you'll see what we mean. Also, a guide to the Lower East Side is really a guide to the roots of the American Jewish community. As for L.A., well, perhaps its inclusion will silence at last the charge that the *Jewish Catalog* is an "East Coast book"!)

SOME GENERAL NOTES

1. Many cities have Jewish guides written about them. Get them whenever possible before or immediately upon arrival in a city.

2. Some general guides are

Postal, Bernard and Koppman, Lionel. *A Jewish Tourist's Guide to the United States.* JPS, Philadelphia, 1954 (out of print); comprehensive but requires some updating.

Postal, Bernard and Koppman, Lionel. *A Guide to the Jewish Landmarks in the United States.* New York: Bloch, 1978.

Green Flag, compiled by *The Jewish Travel Guide*, Jewish Chronicle Publications, 1974/5. This lists synagogues, kosher restaurants, organizations, etc., worldwide. Updated yearly.

3. For cities not listed here

a. Check the phone book (after you've arrived) under "Jewish," "Hebrew," or "Israel."

b. Try to find a central address (e.g., the federation, community center, synagogue, etc.). Most people will be glad to give you advice.

c. Smaller towns, which have fewer guests, usually try to make you feel especially welcome. Whether you find yourself in a small or large town, people will often open their homes to you—especially for Shabbat. Contact the local synagogue for such hospitality.

d. Check the guidebooks listed above.

4. If you aren't certain whether Jews live in Halifax, Nova Scotia, or Sioux City, Iowa (the answer is yes to both), try finding out by dipping into the *Encyclopaedia Judaica.* It has articles on many cities (it should be referred to

anyway if you're interested in finding out about the Jewish history of the places you're visiting) with short bibliographies. Also, if you own one of the pocket engagement calendars that so many Jewish organizations use, you can check the front of the book where there is a list, state by state, of all the cities in America with any significant Jewish population. In addition, any of the synagogue movements should be able to tell you if they have an affiliated synagogue in the area you are visiting. Finally, the *American Jewish Year Book*, published each year jointly by the American Jewish Committee and the Jewish Publication Society, has a list of affiliated federations (and addresses), as well as a list of Jewish periodicals in the U.S. and Canada.

5. There also exists the *American Jewish Organizations Directory*, distributed by

Frenkel Mailing Service
24 Rutgers St.
New York, NY 10002

This lists synagogues and organizations in most communities in the United States and is updated every few years; it's well worth owning.

6. If given a choice between many organizations, contact the ones that are most likely to have the information you want, e.g., a synagogue if you want to find out where to buy kosher food.

7. We have found that there are generally three types of organizations who seem to be interested in guides to their communities or in local Jewish history, so contact them first:

(a) student groups, Hillels, and others (it was these groups that pioneered the spate of Jewish guides to Mezritch, etc.)

(b) the local branch of the American or Canadian Jewish Congress

(c) the local federation of Jewish philanthropies, which increasingly is the central organizational address in any American Jewish community

Also: Check in the Jewish Yellow Pages in *Catalog 2.*

HAPPY VISITING!

Walking tour of the Lower East Side

Don't go to the Lower East Side looking for great sites and beautiful monuments. Mid-Manhattan it's not. If you want tourist attractions you're better off at Radio City or the Empire State Building.

The Lower East Side was settled by poor Jewish immigrants who came over from Eastern Europe between 1880 and 1930. They landed in New York, took up residence in the Jewish ghetto, established themselves in work and business, and eventually moved out of the neighborhood when they became middle class in wealth and outlook. While in the area, the immigrant Jews gave rise to a culture composed of both traditional Jewish motifs and novel American additions. It is for evidence of this Yiddish-American culture that one must search in touring the Lower East Side.

The Jews who lived here were poor, and many spots in the Lower East Side reflect their poverty. But they also produced a culturally rich community. Fortunately for the tourist, many examples of that cultural life remain to be seen and explored. What we will try to do, then, is to recapitulate the lifestyle of turn-of-the-century Jewry by looking for physical evidence of their everyday lives.

Of course, the Jews are not the only group who ever lived on the Lower East Side. Although this area constitutes the motherland of American Jewry, the Jews took it over from other ethnic communities who preceded them and are now giving it up to more recent arrivals to America. Before the 1890s, the area housed a basically German and Irish population. At present, Chinatown is encroaching on the Jewish settlement from the west, Puerto Ricans increas-

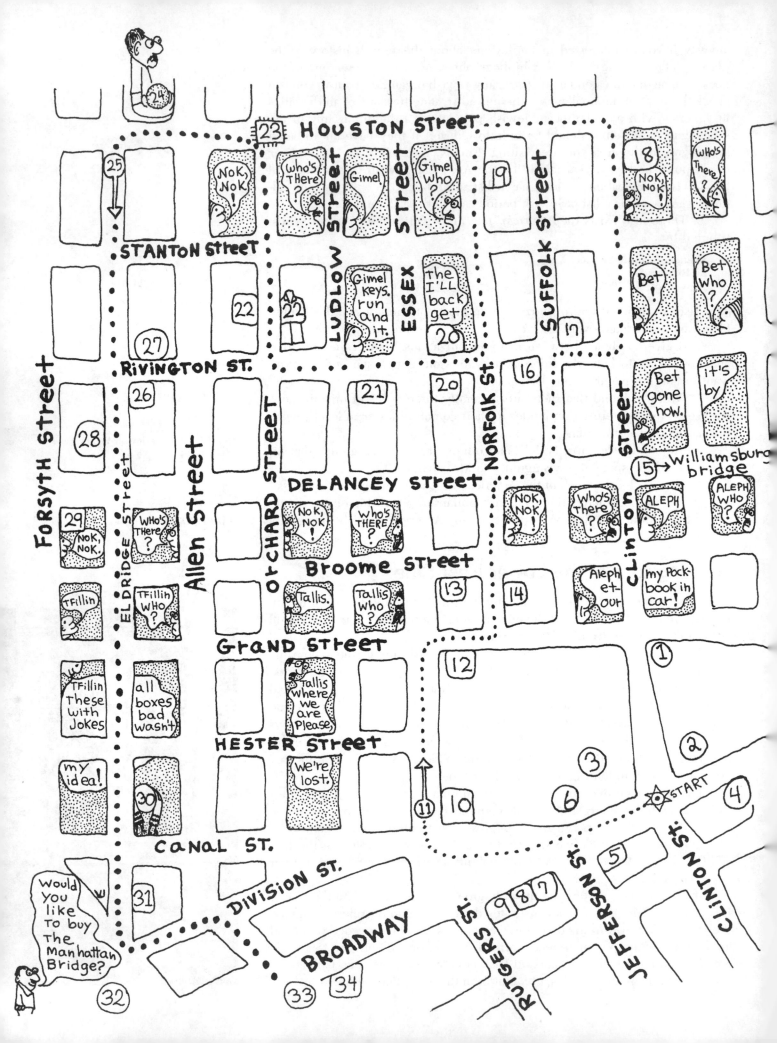

ingly occupy tenements and housing projects that once contained mostly Jews, and a newer community of East Indians is entering into the area.

Our tour is divided into roughly two parts. It begins in the section where Jewish institutions and economic enterprise remain strong, along East Broadway and Essex Street. It then proceeds toward areas that reflect the destruction of the Jewish community in the Lower East Side along Norfolk and Eldridge Streets. Both parts of the tour truly reflect the condition of Jewry in the modern inner city. Pockets of the culturally resonant Jewish settlement remain. But most areas have been abandoned by Jews; consequently their synagogues, stores, and social meeting places suffer neglect. The Jews who still live there—often poor and aged, unable to move—must endure this terrible and lonely urban blight.

These, then, are what we will stress in touring the Lower East Side. We will look for examples of how poor Jewish immigrants used to live. We shall sample their cultural and economic life-styles. Notice will be taken of landmarks that Jews inherited from Germans and Irish and have given up to more recent immigrant groups. The community will be examined for both its remaining pride and its present shameful destruction. We will look at the area as a mosaic of old and new, beauty and ugliness, joy and sorrow.

The tour begins at the corner of Clinton Street and East Broadway. You can see four important locations from this intersection, all of which represent significant experiences in the history of American Jewry. First, look one block north, to the corner of Clinton and Grand Streets. Located there is the original site (now destroyed) of *Temple Emanu-El* (1). Founded in 1843 by German Jews who lived among their countrymen on the Lower East Side, it was at first a struggling congregation. At its initial fund-raising meeting, it collected the grand sum of $28.25, in contributions ranging from 25¢ to $2.50. This institution, now moved to Fifth Avenue and Sixty-fifth Street, went on to become the wealthiest and most prestigious Jewish house of worship in the country, demonstrating early on a classic pattern: many organizations would take root in this area but move to other locations when they achieved success.

Next, turn to the *Bialystoker Nursing Home* (2) on the northeast corner of East Broadway and Clinton, which represents the success story of Eastern European Jews in America. The Bialystoker landsmanshaft—the community of Jews in New York who originated from the East European town of Bialystok—established one of the strongest immigrant organizations in America. They still operate a nearly hundred-year-old synagogue (not on the tour), as well as this magnificent nursing home structure (this is not one of the homes touched by the New York nursing home scandals). That East Europeans could arrive in the United States in poverty and be successful enough to build impressive institutions like this one served then as now to confirm America's status as the promised land for the immigrants. But while this nursing home remains an obvious credit to the East European Jewish community, it is also one of the last major East Side institutions still operated by the immigrant Jews.

Across the street, on the northwest corner of East Broadway and Clinton stands another example of Jews' success in the United States, the *Seward Park Houses* (3). These modern apartment buildings, which were erected by a corporation of the International Ladies' Garment Workers' Union, operate on a cooperative plan. The ILGWU, a union which once consisted mainly of Jews, believed in certain socialist principals for changing society. These political and economic beliefs influenced the decision to operate the apartment complex as a cooperative venture in which all tenants would also be owners. The Seward Park Houses should be viewed as a manifestation of both the

A practical hint. Although there is no great danger in touring the Lower East Side, it is a high crime area. Go in daylight hours and take some friends. Don't wear expensive jewelry. If you are circumspect and act intelligently, you should have nothing to worry about.

Key to Map

1   Former site of Temple Emanu-El
2   Bialystoker Nursing Home
3   Seward Park Houses
4   East Broadway institutions
5   Educational Alliance
6   Seward Park Branch, New York Public Library
7   Former offices of Tog-Morgen Journal
8   Forward Building
9   Garden Cafeteria
10 Seward Park
11 Essex Street
12 Hot bialy store
13 Seward Park Extension
14 Beis HaMedrash HaGodol
15 Williamsburg Bridge
16 Public School 160
17 Streit Matzoth Co.
18 Chasam Sofer Synagogue
19 Former Congregation Anshei Slonim
20 Rivington Street food shops
21 First Romanian synagogue in America
22 Orchard Street garment retail center
23 I. L. Peretz Square
24 Boccie courts
25 Eldridge Street
26 University Settlement House
27 Former First Warsaw Congregation
28 Former Anshei Monaster Congregation
29 Former Forsyth Street Synagogue
30 Zion Talis
31 Congregation Adas Jeshurun–Anshei Lubz
32 Manhattan Bridge
33 Former site of Second Avenue el
34 Former Pike Street Shul

ILGWU's achievement in raising the living standards of immigrant Jews and the perpetuation of its progressive ideology.

The fourth important site to notice on the corner of Clinton and East Broadway are the many *small synagogues, yeshivas,* and *charitable offices* on the south side of *East Broadway* (4). Almost all of these organizations occupy less than one building and some operate in just one apartment. Immigrants coming over to America were often too poor to erect large buildings or even to buy existing structures for their schools and religious institutions. They had to settle for what they could afford—small rooms or sections of a building. A few decades ago one could find these tiny cells of Jewish life spread out over the entire Lower East Side. As the northern and western parts of the area have increasingly come under Puerto Rican and Chinese influence, however, these organizations have tended to concentrate in the remaining section of Jewish strength along East Broadway.

Now walk a block west along East Broadway, to Jefferson Street. On the southwest corner of Jefferson and East Broadway stands one of the most famous of Lower East Side landmarks, the *Educational Alliance* (5). When it was founded as the Hebrew Institute in 1889, this institution, commonly called the "Palace of Immigrants," aimed to assimilate Yiddish-speaking Jews into the American culture. In 1893 the acculturated German middle-class Jews who founded the Hebrew Institute changed its name to the Educational Alliance to banish any hint of sectarianism in the institution's goals. Its purpose was clearly Americanization, not the perpetuation of Jewish life and culture. The Yiddish immigrants were in no mood simply to give up their traditional heritage, but they did want to benefit from the Alliance's educational and recreational events. A long struggle over programming ensued, as might be expected in an institution that was supported by German Reform Jews but aimed to serve Yiddish and traditional coreligionists. The situation was further complicated when immigrant workers wanted to use the building for union meetings—which the business-class-dominated board of directors opposed. Finally these issues were compromised, and the Educational Alliance carried out a dual program of acculturation and preservation of traditional elements of Jewish life. It now serves as a center of social, educational, and recreational activities for the Lower East Side's population, both Jewish and non-Jewish. Many of the remaining landsmanshaften meet here, and a housing development for the aged is maintained as well.

Across the street from the Educational Alliance, still on East Broadway, you can see the Carnegie-built *Seward Park Branch of the New York Public Library* (6). Ambitious young Jews on their way up the American social scale could come in and use this library, as well as the collections of the Educational Alliance and other settlement houses in the area, to educate themselves.

Farther west, at 187 East Broadway (now the Chinart Gallery), is where the *Tog-Morgen Journal* (7), the Yiddish Orthodox newspaper, used to have its editorial offices. If the public library on the other side of the street helped young Jews to make their way in the wider American society, the *Tog-Morgen Journal*, before its demise, served to retain the vitality of traditional Yiddish culture. Both aspects of the immigrants' lives are accurately mirrored at these two sites.

A few more doors west, at 175 East Broadway, you will see what is probably the most prominent of all Lower East Side institutions, the *Forward Building* (8). This structure housed not only the famous Lower East Side Yiddish socialist newspaper, the *Forward* (still published, but not in this building), but also almost every Jewish socialist organization in New York. Etched over the entrance to the building are busts of Karl Marx, Friedrich Engels, and Ferdinand Lassalle. The picture of the Statue of Liberty's arm

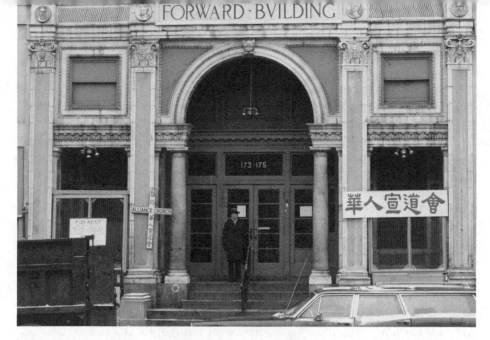

holding the torch, located above the front door, was once the symbol of the New York Socialist party. In keeping with the socialist decor of this edifice, the *Forward* newspaper's masthead still carries every day two Socialist party slogans, "Workers of the World, Unite," and "The Liberation of the Workers Depends on the Workers Alone."

To the Yiddish population of the Lower East Side the Forward Building symbolized something more than a publishing house or a political party. For the immigrant Jew this towering edifice served as a graphic demonstration of the power and ability of the Yiddish-speaking population to prosper in the United States while still maintaining its beloved culture. The recent sale of the Forward Building to a Chinese church serves to illustrate the decline of Yiddish New York. To the aged Jews who still populate the Lower East Side this sale only confirmed the passing of their cherished institutions and life-style.

At the western end of this block, on the corner of Rutgers Street and East Broadway (southern side), is located one of the most famous dairy restaurants in the world, the *Garden Cafeteria* (9). The importance of the Garden lies not only in its age (it goes back to the turn of the century), but also in what it represents. The Garden is one of the few remaining cafés and bars of the many that liberally dotted the Lower East Side in the period of dense Jewish residence. In fact, progressive reformers estimated that in 1894 there existed one bar for every 208 residents of the Jewish section of the Lower East Side. These small cafeterias and saloons were characteristic of ethnic neighborhoods. The residents of the area were not rich enough to have their own clubhouses, much less to build new halls. Nor could they meet in their apartments, which were often given over to sweatshop labor during the day. The only place where they could get together were the bars and cafés of the district, such as the Garden, where for the price of a small bit of food they could find companionship and social warmth. The Garden is one of the few remaining restaurant–meeting places in the entire area.

Across the street from the Garden, on the corner of East Broadway and Essex lies *Seward Park* (10). When the Jews settled in the Lower East Side, not a single park existed in this area of concrete and tenements below Eighth Street. Progressive reformers of the turn of the century, believing that parks would greatly enhance the immigrants' lives and health, agitated for the construction of play areas in the midst of the ghetto. Seward Park is one result. If you go through it on a nice day, you can still see peddlers hawking their secondhand goods, just as their predecessors did fifty years ago.

Incidentally, don't miss the mural inside the Garden, on the left wall as you enter, which depicts the corner of East Broadway and Rutgers Street as it existed in 1906, when the mural was painted by the cartoonist of the *Forward*.

Before you leave East Broadway glance west for a second. You can easily see the Municipal Building and the World Trade Center. The Lower East Side, though the home of many immigrant cultures, is not in some isolated spot in Manhattan. Rather, it is literally right down the street from New York's financial, administrative, and business section.

Now, turn north and take a leisurely stroll up *Essex Street* (11) to Grand. You will pass a plethora of small food and religious shops. Stop to buy a pickle right out of a barrel or a fresh piece of cake or kosher cheese. Notice the extremely small size of each of these stores. When Jews came to shop here they wanted not only to buy goods, but also to carry on intimate conversations with the shop owners and clientele. Shopping constituted a social as well as an economic activity. These closely knit social groups could best exist in the very small shops that still line Essex Street. Although two large department stores did move into the Lower East Side, the area's economic style was defined by the small, intimate shops and peddlers' pushcarts, not by the bigger operations. Incidentally, when you get to Grand Street, turn east (right) and go buy a *hot bialy* (12), a version of the bagel brought to America by the East Europeans.

On Grand Street (north side), between Essex and Norfolk, stands the *Seward Park Extension* (13). This structure, which architecturally represents a significant advance in low-income housing, was the site of a bitter battle between the Jews and Puerto Ricans of the area when it was completed in the early 1970s. Each community wanted a large portion of its own ethnic group to occupy the building, and for a time the completed apartment house remained vacant while the conflict was debated in the courts. Though the issue has been settled by an out-of-court compromise, the Seward Park Extension still serves as a spatial symbol of the tension between Jews and Puerto Ricans as these two groups fight for residential dominance of the area.

Walk around the Seward Park Extension and take a left onto Norfolk Street. In the middle of the block on Norfolk between Grand and Broome, you will come across the *Beis HaMedrash HaGodol* (14). Like many other synagogues in this part of the Lower East Side, the Beis HaMedrash HaGodol was originally a Christian church. Indeed, this structure carries a New York City landmark designation as an outstanding example of nineteenth-century church architecture. To the greatest degree possible the front of the synagogue has been changed to appear Jewish, but if you walk far enough to see the left (north) side, you will recognize Gothic windows and five-pointed stars that still make the building look very much like a church. This synagogue houses

the oldest Russian Orthodox congregation in the United States. Together with the Seward Park Extension, the Beis HaMedrash HaGodol exemplifies the mobility of different groups through the neighborhood. When the synagogue took over the church building in the late nineteenth century, it signaled the growing dominance of East European Jews. The fight over the housing complex reflects the recent weakening of the Jewish hold and the increasing strength of newer ethnic groups.

Continue north on Norfolk Street to Delancey Street. Cross Delancey and walk a block east (right) to Suffolk Street. Standing on this corner you can't miss the *Williamsburg Bridge* (15), connecting the inner city of the Lower East Side to the Jews' first suburban location in Brooklyn: Williamsburg.

Turn north and go up Suffolk Street one block, to the corner of Rivington. On the southwest corner of Suffolk and Rivington you will notice one of the outstanding structures on the Lower East Side, *Public School 160* (16) (no longer in use). We mentioned before that the founders of the Educational Alliance sought to Americanize the immigrants. But it was soon recognized that adults brought up in an Eastern European culture could not adapt completely to American mores. However, if the children of the immigrants could be immersed in an American milieu such as the public school early enough, they could grow up to idealize the American rather than an alien way of life. Such, at any rate, was the ideology of the progressive educators who built this school in 1897. The building was to house not only an educational effort to teach children the basic skills of reading, writing, and arithmetic, but also a spiritual quest to imbue the youngsters of the Lower East Side with the American ethos. The architecture of the structure renders this quest obvious. The place looks like a religious building with its Gothic windows and French chateau roofs. This style represented the builders' desire to construct not only a school but a cathedral to American education.

Diagonally across from the public school is the *Streit Matzoth Co.* (17). As you walk west on Rivington Street (which we will do after a brief detour), you will pass a number of Jewish food places.

Take a right and walk along Rivington Street one block east to Clinton Street. Turn left (north) and walk a block and a half and you will come, on your right, to the *Chasam Sofer Synagogue* (18). This building was erected by the German Jewish congregation Rodeph Shalom in 1853. This German congregation was originally Orthodox, as can be seen by the two street-level doors, which originally led to the separate women's galleries and flank the main entrance that opens to the men's section. Rodeph Shalom moved out of the area, however, became a leading Reform temple, and now occupies a large building on West 83rd Street. The acquisition of this building by the Hungarian synagogue that now owns it was another symbol of the change in the character of the neighborhood in the late 1800s: from German to East European. This structure has recently been beautifully renovated.

Not so lucky was Congregation *Anshei Slonim* (19) which you can reach by walking north to Houston Street, then left (west) two blocks to Norfolk Street and then left again (south) for half a block. This is one of the saddest sights to behold. This once-magnificent structure is now horribly vandalized and partially destroyed, but you can still discern the outline of the beautiful building it once was. Thugs and drug addicts have ravaged this shul too much for prayer to be carried on there; the building had to be abandoned about five years ago. Before its demise this structure was the oldest existing synagogue building in New York City. It was erected in 1850 and at that time was considered the most prestigious synagogue in New York. Like Rodeph Shalom, it passed from German Jews to East Europeans as the ethnic makeup of the area changed after 1880. But all the historical data and the architectural

If you happen to like broken matzot, you can buy a bag in Streit's for bargain rates.

beauty of the edifice must recede in one's consciousness as one views the terrible destruction the building has undergone. If any one place in the Lower East Side symbolizes the problems of neglect and destruction that the Jewish community suffers here, this is it. The fact that this spot is largely unknown to nonresidents of the area speaks volumes about the general Jewish community's lack of concern with its inner-city members.

Now, continue to walk south on Norfolk Street to Rivington. On Rivington Street, turn right and walk west toward Orchard. First you will pass the remainder of the *food store district* (**20**) (including Schapiro's Wines, with its sign, THE WINE YOU CAN ALMOST CUT WITH A KNIFE). As you continue along Rivington, between Essex and Ludlow Streets, you can also see the synagogue of the *First Romanian Congregation* (**21**).

When you get to Orchard Street, turn right and walk up to Houston Street. This part of Orchard Street contains probably the Lower East Side's best-known section, the *clothing stores* (**22**). Again, notice the very small size of the shops. In the early part of this century garment manufacturing (done mostly as piecework within the laborers' apartments rather than in large factories) was the area's chief industry. This clothing shop district is the major link in the area to its past as New York's most important clothing center. On Sunday this section of Orchard Street is turned into a pedestrian mall. The quality of clothes here is quite high and you can get some good bargains— and maybe haggle about the prices with the store owners.

The corner of Orchard and Houston Streets, at the end of the clothing store section, is called *I. L. Peretz Square* (**23**). The name derives from that of the famous Yiddish poet, who wrote, among other things, the words to the Yiddish socialist theme song, "All Men Are Brothers."

At Houston take another left turn and walk west to Eldridge Street. Just before Eldridge, on the north side of the street, you can take in some exciting *boccie matches* (**24**) on the dirt alleys in the middle of the street. (Boccie is an Italian form of lawn bowling.) Interesting social interaction among men of different ethnic groups can be observed here.

When you get to Eldridge Street, take a left and walk south. Although we will be pointing out different sights along *Eldridge Street* (**25**), we should say something about the street in general. You will observe many gutted buildings; some have been destroyed by fire, others just abandoned. This not only makes for unsightly blemishes in the street's facade, but it also drastically lowers the quality of life in the remaining buildings. Aged Jews live in almost every block of this horrible street. They share the problems of filth, discomfort, and vermin with the other ethnic groups who inhabit the area. But they also suffer from the unique neglect by the rest of American Jewry of their lonely plight.

After walking two blocks south on Eldridge Street you will come across the *University Settlement House* (26), on the southeast corner of Rivington Street. When the Lower East Side was inhabited by a largely East European population, young Protestant and German Jewish men and women (mostly women) came to live among the immigrants, both to meet them and to introduce them to the American way of life. Although these settlement workers attempted to foster respect for the recent arrivals' culture and human rights, their basic goal (like that of the public school that they supported) was Americanization. For example, the University Settlement stated in its 1898 report that one of its main aims would be to get young local residents out of their candy-store hangouts and into the settlement's parliamentary club. The major settlements in the Lower East Side, beside the University, were the Henry Street and College Settlement Houses.

Before you leave this corner, turn around; you will see on the north side of Rivington Street, between Eldridge and Allen Street, the *First Warsaw Congregation* (27), another formerly beautifully synagogue that had to be abandoned because of continued vandalism and attacks on its members.

Continue walking south on Eldridge Street for half a block. On the west side of the street, at number 178, used to hang a small sign carrying both English and Hebrew script. This sign designated the location of the *Anshei Monaster Synagogue* (28), one of the last Sephardic congregations on the Lower East Side. If you went in the door under the sign when the congregation still existed, you would pass through the hallway of an apartment building to an outside courtyard, in which a small three-story, undecorated gray building still stands. This structure was the Monaster shul. You can also see it from Eldridge Street if you look for it through the empty lot next to the building with the sign. When religious Jews occupied the Lower East Side in force, many more of them prayed in small unimpressive synagogues like this one than in the large edifices that you have observed on the rest of the tour.

Now explore a little for yourself. Almost every street in the vicinity possesses the power to delight you with its beauty or disturb you with its deterioration. Glory and destruction vie with each other for dominance in every block. So go look for yourself. Make your own tour. Get involved in the Lower East Side, for it contains much of your own history and will tell you a lot about yourself.

Continue down Eldridge Street for half a block to Delancey Street. At the intersection, look to your right one block to the southeast corner of Delancey and Forsyth Streets. There stands the former *Forsyth Street Synagogue* (**29**), which is unique because its Delancey Street side has stores built into it, making for a most interesting combination of secular and holy. This structure is now occupied by the Seventh-Day Adventist Church. One may regard this ownership change as the opposite of the process we noticed operating with the *Beis HaMedrash HaGodol* (**14**). Just as that building turned from a church into a synagogue when Jews moved into the area and Christians moved out, now many shuls are being taken over by churches as Jews abandon the Lower East Side and other communities come in.

As you continue south along Eldridge Street, you will go through several different economic areas. First, you will notice a large textile and drapery district. Then you will come to a row of stores selling Jewish religious articles, the most prominent of which is *Zion Talis* (**30**). Finally, as you approach Canal Street, you will be dazzled by a collection of fairly fancy jewelry stores.

Across Canal Street, halfway down the Eldridge Street block toward Forsyth Street, you will view with a mixture of pleasure and pain the magnificent *Eldridge Street Shul, Adas Jeshurun–Anshei Lubz* (**31**), built in 1886. In our opinion this is the single most impressive structure on the Lower East Side. Its complex Romanesque, Gothic, and Moorish facade makes it one of New York's handsomest houses of worship. Its beauty and glory only heighten one's sadness at observing the synagogue's smashed windows and broken detail work. This building reflects the history of Jewish residence in this area. When it was erected it demonstrated the wealth of its sponsors and proved that immigrant Jews could advance far in the United States. Its present dilapidated state mirrors the destruction of the Jewish settlement in the neighborhood—one more symbol of the neglect of the wider Jewish community of its origins.

At the end of Eldridge Street, on the corner of Forsyth Street, you can't miss the *Manhattan Bridge* (**32**). This site combines with the *Williamsburg Bridge* (**15**) to so dominate their surroundings that on many city planning maps this section is called the Two Bridges Area rather than the Lower East Side. Bridges inevitably bring noise, and these two huge structures, built when Jews swarmed over the Lower East Side, have greatly added to the crowded and run-down nature of the district.

When you get to the end of Eldridge turn left (east) on Division Street, and after one block walk south (right) to Pike Street, just below East Broadway. Stand on the island in the middle of the street. This is the former location of the *old Second Avenue elevated tracks* (**33**). Because the terminus of this line was in Harlem, many Jews moved to that neighborhood as their first step out of the Lower East Side.

On your left (east) you will see the former site of the *Pike Street Shul* (**34**), the last stop on the tour. It is yet another of the Lower East Side's seemingly endless string of once-proud but now dilapidated synagogue structures. Because of dwindling attendance and vandalism it no longer holds services. Like many other Jewish institutions in the area it has passed into memory.

This ends our tour of the Lower East Side, but it by no means exhausts the area's many treasures and surprises. By now you have been walking for close to two hours. But you still haven't seen the Bialystoker Synagogue (Willett between Grand and Broome) or any of the district's many public housing projects, which form a distinct section of the Lower East Side.

Still, you have seen enough to get a flavor of what the Lower East Side was and is.

Los Angeles

Los Angeles has the second largest Jewish population of any city in the world. Unlike many other cities with large numbers of Jews, however, Los Angeles is a very pleasant place in which to live: it has a relatively low crime rate, and both its climate and its people are usually warm and almost never harsh. For Jews there is an additional advantage: the climate and vegetation are remarkably similar to those of Eretz Yisrael, enabling the Jewish Angeleno (or Angelena) to begin to praise God for rain at the same time that the rainy season begins in Israel, just after Sukkot. If you're going to live in the Diaspora, therefore, you might as well live in a city where deserts, mountains, palm trees, and a powerful sea remind you of the places where our ancestors first met their God, and invite you to share the encounter they discovered.

It is not recorded whether the first Jews came to the City of Angels seeking encounters with the divine. Historical evidence indicates that they trekked westward in the mid-1800s as suppliers to gold miners and rancheros; the next generation came around the turn of the century to be cured of tuberculosis; and the post-World War II generation came in search of the open spaces and the sense of personal freedom that the East Coast could no longer provide.

It is this generation that has most clearly left its stamp on the city's Jewish population. While Los Angeles is one of the best organized Jewish cities in the country, the lay and professional leaders of communal organizations are not as deeply entrenched as they are in older Jewish communities, and so creative ideas can frequently be acted upon very quickly, and newcomers interested in Jewish involvement find it relatively easy to integrate on both the countercultural and establishment levels.

In planning your trip it is useful to know the location of the major Jewish areas of the city. First, you should know that Los Angeles is cut almost in half by a mountain range, the Santa Monica Mountains, which divides the San Fernando Valley (generally called "the Valley") on the north from the City to the south. Downtown Los Angeles is somewhat in the center of the City, but since the major Jewish areas are located to the west of downtown or in the Valley, most Jews consider downtown the eastern border of their Los Angeles.

It wasn't always that way. Around the turn of the century downtown was the center of Jewish life. Later large numbers of Jews settled in Boyle Heights, just east of downtown. In the late 40s and 50s, Jews began a westward mi-

This guide is intended to lure you out to the City of the Malachim—Angels—and help you find your way between the ocean and the mountains and the desert and the valleys.

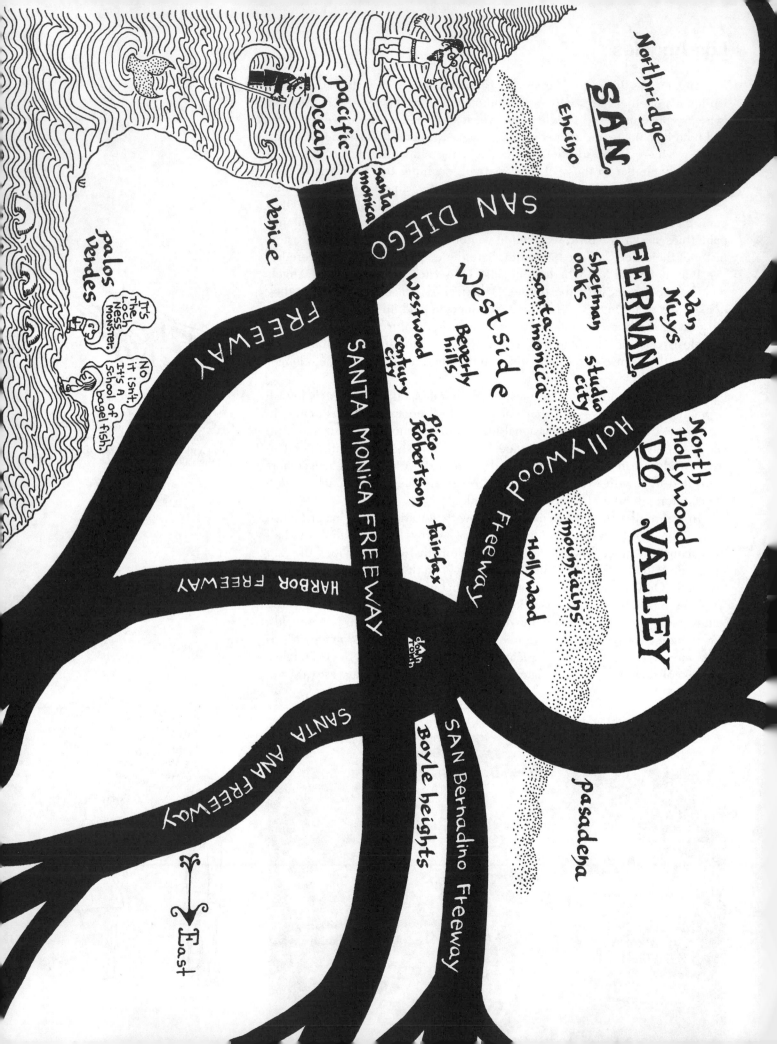

gration that has not stopped, leaving Boyle Heights with but one remaining synagogue, the Breed Street Shul, which has become a museum piece in an area almost completely Mexican-American.

The Jewish settlement in downtown Los Angeles has been all but obliterated in the urban renewal program that has brought wealthy Angelenos back downtown for business and cultural pursuits but driven the original residents away. The major downtown's Jewish area today is Fairfax, the streets to the east and west of Fairfax Avenue.

FAIRFAX AVENUE

The best place to park while spending an afternoon on Fairfax is at *Farmer's Market*, a multiethnic outdoor potpourri of shops, restaurants, produce, and (nonkosher) meat markets. You can also buy fish meals at *Ocean Foods*, fruit and vegetable plates at the *Juice and Salad Bar*, and delicacies at *Michael's Blintzes and Pastry*.

Just across from the Farmers Market, at 163 South Fairfax, is one of the city's more creative Jewish institutions, *Bet Tzedek*. Bet Tzedek is the city's Jewish legal services office, begun a few years ago by a group of young rabbis (of all three branches), lawyers, and law students. It was created to enhance the role of Jewish law in the Los Angeles community by providing free legal services to the Jewish poor and by encouraging greater use of the area's batei din—courts dealing with matters of Jewish religious law (among them, an Orthodox court presided over by Rabbi Samuel H. Katz, *Congregation Ohev Shalom*, 525 South Fairfax, and the Conservative court at the *University of Judaism*, 15600 Mulholland Drive, of which Rabbi Ben-Zion Bergman is the secretary). Bet Tzedek also developed the Jewish Conciliation Board, a community court made up of a wide variety of members of the Jewish community, to bring the settlement of legal matters between Jews back to the Jewish community. Bet Tzedek depends a great deal on volunteer lawyers and law students, and has helped raised Jewish consciousness along with the level of Los Angeles justice.

Moving north on Fairfax from the main intersection of Beverly Boulevard you'll see, on the east side of the street, a remarkable showplace of Jewish ritual objects, *Gifts by Esther*, run by Esther Fekete and her husband, Barish, former residents of Brooklyn's Williamsburg, who import lovely contemporary etrog boxes, Havdalah sets, Kiddush cups, and the like, along with copies of marvelous antique menorahs. While some of the objects are carried in other book-and-ritual stores on Fairfax, what is remarkable about the Feketes' shop is its lack of clutter, its elegant displays, and the high quality of its merchandise. Schlock, evident elsewhere, is nowhere present here.

Keep walking and you reach the first of several bakeries on Fairfax Avenue, *Famous*, a shomer Shabbat establishment, which urges you to "Count Your Blessings, Not Your Calories." On the other side of the street are some other bakeries: the *International*, which sells such Mediterranean delicacies as homemade pita, goldfingers, sabra, and baklava; *Schwartz's*, the biggest bakery on the block, also shomer Shabbat; the *King David Bakery* (ditto); *Diamond Bakery*; and the *Fairfax Bakery*. One local maven of the Avenue recommends Schwartz's for cakes and kichel, Fairfax for breads (rye, date nut, etc.), and Famous for hallah.

The *S and D Market* is one of several stores carrying large collections of kosher foods (including eight different brands of gefilte fish). Before you reach the grocery section there is a large open-air produce market, similar to the *People's Kosher Market* across the street. (If you want really fresh, but also

New Yorkers nostalgic for the Lower East Side and its past will find it rewarding to spend a day in the Fairfax Avenue environs. Like Little Tokyo, Chinatown, Watts, and the Korean areas of the city, Fairfax is a lively ethnic community, filled with pedestrians (a rarity in non-ethnic Los Angeles), mostly elderly people in sweaters, with canes and frayed coats, going determinedly about their business or staring vacantly into space in search of memories of the lives they once lived.

You can also buy what the *Feed-Rite Pet Shop* calls "yamakas"—houndstooth red or Magen David-adorned kippot—for your dog.

more expensive, fresh fruits and vegetables, however, Farmer's Market has much better selections.) The market best stocked with prepared kosher foods is the *Fairfax Kosher Food Market*, at number 439, which sells nothing but kosher foods, American and Israeli, including halav Yisrael.

On the corner of Fairfax and Oakwood is a large *open-air bookstand*, where you can purchase Israeli newspapers and magazines, Yiddish papers, and periodicals published in New York.

Continuing north up the east side of Fairfax, you approach the first of several Israeli restaurants, the *Tel Aviv Kosher Restaurant*, small, clean, and shomer Shabbat. Others on the Avenue (not all kosher) are the *King David*, *Eilat*, *Café Tel Aviv*, and *Mi-Va-Mi*, the last a little stand with outside tables under umbrellas. South of Beverly Boulevard is a kosher Italian restaurant, *Kosher Nostra*. There are "Jewish" (but nonkosher) restaurants also, of which the most famous is *Cantor's*, a large, 24-hour-a-day establishment offering such sandwich concoctions as Mickey Katz Gourmet, Eddie Cantor's Delight, Las Vegas Special, and Brooklyn Avenue (a remnant of Boyle Heights).

Back on the east side of Fairfax, you soon arrive at a red-and-white sign on the sidewalk commanding passersby to STOP: PUT ON TEFILLIN, which can mark none other than a Habad establishment, this being the *Lubavitch Habad Mid-City Center*. Books on Habad Hasidism and related text abound in a very large, very neat store, along with people eager to assist you in doing mitzvot. This is one of a myriad of bookstores on the Avenue: *Herskovitz*, a small but friendly bookstore selling paperbacks and sefarim as well as ritual objects; *Atara's* (formerly Sojcher's), a larger store with more books and objects, including some old and unusual ones; and *Solomon's*, the largest and most crowded of all, filled to overflowing with sefarim, ritual objects of both quality and mediocrity, sifrei Torah, and English hardcover books and paperbacks of Jewish interest. There is a plethora of synagogues on or near Fairfax Avenue, to which the Los Angeles Jewish *Guide*, local Jewish newspapers, or a friendly Fairfax bookseller can lead you. The avenue also has a remarkable Jewish record shop, *HaTaklit*, run by Carmella and Tziporah, who boast that their collection of Israeli and Jewish records is more complete than any that can be found in New York or Israel. Judging by the size of their stock, it is hard to disagree.

To the question, "Is it possible to live a complete Jewish life in the Diaspora?" Fairfax Avenue provides a convincing, "Yes."

Should you decide to spend some time in the area, or in Los Angeles in general, there are other places on the avenue that you will find useful. The *Freda Mohr Center*, at 351 North Fairfax, a branch of Jewish Family Service, helps older residents of the area find apartments, rooms to rent, kosher meals, as well as volunteers to help out with many kinds of problems. If you are in need of threads and your money is in short supply, you might find it convenient to wander into *Bargain City*, a large cut-rate dry goods store that sells pharmaceuticals, clothing, stationery supplies, etc. Dignified elderly people throng the aisles, and you will find good bargains, as you will at *Honest Max Bargains* or at the *Council (of Jewish Women) Thrift Shop*, at 533 North Fairfax. If you're looking for a place to stay, you might check in at the *Fairfax Motel*, which offers rooms with kitchenettes if you wish to cook your own kosher meals.

PICO-ROBERTSON

Slightly to the west of Fairfax is the Pico-Robertson area, a newer Jewish district, whose blessings are more spread out and less abundant than the delights of Fairfax. Some of the larger synagogues are located here—*Beth Am*, Conservative, 1039 South La Cienega; *B'nai David-Judea*, Traditional, 8906 West Pico; *Mogen David*, Traditional, 9717 West Pico.

A jewel in the modest crown of Pico-Robertson Jewish establishments is *J. Roth Booksellers*, the best-stocked Jewish bookstore in the city, run by one of the gentlest and most unassuming merchants in the world, Jack Roth. The store has an excellent supply of hardcover and paperback Judaica (primarily in English) and keeps up-to-date with new books. It also has an outstanding collection of educational materials and some beautiful ritual objects.

Day schools also flourish, along with kosher (though not shomer Shabbat) bakeries, kosher meat markets, and kosher restaurants—*Kosher Gourmet* (8971 West Pico); *Kosher Kolonel* (9301 West Pico); and the *Pico Kosher Deli* (8826 West Pico). Dominating Beverly Boulevard is a kosher kitchen run by a hospital—*Cedars-Sinai*, surely one of the most elegant places in which to be sick in the world. Cedars—which started out as a hospital for the TB patients who once formed a sizable part of the Los Angeles Jewish community—in recent years has come to reemphasize its Jewish roots, with a Bris Room, a synagogue, and a resident rabbi.

WEST SIDE

A new center of Jewish life on the West Side of town has developed in the past two or three years. It is located on Wilshire Boulevard, the Main Street

If you're thinking of getting out of town, you might visit *Pedroza Travel*, run by an active Sephardi family, whose signs welcome you in English, Hebrew, and Spanish.

of Los Angeles, just a jump over the border of Beverly Hills. At 6505 Wilshire you'll find the home of the *Jewish Community Building,* which has continued to move whenever the Jewish community did so—from Boyle Heights to Hollywood (590 North Vermont) to this modest high-rise not far from Fairfax and Beverly Hills. Incidentally, 6505, whose offices afford sweeping views of the city and the mountains, is sometimes affectionately referred to as the "Jewish Pentagon," in part because the "official" strategies of the Jewish community are worked out in the offices of the federation's Community Relations Committee and the local offices of the American Jewish Committee, the Anti-Defamation League, and the American Jewish Congress. The Jewish Free Loan Society lives there, willing to provide interest-free loans to students and others who are temporarily down on their luck; the Youth Department is there, too—it maintains lists of activities for high-school students throughout the city and helps to plan many of them; and the Jewish Vocational Service is also on the premises (contact them in case you decide to stay in L.A. and need a job to provide you with vegetables). On the top floor are the Jewish Community Library and a memorial to the Martyrs of the Holocaust; in the basement is a tiny, but tasty, kosher restaurant. In fact, 6505 deserves a day in itself to enable you to pop in on all the offices that give visible evidence of the many facets of official Los Angeles Jewry. The ability of so many Jewish organizations to live under the same roof is reflected in the remarkable cooperation that has long existed between secular and religious, official and countercultural, Reform, Orthodox, and Conservative groups in the Los Angeles area. While there are more strains in this harmony than there used to be when the institutions were of more modest size, there is still an uncommon degree of congeniality among very disparate brands of Jews.

Just across the street from the Jewish Community Building, at 6380 Wilshire, are the offices of the *Israeli Consulate,* and a few buildings down, at 6300 Wilshire, are the District offices of *Bnai Brith.* A few long blocks to the south is the *Westside Jewish Community Center,* on Olympic Boulevard near Fairfax and San Vicente (Los Angeles's equivalent to New York's Broadway), cutting a transverse swath through the western part of the city. Westside boasts a marvelous pool and other athletic facilities and a bevy of very nice people planning increasingly Jewish-oriented programs for all age groups. The headquarters of the *Jewish Centers Association* is in that building, too, from which you can find your way to the five other Jewish centers around the city (Valley Cities, Bay Cities, Hollywood–Los Feliz, North Valley, and West Park).

BEVERLY HILLS

Beverly Hills is a Jewish area more in terms of people than institutions. The city has a very large Jewish population, frequently elects a Jewish mayor, and boasts "Jewish" (albeit nonkosher) restaurants such as *Nate-n-Al's* on 414 North Beverly Drive. Among the synagogues in Beverly Hills are *Beth Jacob* (Orthodox) at 9030 West Olympic, and *Temple Emanuel* (Reform) at 8844 Burton Way.

WESTWOOD

A newer and still developing West Side Jewish community, one almost devoid of visible Jewish institutions, is Westwood, the community surrounding UCLA. The Westwood Jewish community centers around 900 Hilgard Avenue, which is the address of the *University Religious Conference* (URC), an interreligious building whose most active occupant is *Hillel Council at UCLA.*

There you will find Wednesday-night folk dancing, a tradition among the Los Angeles folk-dance community; regular Friday-night services, often with dinner and a speaker; lectures and classes, social and cultural programs on campus and off. Aside from these activities, Hillel has also given birth to some of the countercultural activities that have made Westwood a center for young Jewish life. Among these are the *Westwood Free Minyan*, an autonomous egalitarian group that meets weekly at the URC and features a traditional service led by a Hebrew and an English hazzan, discussions on the Torah portion and other subjects, Kiddush, and lunch. Men and women participate equally in the service. The Minyan is populated by students, young faculty, and young professionals, often with small children, who have developed a well-integrated religious, social, and intellectual existence. The Minyan has had a considerable effect on the religious life of the Jews of various ages who are familiar with it.

Other scions of 900 Hilgard are the *Beit Midrash*, which offers courses similar to those in other cities, and the various and changing programs of the *Organizing Project*, an outreach program at UCLA Hillel.

Ha'am is a Jewish student newspaper funded by the Communications Board of the Associated Students of UCLA, which appears twice each academic quarter. Across the campus from Hillel at 741 Gayley Avenue is *Habad House*, peopled by several rabbis from Lubavitch who gladly study with individuals or groups and hold regular daily and Shabbat services, and whose Purim and Simhat Torah bashes are renowned for miles around. A few blocks away, at 617 Levering Avenue, is the *Westwood Bayit*, an old fraternity house transformed into a kosher living cooperative of nearly twenty-five students, who observe Shabbat and the holidays together and help lead Jewish activities on campus. The groups associated with Hillel, the Organizing Project, *Ha'am*, the Bayit, other independent groups, and Habad have formed the *UCLA Jewish Union* (UJU), which sponsors its own activities and maintains an office in the student activities building on campus (Kerckhoff Hall). The office of *Ha'am* is also located in Kerckhoff.

UCLA has a flourishing major in *Jewish Studies*, housed in the Near Eastern Languages Department, and utilizes the considerable bibliographic resources of the *Jewish Studies Collection* of the University Research Library on campus. While the nearest Jewish bookstore is J. Roth, twenty minutes away, the Student Store in Ackerman Union and the large number of bookstores in Westwood Village, proper and all along Westwood Boulevard, often have some Jewish books for sale. (*Ken Karmiole*, at 2255 Westwood Boulevard, even specializes in old or used Judaica.) Attractive Jewish ritual objects, in limited quantity, can be obtained at the *World Center* at 1048 Westwood Boulevard.

While there are no kosher restaurants or meat markets in Westwood, "Jewish" food can be obtained at *Junior's*, 2379 Westwood Boulevard, and, for excellent falafel, *Jason's* at 918 Broxton, *Me and Me*, 10975 Weyburn, and *Falafel King*, 10940 Weyburn. Nonkosher shwarma is also available at the last two. The *Bomb Shelter*, an eating place in the Science Quadrangle at UCLA, has lox and cream cheese, falafel, and other such delicacies.

There are only two synagogues in Westwood proper—*Sinai Temple* (Conservative), 10400 Wilshire Boulevard, and *Tifereth Israel* (Sephardic Temple), 10500 Wilshire Boulevard. There are, however, in addition, several others on the West Side: *Leo Baeck Temple* (Reform), 1300 N. Sepulveda Boulevard; the *Jewish Congregation of Pacific Palisades* (Reconstructionist), 16019 Sunset Boulevard; *University Synagogue* (Reform), 11960 Sunset Boulevard; and *Adat Shalom* (Conservative), 3030 Westwood Boulevard at National. Leo Baeck is a particularly fine place to hear good music and provocative sermons.

Sephardic congregations in the city are: *Congregation Kahal Joseph*, 10505 Santa Monica Boulevard; *Sephardic Hebrew Center*, 4911 W. 59th Street; *Magen David Congregation*, 7454 Melrose. There is also a Sephardic Young Adult group about whose activities the synagogues can inform you.

VENICE

Farther west, in the decaying beach community of Venice, is one of the most colorful, bizarre, and poignant of all the Los Angeles Jewish communities. Built originally as a replica of the Italian city of the same name, it has suffered the filling in of all but one of its canals (the Grand Canal) and the transformation of its ersatz Doge's Palace (at Windward and Pacific) into a flea market. Because the rents are low and the beach is warm, elderly and less affluent Jews have migrated there; they add a distinctly Jewish flavor to a community that probably boasts more ethnic groups living together than any other in ethnically segregated Los Angeles. The present main center of Jewish life—cultural, social, and occasionally political—is the *Israel Levin Center* on the boardwalk. Yiddish and literature classes are offered, heated discussions fill the air, and programs that bring together students and the older residents—for example, oral history projects and the like—have been under way for some years. Several bakeries with Eastern European Jewish food fill the air with a pleasant complement to ocean salt. There used to be several synagogues on the oceanfront, but as a result of attrition, death, and internal squabbling, only two remain: *Mishkon Tephilo*, and the *Pacific Jewish Center*, a dynamic young congregation whose members have moved into Venice from other parts of the city to study and daven with their rabbi, and who have offered considerable assistance to the beleaguered elderly community in their midst.

The history of Venice, Los Angeles, Europe, and Israel can be learned just by sitting in the sun on the benches of any day of the week. The people whose lives have been part of that history will be glad to share them with you, even as they are battling landlords who are trying either to raise their rents or to evict them to make room for high-rise condominiums; but they have begun to find allies from other groups who have convinced them that in numbers and determination there is strength. Venice itself is a community always under siege; it is a very friendly amalgam of old people, blacks, Chicanos, and student types, and one of those groups is usually under attack from someone. It's a great place to find what is so sorely lacking in Los Angeles: a sense of the past, as well as an excitement about the possibility of consolidated human effort in the future.

JEWISH VALLEY

We've left the Jewish Valley for last only because, like the rest of the San Fernando Valley, its Jewish life is terribly spread out, and an automobile is generally required for travel from one site to another. Some very distinguished and creative synagogues abound there, particularly **Valley Beth Shalom** (15739 Ventura Boulevard, Encino), a synagogue filled with active havurot, which also pioneered the now widespread Los Angeles tradition of Israeli dancing after (and even before) services. Other synagogues of particular note are: Conservative—**Adat Ari El**, 5540 Laurel Canyon Boulevard (North Hollywood), and **Ramat Zion**, 17655 Devonshire (Northridge); Orthodox—**Valley Mishkan Israel**, 12822 Victory Boulevard (North Hollywood); Reform—**Beth Hillel**, 12326 Riverside Drive (North Hollywood), **Emet**, 20400 Ventura Boulevard (Woodland Hills), and **Judea**, 5429 Lindley Avenue (Tarzana).

An active **Hillel** foundation is maintained at **Cal State University at Northridge** (17729 Plummer Street), which, in addition to the usual activities, boasts summer programs, various singles and couples havurot, a Jewish newspaper (*B'Yachad*), and a burgeoning relationship with the Jewish studies program at CSUN, which operates through the Religion Department.

Other places to visit are the **House of David Bookstore** (12826 Victory Boulevard) and the **Valley Cities Jewish Community Center** at 13164 Burbank Boulevard, attached to which is the **Hillel House at L. A. Valley College**, 13162 Burbank Boulevard—both places of thriving activity. Valley College boasts a large and well-attended Jewish studies program, perhaps the most extensive of any community college in the country.

The Valley is the fastest growing Jewish area in the city, and of all the Los Angeles communities with sizable Jewish populations, it is the only one, a recent study indicates, to which people indicate specifically that they want to move for "Jewish reasons." More and more of the city's Jewish leaders come from the Valley. New day schools are opening there (in addition to a respected Orthodox one, **Emek**, and a fine "community" school, **Abraham Joshua Heschel Day School**).

More information about Valley Jewish life can be obtained at the Valley office of the Jewish Federation Council at Encino, or the Valley Storefront at 12821 Victory Boulevard, North Hollywood.

JEWISH INSTITUTIONS

Some of the most distinguished Jewish institutions in Los Angeles are quite outside the Jewish areas, yet they are very influential. The **Hebrew Union College-Jewish Institute of Religion**, the **Jewish Theological Seminary**, and **Yeshiva University** all maintain branches in Los Angeles. The California School of HUC (3077 University Mall) is located adjacent to the University of Southern California, near downtown in a primarily black and Hispanic neighborhood that is now going through a vast urban-renewal program. The school offers the second and third years of the rabbinic program, as well as schools of Jewish Communal Service, Jewish Education, and Judaic Studies. It has an excellent faculty, fine students, and rapport between both that is unusual. The school has a small but growing library, the **Tartak Learning Center**, overflowing with educational materials, and the **Skirball Museum**; the latter mounts interesting and informative exhibits of its own collection of ritual objects and other aspects of visual Judaica. Beautiful ritual objects, posters, and books can also be purchased in the museum gift shop.

The converted Hollywood athletic club building that used to house the

You will find the Jewish denizens of the City of Angels generally friendly to visitors and hospitable to strangers. After all, like their ancestors in Egypt, most of us were strangers here ourselves not so many years ago.

Come meet us.

University of Judaism, the West Coast Branch of JTS, has now given way to a sweeping modern structure at 15600 Mulholland Drive amid the Santa Monica Mountains, bridging the classical boundary between the City and the Valley. The University of Judaism allows rabbinic students to complete the Mechina program of the Seminary, and also offers programs in general Jewish studies and Jewish education, as well as an extensive series of day and evening courses to those desiring merely to improve their Jewish knowledge. Its young, scholarly, and sensitive faculty help create a very positive atmosphere.

A few years ago Yeshiva University moved some of its brightest and most dynamic teachers and alumni to Los Angeles to establish *Yeshiva University of Los Angeles* (YULA), at 9760 West Pico Boulevard. Its offerings include adult courses, initial training in the Isaac Elchanan Theological Seminary rabbinic program, and the Simon Wiesenthal Center for Holocaust Studies. YULA provides many programs to the community and encourages its students to reach out to young people in the city to demonstrate the beauty of Orthodox Jewish practice. YULA has also assumed supervision of its own high school at the YULA site.

Other day schools in the city are: *Hillel Hebrew Academy*, 9120 West Olympic Boulevard; *Akiba Academy*, 10400 Wilshire Boulevard; *Herzl Academy*, a high school at 1027 South La Cienega Boulevard; and *Emanuel Day School*, 8844 Burton Way, Beverly Hills. The Conservative and Reform movements also each run a Hebrew high school. The Federation's *Bureau of Jewish Education* offers such creative enrichment programs as Havurat Noar for ninth graders, Chalutz for tenth graders, and an Ulpan in Israel. In all these, as well as in the synagogue schools, there are many opportunities for employment.

Unique to Los Angeles is the distinguished institution in the Santa Susana Mountains known as the *Brandeis-Bardin Institute*, which, under the guidance of the late Shlomo Bardin, developed an intensive summer program for college students from around the country (BCI, the *Brandeis Camp–Institute*); an adult support and education group known as the *House of the Book*, which sponsors lectures and weekends featuring eminent Jewish personalities; a summer camp for children, *Camp Alonim*; and now in-town lectures featuring discussions with the Institute's new leaders, Dennis Prager and Rabbi Joseph Telushkin. Los Angeles is also developing a growing number of synagogues intended for particular groups of people: the *Synagogue for the Performing Arts*; *Beth Chayim Chadashim*, whose members come primarily from the gay community; *Temple Beth Solomon of the Deaf*; and the *Los Angeles Singles Synagogue*. The addresses of these groups, as well as a wealth of other information about the Los Angeles Jewish community can be found in another special Los Angeles Jewish institution, *Jewish Los Angeles: A Guide*, an informative but good-humored publication of the Jewish Federation–Council.

With all that we have told you about the City of the Angels, we have said nothing about that particular Jewish institution from which you, dear readers from the East and Middle West, probably heard about Los Angeles in the first place: Hollywood. The movies were founded in great part by Jews, but you would never know it from the themes of the films produced here, or the (often negative) manner in which Jews are portrayed on the few occasions when they appear as characters on the screen. Now that Los Angeles has finally succeeded in luring the Eastern Jewish institutions out West, perhaps the next frontier to be conquered is to make the Jews of Hollywood aware of the vibrant Jewish world that lies just outside their doors. We who live in that world, unoppressed by snow and winter winds, welcome all who live in frostier climes to join us here in the climate of the Eretz Yisrael of the West.

A guide to the world of Hasidim

YOU SHALL BE EXTOLLED WITH THE WORDS OF THE RIGHTEOUS
Prayer Book ובלשון חסידים תתרומם

The purpose of this guide will be to direct the seeker and uninitiated to some of the Hasidic communities located in the United States. Hasidic communities are not all alike. Some, like Lubavitch (Habad) or the Bostoner, openly seek to attract followers. Others, like Bobov and Skver, neither encourage nor discourage potential followers. Still others, Satmar and Munkatch, for example, discourage any outsiders. Obviously Hasidic groups also differ from each other in other respects: beyond social distinctions, for instance, they will each stress different aspects of Hasidism, and generally there are strong differences in personality among the various Hasidic rebbeim.

Lubavitch

Of all Hasidic groups, Lubavitch is the best known, although not the largest (Satmar seems to have won that distinction). Lubavitchers are not insular and seek to convert their fellow Jews—not just to Orthodoxy but to their brand of

Local Lubavitcher representatives are to be found in most U.S. cities with a sizable Jewish population. A complete list is to be found in *Catalog 1*.

Hasidism. They are extremely outgoing and friendly. Hence they are usually the outsider's first contact with Hasidism.

The main Lubavitch Shul is located at 770 Eastern Parkway (which equals uforazto [and you shall spread out]—the tenet of Lubavitch—in gematria), and arrangements can be made to spend a Shabbat or longer there by contacting

Lubavitch College and Youth Council
770 Eastern Pkwy.
Brooklyn, NY 11213
(212) 778-4270

A rather recent phenomenon in Lubavitch is the creation of Habad houses. These are usually located near college campuses and serve as centers of Jewish activities for the local colleges. They are frequently run by young Lubavitcher couples whose full-time work is running the house. Activities include Shabbat services, classes in all areas of Judaism, living space for crashing, rap sessions, and similar activities.

The Habad houses are rapidly expanding and for the most part have achieved great success. Each house varies in many ways from the next. Some are spacious and comfortable, others are fairly rundown. Most, however, are run by energetic dedicated directors. The following is a list of Habad houses:

1536 E. Maryland
Phoenix, AZ 85014
602-274-5377

2340 Piedmont Ave.
Berkeley, CA 94704
415-845-7791

741 Gayley Ave.
Los Angeles, CA 90024
213-272-7113

4915 Hayvenhurst Ave.
Encino, CA 91436
213-784-9985

627 Broadway
Santa Monica, CA 90401
213-395-4470

24412 Narbonne Ave.
Lomita, CA 90717
213-326-8234

6115 Montezuma Rd.
San Diego, CA 92115
714-286-4747

85 Forest Rd.
Denver, CO 80220
303-393-0112

Yale Habad House
198 York St.
New Haven, CN 06511
203-562-2227

1401 Alton Rd.
Miami Beach, FL 33139
305-672-8947

1540 Albenga Ave.
Coral Gables, FL 33146
305-661-7642

5721 Park Heights Ave.
Baltimore, MD 21215
301-578-0338

3330 Peachtree Rd. NE
Atlanta, GA 30326
404-237-1000

2014 Orrington
Evanston, IL 60201
312-869-8060

2932 University Ave.
Des Moines, IA 50311
515-277-2039

7037 Freret St.
New Orleans, LA 70118
504-866-5164

311 W. Montgomery Ave.
Rockville, MD 20850
301-340-6858

30 N. Hadley Rd.
Amherst, MA 01002
413-253-9040

42 Kirkwood Rd.
Brighton, MA 02135
617-254-0352

14000 W. Nine Mile Rd.
Oak Park, MI 48237
313-548-2666

715 Hill St.
Ann Arbor, MI 48104
313-995-3276

1910 Michigan N.E.
Grand Rapids, MI 49503
616-458-6575

15 Montcalm Ct.
St. Paul, MN 55116
612-690-1395

8901 Holmes St.
Kansas City, MO 64131
816-333-7117

226 Sussex Ave.
Morristown, NJ 07960
201-267-9404

184 Hallock Rd.
Lake Grove, NY 11755
516-588-5832

2501 N. Forest Rd.
Getzville, NY 14068
716-688-1642

2004 S. Green Rd.
Cleveland, OH 44121
216-721-5050

1636 Summit Rd.
Cincinnati, OH 45237
513-821-5100

57 E. 14th Ave.
Columbus, OH 43201
614-294-3296

7622 Castor Ave.
Philadelphia, PA 19152
215-725-2030

48 Savoy St.
Providence, RI 02906
401-273-7238

2101 Nuences Ave.
Austin, TX 78705
512-472-3900

10900 Fondran Rd.
Houston, TX 77096
713-777-2000

6145 Sylvan St.
Norfolk, VA 23508
804-423-3983

5311 W. Franklin
Richmond, VA 23226
804-288-0588

4541 19th Ave. N.E.
Seattle, WA 98105
206-527-1411

613 Howard Pl.
Madison, WI 53703
608-251-6022

3109 N. Lake Dr.
Milwaukee, WI 53211
414-962-0566

Canada

497 W. 39th Ave.
Vancouver, B.C.
604-324-2406

532 Inkster Blvd.
Winnipeg, Man.
204-586-1867

44 Edinburgh Dr.
Toronto, Ont.
416-633-8020

3429 Peel St.
Montreal, Que.
514-842-6616

The Lubavitch House in St. Paul has an additional unique program: Beth Hannah, a school that offers beginners' instructions in Judaism for women. Sessions are usually held during December or January and in the summer vacation period.

A must for everyone interested in Hasidism is to attend a farbrengen, a Hasidic get-together where there is singing and socializing interspersed with words of Torah and Hasidic mystical discourses from the Lubavitcher rebbe—all in Yiddish, of course. The farbrengens are held every Shabbat Mevorkhim—the Shabbat before Rosh Hodesh, the festival of the New Moon—and on the eve of festivals, as well as on the following special occasions:

19th day of Kislev:	anniversary of the release of the founder of Habad, Rabbi Shneur Zalman of Ladi, from prison
10th day of Shevat:	Yahrzeit of Rav J. I. Schneersohn, predecessor and father-in-law of the present rebbe
11th day of Nisan:	the rebbe's birthday
12th day of Tammuz:	day of release of R. J. I. Schneerson from the Communist prison Spalerna (Moscow) in 1927
20th day of Av:	Yahrzeit of the rebbe's father, R. Levi Yizhak Schneersohn, chief rabbi of Dnepropetrovsk, USSR

And on other days, when the rebbe so wishes

If you're a New Yorker and can't come down, most weekday farbrengens are broadcast live on WEVD, 97.9 FM, with English summaries by Rabbi Jacob J. Hecht. These broadcasts can be very interesting and at times can beat the real thing—especially for the meek and those who don't understand Yiddish.

All farbrengens on weekdays start exactly at 9:30 P.M. and end early in the morning (2–4 A.M.). Pushing is the order of the day: come early to get a seat; otherwise be prepared to stand, crane, and struggle. Women are seated in a balcony and are most welcome.

Lubavitch runs three schools for baalei teshuvah—people who have "returned" to Judaism (see *Catalog 2*, pp. 253–61)—and for newcomers to Judaism; these schools teach not only Orthodox Judaism but also Habad Hasidic thought. They have part-time programs and are very loosely structured.

1. **Hader-Hatorah**
   824 Eastern Pkwy.
   Brooklyn, NY 11213

caters to men over twenty. Most of its students are either college graduates or men who have gone to college. This school has guided several of its students from alef-bet to ordination.

   Makhon Hannah
   1367 President St.
   Brooklyn, NY 11225

is the women's counterpart to Hadar-Hatorah and offers a full range of courses in Judaism.

2. **Morristown Yeshiva**
   Sussex Ave.
   Morristown, N.J. 07960

has a beautiful campus and houses not only a regular branch of the Lubavitcher yeshivah but also a newcomer branch, directed by R. Abraham Lipsker. This is designed for teenagers first coming to Judaism. Contact

   Rabbinical College of New Jersey
   Morristown, NJ 07960

3. **Machne Israel House**
   1408 President St.
   Brooklyn, NY 11213

offers dorm space for visiting young people, as well as classrooms and a library created in response to a call by the rebbe for the creation of Jewish libraries throughout the world.

The Lubavitcher rebbe, Rabbi Menahem Schneersohn, is probably among the most outstanding Jewish personalities in post-Holocaust Jewish life. He was Jewishly trained under his father, a great scholar. He also attended the Sorbonne and holds an engineering degree. He practiced as an engineer until his elevation to the rebbe's chair in 1950. The rebbe is an exceptionally brilliant man, and among his many callers have been scholars, philosophers, artists, novelists, politicians, Israeli generals, Jewish lay leaders, and others, a list that reads like a Who's Who in World Jewry. Currently the rebbe is directing a five-pronged battle on these fronts: 1. increased Torah learning, 2. mezuzot, 3. tefillin, 4. Shabbat candles for women, 5. Jewish books in every home.

Unfortunately it is now almost impossible to see the rebbe, and appointments entail a six-month to one-year waiting period. While writing a letter is suggested by Hasidim as an alternative means of contacting the rebbe, it is known that in many cases this is not effective.

Lubavitch also publishes many pamphlets, books, records, etc. on Habad, many in English. For a full catalog write to

Kehot Publication Society
770 Eastern Pkwy.
Brooklyn, NY 11213

Another interesting Lubavitch-initiated venture is Chai Institute, an art gallery that was opened fairly recently by some Lubavitcher Hasidim. It displays works by non-Lubavitchers and has some interesting pieces. Hours are Monday through Thursday 12–5 P.M. and Sundays 11 A.M.–6 P.M.

Chai Institute
375 Kingston Ave.
Brooklyn, NY 11213
(212) 774-9149
(212) 778-8808

One of the more interesting Lubavitcher Hasidim is Meir Abehsera, well known to people who go in for macrobiotics. Although born to an Orthodox Sephardic rabbinical family, he drifted away from Judaism but found his way back through the rebbe. In a way Abehsera functions as a minor rebbe, as he has attracted many of his former macrobiotic followers and health-food freaks to Lubavitch. Abehsera loves to talk to visitors, and his house is open for Shabbat. Contact:

M. Abehsera
1852 E. 7th St.
Brooklyn, NY 11213

Bostoner

The only other Hasidic group that actively strives to attract outsiders is the Bostoner, led by the Bostoner rebbe, Grand Rabbi Levi Yitzhak Horowitz at

1710 Beacon St.
Brookline, MA 02146
(617) 734-5100

Most Hasidic rebbes are called after towns in Europe, but Rabbi Horowitz's father, one of the first rebbes to come to the U.S., established the first American Hasidic dynasty when he came to Boston in the pre–World War I years; hence the name.

The rebbe is American born, speaks English, and is thoroughly familiar with the current American scene. Naturally Bostoner Hasidut is centered in Boston, but there are some Bostoner Hasidim in New York and Israel as well.

Among the activities of the Bostoner rebbe are college Shabbatons (Shabbat programs held at the center), the New England Torah Institute (a school for the male beginners), and the Lionel Goldman Seminary of Jewish Studies (a similar school for women). Both offer a variety of courses and have summer programs. The Bostoner rebbe is known for his tremendous hospitality, and students and others are always welcome to spend Shabbat at the rebbe's home. Recently the Bostoner rebbe has begun to visit other cities (Washington, Baltimore, and Providence) to hold Shabbatons.

The rebbe has had a great deal of success; not only has he attracted many students to Orthodoxy, but some have even become full-fledged Hasidim of the rebbe. Many of the rebbe's Hasidim are professional men and women with advanced degrees and successful careers. Unlike the Lubavitch, the Bostoner rebbe does not discourage his Hasidim from academic or professional achievement. The Bostoner rebbe is also very accessible, and there is usually only a short waiting period for personal appointments to be arranged.

Bratslaver Hasidim

The Bratslaver Hasidim have not had a rebbe since the death of their first and only rebbe, Rabbi Nahman of Bratslav, a great-grandson of the Baal Shem Tov, the founder of the Hasidic movement.

Like the Lubavitcher, the Bratslaver also actively seek to spread their own teachings to other Jews. The main center of the Bratslaver is in Jerusalem, where leading Bratslaver teachers like Rabbis Levi Yizhak Bender and Gedalya Kenig reside.

In the U.S. there are Bratslaver synagogues in various parts of the greater New York area. The most active of these is

Congregation Heichal Hakodesh
851 47th St.
Brooklyn, NY 11219
(212) 438-9097

Also located here is a yeshivah catering primarily to baalei teshuvah, as well as a dormitory. This synagogue also publishes Rabbi Nahman's works and distributes them at a very low cost. This center is headed by Rabbis Eliezer S. Schuck and Samuel Jungreis.

Although the Lubavitcher, Bostoner, and Bratslaver communities are the only ones that openly seek to attract outsiders, most other Hasidim, while they do not actively propagandize, receive visitors hospitably and go out of their way to make them feel at home.

Brooklyn

Since Brooklyn, New York, contains the largest Hasidic community, that community will be treated more extensively.

BORO PARK

This Brooklyn neighborhood contains numerous Hasidic shtiblech, etc. of all types. Here are a few of the more interesting ones:

Bobover Bet Medrash
1533 48th St.
The Bobover community is a very friendly one and the rebbe, Solomon Halberstam, is an extremely personable man. Bobov is especially recommended for its Friday night tishen—literally, tables, where students are invited to eat, sing, and learn with the rebbe—and Saturday evening melave malkahs. On Purim, a Purim spiel—play—is performed, which is an event worth attending. Bobov is the third largest Hasidic group in the U.S.

Stoliner Bet Medrash
1818 54th St.
The historic Karlin-Stolin dynasty is today headed by a twenty-five-year-old American-born rebbe, Barukh Shochet. The community is currently investigating the possibility of relocating to Staten Island, N.Y.

Kapishnitzer Bet Medrash
1415 55th St.
is the shtibel of the late Kapishnitzer rebbe, Moshe Mordechai Heschel, who was well known for his many acts of kindness and charity.

Bostoner
1535 49th St.
is the shtibel of Rabbi Moses Horowitz, the older brother of Boston's Bostoner rebbe.

Chuster Bet Medrash
1259 56th St.
has as its new rabbi Pinhas Horowitz, the son of Boston's Bostoner rebbe. In the winter months the Chuster rav has tishen, which are conducted in English and attract young people.

Rabbi Sheingarten's Shtibel
1520 48th St.
is a very small synagogue with a heterogeneous group of worshipers. It is renowned for its friendliness.

Adas Yakov
1569 47th St.
Brooklyn, NY 11219
is the synagogue of the Novominsker rebbe, Rabbi Yakov Perlow. This is a very friendly synagogue where a guest can easily feel comfortable.

Belzer Bet Medrash
4814 16th Ave.
Brooklyn, NY 11219

Munkatcher Bet Medrash
5306 13th Ave.
Brooklyn, NY 11219
is the synagogue of the Munkatcher rebbe, Rabbi Moshe Leib Rabinowitz. There are tishen here every Friday evening.

Sigeter Bet Medrash—Azei Chaim
4915 15th Ave.
Brooklyn, NY 11219
is the synagogue of the new Satmarer rebbe, Rabbi Moshe Teitelbaum, who is also known as the Sigeter rav.

Skolyer Bet Medrash
1335 48th St.
Brooklyn, NY 11219
is the synaogue of the new Skolyer rebbe, Rabbi Yakov Rabinowitz, who is eighteen years old and succeeded his grandfather in 1979.

Stuchiner Bet Medrash
1266 50th St.
Brooklyn, NY 11219
is the synagogue of the Stuchiner rebbe, Rabbi Judah Horowitz, one of the senior Hasidic leaders in the United States.

Tchernobler Bet Medrash
1520 49th St.
Brooklyn, NY 11219
is the synagogue of the Tchernobler rebbe, Rabbi Jacob I. Twersky. It is particularly lively on Simhat Torah.

WILLIAMSBURG

Williamsburg contains the largest and most insular Hasidic community in the world. The Satmar community dominates and controls the area. Satmar is best known for its fight against Zionism. Yet its activities include a Bikur Holim to visit the sick, a community clinic and pharmacy, an employment agency, aid to Soviet Jews in Russia and to new Russian immigrants, and the largest Jewish school system in the United States. Besides their central synagogue in Williamsburg, they maintain branch synagogues in Boro Park, Crown Heights, Lakewood, N.J., Monsey, and Monroe, N.Y., where the Satmarer have built a self-contained community that includes the residence of the late Satmarer rebbe. Visitors are not advised to go to Satmar, as outsiders are generally not very welcome except in rare instances.

Williamsburg is particularly interesting to visit during Purim, when the Hasidim dress up in absurd costumes and don delightful masquerades. Other good times to visit are during Hol ha-Moed—the intermediate days of Passover and Sukkot. These days are semifestivals, which means that the Hasidim dress in their holiday clothing; yet travel is permitted during these days so

that your traveling to visit Williamsburg will not be seen as a violation of Jewish law by the Hasidim. On Hoshana Rabba (the seventh day of Sukkot) there is an elaborate synagogue service that can be worth seeing.

SEA GATE

The Ribnitzer rebbe, Rabbi Chaim Zanvil Abramowitz, arrived in the United States from the USSR in 1974. In Russia he resided near Kishinev and was regarded as a tzaddik—righteous person—and a baal mofes—performer of miracles—by religious Jews throughout Russia. Since his arrival in the U.S. he has gained a similar reputation here. His current address is

5134 Ocean Ave.
Brooklyn, NY 11235
(212) 946-7706

CROWN HEIGHTS

Besides Lubavitch, there are several other Hasidic groups residing in Crown Heights. Only ten years ago dozens of rebbes and many Polish, Galician, and Hungarian Hasidim lived in Crown Heights. Because of neighborhood changes and the ensuing panic, however, today only a few rebbes and Hasidim (besides the Lubavitch community) are left.

Hasidic synagogues

BROOKLYN

Williamsburg
Congregation Yitav Lev of Satmar
152 Rodney St.
Brooklyn, NY
This is the main Satmar synagogue. There are seven more Satmar synagogues in Williamsburg as well as six in Boro Park.
Arugoth Ha-Bosem
559 Bedford Ave.
Brooklyn, NY
This synagogue is headed by the Zehlemer rav, Rabbi L. Y. Gruenwald.
Boyaner Kluiz
260 Marcy Ave.
Brooklyn, NY

Galanter bet Medrash
287 Hewes St.
Brooklyn, NY
Rabbi Yitzhak Eichenstein is the Galanter rebbe.
Kehillath Yakov of Popa
656 Bedford Ave.
Brooklyn, NY
This is the synagogue of the Poper rav, Rabbi Joseph Grunwald, and represents the second largest Hasidic community in Williamsburg.
Nesivot Olam Bet Medrosh
150 Hewes St.
Brooklyn, NY
This is the synagogue of the M'lochim (Angels), a native American Hasidic group whose spiritual leader is Rabbi Jacob Schorr.

Toales Yakov Bet Medrosh
99 Wilson St.
Brooklyn, NY
This is the synagogue of Rabbi Chaim Mertz, considered by many to be a baal mofes—performer of miracles.
Payer Bet Medrash
296 Marcy Ave.
Brooklyn, NY
Rabbi M. D. Weinberger is the Payer rav.
Sigeter Bet Medrosh
152 Hewes St.
Brooklyn, NY
Minchas Elozor Bet Medrash
137 Hooper St.
Brooklyn, NY

Karlsburger Bet Medrash
609 Bedford Ave.
Brooklyn, NY
Rabbi Baruch Kahana is the Karlsburger rebbe.

Crown Heights
Belz
662 Eastern Pkwy.
Brooklyn, NY
Minhat Osher
552 Montgomery St.
Brooklyn, NY

MANHATTAN

Upper West Side
Boyaner Shtibel
441 West End Ave.
New York, NY
This group is very friendly.
Congregation Heichal Moshe
303 W. 91st St.
New York, NY
Rabbi Zev Vorhand is the Praguer rav.
Sassover Shtibel
254 W. 103rd St.
New York, NY
Rabbi David Rubin is the Sassover rebbe.

Upper East Side
Congregation Akh Pri T'vuah
163 E. 69th St.
New York, NY
This is the synagogue of the Lisker rebbe, Rabbi Solomon Friedlander.

Lower East Side
Boyaner Shtibel
247 E. Broadway
New York, NY
Belzer Bet Medrash
255 E. Broadway
New York, NY

METROPOLITAN NEW YORK

Lakewood, NJ
Congregation Yetav Lev—Satmar
10 First St.
Lakewood, NJ

Monroe, NY
The late Satmarer rebbe established a community of his followers here in 1972 and spent the last years of his life there. The rebbe is buried there, and his wife, Rebbetzin Feiga Teitelbaum, continues to reside in the community, which is known as Kiryat Joel. The main Satmarer yeshivah is located in Kiryat Joel.

Monsey, NY
Monsey has quite a large Hasidic population, including numerous Hasidic synagogues. Among these are the following:
Vishnitzer Bet Medrash
Phyllis Terrace
Monsey, NY
This is the synagogue of Rabbi Moteli Hager, the Vishnitzer rebbe in the U.S.
Stanislower Bet Medrash
55 W. Maple
Monsey, NY
Rabbi Israel Rosenbaum is the Stanislower rebbe.
Satmarer synagogue
25 S. Maple
Monsey, NY

New Square, NY
This community of over two hundred families was established in 1959 by the late Skverer rebbe, Rabbi Jacob Twersky. It is currently headed by its founder's son and successor, Rabbi David Twersky. This community is located about three miles from Spring Valley, N.Y.

THE REST OF THE COUNTRY

California—Los Angeles
Congregation Ohel David
7967 Beverly Blvd.
Los Angeles, CA
This is the synagogue of Rabbi Eliezer Adler, the Zhviler—Los Angeleser rebbe. This very friendly and hospitable place numbers one of the Warner brothers among their regular daveners.
Congregation Adath Ha-Charedim
221 S. La Brea Ave.
Los Angeles, CA
Congregation Atzei Chaim
8018 W. Third Ave.
Los Angeles, CA
This is the synagogue of the Rudniker rebbe, Rabbi Hershele Halberstam, a nephew of the late Satmarer rebbe. A mikveh is located on the premises.
Congregation Kehillath Yizkoh
7709 Beverley Blvd.
Los Angeles, CA
Congregation Mogen Avrohom
356 La Brea Ave.
Los Angeles, CA
This synagogue was founded by the late Rabbi Yudele Isaacsohn, a nephew of the late Satmarer rebbe. It is currently headed by Rabbi Isaac Lev.
Bet Medrash Chasidei Gur
7575 Melrose Ave.
Los Angeles, CA
This is the synagogue of the Gerer Hasidim in L.A.

Colorado—Denver
Rabbi Shlomo B. C. Twerski
4634 W. 14th Ave.
Denver, CO
Rabbi Twerski has a large following throughout the United States and is a psychologist as well as a rabbi. He is particularly active with baalei teshuvah.

Illinois—Chicago
Congregation Bnai Reuven—Nusach Ari
6350 N. Whipple Ave.
Chicago, IL
This synagogue, led by Rabbi Harold Shusterman, has strong Lubavitch leanings and has an exclusively Hasidic service on Shabbat as well as modern Orthodox services.
Congregation Agudath Anshei Lubavitch
7424 N. Paulina
Chicago, IL
This is a Lubavitcher synagogue.
Congregation Nusach Ho-Ari
4706 N. Monticello Ave.
Chicago, IL
This synagogue has a strong Lubavitch leaning. Its last rabbi was the late David Winchester, a kabbalist.

Congregation Lev Someach
5555 N. Bernard St.
Chicago, IL
This synagogue was founded by the late Maliner rebbe, J. Twersky, and is currently headed by his son, Rabbi Eshia Twersky.
Congregation Tiffereth Moshe
6308 N. Francisco
Chicago, IL
This small synagogue was founded by the late Rabbi Moshe Goldzweig, a kabbalist. It is currently headed by his son Rabbi Chaim Goldzweig, the Ⓤ supervisor for the Midwest. It is a very friendly synagogue.
Congregation Chesed L'Avrohom Nachlas David
6342 N. Troy St.
Chicago, IL
This synagogue is headed by Rabbi Yehoshua H. Eichenstein, the son of the late Zidichover rebbe. Rabbi Eichenstein is a charming and friendly man who takes a personal interest in all the congregants. The synagogue is very friendly to newcomers and students. A mikveh is located on the premises.
Congregation Khal Charedim
100 N. Bernard
Chicago, IL
This is the synagogue of Rabbi David Meisells, a son of the Waitzner rav of Chicago. Rabbi Meisells is also a son-in-law of the new Satmarer rebbe, Rabbi Moshe Teitelbaum. Of the Chicago Hasidic synagogues, this one most closely resembles its Brooklyn counterpart.

There are also several smaller Hasidic synagogues in the Chicago area.

Maryland—Baltimore
Congregation Arugath Ha-Bosem
615 Park Heights Ave.
Baltimore, MD
This is the synagogue of Rabbi Amraam Taub, the Kaliver rebbe of Baltimore. Among the worshipers here are quite a few baalei teshuvah.

Congregation Shearith Ha-Pleitah
6216 Biltmore Ave.
Baltimore, MD
This is the synagogue of Rabbi Isaac Sternhell, the late rosh bet din—ecclesiastical judge—of Baltimore's Rabbinical Council.

Massachusetts—Brookline
Besides the Bostoner rebbe, the following synagogues function in the Boston area.

Talner Beth David
64 Corey Rd.
Brookline, MA
This is the synagogue of the late Talner rebbe, Rabbi Meshulom Z. Twersky, and is currently headed by Rabbi Dr. Isadore Twersky. Dr. Twersky is the Littauer Professor of Jewish Studies at Harvard University. (Incidentally, he is also the son-in-law of Rabbi Dr. Joseph B. Soloveichik, a leading Mitnaged!) Since his father's death Dr. Twersky has accepted a limited rebbe's role and has been quoted as saying that if people consider him a rebbe and consult him, then he is in fact a rebbe.

Lubavitcher Bet Medrash
239–241 Chestnut Hill Ave.
Brighton, MA
This Lubavitch synagogue is directed by Rabbi Pinchos Krinsky.

Michigan—Detroit
Rabbi Zvi Deutsch
200 Kenosha
Oak Park, MI
Rabbi Deutsch is the Vienner rebbe.

Ohio—Cleveland
Congregation Heichal Ha-Brocha
1771 S. Taylor Rd.
Cleveland Hts., OH
Congregation Khal Yereim
1711 S. Taylor Rd.
Cleveland Hts., OH
Congregation Zemach Zedek
1922 Lee Rd.
Cleveland Hts., OH
This is a Lubavitcher synagogue.

Pennsylvania
Rabbi Ephraim Eliezer Yolles
7926 Algon Ave.
Philadelphia, PA
Rabbi Yolles is the chief Orthodox rabbi in Philadelphia. His father was the Sombover rebbe. A synagogue is located in Rabbi Yolles's home.
Congregation Zemach David
4900 N. 8th St.
Philadelphia, PA
This is the synagogue of the late Talner rebbe of Philadelphia.

Wisconsin—Milwaukee
Congregation Beth Jehudah
2700 N. 54th St.
Milwaukee, WI 53210
This is the synagogue of Rabbi Michel Twerski, a son of the late Hornistaypler rebbe of Milwaukee, Rabbi J. I. Twerski. Rabbi Twerski has an MA in psychology. This congregation is very friendly and hospitable.

Meeting the rebbes

The following rebbes are easily accessible and speak English.

Bobover Rebbe
Rabbi Solomon Halberstam
1533 48th St.
Brooklyn, NY
(212) 854-2444
contact: Rabbi Horowitz
Bostoner Rebbe
Rabbi Moses Horowitz
1535 49th St.
Brooklyn, NY
(212) 851-0500

Monoshtritzer Rebbe
Rabbi J. I. Rabinowitz
40 Paerdegat 4
Brooklyn, NY
(212) 531-3539
Novominsker Rebbe
Rabbi Yakov Perlow
1569 47th St.
Brooklyn, NY
(212) 436-1133

Skverer Rebbe
Rabbi David Twersky
New Square, NY 10977
(914) 562-9562
contact: Rabbi Ungar

Hasidic Clothes

Hasidic garments such as tish bekeshes (Hasidic-style smoking jackets), chalats (long coats worn on Shabbat), kapotes (Prince Albert-style frock coats), and reklechs (overcoats) can be purchased in many clothing stores in Williamsburg, Boro Park, and Crown Heights. Among these stores are the following:

JJJ Clothier
    333A Kingston Ave.
    Brooklyn, NY
    This store specializes in Lubavitch-style kapotes.
Marcy Clothing Center
    210 Broadway
    Brooklyn, NY
Reinhold Clothier
    4421 14th Ave.
    Brooklyn, NY
    This store has an excellent selection of all types of Hasidic coats and has friendly, prompt service.

Shtreimlech—fur hats worn by most Hasidim on Shabbat and holidays (cost is $500–$800)

Shmuel Kraus
    202 Keap St.
    Brooklyn, NY
Israel Schwartz
    190 Ross St., Apt. 5B
    Brooklyn, NY

Hasidic hats

Bencraft Hatters
    236 Broadway
    Brooklyn, NY
Hat Rack
    5416 16th Ave.
    Brooklyn, NY
Kova Hatters
    4311 13th Ave.
    Brooklyn, NY

Selco Hatters
    228 Broadway
    Brooklyn, NY

Books

PUBLISHERS

Jerusalem Book Store
    156 Wilson St.
    Brooklyn, NY
    This publishes the works of the late Satmer Rebbe, Rabbi Joel Teitelbaum.
Kehot Publication Society
    770 Eastern Pkwy.
    Brooklyn, NY
    This is the publishing arm of the Lubavitch movement. It provides works in many languages including English. Write for a free catalog.
Mesivta Heichal Ha-Kodesh
    851 47th St.
    Brooklyn, NY
    This is the publishing arm of the Bratslaver movement. Write for a free catalog.
Yeshivath Ohel Shmuel
    Haines Rd.
    Bedford Hills, NY
    They publish the works of the Kashever rav—Rabbi Raphael Blum.

BOOKSTORES

The following bookstores have an extensive selection of books dealing with Hasidism.

J. Beigeleisen
    83 Division St.
    New York, NY
Blum's Book Store
    169 Ross St.
    Brooklyn, NY
Drimmer's
    329 Kingston Ave.
    Brooklyn, NY
    This store specializes in Lubavitch publications.

Frankel's Hebrew Book Store
    4904 16th Ave.
    Brooklyn, NY
Grunfeld Hebrew Books
    4624 16th Ave.
    Brooklyn, NY
    The proprietor of this store is one of the Bobover rebbe's secretaries.
Jerusalem Book Store
    156 Wilson St.
    Brooklyn, NY
    This store specializes in the works of the Satmarer rebbe and other Hungarian Hasidic leaders.
M. Parnes
    41 Essex St.
    New York, NY
    This store specializes in Lubavitcher publications.

Tapes

The following stores carry cassette tapes in Yiddish with sermons and teachings of various Hasidic leaders:

Drimmer's
    329 Kingston Ave.
    Brooklyn, NY
    They sell tapes of talks by the Lubavitcher rebbe.
Joseph Kaufman
    1234 47th St., 2nd fl.
    Brooklyn, NY
S. Sandel
    Monroe, NY
    This store carries an extensive selection of tapes of sermons by the late Satmarer rebbe.
WLNS
    770 Eastern Pkwy.
    Brooklyn, NY
    They carry tapes of the farbrengens of the Lubavitcher rebbe.

The following photographers sell wallet-size color photos of Hasidic leaders:

Drimmers
329 Kingston Ave.
Brooklyn, NY
They carry photos of the Lubavitcher rebbe.

Elite Photographers—Kalman Zeines
516 Kings Hwy.
Brooklyn, NY
This studio has the largest selection of photographs of Hasidic rebbes in New York. Zeines is very friendly, courteous, and helpful.

Focus Studio
4419 13th Ave.
Brooklyn, NY

Morgan Studios
5101 New Utrecht Ave.
Brooklyn, NY

Newspapers

The following newspapers carry news and advertisements of Hasidic interest:

Algemeiner Journal
404 Park Ave. South
New York, NY
Gershon Jacobson—editor. Subscription—$25 a year.
This Yiddish weekly is published by interests close to the Lubavitch movement. It gives extensive coverage to news of Hasidic interest, especially of Lubavitch. Among its contributors are writers close to the Bobov, Ger, and Lubavitch Hasidim.

Der Yid
260 Broadway
Brooklyn, NY
Subscriptions—$20 a year
This Yiddish weekly is published by the Satmarer community. It contains detailed coverage of the activities of that community as well as other news and articles of Hasidic interest. Many of its articles are fiercely anti-Zionist, reflecting the Satmarer position on Zionism. It is the only Yiddish newspaper whose circulation increases every year.

The Jewish Press
338 Third Ave.
Brooklyn, NY
Shalom Klass—editor. Subscription—$16 a year.
While not Hasidic, this English weekly often has material about the Brooklyn Hasidic communities.

World Jewish Tribune
1133 Broadway
Brooklyn, NY
Subscription—$18 a year.
This English weekly was launched in 1979 by interests close to the Satmarer Hasidim.

Zohar
P. O. Box 5430
Jerusalem, Israel
Editor—Chaim Saulson. Subscription—$40 a year.
This Hebrew weekly covers the Hasidic community in Israel and is well illustrated.

Journals
Di Yiddishe Heim (The Jewish Home)

770 Eastern Pkwy.
Brooklyn, NY
Editor—Mrs. Thema Gurary. Subscription—$3 a year.
This Yiddish-English quarterly is published by the Lubavitch Women's Organization. Among its past features was an extensive biography of the Lubavitcher rebbe.

Ha-Moed Ha-Moer
5010 18th Ave.
Brooklyn, NY
Editor—Rabbi Mayer Amsel.
This is a monthly Hasidic rabbinical journal.

The Jerusalem Idishe Licht
193 Hewes St.
Brooklyn, NY
Editor—Rabbi Rochman.
This Yiddish weekly is designed for Hasidic women.

Kol Machzikei Hadas
c/o A. Laub
5023 14th Ave.
Brooklyn, NY
This Hebrew quarterly is published in Jerusalem by the Belzer Hasidim and is designed for the whole family.

The U'foratzto Journal
770 Eastern Pkwy.
Brooklyn, NY
Editor—Mayer Rivkin. Subscription—$6.40 a year.
This English quarterly, published by the Lubavitch Youth Organization, is well illustrated and designed.

Tziyunim—prayers at the grave of tzadikim

It is a Jewish custom in general, and a Hasidic custom in particular, to pray at the graves of tzadikim—holy men. Since most of our tzadikim are buried in Europe and Israel, this custom is not generally well known or kept up in the U.S. However, there are graves of rebbes here that attract many people. Rabbi Joseph I. Schneersohn, the sixth Lubavitcher rebbe and father-in-law of the present rebbe, died in New York on the tenth day of Shevat in 1950 and was buried in the Lubavitcher section of the Montefiore Cemetery in Queens, N.Y. Hundreds of people visit his grave annually, especially on his Yahrzeit—the anniversary of his death. For information on how to get there, contact Lubavitch at

770 Eastern Pkwy.
Brooklyn, NY 11213

The Skverer rebbe, Rabbi Jacob Twersky, died in 1968 in New Square and was buried in the cemetery there. His grave attracts many Hasidim annually, not all of them Skverer Hasidim.

Hasidism has gone through a renaissance in the U.S. since World War II, and offers a good deal to the native American Jew, especially to the person who is spiritually "searching." By all means, try at least to taste the Hasidic life-style.

Kosher Camping

Shabbat and davening outdoors is an experience that speaks directly to the soul, with no intermediary of walls or chairs or ceilings. You feel as if the world has been waiting for this very moment, and you enter with the newly discovered words of the rabbis on your lips.

> Were our mouth filled with song as the sea (is with water) and our tongue with
> ringing praise as the roaring waves;
> Were our lips full of adoration as the wide expanse of heaven, and our eyes spar-
> kling like the sun or the moon;
> Were our hands spread out in prayer as the eagles of the sky, and our feet as swift
> as the deer,
> We should still be unable to thank Thee and bless Thy name, Lord our God and
> God of our ancestors,
> For one-thousandth of the countless millions of wondrous favors which Thou hast
> conferred on our ancestors and on us.

    The experience of Shabbat with nature is a process freed from so many of the halakhic situations found during Shabbat at home. There's no need to remember to turn on the stove or to refrain from touching the electric light switch. There are no gadgets, telephones, cars, buses—nothing to distract you from the essence of the day. There's only you and the real world, as Shabbat was meant to be celebrated.

    And if there is reason behind the halakhot—laws—for Shabbat, it is to recapture this real world and to remind us that a world of beauty and richness does indeed exist and we have only to be willing to stretch ourselves wide open to receive it. The planning we need to do to move ourselves to the outdoors for Shabbat is effort superbly invested. For above all Shabbat with nature is, we think, the truest celebration of Shabbat.

General planning

Kosher camping and camping on Shabbat are events so spiritually fulfilling that they should be experienced by all. The preparation may seem burdensome or even forbidding because of the apprehension of entering a new situation with new problems, calling for solutions that differ from those encountered at home. Yet with adequate foresight kosher camping and Shabbat camping should not create any problems at all for most people; on the contrary, they should prove a beautiful and soul-satisfying experience.

Kosher camping is no different from kosher living: the rules and practices followed at home are merely repeated in the outdoors. (For an explanation of kashrut, see *Catalog 1*, pp. 18–36.)

Many problems can be avoided if you use paper plates, paper cups, and separate reusable plastic flatware that is designated meat or milk. An alternative for the more serious camper is to use two different mess kits, similarly designated.

Food is most easily stored during camping in a metal or Styrofoam ice chest. Dairy foods generally cause no problem for short trips if you use five pounds of dry ice in a standard chest; that should easily last at least two days.

In choosing kosher meats you'll find that it is most practical to purchase packaged processed meats (frankfurters, salami, bologna), as these are easier to keep fresh than other kosher meats. For weekend camping take fresh frozen chicken, which is left outside the chest and allowed to defrost during camping preparations. If you cook a substantial amount of chicken for Friday evening, you'll have cold chicken for lunch the following day.

Kosher food in the wilds

Obtaining kosher food becomes more of a problem the farther you get away from "civilization." Unfortunately, Jewish communities don't exist in the Grand Canyon or the Canadian Rockies. So expect to go for some time without meat unless you have a camper or trailer with a freezer. However, don't be discouraged too quickly. Check around, because there are frequently kosher butchers in seemingly unlikely places like Halifax, Nova Scotia. Remember that most kosher meat comes from the Midwest, and thus places like Sioux City, Iowa, have small Orthodox communities populated partly by shohetim—slaughterers—for the local slaughterhouse.

One obvious solution is to eat fish. But it is often difficult to obtain fish in mid-U.S.A. (Remember, you Easterners, no oceans!) It is probably a good idea nonetheless to "bone up" on the types of freshwater fish that are kosher.

It is sometimes very difficult to obtain kosher processed foods. Brands often differ across the country, and the ⓤ and similar labels are not always available, especially on local brands. It might take a little searching. You also might want to use those food products that you feel do not require rabbinic supervision. Otherwise, stock up ahead of time on those processed foods that you feel do require rabbinic supervision. Some foods such as kosher cheese

Call the synagogue (check the "Congregation" or "Temple" listings in the phone book or look under "Churches" in the Yellow Pages).

Wait a minute. Does it say ⓤ

and wine are very difficult to get in the boondocks; one of the most difficult is bread, especially if supervision is desired. In Jackson Hole, Wyoming (near Grand Teton and Yellowstone), it is unlikely that you will find national or Eastern brands that carry the . Again, it is fairly easy to find bread without shortening, etc.—especially the ubiquitious sourdough bread. (I tried for three weeks to develop the proper palate for the enjoyment of sourdough bread, but it was hopeless! However, we did find in Jackson Hole a health-food store that baked its own bread. Since it was a local product, we could ask questions about ingredients and the baking process.)

Remember to bring other religious paraphernalia such as matzah (easily portable for ha-Motzi on Shabbat), Shabbat candles and candlesticks, Kiddush cup, siddur, Havdalah candle, wine, hallah cover, etc.

Health-food freaks don't use chemicals and are careful about what ingredients they do use; most important, they *like* to spend time explaining what they cook or bake—so hunt out the food-freak places of the world.

Preparation for Shabbat

As with Shabbat at home, preparation for Shabbat in nature should be a busy, bustling, and even tiring activity. As at home, all needs anticipated for the next day must be provided for beforehand. Yet while camping you become responsible not only for your meals, prayers, study, and leisure, but also for your very shelter—in a sense, your survival.

The following are some details to be concerned with for Shabbat camping:

1. *Choosing a campsite*: In deciding where to settle for Shabbat, be attentive to the moods and forms of nature and the land surrounding you. Set up camp in an area you are particularly fond of: by the water, high on a mountain or hill, in a field or a pine forest, or in an expanse of milkweed during early fall. If you are in a campground or national park, try to find a campsite that is somewhat secluded or surrounded by trees. Be aware of what you will see when you look out of your tent, to make yourself more sensitive to what surrounds you. Have your tent face a direction that will let you view

Note: Some of the material given here will not be of concern to you, depending upon how you observe Shabbat. We have included suggestions for those who are very strict as well as more general comments. Ignore those that do not apply to your situation.

either the afternoon sun followed by sunset or a glowing moon or sunrise.

2. *Carrying*: Traditionally, on Shabbat it is forbidden to carry any object, no matter how small, from an enclosed area (a private area) to a public domain and vice versa. If it is established, however, that all of an enclosed area is really a private area owned by one person or by a group of people who are shareholders in the property, then you may carry *within that enclosed area*. If you rent a campsite you become the temporary "owner" of that site and can establish the ownership and permission to carry by creating an eruv.

To make an eruv around your domain:

a. Station four poles (or use available substitutes such as trees, bushes, your car, etc.) at the four outer limits of your campsite. The poles, trees, bushes, whatever, should be ten handbreadths high (about five feet) and must be able to withstand a strong wind.

b. Stretch wire, string, or rope from pole to pole, thereby forming a stringed enclosure to your site.

c. Natural barriers such as a lake or a cliff can be used for an eruv. If your campsite goes right up to the lake's edge, it is not necessary to string wire on that side.

d. In order to maintain the legal fiction of an enclosure, you must create a doorway in the eruv. If you are using trees, create a semblance of a door frame by tying a stick to one tree and a second stick to a second tree and running your string between them. In order to make a door frame you must place the string at the top of an object—which is why a tree without a recognizable top (or one that's too high) can't be used and a stick must be attached instead. It's easy to hammer a nail to the top of the sticks and attach the string to them.

e. Be sure to include all necessary areas within the enclosure, such as your actual tent and eating areas, as well as water, shade, open spaces, and whatever else you may value as part of your home away from home. However, it is important to put the eruv wire high enough so as not to decapitate neighbors stumbling to the bathroom in the dark.

f. On long camping trips your car is an important storage area at night, so include the car in the eruv or use it as part of the eruv. Remember that some cars have inside lights that go on when the doors are opened. Either unscrew the bulb or plan to use those doors (rear doors, passenger

side) that are not connected to the light. Make sure in the latter case that the doors open *inside* the eruv—otherwise you'll be gazing wistfully all Shabbat.

g. The same is true of the trunk and glove compartment, which are good places for storing "valuables." The trunk should open *into* the eruv. And check to see if either the trunk or glove compartment has a light.

h. One of the problem areas in public campgrounds is that facilities such as water fountains and bathrooms will frequently be outside your eruv (because of the distance between these facilities and the problems involved in stringing an eruv through other people's campsites). The problems are both halakhic (someone else's property) and practical (trying to explain to the park rangers). So (1) fill up a five-gallon water jug before Shabbat; this should be enough for both washing and drinking; if your site is right *on* the water this helps; (2) if you're concerned with the prohibition against watering plants on Shabbat, make sure the water falls on plain earth or a plate or board left on the ground under the water so the water reaches the ground only indirectly; (3) the bathroom can be used, but nothing may be carried there. Washing and brushing your teeth can be done at the campsite. The main problem is toilet paper. You can try leaving a box of tissues in the bathroom with a sign reading, DO NOT REMOVE or PROPERTY OF —— (you don't want everybody to use the box up).

i. On Friday remember to pay for the site two days in advance to avoid hassles on Shabbat.

3. *Collecting Wood*: On Friday afternoon sufficient wood must be collected for three different fires: a fire on which to prepare dinner for Shabbat evening; a fire on which to warm food for Shabbat lunch (see below); and the campfire you may want to have Saturday evening after Havdalah. (Collecting wood in the dark is difficult and dangerous, so don't put off collecting wood for this last fire until Saturday night.) Of course, if you are using a camping stove (white gas or propane) everything is simplified. Food can be warmed and the stove shut off before Shabbat. If wrapped well in foil, all food will stay warm until the Friday night meal.

4. *Fires*: A fire prepared Friday afternoon well before sunset can be used for cooking, warming food, light, and personal warmth. For the more ambi-

Kosher camping

In general, however, cold food can be more than adequate for Shabbat lunch. For milchiks, yogurt, cheese, fresh fruits and vegetables, hallah and butter, tuna-fish, egg salad, etc. are good. For fleishik, the cold chicken you made Friday or any cold meat with a salad will do nicely.

tious, the following procedure will allow the heat of an original fire prepared Friday afternoon to keep food warm at least until Shabbat lunch the next day. Dig a hole two feet deep and line the bottom of it with stones. Cover these stones with a layer of dirt. Build a mighty fire in your fireplace and cook your food thoroughly until it is steaming. Place the securely covered pot of food (such as cholent) in the hole and then cover the pot with soil, completely filling the hole and marking the spot. When you're ready for Shabbat lunch, pull out your pot and enjoy.

If you are less stringent in your Shabbat observance, you could build the fire in the hole. As the fire subsides you can bury the pot directly on top of the coals at the bottom of the hole. Because of the fear that you might stir the coals (something that is prohibited traditionally), you must not leave food *directly* on the heat; by strict halakhah this procedure is inadvisable.

5. *Setting up camp*: In setting up your tent and campsite, be certain that your tent is firmly secured to the ground. In addition, try to create as much comfort in your campsite as possible by taking advantage of nature's gifts of soft grass or pine needles, etc. Since you will probably have little light later, set up your sleeping bags, sleeping attire, and anything else you might need for the evening. Be sure to allow enough time to do this properly so as to ensure a secure and comfortable Shabbat.

6. *Washing for Shabbat*: With the fires going, the food cooked, the campsite and tent secured, and the sun beginning to lower in the western sky, it is time to wash for Shabbat. Take advantage of the nearby lake, river, or stream. Do not hurry this part. Given the extent of your privacy, wear as few clothes as possible and slowly immerse youself totally in the water. Let it flow over you, cleansing and purifying, seeping away tensions and tiredness. Float gently. Relax. Dry yourself slowly, lovingly. Dress with care.

7. *Kindling the Shabbat candles*: This step, seemingly the simplest after a busy period of preparation, can be most troublesome outdoors. As most tents are flammable, lighting candles inside them can prove to be quite dangerous unless supercareful precautions are taken—and even then it is inadvisable. When kindling outside, check the wind direction and provide a sheltered spot for the candles. Use natural shelters or even such things as ice chests and boxes to surround the candles. Another possibility, one that is permissible under Jewish law, is to use a camping lantern fueled by white gas. Some of these are double-manteled and so have two separate flames. With a little practice you'll learn how much fuel the lantern needs to burn a few hours rather than all night. A lantern will also give you light to read by, especially if you don't have a fire. However, the light will attract many kinds of bugs, so beware. You should also be careful to ensure that the light doesn't disturb people at other campsites—another reason to carefully limit the amount of fuel you put in the lantern.

8. *Receiving Shabbat*: You are now ready to greet Shabbat as she was greeted four centuries ago by the Jews of Safed. They left the confines of the town and entered the surrounding fields to bow in greeting to the Shabbat bride. For them

the synagogue was not grand enough to receive the Shabbat; its walls were too limiting; its presence too confining. So they would go out into the open fields, dressed in white, the color of the wedding garment, and there chant psalms and sing L'Kha Dodi (Samuel H. Dresner, *The Shabbat*).

So too with you. You must take care to choose a holy spot for prayer. Davening outside, in the world of nature, is a very special, very fulfilling experience, and the words of the psalms become imbued with new beauty:

The fields and everything in them exult;
then shall all the trees of the forest shout for
joy at the presence of the Lord, for He is coming,
for He is coming to rule the earth (Psalms 96:12–13).

Let the sea and all within it thunder, the world
and its inhabitants; let the rivers clap their hands,
the mountains sing joyously together at the presence
of the Lord, for He is coming to rule the earth (Psalms 98:7–8).

And the words of the Hallel ring so true and clear when surrounded by simple nature:

This is the Lord's doing; it is marvelous in our sight.
This is the day that the Lord has made—
let us exult and rejoice on it (Psalms 118:23–24).

9. *Activities for Shabbat:* Shabbat is a day devoted to learning and rest. Bring books but do not devote all your time to the study of a book. Study all God's world—His gift to us. It's all around you—the perfect "subject."

Study, however, is important and time should be spent with some sacred text and/or scholarly treatise, serious article, or novel. Yet the nature surrounding you beckons you, and you only celebrate Shabbat fully by participating in God's creation.

Take a walk, and just look and listen. Smell. Touch. You will discover new things, things that far surpass in sensual quality anything you have ever known. To sharpen your senses take a walk blindfolded, guided by a partner. Without sight, you will experience more fully all that nature offers.

Based on your own level of Shabbat observance, you might want to swim, picnic, or engage in a sport. Consult a rabbi and your own feelings to help you figure out your "comfort level."

If possible, try to daven beside the ocean. It is a tremendous, awe-full experience. For those on the West Coast the thrill lies with Maariv—the evening prayer; for the Easterners it is with an early morning Shaharit. Davening, when accompanied by a rising or setting sun, allows the words of the siddur to come alive and to embrace and enwrap the moment.

Above all, give yourself over fully—joyously—to the experience. *Feel* the sun beating down on you. *Smell* the warm earth. *Watch* an ant, a mosquito, a butterfly. And understand the poem Moses recited to the people of Israel before his death:

Give ear, O heavens, let me speak;
Let the earth hear the words I utter!
May my discourse come down as the rain,
My speech distill as the dew,
Like showers on young growth,
Like droplets on the grass,
For the name of the Lord I proclaim;
Give glory to our God! (Deuteronomy 32:1–3).

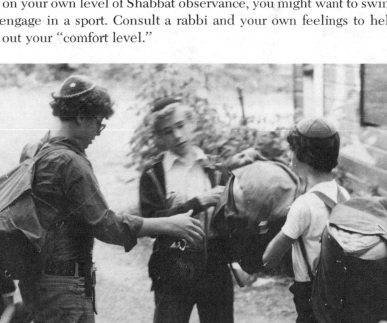

EXILE

FOR I WAS A STRANGER IN A STRANGE LAND

גר הייתי בארץ נכריה Exodus 2:22

Intermarriage and conversion

Intermarriage

Richard Israel, director of the Bnai Brith Hillel Foundation of Greater Boston, shares his thoughts on the subject.

Gee, you don't look Jewish.

For almost seventy years the "Bintel Brief" column in the *Jewish Daily Forward* has served as the "Dear Abby" column of the Yiddish-speaking world. A few years ago Isaac Metzker edited a representative collection of those letters from the years 1906–67 and put them together in a book entitled *A Bintel Brief* (Doubleday, 1971, $6.95). Aside from the fact that the letters are a fascinating sampling of Jewish life, they also cast light on the problems and concerns of Jews throughout this period—perhaps throughout all history. For example, a letter from 1928:

Worthy Editor,

I consider myself a progressive woman who thinks there should be no difference between Jews and Christians. Years ago when I was a girl and sometimes heard that parents would not allow their children to marry a Christian, I maintained that they should not interfere. I believed that a fine Christian was as good as a fine Jew.

Now, however, when my daughter has fallen in love with a gentile, I have become one of those mothers who interferes because I am against the match. I am not one of those fanatic parents who warn their children that they will disown them because of it, but I'm trying with goodness to influence my daughter to break up with the boy.

My daughter argues with me: "Why? You always used to say that all people are equal." She is educated, she knows how to talk to me, and often I have no answers to her arguments. But I feel this is no match for my daughter. Her friend comes here often and as a person he appeals to me, but not as a husband for her.

I don't know how to explain it. He is intelligent, quiet, and gentle, but somehow his nature and his way of thinking are different from that of a Jew. His parents are American Yankees, never miss a Sunday at church, and speak with reverence of President Coolidge. When I think that they might become my in-laws and their son my daughter's husband, I tremble. I feel—a mother's heart feels—that my daughter could never get used to these people.

When one is young and in love, one is in the clouds and sees no flaws. But when love cools down, she will see it's no good. I see it in advance. True, it could happen that she could marry a Jewish man and after the wedding not be able to stand him. But with a Jew it's still different.

I would very much like to hear your opinion about this.

> Respectfully,
> A Mother

The intermarriage rate is up. No one agrees by how much or precisely what the implications of the statistics are, but it is clear that Jews are marrying non-

Jews at an increasing rate. There are few phenomena of Jewish life today that cause as much angry debate, pain, and bewilderment as intermarriage.

We live in a society that usually says, Make your own decisions as best you can and then be prepared to live with the consequences. Couples who in good faith decided to intermarry often wonder why the rules seem to have been changed in this instance. They are puzzled as to why the rabbi complains about people like them from the pulpit, why their parents are either furious or despondent. After all, it was supposed to be *their* decision.

Why do people decide to intermarry? Ultimately there are as many reasons as there are people. But certainly it is one of the natural outcomes of living in an open society. Thus in some ways it is extraordinary that there has not been a lot more intermarriage. For some people the question about why people decide to intermarry is really the question of why not? Often the Jewish partners have never seen Jewishness as a salient feature of their families' lives. They may be Jewish universalists who believe that ethnic and religious particularities stand in the way of human progress. Thus their marriage choices were not affected by questions of religion in any essential way.

In other cases the Jewish partners are intellectually committed not to intermarry, so thoroughly committed that they feel free to date whomever they like since they believe dating can never lead to anything serious. They will obviously only marry within the Jewish community. Surprisingly, many dates later, when they are deeply committed to non-Jewish partners, they find that the immediate claims of love greatly outweigh the more distant and impersonal claims of the tradition.

Then there are the more complicated people—those who are angry at their families or their first spouses and want to marry people as unlike them as possible. (Sometimes, years later, when they are not so angry, they discover that anger alone is not an adequate justification for marriage.) With surprising frequency it happens that those who "marry out" in order to leave the Jewish community, which they find too parochial, marry non-Jews who need a little more parochiality and want to join that community. Unless they are careful, the mates in such cases can become to each other only ships passing in the night.

It is easy to understand why parents who are themselves deeply committed to Jewish life should be crushed when their children reject this very important part of them by marrying out. The children's implicit rejection of their values hurts, and they feel like failures as parents. For many parents in this generation there is a special kind of survival guilt and anger: "I survived the Nazi era only to have my children do to my family what Hitler could not: bring my family's Jewishness to an end." That is a stark formulation but not altogether unjustified. Those who intermarry should recognize that they are in all likelihood "terminal Jews," the end of the Jewish tradition to all who come after them. Jewishly committed parents and institutions of the Jewish community are concerned about intermarriage because if there are no Jews, neither will there be any Judaism.

Distraught parents who have never had much to do with things Jewish are more of a puzzle to their children. Why should they be upset with a child's decision to intermarry? They themselves are frequently the last people to be able to articulate the reasons they are distraught.

What most often troubles them in fact is their deep, if seldom stated, loyalty to the Jewish people and community. Though that loyalty may never have been expressed institutionally, it is an important part of them. Not having expressed it often, they know they have no clear answers for their infuriatingly logical children. No, they were not very enthusiastic about the synagogue and their life-style didn't require them to become involved in the Jewish center

If it is legitimate for Jews to be concerned about the survival of the whooping crane and the blue whale, it is certainly no less legitimate for Jews to be worried about their own group's future. The world will not be richer if any of them vanish, though my own value system would put the Jews ahead of the cranes and the whales.

or even the Jewish country club, but that doesn't mean they are prepared to accept non-Jewish grandchildren with equanimity! Hardly an argument. They know it. Their children know it. And it is an agonizing situation.

When parents and children are at loggerheads, what should they do? Some parents will occasionally call in a rabbi they haven't seen for twenty years in the hope that a rabbinic miracle will put an end to the match. Sometimes they will flail about with bizarre warnings regarding the ultimately anti-Semitic character of the non-Jewish partner. Perhaps they will just silently nurse their wounds.

To the parents I would say, Don't bother to call in the experts. Your views are more relevant to your children than other people's are. They may not listen to you—but they are more likely to listen to you than to anyone else. If you send them to see the rabbi, they will usually go in order to keep peace, but not very much is likely to come of the conversation.

To determined children who ask if their parents will ever accept their decision, there is no clear answer. Some parents do become reconciled when they are convinced that their choices are either to accept the non-Jewish partner or to risk losing their own child. Some will accept the match when they conclude that their child's choice of partner may be wrong from their point of view but is not crazy, that it would have been an acceptable match if the partner were Jewish. Some become reconciled when the wedding invitation arrives, some at the first baby. Some never become reconciled, though there is a wide range of degrees of estrangement. Mourning the intermarried child as if dead is an extreme reaction that, though it's frequently referred to in Jewish popular culture, is one I have never witnessed. I have reservations about the reliability of many of the third- and fourth-hand reports of such mourning that circulate.

To both children and parents locked into these difficult situations, I would counsel compassion, not all-out war. I have seen a few cases in which parental threats to cut off school tuition or children's threats to break off contact forever had the desired effect, but these were the exceptions. Threats of this sort are more likely to bring about stiffer resistance from the other side. The feelings that are present on both sides are real and deep.

> Let your parents/children know what those real feelings are. You are most likely to be heard if you come through with all of the honesty you can muster. Describe where *you* are, anguish, anger, and all, not where *they* ought to be. Don't try to talk them out of their feelings. It doesn't work.

Even in Paradise, it is not good to be alone.
Yiddish Proverb
Trans. Reuben Alcalay

Once they have decided to marry, some couples contemplating intermarriage seek a marriage officiated at by a rabbi, even though the non-Jewish partner has not converted. They want to marry with dignity. A justice of the peace doesn't seem adequate for the job. If the Jewish parents really want a Jewish wedding and one can be worked out that is not too heavily religious, why not?

Traditionally, what makes a Jewish marriage ceremony is a Jewish man giving a ring to a Jewish woman in the presence of the official notary public and representative of the Jewish community, the rabbi. What binds their lives is the couple themselves who create the event and perform the acts, not the rabbi. If one of the partners is not Jewish, therefore, s/he cannot participate in the marriage for the same reason that an alien without citizenship cannot vote and a minor cannot sign a legally binding contract: the non-Jewish partner is technically not competent to participate in a Jewish ceremony. Substantially for these reasons, all the major rabbinic groups of all denominations have taken public positions opposing rabbinic officiating at intermarriages.

Nevertheless, there are some rabbis in the liberal camp who feel that Jewish law is no longer binding. If the couple believes the addition of Jewish ceremonies to their wedding would be meaningful and enriching, and perhaps even bring them closer to the Jewish tradition, then these rabbis are prepared to officiate. Some will only do so if they are convinced the couple can make a serious Jewish commitment (even if it is short of conversion) or will agree to raise the children as Jews.

There are a few charlatans who will officiate upon payment of large fees or who officiate at intermarriages as their major rabbinic activity. I believe, nonetheless, that most rabbis who so officiate do so out of integrity and concern for the people who seek them out. They also believe that by refusing to perform these weddings they may be driving people away from Judaism. And they believe that they are doing right by the Jewish tradition. Nevertheless, if you are considering seeking out such a person, I would like to take a hard line and urge you not to do so.

There is a story of a classic vulgar American tourist visiting one of the great cathedrals of Europe, falling in love with it, and asking, "How much would it cost to rent this place?" The point is, you *can't* rent it. Either it is free and yours or you can't have it at all. I don't believe that you can rent the Jewish tradition either. If you can accept it on its own terms, it's yours. If you can't, why make it be something it's not?

If you are grown up enough to live with the implication of your decisions, you should be willing to accept the fact that your decision to intermarry does not receive the formal blessing of the Jewish tradition. You shouldn't try to have it both ways. If you still feel yourself committed to the Jewish tradition in spite of intermarrying, then why should you want to falsify it? If you are not committed to it, then why use it? A spurious act is no less spurious because your parents want it.

You have real positions about the things that are important to you in this world; if you are about to intermarry, the two of you can work out a ceremony that says them. The ceremony may even contain Jewish dimensions, but it will at least have the virtue of being your ceremony and not one that you are pretending about for this occasion. Marriage is too important an event to begin with a lie.

It is not hard to find a justice of the peace or a judge to read your ceremony. If your situation later changes, through conversion, and a Jewish ceremony becomes a possibility as an authentic event, that is the time to have a rabbi officiate.

Another view

Al Axelrad, who serves as Hillel rabbi at Brandeis University, has spent some time thinking about the problem of intermarried couples and offers these observations.

Because of the number of inquiries I have received about officiating at mixed-marriage ceremonies, I have spent some time thinking about mixed marriages and their import for the Jewish community. I have arrived at a personal position that diverges in many ways from the position maintained by my colleagues but could, I am convinced, set the stage for a radical rethinking of how the Jewish community can begin to relate to intermarried couples.

I have discovered that there are a significant number of couples who, while not ready for the non-Jewish partner to convert, are ready to commit themselves to studying Judaism together (either in a course or in an open-ended and individualized tutorial), experiencing and practicing the Jewish tradition. The couple is committed to having a Jewish home and family life and to raising their children actively and conscientiously as Jews.

Why would the non-Jewish partner of such a Jewishly committed couple stop short of becoming a Jew prior to the wedding ceremony? The reasons can be many: the desire to be away from or entirely independent of one's parents' household and involved in one's own family life before converting; the need to make certain that the conversion is separate from the marriage and not merely an accommodation under pressure to the Jewish mate and/or his/her family; the desire to become still more knowledgeable first; the need to feel more a part of the Jewish people in spirit—thinking more naturally and instinctively of the Jewish people as "we" rather than "they."

If such a couple wants a religious ceremony colored Jewish, I am prepared to participate in such a ceremony, making it clear that I will not conduct the standard normative Jewish ceremony. Certainly they must understand that any marriage between a Jew and a non-Jew lacks any standing in Jewish law. And yet I believe that it is my responsibility as a member of the Jewish community to open a Jewish door to such a couple with the hope that they will one day be able to walk through that door together as Jews.

Although historically the Jewish community has gone out of its way to reject intermarried couples (and sometimes, despite halakhic exhortations to the contrary, to shun converts), I believe the time for this "luxury" has passed. Practicality alone (given the enormous upsurge in intermarriages) should teach us what mentshlikhkeit may not. It is no longer in our own best interest to ignore the intermarried couple. The erosion has gone too deep.

Additionally, we are perhaps facing a different kind of intermarried couple than ever before. We are finding that for many such couples there is an interim stage—after the marriage but before the conversion—during which the couple is feeling their way in the Jewish community. They are very tentatively seeking ways of entrance, ways to feel at home and comfortable in a community that they know has historically been hostile to them.

We must seek for ways to open our doors to those couples who are already practicing as Jews and those couples whose non-Jewish partner is altogether removed by practice and belief from any other tradition but whose Jewish partner is a committed Jew. It has been my experience that such couples abound and would be receptive to and indeed grateful for any reaching out to them by the Jewish community, in ways that are neither condemnatory nor slyly self-serving.

There is a world of pain in Abraham's statement, "I was a stranger who dwelt in your midst." Perhaps the time has come to rethink the ways in which we treat the strangers that are in our own midst.

Dick Israel resumes the discussion with some observations on the process of conversion.

Conversion

The question of conversion is one that should be carefully considered by any couple considering intermarriage. In Jewish law, conversion for the sake of marriage is discouraged. That is a view I support. Conversion should be thought of as an end in itself. Being Jewish is sufficiently important that you must be a Jew for yourself, not for others—not even if the others are your spouse or your in-laws. But there are now many apparently nominal Christians who are, in fact, traditionless non-Jews, and they welcome the opportunity to be part of the Jewish tradition and community. These are people seeking spiritual roots whose choice of a Jewish partner is often not accidental. They are people who, given the character of the world in which we live, would not be likely to convert were they not contemplating marriage to Jews, but whose conversion may nevertheless be sincere and real.

After conversion there is no longer a question of intermarriage since a convert is in every respect a full Jew. In Jewish law it is even prohibited to refer to a person who has converted as a convert. Ordinary Jews frequently forget this nicety, but we should recognize that this is our problem, not the convert's. One of the virtues of the conversion process is that the intensive study that is required frequently makes it possible for the potential convert to acquire a body of knowledge that the new Jewish in-laws do not possess. Such knowledge often has a very salutory effect on the family. It becomes difficult even for rather closed-minded Jews to reject the authenticity of the conversion.

There was a time when Jews devoted a considerable amount of energy to proselytizing. Though this activity was never considered an essential feature of Judaism, many felt that if the Torah was a good thing it was wrong not to let others in on it. (On the other hand, some rabbis took the position that Torah was such a good thing that sharing it with non-Jews was a waste.) The whole question was mooted when early Christian rulers prohibited conversionary activity and put to death offending converts and proselytizers.

In later periods and in non-Christian cultures a number of factors continued to militate against conversion to Judaism. There was no agreed-upon Jewish mandate that required Jews to proselytize. Because they were so frequently persecuted, Jews were deeply suspicious of the non-Jewish world and desired to have as little as possible to do with non-Jews. Because of the pariah status of the Jew, few non-Jews wanted to join them anyway. There were periods of Jewish history in which the relations between Jews and non-Jews were relatively open and friendly, and there are famous examples of individuals and even entire communities of non-Jews converting to Judaism. Still, until modern times, conversion to Judaism was rather rare.

Recently, however, Rabbi Alexander Schindler, president of the Union of American Hebrew Congregations (Reform), called upon Jews to try to reach "the unchurched" of America and convert them to Judaism. The Reform movement has begun a program of outreach both to Jews and non-Jews. Others in the American Jewish community feel that an effort should be made to attract intermarried couples to Judaism. They quote studies showing that many converts to Judaism have a higher-than-average sense of identification with Judaism and with the Jewish community. Therefore some believe it may be possible to increase the number of Jews (or at least not lose ground) if efforts are made to convert the non-Jewish spouse, either before or after the marriage. Others believe that even when the non-Jewish spouse does not convert to Judaism, if s/he has positive experiences with the Jewish community, the likelihood of the children of such a marriage being given a Jewish education will be greatly increased.

THE CONVERSION PROCESS

The process of conversion is described rather simply in the Talmud. The prospective convert is asked: "Do you wish to convert in spite of the difficult and often desperate situation of the Jews?" If the answer is yes, the candidate is then taught some easy commandments and some hard ones; if male, circumcised; and then, whether male or female, ritually immersed in water and declared Jewish.

A phrase in early rabbinic literature expresses a decidedly negative attitude toward converts: "Proselytes are as hard for Israel (to endure) as a sore" (Yevamot 47b). One explanation of the passage is that the rabbis had had bad experiences with converts who became informers against the Jews. Another interpretation is that they make natural-born Jews look bad since the converts are so much more pious and knowledgeable than they. My experience sustains the latter explanation. The opposite attitude is also found in rabbinic literature: "Proselytes are beloved; in every place He considers them as part of Israel" (Mekhilta Va-Yehi 2). In the daily Amidah, converts are singled out as meriting God's special blessing.

Contemporary practice does not differ a great deal. The biblical Ruth, who is frequently held up as a model convert, was told three times by her mother-in-law, Naomi, to return to her own people, the Moabites. Ruth persisted, joined the people of Israel, and started a line that ultimately gave birth to King David. There is a tradition that grew up around the conversion process which maintained that anyone who inquires about conversion should, like Ruth, be rejected three times and that serious conversation about conversion should take place only if the person persists. So don't be surprised if you experience a singular lack of enthusiasm about your conversion from the first rabbi you approach. Since Judaism clearly does not demand conversion as a prerequisite to finding divine favor, much of the initiative for pursuing the process must rest with the potential convert.

Finding a rabbi should be considered the first step in the conversion process. Before you go for such an interview, find out what you can about the rabbi. Is that rabbi likely to assist people to convert? Some rabbis will not. Does the rabbi have a reputation as a sympathetic person? Is s/he knowledgeable? Is there someone you trust who has been helped by the rabbi in the past? (I think doctors, dentists, and psychiatrists should be checked out the same way.)

At your first visit, assuming that the rabbi does not chase you away and that the two of you get along well, several things are likely to happen. You may be taken on as a student. You will then be told what the requirements for conversion are, how long you are expected to study, what material you must learn, whether you must attend services on a regular basis or participate in some other aspects of Jewish life. To some extent each rabbi's requirements are different. In a large city you may be sent to a class for converts, at which your rabbi or some other rabbinic colleagues teach. You may be sent to an individual whom your rabbi trusts to instruct converts. The process that aids people to become Jews is a mysterious one which, though I have participated in it often, I do not fully understand. It makes great demands upon a rabbi's time and energy. Given the nature and extent of their responsibilities, many rabbis cannot personally instruct every convert.

A word of caution about classes: some converts find classes enormously helpful—more helpful than individual instruction, since you will find not only information, but a group of people who share many of the same problems and questions you do, people with whom you can talk. On the other hand, some of these classes are organized like continuous-run feature movies, with a specific number of lectures offered in sequence throughout the year so that the students can drop in and out at any point along the way. Classes of this sort often never congeal as groups, are instructed at the level of the most unsophisticated student in the class, and are not very edifying. If you are a serious reader confronted with such a situation, try to get a supplementary reading list from your instructor or the rabbi who sent you and then try to get some appointments with one or the other to discuss the material you've read (see the sections entitled "On Teaching Converts" and "On Being a Convert"). If you have done your homework, few people will turn down your request for additional instruction. Try to move into the tradition with earnestness and diligence, but move at a rate that feels right. Push yourself forward, but don't overwhelm yourself. Take care to move step by step and avoid a serious case of spiritual indigestion.

Once the instruction period is over and your teacher feels that you have acquired knowledge and commitment, it is time for the formal conversion procedures. This is another point at which many people become alarmed. The rabbi may feel you are ready, but you don't. You are a fraud. You don't know enough. You aren't committed enough. You will be discovered for what

Some potential converts are reluctant to enter into the period of learning, feeling that they are not yet sufficiently committed to conversion to begin learning. That is an appropriate feeling since they do not yet know enough to convert. It may be an appropriate course of action to refuse such instruction: the instruction is intended to help you toward that commitment. If you later find it impossible to convert, well and good. But that decision is better built on knowledge than on early apprehension.

you really are the first time you open your mouth in a gathering of Jews. By way of consolation you should know that most lawyers, doctors, and rabbis feel like fakes too when they first receive their new titles. Most married people don't feel much more married after the ceremony than they did beforehand. When you receive a new set of major responsibilities, you have to live your way into them before they begin to feel natural and real. If your rabbi thinks you are ready, you should probably accept that judgment. The rest will come in time.

Your sponsoring rabbi will assemble a rabbinic court of three rabbis (or if other rabbis are not available it might be the rabbi and several of the more learned laypeople in the community) to question you about your readiness for conversion. The questions they ask will generally include matters of (1) straight information: Who was ——?; On what holiday do you ——?; (2) matters of opinion: What do you understand by the term Messiah? by the authority of Torah? Who is your favorite figure in Jewish history?; (3) the nature of your commitment: Why do you want to be Jewish? What type of Jewish life do you intend to lead?

We assume that your answers will be satisfactory. Few rabbis will present a candidate before a rabbinic court without a strong degree of confidence in the readiness of the candidate. (Nevertheless, don't be surprised if your rabbi is more nervous about the whole thing than you are. By this time it is not just you who have a stake in the outcome.)

Next, traditional rabbis (Orthodox and Conservative) will require circumcision (anesthetized, of course) for the male convert. Traditionalists also require a symbolic circumcision—a drop of blood being let—for males who are already circumcised. The rabbi will make the arrangements to bring the professional called a mohel who performs this rite. (See Birth in *Catalog 2*, pp. 23–30.)

Immersion in the mikveh—ritual bath—comes next, for both men and women. Though a natural pond or lake is also permissible, the mikveh is used more frequently because of its convenience. The mikveh will usually be a sort of tile-lined king-sized bathtub with steps leading into it. Either you or the rabbi will call beforehand to be sure that the water is heated. A small fee is generally paid afterward to the woman who is in charge of the mikveh in gratitude for that absolutely essential service and also to defray the overall costs of the mikveh. (Regarding preparation for the mikveh, see *Catalog 1*, the article Tumah and Taharah, p. 171.) When you are in the water the rabbinic witnesses (who will be standing outside the door of the mikveh room, close enough to know that you are there but far enough not to be able to see you) will ask you to say the required blessing and then immerse yourself.

After you dry off they will give you the Hebrew name that you agreed upon earlier. They will give you a new parent as well: you will become a child of Father Abraham because according to the tradition he, the first Jew, is the first convert to Judaism and therefore the spiritual father of all converts. A brief ceremony may then be held, in which the convert is often asked to recite the Shema and accept a blessing. Since there are frequently minor variations, you may wish to ask your rabbi to detail the ceremony for you in advance. Documents attesting to the event will be read and everyone will wish you a mazel tov.

Liberal rabbis are much less likely to insist upon circumcision and mikveh than are the traditionalists. They are more likely to suggest a public conversion ceremony as one of your options, perhaps as part of a congregational service. Anyone who chooses the more liberal modes of conversion should know that they could run into difficulties with traditionalists later on. Traditionalists are unable to accept as authentic those conversions that have not included circumcision and mikveh, and thus the convert's status as a Jew, as well as that of her children if she is a female convert, may be called into question at some future time—when the child is ready to become Bar/Bat Mitzvah, to be married, or, to settle in Israel, for example. (These days the Israeli rabbinate tends to accept as valid *only* Orthodox conversions.)

Another way to welcome a convert

Everett Gendler has experimented with alternative ways to welcome converts to Judaism. He shares his experiences here.

Two colleagues, or, if that is infeasible, two qualified laymen in the community, should be made acquainted with the particular case and invited to join the rabbi in constituting a bet din. The bet din examines the knowledge and attitude of the prospective convert and presides over his or her admission into the Jewish faith (*A Rabbi's Manual*, Rabbinical Assembly, 1965).

There is something to be said for the traditional bet din in cases of conversion. There is some assurance of halakhic correctness and an acknowledged source of authority to verify the conversion. On the other hand, there may be a formality verging on the formidable and a suggestion of secretiveness about the whole procedure. Though representing the community, the bet din is often rather separate from it.

Recently we participated in a conversion ceremony in which an entire subcommunity of eight families, away on a religious retreat weekend, "examined the knowledge and attitude of the prospective convert and presided over her admission into the Jewish faith." It was such a beautiful and moving occasion that we think it deserves some description.

The person who was "converting"—"affirming her Judaism" would be more accurate—was a young woman who had been involved with Judaism for some years. She had read extensively, had thought about and spoken of affirming her sense of being Jewish, and had attended services regularly for a couple of years preceding this particular weekend. She was thus acquainted with many of the people present, and we knew her.

All of us, adults and children, gathered at dusk in the living room of the house where we were spending the weekend. It was apparent that Havdalah was rather special that night. Having spent Shabbat together, all of us felt quite close to one another. In addition, the presence of hallah and honey along with the wine of Havdalah made visible what we all knew: that at the end of the ceremony concluding the Shabbat we would ask Vivian to share her feelings and intentions about Judaism with us and that most likely we would receive her into the wider community of the Jewish people.

After first hearing from those who had witnessed her ritual immersion in a spring-fed mountain lake, we listened as Vivian told us a little about her growing up, her association with and increasing interest in Jews and Judaism during adolescence, her subsequent study, her explorations, her questions, her marriage (two years earlier), and her growing comfort with this step she was taking. Her words were simple, direct, personal, and very touching.

Her words prompted a couple of question—but more important, they evoked personal responses from almost everyone present. Several shared appreciations of Vivian and her attitudes; some told how happy they were that she was joining us; another person, herself a convert, shared some of her feelings when she had undergone conversion; two or three remarked how warm they felt and how right the setting seemed. Again, the words were simple, direct, personal, and very touching.

Vivian read from the Book of Ruth and sang the Shema. We as a community sang the lovely Debbie Friedman musical setting of "And thou shalt love the Lord thy God." Vivian received her chosen Hebrew name, Chaya bat Avraham Avinu v'Sarah Imenu—Chaya the daughter of Abraham our father and Sarah our mother. There was more singing, the traditional priestly blessing, and finally, as the Havdalah candle burnt low, Chaya ate of the hallah and honey, which bore out our wishes for sweetness and satisfaction—most especially for her, but also for Mark, her husband, and finally for us, for all Israel, and for all humankind.

On being a convert

Although each individual's conversion is unique, I believe that there are several experiences that many converts share. I will talk briefly about three of them—three that are certainly a part of my own conversion and have been common to several of my friends who are converts. I should emphasize that these experiences occur (if, indeed, they do at all) over a long period of time, not the moment one steps from the mikveh or recites the Shema. My conversion ceremony took place over fifteen years ago, and each succeeding year new aspects of being Jewish have presented themselves to me. I think of the conversion ceremony as a promise to assimilate Jewish life, ethnicity, viewpoint, religion, and so on; and this can only be a gradual process. I expect it to continue throughout my life.

Lynn Andrew Ellenson writes about another point of view.

The first problem most converts face is this: How can I honor my father and mother when I have, in many ways, left behind the upbringing they gave me? (I am, of course, assuming that the convert *wants* to maintain a relationship with his/her parents or family.) This question usually takes two forms. The first is, How do Jewish customs operate for the non-Jewish members of a convert's family? I remember, for example, wondering whether I should light a Yahrtzeit candle for my grandmother. Should I say Yizkor, since none of her children were doing it for her?

The second form is, How do non-Jewish customs, especially holidays, affect the convert? Should a convert who was previously Christian visit his/her parents over the Christmas holidays, for example? Emotional levels run high in homes where Christmas is being celebrated, so no matter how secularized the mode of celebration, a convert and his/her parents are likely to feel moments of tension. Children, of course, complicate such problems. Obviously there are no easy answers, and such situations must be worked out by the people involved.

The second area of experience that many converts share is the assimilation of a new ethnic identity. I have found myself using Yiddish English, which was never a part of my vocabulary as a non-Jew, with a relish and excess of gesticulation that I have seen very few born Jews use. Converts tend to feel a tremendous surge of unreasonable pride when a Jew accomplishes something noteworthy, or upon the discovery that an excellent author (or some other famous person) you've admired for a long time without knowing his/her background is Jewish. In my case Norman Mailer was a notable example. I have loved his writing but did not like him "personally" (if an anonymous fan can use such a word) until I discovered that he was Jewish. Since then I have thought of him with irrational (and amusing, I think) affection.

If a convert has been a Wasp, and therefore relatively invulnerable to the slings and arrows of American anti's, it is especially difficult to learn ethnicity, to develop a sense of solidarity with a group of people who share a common experience by virtue of their position as a religious, cultural, and intellectual (to choose three adjectives from the many available) minority. Learning ethnicity is difficult but certainly not impossible; it is a feeling acquired little by little, day by day. To aid in this acquisition of Jewish ambience, I believe it is helpful (in the way literature always helps one simulate an experience) to read novels and autobiographies by Jewish men and women, even if their references to being Jewish are relatively obscure. This experience, the acquiring of an ethnic identity, is an exciting one—and incidentally an experience converts share with previously assimilated Jews.

The third problem is related to the second experience, but is an emotion a convert cannot share in its full intensity with anyone because it is Jewish experiences, past and present, that are responsible in large part for Jewish ethnic solidarity. Of course, the major example is a convert coming to terms with the Holocaust. A convert must usually experience this, or *any* ill-treatment of Jews by non-Jews, on two levels: (1) the sometimes overpowering guilt felt by those born into the "oppressor" group (loosely defined) and (2) the absolute horror of the victim. A convert knows that had s/he lived in Germany during the 1930s and 1940s a tremendous amount of courage would have been required to take a stand against the Nazis, and many converts spend considerable time wondering, with great anguish, whether or not they would have been capable of such heroic action. There is also the awful knowledge, which often accompanies bearing a Jewish child, that this child's life would have depended on just such efforts. I found it debilitatingly painful to visit Yad Vashem—the Holocaust memorial in Jerusalem—and I do not think I could go back again. Yet I believe a visit, or some equivalent sensitizing experience, should be required for every person who has any connection at all to Western culture—Jew and non-Jew alike.

In addition to these three areas of experience, which represent a small portion of the process of becoming Jewish, I would like to offer three or four "helpful hints" to potential converts:

1. Do not balk at learning Hebrew, even if by rote. It will make you feel so much more at home in any Jewish service.

2. Find someone to teach you some Hebrew songs for the same reason—plus the fact that they're fun.

3. Try to visit, or make plans to visit, Israel.

4. Shelve, as much as possible, your tender feelings. If you are used to converts being sought and catered to as they are in the Christian tradition, you may be puzzled not to have a red carpet rolled out for you. Try to talk about this attitude (if it occurs) and understand it from several points of view, especially the theological and the historical.

One of my friends who converted told me that she heard a rabbi say once that he thought each convert represented the soul of one of the six million who died. This is the most complete welcome anyone could have.

On teaching converts

Barry Holtz writes about his experiences in instructing prospective converts.

During the past few years I've had the experience—generally a fascinating one—of tutoring people for conversion to Judaism. I say tutoring because I have never taught a *class* of converts, nor do I think that I ever would. To my mind the peculiarly private nature of the event of conversion lends itself ideally to the situation of individuals working together in learning, and, for me at least, it is in this private interaction that the growth of convert *and* teacher takes place. To be sure, there are classes offered by synagogues and rabbis, but this section is for those who either want to teach converts or want to learn themselves; for my purposes here I assume a tutoring atmosphere rather than a classroom atmosphere.

MOTIVES

When I first began to work with converts I insisted that I would only take on those who sincerely wanted to convert, not those who were being forced to convert because of various "external" factors—usually family pressures before a wedding. But as time has passed the distinction between the "sincere" and the "compelled" convert has blurred considerably for me. The simple fact is that motivations for conversion are extremely complex and are subject to subtleties too difficult for any outsider (and often for the convert him/herself) to unravel. Nowadays I play it by ear and let my instincts and experience guide me.

One factor, however, is interesting to note. Many people who convert do so *ostensibly* for reasons of family and marriage, yet for many years before have been thinking (with varying degrees of seriousness) about conversion to Judaism. What happens often, I think, is this. Conversion—for whatever reason—fascinates and interests these people, but the act of conversion itself seems so mysterious, difficult, or psychologically radical that to do so for purely religious reasons seems out of the question. Therefore they put themselves in social situations—with Jewish friends, particularly boyfriends or girlfriends—that destine then eventually to confront the social necessity or acceptability of conversion. Most striking to me is the number of men and women converting to Judaism who tell me that they had often considered conversion and that their impending marriage to a Jew is giving them the opportunity to do so.

BEGINNING THE PROCESS

So much for the subtleties of motivation. Now—what actually happens? To begin with, I should explain that although I am a teacher of converts, I do not consider myself directly responsible for the conversion ceremony or process itself. I am usually referred to a prospective convert by a rabbi, and it is the rabbi who has the ultimate authority as to matters of halakhah and readiness. In my experience this has always worked out well. The convert, rabbi, and I mutually decide when the time for the conversion has come. But the convert understands from the beginning that we can make no hard-and-fast agreement as to when s/he will be "ready." I have never had any difficulty about this matter, but it should be made clear from the beginning.

I can and do, however, give an estimate about the time that will be involved when I first meet with the prospective convert. This first meeting is important for both the convert and me because it is then that we decide whether we would get on well enough to study together over this length of time. Later we can work out the technical matters (how long, how much work, etc.).

If there is a future spouse involved, I suggest that the three of us meet. It is important to get a sense of the attitude of this highly important "third party" since his/her feelings about Judaism often become relevant to future discussions. Ideally, I prefer to meet with both the convert and the future spouse at all sessions, and, although I do not insist upon it, I encourage them to read and discuss and study the material together as we proceed.

I usually begin this meeting by telling them about my own background, both academic and religious, and I share a little bit about my own struggles with Jewish learning and Judaism. I then ask the convert (and the spouse, if there is one) to tell me something about his/her religious training and attitudes toward Judaism. This gives me a sense of the kinds of issues that might arise and the kind of entrée into Judaism that would make sense for such a person. (For example, a person from a nonreligious Protestant background might need a different approach from a person who came out of a strongly Catholic home. Likewise, the emphasis for a person interested in Eastern mysticism might differ from the emphasis for one who is studying rationalist philosophy.)

GUIDELINES

I usually meet with students once a week for about an hour and a half and expect them to do a healthy amount of reading between sessions. I don't require any halakhic observance from future converts, but I do ask that they try to attend two or three different Jewish services (usually on Shabbat) each month. "Different" is important because I want them to get a sense of the variety of choices within the Jewish community—Reconstructionist, Reform, Conservative, Orthodox; large synagogues, small synagogues; havurah-style services, Hasidic services, etc. Meeting once a week and reading with seriousness and voraciousness, a convert can be "ready" in about five to eight months; as I've said, the figure has to remain flexible. I make one further stipulation: during this time the convert must learn to "read" (i.e., read out loud, not comprehend) Hebrew. I *encourage* converts to take a course in the Hebrew language, but I *require* them to know how to read aloud from a prayer book.

BOOKS

A Jew should own Jewish books, and I usually ask converts to begin by buying some basic books. There will be others later (some they might want to take out of the library), but we begin with the following: A Bible (the Jewish Publication Society's Hebrew/English in two volumes is a good basic suggestion; they might also want to buy the JPS *Torah* translation [1962] and *The Prophets* [JPS, 1978]); a prayer book (I recommend the Birnbaum *Daily Prayerbook*, which is complete and has explanatory notes [Hebrew Publishing Company, 1949]); a basic popular history like Cecil Roth's *History of the Jews* (Schocken, 1961); four books on ritual and life cycle: Theodore Gaster's *Festivals of the Jewish Year* (William Sloane, 1952), Hayim Donin's *To Be a Jew* (Basic Books, 1972), and (of course!) *The First Jewish Catalog* (JPS, 1973) and *The Second Jewish Catalog* (JPS, 1976). As an introduction to Judaism, I recommend Jacob Neusner's *Way of Torah* (Dickenson, 1965).

AREAS OF CONCERN

In teaching I try to work within three very large areas of concern: ritual and practice, history of thought, and peoplehood. It is impossible to talk about one of these areas without talking about all three, and it is impossible to develop a step-by-step approach to the vast amount of material we might want to examine. All we can do is to try. The Talmud, as they say, is the only book that assumes that you've studied all of it before you've studied *any* of it!

The issue of "belief" in Judaism is often an issue of some anxiety for converts, particularly those coming out of traditional Catholic backgrounds, and so I always begin there. "What do I have to believe, what is the creed?"

is a question frequently asked early in the conversion process. I try to discuss this question particularly in the light of Christianity by pointing out that the "belief orientation" of Christianity is very different from the "action/mitzvah orientation" of Judaism. I discuss the difference between the idea of "creed" in Christianity and the same idea as it appears in the history of Jewish thought. Good reading suggestions for this area are "Torah and Dogma" by W. D. Davis (*Harvard Theological Review*, April 1968) and Section III of Abraham Joshua Heschel's *God in Search of Man* (Farrar, Straus, 1955). The discussion of belief in Judaism leads naturally to studying the ideas of halakhah, mitzvah, and Torah. We discuss these terms and read the first fifty pages of Jacob Neusner's *Way of Torah*.

At this point we might consider what has happened and why teaching for conversion is so complex. Here we are talking about Torah and halakhah and I haven't even asked them to read anything in Bible! They know nothing about Jewish history! We are talking about major ideas in rabbinic Judaism and they know nothing about the rabbis! And yet to begin with Bible, move on to rabbinic Judaism, and right on through Buber, Heschel, and Kaplan seems too diachronic. I have considered this problem frequently and I think the answer is—there is no answer. You will end up jumping around a lot and questioning your own methodology, but this is inevitable. When do we talk about the laws of Shabbat? When do we look at a prayer book? When do we study the holidays? These are questions you constantly will be asking yourself. And they are part of the excitement as well as the frustration of this kind of studying. Everything will seem essential and everything will seem more basic than everything else. Accept it; there is nothing you can do about it. I offer the rest of the "course" with that advice and these suggestions:

Texts: I believe that converts should be exposed to different types of traditional Jewish texts, that it is the best way to get at fundamental concepts and ideas:

   1. Bible: Genesis; Exodus 1–25, 30–34; Deuteronomy, Amos, Jonah, selections from Isaiah; Esther (for Purim); Job; selections from Psalms. Nahum Sarna's *Understanding Genesis* (McGraw-Hill, 1966) is well worth looking at as well.

   2. Rabbinic: Converts should have some exposure to Midrash—Nahum Glatzer's *Hammer on the Rock* (Schocken, 1960), for example. They should see what a page of Talmud looks like in the original and read some selections in English.

   3. Medieval: Converts should also read some of Maimonides' *Guide of the Perplexed,* ed. Shlomo Pines (University of Chicago, 1963) to get a taste of medieval philosophy. Gershom Scholem's selections from the *Zohar* are of interest. Looking at translations from one of the Codes is also very important.

Ritual and practice: Along with the *Jewish Catalogs,* converts should read Gaster's *Festivals of the Jewish Year,* A. J. Heschel's *The Sabbath* (Meridian, 1963), and Samuel Dresner and Seymour Siegel's *The Jewish Dietary Laws* (Burning Bush, 1959). Moreover, the convert should deal with A. J. Heschel's *God in Search of Man* (Farrar, Straus, 1955), Neusner's *Way of Torah,* as well as the section on Torah in Louis Jacobs's *Jewish Thought Today* in the "Chain of Tradition" series (Behrman House, 1964).

History of thought: Leo Schwartz's *Great Ages and Ideas of the Jewish People* (Modern Library) is an excellent book, as is Louis Finkelstein's *The Jews* (JPS, 1949). I would recommend the essay on the Bible by Yehezkel Kaufmann in *Great Ages.* For rabbinic Judaism, Judah Goldin's introduction in *The Living*

Talmud is a good place to start, Gerson Cohen's essay on the talmudic age in *Great Ages* is superb, Milton Steinberg's novel *As a Driven Leaf* is a nice way to begin, and Nahum Glatzer's *Hillel* is easy going. Neusner's *Way of Torah* should be required, and I also like his introductory chapters in *Invitation to the Talmud* (Abingdon). As should be obvious, I feel that the crucial period in Jewish thought for converts to grasp is the rabbinic period, and I spend a good deal of time working on this one area. After that it is up to the teacher and convert to decide on emphasis. The Schwartz and Finkelstein books both have excellent essays on some of the later periods. Converts should be familiar with the development and progress of Jewish thought after the rabbinic period. But much of the emphasis on study will depend on the student's interests. Converts should know something about Jewish mysticism, for example, but whether that something will come from Gershom Scholem's introduction to *Major Trends in Jewish Mysticism* (Schocken, 1961) or Heschel's "Mystical Element in Judaism" (in *The Jews*, vol. 2) will depend on his/her interests and abilities. The same is true about Hasidism, the rise of Reform Judaism, modern theology, or any other issue that is deemed significant.

Peoplehood: This is usually the most difficult area of all to do well. The whole cultural and ethnic side of Judaism, the sense of belonging to a people, the idea of am Yisrael—all this is crucial and yet extremely hard to communicate. Under this topic I include such issues as persecution, the State of Israel, the Holocaust, the shtetl. This will take a lot of work and a lot of personal sharing of your own feelings. Books will help, but ultimately much depends on the teacher. Zionism is crucial and for the history of Zionist thought Arthur Hertzberg's introduction in *The Zionist Idea* (Doubleday, 1959) is excellent. For all its schmaltz Leon Uris's *Exodus* has a good deal of power, and after all this whole topic of peoplehood is highly emotional. Reading fiction at this point can be very useful: Elie Wiesel's *Gates of the Forest* (Holt, Rinehart & Winston, 1964), André Schwartz-Bart's *Last of the Just* (Atheneum, 1960), Irving Howe and Eliezer Greenberg's *Treasury of Yiddish Stories* (Viking, 1954). Read Elie Wiesel's *Night* (Hill and Wang, 1960) about the Holocaust and his *The Jews of Silence* (Holt, Rinehart & Winston, 1966) about Soviet Jewry—they are important and moving. For Eastern Europe I recommend Mark Zborowski and Elizabeth Herzog's *Life Is with People* (International Universities, 1962) despite its flaws and Heschel's *The Earth Is the Lord's* (Abelard-Schuman, 1960) for its emotional power.

Prayer: This too is an area that will require a good deal of personal talking. Selections from the prayer book are one's primary source, and it is essential that converts know about the structure *and* mechanics of the Jewish service (when is the Torah read, the Amidah, when to rise, etc.—see The Geography of the Synagogue in *Catalog 2*, pp. 264–95). Also it is important to stress and talk about the rituals of the home (candlelighting, Kiddush, mezuzah, etc.), if this has not been done before.

This basically is my way of approaching conversion. I do a good deal of talking about my own relationship to Judaism, but I try to show a convert that there are many different ways of being Jewish. Perhaps the hardest thing of all in working with a convert is walking that delicate line between being *honest* about your own personal beliefs and practices and *propagandizing* for your own point of view. I have had converts choose to practice Judaism in ways that are different from my own, and that is at times hard to accept. In the long run the most important thing you can do is to open up different possibilities. And doing that can give you a great sense of joy.

Living in a small town

We have become a mobile society, so one day you may find yourself living in a small town with few coreligionists—or none. Can you survive as a Jew? My view is YES—and you may come to appreciate Judaism even more.

Moving from a large metropolitan area (New York) to a comparatively small Texas town was a cultural shock. We arrived a few weeks before Rosh ha-Shanah and, having found a house, began to scout the neighborhood. I remember driving down the highway scanning the stores—Jewish meat market, NO, Jewish bakery, NO, nope, negative—and inquiring for the Jewish population, which seemed to be invisible.

Missing family and the familiar, I decided to model Rosh ha-Shanah as closely as possible on our former life-style, so easily achieved in New York. I started by trying to make the elaborate double-braided hallot traditionally associated with the holiday. My next-door Baptist neighbor visited just as I finished coating the tops with egg white, and so admired the artistic look of the loaves that she asked for a spare one (the beginning of interfaith dialogue!). To my horror the finished product was hard as a rock—I'd yet to learn the technique of yeast breads. As I despaired the doorbell rang, bringing a stranger to the house with the answer to my prayers. "Welcome to our town," she said. "I heard another Jewish couple arrived here, so I brought you a hallah."

She couldn't stay long but was able to tell me that services for Yom Kippur were being held in the YMCA building on the campus ten miles from our home. Yom Kippur found me walking in the direction of the Y, minus nourishment, an uncomfortably hot sun beating down. Dripping sweat all the way, I arrived in time for the services feeling weak and dehydrated. The room assigned for the service was empty, so I inquired of the desk clerk—only to find that the service had been canceled without explanation. Convinced that I could not make it home in reasonably good shape, I rode back, demoralized and missing the old ways very much. My opinion of the town's Jewish families, with the exception of the "hallah lady," was not flattering, and it decreased with further encounters.

In time I learned that there was a temple in town. Formerly a church, the building had been the gift of a Methodist gentleman in a beautiful ecumenical gesture. Friday night services were occasionally held there—if a card game wasn't in progress somewhere else. Religiously things looked glum, but it was the beginning of deep self-examination. With memories of a happy, close-family Jewish childhood, I soon realized that Judaism was a vital part of my being. If I had to go it alone, so be it; I would learn.

During those years we began our self-instruction in survival Judaism, armed with books in our home library and an increasing knowledge of the available resources. A chain of supermarkets known as "Weingartens" could be found in most large towns throughout Texas, and there was one where we lived that carried familiar foods (mostly delicatessen and bagels) in specially designated areas in the freezer section. (This was on strict orders from the founder, the late Joe Weingarten, who started this supermarket chain with one small grocery in Houston years ago. He gave further orders that holiday foods were to be shipped to any store at the request of a customer if reasonable advance notice was given, so it was possible to order Pesah goods without having food shipped long distances by freight.)

By and large, one can live any Judaism with certain basic knowledge: kashrut observers can order meats—solid-packed and shipped in by Greyhound bus—from the kosher butcher shop in the nearest large city, or friends driving into the city can pick up your order for you. You may also decide to become a vegetarian, eliminating the elaborate preparation and costlier merchandise.

Be sure to investigate the nearest city thoroughly; if you want to live Jewishly, its resources will be as important to you as those of your own town. You may already be buying your meat there. Remember, too, that a city able to support a kosher butcher probably offers other useful supplies. Many synagogues and temples have gift shops that carry a variety of religious items, cards, and books. The Jewish community center—if there is one—may also stock gifts. In a city with a sizable Jewish population the larger bookstores may have works of Jewish interest. Also find out from local Jews about special features—Houston's Jewish center has a kosher snack bar, with meat segregated from dairy products.

My Christian friends have become accustomed to my routine. Some even ask if they may bring others to see my Shabbat or holiday table—they are impressed that we do all this on our own. Close friends are sure to show up at the appropriate holiday time to enjoy the goodies they know they'll find awaiting them. I cook for a mob and seldom have much left over. During the Shavuot celebration, for example, goodly amounts of blintzes and cheesecake were sampled by my visitors. Occasionally I'm asked to give lessons in the art of blintz making, which I'm glad to do if there's time to spare. When the Department of Parks and Recreation in the town we now live in held a Bread Seminar, my hallah recipe—by this time fully mastered and tested—was there, along with a note explaining the significance of bread in Jewish tradition.

In our home we observe the Shabbat from start to finish, as well as all the holidays, for we love our Jewish way of life and take comfort from the joys of our faith. Preparation for Shabbat usually begins on Thursday, when the silver gets a good polishing. (The hallah is baked in large batches and wrapped for the freezer, eliminating the need to bake it weekly.) If there's time, on goes the lace tablecloth and the napkins; otherwise, I do that in the early hours of Friday morning. The evening meal is also completed before noon, which is the deadline I set for myself. Then I can relax and set my mind in a Shabbat mood. By the time our daughter comes home from school and my husband from work, I'm in a happy, peaceful frame of mind, and all of us arrive at the Shabbat table with pleasure. When the candles are lit, our daughter says the blessing. This is the way we taught her, so she will never forget the ritual. For the same reason it is she who says the ha-Motzi after my

In many towns, particularly in the South, food is the occasion for social exchange. Do not feel that keeping kosher prevents your sharing your life with your neighbors. Most people are interested in the customs of others; instead of widening the gap, your table can often help ease misunderstandings without intimidation.

husband has recited the Kiddush. Then we enjoy the meal, harmonizing on many of our favorite zemirot—table hymns—during the evening.

I have discovered that you must continue in custom and spirit most of what you remember of a joyous Jewish childhood if you want your children to enjoy some of the same memories. Think for a minute about how it all happened to be there: our European-born parents brought with them a way of life that they continued in new surroundings. They tended to live near one another, building places of worship as they did in "the old country"—perhaps a simple converted store (front part set for the men, rear room for the women's section) trying to duplicate the close-knit communities they had left behind.

In today's very mobile society the landsleit community is almost gone, and more Jews are finding themselves in situations where they have to go it alone. The memories their children will have depend on what they choose to give them. It is all too easy to avoid the fuss and the extra effort, to just coast—you have your wonderful memories to think back on. Remember, though, that your children will have none. There are families in this situation who are unable to answer the simplest questions about Judaism. The problems increase where young children are involved. Not able to teach them, the parents' suffering is doubled as they watch their children, ignorant of their own wonderful heritage, reach for another that has dimension and "glamor." Sometimes, not often, they will ship their child off to another city to learn what they really should have learned at home.

I made the decision a long time ago to bring into our daughter's life all that was possible of the treasures that were so easily given me by my parents and grandparents. It wasn't really hard, as I am (in my own definition) a joyous Jew. I love Shabbat and the holidays and immerse myself in activities concerning them. In addition, my husband and I painted our own childhood word pictures of holiday time and family. Our daughter was kept busy making her own crayoned holiday greeting cards or helping to prepare holiday sweets (and tasting en route!). We'd sing songs days before each holiday to invoke the mood. We bought Simhat Torah flags—a pretty apple stuck into the top of the dowel to which the paper flag was glued—while we recounted stories of childhood days when a loving and wise zaydeh would prepare them for an excited group of hovering grandchildren. Our daughter experienced this joy with the pictures evoked by our spoken remembrances. In the gift shops I found a child's megillah and brought it home. We inscribed our daughter's name on it and would read for her when she was quite little. We played niss—nuts—at Pesah, and she got quite adept at this early form of marbles and won a mighty amount.

Absences from school at appropriate holiday times were never questioned. All it took was a note to the teacher a day or two ahead of time. Often her teachers asked her to explain the holiday to the class, as they were interested in knowing about her religious observances. Sometimes she would bring holiday food to class to share with her teacher and classmates, often resulting in a request for the recipe. (Rosh ha-Shanah's honey cake was a favorite of the consumers.) We took care to show her that our holidays are not a burden—or a means of exclusion—but a source of joy.

A good example was the celebration of Hanukkah, child-style. The windows and rooms were decorated in the holiday spirit, and latkes and applesauce pleased the palate. Appropriate songs were learned, sung in Hebrew, and translated into English so that their meaning was clear. Each day brought another gift to commemorate the holiday. Our daughter had her own menorah with miniature candles to light. Young friends who visited at that time not only gobbled the latkes happily but remarked that it was great to get a present

on each of the eight days. When she was twelve the eight gifts were reduced to one, given on the first day—our daughter had entered the adult world gracefully.

Of course, there have also been many unhappy moments, starting when she entered nursery school and encountered children whose minds were already warped by prejudices taught at home. Although she was quite young, we discussed the hurt of anti-Semitism and how to handle it. Each negative encounter was dealt with according to the deed, and it was soon obvious that she gained strength as her knowledge of Judaism increased. Though the incidents often brought tears of anger and frustration when she told them to us, they also reinforced the Jewishness in her own mind and heart. As some of her peers became friends, an acceptance by many of them of her distinct and different way of life developed. Oddly enough, the early teen years brought a resurgence of anti-Semitism, probably a result of the gung-ho approach in Sunday School classes—each one promoting the belief that we should be saved from the "sin" of not following their way. Though annoying and disturbing to our daughter, their efforts were, we believe, really an expression of their concern for her; they did not realize that their behavior offended and hurt. Perhaps she would have done the same if Judaism taught her that she must persuade others of the truth of her faith.

As our daughter approaches her fifteenth birthday the matter of dating is becoming a reality. She will be going out with Christian boys, which is quite all right since we believe it is necessary to her social growth. She already has a distinct Jewish identity based on both home teaching and her encounters with classmates at school. We have taught her ourselves using books from the Jewish Publication Society and from Ktav and Bloch publishing houses, with related workbooks and projects as well. There are now 360-odd books relating to things Jewish in our library, not to mention a large record collection that includes liturgical gems, Hebrew-language records, Israeli, Hebrew, and Yiddish favorites, and holiday material. Besides umpteen dictionaries, we have the twelve-volume set of the *Jewish Encyclopedia*, the two-volume *Encyclopedia of Zionism and Israel*, and all the Soncino collection. Our local library has the entire sixteen-volume set of the *Encyclopaedia Judaica*, along with some new books just ordered and several we donated. It also has some wonderful children's books, like I. B. Singer's delightful *Mazel and Shlimazel*.

Frequently friends involved in teaching church Bible classes have asked me to visit their group and inform them about some form of Judaism, ranging from a capsule "Jewish way of life" to a description of a particular holiday. I usually comply because it helps reduce stereotyped misconceptions about our faith, and because I enjoy talking about how we live. It also keeps me "cracking the books"—reviewing and adding to my own knowledge. The questions posed are often weightier than you would expect, so I learn with each reference-hunt that I undertake. A number of times Bible classes have come to our home to see more concretely how we follow our faith; visible symbols are explained, beginning with the encounter with the mezuzah on our door. Appropriate refreshments are offered to our guests with an explanation of the food, especially if it relates to a particular holiday.

I'd love to help with the hannukah party; but I'm just so busy with the AAUW executive committee, and the school board; ...

Believing that the world is large and that one lives a vital and active part in it doubles the meaning of holidays for me. I remember my friends at their holiday time with appropriate cards and gifts, the latter usually handmade because I feel you really give more when you put your own creativity into it. One Christmas I made gift batches of sesame-seed candies, enclosing a note explaining that this sweet was probably enjoyed by Jesus as a child (research helped!); they were warmly received. Shoe on the other foot, you'd be astonished at the number of cards and beautiful gifts we've received at our holiday time. Every Rosh ha-Shanah a beautiful floral arrangement, suitable for placing upon the festive table, arrives from one of our cherished friends. Religious cards flood the mail to add to our holiday joy. The local card shop now stocks them after I inquired for them just one time—the dealer thoughtfully remembered to order them from the supplier and continues to do so. We moved into our present home during Hanukkah, and on the last evening, while the candles glowed and we sang "Maoz Tzur," the doorbell rang. We opened the door to find another dear family, laden with holiday cookies and handcrafted gifts, wishing us joy on the last night of the holiday. A beautiful embroidery, specially created as a personal tribute, hangs in the kitchen near the breakfast table, where it still brings joy to my heart, as does the Shalom tile that another friend ordered as a special surprise for us. As friends learn more about my faith, they seem to remember what is taboo for me and honor the observance accordingly.

Living in a small town requires a reevaluation of your religious priorities, and answers depend on your own rationalization of Jewish law. Time has tempered my decisions on every aspect of my Conservative persuasion—time and experience.

It is not difficult to live Jewishly here unless you do not drive on Shabbat, since our town lacks a synagogue or temple. Oddly enough it boasts a Jewish cemetery, mute evidence that at one time a fair number of Jews called this town home and put down roots. Today I count five Jewish families, each with a different view of Judaism. So far I have witnessed a brit and a wedding. *Catalog 1* saw service in helping plan the marriage of a Christian girl who converted to Judaism. The beautiful and impressive ceremony was conducted by two rabbis to an assemblage of 90 percent Christian and 10 percent Jewish guests. I haven't attended a funeral yet for various reasons—one of which is that they are, thank God, very few. But the funeral director has told me that he is quite able to take care of the somber details properly; he even has a key to the local Jewish cemetery. He uses three comprehensive information manuals and can supply coffin, etc. in as little as two hours. The only thing he can't provide is the shroud, but if requested he would send someone to pick one up. (What comes to my mind is the use of a clean sheet, for want of anything else; that, or reverting to the old European custom of sewing one's own in advance of need—an idea I got from an I. B. Singer story.) So it is possible, even in a small town, to welcome and depart from life in the Jewish way.

Of course there are moments of alienation, when you begin to wonder whether all attempts to share your differences are hopeless. Yet you must assume that however thoughtless they are, most people are not deliberately malicious. Our Baptist neighbors, for example, had always treated us like family. When Christmas Day arrived it was natural that we were invited next door to sample the sweets. Their young son and infant daughter played happily with the just-opened presents while we chatted with the parents. The talk was of how expensive Christmas presents could be and how they had tried to cut corners by bargaining with the vendor. They used an expression we'd never heard before, "to jew him down," to describe this process. We

were taken aback when we heard it—both initially offended by the term and at a loss to equate their casual use of it with their warm friendship. An awkward silence followed, and we shortened our visit without appearing rude, no longer able to maintain easy chatter. Discussing the meaning of this colloquialism and how it was intended, we wondered whether the friendship was now lost. Having a direct nature, I visited my friend the next day and asked her what the term meant. While explaining that it meant "bargaining for a lower price" she became embarrassed, suddenly realizing that *we* are Jews and therefore might see this as an offensive term. She apologized for inadvertently hurting us.

After the immediate pain of betrayal in such incidents, you begin to realize that although prejudice and exclusion may always be with us, you can still influence people to change their assumptions in small day-to-day ways. When our daughter was in junior high school she brought home an orientation booklet containing the student pledge for high school. It read, in part, "to live and act in good Christian ethical/moral code." Visiting the high school principal, I explained that we had a problem: I wanted my daughter to be a good member of the high school student body, but it was not possible to adhere to the code as given in the booklet. "What is the trouble?" the principal inquired. "According to the code, our daughter must live a moral Christian life," I replied, "and this she cannot do, as we are Jewish." The dear man was embarrassed and apologetic; he had formulated the code years ago, when minority points of view—religiously speaking—had not been obvious. He promised to change the wording to read "good moral life" in the next printing. That was just before summer vacation. When school resumed in the fall the new booklet had been printed and distributed—as amended.

There are other redeeming moments. A few years ago a good friend asked me to attend her "Share" group meeting. It was essentially a prayer group (prayer—silent or vocal—went around the circle at a designated time, and one could join in or decline at one's preference). Many church affiliations were represented in the membership, and I added a Jewish voice. Experiences and problems relating to our spiritual selves were freely discussed. At first I shied away from speaking and offering my point of view frankly, but encouragement on all sides broke the barrier. I remember particularly the meeting a few days after the Munich massacre, when I poured out my feelings in a plea that tolerance in religious teachings, not prejudice, should be taught in the home. Remembering that joyless day when the morning hours revealed the deaths of Israel's representatives at the Munich Olympiad, I recall too the touching actions of those friends. One insisted I come to her house for lunch. I wanted to refuse, to go home and privately cry out my anguish at the horror. But she would not hear of it. In her house the bitter feelings spilled forth for hours. She listened with great patience, sympathy, and understanding, which eased the pain. That evening a card was delivered by hand to our home. Signed by an impressive number of friends, it expressed sympathy for our sorrow. We were moved to tears by this display of sensitivity; their concern helped soothe our grief. That card remains in our file to this day—a very precious piece of paper.

In a small town it is tempting to abandon your distinctive customs in order to adjust, because differences are far more noticeable here than in a big city. Don't feel that it's necessary—you will always be Jews to the non-Jews anyway, and you'll be much more respected if you define your identity from the beginning instead of letting it be defined for you. In a small town, unlike a larger, more diversified community, you are never anonymous; people's religious and cultural allegiances are common knowledge. Your attitude to your faith will set the tone for others.

Ultimately, your Jewish way of life rests on your conception of what it should be for you. If your needs are great, you'll make the effort and never feel the price too high; if you don't really care, you and your children will soon forget what it's all about—the choice is yours. Whether you live in a city with a large Jewish community and easily obtained resources or if you are the only follower of your faith in a small town, the results will always be in direct proportion to your involvement.

Surviving the army

It is difficult to remain a positively identified and practicing Jew as a member of the American armed forces—difficult but possible. To some degree the challenge is similar to that of a Jew in a small town. S/he lives without the support, models, and resources of a larger Jewish community and must compensate with a strong, self-reliant commitment that will not easily erode. Yet the situation in the service is both better and worse at the same time. It is better in that the military command *expects* a Jewish program to exist and is *obligated* by regulations to enable a Jew to fulfill his/her religious needs. Regardless of the sympathies of the individual unit commander, those regulations will govern the officer's response to expressed Jewish concerns. The installation chaplains, even in the absence of a rabbi, are in turn vested with the responsibility for maintaining a Jewish program. Generally they will take pride in such a program and will lend their support and resources. The gov-

ernment in fact prints a siddur, produces a certain number of essential ritual objects, and will appropriate funds for essentials.

On the other hand, the Jew in uniform must face some stark facts. The military is a leveler. Only under intense, persistent pressure does it make room for individual differences. It rewards conformity and expects uniformity. The overriding concern is the primary mission of the unit, and particular needs will, at times, be submerged. Jews who wants to maintain a good standard of observance will be very much in a minority. They must step forward to identify themselves—and thus will call attention to themselves. Their special requirements can bring a certain amount of disapproval or even derision by peers and private distrust by superiors. Furthermore, whatever success they have in asserting their identity will have to be continually reestablished as they move from post to post. Whatever Jewish community a Jew manages to find or create will have to be continually rebuilt as people flow in and out. Much personal strength is required, but leading a satisfying religious life can be accomplished.

Some guidelines

The following are some suggestions for insuring maximum realization of personal needs and for maintaining a community:

1. *Establishing credibility*: The first step is to make your needs known immediately upon entering the military. Special requirements will receive a more sympathetic hearing if there are no sudden surprises along the way, if you are consistent in your behavior. Arrangements for kashrut, for example, will be facilitated if you make your dietary needs clear from the outset.

2. *Contacting allies*: Contact local chaplains immediately. There are approximately fifty full-time rabbis on active duty, more in the active reserve,

and many more civilian rabbis who service military installations. They will give much guidance and provide support. Any rabbi connected with the military will try to serve the needs of every person, regardless of his/her personal stance. Non-Jewish chaplains, much more than their civilian counterparts, are generally acquainted with the special requirements Jews might have and will often go out of their way to assist. The Jewish Welfare Board and its Commission on Jewish Chaplaincy in New York, with regional offices and field workers, while more distant, can be counted on to respond and carry much clout with the command. The JWB Commission is the official liaison between the Jewish community and the armed forces.

3. *On keeping kosher*: The problem will be most acute for anyone in basic or advanced training, during wartime, or in an overseas assignment where most people eat in the mess hall or field kitchen. Even for the very strict, there are some readily available foods, such as cold juices, cereals, fresh vegetables and fruit, canned tuna, and canned salmon. Such a diet will of course have to be supplemented. By special arrangement, a cooperative mess officer or sergeant will allow you to have foods heated and brought into the mess hall. The JWB supplies limited quantities of canned meats to single Jews or those serving overseas without their families. (What observant Jew in the last generation does not remember Hebrew National rice with braised beef!?) Packages from home are a must.

Even a better arrangement is the provision for "separate rations": you apply for a modest extra sum of money to purchase your own food, bypassing the mess hall entirely. You might persuade the local commissary to order and stock some kosher foods. Make arrangements to heat and cook meals at the Jewish chapel or elsewhere.

Under wartime conditions or in otherwise remote and difficult situations there are provisions for some easing of the requirements of Jewish law. No less an authority than the Hafetz Hayyim, in his classic *Mahaneh Yisrael* (The Camp of Israel), has written that if you cannot keep all the details of the mitzvah of kashrut, you should do the best you can. In 1943 Rabbi Moses M. Yoshor published *Israel in the Ranks: A Religious Guide of Faith and Practice for the Jewish Soldier,* based on the Hafetz Hayyim's work. In it he writes (pp. 70–71):

When kosher meat is unavailable, it is well to remember that one can frequently subsist on a purely vegetarian diet and that people who live on a meatless diet prove to be no less strong or courageous than those who dine on meat. Even a soldier may at times select a variety of vegetables and other heathful foods on which he can subsist.

However, there are different degrees in the prohibition of nonkosher foods. Some food articles are under a more stringent ban than others. In reference to animal food, the eating of meat of a forbidden animal is considered a more severe transgression than the meat from animals allowed for food, but prepared in a nonkosher manner; or the drinking of trefa (nonkosher) soup is less a violation than the eating of trefa meat.

Hence, when the soldier is in a condition that he cannot subsist on a restricted diet, he should try to minimize as much as possible the violation which he feels compelled to commit.

It is advisable for him to consult a person well-versed in the Jewish ritual whenever he has the opportunity.

Of course such allowances should be used only when no other options are available.

4. *Shabbat and holidays:* The military is familiar with "days of religious obligation" for all religious groups. These days in the Jewish calendar are generally well-known in the chaplain's office. Before the High Holidays or Pesah, command letters from the highest echelons will often circulate, informing all units of the special requirements Jewish servicepersons might have. Leaves can be arranged, and passes that do not count against leave time are often liberally granted. If you show a readiness to reciprocate, to take extra duty assignments in order to make up for your absences, to stand in for others

on Christian holidays or on national holidays, you will often find your special requests granted without acrimony.

Shabbat is potentially a more difficult problem. Although the military is normally on a five-day work week, there are circumstances when weekend duties will arise: the period of basic training, wartime, periods of alert, and normal duty rotations are among them. Once again, willingness to reciprocate by taking Sunday and holiday rotations will help pave the way to keeping Shabbat sacred. Yet almost inevitably there will be times when it will be impossible to observe a Shabbat or part of a Shabbat. This sacrifice is part of the price paid within the military context. Your freedom is circumscribed, but the extent of the limitations can be minimized. Even if some part of Shabbat might be given up from time to time, do whatever you can. Thus even while on duty, avoid as many prohibited kinds of work as possible. Further, there is no reason not to arrange a Seudah Shelishit (third Shabbat meal) and recite Havdalah even if you have had to work at the beginning of Shabbat.

5. *Becoming a chaplain's assistant:* For a few, the ability to observe and even foster observance among others can be enlarged greatly by becoming a Jewish chaplain's assistant. A special military school trains assistants, who then work almost exclusively in promoting the Jewish program—generally under the guidance of a rabbi. Others become assistants after a period of on-the-job training when there is an opening. A chaplain's assistant can escape most of the limitations others are bound to face.

6. *Establishing a community:* A community is terribly important in the armed forces: to provide mutual support, strength, and sharing of Jewish concerns. A Shabbat spent alone can be devastating. Holiday periods can be the worst of times—with past pleasant associations in painful relief against present emptiness and loneliness. Every effort should be made to nurture a small community.

If a rabbi serves an installation the community will usually center around him, and his lead should be followed. In larger installations, an ongoing program will most likely be found. If rabbinic coverage is limited or nonexistent, someone will have to take the initiative. Lay leadership is encouraged in the military, and support from various sources can be counted on. It is important that the lay leader be approved by the Commission on Jewish Chaplaincy of the JWB and be known to non-Jewish chaplains as well. The JWB publishes

Listen Cohen, I don't care what it says in the Talmud, get those damned strings off your uniform.

a *Jewish Program and Resource Guide,* which is available on request. It is a step-by-step guide encompassing Jewish needs, problems, and resources. Periodically in almost every part of the world where troops are stationed, the JWB Commission conducts lay-leadership training conferences where new skills are learned, common problems analyzed, and important contacts made. The non-Jewish chaplain and his assistants will be helpful, providing advice, facilities, and logistical support. Local Armed Forces Committees exist in many parts of the country, which provide some funding and important liaison with nearby communities and their resources. Nearby civilian congregations and their rabbis will usually welcome servicepersons and provide rich programming resources into which a military community can be plugged. The lay leader should also establish a relationship with a rabbi s/he respects so that rabbinic advice can be readily available, particularly in an emergency.

The building of a military community can be a very rich creative opportunity. Because of the constant flow of people, there will be little established tradition. The lay leader will find most Jews anxious to pitch in because most will feel the need for some Jewish contact and sharing. The lay leader will have to keep in mind that the needs of all must be served, and military communities usually take a middle-of-the-road stance. Activities generally focus around Shabbat but alternative arrangements are possible, depending on when most people can come together.

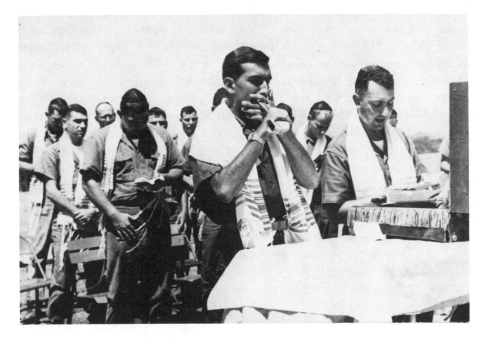

The tendency in many synagogues today to create havurot—small, intimate groupings of complete families who study and partake together in Jewish experiences—seems to be an idea readily translatable into a military context. Moving activities into homes and allowing compatible small communities to grow up can provide some of the intimacy and friendship that more traditional public chapel activities could not approach. The home setting can also provide some welcome relief from the military trappings outside.

If there is a sizable group of children at an installation, Jewish education will have high priority. The Department of Defense and the JWB Commission publish a *Unified Jewish Religious Education Curriculum for the Armed Forces,* which gives guidance on goals, methods, and recommended texts that can be adapted under virtually all circumstances. The curriculum was designed so that children moving from post to post would find a certain amount of continuity. Especially if an installation is small, children might be enrolled in a local synagogue's school so that peer relationships and committed adult models can be multiplied.

The creation of such a community and school requires funding. Government or "appropriated" funds as well as "nonappropriated" welfare or sundry funds can be tapped for basic needs. In the absence of a rabbi, the installation chaplain can give guidance in obtaining the funds. In addition, military congregations maintain a Jewish Chaplain's Fund to which members give voluntary contributions.

Resources and Bibliography

1. Available on request from

Commission on Jewish Chaplaincy
Jewish Welfare Board (JWB)
15 E. 26th St.
New York, NY 10010
(212) 532-4949

   a. *Jewish Program and Resource Guide*

   b. *Kashrut Observance in the Military Establishment*

   c. *JWB Calendar*

   d. *Haggadah*

   e. *Elegies for Tishah B'av*

   f. *Machzorim*

   g. *Jewish Songsters (Armed Forces Edition)*

   h. *Religious Message* (sermon ideas)

   i. *Responsa in Wartime*   (collections of questions and rabbinic

   j. *Responsa to Chaplains*   answers peculiar to the military context)

   k. canned kosher foods

   l. tefillin, tallitot, kippot

2. The U. S. Government issues certain Jewish religious articles:

   a. daily and Shabbat prayer book

   b. ark set (miniature ark)

   c. Bible (JPS)

   d. Kiddush cup, candelabra, etc.

Jews in prison

Of course, not every Jewish prisoner is a saint and not every prisoner tells the truth to visitors. But what is needed most is human contact with people from the outside world.

The Jewish community has long been out of touch with its members behind bars. The last few years, however, have seen a heightened awareness of Jewish prisoners and their needs, and a wide variety of programs designed to address some of those needs have begun to emerge.

In addition to being aware of the needs of the prisoner him/herself, we have also begun to realize that the imprisonment of one family member creates an instant crisis for the entire family. A woman in a predominantly lower- to middle-income Jewish neighborhood in Brooklyn described her situation this way; "I'm a prisoner in my own home. I have to stay home and watch the baby with no one to talk with. I don't get enough money from welfare for my baby and me to live on. And I have to put up with the pettiness of the Welfare Department until my husband is released. I see no movies and can't afford to eat out at all. On top of that, I have to keep my husband's situation a secret from the neighbors and most of the relatives. So the families are punished along with the prisoners."

This woman's husband had a short sentence and the family made it through this difficult period on its own. However, some husbands and wives stop communicating in this situation, and many families are confronted with even greater problems, which require outside help.

In addition, the situation of the prisoner who is interested in/committed to Jewish life creates another whole host of problems.

One thirty-five-year-old Jewish ex-offender has spent the last year living, working, and studying in the Lubavitcher Hasidic community after serving ten years in the California state prison system. He became an observant Jew in prison after reading a Lubavitcher pamphlet and receiving a moving letter from a young yeshivah student. "I've spent the year building my new life on three pillars," he said. "They are Torah, counseling, and a self-help group.

It's difficult to be an observant Jew in prison. One guard stomped and spit on the Jewish religious articles he found, and prisoners would warn me when the guard was coming so that I could hide my yarmulka, because wearing it was punishable by a short stay in 'segregation.' "

Below is a list of programs that seek to help prisoners and/or their families.

Lubavitch Hasidic Organization—Habad
770 Eastern Pkwy.
Brooklyn, NY 11213

has organized many programs for Jewish offenders. In Los Angeles they have worked with young drug offenders and in San Francisco, in cooperation with

Committee for Jewish Prisoners
P.O. Box 31265
San Francisco, CA 94131

they have raised money to send books and religious articles into the prisons. Habadniks have also visited prisons in many areas to offer Jewish religious programs, and they have been visited in Crown Heights by Allenwood Federal Prison's Jewish congregation.

Several outside Jewish congregations across the country have arranged for similar furlough programs from low-security prisons, and a group of families from a Reform congregation in California have Jewish prisoners from the nearby Lompoc honor camp as houseguests during Jewish holidays. Millie Rosenblatt, a UJA fund raiser who is a member of one of the families, said that many of the Lompoc visitors "made good company." She noted that Jewish prisoners from another nearby facility "contributed over $500 for Israel during the 1973 war. My daughter, Racelle, collected the money, which amounted to more per capita than the local outside Jewish community contributed until we launched our fund-raising drive."

There have been a number of efforts in recent years to broaden Jewish religious rights in prison. Several campaigns by Jewish convicts, sometimes conducted with outside support from members of the Orthodox community, have won for observant Jewish prisoners the right to have kosher food, wear beards, and use religious articles in the federal prisons.

One organization that has been active in efforts to protect Jewish religious rights is

COLPA
The National Commission on Law and Public Affairs
66 Court St.
Brooklyn, NY 11201

which functions as the legal arm of Orthodox Judaism.

The Bnai Brith Commission on Community and Veterans Services
1640 Rhode Island Ave. NW
Washington, DC 20036

is another group helping prisoners. In 1972 Connie Giniger, a schoolteacher and member of Atlanta Bnai Brith Women, learned through a chance conversation about a former Bnai Brith Youth Organization member incarcerated in the federal prison in Atlanta. He had asked Bnai Brith for some prayer books. After her initial visit to the Atlanta Penitentiary, she started a volunteer program that eventually embraced a wide variety of activities with Jewish prisoners, including rap sessions, Jewish study classes, and Jewish holiday celebrations. The program also works for prison reform and crime prevention.

The vast majority of prisoners will be rejoining our communities. But recidivism is high and a volunteer program can make the difference. Mrs. Giniger's pamphlet, "All Men Are Responsible for One Another" (the title is from a quotation in the Talmud), states: "There are national organizations at present who have programs within the prisons and the participants of these programs have a return rate of 15 to 20 percent, as compared to the national rate of 60 to 80 percent."

A series of pamphlets are available, some based on experiences at the Atlanta Federal Penitentiary, to aid in designing programs to meet the needs of Jewish prisoners. Besides "All Men Are Responsible for One Another," they include "Reach Out and Touch" and "Clusters of Concern." Single copies are free. A more comprehensive publication is now being prepared.

One individual who conspicuously extended himself in behalf of isolated Jewish prisoners in recent years was the late Rev. William Jackson Jarman of New York's Park Avenue Christian Church, which shares its facilities with a Jewish congregation.

In 1977 Jarman arranged for a rabbi to visit after Jewish inmates began to attend the minister's Christian fellowship group at the federal prison where he was a volunteer. They told him that their Jewish chaplain ignored them. "I felt," he said, "that Jewish prisoners should be seen by a rabbi. The warden, a good man, can't do anything about it, he explained to me, because he is not in charge of hiring for that position."

In 1975, when he was informed that Jewish prisoners in the Marion Federal Penitentiary were denied a break-the-fast meal after Yom Kippur, Jarman obtained for them the support of the National Council of Churches.

And when he heard of two separate incidents where two outspoken Jewish prisoners, Allan Berube, a lay leader of the Jewish inmate congregation at Marion, and Robert Levy, a Vietnam veteran who gave free legal assistance to fellow prisoners, had apparently repeatedly been harassed by prison officials, Jarman wrote the warden, involved his congressman, and requested that the urban and rural churches of his denomination across the country assist these men wherever they might be transferred.

Several times, including the day before a heart condition claimed the German-American minister's life, a concerned Reverend Jarman told me that both the warden, who was in conflict with some of his Jewish prisoners, and Allan Berube had been transferred—apparently by chance—to the same prison. "Allan has no luck," he said. Is 'shlimazl' your Yiddish word for that? I've asked my church to support Allen and pray for him because I'm afraid that, unless something is done, Allan might eventually be permanently damaged by his prison experiences."

Mrs. Giniger emphasizes that although it is not for everyone, when you're working with prisoners you just might receive as much as you give—or more.

He doesn't know many Jews behind bars, but he's sure met a lot of Jews in bars.

Robert Levy was recently released from prison and now heads a neighborhood renewal project for his local Chamber of Commerce. His articles about Jewish prisoners have appeared in the *Jewish Post* and *Opinion* and, most recently, in the Autumn 1977 issue of *Present Tense*. He writes the following account of an unusual friendship between a Jewish prisoner and a concerned outsider.

A Jewish ex-prisoner's account (by Robert Levy)

I learned this weekend of the passing of the Reverend William Jackson Jarman of the Park Avenue Christian Church in New York City.

I first met Jack, as he preferred to be called by those of us honored enough to call him friend, through the mail while incarcerated in the state prison system in Virginia. I was a prison librarian in Culpepper, Virginia, and my friend David Rothenberg had a letter printed for me soliciting book contributions in *Fortune News*. Jack read the letter and wrote. I responded, and that began over a two-year period during which we wrote at length on a daily basis. Such was his need to know, and such was my willingness to tell. Over the next nine months through the efforts of Jack and his church, almost two thousand volumes of books were shipped to this small road camp in Virginia. This began his books-for-prison project through his church, and he continued shipping books throughout the country to prisons until his death.

Broad ethnic channels were crossed between Jack and me—he being of the Disciples of Christ faith and I of the Jewish faith—yet there was never any difference. He always signed his letters to me "Shalom"; in fact, once wrote a letter of protest to a warden at the Lewisburg penitentiary signed SHALOM.

Through my involvement in prison reform, Jack's knowledge increased. He became involved in the truest sense of the word. When the warden at Marion Federal Penitentiary refused the Jews a break-the-fast meal and my friend Al Berube was threatened with disciplinary action over his protests, Jack involved the National Council of Churches in the fight. Jewish organizations did not come forth with help when solicited—but Jack

Committee for Jewish Prisoners
Box 31265
San Francisco, CA 94131

works to enhance Jewish consciousness among Jewish prisoners. They send Jewish books and religious items into the prisons and visit Jewish convicts in California.

Jewish Board of Guardians
Volunteer Services Dept.
Jewish Big Brothers and Big Sisters
120 W. 57th St.
New York, NY 10019

was established as the Jewish Prisoners' Aid Society in 1893. It now serves Jewish juvenile offenders and/or emotionally troubled youths through court clinic and court referral and liaison programs, counseling programs, and the Hawthorne Cedar Knolls School. The Jewish Big Brothers and Sisters program seeks volunteers to provide companionship for children who need emotional support. Sometimes this includes children with parents in prison.

Jewish Identity Center
Union of Jewish Prisoners
1133 Broadway, Suite 302
New York, NY 10010

founded by Rabbi Meir Kahane, sponsors the Union of Jewish Prisoners, which seeks lawyers to press claims in behalf of Jewish prisoners and encourages synagogues and other organizations to supply religious articles of all kinds to Jewish prisoners. The union also publicizes issues involving Jewish prisoners.

National Council of Jewish Women
Justice for Children Task Force
1 W. 47th St.
New York, NY 10036

had its beginnings in the 1970 White House Conference on Children. NCJW conducted a year-long survey of the system of juvenile justice in thirty-four states. The study phase of Justice for Children enabled them to identify places where input was needed and where it would provide significant benefits. As they became knowledgeable about the subject, they were tapped for membership on boards and commissions concerned with children on the state and local levels where they could make policy changes. They volunteered in the probation department in Wilmington, Del.; worked to set up a group home for runaway girls in Teaneck, N.J.; and engaged in about two hundred other projects in 123 communities. Their eye-opening conclusions are presented in Edward Wakin, *Children without Justice* (National Council of Jewish Women, 1975). Praised by both government leaders and prison reformers, the task force showed that "the system" can be changed.

Roberta Kalechofsky
North Shore Jewish Community Center
2 Community Rd.
Marblehead, MA 01945

is organizing a library of prison literature, eventually to include a section on Jewish prisoners. Relevant literature is being sought from people on both sides of the bars.

Shalom Sisterhood
California Institution for Women
Frontera, CA 91720

is a self-help group formed by prisoners at Frontera, the largest institution for women in the country. It is composed of Jews and non-Jews who enjoy Jewish cultural and religious activities. They have enjoyed a wide variety of programs, including a program on Israel prepared with the assistance of a visitor from the Israeli Consulate. They are also assisted by a local Jewish congregation.

The prisoners collect what little money they have to contribute to their members upon release. This helps them overcome some of the economic hardships that help send many ex-cons from Frontera back into prison. Once released, some of the women maintain close ties with those still inside.

Probably the most important are self-help efforts. People on the outside can assist these efforts in many ways, such as finding jobs and temporary housing for the ex-offenders.

Richard Summers, Head Chaplain
Federal Bureau of Prisons
HOLC Bldg.
101 Indiana Ave. NW
Washington, DC 20534

says there are no full-time Jewish chaplains in the prisons at present and he has never had an applicant for the position of full-time Jewish chaplain. "I would love for someone to apply," Summers said. He stressed that the requirements include an extensive Jewish education and broad experience working with people.

Rev. Washburn, Chaplain
Federal Prison
P.O. Box 1000
Montgomery, PA 17752

The institution with one of the highest proportions of Jewish convicts is Allenwood Federal Prison: forty-six Jews as of January 1976, or 10 percent of the inmate population. (There are 378 Jews in all federal prisons, or nearly 2 percent of the total federal prison population. The percentage of Jews in state and local prison systems is usually significantly lower.) Jewish books for the Allenwood Jewish congregation may be mailed to the above address.

Jewish Family Service
Social Rehabilitation Dept.
186 Montague St.
Brooklyn, NY 11201

is another attempt to improve the situation of prisoners and their families. The Jewish Family Service's Social Rehabilitation Department had its beginnings at the turn of the century, with the establishment of the Society for the Aid of Jewish Prisoners, later called the Jewish Board of Guardians. Some of its early activities were later absorbed by other agencies, such as the Division of Probation and Parole. In recent years the JBG's work with adult offenders was absorbed by the JFS. In addition to concrete services, these agencies moved in the direction of offering a more intensive counseling experience.

The JFS is a licensed mental health clinic and is able to provide counseling and psychological help for those in need. Fees are on a sliding scale determined solely by the income and available resources of the family. Upon release, men and women can receive counseling to help with the difficulties of readjustment back into the community. Psychotherapy is also available.

Prisoners' wives are assisted either through individual counseling or by participation in a women's group. It has been observed that a prisoner's spouse, confronted with the negative responses of other family members and the community, may suffer a complete emotional collapse. Some prisoners' families may become incapacitated. Some of these families are assisted through an outreach program.

Referrals are generated by the rabbis of the prison chaplaincy and readers of publications such as this.

Visits to most New York State prisons are made by Max Hirschberg, the coordinator of the program. Visits are made annually upstate; prisons near New York City are visited more frequently.

On a more concrete level the Social Rehabilitation Department works closely with a part-time worker on the staff of the Federation Employment and Guidance service to provide job counseling and placement services. To be eligible for release an inmate must have had an approved job offer in advance of his/her parole, or else may be released through the "Reasonable Assurance" program offered through an agency such as JFS. This is vital because many jobs are closed to offenders.

As to financial assistance, the Social Rehabilitation Department reports that there is an extremely limited budget. It basically provides limited interim assistance to individuals recently released from prison and therefore cannot supply any real level of support for maintenance in the community.

American Association of Jewish Correctional Chaplains
10 E. 73rd St.
New York, NY 10021

should be contacted for information about the Jewish prison chaplaincy. This organization shares an address with the New York Board of Rabbis, which directs New York State's Jewish chaplaincy program. Until a few years ago, the community at large could have little direct contact with prison inmates. Today, some Jewish chaplains work with volunteers who come in to conduct discussions, teach courses, and provide entertainment.

Two important articles written about Jews in prison deserve notice:

1. The Autumn 1977 issue of *Present Tense* featured an article by Robert Levy, a former prisoner (*Present Tense*, 165 E. 56th St., New York, NY 10022).

2. *Lilith* magazine's issue no. 5 featured an article by Susan Weidman Schneider entitled "Jewish Women in Jail" (*Lilith*, 250 W. 57th St., New York, NY 10019).

was right there protecting Allan's right to break-the-fast in the traditional manner of Judaism.

When Jack asked for permission to visit me at Lewisburg—he was denied [permission] by my case manager. Jack went to the highest authorities in the prison system and fought like a tiger until he was granted permission to visit—and was personally escorted into the prison by the Catholic chaplain at Lewisburg. I'll never forget when the Father asked Jack not to push the issue because the administration was caught with egg on their face—and Jack looked at him and said that as a priest and a man of God, he had no choice but to pursue it.

When things got bad for me and four years of pushing prison administrations and litigation came to a head—when it was reduced to me versus one warden—there was Jack, going to Washington to gain Congressional assistance in the fight to help me and finally, coupled with other efforts, I was removed literally from Lewisburg and phased out of the system by "bus therapy."

Jack wrote just last week: "Criminal justice reform continues to be a major interest. I write regularly to men in various prisons and every Monday night go to the Federal Correctional Center here in Manhattan for a Yokefellowship meeting. The longer I work with prisoners the more insane the whole system seems. I have found that the crime, the sentence, and the person have no rational relationship. The experience has helped me to become far less judgmental than ever before. I have met some fine people among the inmates and the prison staff, and also some phonies, mentally sick, and just plain mean ('ornery as pond water' my grandfather would have called them) both among inmates and staff. People aren't much different. There have been amusing incidents, saddening ones, and deeply moving and heart-lifting times."

These were the last words I heard from Jack before learning of his passing. Perhaps the greatest tribute is for all of us who are or were prisoners whose lives he touched to strive for justice and universal understanding. His efforts came from the heart and it is in our hearts that friends mourn his loss. Goodbye to a friend—rest in the peace you sought on earth.

SURROUNDINGS

THE EARTH IS THE LORD'S

ליהוה הארץ ומלואה Psalms 24:1

Kindness to animals

An American journalist in the Soviet Union came to a small town in Siberia and looked up a contact. After some general talk, they got around to the "Jewish question."

"There are three Jews in this town," said the Russian in an authoritative tone.

"How do you know?" asked the American in surprise. "After all, there are no synagogues here, no Jewish schools, no Jewish theater, no newspapers. How can you be so sure there are three Jews here?"

"It's very simple," grinned the Russian. "They're the only ones who don't go hunting."

Jews have a long heritage of compassion for animals and concern for tzaar baalei hayyim—preventing and alleviating the unnecessary suffering of living creatures. This compassionate attitude runs through the Torah and the Midrash, the legends of our people, rabbinic commentaries and codifications of Jewish law, and stories and poetry by some of our greatest writers.

Concern for animals' suffering is rooted in the concepts of tzaar baalei hayyim and baal tashhit—the prohibition against wanton destruction of matter (discussed in detail in Ecology). Killing an animal when it is not for legitimate human need is strictly forbidden; torturing an animal is regarded as a criminal act. Taking pity on a suffering animal is a duty that the greatest leaders and scholars performed; in fact, it was often regarded as a sign of their greatness. Two examples out of many:

Once when Moses was a shepherd for his father-in-law, Jethro, he tracked a runaway lamb to a pool of water. Seeing that the lamb was exhausted, he placed it on his shoulders and carried it all the way back to the rest of the flock. God, seeing this, declared: "You who have compassion for a lamb shall now be the shepherd of my people Israel" (Exodus Rabbah).

Another story is told in the Talmud about Rabbi Judah the Prince. A calf being led to slaughter thrust his head in Rabbi Judah's sleeve and wept as if begging for refuge. Rabbi Judah said to the calf, "Go! For this [slaughter] were you destined." Because Rabbi Judah lacked compassion, he was punished with a painful illness. One day his servant was about to sweep out a litter of kittens from their corner. Rabbi Judah told her to leave them alone, saying, "It is written: 'And God has compassion for all His creatures.'" His illness ended exactly at that moment (Bava Metzia 85a).

While Judaism does not consider animals equal to humans in essence or rights, it rejects the view of animal as hefker—valueless, the object of an eternal open season to be misused or abused with impunity. It is precisely because the animal is inferior in intellectual potential, an unfortunate and helpless creature that awaits aid from humans, that humans must show it compassion in emulation of God, whose "mercy is upon all His works" (Psalms 145:9). As Maimonides wrote, "We should not learn cruelty and should not cause unnecessary and useless pain to animals but should lean toward compassion and mercy" (*Guide of the Perplexed*). Rejoicing cannot occur when it is at an animal's expense. Therefore, the blessing of She-heheyanu, thanking God for allowing us to reach a special occasion, and the greeting of Tithadesh (May you be renewed in your garment) are not recited when a person first dons leather shoes or furs because this enjoyment cost an animal's life (Orah Hayyim 223:6).

Rabbi Samson Raphael Hirsch, a nineteenth-century Orthodox scholar, wrote:

There are probably no creatures that require more the protective divine word against the presumption of people than the animals which, like human beings, have sensations and instincts, but whose body and powers are nevertheless subservient to people. In relation to them, human beings so easily forget that injured animal muscle twitches just like human muscle, that the maltreated nerves of an animal sicken like human nerves, that the animal being is just as sensitive to cuts, blows, and beating as people. Thus the human being becomes the torturer of the animal soul, which has been subjected to him only for the fulfillment of humane and wise purposes; sometimes out of self-interest, at other times in order to satisfy a whim, sometimes out of thoughtlessness—yes, even for the satisfaction of crude satanic desire.

Here you are faced with God's teaching, which obliges you not only to refrain from inflicting unnecessary pain on any animal, but to help and, when you can, to lessen the pain whenever you see an animal suffering, even through no fault of yours.

Oppressed and hounded as Jews were throughout history, they outlawed the abuse of animals. Even more than that, a feeling for animals beyond compassion, a feeling bordering on kinship, of being a comrade in distress, permeates the works of some of the greatest Jewish writers. Animals were hunted down, fled for their lives, lived in fear. Jews too were hunted down, fled for their lives, lived in fear and anxiety. Perhaps because Jews lived in fear for a great deal of the time, it was not hard for them to imagine the helplessness and terror of animals.

It is no wonder, then, that Mendele Mocher Sforim's *Mare* is a metaphor for the beaten, broken nation of Israel or that Isaac Bashevis Singer writes that "for animals it's an eternal Treblinka."

But, one might ask, if Judaism is so compassionate toward animals, why does it allow people to kill them for food? The Torah relates that when the world was created, both humans and animals were vegetarians. Only after the Flood was there a concession permitting people to eat meat. The tradition sought to elevate the eating of meat by sanctifying the method of slaughter and by placing restrictions on what could be eaten. Rabbi Abraham Kook, chief rabbi of prestate Israel and a vegetarian, considered the change after the Flood to be evidence of humanity's moral deterioration and felt it constituted "an estrangement from the world of animals" that would be repaired in the messianic era.

The prophets looked forward to a time when all—even wild beasts—would be vegetarians: "The wolf shall dwell with the lamb/The leopard lie down with the kid; . . ./And the lion, like the ox, shall eat straw" (Isaiah 11:6–7).

The Shulhan Arukh, the accepted code of law compiled by Joseph Caro in the sixteenth century, says that if one comes upon horses who cannot pull their load in a difficult spot or up a mountain, "it is a mitzvah to help even a non-Jew because of tzaar baalei hayyim, to prevent the non-Jew from beating his animals to make them work harder."

If an animal kills a human, it is tried before a court of twenty-three (as any murder suspect would be). If it is established that the cause of death was accidental—for example, a cow bumping against a wall, which then collapsed on a person—the animal is set free.

Even in extremis—during the Holocaust—Jews remembered their animals, as seen in this story reported by Rabbi M. Weissmandel:
Itzik Rosenberg was a Jew from somewhere in Slovakia. He made his living by raising poultry. One day he and his family were squeezed into the cattle cars. . . . In the car there was despair all around him. Outside a celebrating population of former neighbors was jeering at him. . . . He begged them, "Please go to my house and give water and food to the poultry. They've had nothing to eat or drink all day."

"A righteous person knows the soul of his beast" (Proverbs 12:10).

"A human being's animal is his life" (Mekhilta).

Tradition shows some sensitivity to a species outgrowing its food supply. After Creation, according to the Baal Haturim, God blessed ("Be fertile and increase") only those species whose food sources were bountiful. Other species were not blessed so that their propagation should not outstrip the earth's ability to sustain them.

"For in respect of the fate of man and the fate of beast, they have both one and the same fate; as the one dies so dies the other, and both have the same life-breath; man has no superiority over beast. . . ." (Ecclesiastes 3:19).

Hugh Nissenson's story "In the Reign of Peace" is about an atheistic young kibbutznik who does not believe in the coming of the Messiah, and Chaim, the Moroccan laborer who does. One day Chaim drags the kibbutznik to the flagstone path to see an injured field mouse being devoured alive by ants:

"Ai, habibi," says Chaim, "Things like that must happen all the time, don't you think?"

"I imagine so."

"Yes," he said, "but not in the reign of peace."

"When the Messiah comes . . . not then . . ."

I understood. On the flagstone path under the eucalyptus trees, he had shown me what he expected to be redeemed.

Jewish law on preventing cruelty to animals is derived directly from a biblical verse, and thus is said to be de-oraita—to have the force of the Torah behind the injunction (Bava Metzia 32b). Indeed, Jewish law regarding animals is derived from a number of biblical verses. "When you see the ass of your enemy lying under its burden and would refrain from raising it, you must nevertheless raise it with him" (Exodus 23:5). The Bible's choice of your enemy's animal is meant to emphasize the importance of the animal and relieving its pain. "You shall not muzzle an ox while it is threshing" (Deuteronomy 25:4). Under the Jewish legal system the punishment for muzzling a working animal is more severe than that for preventing a human laborer from eating as he works—presumably because an animal is defenseless (Tur Hoshen Mishpat 338). The Shulhan Arukh also forbids tying the legs of an animal, beast, or fowl in such a way as to cause them pain and prohibits making a bird sit on eggs that are not her own (Kitzur Shulhan Arukh, vol. 5, ch. 191/3). Similarly, *Sefer Hasidim* (twelfth century) warns against the spurring of horses, a common practice in the Middle Ages (and today).

"You shall not plow with an ox and an ass [or any other two species] together" (Deuteronomy 22:10). Among the reasons commentators gave for this law are the following: (1) the ox will suffer because it is the stronger of the two (Ibn Ezra) and (2) the ass will suffer because the ox chews its cud and the ass will think that the ox is eating while it is not (Baal Haturim).

The law of shiluah ha-ken is that a person who comes across a bird sitting on her young eggs or young in a nest is not permitted to take them unless the mother is first sent away (Deuteronomy 22: 6–7). According to Abarbanel, the concern is with the preservation of the species for the long-term good of humanity (the mother must live to lay more eggs). Nahmanides understands this mitzvah in terms of education to mercy: by not being allowed to take the offspring in the mother's presence, by practicing compassion to animals, we

become even more compassionate to human beings. This mitzvah reminds us that animals, like humans, suffer emotionally. Just as we cannot wantonly cause them physical pain, so we cannot add to their emotional anguish. Two other commandments reinforce this constraint:

> When an ox or a sheep or a goat is born, it shall stay seven days with its mother, and from the eighth day on, it shall be acceptable as an offering by fire to the Lord. However, no animal from the herd or from the flock shall be slaughtered on the same day with its young (Leviticus 22:27–28).

> You shall not boil a kid in its mother's milk (Exodus 34:26).

Rabbi Samson Raphael Hirsch points out that this

law which asks us to remember that animals and their young have a bond is a good starting point for teaching our own children compassion. Above all, those to whom the care of young minds has been entrusted should see to it that they respect both the smallest and the largest animals as beings which, like people, have been summoned to the joy of life. . . .

Toward a halakhic approach to current issues

The laws and spirit of the tradition regarding tzaar baalei hayyim are relevant to many problems regarding cruelty to animals today. Here we shall discuss experiments, hunting and other "sports," furs and cosmetics, zoos, and pets and strays.

Since Jewish law unequivocally forbids causing pain to animals when it is unnecessary for human benefit or need, we can establish a benefit/pain ratio and group cruelties in four categories: (1) benefit to humans: great/pain: great; (2) benefit to humans: small, nonexistent, or dubious/pain: great; (3) benefit to humans: great/pain: small; (4) benefit to humans: small or dubious/pain: small. The cruelties we will be concerned with here fall into the categories of (1) and (2).

EXPERIMENTS

Every year millions of cats, dogs, primates, rabbits, and rodents (63 million in the United States alone) are subjected to untold numbers of experiments—for medical, psychological, and cosmetic testing and as "learning tools"—all in the name of science and progress. The primary source on this issue is the Ramah (Rabbi Moses Isserles, cited in the Shulhan Arukh), who says that the laws of tzaar baalei hayyim can be waived for anything needed for "medicine or other purposes." There is little dispute that when a direct cause-and-effect relationship can be established between animal experimentation and medical benefit for human beings, the experiments are halakhically permitted, provided all steps have been taken to eliminate unnecessary and avoidable pain.

The problem arises with "general" research. Does it fall into category (1) or (2)? Are animals to be tortured and sacrificed in the hope that ultimately knowledge leading to a medical cure may be discovered? Jewish law has not drawn clear lines in this gray area. There is also research that clearly has no medical value but is supposed to increase our knowledge of the universe. Are animals to be sacrificed or tortured for our "enlightenment"?

The key to a halakhic approach may lie in the interpretation of the second half of the Ramah's statement "for medicine or *other purposes.*" What "other purposes" could set aside the laws against cruelty to animals? The Imrei

One day Rav Hiya Bar-Ada was learning Torah from Rav but was not paying attention. When Rav asked him why, Rav Hiya answered: "My donkey is about to give birth and I'm worried she'll catch cold and die."

Humanity was created Friday, before Shabbat and after the creation of the animals. Therefore, in the event of human arrogance, one can reply, "A mosquito took precedence over you" (Sanhedrin 38).

A man was jogging along a road with his donkey trailing behind him. He carried on his shoulder a small bundle of corn so that the donkey followed, hoping to eat it. Upon arriving home, he put the donkey inside and tied the corn at a point above his head. He was rebuked: "Villain—the poor animal ran all the way for that corn and you refuse to feed it to him!" (Exodus Rabbah 31).

Shefer uses "medicine" as a guideline for determining these purposes: they must be as important to humanity as medicine.

This guideline can be used to gauge the importance of a whole variety of experiments being done. Are these experiments beneficial or do they fall into category (2)—benefit: small/pain: great? For example, stress tests, which involve subjecting animals to extreme temperatures, pressure, shock, gas, and addictions, are extremely questionable according to this guideline, especially when the experiment has already been done hundreds of times before. Are experiments performed on animals to test cosmetics really a human need? Some scientists are questioning the benefit of medical and psychological experiments, given that many results are not applicable to humans (e.g., Thalidomide was thoroughly tested on animals before going on sale). Moreover with time, alternatives—computer and mathematical models, tissue and organ cultures—are becoming increasingly available. Shouldn't these then be consistently used instead of animals?

What about using live animals in high school biology classes? Can't teaching biology by using films and plastic models be just as effective? By using live animals aren't we teaching that animal life is hefker—valueless? This is an issue that schools, especially Jewish schools, must face.

The answers to these questions and others like them are not always simple, but too often many things are done without carefully considering the value of experiments versus the cruelty inflicted upon the animals.

HUNTING

Hunting for sport is prohibited by Jewish law. Yehezkel Landau, rabbi of Prague (d. 1793), wrote the classic responsum on the subject:

How can a Jew kill a living animal for no other purpose than to satisfy the cravings of his time . . . [and if one attempts a rationalization and says] it is because bears and wolves and other violent animals are liable to cause damage, [such an argument might make sense] in cases when [those animals] came into a human settlement . . . but to pursue them in the forests, their place of residence, when they are not wont to come to a [human] settlement, is no mitzvah and you are only pursuing the desires of your heart (Noda B'Yehudah, Mahadurah Tenina).

Sports using animals are forbidden. The Talmud condemns bullfighting in no uncertain terms: "One who sits in a stadium spills blood" (Avodah Zarah 1). Obviously today's cruel rodeos, dogfights, cockfights, coonbaiting, etc. (as well as the "training" for these inhumane events) fall into this category, as does making films in which animals are tortured for the audience's entertainment.

FURS

Jewish law states that when hunting is necessary, it must be done with a minimum of cruelty. The Talmud, for example, forbids association with hunters who set dogs on the trail of hunted animals. The method of killing animals (including endangered species) for their pelts is cruel, whether they are killed in traps, in the wild, or on fur farms.

Wild animals are caught in bone-crushing leghold traps (banned long ago in England and Norway, where instant-kill traps are used instead). Baby seals are clubbed and often skinned alive—in full view of their mothers (remember the law of shiluah ha-ken?). Rabbits and raccoons raised on fur farms are hung by their tongues until they die to ensure a scar-free pelt.

I believe that the use of furs, particularly those made from sealskin and the pelts of animals caught in leghold traps, is against the Jewish tradition. It is questionable whether furs should be worn at all, especially now that artificial furs can provide the same warmth and attractive style. The wearing of furs to synagogue especially on Yom Kippur (when wearing leather is prohibited) should be forbidden. People can give away their furs to the Fund for Animals which sends them to Arctic peoples, who really need them. People should buy only fake furs and nylon-stuffed toys from now on.

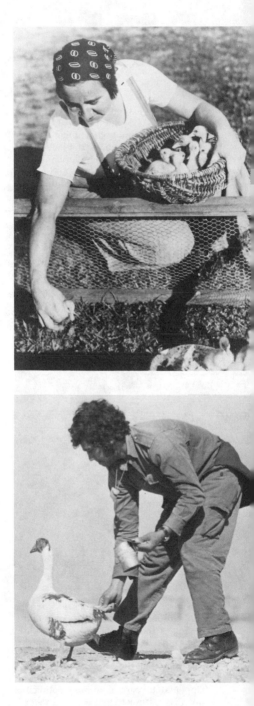

COSMETICS

Popular ingredients in many perfumes are civet, musk, and castoreum, which are scraped from a gland on the genitals of caged deer, civet cats, beavers, and rats—an excruciating procedure. Some elements in perfumes and lipsticks are extracted from endangered whale species. And as pointed out above, experiments to test cosmetics on animals are excruciating. Looking at these substances from the benefit/pain ratio, there is little doubt that their use is against Jewish tradition. There are cosmetics on the market that contain no animal substances and are not tested on animals. Beauty without Cruelty can send you a list.

ZOOS

Zoos are a subject of argument between humane and conservation circles. The Mekhilta (see the section on "Shabbat" below) says that keeping animals pent up constitutes a form of tzaar baalei hayyim (this should also be a concern for those who eat meat produced on feedlots and in large-scale chicken coops). On the other hand, zoos are becoming "stationary arks" for endangered species and centers for educating the public on the need to protect wildlife. Confining animals is an exercise of our power over other life forms. As in the law regarding household pets (below), we may not assume responsibility for other creatures unless we care for them in kindness. Zoos whose animals are not adequately provided for must be immediately improved or closed down.

PETS AND STRAYS

Jewish tradition requires that we care responsibly and kindly for the animals entrusted to us. Rabbi Eliezer ha-Kapar states that "a person is not permitted to buy cattle, beast, or bird unless he can provide adequate food" (Yevamot

Jonah was rebuked by God for refusing to go to Nineveh to warn that city of its impending destruction: "And should I not care about Nineveh, that great city, in which there are a hundred and twenty thousand persons who do not yet know their right hand from their left, and many beasts as well!" (Jonah 4:11).

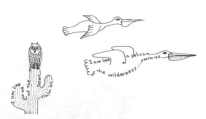

National Wildlife Foundation
Washington, DC

Dear Sir:

My name is Joshua David Rovin. I am 4½ years old. I do not think that bad people should kill mountain lions, not any animal, not fish, not bees, not hamburger animals, not pigs and not elephants. Not any kind of animal. Eskimos and people that don't have any other food, that's all right. But we can eat other things—blueberries, cereals, milk, cheeses.

I have 4 cats. I do not want them to eat food with dead animals in it. What kind of cat food can I give them?

I will write to you again.

The story is told of a pious Jew whose whole life was lived in expectation of the coming of the Messiah. One day while at work he heard the sound of a shofar. He rushed into the street, very excited, assuming that the shofar had signaled the arrival of the Messiah. As he ran he happened to pass a farmer beating his mule. "Ah, I must have been mistaken," he thought, "If the Messiah were truly here, such a thing could never occur."

When a Jew sees a beautiful animal, s/he is commanded to respond with the words, "Blessed be the One who created beauty in the world's living things" (Jerusalem Talmud, Berakhot 9).

15). Rabbi Yehudah, in the same vein, says that one is not permitted to eat anything until after feeding one's animals (Gittin 62a); Maimonides codified this statement as an action befitting the righteous.

When we keep animals as pets we must not only provide them with good food, shelters, and veterinary care, but also those intangibles that come under knowing the "soul" of your animal. Knowing an animal's "soul" or nature means, for example, not leaving a dog alone all day when it is in its nature to need human company. It means not keeping exotic animals in city apartments when their nature is to roam the wilds. It means not declawing your cat when the cat's nature is to scratch—and providing him/her with a scratching post.

Caring responsibly for an animal means not getting rid of your pet without ensuring that it has a good new home. Abandonment of pets is one of the most rampant abuses of animals today. Living in an age when everything is disposable, we increasingly encounter the tragedy of the disposable pet. People buy pets from irresponsible breeders ("puppy mills") or adopt animals while on vacation without considering whether they can afford them financially, emotionally, or logistically. Too often the pets are later simply thrown out into the street. As a result, millions of stray dogs and cats roam the streets and alleys of our cities, most of them starving and ill, the object of children's torture and often a danger to human health and well-being as well.

One solution is to neuter pets at cheap prices at municipal clinics. While we must consider that halakhah forbids the "castration" of male animals (females can be given a sterilizing potion), this should be weighed against the pet population explosion, which is harmful to both animals and humans. Perhaps the solution lies in the development of "the pill" for pets. Certainly education about responsibility for pets, promoting zero pet population growth, and rescuing strays are in the spirit of Jewish law.

Shehitah—ritual slaughter of animals for meat

Although a separate chapter has been devoted to the question of shehitah, it is necessary to deal here with what happens before shehitah, a practice that is not covered by halakhah but does, in fact, violate its whole purpose.

American slaughter laws promulgated at the turn of the century required (for sanitary reasons) that the animal not be slaughtered on the ground, as was done before (and is still done in Israel). The substitute was shackling and hoisting—that is, suspending the animal upside down on a fast-moving ceiling conveyor belt until it approaches a certain point, where it is slaughtered. Humane legislation has required that animals slaughtered by this method be unconscious at the time of slaughter, but because Jewish law demands that the animal be conscious, kosher slaughter has been exempted from this requirement.

The tragedy is that shackling and hoisting is not necessary. Since the early 1960s, the ASPCA has made available, at no charge, its patent on animal pens. These pens eliminate the necessity for S&H because they both take the animal off the floor *and* allow it to be conscious. The use of the ASPCA pens conforms to Jewish law and was supported by the Rabbinical Council of America. The RCA recommendation, however, was unenforceable. Laws should therefore be passed that require use of the ASPCA pens when shehitah follows, and in all cases where the animal cannot be rendered unconscious before S&H. Jews should be in the forefront of campaigns for such laws.

One obstacle has been the unfortunate position taken by a few groups, which cannot or will not differentiate between shehitah itself and preshehitah

S&H, and keep promoting package laws to eliminate both. Communication between Jewish and humane groups could relieve misunderstandings and lead to the passage of these necessary laws.

Animals in Israel

It is tragic that Jews, with their long and beautiful tradition of kindness to animals, are letting cruelties in Israel persist, despite the laws on the books against them.

Municipalities handle the problem of strays in cruel and inefficient ways (such as strychnine poisoning). Israel has some bad zoos, fur farms, and a great deal of animal experimentation of dubious value. Children routinely torture street and road animals without interference. Hunting is permitted, although there are some excellent nature reserves set aside to "ingather exiled animals" extinct in the Israeli wild.

The Federation of Societies for the Protection of Animals in Israel and its most active member, the Tel Aviv–Jaffa ISPCA (30 Salome St., Jaffa), need funds and volunteers to combat cruelties. Most other cities, such as Jerusalem, don't even have a shelter, although Haifa has a Cat Lovers' Society (13 Einstein St.). Nor are there any humane education programs for children in schools or youth movements.

England has a very excellent Society for Animal Welfare in Israel

SAWI
4 N. Mews
Nothington St.
London, England WC1N 2JP

which raises and distributes funds to proanimal societies and projects in Israel. It is knowledgeable, fair, and accountable. The United States would do well to create a similar group.

Shabbat: in anticipation of the messianic era

Adam was commanded by God to guard and preserve the garden of Eden (Genesis 2:15). Within the hierarchy of creation, human beings have a dual responsibility—to preserve nature and to use nature in the service of God. People are thus caretakers of the world, not owners of it. An owner may exploit; a caretaker preserves. An owner serves him/herself; a caretaker serves others.

Since we are in a position of power, it is even more important for us to remember that we share the world with other created beings. That animals have their own independent sanctity is taught in the commandment, "Six days you shall do your work, but on the seventh day you shall cease from labor, in order that your ox and your ass may rest" (Exodus 23:12; see also Exodus 20:9–11). We are therefore prohibited on Shabbat from placing any burden on an animal, whether it be sack, saddle, or ornament. A person may not even lean on an animal. But a blanket to keep it warm is naturally permitted, and the Talmud (Shabbat 53a) also allows us to suspend a basket with fodder around the necks of calves or foals. (Because of their short necks, says Rashi, they might suffer discomfort in reaching for food on the ground.) A full chapter in the Talmud (the fifth chapter, Tractate Shabbat) and in the Shulhan Arukh (Orah Hayyim 305) deals exclusively with laws against burdening an animal on Shabbat. Elsewhere in the Talmud and Codes there are a multitude of laws guarding an animal's day of rest. For example, one may not hire out one's

Rabbi Mosheh Leib of Sassov saw that the cattle merchants had been gone from the marketplace a long time, leaving their animals without food and water. He took a bucket and gave them water to drink. When one merchant returned and saw him so engaged, he ordered the rabbi to water the calves too—and the rabbi did so.

They who go to hunt [or] to kill fowl are violating the mitzvah of "Do not destroy" (Maimonides, Hilkhot Milahim 6).

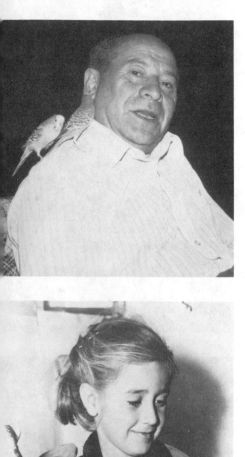

animal to a non-Jew unless it is stipulated that s/he return the animal before Shabbat.

Shabbat was given as a gift from God to His creatures so that each created being can rest according to its nature. For human beings, Shabbat limits our physical actions to encourage spiritual growth; for an animal, on the other hand, rest has a purely physical dimension. Because the concept of rest differs between person and animal, animals are permitted to uproot grass whereas people are not. The Mekhilta makes it clear that animals are not to be penned up in the stables on Shabbat (Exodus 23:12). For them, "rest" means being able to roam freely in the fields, chewing on grass to their hearts' content.

Letting an animal rest is only a reflection of Shabbat's general theme. On Shabbat we tune in to the primal glory of creation, relinquishing our domination over nature to stand back and appreciate it. The special perspective we gain from Shabbat corresponds to the messianic ideal portrayed by the prophets. In the messianic era all the diverse elements of creation will discover their underlying relationship. As humanity and nature discover their common roots, humankind will come to deserve their unique position in creation. We will no longer indulge in cruelty and war—the products of a distorted perspective—"the calf, the beast of prey, and the fatling [shall lie down] together/With a little boy to herd them" (Isaiah 11:6). Person will be in harmony with person, beast will be in harmony with beast, and both will be in harmony with each other.

The laws of tzaar baalei hayyim and Shabbat direct our energies toward the realization of the ideal. As we heighten our sensitivities toward animals and their pain and toward our fellow human beings, we bring ourselves closer to the messianic era.

What you can do

If you feel strongly that there is a Jewish imperative to stop cruelty to animals and that Jews have a unique tradition to contribute to the struggle, there are various humane societies you can join; even if all you do is pay dues, it's a good beginning. Activities fall into two main categories: (1) increasing public awareness of problems and getting legislation passed and (2) direct rescue work.

If you are interested in raising consciousness and passing legislation, the humane societies below will send you literature. Write letters; legislators are sensitive to their constituents' views. And get your Jewish organization to act on the issues too.

1. **Fund for Animals**
   140 W. 57 St.
   New York, NY 10019
   supports local and national anticruelty and legislative campaigns

2. **Beauty without Cruelty**
   175 W. 12th St.
   New York, NY 10011
   combats fashion cruelties

3. **Society for Animal Rights**
   421 S. State St.
   Clarke Summit, PA 18411
   concentrates on legislation and court cases

4. **National Cat Protection Society**
   340 W. Willow St.
   Long Beach, CA 90806
   has pioneered in the humane education field

HASiDUCK

5. **International Association against Painful Experiments on Animals**
   51 Harley St.
   London W1N 1DD, England
   is active in many countries and makes available studies on alternatives

6. **International League for Animal Rights**
   POB Sta. C.
   Ottawa, Ont. K1Y 4J6, Canada
   has the support of world-renowned scientists and philosophers

For rescue work, you have to join a local humane society. Check yours carefully—see if they actively go out to pick up strays, take care of adoptions and do followups, insist that people who adopt animals neuter them, investigate cruelty cases, and refuse to turn over animals to labs, race tracks, etc.

Finally, there is a Jewish humane society-in-formation
Jewish Committee to Help Animals —CHAI
225 W. 106th St.
New York, NY 10025
It has done a limited amount of work and needs active members to really get off the ground.

Jewish sources

Tzaar Baalei Hayyim: The Prevention of Cruelty to Animals. Its Bases, Development and Legislation in Hebrew Literature was a PhD thesis by Noah J. Gordon that's available in paperback from

Philipp Feldheim Inc.
96 E. Broadway
New York, NY 10002

This is an excellent secondary source with elaborate footnotes but no index. Highly recommended. Two books in Hebrew by Dr. Aryeh Shoshan, DVM, are highly recommended too: *Animals and Us* (Jerusalem, 1963) and *Animals in Jewish Literature* (Rehovot: Shoshanim, 1971). The second book is an excellent secondary source with an English synopsis. Shoshan has delved deeply into Jewish law and literature and cites many relevant and ignored materials.

Louis Gompertz's *Moral Inquiries on the Situation of Man and Brutes* (1824) is a philosophical essay by a Jew who was a founder and a leading activist in England's RSPCA, the world's first humane society. It is currently out of print but available on microfilm from the British Museum.

The Carp in the Bathtub by Barbara Cohen, with illustrations by Joan Halpern (New York: Lothrop, Lee and Shepard, 1972), is a wonderful children's book infused with the Jewish attitude toward animals.

General sources

1. Amory, Cleveland: *Man Kind?* (New York: Harper & Row, 1974).
2. Carson, Gerald: *Men, Beasts, Gods: A History of Cruelty and Kindness to Animals* (New York: Scribner, 1972).
3. Diole, Philippe: *The Errant Ark: Man's Relationship with Animals* (New York: Putnam, 1974).
4. Godlovitch, Stanley; Godlovitch, Roslind; and Harris, John, eds.: *Animals, Men and Morals* (New York: Grove Press, 1971).
5. Morris, Richard Knowles and Fox, Michael, eds.: *The Fifth Day: Animal Rights and Human Ethics* (Washington, D.C.: Acropolis, 1978).
6. Morse, Mel: *Ordeal of the Animals* (Englewood Cliffs, N.J.: Prentice-Hall, 1968).
7. Regenstein, Lewis: *The Politics of Extinction* (New York: Macmillan, 1975).
8. Regan, Tom and Singer P.: *Animal Rights and Human Obligations* (Englewood Cliffs, N.J.: Prentice-Hall, 1976).
9. Reusch, Hans: *Slaughter of the Innocent* (New York: Bantam Books, 1978).
10. Singer, Peter: *Animal Liberation: A New Ethic for Our Treatment of Animals* (New York: N.Y. Review of Books/Random House, 1975).

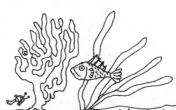

This great and wide sea, wherein are things creeping innumerable, both small and great beasts. —Psalm 104

Shehitah

Rav said: The commandments were given only in order that a person might be refined by them (Genesis Rabbah 44:1).

Through the mitzvot, Jews try to raise the common everyday to a higher level of meaning—to grant special significance to what by its very nature is devoid of such significance. Not only do mitzvot sanctify our actions, we become more godlike in performing them.

The laws of kashrut are one example of how an everyday act is transformed and hallowed (see *Catalog 1*, Kashrut). We realize that our eating involves taking of God's bounty; the laws of kashrut and especially those concerning shehitah (ritual slaughtering of animals for food) are a compromise between the ideal of vegetarianism and our basic urges. Kashrut demands that we have reverence for the life we take in order to eat. The principle of reverence for life is also translated into the mitzvah of slaughtering an animal in the swiftest, most painless and humane way possible by making a horizontal cut with an extremely sharp knife across the throat of the animal to quickly sever the esophagus, trachea (windpipe), jugular vein, and carotid arteries, killing the animal instantly.

Laws of shehitah

The mitzvah of shehitah is given in a biblical verse: "You may slaughter any of the cattle or sheep that the Lord gives you, as I have instructed you" (Deuteronomy 12:21). Rabbinic tradition teaches that the laws of shehitah were given to Moses on Mount Sinai as part of the oral law. Shehitah is therefore one of the oldest and most sacred of Jewish rituals.

There are three basic requirements for shehitah: a qualified and trained shohet—slaughterer, the proper instrument (halaf), and the correct procedure.

The shohet

The shohet must be a pious, observant, and sensitive Jew who has been instructed in the laws of shehitah. The physically or mentally impaired, minors, apostates, drunkards, and those whose hands are unsteady are excluded from becoming shohetim. There is a difference of opinion as to whether women can be shohetim. In some Sephardic communities women were permitted to sheht, and many did. In almost all Ashkenazic communities however, the profession of shohet was closed to women.

The potential shohet must undergo rigorous training before receiving a kabbalah—license. The shohet must first study the laws of 1) shehitah, 2) nevelah—literally, "carrion," an animal who has died a natural death; here referring to an animal not slaughtered in the correct manner, and 3) terefah—literally, "torn," an animal torn by a beast of prey, but used here of an animal afflicted with a (fatal) organic disease, the discovery of which, after slaughtering, makes the animal forbidden for eating even if slaughtered properly. These laws are found in the talmudic tractate Hullin and in the Shulhan Arukh, Yoreh Deah, chapters 1–28. The shohet then learns about the knife—how to sharpen it, how to test it, etc. Finally come the essentials of the slaughter: how to perform the act of shehitah and how to examine the animal after it is slaughtered. In order to receive a kabbalah the potential shohet must be tested on the laws of shehitah and must correctly perform shehitah three times in the presence of rabbinic authorities. Even after receiving the kabbalah, the shohet is required to review the laws periodically and submit his knives for periodic inspection.

Halaf—the knife

The knife the shohet uses is called a halaf, from the Hebrew word meaning "to change over," and refers to the changing over of an animal from a living being to a dead carcass. The halaf must be at least twice as long as the diameter of the animal's neck and cannot be pointed at the end. In order to slaughter the animal as quickly and painlessly as possible, it must be extremely sharp and clean, without any nicks, dents, or other imperfections. The shohet tests the halaf to make sure it is perfect by passing a fingernail over the blade. If there are any imperfections the fingernail will catch in the nick or dent, and the instrument will have to be resharpened. The knife must be checked both before and after shehitah.

The procedures

Since shehitah is such a holy act, the shohet must make a blessing before it is performed: "Praised are You, O Lord our God, King of the Universe, who has sanctified us with His commandments, and has commanded us concerning shehitah."

After the shohet has checked the halaf to make sure it's in perfect condition, the animal is brought in and raised. While an abattoir worker holds the animal's head still, the shohet makes a quick cut in one or more *uninterrupted* horizontal slices across the animal's throat. The act of shehitah takes no more than a second and renders the animal senseless immediately. In animals the cut must sever the esophagus and trachea (the two simanim—signs), or at least a majority of both parts; in fowl it is sufficient to cut one of the simanim or at least a majority of the larger one.

There are five special laws concerning the act of shehitah, all designed to ensure that shehitah is performed swiftly and painlessly.

1. *Shehiyah—delay*: There must be *no* delay or interruption while the shehitah is being performed. The knife must be kept in continuous backward and forward motion. The slightest delay—even for a moment—renders the animal unfit for food.

2. *Derasah—pressing*: The knife must be drawn gently across the throat without any undue exertion on the part of the shohet. It must not be pressed into the neck of the animal. The least pressure makes the animal unkosher.

3. *Haladah—digging*: The knife must be drawn across the throat, *not* stabbed into the neck of the animal. It must be visible at all times.

4. *Hagramah—slipping*: The limits across which the knife is drawn are from the large ring in the trachea to the top of the upper lung when inflated. If shehitah is performed anywhere else the animal is not kosher.

5. *Ikkur—tearing*: If either the trachea or the esophagus is torn out or removed from its regular position during the shehitah the animal is not kosher.

After the shehitah of birds and undomesticated animals, the blood is covered with ashes and the blessing "on the covering of the blood" is said. It has been suggested that the reason for this is that unlike domesticated animals, which are fed and cared for by human beings, birds and wild animals have gained nothing from us; therefore the slaughtering of these living things is a more reprehensible act. As a sign of this the blood—the symbol of life—is covered.

After shehitah the shohet again inspects the blade. If any imperfection is found, the animal just slaughtered is not kosher. If the knife is still in perfect condition, the slaughtered animal undergoes bedikah.

Bedikah

Bedikah means "examination." After the animal is slaughtered and allowed to bleed for a few moments and after any postmortem movements have ceased, the shohet must examine the animal's lungs to make sure that the animal was neither suffering from any fatal disease nor deformed.

The reason for bedikah is twofold: (1) it is a health measure to ensure that no diseased meat will find its way to someone's table; (2) as the Midrash makes clear, the act of shehitah is connected with the ritual sacrifice of animals in the Temple. (In fact, animals used to be slaughtered for sacrifice in the

same way as shehitah is performed.) Just as the animal brought to the Temple for sacrifice had to be a perfect specimen without blemish or disease, so too the meat we eat must come from an animal without blemish or disease. The lungs are the focal point of bedikah because the most common maladies of cattle are pulmonary—that is, afflicting the lungs.

There are two parts to bedikah. First comes the investigation by touch (internal examination). A ventral incision is made in the animal's chest cavity. The shohet inserts his hand through this opening and examines the lungs by touch, searching for telltale signs of disease and defects such as improper texture or consistency, missing or mislocated parts, lumps, perforations, or adhesions. In this part of bedikah the lungs are examined while still intact inside the carcass, because removal before examination might tear away any adhesion that would cause an animal to be declared terefah (not kosher).

The second part of bedikah is visual. The lungs are removed from the carcass of the animal and inspected by the shohet for discoloration and other defects that might render the animal unfit for consumption.

Bedikah, like the act of shehitah, demands that the shohet be very well versed in the laws of kashrut. Since not every kind of adhesion or dislocation makes an animal unfit, the shohet must be able to distinguish between those defects that render an animal terefah and those that do not. This requires a tremendous amount of knowledge and experience.

Bedikah is an essential part of the shehitah process. No meat is considered kosher without it because it is bedikah that changes the status of the meat from being forbidden to being permitted.

Glatt kosher

Especially in recent years, certain Hasidic and other right-wing Orthodox groups have required their followers to eat only glatt kosher meat. The word "glatt" is Yiddish for "smooth" and refers to the smoothness of the slaughtered animal's lungs.

Remember that the act of bedikah is a two-stage process during which the shohet examines the lungs to determine whether there are any (pathological) defects in them. One of the signs the shohet looks for is the presence of cysts and scabs (called lesions). Some cysts and scabs do *not* affect the kashrut of the animal; others render an animal nonkosher. The shohet is trained and qualified to differentiate between the two.

For meat to be glatt kosher, however, there can be *no* cysts or scabs—not even those that do *not* make an animal nonkosher. To determine whether an animal's meat is glatt kosher or not, the shohet feels the lungs while they are still inside the carcass. If the lungs contain no cysts or scabs and are perfectly smooth to the touch, the meat is glatt kosher. If the shohet does detect cysts or scabs, the lungs and testes are removed and examined to see whether they are the kind that leaves an animal kosher or not.

The question immediately arises: Is glatt kosher meat more kosher than regular kosher meat? The answer is an emphatic *NO!* First of all, the cysts and scabs that the lungs of a regular kosher animal are allowed to have are *not* pathological. They are usually the result of such natural processes as food going down the animal's esophagus and pricking the lungs very slightly. These small pricks are *completely* healed in a kosher animal. Second, the concept of glatt kosher meat goes back over two thousand years; it is discussed in the Talmud and was therefore known to all Jewish religious authorities. Yet *the Talmud itself and ALL the major Jewish law codes* (such as the Mishneh Torah of Maimonides, the Arbaah Turim of Jacob ben Asher, and Shulhan Arukh of Joseph Caro, to mention only the three most important) *REJECT glatt kosher as the standard for determining whether or not meat is kosher.* The insistence upon only glatt kosher meat is therefore a humrah—a stringency far above the letter of the law—which certain superobservant groups have taken upon themselves. It is indeed unfortunate when such groups imply that regular kosher meat is not really kosher enough, for such is not the case.

GLATT KOSHER

Actually, we're so kosher all we sell is water!

The fact remains that all the major Jewish religious authorities have maintained that *regular kosher meat is one hundred percent kosher.*

Antishehitah laws and movements

As we have seen, the purpose of shehitah is to kill an animal as quickly and painlessly as possible. Utmost care is taken under Jewish law to ensure that this is so.

Yet over the past one hundred years, both in Europe and in the United States, attempts have been made in the non-Jewish world to effectively ban shehitah. The first ban was put into practice in Aangau, Switzerland, in 1891. Two years later a national plebiscite in Switzerland resulted in the prohibition of shehitah, and this became part of the Swiss constitution. In the 1930s several other countries followed suit. In almost all of these cases shehitah was not outlawed outright; rather, laws were passed to establish conditions that made the practice of shehitah impossible. This was done by requiring that all animals be stunned (usually done by a blow to the head or by electric shock) before slaughtering. Stunning is forbidden under Jewish law; if an animal is stunned it cannot be considered kosher.

Movements to ban shehitah in the U.S. have arisen from time to time, some as recently as four years ago. Fortunately, these groups have failed, and the right to perform shehitah is protected by the laws of many states. Similar laws exist in Great Britain, Ireland, South Africa, and other countries.

Most antishehitah movements have claimed humanitarian motives. They allege that shehitah is a pain-inducing process and therefore inhumane. However, a closer examination shows that anti-Semitism is at the root of almost all antishehitah movements. This statement is not an overreaction by Jews to a sensitive issue. It can be proved for example, by analysis of the voting patterns in the Swiss national plebiscite of 1893, by examination of the contents of the publications of various anitishehitah groups (they're not only against shehitah!), and by the fact that many of the people involved in such movements were also involved in other anti-Jewish activities. Unfortunately, this is not just history; such persons and groups still are active today.

Is shehitah the quickest, most painless, and humane way to slaughter animals?

The answer to this question is an unqualified yes. Doctors and scientists, both Jewish and gentile, have attested to this time and time again. Modern medical technology has enabled us to test the validity of shehitah's claim to painlessness. In all cases it was proven that shehitah is the swiftest and most painless method of slaughtering.

I have seen both nonkosher slaughtering as well as shehitah, and the difference between the two is enormous. In the nonkosher slaughtering the slaughterer shows no concern for the animal. The worker plunges the knife into the animal's neck, stabbing, hacking, and slicing through the throat. The animal shrieks in pain, its whole body twisting in agony, its face and its eyes screwed up. Death is not only drawn out, it certainly is excruciatingly painful. The shehitah I witnessed was exactly the opposite. The shohet was quick: in less than a second he was done. The animal did not cry out. Its body and face were not contorted in agony.

Shehitah is effective for several reasons: first, the shohet is not a slaughterhouse worker but a specially trained, tested, supervised, and sensitive individual who knows exactly what has to be done and how to do it; second, the knife used is more than razor sharp so the animal does not feel any pain when the shohet draws the knife across the animal's throat. (This is similar to what happens to a person who shaves with a razor blade. If he uses a fresh sharp blade, he may accidentally cut himself without realizing that he has been cut. And the halaf is sharper than the typical razor blade.) Most importantly, the act of shehitah not only severs the trachea (thus cutting off the animal's air supply) and esophagus but it also severs the jugular veins and carotid arteries. The result is a sudden and voluminous outpouring of blood (as much as 70 to 90 percent of the animal's total blood supply) and immediate acute anemia of the brain (since the blood in the brain rushes out through the severed jugular veins and it can no longer receive a fresh supply of blood from its primary source, the carotid arteries, as they too have been cut)—thus rendering the animal senseless instantaneously.

Stunning

We have already seen that most of the antishehitah laws require the preliminary stunning of the animal before actual slaughtering. Two methods of stunning an animal are most common today: a blow to the head of the animal and electric shock.

Stunning by a blow to the animal's head is prohibited under Jewish law for several reasons. First, there is a very real possibility that the animal will feel pain when the blow is administered. The person who deals the blow might not strike hard enough or might err and hit the animal in the wrong place or might not take into account that the structure of animals' skulls varies from specimen to specimen. All of these factors might result in a blow that would not render the animal unconscious in time to avoid pain. Unfortunately these are not remote possibilities; they happen all too frequently.

The second reason that stunning is not allowed under Jewish law is that the blow damages the animal's skull and brain. Since shehitah is analogous to the Temple sacrifices, an animal whose meat is to be used for food must be without blemish or injury. Because it damages the perfection of one of God's creatures, a blow to the head disqualifies that animal from being kosher.

Finally, striking the animal on the head and rendering it unconscious impedes the normal flow of blood. Since in kashrut nothing that hinders the evacuation of the animal's blood is permitted, stunning is not permitted. One reason we are concerned with the unrestricted outpouring of the blood is for health. More important, since blood is the symbol of life, Jewish law demands that we remove as much of the blood as possible before we eat meat. Therefore anything that prevents or hinders the removal of the blood is not allowed (see *Catalog 1,* pp. 21–22).

This point also pertains to stunning by electric shock, since shock frequently affects animals in such a way as to cause the formation of small blood clots, hemorrhage, and disfigurement of the muscles. Also, differences in the body chemistry of animals might prevent the electric shock from rendering some animals unconscious without unnecessary pain.

Slaughtering an animal by shooting is not allowed under Jewish law for the same reasons: it happens *very frequently* that the animal is not killed by the first bullet and therefore suffers severely; shooting damages the perfection of the animal; the animal's meat might prove unhealthy; and it does not allow for the proper outflow of blood. (If hunting even for food is not permitted, taking animal life for sport is certainly forbidden.)

I'm sure there would be a big market for kosher blubber, but whales just aren't kosher no matter how you slaughter them.

Shackling and hoisting

There is some question about the method used to restrain the animal as it is being slaughtered. The most common method today is called "shackling and hoisting." Just before the animal is brought onto the slaughterhouse floor, its rear legs are shackled. A few seconds before the shohet administers the cut, the animal is raised by its hind legs. Then its head is held by an abattoir worker while the shehitah is performed. Although the actual pain and fright caused to the animal have been greatly exaggerated (the animal is hoisted only for a few seconds, its hind legs are strongest, and no damage to the animal results from shackling and hoisting for if any injury did occur the animal would not be kosher), and although shackling and hoisting represents an improvement over previous methods, it seems to me that we should seek to replace this practice, about which there is some question, with a method that we are sure causes the animal absolutely no pain.

Several years ago a number of Jewish groups, recognizing that shackling and hoisting were not ideal, joined together with the American Society for the Prevention of Cruelty to Animals (ASPCA) in underwriting research into the development of an improved way to restrain the animal for shehitah. The result was the so-called ASPCA pen, which is designed to meet all the requirements of Jewish law and to eliminate the possibility that the animal might endure any pain just prior to shehitah (see Kindness to Animals).

Unfortunately, because of the expenses involved conversion to the ASPCA pen has not been universal, although it is being used in more and more kosher slaughterhouses. It is our responsibility to see that all such establishments use the ASPCA pen or a similarly painless method. If, as we have seen, Jewish law requires that the animal be *slaughtered* painlessly, then we ought to ensure that the animal is also restrained painlessly.

Like our own lives, animals partake of the sacred and may be extinguished only by the sanction of religion at the hands of one of its servants.

Bibliography

The source for most of the laws of shehitah is the Talmud tractate of Hullin. An English translation is published by Soncino. It should be noted that Hullin is one of the more difficult tractates of the Talmud.

The laws of shehitah are codified in all of the Jewish law codes. The most authoritative and most widely used today in matters of religious law is the Shulhan Arukh of Joseph Caro. As mentioned, the laws of shehitah are found in the section called Yoreh Deah, chapters 1–28.

Almost all introductory books to the study of Judaism and its laws and rituals contain a section on kashrut and briefly discuss the laws of shehitah. For fine, concise treatments of the topic, however, the reader is referred to the articles on "Shehitah" to be found in the *Jewish Encyclopedia* (1905; vol. 11, pp. 253–56) and in the *Encyclopaedia Judaica* (1971; vol. 14, pp. 1337–44).

Other works of interest include the following:

Dresner, Samuel H., and Siegel, Seymour. *The Jewish Dietary Laws: Their Meaning for Our Time.* New York: Burning Bush, 1959. This is by far the best work on the significance and higher meaning of kashrut.

Berman, Jeremiah J. *Shehitah: A Study in the Cultural and Social Life of the Jewish People.* New York: Bloch, 1941. In addition to a study of the historical and sociological development of kashrut institutions, this book contains a very good survey of antishehitah legislation as well as ample evidence (scientific and medical) as to the humaneness of kashrut. Excellent summary of laws of shehitah and bedikah.

Lewin, I.; Munk, M.; and Berman, J. J. *Religious Freedom: The Right to Practice Shehitah.* New York, 1946. Another thorough discussion of antishehitah movements and rebuttals to their allegations.

Freedman, Seymour E. *The Book of Kashrut.* New York: Bloch, 1970. A very accessible treatment of all aspects of kashrut and shehitah: rationale, humaneness, institutions, abuses, and guide for homemakers.

It was told to me by Rabbi Shmuel Arieh: In my youth I lived in the village of Koshilovitz, the same Koshilovitz which gained world renown because of the Baal Shem who was a shochet there before his greatness was revealed. I met a shochet there—an old man over eighty. I asked him, Did you perhaps know someone who knew the Baal Shem? Said he, I have never met a Jew who saw the Baal Shem, but I have met a gentile who saw him. When I was a young man I used to lodge with a gentile farmer. Whenever I would pour water on a stone before whetting my slaughtering knife the farmer's grandfather, an old man of ninety or a hundred, would shake his head. I used to think it was due to his age. One time I sensed that he was doing it out of disapproval, I asked him, Why do you shake your head while I work? Said he, You are not going about your task in a nice way. Yisroelki, before he whetted his knife, would dampen the stone with tears (S. Y. Agnon, "Tears," translated by Jules Harlow [Shocken, 1966]).

Ecology: bal tashhit

When in your war against a city you have to besiege it a long time in order to capture it, you must not destroy its trees, wielding the ax against them. You may eat of them, but you must not cut them down. Are trees of the field human to withdraw before you into the besieged city? Only trees which you know do not yield food may be destroyed; you may cut them down for constructing siegeworks against the city that is waging war on you, until it has been reduced (Deuteronomy 20:19–20).

The reason for this law is implied in the rhetorical question: "Are trees of the field human to withdraw before you into the besieged city?" It is abominable to attack the defenseless, and a growing tree yielding fruits that sustain life is an acute example of vitality and innocence.

The rabbis explain this passage as the source for the prohibition of any wanton destruction, extending bal tashhit—the principle of "you must not destroy"—to include every situation and interpreting "fruit tree" as symbolic of any useful object. The obligation to preserve property appears in the Torah as one of the rules of war, to remind us that even in the most extreme case of violence we—as God's co-partners in Creation—are responsible for the protection of the earth.

The rabbis applied this principle of bal tashhit in numerous specific cases reflecting four areas of concern:

1. A general prohibition against being wasteful. For example, they felt that one should not adjust a lamp to burn too quickly, for this would be wasteful of the fuel (Shabbat 67b).

2. Excessive wastefulness. Even when commanded by the Torah to destroy, we are warned not to exceed what is commanded. Thus while one should tear one's garment when hearing of a death in the immediate family, one should not tear the garment too much because that would be bal tashhit (Bava Kama 91b). Another case involved Rav Huna, who wanted to see if his son would become angry so he tore a silk purse in front of the son. The rabbis questioned this act because of bal tashhit, but Rav Huna answered that he had been careful to tear it on the seam (Kiddushin 32a).

3. Bizayon ha-okhel—spoiling (literally, "demeaning") food. This area was singled out for special attention. For example, one is not allowed to throw bread nor is one allowed to pass a cup full of liquid over bread; in both cases the bread could be ruined (Berakhot 50b). Bread especially received attention, since traditionally it represents the essence of all food.

4. A general concern for the environment. The following two verses illustrate this concern: "I will not drive them out before you in a single year,

lest the land become desolate and the wild beasts multiply to your hurt. I will drive them out before you little by little, until you have increased and possess the land" (Exodus 23:29–30). The Talmud tells us that tanneries, cemeteries, and places for threshing grain were situated forty cubits outside the walls of Jerusalem so as to protect the environment.

This concern with not destroying is connected with the hope for the return of the pristine state of the garden of Eden—the desire for return to a time when man and nature were at one rather than in conflict. It is written in the Prophets:

> For whoever blesses himself in the land
> Shall bless himself by the true God;
> And whoever swears in the land
> Shall swear by the true God. . . .
>
> For behold I am creating a new heaven and a new earth; . . .
> Be glad then and rejoice forever
> In what I am creating. . . .
> The wolf and the lamb shall graze together,
> And the lion shall eat straw like the ox,
> And the serpent's food shall be earth.
> In all My sacred mount
> Nothing evil or vile shall be done,
> Said the Lord (Isaiah 65:16, 17, 18, 25).

Judaism, the environment, and you/I/we

The first thing to notice about the biblical approach to the environment is that it permits no sharp distinction between the so-called natural and the so-called historical or societal. The classic proof-text (Deuteronomy 20:19–20) for (bal tashhit, Deuteronomy 20:19–20) is presented as one of the restrictions in waging war, and the major text (Leviticus 25) prescribing rest for the land (shemitah and yovel) is given as part of radical social legislation to redistribute concentrated land holdings. "Nature" and "history" may be separable in

thought but not in fact: since the advent of human beings on this planet one is dependent on the other.

Consider the plants that surround us. They seem to be examples of the natural sphere unaffected by human history, yet intervention and selection have produced plants that are quite different from their wild origins, as Franz Schwanitz shows in *The Origin of Cultivated Plants* (Cambridge, Mass.: Harvard University Press, 1967). Nature, in this sense, has a history. On the other hand, no study of any civilization is complete without careful attention to the conditions of hunting and food growing, topsoil and mineral resources which affected that civilization. There is no history without nature.

Obvious, of course, yet rather easily overlooked. Haven't most of us in this civilization at this period of history lived as though history were all, as though technology had finally made us independent of nature?

Part of our task, then, is to establish a keener sense of the natural context within which history unfolds, remembering too that for our human consciousness nature itself is not pristine but partially a result of historical process.

For this perspective to inform both our personal lives and our policy decisions, we need practical suggestions more than philosophical speculations. Not that thought is irrelevant; rather, naaseh venishma—let us do, that we may hear and comprehend—applies here as elsewhere; and thoughts, fantasies, and feelings will emerge from the doing. Besides, there are already good discussions of Jewish texts about Judaism and the environment, some of which are listed at the end of this section, so there's no need to repeat them here.

One other preliminary: any discussion that tries to reawaken our sense of nature must in good conscience be brief. Fewer words mean less paper, and less paper means fewer trees felled. Therefore, summary suggestions rather than full statements will follow; not prescriptions for getting out of the city and onto the land—though that may happen—but rather ways of reconnecting with the environment here and now, in cities and suburbs as well as in the country.

The daily sequence

Sun sighting and moon watching are good habits to develop, Have you a morning prayer about the sun? If not, try Psalms 19:2–7:

> The heavens declare the glory of God,
>   the sky proclaims His handiwork;
> Day to day makes utterance,
>   night to night speaks out.
> There is no utterance,
>   there are no words,
>   whose sound goes unheard.
> Their voice carries throughout the earth,
>   their words to the end of the world.
> He placed in them a tent for the sun,
>   who is like a groom coming forth from the chamber,
>   like a hero, eager to run his course.
> His rising-place is at one end of heaven,
>   and his circuit reaches the other;
>   nothing escapes his heat.

Too formal? Then how about this brief excerpt from a lovely children's poem by Miriam Yalan-Shtekelis:

Shemesh shemesh bamarom,	(Literally: Sun, Sun in the sky,
Boker tov lakh, rav shalom.	Good morning to you, Great peace.)
	On the horizon the Sun appears.
	I greet the day! Away with fears!

Moon watching? New Moon, full moon? Check *Catalog 1* under The Calendar (pp. 96 ff.).

Star gazing? Constellation? Don't miss them—they're glorious! And combine them with Psalm 8 or Job 38 (or 37, 39, or 40).

In some way welcome the gift of the sun gratefully.

You might also try to catch the sun at zenith as well as at setting, and meditate on that great triangle.

Walking among grass and trees is another habit worth cultivating; and throughout the growing season, from earliest spring to late autumn, you're certain to come across various signs of life that are eloquent testimonials to the power of Hei Haolamim—the Life of the Universe. When struck by such evidence of the Great Life Stream, why not celebrate by chanting three or four times "Hei Haolamim—Life All Around" (a phrase from the prayer book).

Or try this prayer:

> Master of the Universe,
> grant me the ability to be alone;
> may it be my custom to go outdoors each day
> among the trees and grass, among all growing things,
> and there may I be alone, and enter into prayer,
> to talk with the One that I belong to.
> May I express there everything in my heart,
> and may all the foliage of the field
> (all grasses, trees, and plants)
> may they all awake at my coming,
> to send the powers of their life into the words of my prayer
> so that my prayer and speech are made whole
> through the life and spirit of all growing things,
> which are made as one by their transcendent Source (Rabbi Nahman of Bratslav
>   [1772–1811]; translated by Rabbi Shamai Kanter).

But the Great Round of Life is not all life. Death, too, has its function, returning to the earth that which has reached the end of its life cycle. Yet from the earth, nourished by that which was once living, now life springs forth—and so the cycle continues and is renewed. Melekh meimit u-mehayeh—the Sovereign who slays and enlivens—is the way the prayer book explains it. Why not chant that when confronting a tree decaying, fungi growing, or fragrant piles of late autumn leaves? Prayers, after all, are not confined to the prayer book. Here's how Ecclesiastes says it (3:1–3):

> A season is set for everything, a time for every experience under heaven:
> A time for being born and a time for dying,
> A time for planting and a time for uprooting the planted;
> A time for slaying and a time for healing,
> A time for tearing down and a time for building up.

Walking along the seashore is another privilege; nor is a lakeshore to be ignored. Have you tried Psalm 93 or 98 in such a setting? Or 107:23–32? Perhaps they'll add a dimension to your walk.

Seasonal shifts

Don't let seasons slip by unnoticed and uncelebrated. Sukkot for autumn and Pesah for spring, with their traditional readings of Ecclesiastes and Song of Songs respectively, are ideal for seasonal as well as historical celebrations. But they can become much more. Pesah, our festival of deliverance, occurs at the beginning of the spring grain harvest in the Mediterranean. Barley starts growing when it's planted in the autumn, survives the winter, spurts ahead in early spring, and is ripe enough by Pesah so that the cutting season can begin—culminating seven weeks later in Shavuot. All through that seven-week period there is a special counting, sefirat haomer, connecting Pesah to Shavuot and binding the days of that period together like the sheaves of wave offering mentioned in Leviticus 23:9–17.

> For now the winter is past,
> The rains are over and gone.

The blossoms have appeared in the land,
The time of pruning has come;
The song of the turtledove
Is heard in our land.
The green figs form on the figtree,
The vines in blossom give off fragrance.
Arise, my darling;
My fair one, come away! (Song of Songs 2:11–13).

It must have been beautiful to take an additional stalk of ripening grain each day and wave it in celebration of the increasing harvest and promise of bounty to come. How fortunate they were to harvest so fully, discovering in the growing grain secrets of their own unfolding.

"They." Why not "we"? In the wheat belt of the U.S. winter wheat is grown widely, corresponding to Mediterranean barley in its planting and ripening cycle. In the American northeast winter rye follows the same pattern. Depending on the climate, barley would probably do the same.

From all of this, a suggestion: near the end of Sukkot get a pound of barley or winter rye or winter wheat at a feed and grain store. Ask for planting suggestions (similar to seeding a lawn); then go dig up a small patch (10′×10′ might be enough) of the grass surrounding your temple, and plant some of the seed (one pound should do 400 square feet). Mark the patch off so that it doesn't get trampled, then watch the seed germinate soon after planting (ten days to two weeks depending on sun and moisture). It should winter over, to resume its growth early in the spring. Let it grow.

Beginning the second night of Pesah, cut some for use at second Seder, at services, at celebrations. As you number the days between Pesah and Shavuot, increase the size of the bundles you wave. For services, work out dances, waving motions, stretching motions. Involve the religious school students and high schoolers. Include yourselves—kids shouldn't have all the fun! Watch the grain begin to fill out. Follow its growth closely over those weeks. Have

a big Lag b'Omer—May Day celebration, then decorate the shul on Shavuot with sheaves of grain.

These seven weeks of ripening grain are also a most appropriate occasion for giving thought to world hunger and for finding ways to share what we have with others. Our own diets, food monopolies, distribution of world wealth, ways in which we share responsibility for hunger elsewhere in the world—all of these are part of a full approach to the omer. Again, no nature without history, no history without nature.

An omer proposal

1. Fast on Mondays and Thursdays during the seven weeks. The fast, lasting from Sunday evening through Monday afternoon, would consist of abstention from (a) all meat, (b) alcohol made from grains (e.g., beer and whiskey), (c) products whose production and consumption are wasteful (e.g., convenience foods, fancy cakes, imported delicacies), (d) food products whose packaging is wasteful, and (e) food or any other products not required for a simple life-style.

2. Conservation of natural resources necessary for the production of food. This would include (a) no unnecessary travel and greater reliance upon public transportation (at least on Monday and Thursday—the traditional days when the Torah is read during morning services), (b) no exorbitant use of electricity (e.g., no electric canopeners, toothbrushes), (c) no purchase of or use of gimmicks or labor-saving devices without serious reflection as to their necessity, and (d) no waste of water, gas, materials, or food.

3. Involvement in some efforts at alleviating world hunger:

a. Each day at the time of the counting of the omer, place one dollar in a pushke to be given *after* Shavuot to a group involved in relief efforts or political action directed at the problem. Examples are your local Jewish social-service agency and

Oxfam
302 Columbus Ave.
Boston, MA 02116

UNICEF
331 E. 38th St.
New York, NY 10016

United Farm Workers
P.O. Box 62
Keene, CA 93531

Food Day
1785 Massachusetts Ave. NW
Washington, DC 20036

American Jewish Joint Distribution Committee, Inc. (JDC)
60 E. 42nd St.
New York, NY 10017

Tzedek, Tzedek
1713 Hobart St. NW
Washington, DC 20009

b. On Tuesdays and Wednesdays devote at least one hour to studying Jewish traditional literature on food (kashrut), famine, collective responsibility, tzedakah, or tzedek—justice.

c. Once a week bring an offering of food or money directly and personally to a local distributive center for gifts to poor people.

d. At least once a week explain both the nature of the world food crisis and your response to it to somebody. Other efforts at education and publicity are considered meritorious.

From liturgy to life (and back again)

Why grow only for synagogue ceremonies? Why not for your own consumption? Gardening is great for the muscles as well as for the digestive system, and helping food grow will quickly attune you to the rhythms of the vegetation cycle—"seedtime and harvest, cold and heat, summer and winter, day and night" (Genesis 8:22).

There is also a special satisfaction in eating what you have helped grow, a sense of connection with the Life Flow that cannot be purchased in any market. There is an intimate mingling of self with soil, that substance from which we all emerged and to which we are destined to return.

> Rabbi Ahai ben Josiah states: He who purchases grain in the market place, to what may he be likened? To an infant whose mother dies; although he is taken from door to door to other wet nurses, he is not satisfied.... He who eats of his own is like an infant raised at its mother's breast (Avot de Rabbi Natan, ch. 30).

If you do some gardening, be sure to notice seeds. We read phrases such as "seed of Abraham" or "seed of Sarah," but rarely do we focus on the image itself. Yet consider the seed: always small, sometimes tiny, it contains within it both the energy to initiate new life and the wisdom to shape and direct it. As its caretakers we can water and enrich the soil it seeks, and so provide it with surroundings that help it unfold; but we are not its creators. The life in it began elsewhere and flows onward, producing further seed in its turn. It may pass near us—even through us—but we are neither its source nor its ultimate destination. Tiny though it be, a seed is eloquent witness to the Great Life Stream, receiving and transmitting that precious substance.

Seen in these terms and applied to ourselves, what does it mean to be "seed of Abraham" or "seed of Sarah"? What does it mean to be "seed of our parents"? "Seeds of our children"? (Note: the seed is both receiver and transmitter.) There is great richness in just such simple images as these.

Diet

Diet should also be reconsidered. Dietary discipline in the form of kashrut has a long history in Judaism; perhaps we should now look at the pre-Noahitic diet:

Every seed-bearing plant that is upon all the earth, and every tree that has seed-bearing fruit; they shall be yours for food. And all the animals on land, to all the birds of the sky, and to everything that creeps on earth, in which there is the breath of life, [I give] all the green plants for food (Genesis 1:29–30).

The considerations favoring vegetarianism are several. For one, a unit of land can feed many more people when its produce is consumed directly by human beings rather than mediated by animals. For example, a cow must be fed twenty-one pounds of protein in order to produce one pound of beef protein for human consumption. (The conversion ratio for chicken is 5.5 to 1; for milk 4.4 to 1; for eggs 4.3 to 1.) These and many other telling facts, along with "a guideline for eating from the earth that both maximizes the earth's potential to meet man's nutritional needs and, at the same time, minimizes the disruption of the earth necessary to sustain him" may be found in Frances Moore Lappe's *Diet for a Small Planet*.

Second, tzaar baalei hayyim—the pain of living creatures (see Kindness to Animals as well as Exodus 20:10, 23:12; Deuteronomy 22:1–4, 6–7, 10, 25:4; Bava Metzia 32a–b, 33a)—is a consideration frequently invoked by the rabbinic tradition to encourage kind treatment of our fellow creatures, and is the traditional rationale for shehitah—Jewish ritual slaughter. To some the logical extension of this is basing our diets on foods that do not require taking the lives of these fellow creatures.

Even short of vegetarianism, however, there are further questions we

need to ask about our diets. Tzaar baalei hayyim poses serious challenges to "factory farming" or "intensive rearing"—the uncritical application of technology to animal rearing with a total disregard for their own creaturely needs. Is this definition of a chicken, quoted from a technical journal, acceptable?

The modern layer is, after all, only a very efficient converting machine, changing the raw materials—feeding stuffs—into the finished product—the egg—less, of course, maintenance requirements (Ruth Harison, *Animal Machines* [Vincent Stuart, 1964], p. 50).

What does it mean in practice?

Day-old chicks are installed, eight or ten thousand at a time, sometimes more, in long, windowless houses punctuated only with extractor fans in serried rows along the ridge of the roofs, and air intake vent along the side walls. . . . Inside a house the impression is of a long, wide, dark tunnel disappearing into the gloom, the floor covered with chickens as far as the eye can see (ibid., p. 12).

And the results?

The battery chickens I have observed seem to lose their minds about the time they would normally be weaned by their mothers and off in the weeds chasing grasshoppers on their own account. Yes, literally, actually, the battery becomes a gallinaceous mad-house. The eyes of these chickens through the bars gleam like those of maniacs. Let your hand get within reach and it receives a dozen vicious pecks, not the love peck or the tentative peck of idle curiosity bestowed by the normal chicken, but a peck that means business, a peck for flesh and blood, for which in their madness they are thirsting. They eat feathers out of each other's back or, rather pull out each other's feathers and nibble voraciously at the roots of the same for tiny blocks of flesh and blood that may adhere thereto (ibid., p. 154–55).

Thus feather pecking and cannibalism replace the normal "pecking order" of the farmyard. And the "solutions" to these technologically created problems? Not the reestablishment of conditions of life considerate of the instinctual needs of these creatures, but rather debeaking, reduced light, the fitting of opaque "specs" that prevent the chicken from seeking directly in front of it, cages, etc.

By our alienation from our surroundings we have—quite unknowingly for the most part—completely disregarded the simple but basic biblical-rabbinic principle of consideration for our fellow creatures:

If, then, you obey the commandments that I enjoin upon you this day, loving the Lord your God and serving Him with all your heart and soul, I will grant the rain for your land in season, the early rain and the late: you shall gather in your new grain and wine and oil, and I will provide grass in the fields for your cattle; thus you shall eat your fill. Take care not to be lured away to serve other gods and bow to them. For the Lord's anger will flare up against you, and He will shut up the skies so that there will be no rain and the ground will not yield its produce; and you will soon perish from the good land that the Lord is giving you (Deuteronomy 11:13–17).

The consequence is an unprecedented violation of the needs of other animals:

To some extent . . . farm animals have always been exploited by man in that he rears them specifically for food. But until recently they were individuals, allowed their birthright of green fields, sunlight, and fresh air; they were allowed to forage, to exercise, to watch the world go by, in fact to live. Even at its worst, with insufficient protection against inclement weather or poor supplementation of natural food, the animal had some enjoyment in life before it died. Today the exploitation has been taken to a degree which involves not only the elimination of all enjoyment, the frustration of almost all natural instincts, but its replacement with acute discomfort, boredom, and the actual denial of health. It has been taken to a degree where the animal is not allowed to live before it dies (*Animal Machines*, p. 3).

Any serious consideration of our surroundings requires attention to the question of how our animal food is raised. It also requires a critical look at environmental degradation by present chemicalized production methods for grain and produce as well as an examination of food monopolies. Barry Commoner's *The Closing Circle* and current periodical coverage help, so be on the lookout.

The earth in its fullness

There is a final area of our relationship to the environment that must at least be mentioned—the distribution of wealth, power, and population. At the heart of the sabbatical and jubilee legislation (Leviticus 25; Exodus 23:10–11; Deuteronomy 15:1–18) seems to be the notion of inalienable ancestral subsistence land, a small holding where each person could dwell "under his own vine, under his own fig tree, undisturbed" (cf. Micah 4:1–4; Isaiah 2:1–4; Zechariah 3:10; and others). This decentralized, agriculture-based model from biblical times, with the (extended) family unit that was assured a means of basic subsistence in the form of a small holding of land sufficient for its basic needs, is the "liberty" that was to be proclaimed "throughout the land to all the inhabitants thereof." Applied seriously to our own time and place, it would result in a considerable redistribution of wealth, a decentralization of power, and a redistribution of population toward more rural areas—resulting in an immediate and direct relationship to land and surroundings.

Are there others who feel that some such social policy, seriously implemented, would be a fitting way for the U.S. to enter the 1980s, to provide the possibility—now denied millions of us—to again respect our God-given earth in all its fullness?

> Fear not, O beasts of the field,
> For the pastures in the wilderness
> Are clothed with grass.
> The trees have borne their fruit;
> Fig tree and vine
> Have yielded their strength.
> O children of Zion, be glad,
> Rejoice in the Lord your God.
> For He has given you the early rain in [His] kindness,
> Now He makes the rain fall [as] formerly—
> The early rain and the late—
> And threshing floors shall be piled with grain,
> And vats shall overflow with new wine and oil. . . .
> And you shall eat your fill
> And praise the name of the Lord your God (Joel 2:22–24, 26).

In his heart, the proud man says: "I am a writer, I am a singer, I am a great one at studying." Since such men will not turn to God, not even on the threshold of hell, they are reborn again as bees, which hum and buzz: "I am, I am, I am."

—Rabbi Raphael of Bershad

For further reading

1. *Judaism and Human Rights*, ed. by Milton R. Konvitz (New York, 1972), has a section on "The Earth Is the Lord's," with articles by Samuel Belkin, Samson Raphael Hirsch, and Eric G. Freudenstein—all of them with numerous traditional citations.

2. *Keeping Posted* (a publication of UAHC), vol. 16, no. 3 (December 1970), is devoted to ecology and includes an essay by Robert Gordis on "Judaism and the Spoliation of Nature." This one also has many traditional references.

3. "On the Judaism of Nature," in *The New Jews*, edited by Sleeper and Mintz (Vintage Book V-669, 1971); and

4. "The Return of the Goddess," in *Ecology: Crisis and New Vision*, edited by Richard E. Sherrell (Richmond, Virginia: John Knox, 1971) were written by the author and may be of some interest.

5. Some further reflections on treatment of animals may be found in "The Life of His Beast," also by the author, obtainable from

> **Society for Animal Rights**
> **900 First Ave.**
> **New York, NY 10022**

6. From the same place one can obtain reprints of "A Mother's Tale" by James Agee, an incredible and deeply moving story of significance.

ISRAEL

TO BE A FREE PEOPLE IN OUR OWN LAND

Hatikvah להיות עם חפשי בארצנו

Traditional attitudes about Israel

The Catalog's usual style incorporates the practical and the mystical, the realistic and the idealistic, but in an article about how tradition sees the land of Israel, Eretz Yisrael, that's impossible. The section reads like a love story because this is precisely how Jews have traditionally related to Israel. Romance, yearning, passion, this is not the major attitude adopted by traditional Jews; it is the *only* attitude.

The source

The Midrash has it that when Israel went into exile the Divine Presence joined them to comfort them in their homelessness. But in fact the Jewish people never really left Eretz Yisrael; for wherever they went they carried with them the tangible memory of Zion and the love of Jerusalem. In a thousand different ways this memory and the ardent desire and impatient hope for restoration have become part of the Jewish way of life, so that, spiritually and ideationally, Jews have never stopped breathing the air of Israel. They went into exile but carried along with them the spiritual harvest they had gathered on their own soil, a spiritual motherland no enemy could deprive them of. In due course this "portable motherland" became a potent mainstay that upheld and gave them strength to survive until the day of "the Return."

Jewish literature of all times and all countries is, to a very large extent, a paean singing the praises of Eretz Yisrael—in keys and notes of limitless variety. Singer and sage, rabbi and scholar, rationalist and mystic, statesman and financier—all these as well as the large mass of anonymous though articulate Jews have built monuments to Zion fashioned in verse and prose.

There is not a trait or quality of beauty, goodness, and excellence that has not been woven into the tributes paid by generations of creative lovers of Zion to their dearly beloved. Nor did this exaltation of the qualities of the homeland begin in exile.

In the Bible itself we find the seeds that flower into the love that Jews bear the land of Israel.

Keep, therefore, all the Instruction that I enjoin upon you today so that . . . you may long endure upon the soil which the Lord swore to your fathers to give to them and to their descendants, a land flowing with milk and honey . . . the land you are about to cross into and occupy, a land of hills and valleys, soaks up its water from the rains of heaven. It is a land which the Lord your God looks after, on which the Lord your God always keeps His eye, from year's beginning to year's end (Deuteronomy 11:8–12).

I have marked well the plight of My people in Egypt. . . . I have come down . . . to bring them out of that land to a good and spacious land, a land flowing with milk and honey (Exodus 3:7–8).

For the Lord your God is bringing you into a good land, a land with streams and springs and fountains issuing from plain and hill; a land of wheat and barley, of vines, figs, and pomegranates, a land of olive trees and honey; a land where you may eat food without stint, where you will lack nothing; a land whose rocks are iron and from whose hills you can mine copper (Deuteronomy 8:7–9).

The Talmud and rabbinic literature elaborate on these biblical tributes to the land of Israel. The talmudic tractate Kiddushin asserts that "ten measures of beauty were given to the world, nine of these went to Jerusalem and one to the rest of the world." Another rabbi commented enthusiastically, "Eretz Yisrael does not lack a thing!" (Berakhot 36b). Even its "fruit is easier to digest than the produce of other countries" (Sifrei, Ekev). Small wonder, therefore, that the rabbis felt that "happy are those who live in Eretz Yisrael," where, according to the Zohar, "all the splendor and all delight are found."

Our sages perceived a preordained and inseparable tie between the Jewish people and their country. They mused about this unique relationship: "God measured all the countries and found only Eretz Yisrael suitable for Israel" (Leviticus Rabbah 3). Another rabbi declared that the iron bond between the people and their land began with the love of God who said: "I love Israel and I love Eretz Yisrael. I shall, therefore, give my beloved country to my beloved people" (Numbers Rabbah 23).

The spiritual qualities and the inspiration of Eretz Yisrael were even more elaborately exalted. Nahmanides, the famous scholar and biblical commentator who powerfully stimulated the "love of Zion" among thirteenth-century Jewry, summed up the conviction of every Jewish scholar when he stated that "Eretz Yisrael is destined for the Torah—and the Torah can be complete only in Eretz Yisrael." To other rabbis it was "the holiest of all countries" and the abode of the Shekhinah—the Divine Presence—which, according to Rabbi Yosi ben Halafta, rests upon the person who combines the study of Torah with living in Israel.

The intense love for Eretz Yisrael that inspired the sages of the talmudic era has been expressed in many passages of touching fervor and in stories of great emotional quality. In order to give concrete expression to their love for Eretz Yisrael, "Rabbi Abba used to kiss the stones of Acco, while Rabbi Hanina would mend the roads, and Rabbi Hiya, the son of Gamda, would lie down in the dust of the Holy Land. All this to fulfill the passage, 'For Thy servants take pleasure in her stones and love her dust'" (Ketubbot 112a).

Another sage held that "he who dwells in Eretz Yisrael and speaks Hebrew is assured of his share in the world to come" (Jerusalem Talmud, Shabbot 1, 3). And elsewhere it is written: "It is better to dwell in the deserts of Eretz Yisrael than in the palaces of other countries" (Genesis Rabbah 39). In fact, God Himself is said "to prefer a small group of scholars in Eretz Yisrael to the Great Sanhedrin abroad" (Jerusalem Talmud, Nedarim 6, 8).

S/he who adds the glory of Eretz Yisrael thus atones for his/her sins. The

rabbis illustrated this with the following homily about Omri, one of the idolatrous and unrighteous kings of Israel. Wondering at the fact that Divine Providence led him to the throne despite his many transgressions, they explained his merit by stating: "He added one town to Eretz Yisrael," namely, he bought the site and build the town of Samaria (Sanhedrin 102b).

Going beyond even this, some Hasidic rabbis identified Eretz Yisrael with the Divine Presence. The very boldness of this comparison of pure spirituality with a concrete and real country attested to their mystical idealization of the Holy Land.

The Diaspora relationship to Eretz Yisrael

Jews in the Diaspora have always lived according to the calendar of Israel, celebrating the spring and the harvest when *Israel* celebrated its spring and harvest. They toasted the Shabbat and the holy days with wine pressed from grapes of the homeland and forwent other necessities to be able to afford the etrog—the fruit used in celebration of Sukkot—whose sweet aroma was synonymous with the air of the Holy Land. A little soil from Eretz Yisrael was among the most precious possessions of Jews, who dreaded nothing more than being buried in foreign soil without the comfort of a bit of Eretz Yisrael under their heads. At prayer and even in the grave our faces were turned toward Zion.

Such underlying love of Eretz Yisrael betokens the extraordinary loyalty and devotion that Jews have always felt for their homeland. This tiny land has been home to the Jewish people less than one-third of their historical career thus far. Yet in all countries and under many skies for twenty-five centuries Jews have prayed three times a day for the restoration of their ancient homeland.

In later centuries, as the exile dragged on and weighed ever more heavily upon those who were longing and hoping impatiently for the promised return to Eretz Yisrael, the country became the idealized beloved of Jews everywhere. Nearly all the great thinkers, commentators, and poets of the Middle Ages acknowledged their burning desire to behold Eretz Yisrael and its glory, Jerusalem. Many left home and family to journey to the Holy Land despite the hazards and difficulties they encountered. Yehudah Halevi, the poet and philosopher, whose pilgrimage to Eretz Yisrael is often held up as a shining example of the love for Zion, was only one of many who embarked on the perilous journey. Nahmanides, who agitated feverishly for the resettlement of the Holy Land, expressed the sentiments and feelings of all medieval Jewish pilgrims, both the famous and the nameless ones, when in the introduction to his Bible commentary he wrote that the separation from his family and friends, the hardships of his lonely life far from them, and the sufferings and perils of the journey to Eretz Yisrael are "easy to bear and it is easy to give up all the good that may be my share, for it is agreeable to dwell even one day within your precincts, to visit your destroyed palace, to behold your forsaken sanctuary." He, like all other lovers of Zion, felt that "abroad, even if everything is done to conform with God's honor, complete purity is still lacking." And so he and all the many who were of his persuasion went in search of this purity—the consummation of their Jewishness.

Even those who opposed one another on their understanding of the nature of Judaism were in agreement on the issue of Eretz Yisrael. The Baal Shem Tov—the founder of Hasidism—regarded his pilgrimage to Eretz Yisrael as the fulfillment of his life; his opponent, the rationalist Mitnaged—the

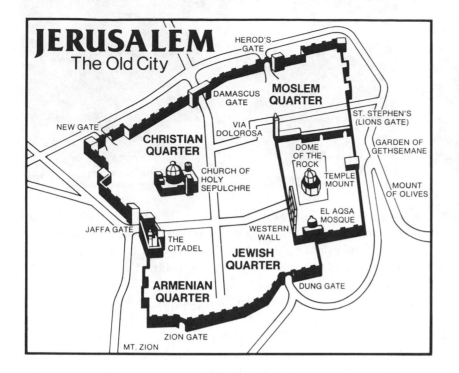

JERUSALEM
The Old City

Gaon Elijah of Vilna—wrote to his family upon leaving for the Holy Land: "I beg of you, do not grieve over my departure for Eretz Yisrael, may it be rebuilt and reestablished! I am, God be thanked, on my way to the Holy Land, which all are eager to behold. It is the desire of all Israel, yea the desire of God for which all are yearning in heaven and on earth."

There is very little difference between the tenor and mystical fervor of the Gaon's letter and the Hasidic Rabbi Nahman of Bratslav's touching prayer:

Please God, may it be Your will to grant me in compassion and love—and as special favor—to become speedily worthy of reaching Eretz Yisrael—the Holy Land which our fathers inherited, the country desired and longed for by all those who are truly pious. And most of them came there and improved and accomplished whatever they were capable and worthy of all this thanks to the sacredness of Eretz Yisrael—the holiest place on earth.

The lovers of Zion demanded that she be desired for her own sake, and not for ulterior motives: "Only he merits to dwell in Eretz Yisrael," remarked the Bible commentator Moses Alshach (sixteenth century), "who journeys there out of love for the country and not because of ulterior motives." Three centuries later the Hasidic Rabbi Shneur Zalman of Ladi declared: "The love for Zion must be like a fire burning in the heart of every Jew. He who wants to live truly as a Jew must go to Eretz Yisrael. . . . If there are obstacles in his way, he must overcome them—go he must."

Because of a statement that "those buried in Eretz Yisrael will be resurrected first in the days of the Messiah" (Genesis Rabbah 96), burial in the Holy Land was especially coveted by the kabbalists and the later mystics, who speculated a great deal about the temporal differences in the resurrection of the dead of Eretz Yisrael and those of other countries. To enable the largest number to share in the salvation bestowed by the precious soil of Eretz Yisrael, it became customary to put a little earth from the Holy Land under the heads of those who were buried in the Galut—exile—a custom that still prevails.

The unique place Eretz Yisrael occupies in Jewish life is perhaps most conclusively shown by the fact that two of the most important commandments—the sanctification of the Shabbat and the honoring of parents—may be

infringed upon for the sake of dwelling in Israel. The duty to purchase soil and houses in Eretz Yisrael is regarded as so important that it is permissible to have the deed of sale drawn up on Shabbat if it can't be postponed: "He who buys a house in Eretz Yisrael may have the contract drawn up even on the Shabbat" (Bava Kama 80b).

Although children owe obedience to their parents, they may act contrary to their parents commands if the parents interfere with their children's desire to settle in Eretz Yisrael. To dwell in the Holy Land is a "positive commandment" that brooks no interference whatsoever. A husband or wife may sue for divorce if the spouse refuses to settle in Eretz Yisrael. Likewise, a husband has no legal right to ask his wife to move away from the Holy Land, for "the commandment to live in Eretz Yisrael outweighs all other commandments of the Torah" (Sifrei, Reah).

Messianic hopes

Diverse interpretations of Jewish history have considered the meaning of the march of the Jewish people across time. But no matter how you view history, the fact remains that Jewish history is, to a very large extent, the record of the "Love for Zion" translated into action. Jews did not simply pray for the return to Zion and the advent of the Messiah to bring about the redemption. For the first "Zionist movement," led by Zerubbabel, Ezra, and Nehemiah, half a century after the destruction of the First Temple (586 B.C.E.), to the proclamation of the Basle Program (1897), the hope and desire of the national restoration have been among the most important elements shaping Jewish destiny.

In keeping the promise of the prophets, elaborated by the sages of the Talmud, the Jews of all countries and all centuries looked forward to the coming of the Messiah, who would lead the dispersed and homeless sufferers back to the ancestral home in Eretz Yisrael. As the persecutions and tribulations grew fiercer and more difficult to bear, the Jewish people became ever more occupied with speculations and dreams about the days of the Messiah, when Israel's bondage would be broken and its ancient glory renewed.

Because they were feverishly eager for the redemption, it was inevitable that the people and their spiritual leaders should seek consolation by calculating the date of the advent of the Messiah and the redemption. But when time and again the calculations proved disappointingly wrong, the rabbis legislated against such dangerous and idle speculations. Notwithstanding the rabbinic admonitions and prohibitions, the people continued to seek in the texts of certain biblical books, especially Daniel, clues concerning the date of the advent of the Messiah.

Throughout Jewish history the Messiah has been conceived of as the redeemer of the nation who will lead the dispersed people back to their promised land. To be sure, early and latterday mystics associated a variety of supernatural events with the messianic era, but from the authoritative teachers of the Talmud to Maimonides and his successors the prevailing opinion has invariably been that the messianic era will be characterized primarily by the cessation of Israel's servitude and dispersion. In keeping with this, Maimonides warns: "Do not imagine for a moment that the King Messiah will have to perform wonders and miracles, create new phenomena in nature, and cause the resurrection of the dead. . . . The world will go on its usual course."

As a result of the popular preoccupation with messianic speculations, it was inevitable from time to time—and especially in periods of great suffering—that men would arise and lay claim to the crown of the Messiah. The cavalcade of the more important pseudo-Messiahs opened with Bar Kokhba. He led a popular uprising against Roman tyranny but was defeated (135 C.E.) when the enemy destroyed his last stronghold: Betar. The intensity of craving for national liberation in the days of the Hadrianic persecutions may be gauged from the fact that Rabbi Akiba, one of the most astute sages of all time, enthusiastically acclaimed Bar Kokhba as the Messiah—and this over the protest and opposition of his colleagues.

In the following centuries numerous pseudo-Messiahs, whether widely known or obscure, tried to hasten the redemption. Some tried to bring it about by force, some by mystical means, some by political negotiations. One of the last pseudo-Messiahs, and the one who had the widest following among the Jews since Bar Kokhba, was Shabbtai Zevi. His strange and hypnotic character won him many adherents throughout the Jewish world. His apostasy to Islam aroused a widespread attack upon his followers and their mystical doctrines. This dampened the messianic enthusiasm of most Jews—an attitude that has continued into the modern period.

When the influence of mysticism was broken with the advent of the Age of Enlightenment, the Jewish hope for national redemption did not wane. In keeping with the realistic orientation of the time, Jewish hope turned to the original conception of the prophets and the talmudic sages. The talmudic pronouncement that the only difference between the era before the advent of the Messiah and the messianic era would be "the cessation of Israel's servitude" became the generally accepted belief.

Thus it is apparent that the nineteenth-century exponents of the Jewish national idea—those who pleaded for Israel's return to its land by using political arguments fortified by historical and economic proofs—were not the products of Enlightenment thinking. They were, rather, in the direct line of succession to the pseudo-Messiahs. The yearning for restoration that agitated Hirsch Kalisher, Solomon Gutmacher, Moses Hess, Leon Pinsker, Theodor Herzl, and others was identical to what had fired the pseudo-Messiahs of a less realistic age.

Modern Zionism is, therefore, not a break with Jewish tradition but, on the contrary, its logical continuation. All generations throughout the millennia of the Jewish dispersion expressed the hope for national restoration; Zionism is the result of a firmly rooted Jewish tradition. The Jewish national hope, in its many diverse forms of expression and even its perverse vagaries, has kept the Jewish national will alive. Judaism could survive after the loss of the land because the physical Jerusalem was transformed into the spiritual Jerusalem, "the chiefest joy" and the greatest love of every Jewish heart. Spiritually the Jews never left their ancestral soil, and so the physical separation had no serious repercussions on their will to survive. They breathed and continued to breathe "the air of Eretz Yisrael" in all countries and at all times of the dispersion.

Zionism

Note: This chapter is *not* a history of Zionism. The bibliography lists books dealing with this subject. We only attempt to present the background of Zionism and to raise the questions about Zionism that have arisen since the founding of the State of Israel.

All of the history in the preceding section can be seen as the seeds that were sown in the hearts of the Jewish people and began to take root in the nineteenth century—the century that saw the beginnings of modern Zionism. Throughout the nineteenth century, Jewish thinkers such as Leon Pinsker, Ahad Ha-Am, and Moses Hess, who had been influenced by the widespread rise of nationalism throughout Europe, wrote of the need for the return to Israel, for a Jewish homeland, and for Israel to serve as a cultural center for the Jewish people. This same rise of nationalism affected others, and, aided by the Baron Edmond de Rothschild, Jews began to settle in Palestine during the second half of the century.

All these trends were the beginnings of the movement toward modern Zionism that was fathered by the ideas and writings of Theodor Herzl. He launched Zionism as a political movement in 1897 when he called together the first Zionist Congress in Basle, Switzerland. His dynamic personality and unflagging energy lent force and helped gain adherents throughout the Jewish and non-Jewish world (see the chart showing the historical development of Zionism).

The twentieth century saw a slow but miraculous step-by-step movement from the dreams of Herzl to the founding of the State of Israel in 1948 (fifty years after the first Zionist Congress—just as Herzl had predicted). Tragically, the Holocaust gave support and urgency to those calling for the creation of a state that only a dedicated few believed would ever come into existence. Yet it is undeniable that the perseverance and determination of those dedicated Zionists who pursued their dream unrelentingly were important instruments in fulfilling the work begun by the early Zionists.

Zionism after the founding of the State of Israel

Zionism as a movement has succeeded far beyond even Herzl's dreams. And because of this, since 1948 it has become a movement trying to grapple with its success. For people in Israel the question is whether they are Israeli Zionists, Israeli Jews, or simply Israeli citizens. For some people in Israel the absorption of new immigrants and the continued building of the state is seen as true Zionism. For others Zionism ceased to exist with the creation of the

state, and they see themselves, not as part of the fulfillment of a Jewish dream
or even as part of the Jewish people, but as citizens of a country called Israel.

In America, Zionism as an ideology is even more problematic. Israelis
call on Americans to settle in Israel as the real fulfillment of their Zionist
ideals. Yet most American Zionists do not plan to make aliyah. American
Zionism expends its energy in support of Israel, both financially and politically, but much of the force of real Zionist ideology has been dissipated or
lost. Indeed, the differences among the Zionist groups have blurred, and in
most cases these differences have little to do with differing ideologies. And
yet for many American Jews a commitment to Israel, perhaps rather than a
commitment to Zionism, is the cardinal tenet in their identity as Jews.

Such questions and ambivalence—on the part of both Israelis and Americans—will not be successfully resolved in the near future (if indeed they can
ever be). It is clear that the definition of a Zionist in 1897 must of necessity
differ from the definition of a Zionist in 1948 and afterward. The fundamental
question of whether true Zionism can reside within anyone who has no plans
to live in Eretz Yisrael is a post-1948 one. Such challenging and provocative
issues indicate the need for a modern poststate evaluation of Zionism and a
possible reinterpretation of Zionist ideology.

To give you some sense of Jewish history through an overview of the
history of the land of Israel and of Zionism, we include the timeline below
(see the *Encyclopaedia Judaica,* vol. 8, under "History" for a more complete
chart). The first four dates are only approximate.

Zionism

1700–1500 B.C.E.	Patriarchs
1280 B.C.E.	Exodus from Egypt
1250 B.C.E.	Conquest of Canaan by Joshua
1200 B.C.E.	Philistines settle in Eretz Yisrael
722 B.C.E	Samaria captured by Shalmaneser V
720 B.C.E.	Sargon makes Samaria an Assyrian province—mass deportation of Israelites
587 B.C.E.	Destruction of Jerusalem—mass deportation to Babylonia
538 B.C.E	First return under Sheshbazzar
520–15 B.C.E.	Temple rebuilt
458 B.C.E	Second return under Ezra
445 B.C.E	Walls of Jerusalem reconstructed under Nehemiah
428 or 398 B.C.E.	Second return under Ezra
332 B.C.E.	Alexander the Great conquers Eretz Yisrael
301 B.C.E.	Ptolemy I conquers Eretz Yisrael
219–17 B.C.E.	Antiochus III conquers most of Eretz Yisrael
198 B.C.E.	Seleucids take control of Eretz Yisrael
169–67 B.C.E.	Antiochus IV plunders Temple, storms Jerusalem, outlaws Judaism, profanes Temple
166–60 B.C.E.	Judah Maccabee leads rebellion of Hasmoneans, captures Jerusalem, falls in battle; Jonathan assumes leadership
140 B.C.E.	Simeon becomes ruler and high priest of an independent Judea
63–40 B.C.E.	Judea loses its independence to Romans
37 B.C.E.	Herod's rule begins
6 C.E.	Judea, Samaria, and Idumea formed into Roman provinces
66 C.E.	Beginning of revolt against Rome
70 C.E.	Siege of Jerusalem; Second Temple is destroyed
73 C.E.	Fall of Masada
116–17 C.E.	"War of Quietus"
132–35 C.E.	Bar Kokhba war
135–38 C.E.	Persecutions of Hadrian
351 C.E.	Jews and Samaritans revolt against Gallus; destruction of Bet Shearim
614–17 C.E.	Jewish rule established in Jerusalem under the Persians
638 C.E.	Jerusalem conquered by the Arabs
1099 C.E.	Jerusalem captured by Crusaders
1187 C.E.	Jerusalem captured by Saladin
1210–11	Settlement of 300 French and English rabbis
1244	Jerusalem captured by the Khwaruzms
1516	Eretz Yisrael conquered by the Turkish Empire
1700	Judah Hasid and his group arrive in Jerusalem
1742	Hayyim Attar and his group arrive in Jerusalem
1777	Menahem Mendel of Vitebsk and his group settle in Galilee
1808–10	Disciples of Elijah Gaon settle in Eretz Yisrael
1839	Citizenship extended to Turkish Jews
1840	Restoration of Turkish rule in Eretz Yisrael
1852	Confirmation of "status quo" in holy places
1882	Beginning of first aliyah; Rishon le-Zion founded
1883	Baron Edmond de Rothschild begins to help Jewish settlements
1890–91	Large numbers of Russian immigrants settle in Eretz Yisrael
1904	Beginning of second aliyah
1917	British capture Jerusalem
1918	Zionist Commission appointed
1919–23	Third aliyah begins
1920	British Mandate over Palestine; Arab riots in Jerusalem
1920	Histadrut and Haganah founded
1921	Arabs riot in Jaffa
1922	Churchill White Paper

1922	Mandate confirmed by League of Nations
1924–32	Fourth aliyah
1929	Arab riots in Jerusalem, massacre in Hebron and Safed
1930	Passfield White Paper
1933–39	Fifth aliyah; immigration from Germany
1934	Beginning of large-scale "illegal" immigration
1936	Arabs riot
1937	Peel Commission proposes partition of Palestine; Arab revolt; Haganah reunited
1938	Wingate organizes special Jewish units to fight Arab terrorism
1939	MacDonald White Paper
1941	Palmach organized
1944	Ezel and Lehi strike at the British
1945	Bevin's declaration on Palestine; "illegal" immigration intensified as is struggle against British
1946	British deport "illegal" immigrants to Cyprus
1947	U.N. General Assembly decides on partition of Palestine; beginning of Arab attacks
1948	Proclamation of State of Israel; seven Arab states invade; Negev liberated
1949	Cease-fire agreements with Egypt, Lebanon, Jordan, Syria; Israel becomes member of U.N.
1949–50	Airborne transport of 50,000 Jews from Yemen to Israel
1950	Western powers guarantee existing borders in the Middle East; Law of Return enacted in Israel
1950–51	Airborne transport of 123,000 Jews from Iraq to Israel
1951	Mass immigration continues
1953	Beginning of attacks by Arab infiltrators; first Israeli reprisal action
1954–55	Emigration from Morocco
1955	Fedayeen attacks and reprisal actions continue
1956	Jews of Egypt expelled
1956	Sinai campaign
1957	Israel evacuates Sinai; U.N. observers stationed on border with Egypt
1967	Six-Day War; Jerusalem united
1969	War of Attrition at Suez Canal front begins
1970–72	Increase of terrorism by Palestinian terrorist organizations
1972	Eleven Israeli athletes murdered by Palestinian terrorists at Munich Olympics
1973	Yom Kippur War launched by Egypt and Syria
1974	Arafat speaks at U.N.
1975	"Zionism Is Racism" resolution is passed by U.N.
1976	Israel commandos free 104 hostages from hijacked jet at Entebbe airfield in Uganda
1977	Egyptian president Anwar Sadat visits Jerusalem
1978	Camp David summit meeting is held between Egypt and Israel; PLO terrorists kill 38 people on hijacked bus near Tel Aviv; Israel invades southern Lebanon
1979	Peace treaty is signed between Egypt and Israel

ZIONISM

1862	Moses Hess publishes *Rome and Jerusalem*
1882	Leon Pinsker publishes *Autoemancipation*; Bilu organized in Russia
1884	Kattowitz Conference of Hibbat Zion
1887	Druzgench Conference of the Hovevei Zion
1889	Vilna Conference: Benei Moshe founded by Ahad Ha-Am
1890	Odessa Conference
1896	Herzl publishes *Der Judenstaat*
1897	First Zionist Congress in Basle, Switzerland
1899	Jewish Colonial Trust founded
1901	Jewish National Fund established
1902	Mizrachi founded
1903	Uganda project raised at Sixth Zionist Congress
1905	Seventh Zionist Congress rejects Uganda project
1906	Helsingfors program
1920	Keren Ha-Yesod established
1929	Jewish Agency expanded
1931	World Zionist Agency founded
1936	World Zionist Congress founded
1939	United Jewish Appeal founded
1942	American Jewish Conference endorses Biltmore program
1948	Founding of State of Israel

Models for Diaspora–Israel relations

The problems of the relationship between Jewry-in-the-land-of-Israel and Jewry-in-Dispersion did not arise in 1948 with the declaration of Israel's independence. The Diaspora has a history of more than twenty-six centuries. Its first chapter was written by those exiled to Babylonia after the destruction of the First Temple (587 B.C.E.), and the final chapter may never be written. However, the years since the rise of Israel have introduced an altogether new dimension in relationships between the Yishuv—the Jewish community in Eretz Yisrael—and the Golah—the Jewish community in the Diaspora. They are rife with Israeli expressions of doubt about the possibility of Jewish survival in the Golah (especially in the United States), while in the Golah (especially in this country) the "Jewishness" of Israel has been challenged and even denied by some.

All too frequently, however, those who address themselves to the theme of "Israel and the Diaspora" ignore the long history of this relationship. In fact, there are historical models of homeland-dispersion interaction that are more realistic and viable than those delineated in the years since the birth of the Zionist movement and in the years since the establishment of the State of Israel.

In modern Zionist literature the controversy between the affirmers of the Golah and the negators of the Golah is an important theme. In recent years, especially, the two camps have become increasingly articulate—and also increasingly antagonistic. The fact is that the Golah has been the counterpoint of the Yishuv—the Jewish community in Israel—for some twenty-six centuries. As a result, Jewish law and custom developed a modus vivendi for the relationship between the Jews of the Diaspora and those of the homeland. It was a relationship fruitful for both because it was predicated on sound premises:

1. the equal importance of the Golah and Yishuv communities

2. Eretz Yisrael's supremacy over any other country of Jewish settlement vis-à-vis halakhic concern, because certain mitzvot can only be performed in Eretz Yisrael; thus living elsewhere prohibits total fulfillment of traditional Judaism.

3. the acceptance by the Golah of special obligations to the Yishuv, i.e., compulsory and voluntary taxes for maintaining religious, educational, and social-service institutions

4. submission to the religious authority of the rabbis and teachers of the

Yishuv with respect to the Jewish calendar and the specific religious laws pertaining to the land of Israel. (This model is not relevant, since today the Israeli rabbinate is not recognized as authoritative outside the land of Israel.)

Choosing between alternatives is hard and painful, but Yishuv and Golah were never—nor are they now—alternatives pressing for an either/or choice. They are the harmonization of point and counterpoint. Yishuv and Golah *together* are the Jewish people. The Yishuv depends for support upon the Golah, and the Golah leans upon and needs the Yishuv.

This truth has been disregarded by some Zionist ideologists. The Golah cannot be negated in the manner of Ben-Gurion whose sole message to the Golah, "come to Israel," could only mean a cultural, religious, educational, and social death sentence for the distinct and vibrant Judaism represented in the Golah. The sound approach to the relationship of the Yishuv and the Golah is that of the pragmatist Ahad Ha-Am. Jews are naturally negators of the Golah because "exile" is tragic. We pray for the redemption from exile, for the Messiah. But the vast majority of the Jewish people—and this has been the case for two millennia—live in the Golah. They make this choice voluntarily. This means that instead of "negating" the Golah, efforts must be made to merge, at some level, the creativity of the Yishuv and that of the Golah. There must be close ties and cooperation between Yishuv and Golah so that each will contribute according to its capacities and receive in keeping with its needs. This was how Yishuv and Golah were constituted in the past—and this is how we, the generation of the Third Commonwealth, must relate.

Historical relationship between Yishuv and Golah
At the time of the destruction of the Second Temple (70 C.E.) the Jewish nation numbered between 4.5 and 5 million. Only about one million lived in Eretz Yisrael, while about 80 percent of Jewry lived in the Diaspora.

How did the exilic Jewish community of 1,900 years ago and afterward fit Eretz Yisrael into its personal and communal patterns of life? Principally in two ways: financial support and pilgrimage.

Financial support

Interestingly enough, the major physical expression of the Golah's identification with the Yishuv was the shekel—i.e., financial support similar to today's funds contributed to Israel. The history of the shekel, the first universal democratic tax on record, started with the biblical legislation. The shekel, or rather the half-shekel, was the tax every Jew over the age of twenty had to pay for the upkeep of the Tent of Meeting, for the support of the Temple, and later for the religious institutions of the Yishuv. The half-shekel was levied from the poor and the rich. The law stated that "the rich shall not pay more and the poor shall not pay less than half a shekel when giving the Lord's offering" (Exodus 30:15). It was a nominal sum that everyone could afford.

The Golah's eagerness to be action-identified with the Yishuv is attested to by the books of Ezra and Nehemiah. Those who stayed in Babylonia contributed liberally to the building of the Second Temple, and after its dedication the equivalent of at least a half-shekel was collected in the Babylonian Diaspora as a yearly tax for the maintenance of the Second Temple. Even the kohanim—the priests (who are exempt from all levies)—as well as minors without means of their own were obligated to pay the half-shekel. In this manner *every* Jew was involved and action-identified with the spiritual and religious center of the nation.

The dedication of the Golah in desiring identification with the Yishuv through payment of the half-shekel is evident from the fact that when the Romans at one time decreed that the collected sums were to be turned over to the imperial treasury as the *fiscus Judaicus* (Jewish tax), the Jews raised the sum all over again. Later, after the destruction of the Second Temple, the rabbis taking command of the leaderless Yishuv organized the shekel system and used the proceeds to cover the needs of the academies and their students. Their emissaries traveled to all the countries of the dispersion, seeing to the collection of the tax and its safe conveyance to the Holy Land. Like the half-shekel of biblical days, this shekel tax levied for the support of the Yishuv's academies was not regarded as tzedakah or as any form of charity. It was, quite simply, an obligatory tax for every Jew.

It is interesting that at the first Zionist Congress (1897), "shekel" was adopted as the term for the Zionist membership card that served as the certification of voting rights for delegates to Zionist Congresses (until 1968, when a new election system was introduced). In the United States the Zionist shekel cost one dollar. It signified membership and voting rights in the World Zionist Organization.

Pilgrimage

Another means of the Diaspora's physical identification with the homeland was pilgrimage. The Bible itself provided the historical basis for this custom:

Three times a year all your males shall appear before the Sovereign, the Lord (Exodus 23:17, 34:23).

Three times a year—on the Feast of Unleavened Bread, on the Feast of Weeks, and on the Feast of Booths—all your males shall appear in the place that He will choose. They shall not appear before the Lord empty-handed, but each with his own gift, according to the blessing that the Lord your God has bestowed upon you (Deuteronomy 16:16–17).

Such pilgrimages were called aliyah—literally, going up—and they became very important institutions in the lives of Jews. The preparation, financial burden, and the journey itself were severely taxing to the pilgrim. But the gains were enormous. The *Encyclopaedia Judaica* points out (vol. 13, p. 511):

Many of the new trends in Jewish spiritual life were ventilated in Jerusalem, and the pilgrim served as the vehicle for disseminating the ideas that were in constant ferment during the period. The pilgrimage had a considerable influence upon the life of the capital in a number of spheres; in the social sphere, from the presence there of Jews from every part of the Diaspora, and in the economic, from the vast sums spent by the thousands of pilgrims both for their own needs and on charity. It also had a national-political influence. The aliyah from all parts of Eretz Yisrael and the Diaspora strengthened the consciousness of national and social solidarity.

Taking the notion of aliyah seriously even in postbiblical times, hundreds of thousands of pilgrims would travel from within and without Eretz Yisrael to visit the Temple during Sukkot, Pesah, and Shavuot. After the destruction of the Second Temple, the pilgrimages still continued. Rituals sprang up that helped these pilgrims express their pain at the destruction, but the pilgrimages themselves continued. One fifth-century account reported a pilgrimage of over 100,000 Jews!

Such pilgrimages continued during the Middle Ages, despite the fact that Jewish pilgrims were often taxed and victimized by discriminatory legislation that made the pilgrimages difficult in the extreme. In modern times pilgrimages continued; however, they ceased to be restricted to Sukkot, Pesah, and Shavuot. Their main focus before the Six-Day War was the Tomb of David on Mount Zion, from where the Old City of Jerusalem could be seen. Following reunification of Jerusalem the Western Wall was reopened, and it in turn became the magnet for all pilgrims.

Adopting a model of relationship

The given in any further discussion is that while Jewish history proclaims Israel's centrality, the Diaspora has its own inherent value and importance in Jewish life that cannot be denigrated or seen as the reservoir of Israel. There must be an interdependence and mutuality between Israel and the Diaspora that allows for cooperation in a noncompetitive spirit. The historical model mentioned above could very well provide the modern model for how the Diaspora can relate to Israel.

The broad tenets are twofold:

1. There is an obligation to support Israel, which can include other material support besides financial support (which is assumed): the donation of time for political action, etc.

2. There is an obligation to support her emotionally—by making pilgrimages, by making consciousness of Israel part of Jewish life.

The financial, political, and emotional support of Israel provide, we believe, the broad guidelines to bring the Golah and the Yishuv closer.

The Jewish world is faced with the challenge of creating a meaningful and honest Yishuv-Golah relationship that gives honor to both and recognizes each one's importance. We will have to create cultural-religious bases anchored in Israel and other such bases anchored in the Diaspora, each reflecting different needs, each with its own dynamic and creativity. Neither should aspire, however, to be independent of the other, for they will thrive by making the most of interdependence. Israel will be built not at the expense and sacrifice of the Galut but by contributing to its survival. As in the talmudic era, we can build a strong Yishuv and a strong Golah—each creating and creative in giving and in receiving.

As Yishuv and Golah united, we have traversed more than two-thirds of our history thus far. Only as Yishuv and Golah joined together are we the Jewish people.

American-Israeli relations

We have been talking about the ideal models of relationship between the Diaspora and Israel. The fact is that since the founding of the state we have always been in the process of developing this relationship. It is a fluid one—constantly rearranging itself in new patterns and responding to new dynamics and demands. And just as this relationship is not a static one, it is also not an ideal one. There are tensions, problems, and issues that experience has not

prepared us to cope with. And these too are ever-changing and developing, forcing us anew—daily—to reevaluate, redefine, renegotiate.

Israel basically makes two demands on American Jews: financial support and aliyah. The first is a commitment that many American Jews are willing to undertake, but it is, nonetheless, problematic for both parties. The roles of donor and recipient are difficult ones, all the more so in this instance when Israeli reactions to financial support can sometimes fall into two categories: (1) resentment against "rich Americans" who give them money, a feeling of frustration and helplessness over the need to accept the support of "an outsider"—which carries with it the implicit admission of an inability to support oneself; (2) an attitude that this is not charity but rather support owed to Israel because it is the Jewish state. This notion is healthier than the first, but it has its own problems. Americans sometimes resent both the taking for granted of their support and the fact that Israelis do not recognize that Americans voluntarily assume their financial responsibility *by their own choice.* In American terms, the difference between an Israel that accepts funds as its due and an Israel that looks on American Jews as a sort of voluntary "silent partner" is enormous.

There is another tricky matter to negotiate here: a silent partner has the right to make his/her wishes known. It is no secret that while Israel is friendly, warm, and appreciative to American donors, it is firmly unresponsive to American interest in or comments about what it regards as its own internal affairs. The tension between accepting money and retaining independence is a difficult one for Israelis. The tension between giving money and feeling no sense of partnership is an equally difficult one for Americans, however, all the more so since no American Jew wants the whole relationship s/he has with Israel to be based solely on a financial need. We want to feel emotionally involved with, as well as financially responsible for, Israel. Yet staying on a kibbutz, for example, which is the symbol of Israel to many Americans, often reinforces the feeling of alienation from Israel. Kibbutzim that have guest houses for visitors treat those houses, by and large, solely as financial ventures. The accommodations are newer and more luxurious than many of the kibbutzniks' own homes, and, even worse, the guests are served separately in the dining room, often in a section partitioned off from the rest of the kibbutzniks. The kibbutzim don't realize that Jews come to stay there for a couple of days to be *at a kibbutz.* More importantly, very few Americans would balk at less than luxurious accommodations if they could feel a part of Israel. Americans who want an opulent vacation don't bother going to a kibbutz— they go to the Hilton. Generally those who go to a kibbutz sincerely want to meet the kibbutzniks, to dig their own hands into the land, to feel at peace with their Israeli brothers and sisters. Granted that all this might be difficult to accomplish without completely disrupting the kibbutz; still, the feeling that there must be some as-yet-unexplored middle ground remains strong.

American feelings of being exploited extend to the fund-raising apparatus. UJA is caught in the dilemma of trying to raise as much money as it can for Israel yet not being exploitative in the process. Certainly it can be said, however, that UJA has frequently come down too heavily on the fund-raising end of the scale. The misuse of the Holocaust is the most blatant exploitation of all and is felt by many to border on the obscene. UJA missions that tour Maalot and other such sites can only be said to show insensitivity to both the Americans and the people of Maalot. A reaction against these kinds of tours has begun to manifest itself. No one wants to feel like a slot machine where, if the right emotional buttons are pressed, increased financial support will pour forth. This whole area becomes particularly frightening when we realize that large numbers of Jews view Israel/UJA as their primary, if not their sole, identification with Judaism. Thus UJA's obligation to people who support Israel looms large. Because it recognizes this, UJA has established Young Leadership Groups: people who study together, go on missions to Israel together, retreat together, etc. These groups do not simply solicit in UJA's campaign (although there is no doubt that they do this); they are interested in a broader Judaism than perhaps their older counterparts, who found and find fulfillment in fund raising for a cause.

Finally, American fund raising on behalf of Israel faces another problem: the lack of accountability and the accompanying charges of mismanagement of funds. That funds are frequently diverted from their original destination or at times used unwisely is undeniable.

At the seventy-fifth convention of the Rabbinical Assembly of America the Conservative rabbis adopted this resolution on "Financial Accountability in Israeli-Diaspora Relations":

The American Jewish community cannot tolerate a situation which has led to allegations of corruption, mismanagement, and substantial losses of direly needed funds.

We urge, in this time of unprecedented peril for the State of Israel, that vehicles of mutual responsibility and accountability be established between Israel and the Diaspora.

We are especially concerned that no funds collected for strengthening Israel be diverted, under whatever disguises, for support of political parties and other purposes for which they were not originally intended.

We declare that funds for refugee settlement in Israel ought not to be diverted to "educational purposes" in the United States.

We must insist that all who are responsible for the disbursement of the philanthropic funds, whether in the United States or in Israel, be held accountable for the manner in which these funds are spent in the Diaspora.

While such statements acknowledge the problem, they do nothing to create change. It is clear that when vast sums are raised, a monitoring device is needed to protect these funds. There is no question here of "stepping on Israel's (internal) toes" or limiting her ability to make decisions, but simply the need to protect both donor and recipient.

Clearly there is no easy balance; the whole financial relationship lends itself to abuse. "Give till it hurts" is not a bad option and we are not suggesting that UJA politely ask you for your money and that you give whatever spare change you have around. There is a certain kedushah—holiness—in each

dollar raised. But there must be balance. Can we honestly say that any tactic justifies raising that extra dollar? Does UJA and/or Israel have a responsibility to those from whom they solicit? All these questions are problematical and not easily resolved.

As mentioned earlier, the other demand by Israel is for aliyah—immigration to Israel—which is even more problematic than the financial demand. In the first place, this demand has for the most part been ignored by American Jews. Yet when they're in Israel Americans are asked over and over again: When will you come to settle? David Ben-Gurion constantly stressed aliyah and denied the possibility of a viable Diaspora.

However, any large-scale aliyah from the U.S. would not only create difficulties for Israel, it would jeopardize the viability of the American Jewish community. Several years ago an Israeli involved in a project to foster communication between young Israelis and their American counterparts called for a yearly aliyah from America of fifty thousand Jews. In one decade this would strip the U.S. of most of its Jewish leadership and most of its committed Jews, since it is a general axiom that the most committed to Judaism/Zionism and the most adventurous are the ones who immigrate. To those committed to a vibrant Diaspora Jewish community, any large number of Jews making aliyah to Israel would be a serious loss.

There is also the question of whether the Israeli government really believes that Americans will come. It must be said that it probably does not, and yet significant amounts of money are spent in the U.S. encouraging aliyah.

There is at least one case where more than $80,000 was spent in an aliyah office from which not one single oleh emerged. Here is an area where the basic self-interests of Israel and the Diaspora are in conflict. Israel will go on encouraging aliyah, and Americans concerned with U.S. Jewry will try to encourage Jews here to build a vital and creative Diaspora; the tension between these two positions is great and irresolvable.

But there are other sides to all these coins. Diaspora Jewry also makes unrealistic demands on Israel. Many, especially those who are themselves not particularly religious, expect Israelis to be pious Jews and are angered upon finding Israelis who, for example, eat nonkosher food. While Americans want Israel to be a *Jewish* state, there are Israelis who insist that Israel is an *Israeli* state. They insist, therefore, that their commitment is to Israel rather than to Judaism.

In addition, we are shocked to discover financial scandals in Israel. Some people do not believe that there are Jewish criminals in Israeli jails. We somehow want Israel to be the perfect state with perfect people (all young and tanned and good-looking), and we feel betrayed when we learn, as inevitably we must, that the Israeli government is as least as bureaucratic, inefficient, and corrupt as our own and that Israelis are no more the "perfect Jews" than we are.

Worst of all are those who feel that their support of Israel lets them own a piece of the rock. They expect to be treated royally (watch the way some Americans act on El Al—they feel they own the airline!) and want the proper servitude and services to be available on demand. (This is, not so incidentally, the most serious deficiency in the donor-recipient relationship.) In fact, those who make such demands are asking the impossible.

Another issue that complicates the picture is the whole problem of the rabbinate's control over marriage, divorce, conversion, the question of who is a Jew, etc. The angry resentment on the part of many Israelis against this control, a potentially explosive issue, has remained submerged only because of the overriding concern for Israel's security. Primarily because the religious parties are needed in the majority coalition that governs the state (see Understanding Israeli Politics) and also for a number of historical reasons, the religious parties have managed to maintain a hold on all religious-civic functions in the country. Opposition from non-Orthodox Israelis and non-Orthodox Diaspora Jews (and a few Orthodox Jews also) has been of little avail. For the Conservative and Reform movements of America it is a particularly burning issue, since no movement except Orthodox Judaism is recognized in Israel. Indeed, any wedding, conversion, etc. performed by a non-Orthodox rabbi is considered nonlegal in Israel. Jews who refuse to have an Orthodox wedding or who aren't allowed to marry according to religious law (e.g., because a kohen—priest—can't marry a divorced woman or a man cannot marry a woman whose first husband did not give her a Jewish divorce) must leave Israel to be married. The Orthodox defend their position because they see Israel as a Jewish state and therefore a place where traditional Jewish law should be enforced as much as possible. In many cities, for example, stores are closed and buses do not run on Shabbat, though this is the only non-working day for many Israelis. Nontraditional Israelis see this as a curtailment of their rights: they have no other day to travel, shop, etc. For all these reasons, many Israelis have come to view the separation of synagogue and state and the freedom of religion (i.e., any type of Judaism or, indeed, secularism) as essential goals to be achieved.

The effects of this situation do not stop in Israel. They affect most American Jews who plan to live in Israel or who are considering the possibility that they might one day move there. Such people would, for example, have to

The real paradox is that Israel *is* a country like all other countries, while at the same time it *is* the most special of places—where David sang songs to Zion and where the Temple stood, the place toward which Jews have yearned all these centuries. But this specialness transcends—must *always* transcend—pools, central air conditioning, and luxury hotels.

have an Orthodox wedding—even though their preference might be Conservative. The same holds true for converts. Any conversion not performed by an Orthodox bet din—rabbinic court—would not be considered legally binding. In the case of an intermarriage, this issue could provide double misery since both the conversion *and* the marriage would be invalid. Similarly, the issue of the aguna—the woman who was not given a legal divorce by her first husband and so can never marry again (see the chapter on Jewish divorce in *Catalog 2* for full explanation)—is a particularly troubling one for Israel. While the Conservative movement in America has worked out methods for coping with the situation of the aguna, the Israeli rabbinate does not accept any Conservative decision, and so injustice continues to abound in those cases in which the Israeli rabbinate feels it cannot act. For all these reasons, many Americans have taken strong stands on this issue. It is a difficult and vexing problem, no less so for those who feel that Israel must continue to make civil decisions according to halakhah. It is also an issue that is sure to cause great pain, no matter which way the system operates.

For those who consider Israel the center of the Jewish world and look toward it for guidance and leadership in all areas of Jewish concern there is yet another area of tension. Over the years Israel has become the spokesperson for world Jewry. Yet Israel of necessity must be concerned with her own self-interest. What happens when the interests of the Jews of Argentina and the interests of Israel are in conflict? What would happen if the Soviet Union said to Israel, "If you keep quiet about Soviet Jewry, we'll grant recognition and aid to Israel." We Jews in America might decide that the issue of Soviet Jewry is more important than diplomatic recognition and aid. Yet Israel might feel differently. What then? What if it is not a matter of sacrifice but simply a matter of control? For example, should a center for Diaspora education supported in large part by American Jews be located primarily in Israel or in the Diaspora?

Many here believe that a subservient relationship on the part of the Diaspora is not good for either party. Despite this feeling, Israel has continued to oppose any world Jewish organization that it did not control. This has created

many tensions and great conflict. The most recent case, in fact, dealt with Soviet Jewry. A serious question of how to handle the problem of noshrim—those Soviet Jewish immigrants who choose not to live in Israel—has recently arisen. The situation clearly and painfully points out the fact that there are positions Israel must maintain for its own internal needs that are in direct conflict with the wishes and attitudes of Jews outside Israel.

Israel's population problems, which include a significantly lower birthrate than her Arab neighbors as well as a serious (though undiscussed) problem of yeridah—emigration—could be significantly alleviated if she were to be the full recipient of all Soviet Jewish emigration. Currently almost 70 percent of all Soviet Jewish immigrants settle outside of Israel (this contrasts, incidentally, with 1 percent in 1973, 36 percent in 1975, and 66 percent in 1979). Israel maintains that such fallout is inevitable since Israel, with its multifaceted economic, social, and political problems, is in no position to compete with the United States for immigration. Israel maintains that if all Jewish-sponsored transit aid to noshrim were cut off, they would perforce settle in Israel.

American Jews have (at least until now) maintained that Jews should be helped to leave the Soviet Union regardless of their Zionist tendencies—and that furthermore our parents and grandparents had no restrictions placed on their immigration, so to place restrictions on Soviet Jewish immigrants would be unfair and hypocritical (who are *we* to tell anyone to live in Israel?).

The question of interference and noninterference in each other's policies is a tricky one. On the one hand it is clear that a hands-off policy for domestic affairs is desirable; on the other hand, if we are two halves of a whole are we not legitimately concerned with each other's affairs? Negotiating these two positions is quite difficult. Even with the best of intentions, abuse is possible. Yitzhak Rabin, the Israeli ambassador to the U.S. at the time of the American presidential elections of 1972, felt free to urge American Jewry to vote for Nixon because it was in Israel's interest that he be elected president. Rabin maintained this position in *his* country's best interest without seriously considering whether it was in the best interests of America. How beneficial Nixon was to America and the American system is now a matter of history. Similarly, our attempts at intervention in Middle East affairs meet polite but firm resistance. Have we the right to urge concessions on the Israelis in the hopes of achieving a Mideast settlement? Has Israel the responsibility to consider our concerns seriously? All these questions pose difficulties. If we are all lovers of our community, then we should be able to criticize or praise each other. Yet in the final analysis internal decisions always rest with each respective country. No matter how much we might criticize Israeli policies, only Israel can change them. And no matter how much Israel advocates a certain American policy, only Americans can support it. Our leverage is in reality very minor.

The truth is that Israel's influence on us is much stronger than we realize,

but this is only because we want it that way. We choose to let Israel exert great influence on American Jewish affairs, and this choosing is an interesting phenomenon. Why does it exist? It is difficult to say. American Jews are unreasonably insecure. A recent Harris poll showed that a large number of Jews said that they expected to be blamed for any future oil embargo, yet only a minority of gentiles polled said that they would, in fact, blame the Jews. Perhaps in response to our insecurity, we see Israel as our lifeline when we feel threatened. Or perhaps the Holocaust has taught us that anything can happen, and we feel that we must do everything *and* anything to prevent Israel's destruction. It is possible that the old image of a Jew passively accepting defeat threatens us and thus we identify with the new image of the Israeli soldier or kibbutznik. Just as they are strong and fierce, we shall be strong and fierce in our defense of Israel. We drown criticism and fight for unqualified support of Israel. We brook no criticism of Israel; anyone who even slightly criticizes her is suspect of being an anti-Semite. We've attacked senators who have positions resembling some of the dovish elements in Israel's governing coalition. Whereas in Israel recognition of the Palestinians can be debated, here such debate is labeled as self-hating and anti-Israel. Some Israelis resent those who call for the defense of every inch of the occupied territories to the last *Israeli.* This is partly the resentment felt toward any American suggestion (whether dovish or hawkish), for, after all, it is *their* country and *their* lives that are at stake. Yet both our militancy and their resentment of it is more complex than that. In the mainstream American Jewish community today the one factor that can instantly make you a good Jew is loyalty to Israel. To criticize Israel is to risk being ostracized and to risk the loss of all credibility.

The painful and perplexing problem arises when we are faced with the realization that we feel a certain Israeli position or policy or act to be wrong. Do we support Israel anyway because she is deserving of every Jew's support? Do we stand silently by, neither supportive nor condemning? Or must we take a stand at some point, expressing our loving disapproval? And—the most crucial question of all—where, how, and under what circumstances should this stand be taken? Do we save our critical comments only for the Jewish community's ears? Do we acknowledge the probability that our criticism will be more effective if voiced in circles beyond the Jewish community? How do we weigh the need to be effective against the value of not "hanging dirty linen in public"? And—the worst ordeal of all to face—how do we measure the need to be honest with our own personal ideals (perhaps, even, to our perceptions of traditional Jewish values) with every Jew's obligation and need to stand united with the community? How do we live with ourselves either way?

Most of the Jewish community will respond to the above dilemmas in two ways: (1) by thinking that Israel is never wrong (or at least not yet) and (2) by keeping quiet. Israel is in dire danger and needs our support, they argue. Anyone who criticizes her at this time is at best a dupe who is aiding Israel's enemies and at worst a self-hating Jew. For some people who both love Israel and disagree at times with her for her sake, the above responses are inadequate. These people find it vexing that some criticisms voiced by Israelis cannot be voiced by Americans. Such a situation, they feel, borders on needless paranoia.

All of this has been a beginning—a raising of some of the issues and an acknowledgment that neither the Diaspora nor Israel is blameless. But we must strive to bridge these gaps, alleviate the tensions, and cope with the problems. We look, not toward a totally calm sea, but rather toward a dynamic, creative joining together in mutual respect.

Financial support of Israel

Needs have grown. A shekel—if we equate it to one dollar—given by every Jew in the world would produce approximately $14,300,000. In its regular appeal for 1976 (the last year these figures were made available to the public in the 1980 *American Jewish Year Book*) the United Jewish Appeal, and its emergency appeal raised $265,883,000. Clearly contributions of one dollar by all could not match these figures.

There is, however, the precedent in Judaism for each to contribute according to ability. The balance that has to be reached is a delicate one. Given your available "giving-away money," how much do you use to support Israel and how much do you use to support American Jewish (and non-Jewish) institutions? No one can dictate this sort of decision. But if we take seriously the existence of Diaspora Judaism, we must take seriously American Jewish institutional needs and must not, under normal circumstances, let these needs be treated less seriously than the needs of Israel—which is not to say that we can abrogate our responsibility to support Israel. The assumption of this chapter is that each and every Jew must, according to ability, financially support Israel. This is a Jewish obligation that cannot be ignored.

Essentially, you can fulfill this obligation to support Israel in three ways:

1. You can give money directly to your local Jewish appeal (see below) or to the United Jewish Appeal.

2. You can give money to any one of the hundreds of organizations that support specific Israeli or Israel-centered projects.

3. You can become an investor in Israel.

Local Jewish appeals

Your local Jewish federation, welfare fund, or community council performs one or all of the following services:

1. supports local, national, and overseas services

2. coordinates local services to eliminate duplication and strengthen programs

3. in small and some intermediate cities, directly administers some or all local social services

What this list tells you is that when you give money to your local Jewish campaign you are supporting a variety of services that go beyond the local needs of your community. In fact, as a general rule about 45 cents of every dollar is retained for local and national community needs, and about 55 cents goes to support overseas needs, with the large bulk of that going to national UJA, which in turn supports Israel.

If we take into account the money given directly to the Israel Emergency Fund, the ratio changes drastically. *Of the total monies raised in federation and Israel Emergency Fund campaigns, about 68–70 percent annually goes to overseas aid via UJA.*

This figure will, of course, vary with the size of your local community and its local needs, but as a rule of thumb this is an accurate appraisal.

Now let's trace a little more carefully exactly what your giving options are and what happens to the money you give—where it goes, what the overlap is, etc. The accompanying chart will be most helpful if you understand the following preliminary information:

Israel Emergency Fund: The IEF was created for people who don't want to support any local communal institutions but would rather have their money go directly to Israel. United Jewish Appeal statistics maintain that 97 percent of this money goes directly to Israel (i.e., 3 percent is overhead for handling the money).

Israel Education Fund: The Israel Education Fund, which is administered by UJA, accepts minimum donations of $100,000 and accepts such donations only after the donor's normal UJA pledge has been made. These monies go for large capital projects in Israel—i.e., the construction of schools, community

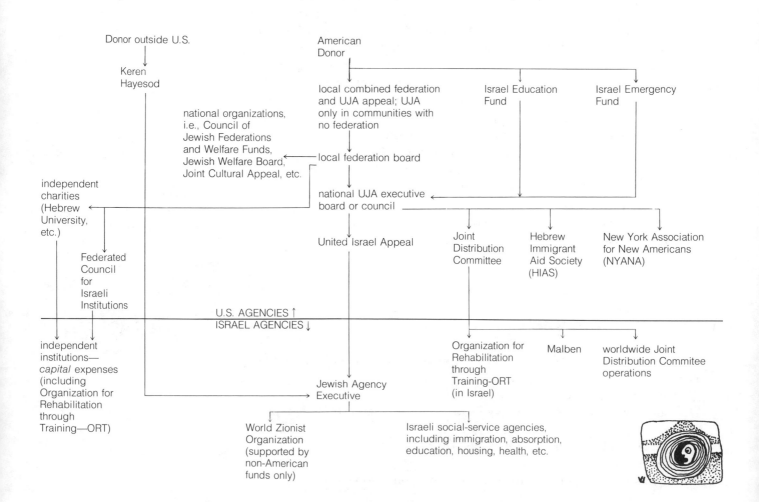

centers, etc.; generally, the donor's name is associated with the newly created institution.

United Jewish Appeal: The national UJA is *solely* a fund-raising body; it has no authority to allocate funds. In addition, funds cannot be raised for support of any non-American political organizations—which explains why American money raised through UJA cannot go to support the World Zionist Organization in Israel. Theoretically UJA is accountable to the federation boards for how its money is spent. Practically, however, such accountability is seldom rendered.

United Israel Appeal: The UIA is the major beneficiary of UJA and in turn distributes funds to the Jewish Agency. It monitors the funds it distributes and is (in theory) accountable to the UJA. The structure described above applies only to the United States, for various political and legal reasons. Outside the United States, in Latin America and Western Europe, there is Keren Hayesod, which is the equivalent of the UJA and UIA combined. In fact, Keren Hayesod is synonymous with UIA but also raises money à la UJA. One major difference is that funds raised by the Keren Hayesod support the World Zionist Organization (unlike UJA funds, as explained above.)

Jewish Agency: The Jewish Agency is a nongovernmental agency that supports the World Zionist Organization and social-service agencies in Israel. It is an implementing agency.

World Zionist Organization: The WZO has a 50 percent partnership in the Jewish Agency. In 1972–73 the WZO budget was about $30 million. Because of the magnitude of its budget it wields considerable power in world Jewish affairs. It is a political-ideological agency that has created a labyrinthine maze of subdepartments in the organization, many of which manage to duplicate one another's work with distressing frequency. Such departments include the Departments of Education and Culture in the Diaspora with (if you can believe this one!) separate religious and secular departments; Youth and Hechalutz (pioneering) Department; the Information and Organization Department; and the Department for Sephardi and Oriental communities.

Independent Israeli institutions

Besides giving through federation or UJA structures, you can support Israeli institutions through American counterpart offices (only if there is an American office will your gift be tax deductible). There are people who are uncomfortable about certain political postures maintained by the Israeli government and/or dislike for various reasons the appeal mechanisms in the U.S. To these people we would say that the following list gives you options to fulfill your responsibility to Israel. Few people would refuse to support an orphanage, a school, an old-age home, or a hospital because of political concerns.

In addition, for many who give to UJA, etc., this list is a way to support a cause that particularly interests you. Some of these institutions also receive money from the Jewish Agency, but usually for specific projects. Capital expenses of these institutions are not supported by the Agency. Many of these organizations must raise money because the funds they receive from the Agency (and other sources) do not fully cover their operating budgets. It is neither desirable nor practical for the Jewish Agency to fully support these institutions. Your donation can be extremely important to them.

America-Israel Cultural Foundation, Inc.
4 E. 54th St.
New York, NY 10022
supports Israeli cultural institutions

American Committee for Shaare Zedek Hospital in Jerusalem, Inc.
49 W. 45th St.
New York, NY 10036
supports hospital

American Committee for the Weizmann Institute of Science, Inc.
515 Park Ave.
New York, NY 10022
supports the Weizmann Institute

American Friends of Bnei Akiva Yeshivas in Israel
41 E. 42nd St.
New York, NY 10016

American Friends of Boy's Town Jerusalem, Inc.
475 Fifth Ave.
New York, NY 10017
supports home for orphans

American Friends of Haifa University
60 E. 42nd St.
New York, NY 10017

American Friends of the Israel Museum
10 E. 40th St.
New York, NY 10022

American Friends of the Jerusalem Mental Health Center–Ezrath Nashim, Inc.
10 E. 40th St.
New York, NY 10016

American Friends of the Kibbutzim in Israel
150 Fifth Ave.
New York, NY 10036

American Friends of Life Line for the Old
1 State St. Plaza
New York, NY 10004
projects for the elderly

American Friends of the Mirrer Yeshivah in Jerusalem
1133 Broadway
New York, NY 10010

American Friends of the Tel Aviv University, Inc.
342 Madison Ave.
New York, NY 10017

American Friends of Yeshivat Kerem B'Yavneh
6 E. 45th St.
New York, NY 10036

American–Israeli Lighthouse, Inc.
30 E. 60th St.
New York, NY 10022
supports education and rehabilitation center for the blind, especially Migdal Or, a center in Haifa

American Mizrachi Women (formerly Mizrachi Women's Organization of America)
817 Broadway
New York NY 10003
supports social-service and Orthodox educational programs

American ORT Federation, Inc.
(Organization for Rehabilitation through Training)
817 Broadway
New York, NY 10003
supports vocational training throughout the world, especially in Israel; has many subgroups, e.g., Women's American ORT

American Physicians Fellowship, Inc, for the Israel Medical Assn.
1622 Beacon St.
Brookline, MA 02146

American Red Magen David for Israel, Inc.
888 Seventh Ave.
New York, NY 10019
supports Israel's equivalent of the Red Cross

American Society for Technion–Israel Institute of Technology, Inc.
271 Madison Ave.
New York, NY 10016

Americans for a Music Library in Israel
220 S. State St., Rm. 1208
Chicago, IL 60604
supports musical education and libraries in Israel

Association for Mental Health Aid to Israel (AMHAI)
30 Michigan Ave., Suite 901
Chicago, IL 60602
sends money to Israel for general mental health needs; tries to bring together Israeli and American professionals

Bar-Ilan University in Israel
641 Lexington Ave.
New York, NY 10022

Bikur Cholim Hospital, Jerusalem
119 Fifth Ave.
New York, NY 10011

Children Day Nurseries
338 Third Ave.
Brooklyn, NY 11215
provides clothing for children in
nurseries in Israel

Diskin Orphan Home of Israel
156 Fifth Ave.
New York, NY 10010

Federated Council of Israel Institutions
(FCII)
38 Park Row
New York, NY 10038
raises funds for a large number of
traditional institutions, receives
allocation from federations

Friends of Israel National Opera, Inc.
150 Fifth Ave.
New York, NY 10011

Friends of Jerusalem–Midrash
Seminary, Ltd.
630 Third Ave.
New York, NY 10017

Friends of Jerusalem College of
Technology
21 E. 40th St.
New York, NY 10010

General Israel Orphans Home for Girls
in Jerusalem, Inc.
132 Nassau St.
New York, NY 10004

Hadassah, the Women's Zionist
Organization of America, Inc.
50 W. 58th St.
New York, NY 10019
supports hospital, schools, youth
aliyah villages

Hebrew University–Technion Joint
Maintenance Appeal
11 E. 69th St.
New York, NY 10021
conducts maintenance campaigns

Israel Music Foundation
109 Cedarhurst Ave.
Cedarhurst, NY 11516
supports the growth of music in
Israel

Jewish National Fund of America
42 E. 69th St.
New York, NY 10021
agency for the purchase and
development of the land of
Israel

Keren-Or, Inc. (Israel Institutions for
the Blind)
1133 Broadway
New York, NY 10010

Keren Yaldenu, Inc.
51 E. 42nd St.
New York, NY 10017
concerned with saving children
from missionaries

Pioneer Women, the Women's Labor
Zionist Organization of America, Inc.
200 Madison Ave.
New York, NY 10016
aids social services in Israel

Religious Zionists of America—Hapoel
Hamizrachi—Women's Organization of
25 W. 26th St.
New York, NY 10010
aids the education and health of
Israeli children

United Charity Institutions of
Jerusalem
1141 Broadway
New York, NY 10001
supports traditional institutions in
Israel

United States Committee–Sports for
Israel, Inc.
130 E. 59th St.
New York, NY 10001
supports sports in Israel, especially
the Maccabiah

Women's League for Israel, Inc.
1860 Broadway
New York, NY 10023
supports the welfare of young
people in Israel

Women's Social Service for Israel, Inc.
240 W. 98th St.
New York, NY 10025
supports aid to the aged

Yeshiva Beth Abraham of Jerusalem
73 W. 47th St.
New York, NY 10036

Yeshiva Chaye Olam of Jerusalem
38 Park Row
New York, NY 10038

Yeshiva Heichal Hatalmud of Tel Aviv
217 E. Broadway
New York, NY 10002

Yeshiva Meah Shearim of Jerusalem
203 Broadway
New York, NY 10007

Yeshiva Petach Tikva Israel
249 E. Broadway
New York, NY 10002

Yeshivath Hanegev
860 W. 181st St.
New York, NY 10033

The organizations listed all maintain American offices, so contributions to them are tax deductible under the American tax system. There are, in addition, many worthwhile projects and organizations in Israel that do not have American offices. The state of Israel Ministry of Social Welfare publishes an annual directory of those agencies that have official recognition by the Israeli government. This directory is available from

Department of Public Institutions
Ministry of Social Welfare
Jerusalem, Israel

They will also answer all inquiries about these institutions.

We make no guarantees or claims either about the organizational list or about the agencies listed in the directory mentioned above because we have no method for evaluating any agency's efficiency, use of funds, or reliability. As with any organization to which you give your money, we urge you to investigate and inquire. Despite this disclaimer, these are certainly among the best-known institutions, although there are many smaller efforts worthy of support (for examples, see Danny Siegel's "Tale of the Shaliah/Messenger" in the Tzedakah chapter).

While some of the goals of these organizations may sound similar, the differences are frequently based on political or religious affiliations. In addi-

Please Note: This list makes no claims to being comprehensive. Every organization (almost) sponsors some activity in Israel. What we chose to include were the more significant of the larger organizations that do have such multipurpose tasks to accomplish. If we have left out any significant group, please let us know.

tion, some of these organizations are solely fund-raising organs, while others have larger purposes and broader scopes of activity (e.g., Hadassah). For a fuller description of many of these organizations, see the *American Jewish Year Book*.

Investment

Finally, you can become an investor in Israel. There are a number of ways to do this, and each has its own different emphasis, result, etc. Recent business scandals in Israel have created a sense of mistrust on the part of potential American investors in Israel. It must be realized that such scandals are inevitable in any country and that the real victims of the resulting mistrust are the Israeli economy and people. We would urge you, as good business sense would indicate, to consider carefully and investigate all aspects of any venture you are thinking of undertaking. But we would urge you to become a supporter of Israel by making a direct investment. Your risks are probably no higher there than they are here, and the gains will be felt far beyond your own personal profit.

DIRECT INVESTMENT

If you are an American businessperson one of the most important ways you can support Israel is through your own or your company's direct investment in Israel, either by setting up businesses or creating partnerships. The Law for the Encouragement of Capital Investments gives special benefits to investors in the form of tax relief and simplified investment procedures; in general, Israel does all it can to encourage such investment. For information, contact

Government of Israel Investment Authority
850 Third Ave.
New York, NY 10022

Government of Israel Trade Center
350 Fifth Ave., 19th fl.
New York, NY 10001

Regional offices for Government of Israel Economic Offices are located at

111 E. Wacker Dr.
Chicago, IL 60611

659 S. Highland Ave.
Los Angeles, CA 90042

Also, the Israel Aliyah Center regularly publishes "Tour Vealeh Business Offers," a booklet of business offers in various fields and at various levels of investment, which are collected in Israel and compiled here. You can get on their mailing list by sending your name, address, and phone number to

Tour Vealeh—Israel Aliyah Center
515 Park Ave.
New York, NY 10022

STOCKS

You can buy shares in the Tel Aviv stock exchange. This is best done through a brokerage firm in the United States:

Leumi Securities Corporation
18 E. 48th St.
New York, NY 10017

They operate some two hundred investment clubs around the country, which are excellent for small investors as well as large ones. As an added bonus the commission that Leumi takes from the sales of stocks is considered small by American standards.

ISRAELI BONDS

Israeli bonds are issued by the Israeli government and they function as government bonds do here. The revenue from these bonds goes directly to the Israel government development budget, which serves as a source for capital investment. Buying Israeli bonds is the most effective way to contribute directly to the Israeli government, since the bonds provide about $370 million out of the $10 billion total government revenue annually. The rate of interest is 4 percent per year for individuals and 5½ percent for institutions; the bonds mature at the end of fifteen years. By law (and business sense) the Israel Bond organization is limited to a maximum 6 percent for overhead, so that your money is of the most direct benefit to Israel. The Israel Bond organization will send you a prospectus. They maintain local offices throughout the United States even in places like Memphis, Tennessee. The main office is located at

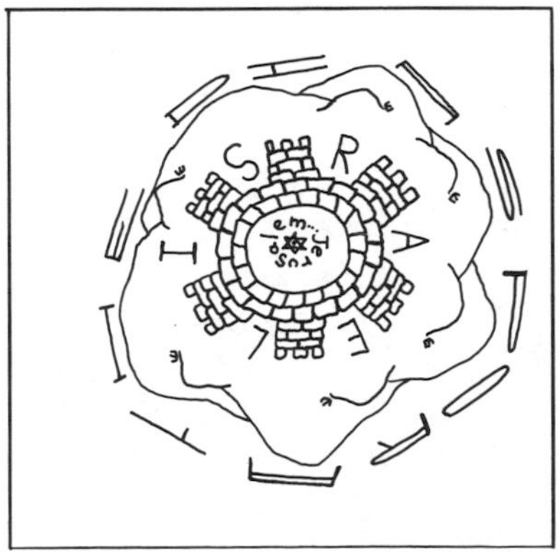

State of Israel Bonds
215 Park Ave. South
New York, NY 10003

Also of interest to investors are two publications. One is a bimonthly magazine published by American Israel Ventures Corp.:

Israel Securities Review
557 Beach 129th St.
Belle Harbor, NY 11694

Dun & Bradstreet has prepared the first official guide to commercial businesses in Israel: *Dun's Guide Israel;* it's available from

Dun & Bradstreet International
99 Church St.
New York, NY 10007

BANKS

You can deposit funds in Israel through four Israeli banks that have branches in New York:

Bank Leumi	**Bank Hapoalim**
579 Fifth Ave.	10 Rockefeller Plaza
New York, NY 10017	New York, NY 10020
Israel Discount Bank	**United Mizrahi Bank**
511 Fifth Ave.	630 Fifth Ave.
New York, NY 10016	New York, NY 10016

Interest rates fluctuate daily and are paid at the rates of the international money market. These banks are not insured by the FDIC but, not unexpectedly, they are backed by the Israeli government. According to Israeli law, there is no withholding tax on interest earned for deposits of three months or more. Also, there are no property taxes, estate duties, or any other interest on these bank accounts.

REAL ESTATE

Buying apartments and commercial real estate in Israel is of direct benefit to the Israeli economy. Recently there has been a growing trend among Americans to forgo buying a condominium in Florida and other vacation spots in favor of purchasing an apartment in Israel.

Besides benefiting the Israel economy by the simple purchase of real estate, you also provide a badly needed rental unit to Israelis who cannot yet afford the very steep down payment necessary to purchase their own apartment. That in itself is a mitzvah, and no one has ever complained that they were unable to find a tenant for their Israeli apartment during the ten or eleven months a year it is vacant. The criticism (a just one) has been leveled that what has been built in Israel are superluxurious apartments to cater to Americans instead of the more moderately priced units necessary for Israeli families who cannot afford American standards of luxury. The answer to such criticism is obvious. There is no need to purchase an apartment that patently mimics American rather than Israeli values. Buy an apartment that will help Israelis too; keep in mind what their needs are and how you will want to "fit into" the country when you are there. Apartments can be bought through relatives or friends in Israel or else through:

Isralom—Israel Home & Real Estate Corp.
800 Second Ave.
New York, NY 10017

Israeli products

If you own any kind of business, selling Israeli products can be an important way of helping the Israeli economy. (It goes without saying that everyone ought to be buying them too! See Bringing Israel to Your Galut.) All Israeli products are priced competitively and are of equal or superior quality to American counterparts. To obtain information about your particular line get hold of: *The Directory of Importers and Distributors of Israeli products in the U.S.*, available for $2 from

The American-Israel Chamber of Commerce
500 Fifth Ave.
New York, NY 10017

In general, for this type of information you should be in contact with the American-Israel Chamber of Commerce, which has offices in New York, Chicago, Los Angeles, Miami, Philadelphia, Detroit and Cleveland.

Also get in touch with the government of Israel Trade Center:

111 W. 40th St., Suite 2202
New York, NY 10018

659 S. Highland Ave.
Los Angeles, CA 90042

111 E. Wacker Dr.
Chicago, IL 60611

BUYING ISRAELI PRODUCTS—IN ISRAEL

While there are many reasons to visit Israel, one of the direct effects of any visit you make there ought to be your purchase of Israeli products, purchases which have a direct effect on the Israeli economy. Tourism in general is an important factor in the health of the Israeli economy. The Israel Government Tourist Office

350 Fifth Ave.
New York, NY 10001

5 S. Wabash Ave.
Chicago, IL 60603

6380 Wilshire Blvd.
Los Angeles, CA 90048

795 Peachtree St. NE
Atlanta, GA 30308

102 Bloor St. West
Toronto, Ont. M5S 1M8

can help you with your plans. Small, intermediate, and large Israeli businesses (although anyone who has been to Israel knows enough to put the emphasis here on "small") will be affected by your patronage. We American Jews stuff our homes full of French, German, Indian, Chinese, and American art—and then add a little green menorah that we stick in a corner somewhere as a memorial to bad Jewish art. Israeli craftsmen are producing magnificent pottery, blown glass, paintings, batik, weavings, etc. And there are Israeli clothes, sandals, perfumes, foods, games, records . . .

COINS

The Israeli government distributes commemorative coins and Israeli State Medals. In the past these coins have increased substantially in value, since they are produced in limited editions. Profits from the sale of such coins and medals are earmarked for restoration and preservation of historical sites. Contact

For stamps, see Judaica Philately in *Catalog 2*, pp. 391–99.

Coins and Medal Dept.
Government of Israel
350 Fifth Ave.
New York, NY 10001

Israel Investment Authority
850 Third Ave.
New York, NY 10022

publishes the following helpful pamphlets:

1. *The Advantages of Investing in Israel (Manufacturing)*
2. *The Advantage of Investing in Israel (Tourism)*
3. *The Encouragement of Capital Investments Law, 5719–1959*
4. *A Word About Taxes*
5. *The Encouragement of Industry (Taxes) Law, 5729–1969*
6. *Israel's Labor Market*
7. *The Advantages of Investing in Israel: Supplement*
8. *How to Sell Duty-Free in Europe and the USA*
9. *Business Organization and Financial Reporting in Israel*

They also publish guides to various industries in Israel, which are available on request.

Bringing Israel to your Galut

The "Israel-consciousness" prevalent all through daily Jewish life has given rise to certain traditions that seek to incorporate this consciousness into ritual life. Among these:

Tu b'Shevat: The holiday of Tu b'Shevat is the festival of the New Year for Trees, celebrated on the fifteenth day of the month of Shevat (see *Catalog 1*, p. 134). It is a minor holiday in the celebratory cycle but one that has certain charming customs associated with it. In the European Ashkenazic communities the custom arose of eating many different kinds of fruits—especially fruits from Eretz Yisrael—and this custom continues today.

Furthermore, in modern-day America and Israel the custom arose during this holiday for schoolchildren to plant trees in Israel. American children take to Hebrew school or Hebrew day school their dimes and quarters, which are collected in slotted cards provided by the Jewish National Fund. When $3 has been collected, it is sent to

Jewish National Fund
42 E. 69th St.
New York, NY 10021

who then plant a tree donated by that class. Needless to say, adults can plant trees too. A nice way to express your feelings of happiness or condolence for someone is to buy a tree. JNF will send a card in your name for each tree you plant.

Burial: As mentioned in the first section of this chapter, it became the custom for Jews to be buried in Israel whenever possible. (Those for whom this was impossible managed to acquire a bit of Israeli earth to be buried with.) In America arrangements can be made through your local funeral director, who can contact any one of the three people in America who are licensed by the Israeli government to handle such arrangements.

Maalin Ba Kodesh Society
Eliezer Gibbs
26 Canal St.
New York, NY 10002

Pincus B. Mandel
175 Lee Ave.
Brooklyn, NY 11204

Solomon Shoulson
2412 E. 14th St.
Brooklyn, NY 11202

Unfinished House: After the destruction of Jerusalem certain customs arose as signs of mourning. The rabbis declared: "A person may whitewash his house, but he should leave a small area unfinished in remembrance of Jerusalem" (Tosefta Sotah 15: 12–14; Bava Batra 60b). This statement was interpreted in various ways. Some people left a corner of their house unpainted. Others left part of the building uncompleted.

Zimrat haaretz

Then their father Israel said to them, "If it must be so, do this: take some of the choice products of the land [zimrat haaretz] in your baggage, and carry them down as a gift" (Genesis 43:11).

Everything grown and produced in Eretz Yisrael is in a special class of "chosenness." Israeli products have always been treasured for themselves. Moreover, "Trade rather than aid" is a popular slogan of Israeli's economists. Israel's economy depends on its exports, which earn much-needed foreign currency. It is, then, a double mitzvah to buy Israeli products:

    1. You help Israel to become self-supporting (some economists have said that if every American Jew were to buy just one piece of clothing made in Israel, i.e., one shirt, dress, suit, raincoat, etc., many of Israel's economic problems would be alleviated).

    2. You strengthen your personal bond with the land.

    The range of possibilities for purchasing Israeli products is enormous, including such diverse products as Israeli

wines and liqueurs	**foods**—including matzah,
automobile parts	Israeli olives, cheese,
jewelry	gefilte fish, soup concentrates, candy
plastics	**fashions**
children's clothing	**home furnishings and furniture**
diamonds	**pottery**
Jewish ritual objects	**Jaffa oranges**
toys	

There are many other ways to make Israel part of your Galut. Plug in wherever you are most comfortable.

Jaffa oranges, in season, are absolutely delicious.

Ben-Azer
4 Park Ave.
New York, NY 10016

will send gift cartons of supreme-size Jaffa oranges anywhere in the United States except California and Arizona. In addition, Trude Weiss-Rosmarin recommends the perfumes and beauty products—especially the avocado face cream. And the *Encyclopaedia Judaica* is an "Israeli product" that can open up whole new vistas in your Jewish life. It's available from:

Keter Publishing Co.   **Shaare Zedek Hospital**
440 Park Ave. South   **49 W. 45th St.**
New York, NY 10016   **New York, NY 10036**

Ta-kol Buyer's Club offers a wide range of gift items and books from Israel. To get their catalog, write

Ta-Kol Ltd.
28 Bar Kokhba St.
P.O. Box 33379
Tel Aviv, Israel

Israel Buy Mail will send you a tallit from Israel. They can be reached at

Israel Buy Mail   **To Israel with Love**
58 Horev St.   **61–08 218th St.**
Haifa, Israel   **Bayside, NY 11364**

provides a gift shopping service that sends fruits, flowers, and candies to Israel.

Mrs. Irving Freistat
1 N. Dawes Ave.
Kingston, PA 18704

provides a meat service that will send twenty pounds of kosher meat to family or friends in Israel.

A complete list of Israeli American importers of Israeli goods is available from

Government of Israel Trade Center
111 W. 40th St.
New York, NY 10018

Also, a booklet called *Made in Israel* includes a complete listing of all Israeli products and services on sale in the United States. Although published in 1973, it is still helpful and, in any case, there is some talk of updating and reissuing it. It is available from $2 from

American-Israel Chamber of Commerce
500 Fifth Ave.
New York, NY 10017
(212) 354-6510

Keeping in touch

NEWSPAPERS

You should keep informed about Israel—what is happening there and what these things mean. You can keep in touch with political developments by reading Israeli newspapers—either in Hebrew or in English.

The Jerusalem Post
110 E. 59th St.
New York, NY 10022

is an excellent weekly published in English in an overseas edition.

2. *Haaretz* is a Hebrew newspaper that is available in either a daily or a weekly edition. It is published in Hebrew only and available from

Israel Communications Inc.
575 Lexington Ave.
New York, NY 10022

3. *Maariv* is another Hebrew newspaper available in a daily or weekly edition from:

Maariv Newspaper
575 Lexington Ave.
New York, NY 10016

4. *Yediot Ahronot, in Hebrew,* is available from

150 Fifth Ave.
New York, NY 10010

5. The Jewish Telegraphic Agency puts out daily and weekly bulletins (in English):

Jewish Telegraphic Agency
165 W. 46th St., Rm. 511
New York, NY 10036

6. American newspapers that cover Israeli news well are the *New York Times* and the *Washington Post*.

MAGAZINES

Numerous Jewish magazines deal with the Israeli scene on a regular basis. Among the best are

Commentary 165 E. 56th St. New York, NY 10022	Moment 462 Boylston St. Boston, MA 02116	Present Tense 165 E. 56th St. New York, NY 10022
The Jewish Spectator P.O.B. 2016 Santa Monica, CA 90406	National Jewish Monthly 1640 Rhode Island Ave. NW Washington, DC 20036	

Each Zionist group has its own house organ. *Hadassah Magazine* and *Midstream* in particular have a wider appeal than their organizational constituency:

American Zionist 4 E. 34th St. New York, NY 10016	Zionist Organization of America
Hadassah Magazine 50 W. 58th St. New York, NY 10023	Women's Zionist Organization of America
Israel Horizons 150 Fifth Ave. New York, NY 10011	Hashomer Hatzair—Americans for Progressive Israel
Jewish Frontier 575 Avenue of the Americas New York, NY 10011	Labor Zionist Alliance
Midstream 515 Park Ave. New York, NY 10022	Theodor Herzl Foundation
Mizrachi Woman 817 Broadway New York, NY 10003	Mizrachi Women's Organization of America
Pioneer Woman 200 Madison Ave. New York, NY 10016	Woman's Labor Zionist Organization of America

A number of Hebrew periodicals are published in America. These, too, are sponsored by constituent organizations and include

Bitzaron 1411 Broadway New York, NY 10001	Hebrew Literary Foundation
Hadoar 1841 Broadway New York, NY 10011	Histadrut Ivrit of America

BOOKS

Buying Hebrew books (a lot of which are published by the Jewish Agency) is also a way of keeping in touch with what's happening in Israel. Just about any Jewish bookstore will carry Hebrew books. Check the list of bookstores in *Catalog 2* (Jewish Yellow Pages) for your local dealer.

Also, more and more Israeli novels, poetry, and nonfiction are being translated and published in the United States. Keep your eyes open for books by Amos Oz, Amos Elon, Yehuda Amichai, Hanoch Bartov, A. B. Yehoshua, Aharon Megged, Shulamith Hareven, etc.

LEARNING HEBREW

You'll never really dig yourself into American culture if you can't understand English, and the same holds true of Israel. If you really want to keep your finger on the pulse of Israel you have to learn Hebrew. It's essential for just about all the Israeli newspapers, for making your stay there successful when you "pilgrimage," for chatting with Israelis here, etc.

There are lots of possibilities for learning Hebrew and you might try some of the following:

1. Contact your local university to see if they have conversational Hebrew courses.

2. Call your local Board of Jewish Education to find out what courses they offer or know about.

3. Try your local synagogue or Jewish community center. They frequently offer ulpan courses.

Less desirable for learning a new language but with definite possibilities are the tape and record sets, which give you a learn-Hebrew-at-home-in-front-of-your-stereo option.

The following are available from
**The World Zionist Organization
515 Park Ave.
New York, NY 10022**

1. *Hebrew through Conversation.* Two-record set accompanied by a student manual. Fourteen lessons in elementary Hebrew. The set is $4.95.

2. *Let's Talk Hebrew.* Cassettes or dual-track tapes. For beginners. It has 40 sessions—15 minutes per session. Price is $25. There is also *Let's Talk More Hebrew* for intermediate Hebrew and *Let's Advance in Hebrew,* each at $25 also.

3. *Takol—Hebrew Home Ulpan.* A series of Israeli ulpan programs through correspondence and cassettes, based on combination of listening, speaking, and writing. Prices vary according to the program you choose.

TELEPHONE

Israel can be called with direct dialing if the area called has internal dialing. To call, dial 011—972—city code—local number. City codes are as follows:

Afula 65	**Akko** 4	**Ashkelon** 51	**Bat Yam** 3	**Beersheva** 53
Dimona 57	**Hadera** 63	**Haifa** 4	**Holon** 3	**Jerusalem** 2
Natanya 53	**Nazareth** 65	**Rehovot** 54	**Tel Aviv** 3	**Tiberias** 67

Israeli culture

You ought also to be paying attention to cultural developments in Israel. A distinct Israeli dance style has emerged (see Dance in *Catalog 2,* pp. 337–51) that's a joy to behold and great fun to participate in.

There is also Israeli-style music, which may sometimes sound uncomfortably like Western imitations (and sometimes not very good ones at that); but there is, if you search, some undeniably good Israeli music floating around.

Most Jewish bookstores carry some Israeli records so, again, take a look at the bookstores list in *Catalog 2*. One company that specializes in carrying Israeli labels such as Hed-Artzi, Gabrau, Isradisks, Isralectra, etc. is

Menorah Records
36 Eldridge St.
New York, NY 10002

Records are also available from

Hebraica Record Distributors
50 Andover Rd.
Roslyn Hts., NY 11577

Songs of Israel on slides are available from

William Swartz
161 Field Rd.
Longmeadow, MA 01106

There are art galleries and stores that specialize in the work of Israeli artists. Some of these are

New England

Pucker–Safrai
171 Newbury St.
Boston, MA 02116

New York

American–Israeli Cultural Foundation
485 Madison Ave.
New York, NY 10022

Ben Ari Arts, Ltd.
11 Avenue A
New York, NY 10009

BLD, Ltd.
301 E. 47th St., Suite 5M
New York, NY 10017

Murray Greenfield Gallery
21 W. 39th St.
New York, NY 10018

Israel Creations
212 Fifth Ave.
New York, NY 10011

Israeli Gift and Ergo Mfg. Co.
29 Canal St.
New York, NY 10001

District of Columbia

Jaffa Gate Imports
5512 Connecticut Ave. NW
Washington, DC 20015

Alpert & Carter
Merchandise Mart
Chicago, IL 60654

West

Bat Sheva Imports
9884 Garden Grove Blvd.
Garden Grove, CA 92644

Embassy Imports
14250 Oxnard St.
Van Nuys, CA 91401

Mizrah

A mizrah is any wall hanging that is hung on the eastern wall of the home as a reminder of the spiritual presence of Eretz Yisrael. It is customarily used to point you in the right direction (toward Jerusalem) for prayers. It is a beautiful symbol even if not used in a ritualistic role—just to serve as a physical Israel-presence in your home.

For details on how to make one, see Symbols of the Home in *Catalog 1*, pp. 16–17.

Tikhun hatzot—midnight prayers

Tradition decreed that special midnight prayers be recited as a symbol that we join the Holy One, blessed be He, in His mourning for Zion. The custom arose because of some lovely aggadot (see the *Sefer Aggadah* sections on Hurban Bayit Rishon and Hurban Bayit Sheni, Dvir Publishing, Israel, 1973) about God's pain at the destruction of His home. For example:

God said to the heavenly angels, "Come and let us go together, you and I, to my home, to see what my enemies have done there." The Holy One, blessed be He, and the heavenly angels went together and Jeremiah led them. When the Holy One saw the Holy Temple, He said: "This is My home and this was My comfort and My enemies came and did whatever was their will." And God cried in pain and said, "My home, My home . . . My children, where have you gone? My priests and Levites, where have you gone? What can I do with you? How many times did I warn you and you refused to repent!"

Also, it is said that during the night God "sits and roars like a lion, exclaiming: 'Woe to the children on account of whose sins I destroyed My home and burnt My Temple and exiled them among the nations of the world' " (Berakhot 3a).

Midnight was chosen because tradition has it that King David used to arise at that hour to study and pray. The kabbalists, especially, adopted such midnight prayers as their practice.

Two separate forms of the service developed—Tikkun Rahel and Tikkun Leah, named for Jacob's wives. Tikkun Rahel consists of Psalms 137 and 79 and tehinnot—poems of lament—on the destruction of the Temple, which are recited on days when Tahanun is said. Tikkun Leah concentrates on the more joyful psalms such as 111 and 126 and is recited on Shabbat, holidays, and other celebrations.

As a dramatic ritual tikkun hatzot has enormous possibilities. Those with some skill at formulating "creative liturgy" could develop this custom into a very moving experience by choosing some selected psalms or parts of Yehudah Halevi's *Zionides* or selections from contemporary writing on Eretz Yisrael, combined with candlelight and the right slow melodic niggunim—melodies—to create a very special Jewish moment.

Visiting Israel

Let's start with one understanding: tourism is *not* aliyat haregel—pilgrimage. If you're looking to be a tourist, you'd better stick to visiting England, France, Hawaii, or China. Tourists are outsiders temporarily visiting the natives. Israel is the *home* of Jews—for some their first home, for others a second home, but a home nevertheless. You don't visit your parents' home as a tourist—you make a pilgrimage there. That's what you do in Israel. You make a pilgrimage to visit your home.

We talked before (under Models for Diaspora–Israel Relations) about obligations to pilgrimage to Israel. This obligation has no relationship to vacations, hobbies, how you do or don't like Israelis, or the state of the humidity there. It shouldn't even depend very much on the state of your finances. It is your obligation—your responsibility—to make periodic visits to Israel.

The issue now is that if you take this obligation seriously you'll be visiting Israel more than the usual once-in-a-lifetime. You're not a tourist. Agreed. What *do* you do there, though?

1. If you go to Israel, steer clear of the usual tourist trek. Do you *really* want to look at hospitals, university campuses (unless you want to register), or community centers—places you probably wouldn't visit if you were home in the States? Even kibbutzim are disappointing—what do you wind up seeing but a lot of fields and workshops, really a lot of minifactories? If you are *really* interested in kibbutzim, hospitals, etc., and you have the time and inclination, why not volunteer to work? *Much* more satisfying for you and everyone else concerned. (See below for agencies that can help you plan this.)

2. Talk to people. If you want to tune into the pulse-and-nerve-center of Israel, talk to the person sitting next to you or across the aisle on the bus, in the cafeteria, at a sidewalk café, in museums, movies, concerts. Sure places to meet people are the university cafeterias, the cafeterias of the Bet Ha-Itonaim—journalists' organization—and the Bet ha-Sofer—the writers' organization in Tel Aviv and Jerusalem, the Tel Aviv sidewalk cafés (beware of pickpockets and Romeos looking for "American passports"), etc. Use your ingenuity.

3. Don't travel in tourist buses—unless you yearn for lots of American company. Also avoid organized group travel—unless you like being herded from place to place on schedule! Israel's public transportation is excellent and

Trude Weiss-Rosmarin offers a variety of ideas for making your stay in Israel a productive one.

economical and goes everywhere. It's not the most comfortable way to travel (crowded hot stations and noisy shoving people), but Israel is not a country of luxuries.

4. Try to meet Russian Jews in Israel. Don't rely on the Jewish Agency's introductions or you'll see walking propaganda. If you really want to understand the problems of Russian immigrants and why tensions have arisen between these immigrants and the native Israelis, find your own Russians and talk to them.

5. If you can't speak Hebrew, learn. Meanwhile, try English or Yiddish. It's best to pick up *some* Hebrew.

6. Compared to the U.S. museums Israel art collections seem insignificant. It can't really be otherwise because these collections are of such recent date. But in terms of archeology there are worlds to be seen that can't be seen elsewhere. Be sure to go to the Israel Museum complex in Jerusalem and see the Qumran (Dead Sea) Scroll of Isaiah. Also, Bet Hatefutsot in Tel Aviv is a fascinating place devoted to the history of the Diaspora communities.

7. Naturally you'll climb Masada. But there are many other archeological sites and quite a few digs in progress. For information about how to volunteer for a dig, see the list of Israel programs below.

8. Go shopping and spend lots of money. If you pass up that menorah or book or dress or piece of pottery while you're there, it's a cinch you'll feel like kicking yourself when you get back home. So spend it. It's good for you and it's good for Israel.

Hints

1. Beware of programs that promise you everything:
see all of Israel · meet the people · do your own thing · cheap

2. Remember
Israel doesn't promise you anything · Israel doesn't owe you anything
Israel is clearly not a utopia · fresh air doesn't puff away personal problems

3. Understand why you ought to join a program rather than come as a loner
it's easier to come as part of a group · there's a program that seems tailored to what you want · it seems cheaper in the long run

4. As soon as you think about Israel
start thinking about Hebrew · and working on it

5. Bring a sleeping bag (lightweight)

6. Before you go contact the Israeli government tourist office for literature, information, etc. They can also give you information about visiting a kibbutz, should you be interested in that aspect of Israeli life. If there is no office in your city, contact the Israel Government Tourist Office at these addresses:

6380 Wilshire Blvd.
Los Angeles, CA 90048

350 Fifth Ave.
New York, NY 10001

5 S. Wabash Ave.
Chicago, IL 60603

795 Peachtree St. NE
Atlanta, GA 30308

102 Bloor St. W.
Toronto, Ontario M5S 1M8

7. **The Council on International Educational Exchange**
   205 E. 42nd St.
   New York, NY 10017

or **777 United Nations Plaza**
   New York, NY 10017

works with

Israel Student Tourist Association
109 Ben Yehuda St.
Tel Aviv
(telephone: 247 164)

They can provide you with a student travel card and lots of advice about student travel. In addition, they sponsor their own student charter flights to Europe and elsewhere. Once you get to Israel, by all means get in touch with ISTA in Tel Aviv for whatever help you need.

8. The Queen Elizabeth II, besides having a gourmet kosher kitchen, also has student rates that are about half the regular fare. There are also cheap and sociable (i.e., crowded) Greek and Italian ships that sail to Haifa.

9. The Israel Camping Union offers a package deal combining fourteen nights of lodging and breakfast at any one of its sites with a fifteen-day Egged bus pass and a half-day Egged tour. This $75 plan is so reasonable that most foreign travel agencies don't bother to handle it for the 25 percent commission they would get. Details are available from

Israel Camping Union
P.O.B. 53
Nahariya, Israel

10. An International Youth Hostel Card can admit you to thirty Israeli youth hostels, located in the major cities as well as at unique historic and natural settings like the oasis of Ein Gedi by the Dead Sea and the gardens of Karei Deshe by the Kinneret.

The Israel Youth Hostel Association
3 Dorot Rishonim Street
Jerusalem

has a number of youth tourist schemes. Get this in addition to the International Student Card. It works wonders in Israel, for a variety of discounts.

11. Call the Society for the Protection of Nature in Israel, Tel Aviv office, at (03) 35063/4/5/6; they sponsor a broad range of one-to-seven-day trips to all parts of the country combining travel and hiking with history and nature study.

12. Take out travel and health insurance policies. This is most important if you want to hike, camp, or work on a kibbutz or at a dig.

13. Have a good trip!

Advice to olim

I think it is fitting to answer those who address inquiries to me because they wish to live in the Holy Land. For this it is necessary to know, and to give information, as to what this land is really like.

Concerning the words, "O Lord, You will favor Your land" (Psalms 85:1), our teachers have said: God changes it again and again, and regards it, and rests His eyes upon it, until it makes its deeds pleasing to Him (Midrash Tehillim).

Many, many changes and events, experiences, and fates befall every single man who comes to this land, until he adjusts to it, has joy in its stones, and loves its dust, until the ruins in the land of Israel are dearer to him than a palace abroad, and dry bread in that place dearer than all delicacies elsewhere. But this does not happen in one day or two, not in a month, and not in a year. Many a year passes before the days of his initiation are over, his initiation into the true life. But then he lives in his native land, and always before God, as it is written, "Indeed, it shall be said of Zion, 'Every man was born there'" (Psalms 87:5), which means that everyone who desires to go to the sanctuary requires a new conception and infancy, a new childhood, youth, etc., until he beholds the land face to face, until his soul is bound up with that of the land.

And that is how it is. He who comes and brings with him his knowledge, each what he has attained according to his degree, does not adjust in the beginning. His mind is bewildered, he is cast hither and yon without finding repose or security, he climbs up to very heaven and sinks into abysses, like a ship that is tossed about on the seas, and he troubles others with his concerns and actions. And of his mode of life in regard to the Torah and the commandments, this holds: What was, is no more—until God shows him the face of the land, and then he will arrive at rest and peace.

But this is something that cannot be definitely gauged: the length of time, how, how much, and when—in each individual, all these matters depend on his affairs and actions and the root of his soul. Therefore let everyone who, with all his being, wishes to enter the Holy Land, consider all these things, and examine himself as to whether he has the strength to surmount everything, lest he lose even what he had up to this time—like the ant (Talmud, Sanhedrin 106) that demanded horns, so they clipped off the ears he had.

Does this sound familiar, timely? Rabbi Abraham Kalisker—the author of this "advice"—was the eighteenth-century disciple of the Gaon of Vilna who switched his allegiance to the Hasidic Rabbi Dov Ber of Mezeritch. In 1777 he settled in Eretz Yisrael, where he became the leader of the Hasidic community in Tiberias in 1788, after the death of Rabbi Menahem Mendel of Vitebsk. This passage is a translation of one section of a long report he sent from Tiberias to the Hasidim in Europe sometime between 1793 and 1797.

Spending time in Israel

A land which a sacred book describes to the children of that land is never merely in their hearts; a land can never become a mere symbol. It is in the hearts because it is in the world; it is a symbol because it is a reality. Zion is the prophetic image of a promise to mankind: but it would be a poor metaphor if Mount Zion did not actually exist. . . . What is decisive for us is not the promise of the land, but the demand, whose fulfillment is bound up with the land, with the existence of a free Jewish community in this country. . . . We need our own soil in order to fulfill it: we need the freedom to order our own life (Martin Buber, *Israel and the World* [Shocken]).

On memory

Much of the heavy stuff of the weave of Israel is the weight of memory. Wherever one turns there is a marker—in the form of a building or a piece of forest, a tombstone, a jutting bit of architecture on a hillside or byway. Our "telling our story" is not restricted to the Haggadah or to biblical readings. It is so present as to haunt; it is as everyday as prayer. Jewish memory has never been linear or progressive but always cyclical and embedding, layer upon layer.

When you partake of Israel you bump into the past at every turn, boldly juxtaposed to the now and openly proclaiming bonds and allegiance to remembering.

You can skim across the surface of Israel as a guest, or you can plunge in, accepting the accountability demanded of one of the family. If it's crashing that is your style, you'll miss most of Israel as you tour the country. A hedonistic searching out of the land is a far cry from a search for self in the land.

Whatever it is that you think you want to find in Israel, what you actually meet will jangle you.

It's helpful to think on your expectancies. And to think on how you want to "do Israel"—crashing into someone else's place . . . visitor . . . guest of honor . . . part of the family. Where you feel yourself to be on this range of hookings—it will determine how much intimacy and responsibility is yours in Israel.

A messianic perspective

Any resemblance between Israel and a messianic reality may or may not be purely coincidental—depending on your religious sensibility. Nevertheless, a certain messianic perspective, a communal and realistic one, can be a helpful way of embracing your experience in Israel. The distinctive and unifying feature of the many messianic conceptions in the Jewish tradition is the centrality of community. Jewish messianism, however formulated, is a communal event in history. It isn't necessarily an apocalyptic or utopian one though. It can be very earthbound. And so our messianic perspective insists on community and realism, and demands responsibility to both. The State of Israel is the messianic opportunity for extended responsibility. It represents the Jewish people—imperfect and even impolite—unapologetically gone public. As a polity the Jewish people is publicly accountable for its actions; and responsible action means clear sight and realistic expectations.

Jewish people, not prophets, walk the streets of Tel Aviv and push their way through the bus lines of Jerusalem. Israel furnishes the opportunity of getting to know the Jewish people as they are—when they are home—after years of good manners abroad. We are no longer on the margins of history and so cannot afford the luxury of serving as a moral presence to the nations. It's not that we wouldn't enjoy continuing that somewhat thankless role, but we simply have neither the time nor the energy. Our energies are channeled inward. We have our own house to construct and clean. Israel is a vital test of self-acceptance—of seeing ourselves as we are—honestly and without apology.

For Jews, then, the spiritual road through Israel is a public thoroughfare; we are responsible for its maintenance; if it is a bumpy one, it is for us to pave it. Travel in Israel is not merely a private trip but a communal commitment. Our messiah is not so much a mystic as a mitnaged.

Such a commitment may require the suspension of individualism as a way of seeing the world. It does not mean, however, the negation of your individual personality. Israel is a place where your personal experiences and insights count, where the total self can be brought to bear on the larger shared enterprise of Jewish community. It is not a place where you seek unique experiences as ends in themselves. It is not where you do your own thing, but where we do *our* thing. Our thing is sharing; what we Jews share with each other is not so much common personal experiences as collective memories and mutual responsibility. Criticism is, of course, a crucial part of discharging our responsibility; yet all criticism is at bottom self-criticism, for it is grounded in the consciousness of who we are and the question of who we are to be. The Jewish people have not yet resolved this question. The reality of a living Jewish community in Israel is a summons for its resolution.

Israel, then, is not a summer camp designed for the satisfaction of private needs but a Jewish collective struggling for life and self-definition in its own terms. Participation in this struggle is what Israel is about.

Israel may not be the garden of Eden, but it does place before us a messianic demand.

Plugged programs

The programs we comment on in what follows have been zeroed in on because of our sense of their sense of purpose and our awareness that there are people involved with them with whom you might be in tune, whose company you might find illuminating.

PARDES

Pardes provides an intensive introduction to the study of Jewish texts in a small, intimate group setting. The basic course of study includes Bible and commentaries, Mishnah, Gemara, Jewish thought, halakhah, and the nature of the oral law. Each area is studied on both informal and formal levels: informal study in pairs or small groups with the help of a tutor, informal discussion seminars, and formal classes led by the faculty. In addition, there are formal lectures given by guest scholars from the Jerusalem community. Informal study concentrates on close textual analysis, with the dual aim of developing technical language skills and uncovering the underlying philosophical assumptions specific to a given text. The formal study emphasizes a broader formulation of ideas and the synthesis of themes. Depending upon student interest, special interest groups may be formed in such areas as the role of the woman in halakhah, hasidut, Torah reading, and calligraphy.

Study is conducted in English to accommodate American and European students, but the texts are mostly in Hebrew. Therefore students are expected to have some knowledge of Hebrew and be willing to increase their proficiency during the year. In addition to the Hebrew instruction offered by Pardes, students who have a deficient Hebrew background may make arrangements through Pardes to take the Hebrew University ulpan the summer prior to the academic year. Most students are college graduates but come from different kinds of Jewish backgrounds; the level and kinds of religious observance varies. Study at Pardes is passionate without compromising the integrity or intellectual maturity of the student. It is a program for those interested in becoming more religious. Unlike most other yeshivot (see below), Pardes is coed. The program begins in October and ends in June. For more information contact

> **Rabbi Larry Laver**
> **Pardes Institute of Jewish Studies**
> **Rechov Gad 10, Baka**
> **Jerusalem, Israel**

OVERSEAS PROGRAM—HEBREW UNIVERSITY

The School for Overseas Students of the Hebrew University has an eleven-month academic program for foreign students who have completed one or two years of university work. Most classes are held in English. A few, however, are conducted in basic Hebrew, for which there is an excellent summer ulpan and Hebrew-language instruction throughout the year. The curriculum, especially in Jewish studies, is extensive but not very intensive. The course load is eight to ten courses crammed into sixteen to twenty hours a week, so you will get more academic credit than hard intellectual currency. There are several unusually fine teachers in the program. It's a good idea to find out who they are before registration. We recommend that you contact an alumnus of the program and get the names of teachers and/or courses that would offer you a meaningful intellectual challenge. There are some—which makes it all the more sad that the curricular framework does not facilitate personal in-depth involvement via several weighty courses in place of the mass cafeteria-style study offered.

There are some very worthwhile extracurricular activities, including discussion groups with leading Israeli personalities, and tours throughout the country. Most students consider this firsthand contact with Israel more valuable than the academic program.

In addition to the eleven-month program there is a two-year program and summer courses offered in two sessions, each of one-month duration.

For more information, contact

American Friends of Hebrew University
11 E. 69th St.
New York, NY 10021

OTHER UNIVERSITIES

Tel Aviv, Bar Ilan, Haifa, and Ben-Gurion Universities also have "overseas programs." If your choice of programs is to be guided by geographical preferences, keep this in mind.

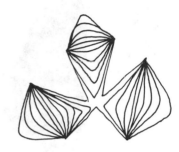

A word about Ben-Gurion University: It is more technically oriented than the others, but it has some of the best young faculty in Israel. If you want to get away from the crowds of foreign students, head for Ben-Gurion University in Beer-sheva.

But even more than Hebrew University's program, some of these programs are to be faulted on how they relate to you as a "foreign student." This will keep you at a distance, at arm's length, and save your Israeli hosts from too much "personal involvement." Pity. We would encourage you to find a less clear-cut pigeonhole for yourself while in Israel.

WORLD UNION OF JEWISH STUDENTS PROGRAM, ARAD

Under the auspices of the WUJS Institute, college graduates under thirty have an opportunity to spend a well-rounded year of study and work in Israel. Apart from some well-guided tours and a ten-day stint on a kibbutz, the first five months are spent in study at the Institute in Arad, a pleasant enough secluded locale. The study program consists of a quality Hebrew ulpan and a sampling of elective courses in Jewish studies taught by a competent staff. In addition, there are social activities such as folk dancing, films, discussion groups, and a lecture series. The remaining seven months are to be devoted to work, for which there is an employment information service that's supposed to help participants locate jobs in their fields at regular salaries. Unfortunately, this service provides little information and help, and participants are usually left to pursue jobs on their own.

For more information, contact

WUJS Institute
Arad, Israel

Spending time in Israel

MIDRESHET JERUSALEM

The Midreshet Jerusalem program is run by the Jewish Theological Seminary and combines classroom study of traditional texts with bet midrash sessions. Courses of study include Bible, Mishnah, Aggadah, Talmud, Jewish thought, halakhah, and Hebrew. Texts are studied in the original language, but the language of instruction is English. This is a nine-month program open to people not currently enrolled at the seminary.

YESHIVOT

Eysh ha-Torah

Aish ha-Torah is directed toward students with no Jewish background and attempts to open up the Jewish tradition to them. The school is centered around the personality of Reb Noah Weinberg. The courses range from basic Jewish ethics to "light" Talmud study. The strong point of the yeshivah is its community. Emphasis is placed more on Jewish practice than study. It is located in the beautiful Jewish Quarter of the Old City.

Or Samayah

Or Samayah is the largest baalei teshuvah—those returning to the tradition— yeshivah in Israel, with an Israeli and an American section. This yeshivah takes both study and religious commitment seriously; therefore time is divided between texts and Jewish ethics. The yeshivah is committed to a halakhic world view and downplays any other approach. Its students feel a strong sense of community. There are programs for both men and women, though the program for women is on a different level. Classes are in English or Hebrew and are given on many levels.

Yeshivat ha-Mivtar (for men), *Michlellet Beruria* (for women, commonly known as Bravender's Yeshivah)

The emphasis of this yeshivah is on an intellectual approach to Jewish learning. While religious observance is assumed, it is really the activity of study that ties the yeshivah together. The instruction is based on a solid grounding in the technical skills of talmudic study. The central figure in this yeshivah is Rabbi Chaim Bravender, whose broad intellectual interests define the scope of the study. Instruction is in English. Separate but equal programs for men and women.

The Diaspora Yeshivah

Located near the Tomb of David on Mount Zion, this yeshivah is centered around the charismatic personality of Rabbi Mordechai Goldstein. Many of its students have made long-term commitments to staying at the yeshivah, and while there they participate almost exclusively in the yeshivah's community. Emphasis here is on the experience of learning more than on the amount of learning. The yeshivah encourages a sincere search for religious meaning via traditional learning and halakhic living. The yeshivah is best known for its student band. Men and women study separately.

> **Rabbi Mordechai Goldstein**
> **P.O.B. 6426**
> **Jerusalem, Israel**

PROGRAM POSSIBILITIES

We hope you won't be confused by the Jewish Agency "feifdoms":

Dept. of Education and Culture of the
World Zionist Organization, American Section
4 E. 34th St.
New York, NY 10016

Torah Education Dept.
Zionist Organization of America
515 Park Ave.
New York, NY 10022

Youth Dept.
Zionist Organization of America
4 E. 34th St.
New York, NY 10016

Youth and Hechalutz (AZYF)
515 Park Ave.
New York, NY 10022

If we've confused them here, we hope that the various personnel will refer you, one to the other, given your needs. We'll also throw in these addresses:

Israel Aliyah Center
515 Park Ave.
New York, NY 10022

Kibbutz Aliyah Desk
575 Avenue of the Americas
New York, NY 10011

and note that Pesach Schindler, United Synagogue of America, Rechov Agron 2, Jerusalem, is a good contact for all sorts of Conservative Jewish-sponsored programs, as are Hank Skirball and his co-worker, David Forman, Hebrew Union College, 13 David Hamelech, Jerusalem, for Reform movement youth programs in Israel.

In the listings below you'll see the variety of program names. Investigate those that appeal to you.

The World Zionist Organization of America
515 Park Ave.
New York, NY 10022

puts out a booklet on these programs, which you can get for the asking.

Programs in Israel

HIGH SCHOOLS

Huleh Valley Regional High School at Kfar Blum
This is a one-year program designed for tenth-graders. Students live with Israeli students at the school and are "adopted" by Israeli families on the kibbutz. For information, contact

America–Israel Secondary School Program
515 Park Ave.
New York, NY 10022

Tochnit Yerushalayim Semester Program
This program for twelfth-graders is located at the Hayim Greenberg College in Jerusalem and is open to students enrolled in day schools. The program runs from January to June. For information, contact

America–Israel Secondary School Program
515 Park Ave.
New York, NY 10022

ORT at Kibbutz Ein Hachoresh
This one-year program is open to tenth- or eleventh-graders. For information contact

America–Israel Secondary School Program
515 Park Ave.
New York, NY 10022

or

Women's American ORT
1250 Broadway
New York, NY 10001

EIE of the Union of American Hebrew Congregations
This program is open to sixteen- to eighteen-year-olds, in either a six month or a one-year option. For information, contact

International Education Dept.
UAHC
838 Fifth Ave.
New York, NY 10021

NFTY Half-Year Work/Study Program
Students who have completed all requirements for high school graduation in January are offered the opportunity to study at an ulpan and take seminars. For information, contact

NFTY Half-Year Program
UAHC Youth Div.
838 Fifth Ave.
New York, NY 10021

Goodman Academic High School of the ZOA
Open to students in the tenth, eleventh, and twelfth grades, this program extends from September to June and is located at the Kfar Silver campus near Ashkelon. For information, contact

Zionist Organization of America
4 E. 34th St.
New York, NY 10016

High School in Israel at Beit Berl
This program, open to high school students in grades 10–12, runs in eight-week sessions in September, November, January, April, and June. For information, contact

High School in Israel
4200 Biscayne Blvd.
Miami, FL 33137

Six-Month Study-Work in Israel
This program has three different options, each of which is a six-month commitment: (1) students live in Jerusalem and study at an ulpan for two months, then spend the next four months living and working on a kibbutz; (2) students study four months at the Hayim Greenberg School in Jerusalem and also travel throughout the country; (3) students spend six months in study as day school students. For information, contact

WZO Dept. of Education and Culture
515 Park Ave.
New York, NY 10022

Yeshivah high school programs for boys or girls
Many of Israel's yeshivot will accommodate American students. Here are some of them:

For girls	*For boys*
Ulpanot Bnei Akiva	Yeshivot Bnei Akiva
Ulpana, Kfar Pines	Netiv Neir, Jerusalem
Amana, Kfar Saba	Kfar Haroeh
Segula, Kiryat Motzkin	Or Etzion, Shafir
	Tikvat Yaakov, Sdeh Yaacov
	Ohel Shlomo, Beersheva
	Natanya
	Yeshivat Shaalvim, Kibbutz Shaalvim
	Medrashiat Noam, Pardes Hannah

For information, contact
Torah Education Dept., World Zionist Organization
515 Park Ave.
New York, NY 10022

Tochnit Yud Gimel for Boys and Girls (separate programs)
For boys or girls who have completed their secular studies at an American school in three and a half years, this program offers five months of intensive study in Jerusalem. For information contact

> **Torah Education Dept., World Zionist Organization**
> **515 Park Ave.**
> **New York, NY 10022**

Kita Tet
This half-year program for ninth-graders begins in April and ends in August. For information, contact

> **Torah Education Dept., World Zionist Organization**
> **515 Park Ave.**
> **New York, NY 10022**

Tochinit Yud Gimel for Boys and Girls
This program offers two options. Option one offers a study-work program to seniors who have completed their academic work by January. This program takes place at a religious kibbutz. Option two offers a study program for college credit at Bar Ilan University. For information contact

> **Torah Education Dept., World Zionist Organization**
> **515 Park Ave.**
> **New York, NY 10022**

Israel Summer Happening
This is a summer program for high school kids. For information contact

> **American Zionist Youth Foundation**
> **515 Park Ave.**
> **New York, NY 10022**

Gesher Summer Seminars in Israel
Open to students between the ages of thirteen and nineteen, this program is designed for teenagers seeking a religious program. For information, contact

> **Torah Education Dept., World Zionist Organization**
> **515 Park Ave.**
> **New York, NY 10022**

Bureaus of Jewish Education programs
Various bureaus of Jewish Education around the country sponsor summer educational programs in Israel. Atlanta, Atlantic City; Baltimore; Brandeis School, Long Island; Cleveland; Dallas; Denver; Framingham, Massachusetts; Houston; Indianapolis; Los Angeles; Milwaukee; New Orleans; Rochester, New York; Syracuse, New York; Temple Israel, Great Neck, Long Island. To find out about them, contact your local bureau or institution or

> **Dept. of Education and Culture**
> **World Zionist Organization**
> **515 Park Ave.**
> **New York, NY 10022**

Bar/Bat Mitzvah Pilgrimage
This six-week program of travel, education, and camping is open to boys and girls thirteen to fourteen years of age. For information, contact

> **Dept. of Education and Culture**
> **World Zionist Organization**
> **515 Park Ave.**
> **New York, NY 10022**

Confirmation Class Study Tour in Israel
This is an individualized six-week program of study, travel, and work. For information contact

> **International Education Dept.**
> **UAHC**
> **838 Fifth Ave.**
> **New York, NY 10021**

Weizmann Institute International Summer Science Program
This four-week program is for science-oriented high school seniors. For information contact

Science Program
> **515 Park Ave.**
> **New York, NY 10022**

The NFTY Israel Academy
This is a six-week tour and work experience. For information, contact

> **International Education Dept.**
> **UAHC**
> **838 Fifth Ave.**
> **New York, NY 10021**

Karen Kupcinet International Science School Summer Work Program
The Weizmann Institute will accept a limited number of juniors, seniors, and graduate students on a research project. For information, contact

> **American Committee for Weizmann Institute of Science**
> **515 Park Ave.**
> **New York, NY 10022**

The NFTY Mitzvah Corps in Ben Shemen, Israel
This six-week program is focused on work and study in the agricultural village of Ben Shemen. For information, contact

> **International Education Program**
> **UAHC**
> **838 Fifth Ave.**
> **New York, NY 10021**

Adventure in Kibbutz
This six-week program for sixteen- to seventeen-year-olds offers three weeks of work on a kibbutz and three weeks of field trips and travel. For information, contact

> **American Zionist Youth Foundation**
> **515 Park Ave.**
> **New York, NY 10022**

Yedid on Kibbutz
Six and a half weeks of kibbutz living and nature study at a center are available in this program for high school juniors. For information, contact

> **American Zionist Youth Foundation**
> **515 Park Ave.**
> **New York, NY 10022**

Israel and Moshav for High School Students
This four- to six-week program consists of touring the land and working on a moshav. For information, contact

> **Histadrut Tours**
> **630 Third Ave.**
> **New York, NY 10017**

Experiment in Kibbutz Living
This is a summer program for students aged fifteen to seventeen. For information, contact

> **Histadrut Tours**   **Kibbutz Aliya Desk**
> **630 Third Ave.** or   **575 Avenue of the Americas**
> **New York, NY 10017**   **New York, NY 10011**

NFTY Archeological Seminar in Israel
In this program the students live in Ben Shemen Youth Village and work at the excavation dig at Tel Afek. Touring is included in this six-week program. For information, contact

> **International Education Dept.**
> **UAHC**
> **838 Fifth Ave.**
> **New York, NY 10021**

ZOA–Masada Teenage Tour in Israel
This is a six-week summer program for kids aged fifteen to seventeen. There are both touring and studying components to the program. For information, contact

> **Zionist Organization of America**
> **Youth Dept.**
> **4 E. 34th St.**
> **New York, NY 10016**

Hebrew University Summer Science Seminar

For those who have completed three years of high school, this six-week program offers a combination of touring and study at Hebrew University. For information, contact

American Zionist Youth Foundation
515 Park Ave.
New York, NY 10022

United Synagogue Youth Israel Pilgrimage

USY Pilgrimage is open to fifteen- to eighteen-year-olds and offers a program of extensive touring and participation in traditional Jewish living. For information, contact

USY Israel Pilgrimage
155 Fifth Ave.
New York, NY 10010

National Conference of Synagogue Youth Summer Seminar

NCSY Summer Seminar is open to students fourteen to eighteen years old and combines an Orthodox life-style with travel and study seminars. For information, contact

NCSY Summer Seminar
116 E. 27th St.
New York, NY 10010

Summer Hebrew-language ulpan programs

Three summer programs—Kfar Galim, Akiva Natanya, and Youth Ulpan—are open to high school students for summer study. For information, contact

Baltimore Hebrew College
5800 Park Heights Ave.
Baltimore, MD 21215

Gratz College
10th St. and Tabor Rd.
Philadelphia, PA 19141

American Zionist Youth Foundation
515 Park Ave.
New York, NY 10022

COLLEGES AND UNIVERSITIES

Hebrew University

Hebrew University offers a variety of programs designed to fit into different university schedules:

1. one-year program—available to sophomores and juniors; includes a university ulpan as well as a nine-month academic period; specialization can be arranged in the fields of natural sciences, business administration, or computer science
2. regular studies program—a course of study for American and Canadian students who have completed at least one year at an accredited institution and want to finish their degree at Hebrew University
3. special cosponsored programs—the Hebrew University cosponsors special programs with the following institutions: Education Abroad Program of the University of California; the California State University and Colleges; the Office of International Education of the University of Colorado; Program of Study Abroad of the City University of New York; the Overseas Study Programs of Indiana University; the International Programs Office of the State University of New York; Spertus College (Chicago); Washington University (St. Louis); the University of Rochester; University of San Francisco; and York College of the City University of New York.
4. graduate programs—Hebrew University offers master's degree programs in humanities, social sciences, mathematics, and natural sciences for students with BA or BS degrees; in addition, special doctoral programs can be arranged in a variety of fields

   For information contact
   Office of Academic Affairs of the American Friends of
   Hebrew University
   11 E. 69th St.
   New York, NY 10021

   Student Affairs Committee
   American Friends of Hebrew University
   1506 McGregor Ave.
   Montreal H36-1B9, Canada

Tel Aviv University

Tel Aviv University also sponsors a plethora of programs designed to fit many needs:

1. college semester for midyear high school graduates—available to high school graduates who are given the opportunity to earn nine to twelve college credits during the semester
2. freshman year program—designed for students who are considering enrolling at Tel Aviv University or who plan to continue studies elsewhere
3. mechina—a year of preparatory courses leading to enrollment on a regular college program
4. ulpan—intensive Hebrew program mandatory for people participating in the Overseas Student Program
5. summer session—four-week program available to English-speaking students who have completed a year of college study
6. archeology program—three six-week summer sessions open to students who have completed at least one year of college
7. one-year program—open to sophomores, juniors, or seniors who wish to study for a year abroad at Tel Aviv University
8. semester program—same as one-year program but shorter
9. graduate regular studies—Tel Aviv University offers a variety of programs leading to graduate degrees

   For information, contact
   Office of Academic Affairs
   American Friends of Tel Aviv University
   342 Madison Ave.
   Suite 1426
   New York, NY 10017

Bar Ilan University

Bar Ilan University is the religious university in Israel. It offers a year-long academic program for freshmen, sophomores, or juniors. The semester begins in October, and an ulpan is offered in July. Qualified male students may combine traditional yeshivah studies in the mornings with the university's college programs in the afternoon. For information, contact

> Office of Academic Affairs
> Bar Ilan University
> 641 Lexington Ave.
> New York, NY 10022

Haifa University

Haifa University offers a variety of programs to fit the needs of different students:

1. semester program—undergraduate program that grants sixteen credits and is available in either the fall or spring semester
2. one-year program—open to all undergraduates; grants thirty-two credits to academically qualified students
3. winter work-study program—eight-week program from January to March. Students are placed in moshavim, kibbutzim, or development towns or various social-welfare institutions and conduct research projects based on their experiences
4. kibbutz university semester—participants spend ten weeks working on a kibbutz while studying Hebrew and doing research, which is then presented as a paper
5. challenge program—permits students with a strong background in Hebrew to attend regular university courses offered in Hebrew
6. graduate regular studies—overseas students can enroll in graduate studies programs in maritime history, marine archeology, and coastal geography

> For information, contact
> American Friends of Haifa University
> 60 E. 42nd St.
> Suite 1656
> New York, NY 10017

COLLEGES FOR WOMEN

Gold College

Orthodox institution for women who will spend a minimum of one year in intensive Jewish study. Special mechina program is available for students with limited program. Stern College for Women cosponsors a credit-transfer program. For information, contact

> Torah Education Dept.
> World Zionist Organization
> 515 Park Ave.
> New York, NY 10022

For women students with limited background

Several Israeli institutions for women sponsor programs designed for the student with little Jewish background. Among them: Neve Yerushalayim, Machon Bruriah, Or Sameach, Diaspora Yeshiva, Bet Midrash L'Nashim. For information on any of these schools, contact

> Torah Education Dept.
> World Zionist Organization
> 515 Park Ave.
> New York, NY 10022

For women students with good Jewish background

The following institutions are designed for women students with good Jewish backgrounds who want to pursue their Jewish studies in an Orthodox atmosphere: Michlala, Machon Sara Schenirer (Beis Yaakov), Midrasha, Bruriah, Bet Midrash L'Nashim. For information on any of these schools, contact

> Torah Education Dept.
> World Zionist Organization
> 515 Park Ave.
> New York, NY 10022

Kibbutz Maaleh Hachamishah

Kibbutz Maaleh Hachamishah sponsors a one-year program for students who wish to combine an academic program with work on a kibbutz. Students enroll in courses at Hebrew Union College–Jewish Institute of Religion while working at the kibbutz. Open to students who have completed one year of college course work. For information, contact

> HUC–JIR
> UAHC Youth Div.
> 838 Fifth Ave.
> New York, NY 10021

Teachers Institute Seminar of the Jewish Theological Seminary

This is an eight-week program of intensive study designed for graduate students working toward their master's degree. For information, contact

> Ms. Sylvia Ettenberg
> Jewish Theological Seminary
> 3080 Broadway
> New York, NY 10027

Hornstein Program of Brandeis University

This four-week program is geared to students who are enrolled in graduate programs to prepare for professional careers as Jewish communal workers. For information, contact

> Dr. Bernard Reisman
> Brandeis University
> Waltham, MA 02154

COLLEGES FOR MEN

For men students with good Jewish backgrounds

Several Israel institutions offer programs designed for graduates of yeshivah high schools. These are Midrasha, Yeshivat Kerem b'Yavneh, Yeshivat Hakotel, Yeshivat Shaalvim, Yeshivat Merkaz Harav Kook, Yeshivat Kol Torah, Yeshivat Har Etzion, Machon HaRaShal, Beit Medrash LeTorah, Dvar Yerushalayim, Yeshivah Chafetz Chaim, Itri, Torah Or, Porat Yosef, Yeshivat Torat Israel, Yeshivat Or Samayeh, Yeshivat Kiryat Arba, Jerusalem College of Technology, Yeshivat Hamivtar, Yeshivat Aish HaTorah. For information on any of these schools, contact

> Torah Education Dept.
> World Zionist Organization
> 515 Park Ave.
> New York, NY 10022

For men students with limited background

The following Israeli institutions have designed programs expressly to suit the needs of men who have a limited Jewish background: Dvar Yerushalayim, Shappel Center, Or Sameach, Diaspora Yeshiva, Aish Hatorah, Yeshivat Hamivtar. For information on any of these schools, contact

> **Torah Education Dept.**
> **World Zionist Organization**
> **515 Park Ave.**
> **New York, NY 10022**

Bet Midrash LeTorah

This Orthodox institution is designed for students who have graduated from yeshivah high schools. Yeshiva University co-sponsors a one-year program. For information, contact

> **Torah Education Dept.**
> **World Zionist Organization**
> **515 Park Ave.**
> **New York, NY 10022**

HEBREW-LANGUAGE PROGRAMS

Israel-America Ulpan at Ulpan Akiva-Hachoff Hayarok

This is an eight-week program open to adults who want to pursue serious language study combined with a tour visit to Israel. For information, contact

> **Dept. of Education and Culture**
> **World Zionist Organization**
> **515 Park Ave.**
> **New York, NY 10022**

USY Autumn Ulpan at Kibbutz Ein Tzurim

Open to recent high school graduates and college students, this program combines kibbutz life with weekend seminars and tours. The program is a five-month program—from September to February. For information, contact

> **USY Autumn Ulpan**
> **155 Fifth Ave**
> **New York, NY 10010**

SUMMER PROGRAMS

Israel Summer Institute

This is a six-week institute for college students and young adults. For information, contact

> **American Zionist Youth Foundation**
> **515 Park Ave.**
> **New York, NY 10022**

Yavneh Israel Summer Tour

This seven-week tour is for traditional college students. For information, contact

> **Yavneh**
> **156 Fifth Ave.**
> **New York, NY 10010**

Kibbutz and Vacation in Israel

This is a four- to six-week program for college students. For information, contact

> **Histadrut Foundation for Educational Travel**
> **630 Third Ave.**
> **New York, NY 10017**

Summer in Moshav

This seven-week program for college students is designed to permit participants to live on a moshav, study at an ulpan, and tour. For information, contact

> **Youth Dept.**
> **Zionist Organization of America**
> **4 E. 34th St.**
> **New York, NY 10016**

Student Summer Tour

This is a six-week program that combines four weeks of kibbutz work with two weeks of touring. For information, contact

> **American Zionist Youth Foundation**
> **515 Park Ave.**
> **New York, NY 10022**

NFTY College Academy

This program consists of a six-week tour of the land. For information, contact

> **International Education Dept.**
> **UAHC**
> **838 Fifth Ave.**
> **New York, NY 10021**

Family Experiment in Kibbutz Life

This summer program for families with children (youngest child must be four years old) involves work on a kibbutz plus an eight-day tour. For information, contact

> **KX Histadrut Tours**
> **630 Third Ave.**
> **New York, NY 10017**

NFTY Kibbutz Summer

This is a seven-week program for college-age students. For information, contact

> **International Youth Dept.**
> **UAHC**
> **838 Fifth Ave.**
> **New York, NY 10021**

Medical Work Summer Program

For students who have completed two years of medical school this program offers an opportunity to spend the summer months in supervised work at Shaare Zedek Hospital. Touring is included. For information, contact

American Zionist Youth Foundation
515 Park Ave.
New York, NY 10022

Summer Seminars for Jewish Center and Camp Workers

In-service training is included in this four-week program. For information, contact

Jewish Welfare Board
15 E. 26th St.
New York, NY 10010

Summer Seminars for Rabbis and Educators

This is a four-week program of workshops and seminars. For information, contact

Torah Education Dept.
World Zionist Organization
515 Park Ave.
New York, NY 10022

College Summer Program

This six-week program for students eighteen to twenty-two years old is designed to allow them to immerse themselves in Israel culture, land, and history. For information, contact

American Zionist Youth Foundation
515 Park Ave.
New York, NY 10022

Summer Ulpan on a Kibbutz

This nine-week summer ulpan for singles or married couples includes working on a kibbutz and studying Hebrew. For information, contact

Kibbutz Aliyah Desk
575 Avenue of the Americas
New York, NY 10011

The Institute for Jewish Youth Leaders from Abroad

This is a leadership development program for youth who have been recommended by their Jewish organizations or movements. For information, contact

Long-Term Programs
American Zionist Youth Foundation
515 Park Ave.
New York, NY 10022

Bnei Akiva Program

Bnei Akiva sponsor a year-long program for members. For information, contact

Bnei Akiva
200 Park Ave. South
New York, NY 10010

Habonim Program

Habonim sponsors a year-long program with a three-month kibbutz stay. For information, contact

Habonim
200 Park Ave. South
New York, NY 10010

Hashomer Hatzair Program

Hashomer Hatzair sponsors a program for its members that includes touring. For information, contact

Hashomer Hatzair
150 Fifth Ave.
New York, NY 10010

Noar Mizrachi Program

This is a one-year program featuring work in an Israeli development town. For information, contact

Noar Mizrachi
200 Park Ave. South
New York, NY 10010

Young Judea Program

This year-long program includes kibbutz work. For information, contact

Young Judea
817 Broadway
New York, NY 10007

For social workers only

There is a two-year program of social work in Israel's development towns. For information, contact

Long-Term Programs
American Zionist Youth Foundation
515 Park Ave.
New York, NY 10022

For chemists only

There is a one-year program for chemists that includes study at an ulpan and then nine months of work at the Technion. For information, contact

Long-Term Programs
American Zionist Youth Foundation
515 Park Ave.
New York, NY 10022

Pardes Institute

This is a two-year program for students who want to engage in serious Jewish study without denominational commitments. For information, contact

Long-Term Programs
American Zionist Youth Foundation
515 Park Ave.
New York, NY 10022

Project Etgar

Open to eighteen- to twenty-five-year-olds, this program combines travel, Hebrew-language study, and kibbutz work. For information, contact

Kibbutz Aliyah Desk
575 Avenue of the Americas
New York, NY 10011

Mate Yehudah

This is a six-month service learning program for people eighteen to thirty-two years old. For information, contact

Long-Term Programs
American Zionist Youth Foundation
515 Park Ave.
New York, NY 10022

Project Development Town

This six-month volunteer program is for nineteen- to thirty-year-olds. For information, contact

Long-Term Program
American Zionist Youth Foundation
515 Park Ave.
New York, NY 10022

SEMINARS

Reform Educators Seminar

This five-week tour features seminars, Hebrew-language study, and lectures. For information, contact

UAHC Dept. of Education
838 Fifth Ave.
New York, NY 10021

Seminars for World Jewish Service

This is a six-week program of seminars and discussions. For information, contact

Office of Academic Affairs
American Friends of Hebrew University
11 E. 69th St.
New York, NY 10021

Middle East Studies Institute for American Educators

This one-month program earns six graduate credits. For information, contact

National Committee for Middle East Studies in Secondary Education
9 E. 40th St., 5th fl.
New York, NY 10016

ZOA-Masada Leadership Training Course

This is a six-week program of work and study. For information, contact

Youth Dept.
Zionist Organization of America
4 E. 34th St.
New York, NY 10016

Hebrew Educators Seminar

Three-week programs are sponsored by the Board of Jewish Education of various cities:

Board of Jewish Education
4650 N. Port Washington Rd.
Milwaukee, WI 53212

Bureau of Jewish Education
2030 S. Taylor Rd.
Cleveland, OH 44118

Jewish Educators Assembly
155 Fifth Ave.
New York, NY 10010

Herzl Institute Study Tour

This is a four-week tour with lectures on Israeli society. For information, contact

Program Coordinator
Herzl Institute
515 Park Ave.
New York, NY 10022

Understanding Israeli politics

UNFORMED AND VOID, WITH DARKNESS OVER THE SURFACE OF THE DEEP

Genesis 1:2   תהו ובהו וחשך על פני תהום

Since its establishment, Israel has been governed under a system of parliamentary democracy. Prior to May 1948, when David Ben-Gurion proclaimed the independence of the Jewish state, Palestine was ruled under a mandate awarded to Great Britain by the League of Nations after World War I. When the British withdrew, following the 1947 U.N. partition plan calling for Jewish and Arab states in the country, Palestinian Jewry—the Yishuv—was able to establish formal governing institutions with relative ease because Jewish communal structures such as the Jewish Agency and the Histadrut had been developed during the Mandate period.

The Israeli political system consists of an executive (the cabinet under the prime minister), a legislature (the Knesset), and a judiciary. Acting under the rule of law, the Knesset is the supreme sovereign body. Owing to various disputes beginning in the early years of the state about religious issues, Israel has no constitution. Instead the Knesset enacts what are known as hokei yesod—basic laws. In addition there are various laws held over from the Mandate period as well as the period preceding that, when the area was part of the Ottoman Empire.

Israel's president is the nominal head of state. S/he is, in reality, a figurehead whose duties are largely ceremonial. The president is elected by a secret majority vote of the Knesset for five-year terms. The current president of Israel, elected in 1978, is Yitzchak Navon. His predecessors were Chaim Weizmann (1949–52), Yitzhak Ben-Zvi (1952–63), Zalman Shazar (1963–73), and Ephraim Katzir (1973–78).

The System

THE KNESSET

Israel's parliament, the Knesset, is a unicameral legislative body consisting of 120 members. The Knesset is elected for a four-year term through direct secret ballot by Israeli citizens over the age of eighteen.

Israelis do not vote for individual members of the Knesset (MKs); rather, voting is based on "proportional representation." This means that Israelis vote

The prime ministers of Israel

1949–54	David Ben-Gurion (Mapai)
1954–55	Moshe Sharett (Mapai)
1955–63	David Ben-Gurion (Mapai)
1963–69	Levi Eshkol (Mapai, Israeli Labor party)
1969–74	Golda Meir (Israeli Labor party)
1974–77	Yitzhak Rabin (Israeli Labor party)
1977–	Menachem Begin (Likud)

The Knesset lineup as of May 1977

Party	Number of Seats
Likud	43
Israeli Labor Alignment	32
Democratic Movement for Change	15
National Religious party	12
Rakach-Democratic Front	5
Agudat and Poalei Agudat Israel	5
Sheli	2
Shlomzion	2
Citizens Rights	1
Independent Liberals	1
United Arab List	1
Flatto-Sharon	1

These are the results of the election to the ninth Knesset, not accounting for later splits.

for a party; each party has a list of candidates presented to the public in numerical order. The number of members a party sends to the Knesset depends on the party's percentage of the popular vote in the election. Thus a party receives forty seats in the Knesset (one-third of the total) if it receives one-third of the vote. MKs are not directly responsible to geographic regions.

THE CABINET (ALSO CALLED "THE GOVERNMENT")

The cabinet of ministers, headed by the prime minister (currently Menachem Begin), is the executive of the Israeli political system. In legal terms the prime minister is not as powerful as the president is in the United States. S/he could better be characterized as "first among equals" in the cabinet. However, the stronger an individual prime minister is, the more "first" s/he tends to be.

The prime minister is generally the first name on the winning party's list; the president invites this person to form a government. For example, Menachem Begin, first on the winning Likud list, became prime minister in 1977.

The cabinet is responsible to the Knesset. Since no party has ever received an absolute majority in an Israeli election, the largest party (the Israeli Labor party and its predecessor [Mapai] before 1977 and the Likud since then) has had to form coalitions with smaller parties in order to guarantee a majority in the Knesset. In exchange for their support the smaller parties receive ministerial portfolios and other political concessions.

If there is a vote of no confidence—i.e., if the prime minister cannot maintain majority support in the Knesset—s/he must either resign or form a new coalition. The resignation of the prime minister may result in the dissolution of the Knesset and new elections. In other circumstances the largest party may choose another member to be its leader and form a new coalition. This was the case when Yitzhak Rabin became prime minister following the resignation of Golda Meir in 1974.

Israel has both civil and religious courts. The highest court, the Supreme Court, is composed of a president, deputy president, and seven justices. The religious courts have jurisdiction over all personal matters, such as marriage and divorce. Thus there are Jewish, Muslim, and Christian courts in addition to the civil ones. Orthodox religious control of personal matters through the religious courts has been the source of much conflict in Israel, since the vast majority of the population are not Orthodox. The largest party in the governing coalitions has always needed the support of the (Orthodox) National Religious party, which is why these conflicts remain unresolved.

THE HISTADRUT

Founded in 1920, the Histadrut is Israel's general trade union federation. Its first secretary-general was David Ben-Gurion, later to become the first prime minister of the independent State of Israel. The current secretary-general is Yerucham Meshel. The Histadrut is actually much more than a trade union federation; under its roof are workers' cooperatives, holding companies, extensive social services, and a health program: Kupat Holim. The various Israeli political parties control the Histadrut through elections in the same way the Knesset is controlled. In the 1977 Histadrut elections the Israeli Labor Alignment maintained its electoral supremacy in the Histadrut despite its defeat in the Knesset elections.

THE WORLD ZIONIST ORGANIZATION AND THE JEWISH AGENCY

From 1897, when the World Zionist Organization (WZO) was created through the efforts of Theodor Herzl, until the British Mandate over Palestine began in 1922, the WZO was an independent organization promoting the Zionist cause. The Jewish Agency, established under the Mandate, was designed to assist in the development of the Jewish national home. The WZO and the Jewish Agency functioned virtually as one until 1929. That year, at the initiative of Chaim Weizmann at the sixteenth World Zionist Congress, the WZO and Jewish Agency separated to allow Diaspora Jews who were not Zionists to support Jewish efforts in Palestine. By 1947, however, little real distinction existed between the two. Most of the non-Zionists had resigned, and the same people sat on the executives of both organizations.

Some Israeli Political Quotes
The State of Israel embodies the national rights and aspirations of the Jewish people, guaranteeing its continued existence and political independence. . . . The national rights of the Palestinian Arab people have never been fulfilled. The Palestinian people has the basic right to self-determination, which includes the right to establish an independent state by the side of, and coexisting peacefully with, the State of Israel (Moked election platform, 1973).

The State of Israel will be open for Jewish immigration and for the Ingathering of the Exiles; it will foster the development of the country for the benefit of the inhabitants; it will be based on freedom, justice, and peace as envisaged by the prophets of Israel; it will ensure complete equality of social and political rights to all its inhabitants irrespective of religion, race, or sex; it will guarantee freedom of religion, conscience, language, education, and culture; it will safeguard the holy places of all religions; and it will be faithful to the principles of the Charter of the United Nations (Israel's Declaration of Independence, May 15, 1948).

I suppose every leader of a state sees his major tasks as those of perfecting his society and making his special impact on the destiny of his people. I do not know that I would use the term architect, but if I stayed with the building idiom I would say that the big difference between Israel and other states . . . was that we had to construct a state edifice almost from the drawing board—laying the foundations and erecting the main structure—whereas other state leaders have inherited the structure and were concerned with renovations, repairs, and the building of new wings, in addition of course to running their "going concern." We are not a "going concern" (David Ben-Gurion; quoted from *Ben-Gurion Looks Back*, with Moshe Pearlman [Shocken Books, 1970], p. 120).

The Jewish Agency, which had been the Jewish governing body and the Yishuv's central institution until the creation of the State of Israel, had taken a back seat to the newly elected government when the country was born. Instead, it became primarily concerned with immigration, absorption, and settlement of immigrants in Israel and the promotion of Zionist concerns abroad. In 1971 the Jewish Agency was "reconstituted" to give 50 percent of its control to the World Zionist Organization and 50 percent to Diaspora leaders (mainly influential and wealthy fund raisers).

Who's who, who's where, and who's what in the Israeli parties.

A scorecard for Israeli politics

THE ISRAELI LABOR ALIGNMENT (HA-MAARACH)

Israeli Labor Alignment = Israeli Labor party (Mapai + Ahdut Avodah + Rafi) + Mapam

The Israeli Labor Alignment, Israel's most powerful political force until 1977, is a joint election list offered by the Israeli Labor Party (Avodah) and the United Workers party (Mapam). The Labor party was formed in 1968 through a merger of several parties, the largest and most prominent of which was Mapai. Mapai (Israeli Workers party) was founded as a Zionist democratic socialist party in 1931 under the leadership of David Ben-Gurion and Berl Katznelson. It was the major component of all government coalitions prior to 1977 and historically was the backbone of the Yishuv and the Zionist labor movement. Famous names associated with Mapai include those of Golda Meir, Pinchas Sapir, Abba Eban, and former prime ministers David Ben-Gurion, Moshe Sharett, and Levi Eshkol.

As mentioned, the former Mapai is the largest element in the Labor party, which is a member of the Socialist International and resembles a West European social democratic party (although it has many internal differences both on foreign and domestic policies). But there are two other components to the party: what were formally Rafi (Israeli Workers List) and Ahdut Avodah (Unity of Labor). Rafi was a small splinter party that left Mapai in the early 1960s, led by David Ben-Gurion, Moshe Dayan, and Shimon Peres. When Rafi merged into the newly formed Labor party, Ben-Gurion refused to rejoin his former allies and disciples in Mapai for political and personal reasons. Dayan and Peres did join the new party, and today Peres is its chairman. Ahdut Avodah was a leftist nationalist party that broke from Mapam in the 1950s. Its leading lights included the late Yigal Allon, Israel Galili, Yitzhak Ben Aharon, and the late Yitzhak Tabenkin. Former prime minister Yitzhak Rabin, while close to Allon during most of his career, is not really identified as a member of any of these factions, which are still visible within the Labor party. Since the 1977 defeat of Labor, there has been reshaping of some of the party's internal constellations.

Mapai and Ahdut Avodah were associated with separate kibbutz movements, the Ichud and Meuchad respectively, which began a process of merger in 1979. The youth movement affiliated with Ichud is Habonim, and Dror is affiliated with Meuchad.

Mapam, the other component of the Israeli Labor Alignment, is a smaller Zionist socialist party and is ideologically to the left of its partner. Much of its strength is rooted in its affiliated kibbutz movement, the Kibbutz Artzi, whose youth movement is Hashomer Hatzair.

LIKUD (NATIONAL LIBERAL UNION)

Likud is a common election list between several right-wing and centrist parties and is the major component of the Israeli government that was formed after the 1977 elections (in which it won more Knesset seats than any other Israeli party). Before taking power it offered the strongest opposition to Labor governments, maintaining an anti-Histadrut, antisocialist line and opposing anything but minimal concessions to the Arabs.

Likud = Gahal (Herut + Liberal party) + Laam + Greater Israel Movement

Gahal, the most important component of the Likud, is an alignment between the middle-class Liberal party and Herut, a vociferous right-wing party led by the current premier, Menachem Begin. Herut was originally formed in 1949 as a successor to the Irgun Zvai Leumi, the underground military organization led by Begin. Gahal was in the National Unity government formed during the May–June 1967 crisis but withdrew in opposition to the Israeli negotiating position on the cease-fire ending the War of Attrition with Egypt (1970).

The other groups in the Likud are Laam (The State List—members of Rafi who refused to rejoin Mapai) and the Greater Israel Movement.

THE DEMOCRATIC MOVEMENT AND SHAI

The Democratic Movement and Shai are the remains of the Democratic Movement for Change (also called DMC or "Dash"), a reformist party founded shortly before the 1977 elections and led by archeologist and former general Yigal Yadin. The DMC became Israel's third largest party—largely by capitalizing on discontent with the previous Labor party governments. It called for reform in many areas of Israeli society, especially in electoral laws, but joined the Likud government without gaining major concessions for its program.

Involved in the formation of the DMC were such disparate elements as the Free Center party of Shmuel Tamir (until recently justice minister), a breakaway group from Herut that later joined and then left the Likud; and Shinui (Change), a reform movement that became prominent in the discontent after the 1973 war, led by a Tel Aviv University law professor, Amnon Rubinstein. In the fall of 1978 tensions within DMC over participation in the Begin government came to a head, resulting in a split. Half stayed in the government and formed the Democratic Movement (led by Yadin), and half called itself Shai and went into the opposition. One Knesset member, Asaf Yaguri, formed his own one-man faction.

NATIONAL RELIGIOUS PARTY (NRP OR MAFDAL)

The NRP is an Orthodox Jewish religious Zionist party whose moderate strength in the Knesset has been enhanced by being needed for government coalitions. Composed of Mizrachi and Hapoel ha-Mizrachi, it essentially wants Israel to be governed on the basis of religious law. In recent years the NRP has become increasingly influenced by its "Young Guard," which in turn has been influenced by Gush Emunim (see below).

AGUDAT ISRAEL AND POALE AGUDAT ISRAEL (THE TORAH FRONT)

The Agudat Israel and Poale Agudat Israel are also religious parties, but they have much less influence than the NRP, which they oppose as too moderate on religious questions; they want Israel to become a theocracy. They are non-Zionist and want a rigid application of Torah to modern society.

SHELI

Sheli is the Hebrew acronym for "Peace and Equality in Israel." It is a peace-oriented movement formed in 1977. Its main component is Moked, a socialist Zionist party led by Colonel Meir Pail. In the 1977 elections Sheli's most famous figure was Arie Lova Eliav, a former secretary-general of the Labor party who split from his party in opposition to its foreign and domestic policies.

Sheli has advocated an Israeli policy of recognizing the Palestinians and supporting withdrawal from territories occupied in 1967 for a full peace settlement with the Arabs.

RAKACH (NEW COMMUNIST LIST)

Rakach, Israel's Moscow-oriented Communist party, receives most of its support from Israeli Arabs as a protest vote. In the 1960s when Maki (Israeli Communist party) split into Jewish (Maki) and Arab (Rakach) factions, Rakach gradually emerged as the stronger of the two. Maki later merged into Moked. In the 1977 elections Rakach ran as part of the "Democratic Front" with several smaller groups, including a section of the Israeli Black Panthers, a protest group of poor Oriental Jews.

OTHERS

There are several smaller parties and independent members in the Knesset. The Independent Liberal party, a splinter group who broke away from the Liberals, has in the past been especially vocal on issues of religion-state relations and has advocated civil marriage laws for Israelis ineligible for marriage according to religious law, an idea the religious parties oppose. Moshe Dayan is an independent member of the Knesset, having been elected on the Labor party list and then quitting his party immediately after its defeat to become the foreign minister in the Likud government. He resigned from the Likud government in 1979 in opposition to its foreign policy.

Shalom Akhshav (Peace Now) is a dovish nonparliamentary movement started by reserve army officers who want Israel to pursue a more flexible foreign policy. With the slogan of "Peace is better than a piece of land," Shalom Akhshav argues that Israel should be willing to trade lands taken in the 1967 war for peace and that security concerns, not religion, should determine policy. They oppose Gush Emunim, a right-wing messianic, religious, nonparliamentary group that tries to establish settlements on the West Bank and does not want Israel to give up lands God promised to the Jews in the Bible, even for the sake of peace.

The Citizens Rights Movement (CRM) is a consumer and reformist party whose sole Knesset member is Shulamit Aloni, formerly of Labor. After the Israel-Egypt peace treaty, Likud members Geula Cohen and Moshe Shamir withdrew from their party in opposition to the treaty. Their new faction, Tehiya (Renaissance), supports a "Greater Israel" ideology that is opposed to Israeli withdrawal from territories taken in 1967 and is vocal as an extreme right-wing group. The United Arab List ran in the 1977 elections as an affiliate of Labor. Shlomo Flatto-Sharon fled France to avoid prosecution for financial crimes, went to Israel, ran for Knesset, won, and thus received parliamentary immunity from deportation. He faces numerous court and Knesset challenges because of the charges against him. Flamboyant right-wing General Arik Sharon (*not* to be confused with Flatto-Sharon), a founder of the Likud, ran on his own Shlomzion ticket in 1977, won two mandates, and rejoined Likud.

Keeping up

Keeping up to date with Israeli daily politics is no mean feat. If you read Hebrew, look at the overseas editions of the Israeli press. In English there is the overseas edition of the *Jerusalem Post*. In addition, you can get up-to-date news from the daily bulletin of the Jewish Telegraphic Agency. For analysis, valuable periodicals include *Jewish Frontier, Forum, Jerusalem Quarterly,* and *Midstream.*

GENERAL DISCLAIMER
By the time you read "Understanding Israeli Politics" from beginning to end, it is highly likely that at least one of the parties you read about will have split. It is also likely that numerous changes and splits took place between the time this chapter was written and the time it has appeared in print. This general hazard that goes with writing about Israeli politics, as problematic as it is, testifies to the vigor of democracy in Israel.

Political action for Israel

Over the years the importance of the relationship between Israel and the United States has grown immensely. At the present time the U.S. is Israel's strongest ally both politically and militarily, and it is important that we encourage such support. The following is a guide for how to create political support for Israel. We begin with the realization that the U.S. policy toward Israel is formulated by the president (with the secretary of state and others) and by Congress.

Exerting political pressure

It is crucial for people who support Israel to try to exert pressure on political figures to support Israel—utilizing politicians' pragmatic/political and idealistic/ideological concerns. Support for Israel can stem from narrow self-interest (Jews vote and give money to campaigns); idealistic concerns ("Israel is right" or "Israel is a small country fighting for survival"); etc. All these factors should be taken into account (though the first is usually unspoken) when you are trying to influence the political process.

The Executive Branch: There is basically only one way to influence the president. Let him/her (may she be elected soon in our days) know how you feel about a presidential statement supporting Israel, a specific bill relating to Israel, etc. The simplest way to do this is either by mail or telegram. (Calling the president results in your being disconnected and is, in general, not an especially good idea unless you're on calling terms with the commander in chief.) Telegrams to the president or your congressperson can be sent at cheaper-than-usual rates.

One suggested method for quick responses to specific events is organizing a telegram bank. This basically involves obtaining the authorization from large numbers of people to send x number of telegrams in their area to the president or a congressperson during one year. For explicit instructions in setting up a telegram bank, see How to Make Waves.

Congressional representatives: The same holds true for contacting congresspeople. Letters, telegrams, and even phone calls to local offices are particularly effective with congresspeople, who are responsible to a smaller constituency. Ergo, representatives are even more affected by their constituents' communications than are senators. And because of their proportionately smaller constituency, other approaches are possible: phone calls and even meetings with congresspeople (or at least their aides) are not impossible to arrange, especially when they return to visit their local districts. Remember that you want to express your concern and have an influence on your congressperson, so be careful not to antagonize him/her.

Congresspeople can be asked to support congressional resolutions or specific bills calling for aid to Israel. Before such a bill is voted on, you should express your support for the measure. Whatever the outcome, after the vote, check to find out how your congressperson voted. (Call his/her local office if it's not in your newspaper.) Send a letter of appreciation if the bill was supported and a critical letter if the bill was not supported.

Remember that the congressional process is a complex one. Accordingly, you should do several things: (1) Encourage your representative to help get the bill to the floor so that it can be voted on. Find out if s/he sits on a committee that is in charge of the bill (i.e., Ways and Means, Foreign Relations, etc.). (2) Realize that cosponsoring a bill means a higher level of support than just voting for it. The Jackson Amendment, with its seventy-six cosponsors in the Senate, had a very different impact (in the short run at least) than it would have had if the amendment had been sponsored by Jackson alone. So encourage any representative to sponsor a bill of support for Israel. (3) Avoid naiveté. To vote in favor of a bill that has no chance of passage or one that's headed for a veto anyway is not nearly as crucial as voting for a bill on a close vote. Voting for a crippling amendment and then voting for the gutted bill is just playing politics. If, for example, an original bill calls for $50 million in aid for Israel, and Senator X proposes an amendment lowering that amount to $2 million in aid, it is not uncommon for slightly unscrupulous politicians to lobby for the passage of the amendment and then agree to vote for the amended bill. Whereupon they loudly claim to be supporters of Israel. Try to be aware of your representative's position from start to finish. The more politically aware you are, the more influence you will have.

REMEMBER: In the last few years Congress has appropriated each year more money for Israel than can be raised by the entire world Jewish community. So by exerting only a fraction of the effort that goes into UJA fund raising, we can potentially arouse significant financial, military, and political support for Israel.

Lobbying: Political lobbying cannot be done by nonprofit organizations (in a major way). Many Jewish organizations have expressed their opinions on certain bills and policies, but it became clear that a more effective lobbying mechanism was desirable. As a result the American Israel Public Affairs Committee (AIPAC) was set up in 1954. Under the chairmanship of Morris Amitai it plays a major role in attempting to foster a close relationship between the U.S. and Israel. It publishes *Near East Report,* a newsletter with information and opinion on the Middle East situation. To receive it and become a member, write

AIPAC
c/o 1341 G St. NW
Washington, DC 20005

It should be noted that similar methods of protesting/influencing can be used with oil companies, big businesses, the United Nations (UNESCO), etc. Any political institution is sensitive to public opinion, although some are more concerned than others and are particularly attentive to mail and telegrams.

AIPAC also puts out a handy aid to the legislative process: *The U.S. Congress: A Guide to Citizen Action.* Since it is a lobbying organization, AIPAC is supported by private donations that are not tax deductible. Naturally the Israeli Consulate also tries to foster good relationships, but this is done through the Israeli ambassador and carried out within the executive, rather than the congressional, branch of government.

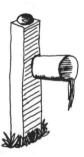

Combating Arab propaganda/making the case for Israel

Another way to foster American support for Israel is to encourage such support among the American public. Obviously this in turn affects the president and congresspeople.

The one thing is clear: to reach the American public you have to make use of the media—through paid advertising on radio and TV, on billboards, and in newspapers. This method, however, can be extremely expensive and is not effective as a response to a specific crisis.

Inexpensive day-to-day methods include the letters-to-the-editor pages, radio talk shows, etc. Some groups have set up watchdog committees, which assign people to read specific newspapers or magazines and respond to any anti-Israel article, editorial, or even letter to the editor. This must be handled tactfully. It can also be done in a more subtle fashion, i.e., a truthful letter praising the brave struggle of a certain group for national liberation could in passing make reference to other such successful struggles in the past— Ireland, Israel, etc.

Similarly, arranging for an honest article about an Israeli sports figure, craftsperson, actor, etc. to appear in the relevant pages of a newspaper or in appropriate specialized magazines such as *Sports Illustrated* is good propaganda. A sympathetic portrayal of an Israeli is worth more than a hundred letters about why Israel can't give back *x* until *y* happens. Such articles naturally require some writing ability. Also, arrange for an articulate spokesperson to appear on a local radio talk show. You might also set up a speakers' bureau and offer speakers and/or films to local schools, civic organizations, lodges, etc. If the library can't or won't buy them, present appropriate books to the local library. Arrange an exhibit in the library during Israel Independence Day week. Set up an Israeli products booth at a local fair. Wear a pro-Israel button on your clothes. Decorate your car with appropriate bumper stickers. It's all free publicity.

Crisis reactions

Many of these actions can also be taken during particularly critical moments in Israel's history. Other things to be done in a crisis include the following:

1. Plan a rally.

2. Set up information booths at shopping centers.

3. Arrange for press conferences by local prominent clergy, politicians, etc., Jews and non-Jews.

4. Set up a hot line with latest information about the situation and advice for volunteers. For the latest teletype readings call UPI or AP and coordinate this so that everyone doesn't call on his/her own. When you have the latest news, use your hot line or newspaper to disseminate it.

5. Get out a local newspaper keeping people and press posted on the latest developments.

6. To get up-to-date information, check the list of newspapers and magazines in Bringing Israel to Your Galut.

All of these can be planned very quickly, given a degree of efficiency and cooperation among the volunteers. But remember—time is of the essence in reacting to a crisis. It is useless to stage a demonstration a week after the crisis has passed. Don't expect to cover every detail as you would under less critical circumstances. Strive to cover as many areas as possible with dispatch, calmness, and efficiency. It is also a good idea to prepare in advance for a crisis. Have a list of volunteers on hand, contingency plans, etc. For more details on political organizing, see How to Make Waves.

The following selection of books dealing with various aspects of Zionism and Israel—grouped according to theme—is hardly comprehensive. It can, however, serve as the start of your own 10-foot Israel bookshelf. Whenever possible, books available in paperback (*) are listed.

". . . the ancient boundary stone that your ancestors have set up (Proverbs 22:28)

1. Aharoni, Yohanan. *The Land of the Bible.* Philadelphia: Westminster Press, 1967.
2. *Albright, W. F. *The Archeology of Palestine,* rev. ed. Baltimore: Penguin/Pelican, 1960.
3. Amiran, Ruth. *Ancient Pottery of the Holy Land.* Jerusalem: Massada, and New Brunswick, N.J.: Rutgers, 1970.
4. Anati, Emanuel. *Palestine before the Hebrews.* New York: Knopf, 1963.
5. Kenyon, Kathleen. *Archeology in the Holy Land.* New York: Praeger, 1961, 1970.
6. *Noy, Dov, ed. *Folktales of Israel.* Chicago: U. of Chicago, 1963.
7. Vilnay, Zev. *Legends of Jerusalem.* Philadelphia: Jewish Publication Society, 1973.
8. *Wright, G. Ernest. *Biblical Archeology,* rev. ed. London: Duckworth, and Philadelphia: Westminster, 1962 (paperback).
9. *Yadin, Yigael. *Masada.* New York: Random House, 1966.
10. ———, ed. *Jerusalem Revisited: Archeology in the Holy City.* Jerusalem: Israel Exploration Society, 1975.
11. ———. *Hazor: The Rediscovery of a Great Citadel of the Bible.* New York: Random House, 1975.

"Your old men shall dream dreams, and your young men shall see visions" (Joel 3:1)

1. Ben-Gurion, David. *Rebirth and Destiny of Israel.* New York: Philosophical Library, 1954.
2. Brenner, Yosef Chayim. *Breakdown and Bereavement.* Ithaca, N.Y.: Cornell U., 1971.
3. Halkin, Hillel. *Letters to an American Jewish Friend: A Zionist's Polemic.* Philadelphia: Jewish Publication Society, 1977.
4. *Hertzberg, Arthur. *The Zionist Idea.* New York: Atheneum/Temple Books, 1969; also Schocken (paperback).
5. *Herzl, Theodore. *The Jewish State.* New York: Herzl, 1970.
6. *Laqueur, Walter. *A History of Zionism.* New York: Holt, Rinehart & Winston, 1972; also Schocken (paperback).
7. *Lowenthal, Marvin, ed. and trans. *The Diaries of Theodore Herzl.* New York: Dial; also Grosset and Dunlap, 1959 (paperback).
8. Shazar, Zalman. *Morning Star.* Philadelphia: Jewish Publication Society, 1967.

9. *Urofsky, Melvin. *American Zionism from Herzl to the Holocaust.* Garden City, N.Y.: Anchor Press/Doubleday, 1975.

10. ———. *We are One! American Jewry and Israel.* Garden City, N.Y.: Anchor Press/Doubleday, 1978.

11. *Weizmann, Chaim. *Trial and Error.* Philadelphia: Jewish Publication Society, 1949; New York: Schocken, 1966 (paperback).

"A time for being born . . . a time for planting . . . a time for building up" (Ecclesiastes 3:2–3)

1. Eban, Abba. *My Country: The Story of Modern Israel.* New York: Random House, 1972.

2. *Kaufman, Gerald. *To Build the Promised Land.* London: Weidenfeld and Nicolson, 1973; New York: Bantam, 1974 (paperback).

3. *Sachar, Howard Morley. *From the Ends of the Earth: The Peoples of Israel.* New York: World, 1964; New York: Delta, 1970 (paperback).

"A time for war" (Ecclesiastes 3:8)

1. *Collins, Larry and LaPierre, Dominique. *O Jerusalem!* New York: Simon and Schuster, 1972; New York: Pocket Books, 1973 (paperback).

2. Herzog, Haim. *The War of Atonement.* Boston: Little, Brown, 1975.

3. *Kurzman, Dan. *Genesis 1948.* New York: New American Library, 1970; New York: Signet, 1972 (paperback).

4. Luttwak, Edward and Horowitz, Dan. *The Israeli Army.* New York: Harper and Row, 1975.

5. Rabinovich, Abraham. *The Battle for Jerusalem.* Philadelphia: Jewish Publication Society, 1972.

6. Schiff, Zev. *A History of the Israeli Army (1880–1974).* San Francisco: Straight Arrow Press, 1974.

". . . and a time for peace" (Ecclesiastes 3:8)

1. Buber, Martin. *Israel and Palestine.* London: East and West, 1952.

2. Eliav, Arie Lova. *Land of the Hart.* Philadelphia: Jewish Publication Society, 1974.

3. *Gendizer, Irene L., ed. *A Middle East Reader.* New York: Pergasus, 1969.

4. *Harkabi, Yehoshua. *Palestine and Israel.* Jerusalem: Keter, 1974.

5. *Laqueur, Walter Z. *The Israel-Arab Reader.* New York: Bantam, 1970.

6. *Shapiro, Avraham, ed. *The Seventh Day.* London: André Deutsch, 1970; London: Penguin, 1971; New York: Scribners, 1972.

7. Schweid, Eliezer. *Israel at the Crossroads.* Philadelphia: Jewish Publication Society, 1973.

"Walk around Zion, circle it" (Psalms 48:13)

1. *Fox, Sarah K. *Footloose in Jerusalem.* Jerusalem: Center for Jewish Education in the Diaspora of the Hebrew University, 1977.
2. *Liebner, Joel. *Israel on Five and Ten Dollars a Day.* New York: Essandess/Simon and Schuster, see latest edition.
3. Orni, Efraim and Efrat, Elisha. *Geography of Israel,* 3d rev. ed. Jerusalem: Israel Universities, 1971.
4. Vilnay, Zev. *The Guide to Israel,* 16th ed. Jerusalem: 15 RaDaK, 1973.

"See what kind of country it is. Are the people who dwell in it strong or weak, few or many?" (Numbers 13:18)

1. Bentwich, Joseph. *Education in Israel.* Philadelphia: Jewish Publication Society, 1965.
2. *Bettelheim, Bruno. *The Children of the Dream.* New York: Macmillan, 1969; New York: Avon, 1973 (paperback).
3. Criden, Yosef and Gelb, Saadia. *The Kibbutz Experience: Dialogue in Kfar Blum.* New York: Herzl, 1974.
4. Curtis, Michael and Chertoff, Mordecai S., eds. *Israel: Social Structure and Change.* New Brunswick, N.J.: Transaction, 1973.
5. Eisenstadt, S. N. *Israeli Society.* London: Weidenfeld and Nicolson, 1967; New York; Basic, 1968.

6. *Elon, Amos. *The Israelis: Founders and Sons.* London: Weidenfeld and Nicolson, 1971; London: Sphere, 1972; New York: Holt, Rinehart and Winston, 1972; an American edition also available in paperback.

7. *Fein, Leonard. *Politics in Israel.* Comparative Politics Series. Boston: Little, Brown, 1967.

8. Halevi, Nadav and Klinow-Malul, Ruth. *The Economic Development of Israel.* New York: Praeger, 1968.

9. Herman, Simon. *Israelis and Jews.* New York: Random House, 1970; Philadelphia: Jewish Publication Society, 1971.

10. Horowitz, David. *The Economics of Israel.* Oxford: Pergamon, 1967.

11. Ichud Habonim. *Kibbutz: A New Society?* (anthology). Tel Aviv: Ichud Habonim, 1971.

12. Lissak, Moshe. *Social Mobility in Israeli Society.* Jerusalem: Israel Universities, 1969.

13. *Spiro, Melford E. *Children of the Kibbutz.* Cambridge, Mass.: Harvard U., 1958; New York: Schocken, 1972 (paperback).

14. *———. *Kibbutz: Venture in Utopia.* Cambridge, Mass.: Harvard U., 1956; New York: Schocken, 1972 (paperback).

"Not . . . on bread alone" (Deuteronomy 8:3)

1. Anderson, Elliott, ed. *Contemporary Israeli Literature.* Philadelphia: Jewish Publication Society, 1977.

2. *Art in Israel.* Tel Aviv: Sadan Press, 1975.

3. *Blocker, Joel. *Israeli Stories.* New York: Schocken, 1962; New York: Bantam, 1971 (paperback).

4. *Burnshaw, Stanley; Carmel, T.; and Spicehandler, Ezra, eds. *The Modern Hebrew Poem in Itself.* New York: Schocken, 1966.

5. Gradenwitz, Peter. *The Music of Israel.* New York: Norton, 1949.

6. *Michener, James. *The Source.* New York: Random House, 1965; Fawcett, 1978 (paperback).

7. *———, ed. *Firstfruits.* New York: Fawcett, 1974.

8. *Oz, Amos. *My Michael.* New York: Knopf, 1972; Lancer, 1973 (paperback).

9. *———. *Elsewhere, Perhaps.* New York: Bantam, 1974.

10. *Spicehandler, Ezra, ed. *Modern Hebrew Stories.* New York: Bantam, 1971.

"It is an ancient nation; a nation whose language you do not know—you will not understand what they say" (Jeremiah 5:15)

1. *Ben Yehuda, Ehud and Weinstein, David, eds. *Ben Yehuda's Pocket English-Hebrew, Hebrew-English Dictionary.* New York: Washington Square, 1966.

2. Chomsky, Zev William. *Hebrew: The Eternal Language.* Philadelphia: Jewish Publication Society, 1957.

3. Horowitz, Edward. *How the Hebrew Language Grew.* New York: Ktav, 1967.

4. *Sivan, Reuven and Levenston, Edward A. *The New Bantam Megiddo Hebrew and English Dictionary.* New York: Bantam, 1975.

In general: Look up relevant articles in the *Encyclopaedia Judaica* and see: *Israel Pocket Library (reprints from the *Encyclopaedia Judaica*) titles: Geography, History until 1880, Jerusalem, Zionism, Immigration and Settlement, Society, Holocaust, Religious Life, Economy, Archeology, Anti-Semitism, Education and Science, Culture, Democracy, Index (Jerusalem: Keter Publishing House, 1973–75).

THE LAST IS THE MOST PRECIOUS

Genesis Rabbah 78 אחרון אחרון חביב

How to be a mentsh

Wise old talmudists know a secret. They seldom talk about it, especially not with outsiders to their world, and may even react somewhat defensively if you bring it up. Nevertheless—sshhh!—they know: there is a fifth section to the Shulhan Arukh!

That great sixteenth-century work, which purports in four sections to cover every aspect of the Jewish behavioral code—ritual, civil, criminal, domestic, and what-have-you—remains in need of a supplement. That fifth section, which *by its very nature cannot be written down,* does not contain any profoundly esoteric doctrines; it rather deals with something that a hypothetical author might have called *Hilkhot Enoshut,* or *How to Be a Mentsh.*

If your particular talmudist is a very wise one, and a little bit open-minded to boot, he may go one step further and admit to you that without this fifth and most intangible portion of the code, the other four sections "teygn oyf kapores" (roughly translated, "are utterly worthless"). I remember that a dear friend of mine once confessed to me that when she was first becoming involved with traditional Jewish life she naturally assumed that all observant Jews must be great and saintly tzaddikim: anyone who performs so many mitzvot could be nothing else. Needless to say, she learned the hard way. The sad fact remains that there are, and probably always were, some people around clever enough to fulfill the letter of the law entirely, while completely missing the point of its edifying spirit. You don't have to be a disciple of Rabbi Saul of Tarsus to know this; the tradition itself has always admitted that there is such a character as the naval bi-reshut ha-Torah—the knave who remains (technically) within the domain of Torah.

Now that the *Catalog* has taught you so much about those first four sections of the Shulhan Arukh, laying out guidelines for interpersonal as well as ritual conduct, we thought the time had come to say a few words about that which really cannot be spoken: what it means to be a mentsh. Or, to put it in other terms, once the details of conduct are all settled, what kind of human being is the Jewish path trying to create? Jewish law allows itself to deal with deeds alone, and it is in the realm of deeds that the Jew believes s/he is ultimately tested. But what of feelings, attitudes, emotions, all of those inner things that go into making a human being? Here the fifth section takes over, and all we can offer are some hints as to what it might say.

WO/MAN IS CREATED IN THE IMAGE OF GOD. This is not an abstract pronouncement, but one that has to be seriously translated into daily living: it means you and me, him and her. Our teacher the late A. J. Heschel used to say that this was the real reason why graven images are forbidden by the Torah. The point is not that there is to be *no* image of God in the world, but rather that *you* as a human being are the only image you are allowed to fashion. Think of this as the starting point of a religious ethic. The most nearly divine thing that exists in this world (far more than any combination of letters on parchment, written by human beings!) is a person. I stand up out of respect for a Torah scroll; I kiss mezuzot; how then should I relate to human beings? When confronted with a difficult interpersonal decision in life, I might do well to ask myself: How should an image-of-God treat an image-of-God in such a moment? LOVE YOUR NEIGHBOR AS YOURSELF; I AM THE LORD, says the Torah. Check out the commentaries on that one.

The fascinating thing about God-images, of course, is that they crystallize in different ways in each human being. Jews are wary of such easy mystical formulations as "All of us are God," in part because that could obliterate the very real differences that exist between us. (Have a look at Martin Buber's writings—he's the one who has best articulated this for us.) In order to know, then, how that image-of-God over there needs to be treated, I first have to recognize that person's otherness and get to know that other as a human being. This might be the first specific in the Jewish "being a mentsh" guide: *Know the Other.* And most particularly, perhaps: *Know the Other's Pain.*

Rabbi Moshe Leib Sassover used to say: I learned from a peasant how to love my fellow-Jews.

Once, at a party, I heard a drunken peasant say to his friend:

"Do you love me or not?"

The other answered, "I love you greatly."

The first peasant went on to ask: "Do you know what I need?"

"How can I possibly know what you need?" was the reply.

"How then," asked the peasant, "can you say that you love me, when you don't know what I need?"

From this Rabbi Moshe Leib learned the love of Israel: Feel their needs, know their pain, be part of their suffering.

This is what it really means to be a Hasidic rebbe, when that institution is functioning at its highest: to know the other in his/her otherness and at the same time to be able to take that person's pains and joys into your own self. In modern times such neo-Hasidic figures as Buber and Heschel were able to carry this way of knowing beyond the bounds of Israel, providing models we would do well to follow.

But this sense of knowing the other's needs is not purely Hasidic; it also functions within the realm of halakhah. Having recently moved into a new neighborhood, I called a local rabbi one Thursday evening to ask about the reliability of a kosher butcher shop I had seen nearby. His first question: "Do you need to eat this meat for Shabbos?" This man, I then knew, was a rav. He began by trying to know my situation. The tradition among the best of halakhic authorities, at least until modern times, was always to be lenient in interpreting Jewish law for others, especially where strictness might cause some hardship, even if the rabbi chose to be more stringent in his own personal conduct. Examples could be multiplied, and in areas much more vital than that of my butcher's meat.

Flowing from this ability to know the other and to identify with his plight is a second principle of Jewish mentshlikhkeit: *Generosity of Spirit*. There is a willingness to give to the other, in both material and spiritual ways of giving, which transcends any of the purely legal norms of tzedakah. "Giving with a good eye" is the way to say it in traditional Jewish language—the best English equivalent is probably "unflinchingly." The "good eye" principle means that it shouldn't hurt when you give even a lot of money to tzedakah, that you shouldn't worry about your "lack of privacy" when you invite guests to your home for Shabbat, that you shouldn't think of yourself as "wasting" time that is spent with someone who needs you to talk or listen (hear, hear, students and professors!). This too belongs to that fifth section of the Shulhan

Arukh because it is the kind of inner attitude that can't be demanded of anyone, but only hoped for. We can't even tell you how to get to that point in your own inner life. What we say is this: if there is an inner stinginess behind your giving, try hard not to let the other know it. We Jews are all behaviorists to a certain extent: generous behavior (and not just with money) may help to develop a true generosity of spirit.

The other side of this coin, perhaps obvious but still worthy of mention, is a deep Jewish aversion to causing pain or harm to others. Our historic experience has taught us that there is enough of suffering in the world without our adding to it. This highly developed instinctual reaction runs all the way from a concern for tzaar baalei hayyim—the pain suffered by animals (see Kindness to Animals and Shehitah), to such refined interpersonal concerns as forbidding malicious gossip and talebearing (see Dissonance and Harmony), because of both the obvious harm they will do to the subject and the moral harm they do to the teller.

Jews don't always treat each other this way, especially when they have some other label attached to their identity ("Orthodox," "Conservative," "Zionist," etc.) that takes on more importance to them than the fact of their Jewishness or mentshlikhkeit. That is why it has been so important to this *Catalog,* and to the new consciousness of the young Jews behind it, that we exist without labels. Some of us are more traditionally observant, others less so; some of us are more-or-less critical of Israeli government policy, others are staunch defenders. One thing we all have in common, however, is a dread of the day when we come to be labeled "Havurah Movement" or "*Catalog* Jews"; we pray that Jews in havurot will never treat Jews in synagogues the way the "Orthodox" treat the "Reform." Jews at their best have always known that "Jew" and "mentsh" are quite enough label-baggage for anyone to lug around.

The most difficult area of this guide to mentshlikhkeit we have saved for last. It is difficult, particularly for moderns, as here the ethic of traditional Judaism seems to fly in the face of much that we are told by others whom we tend to trust. I refer to the value of *self-control,* and especially control of the passions, which has always been seen as central to the Jewish way of moral living. Our contemporary ethic in the West is above all one of self-acceptance and free self-expression: what you feel is really you, what's really you is really good—so learn to let go and say or do it! To put it mildly, this is a far cry from any traditional Jewish vision of what the good life is all about.

The fact that human instincts and passions are both real and powerful is not something that Jewish moralists have generally sought to deny. But the reality of a drive does not itself make for its goodness or even permissibility. If man is created in order to become a mentsh, and if religious teaching exists to edify in that direction, then Torah (in the broadest sense) must have something to say about how we determine the legitimate expression of our passions. We choose one of the most basic and perhaps difficult areas as examples: that of aggression and anger.

Our aggressive drives, in the rabbinic view, are a part of the yetzer ha-ra, that libidinal energy reserve, often associated with eros, which may be called the "evil" urge but which everyone knows we need in order to survive. Aggression runs deep in all of human existence. The task that stands before us is to find the proper use for this aggressive energy. Anger, the most ordinary and natural expression of aggression, is universally regarded by Jewish ethics as a bad outlet. Anyone who shoots off aggressive drives at another human being, even given some provocation, is losing something of the divine image in him/herself. The traditional Jewish way of "learning how to handle hostility" is by converting it into nonhostility. If somebody is doing you (or another) wrong, you have to react; turning hostility inward is not a good corrective. Doesn't the Torah say: "Openly reprove your neighbor, but do not hate him in your heart"? What you have to realize, however, is that reproof will never affect your neighbor's conduct as long as it is done in anger. The violent response can lead to nothing but the escalation of violence. When the aggression bells in you are rung by somebody else's seemingly wrong conduct, find an inner place of calm before you allow yourself to respond. The reproof you are about to offer, it should be remembered, is one of the greatest acts of human love, and its purpose is to call forth a decent level of response in the other, not merely to clear your own head.

Jewish thinkers in our day, it should be noted, have called this ethic seriously into question. It is hardly the basis of Israeli foreign policy. Some have speculated about its psychological implications in creating an overly passive Jewish self-image: the Jew who never fights back. We should note, however, that this ethic is one that Judaism shares with most of the great religious traditions. All we can say is that the struggle between the contemporary and the Jewish ways of dealing with aggression should prove to be a creative one and that the viewpoint of traditional Jewish morals deserves more of a hearing than it usually gets.

Another area in which the traditional ethic of self-control is generally applied is that of love and sexual expression. Here the situation is rather different: love is of course taken by the tradition to be the most positive of all human emotions, though its sexual expression is still contained under the rubric of yetzer ha-ra. Asexual love, agape as the Christian sources call it, is entirely unproblematic: this is the highest of all interpersonal values. Where agape turns to eros, however, traditional Judaism has believed in rather strict self-control and has carefully delimited the areas of legitimate expression. Again, we moderns will have problems with some of the specific limitations. Suffice it to say that self-expression in itself is not the ultimate good and that such other areas of mentshlikhkeit as knowing the other and not inflicting pain might be good guides as to knowing where to exercise the virtues of self-control.

If we are to look for a single word with which to summarize the teachings of this hidden Shulhan Arukh, we would probably do best with an old and good word that is not much spoken in our contemporary vocabulary: humility—shiflut in Hebrew. The prophet Micah, says the Talmud, reduced the commandments to three: "Do justice, love mercy, and walk humbly with God." Humility does not, as some of its contemporary discreditors think, begin with self-abnegation, nor is it necessarily a cover for self-hate. It is rather the recognition that the true "I" in the universe is infinitely larger than my own, that the selfhood which I experience is also known by other humans, and that all of these separate selves are nourished by the radiance of a single "I." Everything else really follows from this. Buber says it well in his *Hasidism and Modern Man*:

The humble man lives in each being and knows each being's manner and virtue. Since no one is to him "the other," he knows from within that none lacks some hidden value; knows that there "is no man who does not have his hour." . . .

"God does not look on the evil side," said one zaddik. "How should I dare to do so?"

He who lives with others according to the mystery of humility can condemn no one. "He who passes sentence on a man passes it on himself."

He who separates himself from the sinner departs in guilt. . . . Only living with the other is justice. . . .

He who lives with others in this way realizes with his deed the truth that all souls are one; for each is a spark from the original soul, and the whole of the original soul is in each.

king of
meleh מֶלֶךְ
the world,
hah·o·lum הָעוֹלָם
... Add
ending ...
bo·ray בּוֹרֵא
pree פְּרִי
hah-aitz, הָעֵץ
ha·mo·tzi
לֶחֶם
מִן
הָאָרֶץ.
gives
bo-ray בּוֹרֵא
pree
grapes
who create
or wine.

After the word

Once there was a nation of people who wandered from place to place. They had been wanderers for so long that they could no longer remember if they had been driven out of their home, or were searching, endlessly searching. They carried with them the vague memory of a better past when they were happier, or at least their purpose was clearer. They also carried with them tokens of their past: an ancient staff, a pair of golden shoes, a tattered purple cloth, and a book filled with ancient, incomprehensible writing. Many had attempted to read the book and there were many theories about what it said, but the voice remained closed to the people.

At last they came to a clearing. Growing in the center was a tall tree, laden with wondrous fruits. They felt the specialness of the place and some imagined that this was their long lost ancient home. One of their number hesitantly approached the tree and picked a fruit.

"What does it taste like?"

"It tastes like the dew waking the grass in the morning."

"No," said another, taking a bite of a different fruit. "It tastes like the cry of a woman in childbirth."

"Quiet!" said a third. "Don't you see? This must be the Tree of Manna?"

Then they remembered the ancient legend of a tree whose heavenly fruit sustains each soul according to its needs.

"Shall we continue to eat?" they asked.
"Eat," came the reply.

The more they ate, the more they knew. They understood that this place was not their ancient home, nor was this the end of their journey. However, they had ended their wandering, for here was the Gate. From now on they would be travelers on the way.

One group picked up the golden shoes and headed north.
A second took the staff, carrying it aloft as they marched to the east.
A third cradled the ancient book in their arms and directed their steps to the south.
A fourth took turns wrapping the purple cloth around their heads as they traveled west.

The journey had begun.

Grateful acknowledgment is made to the following publishers and authors for permission to use copyrighted material:

Doubleday & Company, Inc.: Excerpt from *A Bintel Brief* by Isaac Metzker. Translation and Introduction copyright © by Isaac Metzker. Reprinted by permission of Doubleday & Co., Inc.

Moment: "Irises and Gym Shoes" by Daniel Siegel, vol. 1, no. 2 (July/August 1975). Reprinted by permission of the publisher.

Reconstructionist: "Balance of an Experiment" by Arnold Jacob Wolf, June 1967. Reprinted by permission of the publisher.

Viking Penguin, Inc.: Excerpt from *Old Age: The Last Segregation* by Claire Townsend. Copyright © 1970, 1971 by The Center for Study of Responsive Law. Reprinted by permission of Viking Penguin, Inc.

Index

I refers to *Catalog 1*; **II** to *Catalog 2*; **III** to *Catalog 3*.

405

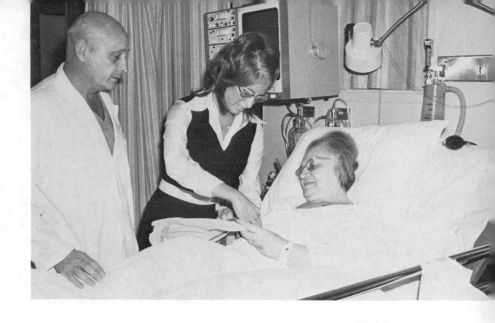

409

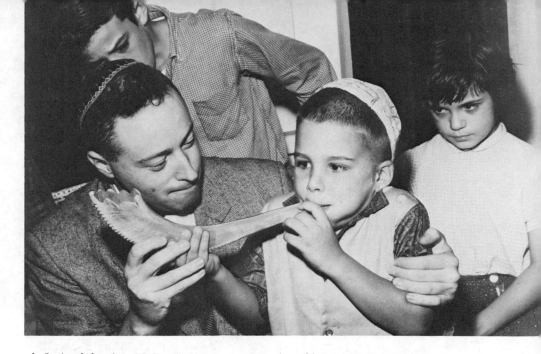

U

V

W

XYZ

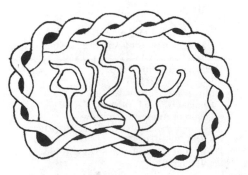